Why Do You Need This New Edition?

If you're wondering why you should buy this new edition of the *The Longman Handbook for Writers and Readers*, here are a few great reasons!

1 Eight new full-length student samples in a range of academic genres model many of the assignments you will be asked to write in college, including the essay exam response, literature review, lab report, portfolio introduction, rhetorical analysis of an advertisement, PowerPoint presentation, cover letter, and a scientific paper written for a general audience.

2 A new chapter, "Ten Serious Grammar Mistakes," will help you avoid making the grammar and usage errors most likely to confuse and distract readers (Ch. 34).

3 Research coverage has been expanded and revised to help you work effectively with the newest technologies and mediums, including a new section on appropriate uses of Wikipedia (Ch. 22), a new section on note taking (Ch. 22), a clearer discussion of avoiding plagiarism (Ch. 27), new guidelines for multimedia as well as traditional presentations (Ch. 28), and new citation models for emerging media.

4 A new chapter offers concrete strategies for effectively integrating text, visual, video, and audio materials in your assignments (Ch. 14).

5 A new chapter on ten serious documentation mistakes will help you avoid some of the most common pitfalls students make when citing their research papers (Ch. 29).

6 The new guidelines from MLA and APA are reflected in instruction, examples, and student model papers to give you the most current citation guidance available (Ch. 30 and 31).

7 A new chapter on assessing writing not only helps you evaluate and revise your own writing but also offers insights into how your readers view your writing and provides tips for giving feedback to your classmates on their own writing (Ch. 8).

8 We've cut 75 pages from the new edition without cutting any topics. Instruction is more succinct so that you spend less time reading about writing, making *The Longman Handbook,* Sixth Edition, a more user-friendly and effective reference tool.

Become a better writer and
researcher—and get better
grades in all your courses—
with MyCompLab!

COMPOSING

● This dynamic space for
composing, revising, and
editing is easy to use
and built to function like
the most popular word-
processing programs.
Store and manage all your
work in one place.

WRITER'S TOOLKIT

This helpful array ●
of grammar, writing, and
research tools accompanies
the Composing space.
The Toolkit includes sample
student papers, access to live
tutoring from Pearson Tutor
Services, a bibliography
builder from Noodlebib,
and so much more!

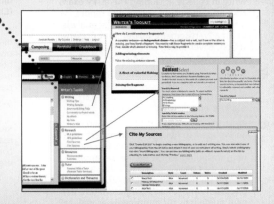

● Access instruction, multimedia tutorials, and exercises in the Resources area to help you master skills and get a better grade.

ADDITIONAL FEATURES

Manage all your written work and assignments online, in one easy-to-use place.

Monitor your writing and exercise scores in the Gradebook area.

Access a Pearson eText of your handbook—search it for key terms, take notes, and more.
Please note: Your MyCompLab account only comes with a Pearson eText if you or your instructor ordered the Pearson eText version.

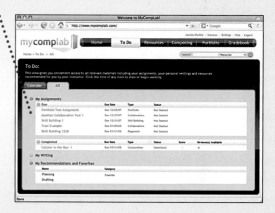

············• Register for MyCompLab today!

Questions? Go to www.mycomplab.com/help.html and click "Student Support."

If this book did not come packaged with an access code to MyCompLab you can purchase access online at www.mycomplab.com/buy-access.html or ask your bookstore to order an access card for you.

The Longman
Handbook for
Writers and Readers

SIXTH EDITION

The Longman Handbook for Writers and Readers

CHRIS M. ANSON
North Carolina State University

ROBERT A. SCHWEGLER
University of Rhode Island

Longman
Boston   Columbus   Indianapolis   New York   San Francisco   Upper Saddle River
Amsterdam   Cape Town   Dubai   London   Madrid   Milan   Munich   Paris   Montreal   Toronto
Delhi   Mexico City   São Paulo   Sydney   Hong Kong   Seoul   Singapore   Taipei   Tokyo

Acquisitions Editor: Lauren A. Finn
Associate Development Editor: Erin Reilly
Senior Supplements Editor: Donna Campion
Senior Media Producer: Stefanie Liebman
Marketing Manager: Susan Stoudt
Production Manager: Jacqueline A. Martin
Project Coordination, Text Design, and Electronic Page Makeup: Nesbitt Graphics, Inc.
Cover Designer/Manager: John Callahan
Visual Researcher: Rona Tuccillo
Senior Manufacturing Buyer: Roy L. Pickering, Jr.
Printer and Binder: RR Donnelley & Sons Company/Crawfordsville
Cover Printer: Phoenix Color Corporation

For permission to use copyrighted material, grateful acknowledgment is made to the
copyright holders on pp. 798–800, which are hereby made part of this copyright page.

Library of Congress Cataloging-in-Publication Data

Anson, Christopher M., 1954-
  The Longman handbook for writers and readers / Chris M. Anson, Robert A.
Schwegler. — 6th ed.
     p. cm.
  ISBN 978-0-205-74195-3 — ISBN 978-0-205-74199-1 (pbk. edition)
  1. English language—Rhetoric—Handbooks, manuals, etc. 2. English
language—Grammar—Handbooks, manuals, etc. 3. Reading
comprehension—Handbooks, manuals, etc. 4. Report writing—Handbooks,
manuals, etc. I. Schwegler, Robert A. II. Title.
  PE1408.A61844 2010
  808'.042—dc22
                                2009044587

1 2 3 4 5 6 7 8 9 10—DOC—12 11 10 09

Longman
is an imprint of

www.pearsonhighered.com

ISBN-13: 978-0-205-74195-3
ISBN-10: 0-205-74195-9

Contents

PART 2

Critical Thinking and Argument   91

PART 5

Researching and Writing   271

PART 6

Documenting Sources 355

PART 7

Grammar 497

PART 8

Sentence Problems   **577**

PART 9

Words and Style   645

PART 10

Punctuation, Mechanics, and Spelling   679

Preface

We have written *The Longman Handbook for Writers and Readers* out of a belief that composition instruction will benefit from an innovative approach that responds directly to recent theory and practice, while still addressing traditional concerns. Our aim has been to offer concrete, helpful advice for writers engaging in a wide variety of writing tasks and audiences.

All writers, whatever their skills and experience, seek at least occasional advice. We've designed the sixth edition of *The Longman Handbook for Writers and Readers* to provide answers to specific questions as well as extended help with larger concerns.

What's New in the Sixth Edition?

The sixth edition of *The Longman Handbook for Writers and Readers* has been revised, reorganized, and improved in a variety of ways. Note the following changes:

- **A new chapter, "Assessing Writing,"** helps students assess their own writing and understand how others read and evaluate it. The chapter also offers guidance on making informed comments on peers' papers and assembling portfolios (Ch. 8).
- **Two new chapters present the most common citation errors and most distracting grammar errors,** offering students brief, easy-to-reference content distilled from over thirty chapters on research and grammar.
  - **A new chapter, "Ten Serious Grammar Mistakes,"** will help students identify and correct the grammar and usage errors most likely to confuse and distract their readers (Ch. 34).
  - **A new chapter, "Ten Serious Documentation Mistakes,"** will help students recognize and avoid making the most common mistakes when citing and documenting sources in researched papers (Ch. 29).
- **Research coverage has been expanded and revised** to include a new section on appropriate uses of Wikipedia (Ch. 22), a new section on note taking (Ch. 22), a more linear and comprehensive discussion of avoiding plagiarism and integrating sources (Ch. 27), new guidelines for traditional and multimodal research presentations (Ch. 28), and new citation models for emerging media—including graphic novels, podcasts, presentations from online conferences, and more. Students have instruction and examples that allow them to work effectively with the newest technologies and mediums.
- **Increased coverage of writing for different audiences across the curriculum** as well as in the workplace and public arena includes expanded instruction and a greater number of sample papers:

- **Eight new full-length student samples in a range of academic genres** model for students many of the assignments they will be asked to write in college, including the essay exam response, literature review, lab report, portfolio introduction, rhetorical analysis of an advertisement, PowerPoint presentation, cover letter, and a scientific paper written for a general audience.

- **Four new Communities boxes that explore "Types of Academic Writing and Disciplinary Writing" in the Humanities, Social Sciences, and the Sciences** introduce students to the kinds of writing they will read and write in the General Education curriculum and in potential majors while also showing how writing differs from one academic discipline to the next (Chs. 17, 18, 19).

- **Four new Communities boxes that highlight differences among academic, public, and workplace writing** help students understand that audience expectations, writing styles, and research conventions shift in different communication environments. New boxes include Citing Research in the Three Communities, Documentation Needs in the Three Communities, Documentation Choices in the Three Communities, and Style and the Three Communities (Chs. 27, 29, 47).

- **Updated documentation coverage** follows style and citation guidelines laid out in the seventh edition of the *MLA Handbook for Writers of Research Papers* and the sixth edition of the *Publication Manual of the American Psychological Association*, ensuring that students have up-to-date instruction and examples for their reference (Chs. 30 and 31). Sample papers have been updated throughout.

- **A new chapter, "Multimodal Presentations,"** teaches students how to read, compose, and evaluate texts that combine textual, visual, and audio content—helping them develop critical twenty-first century composing skills (Ch. 14).

- **An expanded chapter, "Creating a Visual Argument,"** includes new instruction on reading visuals rhetorically as well as new samples, helping students think critically about visual texts they encounter in and out of college and to be more strategic about including visuals in their own writing (Ch. 12).

- **Streamlined and condensed prose throughout** helps key ideas stand out and makes the handbook a more effective reference tool for students.

- **Twenty-five new Strategy boxes** condense discursive instruction into easy-to-read, easy-to-reference lists of practical tips for solving a range of writing problems, helping students adapt their writing for varying rhetorical situations as well as recognize and remedy common grammatical and mechanical problems.

What Makes *The Longman Handbook* Unique?

The new edition of *The Longman Handbook* retains its innovative features while responding to the changing needs of student writers.

- **Writing as social action for communities of diverse audiences.** We emphasize the social nature of writing, especially the ways different groups of readers—in academic, public, and work communities—shape texts and the writing process. We offer specific strategies for responding to these audiences.
- **Critical thinking and reading.** We believe that reading, critical thinking, and awareness of audience expectations are intertwined. For this reason, we emphasize not only the importance of each but also their many interrelationships.
- **A fresh approach to correctness.** We believe that correctness in writing—employing the conventions appropriately and effectively—is largely a matter of social awareness. Errors can undermine the writers' relationship with readers or impede effective, persuasive, and imaginative interaction within a community of writers and readers. Using appropriate conventions of grammar, sentence structure, punctuation, and style is an important part of being able to guide the way readers respond to writing. *The Longman Handbook* treats correctness and understanding written conventions as essential to accomplished writing, helping writers recognize the effect of errors on readers as well as the ways conventions may vary from community to community.
- **Recognize and revise.** We believe that just knowing the definition of an error is seldom sufficient. Writers need *first* to be able to recognize errors. *Then* they need to be able to correct mistakes and internalize the conventions permanently in the process. *The Longman Handbook* helps writers develop the ability to recognize errors in their own writing, an essential step often missing from handbook discussions. Then it provides concrete strategies for revision and correction.
- **Ten Serious Mistakes.** We highlight "Ten Serious Mistakes" in grammar and documentation that are most likely to confuse readers and thus should be avoided. These are covered in two new chapters (29 and 34) and highlighted by icons throughout the chapters.
- **Reader's reaction.** Reader's reactions to unedited examples link the writer and reader and show students how their unedited writing could be perceived.
- **Strategies.** Highlighted "Strategy" sections appearing throughout the handbook provide writers with specific steps they can take to accomplish a task; correct an error; or achieve a goal in expression, critical understanding, or style.
- **Online style.** In writing about online communities, we treat online communication not simply as a matter of technological awareness but also as a setting with its own unique rhetorical and stylistic demands and strategies.
- **Research and writing with critical awareness.** We know that information and ideas lie at the heart of good writing, even writing focusing on personal insights and experience. Our discussions of researching and writing pay special attention to critical reading and evaluation of sources. We also give extended emphasis to techniques of summary,

paraphrase, synthesis, and critical response. We present techniques for personal inquiry, for drawing on print and electronic resources, and for fieldwork, all designed to add depth and interest to writing, both for the writer and for readers. We pay special attention to new resources for writers, such as the ever-growing number of research databases.

- **Integrating sources and avoiding plagiarism.** From our own teaching, we recognize the importance of both these concerns, and we provide advice, concrete strategies, and detailed examples to help students create researched writing that gains strength and depth from sources while appropriately acknowledging the origins of ideas and information.

- **Language variation.** Here we focus on the issue of language variation—home or community language varieties, oral and written dialects, code shifting, the importance of "standard" English in text written for diverse audiences, and the effect that particular choices of personae can have on an audience's reception of a text.

- **Collaboration.** We treat writing, critical thinking, and research as often enriched through collaboration, either with fellow writers and readers or with potential audiences.

- **Speaking.** *The Longman Handbook* offers an entire chapter on speaking, "Speaking Effectively" (Chapter 16).

Supplements

The Longman Handbook for Writers and Readers is accompanied by an extensive package of print and media supplements for both students and instructors. Please see your Pearson representative for details on these and additional supplements.

For Students

The new MyCompLab integrates the market leading instruction, multimedia tutorials, and exercises for writing, grammar, and research that users have come to identify with the program with a new online composing space and new assessment tools. The result is a revolutionary application that offers a seamless and flexible teaching and learning environment built specifically for writers. Created after years of extensive research and in partnership with composition faculty and students across the country, the new MyCompLab provides help for writers in the context of their writing, with instructor and peer commenting functionality, proven tutorials and exercises for writing, grammar and research, an e-portfolio, an assignment-builder, a bibliography tool, tutoring services, and a gradebook and course management organization created specifically for writing classes. Visit www.mycomplab.com for more information.

For Instructors

- The *Instructor's Resource Manual* not only offers instructors support for teaching Parts 1 to 10—with suggested activities, teaching tips, chapter summaries, exercises, and online activities and resources— but also includes opening chapters that discuss other aspects of teaching, such as the student's approach to using a handbook; advice for adjunct instructors and teaching assistants; online teaching in conjunction with the handbook; and designing a course with the handbook.
- An *Answer Key* is available for the exercises in *The Longman Handbook.*
- The *Diagnostic and Editing Tests and Exercises* aids in analyzing common errors and can supplement the handbook's exercises. (Available in both print and electronic formats.)

Acknowledgments

The sixth edition of *The Longman Handbook for Writers and Readers* reflects important improvements in a book that has experienced more than a decade of development. We are grateful to a number of people for helping to keep moving the book forward.

Many of our colleagues have advised us, reviewed drafts, and provided general responses to our ideas. Our special thanks go to the following people who have reviewed this edition of *The Longman Handbook:* Jennifer Ashton, University of Illinois at Chicago; Elizabeth Barnes, Daytona State College; Linda Best, Kean University; Barbara J. Campbell, Quinebaug Valley Community College; Kathryn E. Dobson, McDaniel College; Stacey Floyd, Cardinal Stritch University; Sheryl Holt, University of Minnesota; Amy Hornat-Kaval, DePaul University; Deborah Church Miller, University of Georgia; Marguerite Newcomb, University of Texas-San Antonio; Helen O'Grady, University of Rhode Island; David J. Peterson, University of Nebraska at Omaha; Kristen Schaffenberger, University of Illinois at Chicago; Leah Williams, University of New Hampshire.

Thank you also to those who worked with us as consultants in the development and revision of selected chapters in previous editions of *The Longman Handbook*—Victor Villanueva, Washington State University; Jim Dubinsky, Virginia Tech; Christina Haas, Kent State University; Elizabeth Ervin, University of North Carolina, Wilmington; Gladys Vega Scott, Arizona State University; and Mick Doherty and Sandye Thompson. We are grateful for the expertise and creativity of all these writers and teachers.

An extensive team of editors, producers, and managers at Longman were instrumental in the development and publication of the sixth edition: A special word of thanks to Lauren Finn, acquisitions editor, for her continued support of the project, and to Erin Reilly, development editor, for her excellent editorial management. Thanks also to Mary Ellen Curley, director of development; Donna Campion, senior supplements editor; Megan Galvin-Fak, executive marketing manager; and Jackie Martin, production manager. Lois Lombardo and her team at Nesbitt Graphics Inc. did amazing work on a tight schedule to design and produce the book.

Chris Anson thanks, as always, his wife Gean and sons Ian and Graham for their support and understanding during the revision process, and to the latter for the occasional advice about language, writing, grammar, and contemporary usage that a 12- and 15-year old can provide.

Bob Schwegler would like to acknowledge that he couldn't do any of this work without the advice, insight, and support of Nancy Newman Schwegler, who tolerated with grace and wit the many years the project has taken—and the sunny days spent worrying about comma splices. This and many other projects are the happy consequence of her understanding of readers, reading, and the creative ways writers can represent themselves. He would also like to thank Brian and Tara Schwegler for their advice, Christopher for his smiles, Ashley Marie for her inspiration, Lily for hope, and Kira for imagination.

CHRIS M. ANSON
ROBERT A. SCHWEGLER

PART 1

Writing for Readers

CHAPTER 1

Writers, Readers, and Communities

Someone created the Web page you browsed yesterday—wrote the text, designed the layout, and anticipated readers' reactions. Someone else wrote your housing contract and your student loan forms. Writers worked together to produce the community newsletter you found in your mailbox, and one of them gave a presentation on a community issue to the city council.

Language surrounds us, shaping our lives, choices, responsibilities, and values. This book looks at the roles writers, readers, and speakers play in contemporary culture. It offers concrete strategies for writing, for critical reading and thinking, for oral communication, and for understanding your readers' and listeners' expectations. More broadly, it emphasizes writing and speaking as ways to understand experience and share that understanding.

1a Academic, public, and work communities

Why would a physiology instructor have little patience with a student paper written in the breezy style typical of a column from *Men's Health*? Why would a corporate executive or a city council member frown on a detailed theoretical presentation of a problem but welcome a much shorter report that gets right to the point and proposes a solution?

These audiences' sharply differing needs and expectations offer typical challenges writers (and speakers) face in knowing what style to use, what structure a text should have, and what to include (or not) in its contents. To respond to these many differences, you need to envision a *community* of writers, readers, and speakers. A **discourse community** consists of people with shared goals and knowledge, a common setting or context, and similar preferences and uses for verbal and visual texts.

In this book we focus on three broad and important types of communities: academic, public, and work. We suggest ways you can participate in these communities and in other writing and speaking situations you will encounter throughout your life.

1 Communities in action

Consider this example: In a Denver suburb, pets have been disappearing. The culprits are coyotes, increasingly crowded by new homes and industrial parks. These disappearances are alarming to residents—will a young child be the next victim? Will the wild animals become even more aggressive?

In a situation like this, problem-solving often starts with written and oral presentations. City council members and concerned citizens may turn to discussions produced within the **academic community:** detailed, complex scientific studies and presentations reporting the effects of development on coyotes and other predators. A line from one of their documents looks like this.

> This report summarizes and compares the data from two studies of the habits of predators in areas that have experienced significant population growth and urbanization over the past ten years.

Such scientific information is useful, yet its focus is different from the question of concerned parents, pet owners, and others making up the **public community:** How can we protect our children and pets without harming local wildlife? Drawing on scientific detail and knowledge of residents' perspectives, a neighborhood action group might distribute leaflets and organize meetings.

COYOTE ALERT!

Are your children safe in their own backyards? Coyotes attacked seven dogs and cats last summer. Find out what we can do. Join the Committee to Safeguard Our Children on Tuesday, October 2, at 7:00 p.m. in the high school gym.

Local officials address the problem with writing directed at several **work communities,** in reports and presentations to the city council, the environmental management department, and municipal development offices. The Construction Contractors Consortium, for example, sends out a memo calling attention to the ways that zoning restrictions sponsored by environmental groups could hurt their businesses.

As you can see from this example, writing and speaking will vary in purpose, organization, and style across these different communities, reflecting different expectations.

2 Choices and limits

As you start to write, and then throughout the process, keep in mind four of the most important features of writing/reading (or speaking) communities.

- **Roles** that you and your readers (or listeners) occupy
- **Goals** for communication that you and your audience share
- **Forms** that your audience will look for in writing (or speaking)
- **Characteristics** typical of communication that fulfills a particular set of goals and meets an audience's expectations

THREE MAJOR COMMUNITIES OF READERS, WRITERS, AND SPEAKERS

ACADEMIC	PUBLIC	WORK
Roles Students; teachers; researchers; expert committees; specialized readers	**Roles** Neighborhood groups; potential supporters; public officials; government agencies; local political groups; issue-oriented readers	**Roles** Co-workers; supervisors; management; public relations; clients (current or potential); government agencies
Goals Develop new understandings or policies	**Goals** Persuade people on issues; provide information; participate in public decision making	**Goals** Provide information; analyze problems; propose solutions; promote organization
Forms Analytical report; interpretation of text or event; research proposal or report; lab report; scholarly article; annotated bibliography; grant proposal; policy study	**Forms** Guidelines; position paper; informative report; letter or email to agency or group; flyer or brochure; action proposal; grant proposal; charter or mission statement; letter to editor; Web announcement	**Forms** Informative memo; factual or descriptive report; proposal; executive summary; letter or memo; guidelines or instruction; promotional material; minutes and notes; formal reports; internal and public Web sites
Characteristics Clear reasoning; critical analysis; fresh insight; extensive evidence; accurate detail; balanced treatment; acknowledgment of competing viewpoints; thorough exploration of topic	**Characteristics** Focus on shared values; advocacy of cause or policy; fairness and ethical argument; relevant supporting evidence; action- or solution-oriented; accessible presentation	**Characteristics** Focus on tasks and goals; accurate, efficient presentation; promotion of products and services; attention to organizational image and corporate design standards; concise, direct style

Exercise 1

In groups of four or five, draft a "class charter," that is, a formal statement outlining the principles, purposes, or rules that you think should govern your class. Before you start drafting, discuss the roles, goals, forms, and characteristics of this situation. Which members of the class do you need to address? In what ways might their values or interests be similar or different? What do you hope to accomplish with the document you produce? What does a charter look like? How would you present it orally to the class?

1b Identifying electronic communities

On the Web you can read an article by an academic researcher, then with a click of the mouse find yourself skimming a site sponsored by a major corporation or filling in an online petition circulated by a political or nonprofit organization. To recognize the community to which a site belongs or the expectations you need to observe in creating an electronic document, use the TASALS strategy.

Topic: On what subject(s) does the site focus? Do contributors belong to any organization or share any other kind of affiliation?

Attitude: Does the site have a clear point of view or set of values? Do contributors have similar perspectives or values?

Strategies: Does the writing have a particular tone or style? Does the design of the site have a particular style or emphasis (see Chapter 13 for examples)?

Authority: Does the site support its claims and information? Do contributors reason carefully, offering evidence rather than unsupported opinions?

Links: Do the postings and links refer to related online documents, lists, or resources?

Summarize: On the basis of your answers to these questions, summarize the qualities of the electronic community you encountered.

Exercise 2

A. Find the official Web site of your school or city or of an organization to which you belong. Examine the Web site carefully using the TASALS strategy. How would you characterize the community that sponsors the site? Write out your observations.

B. Use a Web search engine to locate several Web sites maintained by or catering to professionals in your future field of work. Evaluate the Web site using TASALS. Compare your results with those of your classmates.

Visit mycomplab.com for more resources and exercises on reading and writing.

CHAPTER 2

Discovering and Planning

Whether in college, in a public setting, or on the job, you need to explore your task, consider possible subjects, and identify your purposes for writing before you can really get started. Planning before you begin formal writing—often called **prewriting**—helps you move your project forward more smoothly and confidently.

2a Getting started

Whatever your writing task, the strategies in the chart on page 7 can help remind you of what you already know and think about a subject or task. They can suggest a subject worth writing about or help you develop a clear purpose for your writing.

1 Try informal writing

Many accomplished writers use a strategy called **freewriting**—fast, highly informal, unselfconscious writing.

To try freewriting, write quickly for five or ten minutes. Concentrate entirely on *writing without stopping*. Even if you think you have nothing to say, simply writing "I'm stuck, I'm stuck" will at least force you to begin writing. Curiously, you'll find yourself almost magically slipping into more interesting ideas, some of which may suggest possible subjects or purposes for writing.

Focused freewriting involves writing quickly about an idea or topic you already have in mind, or one that you began developing through freewriting. Your first sentence might begin, "Antigambling laws—I guess I'm in favor of them generally," then explore what you know or feel about the topic. Consider stating your topic as an assertion so that you can systematically question that assertion, anticipating a spark that ignites your interest.

2 Use listing

Lists can draw out knowledge already in your mind and *create* new ideas through association. Write your topic at the top of a page and then list ten thoughts, facts, or ideas about the subject. Or adapt listing to generate specific ideas. For example, begin with a general impression or idea, and list supporting details and new associations.

PLANNING IN THREE COMMUNITIES: IDENTIFYING POSSIBLE TOPICS

ACADEMIC SETTINGS	PUBLIC SETTINGS	WORK SETTINGS
Respond to ideas and questions in textbooks, scholarly articles, or class discussions.	**Respond** to ideas, problems, and proposals in newspapers, magazines, or Web sites; listen to local and national news programs or talk shows.	**Respond** to challenges and requests posed in memos or organizational newsletters or to specific requests for reports and other documents.
Ask "Do researchers or experts identify new developments, unresolved questions, or fresh perspectives and techniques?"	**Ask** "What local issues or problems engage my interest (and that of others)? What kinds of information do I and others need? What national or global concerns are worth attention?"	**Ask** "What significant internal or external challenges does the organization face, and how can I respond to them?"
Look up bibliographies or summaries of research as well as newsletters and magazines reporting on current research and discoveries. (See 22c–d and 23c–d.)	**Look up** online archives of newspapers and magazines that cover topics of local, national, and global interest or consult publications and announcements from government agencies, public service organizations, or corporations.	**Look up** articles in business-related journals and magazines for articles, topics, and ideas related to your work; consult professional magazines, Web sites, and newsletters for policy or problem-focused discussions applicable to your work or your organization.

As he started working on his proposal requesting permission to allow local bands to perform in the basement of the community center, Morgan Scott listed some of the subjects the report needed to cover.

Space isn't used for anything else during the evenings.
Will give teenagers a safe place to go, especially on weekends.
Need plans for cleaning the space up and maintaining it.
Noise wouldn't bother neighbors.
Plenty of parking for those old enough to drive.
Recreation department and police could easily provide supervision.
Will provide a creative outlet for local residents.
Low cost.
Will have the support of parents.
Add to the city's reputation as a good place to live.

3 Ask strategic questions

You can generate important information for many writing projects if you try answering the questions *what*, *why*, and *why not* (*where*, *who*, and *how* may also be important questions, depending on your writing project).

2b
plan

Brian Corby used this strategy for his report arguing that his city's zoning board should not allow a high-rise apartment to be built adjacent to a public park.

What?

- Proposed high-rise apt.
- 18 stories, 102 units plus 3 penthouses
- Overlooking east side of Piedmont Park
- Proposal approved by Feb.; Planning by Feb. next yr.; groundbreaking by June
- Finished structure by Aug. of following year

Why?

- Developers profit
- Brings jobs to Lake Walton
- Raises property tax base—supposed to funnel money back into the city and parks
- Provides medium-cost housing in growing area
- Develops ugly vacant property by park

Why not?

- "Citifies" one of the few green patches in Lake Walton
- Increases traffic, crime rate, park use
- Adds to waste; pollution from proposed garbage incinerator in building
- Opens the door to other high-rise development because of new zoning ordinance
- Blocks sunlight from park
- Raises property taxes for longtime and elderly residents

Exercise 1

Begin with the topic, issue, or problem for a writing project you are working on, or choose a topic that interests you. Then try the listing procedure with your topic. Begin by listing ten things you know about your chosen topic. Then choose one item and generate another sublist beneath it. If you can, keep going to a third or fourth level.

2b Keeping a writing/reading journal

A journal is not a diary. Diaries are a record of people's daily activities, thoughts, and personal lives. A **journal** is a place to explore ideas, develop insights, experiment with your prose, write rough drafts, and reflect on your reading. Journals are where ideas, observations, and possible topics for writing can take shape or where responses to reading can be developed.

1 How to keep a writing and reading journal

Keeping a journal may feel strange or artificial at first. After all, you're writing mainly to and for yourself, with no concern about spelling or grammar. The actual shape and size of your journal is less important to its success than what you do in and with it. It helps to have a journal whose pages can be removed or reorganized. An electronic word-processing document will allow you to do this, as will an inexpensive ring binder.

How much and how often should you write? The more you write, the greater your chances to think about a subject. The length of journal entries will (and should) differ. Working half a day searching the Internet or the library might yield fifteen pages of notes, speculations, and interpretations, but an idea that comes to you late at night might yield just a few lines of drowsy prose. At all costs *write regularly.* Journals abandoned for more than a day or two soon wither and die from lack of nourishment.

Use a personal voice. Use your journal writing to express your beliefs, opinions, and reactions in personal terms. Speculate. Instead of writing in abstract terms and formal language, use phrases like "I wonder if . . .," "I think it's wonderful that . . .," or "I can't understand why. . . ." Be conversational. While such sentences would cry out for revision in a formal report, you can feel safe using such a casual tone in a journal.

Use shortcuts. Try writing quickly. Use abbreviations if you're sure you will remember what they mean. Don't worry at this point about grammar, mechanics, or spelling.

2 Thinking, writing, and discovering

Writing in a journal *makes your thoughts visible.* In a journal, you create connections among thinking, writing, and reading.

Translate new knowledge. After reading or hearing about new ideas or information, imagine one or more persons who know little about the topic. Explain your new knowledge to them. You'll find, first, that you'll be forced to *speculate* about the meaning of the information and concepts at places you find difficult to understand. Second, you'll often *clarify and resolve* your confusions in the process of writing.

Brainstorm. Instead of staring at a blank piece of paper or screen, waiting for perfect sentences to roll off your pen or keyboard, use your journal for **brainstorming.** When you brainstorm, you think associatively, letting one idea lead to another or exploring the connections among ideas. You create an exploratory, tentative, and often messy set of responses to reading, issues, and experience that can point the way to a focus and plan for a draft of a paper (see Chapter 4).

Extend your thinking. Imagine that you learn this fact from your reading in a sociology article or textbook: Human aggression increases in hot weather. Recording such an observation in your journal may take a few seconds. But imagine *extending* this idea a little, seeing its implications, wondering about possible solutions and applications. Are people more aggressive in hot regions than in cold regions? If discomfort causes aggression, why aren't people just as aggressive in uncomfortably cold weather? Are workers in hot factories more aggressive than workers in chilly factories? Do Northerners become aggressive on vacations to hot places?

Take issue with ideas. Your journal can be an excellent place to argue with someone else's point of view or criticize a position. Journals let writers "have it out" with an opponent without risking actual confrontation. The result can be a more balanced view of the controversy.

Exercise 2

A. The following journal entry was written by Kelly Odeen, a student in a course on literacy in America. Read Odeen's entry, and then identify specific thinking, writing, reading, or discovering functions for which she is using her journal. What characteristics of her entry suggest these functions?

> Reading about the Amish community left me with very mixed feelings—not sure what to make of them yet. I really admired the family support of Eli's literacy development. Sounded like the older family members did just what we've been encouraged to do as tutors. They gave him positive feedback, etc. Focused on accomplishments rather than failures. But the setting looked sort of ideal. Everyone in Eli's family reads and writes, even more than in my family. I don't think it's possible to make learning totally individualized in the public school system. Choices have to be made that are better for some children than others. I don't have a solution, but I think the author is being too idealistic to think there can be this match like the Amish have. I'd like to look into this more for my project, maybe. Because I do agree that there are many ways of perceiving literacy, each valid, and we have to be sensitive to where kids are coming from *compared* with the school system they're going into.

B. Should animals be used in laboratory experiments for the advancement of scientific, medical, and behavioral knowledge? Write a page or two in your journal on this question, considering as many issues and angles on the topic as you can. Then compare your journal writing in a small group. What ideas did the writing yield? How helpful was it? How would you describe the style, organization, and other characteristics of your writing? Which of the purposes described in the preceding section did your writing serve?

2c Structuring ideas and information

Ideas and information alone won't lead to successful writing unless you can find ways to structure them. Some writing tasks, such as business and research reports, need to follow familiar structures. For many other kinds of writing, you'll often need to identify relationships within the information and ideas you've generated.

1 Draw a cluster

A **cluster** is a diagram of interconnected ideas. When you create a cluster, you will find yourself both exploring what you know about a topic and revealing how that knowledge is related.

To create a cluster, begin by writing a concept, idea, or topic in the center of a page, and circle this kernel topic. Then jot down associations linked to this central idea, circling them and connecting them with lines to the kernel topic, like the spokes of a wheel (see Figure 2.1). As you continue to generate ideas around the central focus, think about the ways the subsidiary

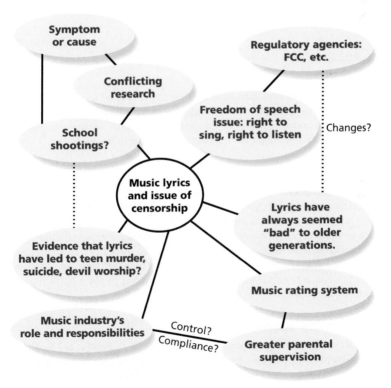

FIGURE 2.1 A simple conceptual cluster

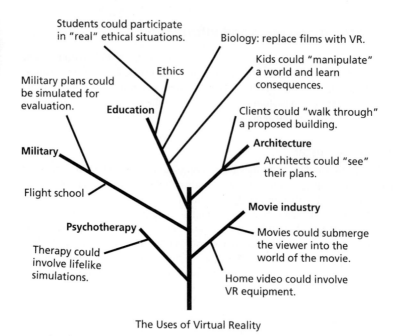

The Uses of Virtual Reality

FIGURE 2.2 A simple tree diagram

ideas are connected, and draw lines to show those connections. You can also create clusters in cycles: each subsidiary idea becomes the central focus on a new page. The nodes or pieces of the cluster will become a visual representation of how your text might be "chunked" into paragraphs or sections.

2 Create a tree diagram

Tree diagrams resemble clusters, but their branches tend to be more linear and hierarchical, with fewer interconnections (see Figure 2.2).

Start with your main focus or topic as the "trunk" of the tree. As you work upward, create primary branches with centrally connected ideas. You can branch off from these with smaller and smaller branches that each relate in a specific way to the main branch. Consider "revising" your tree diagram into a preliminary outline to use when deciding what to place in each paragraph of your paper.

3 Build a time sequence

If you're writing a paper organized chronologically or involving sequences of time, you may find a **time sequence** useful. To create a time sequence, begin by framing each event along a timeline. Then draw vertical lines of thicker or thinner widths depending on how closely connected one event is to the next.

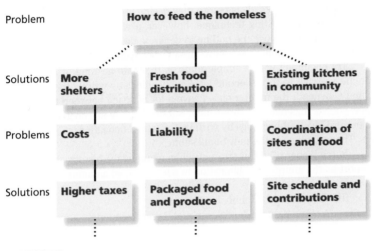

FIGURE 2.3   A problem-solution grid

In planning materials for a self-guided tour of a special museum exhibit on the artist Andy Warhol, for example, James Christenfeld drew a time sequence detailing the history of Warhol's artistic life. With thick connecting lines, he showed how certain pivotal events led to or caused other events or works in Warhol's career. Connections with thin lines were simply chronological.

4 Create a problem-solution grid

In some writing situations, especially in civics contexts, you may need to focus on a problem and then present an argument for a proposed solution. Proposals, reports, position papers, and other persuasive texts often follow this **problem-solution sequence.**

Create a **problem-solution grid** (see Figure 2.3) by putting a statement of the main problem at the top of a page. Make a layer of at least two possible solutions to the problem. For each, name at least one further problem with that solution. "Solve" each subsidiary problem in turn. You can create as many layers as you wish, generating many specifics for your paper or presentation.

As Figure 2.3 shows, Paula Masek identified three temporary solutions to the problem of hunger among the homeless. Using a grid to guide her planning and to identify a structure, Masek discussed each boxed item in a separate section of her draft paper.

5 Outline

The best-known prewriting technique is the trusty **outline,** complete with Roman numerals. Unfortunately, the traditional outline doesn't do much to help writers *generate* ideas before they decide how these ideas should be arranged. As a prewriting technique, however, a **working outline** can be useful. The trick is to use the outline to generate new categories of information rather than to label ones you've already discovered.

Try beginning with a simple topic as the main heading of an outline. Commit yourself to three second-level subheadings by writing the letters *A*, *B*, and *C* beneath the main topics. Leave a lot of space between the letters. Once you've "discovered" three main subheadings, you can try to create three third-level subheadings by writing *1*, *2*, and *3* beneath *each* of your letters. Then try filling in the new blank subheadings.

Mitch Weber tried this strategy when planning the historical section of a report on the nonprofit organization in which he held an internship.

III. Creation of the family health center
    A. Founding work of Susan and Roger Ramstadt
        1. The "vision"
        2. Finding the money
        3. The involvement of the Crimp Foundation
    B. The early years (1980–95)
        1. Building momentum
        2. The great financial disaster
        3. Rebirth
    C. Toward maturity
        1. Fund-raising in the 2000s
        2. State recognition and the big award
        3. Health and sustenance
    D. The future
        1. The new board of directors
        2. The new vision

Exercise 3

Create a list of five topics, issues, or problems. Choose the one that most interests you. Then briefly try out three of the planning techniques discussed in 2c. After experimenting with them, jot down some notes about which one(s) worked worst and best for you. Why do you think this was the case? What sort of topic did you choose, and how did the technique you used affect its development?

2d Planning: Paper in progress

Jessica DiGregorio was assigned a paper in a college course focusing on literacy and its consequences for individuals and societies. The task required her to identify a public or official document (such as a charter, certificate, law, set of guidelines, or official publication) and to discuss its consequences for individuals or groups of people. Other people in the class analyzed the effects of documents such as housing contracts, a parent's death certificate, and a "driving while intoxicated" citation. Jessica had always been interested in sports, perhaps because her father was an accomplished basketball player. She decided to do some preliminary listing to see what specific kinds of documents affect participants in sports—amateur, college, and professional (see 2a). Here is a list of questions and ideas she created.

- Injury reports shape an athlete's participation, the outcome of games, and the emotions of fans and players. Who gives the reports such power?
- Game rules—some rules have serious consequences when broken, but others are less important. Why? Who decides?
- Some sports specify the shape, size, weight, etc., of equipment. What about the sports that have few regulations on equipment? Do the differences reflect something about the nature of the sports or their roles in society?
- Professional sports contracts seem to be in the news often (MLB, NBA, NFL). Can they really determine the success or failure of teams? How do they shape the lives of players? My father's contract.
- Drug regulations. Laws or informal rules. What's the difference?

After deciding on the consequences of professional contracts on players' lives as a focus for her work, Jessica made the following list.

- Contracts in the news—what kinds of things they cover.
- Odd things that some sports stars request.
- My father's NBA contract. What's in it?
- What he had to do as a result of the contract. What the team had to do.
- What it meant for his life. My family. Me?
- Similar to other contracts at the time?
- What if you break a contract?
- What is a contract? Legally. What exactly can contracts do and not do?

Exercise 4

Study Jessica DiGregorio's two planning lists. What other topics on the first list do you think would have been worth developing in ways that addressed her assigned task? What questions would you ask her about the topics on the second list? What advice would you give her for either elaborating her second list or choosing specific items on it to include in (or exclude from) her paper? Generate a list of additional particulars that DiGregorio could use to develop her topic.

Purpose, Thesis, and Audience

Think about what writing actually *does*. It gives you a way to communicate new ideas and information. It can sell, buy, or negotiate. It can do public good and make private profit.

Think about how purposes and audiences for writing can shift from setting to setting and from audience to audience.

PURPOSES AND AUDIENCES IN THREE COMMUNITIES: YOUR CHOICES AS A WRITER		
ACADEMIC SETTINGS	**PUBLIC SETTINGS**	**WORK SETTINGS**
Why write? Present and support interpretations; discuss and explain research results; evaluate others' conclusions; demonstrate knowledge; explore ideas; share information and insight	**Why write?** Persuade people on issues; provide information; participate in public activities and decision making; create groups and organize communities	**Why write?** Analyze problems; propose solutions; provide information; coordinate activities
For whom? Instructors; fellow researchers or scholars; policy makers; public or workplace decision makers; anyone interested in fresh ideas or recent research	**For whom?** Local groups; public officials; potential supporters; agencies and organizations; issue-oriented readers	**For whom?** Co-workers and managers; clients and customers; government agencies; public relations

3a Recognizing your purpose

One of your early steps in planning for any piece of writing should be to analyze the task and setting, taking time to identify what you're being asked (or what you're motivated) to do.

1 Identify the focus

In many writing tasks, your focus or topic may be defined for you in advance. In a memo to the YMCA volunteer tutoring staff, for example, your topic might be an upcoming training session. On other occasions, you may need to identify the topic in a task that's given to you, or even come up with a topic on your own. In all these cases, it helps to articulate for yourself just what it is you're writing about.

Look for key noun phrases. Your written assignment or task description will inevitably contain nouns that signal the main topics you need to address. Underline key nouns or noun phrases in the assignment. Write these nouns in your planning notes and then begin inventing possibilities for your paper's contents (see 2a–c).

In analyzing a writing assignment in his child development course, for example, Dennis Buehler underlined three key noun phrases.

> The purpose of this assignment is to integrate what you have learned in the area of cognitive development. Focusing on the second year of life, what are the most important skills that emerge in different domains (attention, language, and perception)? Give specific examples from the studies we have read so far.

The underlined topics can be stated more simply as *cognitive-developmental skills in the second year of life.*

Create a focus statement. When your writing task isn't an assignment given to you, write your own focus statement. Include key nouns or noun phrases (as in the preceding example). This can help you to keep your writing from straying from the point. Karla Spellman was writing a page for the Web site of a city project called "Green Chair." She wrote the following focus statement and underlined the key noun phrase in it.

> In a page for the City Projects Web site, write a description of the Green Chair project, including its goals, how people can volunteer to build the chairs, and where they can buy one.

2 Define the purpose

Identifying nouns—topics or focuses—gives you a clear sense of what your writing is *about.* But nouns don't act: they're just things that sit, inert, on the page. Your writing doesn't just need to say something; it also needs to *do* something. This "doing" is the rhetorical action—the purpose—of your writing, and it usually appears in a verb or verb phrase.

Look for key verb phrases. In an assignment given to you, the central purpose for your response will appear in key verbs and verb phrases—statements of action and agency. Underline all key verbs or verb phrases that appear in the assignment or task description. Then circle those that appear to be the most important or central—the ones that tell you what to *do* with your writing. Use one or more of the planning techniques (see 2a–c) to generate material for your writing.

In analyzing the second writing assignment in her composition course, Corinth Malletas underlined two key verb phrases.

> *Assignment 2:* Find an advertisement that catches your attention in a popular magazine. Then analyze the ad for its hidden cultural assumptions, being sure to describe exactly what is happening in the ad. Include techniques of camera angle, coloration, and focus.

Create a purpose statement. For self-motivated writing, create your own purpose statement and underline the key verb or verb phrases. In planning an announcement recruiting acoustic bands for a new coffeehouse, Ty Brown wrote the following purpose statement and underlined two key verb phrases.

> Create a flier directed at band members and leaders to <u>encourage their application to audition</u> for the X-Tra Coffee House and <u>explain the process</u> to them as well as details about the coffeehouse.

Notice that these verb phrases contain important assembly instructions for Ty's flier. "Encourage" implies "getting attention" and "advertising." "Explain" implies "giving information" and "being clear." Here are some of the more common verbs used in writing situations, especially in college, along with brief definitions and examples.

VERBS USED IN WRITING ASSIGNMENTS OR SITUATIONS

Describe. Show how something might be experienced in sight, touch, sound, smell, or taste. *Example:* "Describe the obstacles experienced by wheelchair-bound or vision-impaired visitors to historic homes in the area."

Analyze. Divide or break something into its constituent parts so you can analyze their relationships. Begin with careful description and observation. *Example:* "Analyze the causes of increased wildlife roadkill in a suburb."

Synthesize. Combine separate elements into a synthesis, producing a single or unified entity. *Example:* "Synthesize this list of disparate facts about energy consumption."

Evaluate. Reach conclusions about something's value or worth. Substantiate all evaluations with evidence based on careful observation and analysis. *Example:* "Evaluate the proposals submitted by three groups who each want to organize this year's charity auction."

Argue. Argue to prove a point or persuade a reader to accept a particular position (see Chapters 10–11). *Example:* "Write a letter to the college senate arguing your position on the campus-wide ban on indoor smoking."

Inform. Present facts, views, phenomena, or events to inform your reader. *Example:* "Inform homeowners about the hazards of lead paint."

Extend. Apply an idea or concept more fully. *Example:* "Extend the production figures to take into account the mechanics' work slowdown."

Trace. Map out a history or chronology, or explain the origins of something. *Example:* "Trace the development of Stalinism."

Discuss. Provide an intelligent, focused commentary on a topic. *Example:* "Discuss citizens' primary objections to the proposed tax hike."

Show. Demonstrate or provide evidence to explain something. *Example:* "Show how transport problems contribute to operating delays."

Exercise 1

Below are two writing tasks, one in the form of a college writing assignment, the other in the form of a work assignment to an intern at a local nonprofit agency. Locate the noun(s) that indicate the *focus* of each task, and find the verb(s) that indicate its *purpose*. Restate the focus and purpose in your own words if necessary.

Sample Assignment: At some point, most people recognize in themselves a prejudice against another person or group. These prejudices often come from stereotypes—inaccurate generalizations made on the basis of limited experience, rumor, or what others tell us. Choose some past action in your life that came out of a prejudice. What was the cause of the action? If the same circumstances arose today, would you behave differently?

Sample Task: Draft a proposal to the State Board on Aging for our planned ElderHelp Transport System. Refer to the current guidelines for contents of the proposal, length, and format. It would be useful to include some information on actual beneficiaries of our plan, so you will want to conduct a few informal interviews with some seniors—possibly ones who use our center. Rose has written successful proposals to the state board in the past, so get her input early. Of course, you should also run your draft past Jim.

3b Using purpose to guide your writing

Now that you've analyzed the general purpose of a writing task, you can begin to consider more specific effects you want your writing to achieve, or your **rhetorical purposes** for writing: what you want your writing to *do* at each stage. Do you want your first paragraph to grab your reader's attention with something really alarming, or is it more important to begin on a cool note of academic objectivity? Do you want to leave your reader hanging at the end by suggesting unexplored questions, or will you wrap everything up with a really strong, thoughtful conclusion?

1 Rough out a purpose structure

As you think about how you want to affect your reader, it helps to plan a general **purpose structure** for your paper's contents. Begin with a few simple categories that correspond to the main parts of your paper or document, such as "beginning, middle, end," or "introduction, body, conclusion." Then explain what each of your categories will *accomplish*. Use verbs that clarify your purpose: "show," "explain," "disprove."

For a student housing guide, Carol Stotsky specified purposes in a tentative plan for her section on housing options.

BEGINNING	Show students why housing options are important for them.
MIDDLE	Explore advantages and disadvantages of each in detail.
ENDING	Recommend that traditional students move gradually from security (home or dorm) to independence (off campus).

This formal purpose structure gave Stotsky a tentative order and direction for her contribution to the student brochure.

Exercise 2

Roz Dane is a nurse practitioner in a family clinic. Clinic physicians have been seeing many patients who have suffered complications from more unusual body piercings, such as tongue studs. In some cases the patients were not aware of the potential complications or dangers. After some discussion, the physicians who own the clinic have asked Roz to produce a short, informative, and purely factual pamphlet on body piercing, which they can make available to patients before they consider various piercings.

Write a purpose statement for Roz's task, and plan a multipart structure for her pamphlet based on that purpose.

3c Defining a thesis or main idea

Most writing has a point, but if that point isn't clear within the first page or so of a text, readers may become frustrated and give up reading.

One way you can be clear about your purposes and avoid bland, generalized prose is to develop a specific **thesis** for your writing, which you then explore, support, or illustrate using specific examples or arguments. Although you'll hear the term *thesis* almost exclusively in college (with terms like *main idea, message, story,* or *point* being used more often in business and community writing), the principle of the thesis remains the same across contexts: a thesis is the controlling idea of a piece of writing. Many college papers contain a thesis statement, usually a single sentence, that appears somewhere early in the text, most often at the end of the first paragraph. In other writing, the thesis may be more subtle, but it still has the effect of telling the reader what the writing will say and do.

1 Turn topics into theses

To develop a thesis from a topic, first try **narrowing** the topic to a specific angle or perspective. Then begin turning the topic from a noun (a "thing") into a statement that contains a verb. Lynn Scattarelli narrowed her topic in an informational pamphlet she designed for a community parenting group.

VAGUE TOPIC	Ritalin
STILL A TOPIC	The use of Ritalin for kids with attention-deficit disorder
STILL A TOPIC	The problem of Ritalin for kids with attention-deficit disorder
ROUGH THESIS	Parents should be careful about medicines such as Ritalin for kids with attention-deficit disorder.

2 Complicate or extend your rough thesis

Early thesis statements often beg for clarification or elaboration. In Lynn Scattarelli's rough thesis, it's not clear what she's suggesting to parents about Ritalin: that it shouldn't be used? that it should be used judiciously? that it's inappropriate for kids with ADD? Answering these questions led her to a more complex and interesting thesis.

FINAL THESIS	Although Ritalin is widely used as a drug treatment for children with attention-deficit disorder, parents should be careful not to overrely on such drugs until they have a complete picture of their child's problem and have explored all the options for treatment.

Lynn complicated her final thesis by accepting Ritalin as a legitimate treatment for ADD. The main point—a caution about overreliance and the exploration of other options—*qualified* or *extended* her rough thesis.

3 Expand your thesis with specifics

Consider using the planning processes described in Chapter 2 to create a series of points or ideas that extend, support, or illustrate your thesis. Start with a simple list—three items, for example—and then work from there. Each item can form a kind of "minithesis" for its paragraph or section, guiding the ideas and focus of that paragraph.

4 Modify your thesis

Don't force yourself to stick too closely to your original thesis. As you plan, you may find yourself entertaining other ideas, especially those that seem to contradict your main idea or thesis. In such cases, your writing may be more interesting if you can qualify your earlier position or perspective, revising your thesis and its supporting ideas.

3d
thesis

Exercise 3

Turn each of the following topics into two different thesis statements.

EXAMPLE

TOPIC   Saw-blade sabotage in the timber industry

THESIS   Spiking trees to sabotage the saw blades of timber workers is both illegal and dangerous, but it should be understood as a subversive act intended to stop further depletion of virgin forests.

THESIS   Protests that include the illegal spiking of trees to sabotage the saw blades of timber workers actually help the timber industry by suggesting to the public that conservationists are less concerned about human safety and human life than about trees.

Topic 1: Grandparents' visitation rights, which allow them to see grandchildren against the parents' will

Topic 2: Gay rights in the Boy Scouts

Topic 3: Metal detectors at public school entrances

Topic 4: Whose fault is road rage?

Topic 5: Laws declaring English the official language of the United States

3d Kinds of thesis statements

Different writing situations or purposes may call for different kinds of thesis statements. Refine your thesis statement so that it serves your purpose and the expectations of your readers.

THESIS STATEMENTS IN THREE COMMUNITIES		
ACADEMIC SETTINGS	**PUBLIC SETTINGS**	**WORK SETTINGS**
Academic thesis statements generally extend or grow from concerns explored in prior research; they may indicate your conclusion and the ways you plan to explain and support it.	Public thesis statements are generally either argumentative (calling for action or arguing for a policy) or informative (explaining policies, procedures, or useful information).	Workplace thesis statements are generally either argumentative (proposing a policy or solution to a problem) or informative (sharing information or explaining procedures and instructions, for example).

- **General thesis.** Readers will expect to learn your conclusions or special perspective on the topic.

  By the time they are teenagers, children pay more attention to their peers' opinions than to those of their parents.

- **Informative thesis.** Readers will expect to learn why the information is worth knowing and how you'll organize your explanation.

  When you search online for financial advice, you should be aware of the three very different kinds of Web sites that offer help.

- **Argumentative thesis.** Readers will expect you to indicate your opinion (your argumentative proposition), perhaps with an acknowledgment of other views on the issue as well.

  Bioengineered crops have some dangers, yet their potential for helping feed hungry people worldwide justifies their careful use.

- **Academic thesis.** Readers will expect you to indicate your specific conclusion and a plan to support it.

  My survey of wedding announcements in local newspapers from 1970 to 2004 demonstrates the extent to which religious background and ethnicity have decreased in importance as factors in mate selection.

3e Recognizing your audience

Many writing experts use the term **audience** to refer to actual or implied readers or listeners. An audience may be one person (such as the city official you address in a letter complaining about the poor condition of the neighborhood sidewalks), or it may be dozens, hundreds, or thousands of people (such as the readers of the newspaper that publishes your letter about the same problem).

Your first question in any analysis of audience will be, "Whom am I addressing?" Is it a flesh-and-blood person you know well? Or is it a shadowy, unknown reader? Is your reader a single person or a large group?

To begin answering these questions, study Figure 3.1 on pages 24–25. This illustration shows an audience continuum, beginning with the most intimate reader on one end (yourself), addressed in journals, diaries, or plans for a personal project, and ending with the remote and amorphous "general community of unknown readers" on the other.

Audiences themselves can also be multiple. A memo requesting personal leave will be read not only by your direct supervisor but by her supervisor as well. Members of your working group will probably receive a copy of the memo, even though they can't make a decision about your request. If your request is approved, the payroll and personnel departments may also see the memo.

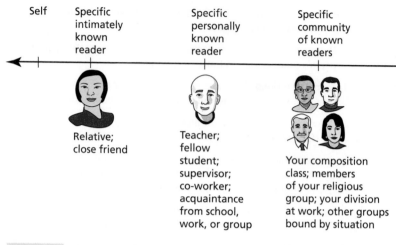

FIGURE 3.1 The audience continuum

Exercise 4

Imagine that you're living on Shell Island, located in a small estuary along the coast of Florida. A favorite winter vacation spot, the area boasts some excellent shelling beaches. But now, after years of ravenous beachcombing, fewer shells appear at low tide, and the area is attracting a more limited variety of birds and other wildlife. The local city council has proposed a general ban on beachcombing and plans to pass an ordinance that would require visitors to obtain a beach permit, at a cost of $30, to use the public beaches. The money would be channeled back into the study and preservation of the local environment.

You're planning to write a position statement on the proposed ordinance. Choose one of the three contexts listed below. Then, referring to the audience continuum, analyze the audience for your position statement. Take a position on the issue, and consider which readers will disagree with your position and why.

Context 1: Surfriders is a small organization for active surfers who visit Shell Island almost daily and are interested in keeping the area clean and safe. Write a letter to Todd Gray, president.

Context 2: Winter Birds is a newsletter sent to retired people who migrate to Shell Island for a few months during the winter. It is published and mailed by a local association for retired people. Write a letter to the editor.

Context 3: Nan Brown is the director of the Shell Island Chamber of Commerce. Business owners, rental agents, and tour operators rely heavily on the Chamber of Commerce for support. Write to Brown.

Specific publicly known reader	Specific unknown reader	Specific community of unknown readers	General community of unknown readers

			Democrats; educated Americans;
Senator Kerry; Ellen Degeneres; president of your university; editor of your local newspaper	Personnel director at Inland Chemicals; editor of the *Journal of Economics*; chair of the university committee on animals in research; others known by title and affiliation	Board of directors at Inland Chemicals; members of the local PTA; the choir's electronic mailing list; readers of *Hunting Magazine;* other groups with shared interests	readers of popular fiction; concerned citizens; working parents

3f Specific readers and communities of readers

Your writing is shaped by how *you* think of your audience and how you understand the communities of interest and purpose to which they belong (academic, public, and work). Constructing audiences also draws on your social and cultural knowledge. For example, if you write to an audience of feminists in a public setting, your knowing that there are many varieties of feminism will complicate your audience, but the result will be a richer and more accurate picture that leads to a better-informed and more incisive piece of writing.

When developing a profile of your audience, be aware that you're dealing with *tendencies.* Not all members of a group or community can be expected to agree with each other, so ask yourself whether you are unfairly stereotyping your reader(s). *Feminism* may suggest one set of policies to some members of an audience (family-friendly workplaces) and a different set to other members (elimination of sexist images in advertising). Or both.

The more specific kinds of knowledge you have (or can gather) about potential readers, the better you can anticipate their likely responses.

ANALYZING YOUR AUDIENCE

Use the following questions to think critically about the nature of your readers as you plan and revise your writing.

1. **Size and relationship.** How large is your audience, and how generalized? How intimately do you know your audience? What sort of relationship do you have to your audience?

(continued)

ANALYZING YOUR AUDIENCE *(continued)*

2. **Prior knowledge.** How much does your audience know about the subject of your writing? Are your readers complete novices or just short of being experts? Do they share your prior knowledge of the subject? Are they young or old? Are they wise or inexperienced and naive?

3. **Physical context.** Where are your readers situated geographically? Is it possible to pinpoint their location? If not, can you generalize about it (e.g., Florida State University, San Francisco, Capitol Hill)?

4. **Social context.** What characterizes your audience socially and culturally? Are your readers educated? poor? middle class? Do they spend their time watching TV or reading books? Do they spend time at singles bars or PTA meetings?

5. **Intellectual disposition.** How would you characterize your readers' way of thinking? Are they highly conservative? radical? apathetic? Where would they stand on certain major issues?

6. **Conditions of reading.** Under what conditions will your audience be reading your writing? Will readers be at home? at school? at the office? Will they be studying your writing closely at a desk or reclining in an easy chair? Will they be busy or distracted? Will time be on their side, or will they be wishing they could buy a few extra hours?

7. **Power.** What is your status relative to your reader? Are you expecting the reader to accomplish something? Is your writing accomplishing something for someone else, such as a supervisor? Is that person also going to read your writing?

Exercise 5

Imagine that your longtime next-door neighbors have sublet their house temporarily. Soon after the renters move in, they begin piling up the yard and driveway with junk cars, old refrigerators, tires, and other debris. The situation becomes so intolerable that you decide to write to the renters, calling attention to the problem. You also decide to write to the local city inspections office, which is responsible for enforcing codes on yard debris.

Write the two short letters, addressing the first to John and Susan Valentine and the second to Betsy Lewis, City Inspections Office. Then analyze the style, tone, and content of your letters. In each case, you were writing to a specific audience. How did their positions on the continuum influence your decisions? What general principles can you infer about the relationship of audience analysis to certain choices you made in your writing style?

3g Adapting to readers and communities of readers

Analyzing an audience can influence many decisions you make as you plan and revise your writing. In particular, consider how audience influences your *genre, content, structure,* and *style.*

- **Genre.** What sort of text should you choose for your writing—what **genre?** People consulting a public handyman site on the Web will not expect a poem or a long philosophical treatise but a clear, concise, and helpful set of tips. Genre choices are especially important because genre often gives you guideposts regarding length, style, structure, and purpose.
- **Content.** What specific information does your audience expect?
- **Structure.** How should you arrange and organize your ideas?
- **Style.** How informal or formal should your writing be? how clinical or emotional? how friendly or hostile? how embracing or adversarial?

Exercise 6

A. Pick a specialized magazine with which you are very familiar (such as *Road & Track, Cooking Light,* or *Wired*). Get a recent copy of the magazine and glance through it, noting the topics, lengths, and formats of its articles; its advertisements; its layout; and its writing style. Then, using the advice outlined in this chapter, select one method for analyzing the magazine's audience. If you can't answer a question definitively, make as educated a guess as possible, and state what further information you'd like to have.

B. Join a group of three or four other students. Briefly describe and compare your magazines, and then discuss your audience analyses. What issues surface about the relationship between the writing and the audience? What problems or questions about audience would you like to discuss?

Visit mycomplab.com for more resources and exercises on purpose, thesis, and audience.

CHAPTER **4**

Drafting

All your planning, purpose, setting, and audience analysis will prepare you to write. But don't expect to sit down and immediately write a smooth, coherent paper simply because you've accumulated a lot of material. **Drafting** is the challenging process of stringing words together into sentences and paragraphs that will make some sense to a reader.

4a From planning to drafting

Your use of various planning strategies should produce enough material to begin drafting. The problem you face at this stage is knowing how and where to begin writing. You need to assess what you have and start turning your material into sentences that move your ideas forward.

1 Draft in manageable parts

The items in your planning materials will usually suggest chunks of text that you can draft in one sitting. Look for specific ideas that suggest paragraphs or sections of your paper. Then choose one idea and write about it, either in draft form or in the form of lists, notes, or sentences. If your fifteen-page paper on the relationship between asthma and ozone levels seems like a daunting task, begin by writing a fairly easy section—for example, two pages summarizing recent research studies.

2 Develop a general structure

The kind of material you're writing may determine the way you organize it. A narrative, for example, will probably be arranged *chronologically* (each event following the previous event in time); an argument may be organized *logically*, by paragraphs supporting some assertion. Whatever you're writing, you need to think about what should come first, second, and third in your paper. Most academic writing will contain at least three parts: an **introduction,** a **body,** and a **conclusion.** This simple structure can help you to make the preliminary decisions about how to group your ideas.

By thinking about this three-part organizing scheme, Amy Burns was able to develop a preliminary structure for a paper on superstition.

INTRODUCTION   Fear; people who believe in superstitions; origins

BODY   Examples of superstitions (black cat, #13, crossing fingers)

CONCLUSION   Truth and falsity of superstitions; mystery surrounding them; concepts of reality

When she began drafting her paper, Burns used this preliminary plan to write an introduction about how superstitions originate in a fear of the unknown.

Many people are superstitious or at least practice some of the bizarre rituals of superstition, but very few know why or have thought about the reason. A lot of people practice superstitions without realizing that what they are doing is superstitious. The biggest percentage of people practice superstition because of a fear of the unknown. You might have heard some superstitions from parents or grandparents, been influenced by school or religion, or perhaps even read about them in books. However or wherever you heard of them, you practice superstitions because you are afraid of what will happen if you do not.

Although the introduction-body-conclusion structure can be helpful, much of the material you will write outside the academic community may require another approach (see the chart on page 30). Petitions, newsletters, sales letters, problem descriptions, status reports, and some Web sites, for example, don't follow a rigid structure with set headings; but readers do have expectations about how such pieces should be organized.

3 Assess your purpose and redraft

Even before you've written a full draft, you may want to stop to think about whether the material is achieving your general purposes for writing (persuading someone of a position, telling a story, explaining how to do something) or your more specific purposes for different parts of your paper (providing information, livening up a paragraph with an anecdote, illustrating a point with an extended example). (See Chapters 3 and 6.) Read your early material and extend, cut, or redraft it to more adequately reflect your intended purposes.

In her paper on superstition, Amy Burns's first *specific* purpose statement was "I want to grab my readers' attention and get them thinking about the nature of superstition." From this statement, she realized that her introduction was informative but too dull. She drafted new sentences and then followed them with her earlier material.

DRAFTING SUGGESTIONS FOR THREE COMMUNITIES

ACADEMIC SETTINGS	PUBLIC SETTINGS	WORK SETTINGS
Consider drafting quickly to set down the links in a chain of reasoning, leaving space to develop detailed discussions, support, and summaries of other interpretations later in the drafting process. Use lists of main points and evidence or informal outlines to maintain the direction of your reasoning as you draft.	Consider creating a list of main ideas and points of information to keep focus on your readers' needs and interests as you draft. Enlist others from your organization or potential audience as respondents during drafting to keep your focus on the ideas and arguments you need to include.	Consider dividing the task according to the conventional sections of a report or other document (see Chapter 21), completing first those sections for which you have the clearest or most complete understanding of information and ideas. When working with a group, consider dividing the work of drafting according to parts of the document or assigning drafts (first, second, etc.) to individuals according to their knowledge and abilities.

Do you knock on wood after making a prediction? Shiver when a black cat crosses your path? Consider the number 13 unlucky? If so, then you have already been swept into the fantasy world of superstitions. Many people are superstitious or at least practice some of the bizarre rituals of superstition, but very few know why or have thought about the reason.

4b Drafting strategies

What makes drafting so challenging? Partly, it's the need to get a complicated job done, finding the right words while you're still figuring out where to begin. It's also dealing with apprehensions, such as feeling the focus slipping away, or thinking your writing isn't working, or revising every sentence instead of moving quickly ahead. You can meet these challenges successfully if you practice some useful techniques for getting words down on the page.

1 Write about your writing

Worrying about your writing probably won't ever go away—even the pros do it. Worrying, however, won't help you write your draft.

Begin drafting not by writing your paper but by writing *about it*. What's foremost in your mind about your paper? What do you hope to do with it? In what possible ways might you start it? As you make these notes, you'll soon find yourself a little less anxious about starting—after all, you *have* started. As your anxiety lessens, you'll find yourself more willing to take risks and try out a few lines.

2 Draft quickly

Another source of frustration comes from the struggle to find the right words. In this situation, you want to gain momentum, to feel that your ideas are smoothly giving way to words.

The solution is to draft quickly. As you begin, don't worry about writing perfect sentences and paragraphs. Just aim to get as much material on paper as you can, right from the start. Writers often find that when they write quickly, they feel a momentum developing, a kind of "flow." If you can type faster than you can handwrite, using a computer may encourage this momentum.

ESL ADVICE: DRAFTING

Paying more attention to grammar, vocabulary choice, and style than to ideas and information while you draft can make your writing harder to do and less effective. As you draft, pay attention first to *what* you are saying and then to *how* you are saying it. You will have time later to revise and correct your grammar and the specific words you have chosen.

3 Semidraft

Some writers can't seem to continue drafting anything for more than a few minutes before they stall out. They can't come up with the words to describe a particular idea, and they get stuck.

Semidrafting is the process of writing full sentences until you feel you're about to stall out. At that point, you simply write the word *etc.* and then continue on to your next point. Or you insert a brief direction to yourself in brackets to remind you what to do when you return to the draft to push that section a little further along.

4 Talk it out or take a break

Sometimes nothing works. You simply can't, at that moment, put coherent sentences together on the page.

Writing isn't like breathing, something you do as a matter of course. It's more like eating, which depends on your appetite. If you simply can't write, no matter how many techniques you try, then don't. Put off your writing until a little later. Just set a time to return to the task—preferably on the same day, but no later than the same time the next day.

STRATEGY   Talk about it with someone

Send an email or talk to someone you know well about your writing project. Expressing your concerns may help you alleviate tension and may even show you some solutions. Your listener may also have suggestions to help you get started.

Exercise 1

Try out one of the Strategies for drafting described in this chapter. Jot down notes about how well it worked. Then compare the results of your experiment in a small group, identifying strategies that seemed to work well.

4c Collaborative drafting

Groups work together in different ways depending on the composition and purpose of the group. A committee formed to revise production standards at a manufacturing plant might consist of department managers who each have an area of expertise, whereas a Sunday school parents' committee might include people who have no experience in running a school but share the goal of increasing enrollment. Each group will distribute writing tasks in the way that seems most efficient for its resources and purposes. If your group is uncertain about how to proceed, consider one of the following suggestions.

1 Do parallel drafting

In **parallel drafting,** your group divides the document so that each member is responsible for drafting a particular section. Members can exchange drafts as they revise and edit. This strategy allows writers with different specializations to work comfortably together yet draw on individual expertise, but it may require one person to act as editor, integrating the drafts.

2 Do team drafting

In **team drafting,** the group agrees on first and second authors for each section. The first author begins drafting and continues until he or she gets stuck. Then the draft passes to the second author, who begins where the first writer stopped. This method works well when the writers share similar ideas and approaches. The drafts are recirculated when the group is ready to revise and edit.

3 Do intensive drafting

Intensive drafting is most successful when you are working with a close friend or colleague. You need to find a location where you can work undisturbed. Decide where each person will start, begin drafting together, and exchange sections at a set time or as each of you finishes a segment. You continue your intensive, undisturbed work—exchanging drafts and reworking the document—until you are both satisfied with the result.

STRATEGY   **Use "track changes" for collaborative drafting**

The "track changes" feature in most word-processing software allows changes to the original draft to appear in a different color on screen. Drafts can be circulated by disk or email, edited by group members using the tracking feature, and returned to the author. Every member's changes will appear (color-coded by editor in some software) in the draft for review.

Exercise 2

Imagine you are part of a student organization that is raising funds for a project in which volunteers read to children in school libraries. Your organization intends to submit a grant proposal to a local philanthropic group. Plan how the members might use the following equipment to draft the proposal collaboratively: telephones, email, computers, fax machines. What steps would be involved in your plan?

4d Drafting: Paper in progress

Recall that Jessica DiGregorio had developed a generalized topic: the consequences of professional contracts on the lives of sports players (see 2d). After listing some possible examples to support this topic, she tried freewriting for a few minutes on selected items in her list. Here is her freewriting passage on the item "What he [her father] had to do as a result of the contract."

- Keep himself fit for five years (meaning?)
- Not indulge in bad habits
- Not stop playing basketball
- Stay clear of strenuous activities to avoid injury

Exercise 3

A. Examine DiGregorio's freewriting. At this point she wanted to use some ideas in her freewriting to begin drafting. What advice would you give her about the ideas she has begun to explore? What other details on the subject of the contract requirements could she include in her rough draft? Is there anything in the freewriting that suggests a good place for this passage in her paper (beginning, middle, or end)?

B. In a small group, compare your responses to Exercise 3A. What elements did the members of your group agree could be profitably expanded from the freewriting as DiGregorio drafts her paper? Was there any consensus about where to place this section of the paper?

Visit mycomplab.com **for more resources and exercises on drafting.**

CHAPTER 5

Revising, Editing, and Proofreading

Because so much of what we read is in a final, published form, we cannot appreciate how many hours the author spent **revising**—considering and reconsidering content and structure, tearing out whole sections and redrafting them, honing and refining paragraphs, polishing the style, and finding just the right words to express a thought. Revision is not simply **editing,** a fine tuning for style, grammar, and problems with sentences and wording. Nor is it **proofreading,** a final-stage cleaning up of typographical errors or a search for missing commas and apostrophes. *Revision* means stepping outside a draft to assess its strengths and weaknesses and then deciding what to expand, clarify, elaborate, illustrate, reword, restructure, modify, or cut.

REVISION HIGHLIGHTS FOR THREE COMMUNITIES OF READERS

ACADEMIC SETTINGS	PUBLIC SETTINGS	WORK SETTINGS
Pay special attention to:	**Pay special attention to:**	**Pay special attention to:**
Clarity of conclusions and thesis statement	Clear statement of policy, cause, or position	Clear statement of problems, solutions, tasks, and goals
Topic sentences and section headings	Relevant and accurate supporting evidence	Explanations and proposals presented concisely and directly
Integration of quotations and supporting information	Direct and clear presentation of ideas and explanations	Factual accuracy
Acknowledgment of competing viewpoints	Fairness of reasoning and in treatment of opposing points of view	Section headings and conventional elements of document
Critical analysis and fresh insight	Focus on actions or solutions	

5a Major revisions

When you begin revising, concentrate on **major revisions,** large-scale changes in your draft. For example, if you've left out a major point, you may need to draft some new material and change your conclusion.

1 Redraft unworkable material

Read through your draft as if you were seeing it for the first time. It helps if you have left your draft alone for a short while so that you can see it afresh. As you read, place a question mark next to sections that seem confusing or garbled. You may need to **redraft** these parts entirely. Go back to the parts you've marked and bracket the specific places where your writing seems to lose its vitality, meaning, or style. Ask yourself what you're trying to accomplish in a particular passage. Then, without even looking at the draft, try again on a new sheet of paper to write what you mean.

Jessica DiGregorio shared with her classmates a draft of her essay reflecting on her father's professional sports contract. They felt the first paragraph didn't capture much tension or create interest, and they placed brackets around sentences that seemed particularly weak. After changing a few words, DiGregorio realized she really needed to redraft the entire paragraph.

ORIGINAL DRAFT WITH BRACKETS FROM PEER GROUP

[A few days ago I decided to go through the musty old cedar chest in my living room and dig up some of the old documents that I had read years earlier.] I came across the Contract marked NBA (National Basketball Association) [that I had looked at before, but remembered that it was very confusing.] It contained words such as: hereunder, however, notwithstanding, and hereof, but when I read this over for the second time it made me realize that my father, [for a total of five years was bound to this document,] and chose to live his life according to what it said.

Jessica's revised introduction appears on page 42.

2 Reorganize poorly arranged paragraphs or sections

Structural problems are common in early drafts. Often you find that you've written your way into your main point, discovering later what you want to say earlier in the draft. Or you may recognize that two paragraphs are making the same point and should be consolidated.

STRATEGY   Summarize your paragraphs

Number each paragraph in your draft. Then, on a piece of paper, explain in a single sentence what each numbered paragraph says (its main point). When you've finished, look back at your list of statements.

- Could any paragraphs be consolidated?
- Are any paragraphs ineffectively ordered?
- Could you arrange the paragraphs or parts of the paper to yield a clearer, smoother flow of ideas?

Keyshawn Williams drafted a section of his paper on the problems of electronic archives. Reading over his draft, he identified the main points of the paragraphs and then arranged the paragraphs in a more logical order. Having done this, he realized that his new paragraphs needed considerable elaboration. He also added a sentence that helped to focus his next two paragraphs.

ORIGINAL

Although most people think that electronic archives can store written documents permanently, they would be surprised to learn that medieval parchment makes a far more lasting medium than computers. In fact, electronic media will begin decaying rapidly.

To create a digital archive that will last without being recopied, you would have to preserve the original system software, hardware, operating manuals, recording devices, and all the other apparatus that did the original archive.

The decay is so rapid that the federal government requires its records to be recopied every ten years and "exercised" once a year. A congressional report notes that there are now only two machines in the world that can read the electronically stored information from the 1960 U.S. Census. Another problem concerns the fact that some records are written in programs that are obsolete, making it impossible to read the data even if the disk is in good shape.

decay

obsolescence

REVISION

Although most people think that electronic archives can store written documents permanently, they would be surprised to learn that medieval parchment makes a far more lasting medium than computers. **There are two main reasons why electronic document storage is highly questionable even as our society plunges into the electronic age.**

First, electronic media will begin decaying rapidly. [Explain why the magnetic medium decays.] The decay is so rapid that the federal government requires its records to be recopied every ten years and "exercised" once a year.

Another problem concerns the fact that some records are written in programs that are obsolete, making it impossible to read the data even if the disk is in good shape. A congressional report notes that there are now only two machines in the world that can read the electronically stored information from the 1960 U.S. Census. To create a digital archive that will last without being recopied, you would have to preserve the original system software, hardware, operating manuals, recording devices, and all the other apparatus that created the original archive.

3 Add new material

Because you may write your first draft quickly, just to get it down on the page, you may find places where something is missing. As you reread your paper, mark any paragraph or sentence that doesn't connect clearly enough to the one before it. Also note any gaps in information or detail. Make a list if you need to add information to your draft (see 2a-2).

Looking over her draft Web page telling employees how to transfer to a new email system, Gina White noticed some gaps and filled them in.

> Your new email address is listed below. It should be easy to remember **because it consists of the first four letters of your name and the last four numbers of your Social Security number.** Our company's address is the same: @Wishfactory.com. You may send your new address to people or discussion groups that send you frequent email, but you don't need to. **Our server will automatically forward any mail directed to your old address.**

4 Delete unnecessary or redundant material

Reread your draft as if an editor has accepted it for publication in a magazine with the stipulation that you trim at least ten percent. Too much prose can be just as distracting or frustrating to a reader as too little. What can you cut? Could some paragraphs be eliminated, perhaps by merging just the essential material from them into another paragraph? (See also 6e.)

Exercise 1

Compare the following drafts of Maureen Lagasse's paper on racism. Describe the nature of Lagasse's changes—did she redraft, reorganize, add, or cut? What do you think motivated her revisions?

FIRST DRAFT

In setting out to write this paper my concept to explain was racism, and in doing some reading and thinking, I realized that racism can't be defined or explained in one simple definition. In the dictionary the definition of racism is "the practice of racial discrimination or segregation, etc." Although this is what racism is, this doesn't fully explain racism. What exactly are races, and how do people actually develop these discriminations against people of different races?

REVISED DRAFT

Have you ever wondered why people view interracial relationships as unacceptable? Have you wondered whether there really is a difference between you and someone of another race? In the dictionary the definition of racism is "the practice of racial discrimination or segregation." Although this is a legitimate definition, it doesn't fully explain racism.

5b Minor revisions

Minor revisions are fairly small changes, mostly in the individual sentences of your prose, with the goal of refining and polishing. Most minor revisions are made for three reasons: *sense* (how clear and understandable is your prose?), *style* (how elegant and smooth is your prose?), and *economy* (how much can you say in the least space?).

1 Revise for sense

Read each sentence of your paper individually and test its clarity: does the statement *make sense* in the context of the paper? Don't let your mind float back into your own construction of ideas; instead, imagine yourself as your intended reader. If you have peer readers, ask them to place question marks next to any statement or group of statements they find confusing or garbled.

2 Revise for style

When you revise for style, you're concerned with the way your prose "sounds"—that is, with its rhythm, complexity, and diction or word choice (see 49b–d). When you read a rough draft, some parts will usually sound better to you than others. Use your intuition as a reader.

In his report on the environmentally threatened wild mustangs of Nevada, Paul Tichey placed an asterisk next to a paragraph he had already revised for sense. Paul liked the clarity of his revision, but the end of his new sentence seemed awkward because so many words began with a *d* ("dehydration and death during the duration of the drought"). He also thought that "during the duration" seemed redundant. Here's his further revision.

The Air Force, which was partly responsible for the demise of the wild mustangs on the Tonopah missile range, has now joined forces with the Bureau of Land Management and a group of wild-horse preservationists to help save the mustangs from **fatal** dehydration ~~and death during the duration of the drought~~ **while the drought persists.**

STRATEGY   Mark paragraphs in need of revision

Place an asterisk in the margin next to any paragraph that seems to need polishing. Then go back to the first paragraph you marked and code each sentence according to what you feel about it: ✦ (positive), ✓ (neutral), ✦ (negative), ? (unsure). Now concentrate on revising the sentences you do not like in that paragraph. Move on to revising the questionable sentences. Reread the entire paragraph. When you are satisfied, go to the next paragraph you marked with an asterisk. If you're still uncertain about any sentence, ask peer readers for their impressions. *When in doubt, try an alternative.*

3 Revise for economy

To revise for economy, read your writing and think about what you can cut from it *without causing it to lose sense or coherence*. In the middle of Paul Tichey's paper, one paragraph included too much material. He decided that half of it could be cut.

5b
revise

SECOND DRAFT

A serious problem confronting groups who want to manage wild mustangs on military sites in Nevada is the relative inaccessibility of the sites, since many require security passes or are fenced off, and environmentalists can't come and go as they please, as they can on public or even some private land. It's simply harder to study or help horses on restricted military installations. Open rangeland has easier access, and inspectors can simply move in and out at will.

THIRD DRAFT

Restricted access to Nevada military sites presents a serious obstacle to successful horse management. In contrast to open rangeland, where inspectors can come and go as they please, military sites are often fenced off and require security clearance.

In the revised paragraph, Tichey said essentially the same thing in thirty-eight words that he had said before in seventy-eight—a cut of over 50 percent!

Exercise 2

Examine the following paragraphs from Anita Jackson's paper on Buddhism. Then characterize the sorts of minor revisions Jackson made. Did she revise for sense, style, or economy? What sorts of changes did she make? How successful were the changes?

EARLY DRAFT

The man who became the first Buddha was named Siddhartha. Siddhartha was a prince in northern India who lived in a large palace. His father didn't allow him outside the palace because he wanted to spare Siddhartha from the miseries of the world.

Siddhartha became curious and one day he went riding outside the palace. What he saw would forever change his life and influence the lives of many thereafter. That which Siddhartha saw has since been named the Four Sights.

REVISED DRAFT

The man who became the first Buddha was Siddhartha, a pampered prince of northern India who lived in a lavish palace. Yet for all his riches his father would not allow him to venture beyond the castle walls because he wanted to spare Siddhartha the miseries of life. Siddhartha grew extremely curious about the outside world and one day went riding beyond the limits of the palace. What he saw that day would forever change his life and influence the lives of many thereafter.

What Siddhartha saw has since been named the Four Sights.

5c Collaborative revising

Professional writers rarely produce a good piece of writing without getting responses from many readers along the way. Follow their lead: *make sure to ask at least one person you respect to read your papers and give you some honest feedback, and promise you'll do the same in return.* Here are tips for getting and giving helpful feedback in **collaborative revision.**

1 Respond helpfully

When you're reading someone else's writing in order to offer constructive criticism, remember that your most helpful role is not as proofreader or editor but as real, warm-blooded *reader.*

- Find out the writer's purpose for the paper. What is the writer trying to accomplish? What sort of paper is this?
- Who is the writer's intended reader?
- What are the writer's main concerns at this point? What would the writer most like to learn from you?

When you have answers to those questions, read the paper through, jotting comments in the margins and keeping track of your thoughts and impressions. Remember you'll need to balance praise with helpful criticism. Don't just say, "I liked it" or give directions like "Move this paragraph up to page 3." Instead, offer diplomatic advice; ask, "What would happen if you moved this paragraph?" or suggest, "I wonder whether that paragraph would fit better on page 3."

2 Make the most of responses

Remember, you're not out to collect pats on the back; you want the most useful, constructive commentary you can get from astute, honest readers. This means accepting even hard-hitting reactions and suggestions with grace and diplomacy. If you react defensively to a peer reader's criticism, that person is not likely to keep giving you much feedback. If a reader questions something you especially like in your draft, *remember that no one can force you to make a change.* You have the final say.

- Give your readers a list of specific concerns you have about your draft. Do you want them to comment on tone? style? structure? logic?

- Keep your apologies to a minimum. You may feel anxious about sharing a first draft, but all writers face the same situation.
- If all of your group members are working on papers at the same time, forming a writer's group and spending time on each of your drafts can be an especially valuable experience.
- Using your readers' responses, *spend some time planning your changes*. A few minutes planning your revisions may save you from fruitlessly experimenting.

3 Workplace collaboration

Collaborative revision is often the norm outside the school setting. However, workplace collaboration may be somewhat different from sharing your draft with classmates.

- In the workplace, many people will have a stake in your text. They are more likely than fellow students to be willing—even eager—to review it for you.
- Supervisors, in particular, may be direct and insistent about making certain changes.
- It helps to solicit responses from individuals with a range of perspectives and kinds of knowledge about your topic or problem.

ESL ADVICE: REVISING WITH A PEER READER

If you are worried about your grammar or spelling, you might want to review these items quickly before sharing your rough draft. Look for a peer reader who is willing to ignore these details. Ask this reader to focus on specific issues (such as the order or development of your ideas) or on problems you often have in your papers (such as weak first paragraphs). Consider sharing your draft with several readers, including native speakers of English, to get a range of responses.

Exercise 3

A. If you haven't done so, form a small revision group and circulate rough drafts of your papers in progress. Using the tips in this section as well as the techniques for major and minor revision described in 5a and 5b, comment on your partners' drafts. Then meet in a revision group to discuss your drafts. Keep track of the group's comments on your own paper.

B. Analyze your group experience. What was helpful? What comments will lead (or have led) to specific revisions? What comments did you choose not to act on? Why?

5d Revising: Paper in progress

After semidrafting several paragraphs about items on her list of particulars, Jessica DiGregorio wrote the following full rough draft of her paper about her father's sports contract.

First Draft of Sports Contract Paper

Jessica DiGregorio

A few days ago I decided to go through the musty old cedar chest in my living room and dig up some of the old documents that I had read years earlier. I came across the Contract marked NBA (National Basketball Association) that I had looked at before, but remembered that it was very confusing. It contained words such as: hereunder, however, notwithstanding, and hereof, but when I read this over for the second time it made me realize that my father, for a total of five years was bound to this document, and chose to live his life according to what it had said. This twelve-page "AGREEMENT" caught my attention from the time I was young, but it did not make sense to me until now.

When I was younger I never took interest in my father's past mainly because I was tired of hearing people telling me "Did you know your father was the best basketball player?!" and "If you could have seen him play!" I used to just smile and not say anything because I never thought my father could be an athlete as good as Michael Jordan or Larry Bird. My perspective on his basketball career changed as I got older, I became interested in watching videos of him and asked him questions on what it was like to be a basketball legend.

"CLUB DOES HEREBY EMPLOY PLAYER AS
A SKILLED BASKETBALL PLAYER"

This statement which was said on the first page of his contract set the setting for all of the other statements that followed. Since the NBA decided that my father was good enough to play the sport, a contract was made to fit the needs of both the Club (the Buffalo Braves) and the Player (my father). After my father read the first line he was honored and knew that all of his hard work and determination had paid off. The Club which drafted him in 1973 knew that he was a person of great charisma and talent including basketball legend Red Auerbach. This contract was the beginning of a five-year long agreement which was taken very seriously.

"HE WILL TO THE BEST OF HIS ABILITY MAINTAIN HIMSELF IN
PHYSICAL CONDITION SUFFICIENT TO PLAY SKILLED BASKETBALL"

This rule stated in the contract meant that my father had to keep himself fit for the next five years, and not allow himself to overindulge in bad habits. The Club made up this rule to insure themselves that they were signing someone who was serious about the game. This meant that my father had to stay physically fit and never stop playing basketball. He was advised to stay clear of skiing, ice-skating, or any other strenuous activity not related to basketball so that he would not get injured. If my father, or any other player disobeyed this part of the contract it stated that, "the club shall have the right to suspend the player for a period of one week . . . and will be examined by a physician."

"IN THE EVENT OF THE DEATH OF THE PLAYER PRIOR
TO THE TERMINATION OF ANY SEASON . . .
THE CLUB SHALL PAY TO THE PLAYER'S HEIRS . . ."

This particular part of the contract interested me the most. It stated that if my father had died, all of the money which was already promised to my father within the contract went to my mother. This was very important to my father since my mother was a housewife and stayed home with my older sisters. The Club added this statement to the contract to give the player's family the proper amount of financial help after the loss of their loved one. Basically after the death of a player the money which was promised throughout the five year term is terminated and the family only received what the player lived for. If there was to be a breach in the contract then lawyers would have had to be appointed to the family of the deceased, and determining where money goes can be a sticky situation if it is not written down and documented properly.

"THE CLUB SHALL HAVE THE OPTION IN ITS SOLE DISCRETION
TO TERMINATE THIS AGREEMENT AND RENDER IT NULL AND VOID"

This final part in this contract stated that the Club had the final say in any of the decisions that would have come along. This meant my father had to follow all of the requirements made within the document which he had signed. If he or anyone else did not follow any of the regulations, then they would have no say if their contract was to be null and void. This left the final power up to the Club and gave them the upper hand in everything that dealt with the players. This was an important part of his contract because it allowed the Club to demonstrate how powerful it really was in the make or break of a person's professional basketball career.

Contracts and legal documents shape our everyday life. Some people underestimate the power of legal documents which bind and connect us to different things. A single piece of paper can determine where we live or how we live our lives. The contract which bound my father to the NBA shaped his life in a major way. For five years he lived by rules and regulations created by the Club to which he belonged. He became a basketball legend and lives in the memories of some people, but to me he is just my dad.

Exercise 4

A. Study Jessica DiGregorio's first draft. Assuming that she has drafted with a loose structure in mind, how would you describe that structure? What is your impression of the draft as a whole, and what suggestions would you make for its organization and its supporting points relative to the main goal of examining her father's NBA contract?

B. In a small group, compare your analyses of DiGregorio's first draft, and try to reach some consensus about what she should focus on in her revision.

5e Editing your own writing

After making major and minor revisions in your writing (see 5a–b), you should turn your attention to editing. **Editing** means fine-tuning your work for a reader—adjusting sentences and words for clarity, for precise meaning and effect, and for correctness. It means identifying problems in grammar and sentence structure as well as glaring omissions or repetitions. And it means looking for consistency in style, punctuation, word usage, and tone.

Successful editing also means recognizing and using the conventions of specific communities. For example, a scientist would use numerals (such as *12* or *84*) for the numbers in a lab report, while an art historian might spell out *twelve* or *eighty-four* in an interpretive paper. Many workplace communities use particular "local" conventions, and you'll need to adapt your writing to those contexts.

Often, editing requires you to keep in mind a certain concern (commas, for example, or sexist language) while you scour your entire text for specific cases. It's hard to look for too many kinds of problems at once. Sometimes you may need to read your text four, five, six, or more times, keeping in mind a different cluster of concerns for each reading.

Editing for style and correctness calls for a special kind of reading, one that shifts away from content (what's being said) and toward form (how it's being said). Focus on each sentence, and scrutinize it for smaller stylistic concerns, grammar, and punctuation. Problems, inconsistencies, and errors will emerge, and you *must* fix them before your paper can be considered finished.

1 Final editing for economy and style

Even after major and minor revisions have tightened the focus, most papers can still profit from some final cosmetic surgery. If any part of a sentence adds little or nothing to style or meaning, eliminate it during a final check for redundancy or wordiness.

NEAR-FINAL DRAFT	In actual fact, the aligned pulleys are lined up so that they are located up above the center core of the machine.
	READER'S REACTION: This seems repetitive and confusing.
EDITED	The aligned pulleys are **positioned** above the **machine's core.**

STRATEGY   Edit for economy and style

- **Are my sentences reasonably easy to read?** Try reading out loud. Whenever you stumble over wording, try rephrasing or restructuring.
- **Do any words stand out as odd or inappropriate for my purpose?** Try to choose a more appropriate word. Consider turning to a dictionary or a thesaurus for help (see 49e).
- **Have I used some sentence structures too often?** Try varying sentence structures. For example, do almost all sentences begin with nouns or with a pronoun like *I*? Then try starting some sentences with prepositional phrases or subordinate clauses.
- **If I had to cut ten words from each page, which ones could I eliminate?** Cut if you can do so without creating new problems in style (such as short, choppy sentences) or meaning.

Exercise 5

In a brochure-writing assignment, Kim Francis drafted the following paragraph for a pamphlet describing tourist attractions and accommodations near her Wisconsin home. Read the paragraph once for meaning and then a second time for editing. During the second reading, ask some of the questions listed in the preceding Strategy. Then edit the paragraph to make it more effective.

> After spending a day exploring the countryside, rest and relax at a quaint country inn, relaxing by the fire and sipping on some mulled wine. After spending a quiet night in a room decorated with beautiful old antiques, wake up to a country breakfast. Then after your pleasant stay at the inn, explore the quaint towns and roads that have made Door County, Wisconsin, such an attractive vacation destination for people who like to escape and get away from it all.

2 Editing for grammatical problems

When you edit for grammatical problems, first you need to *identify* or *recognize* a problem, and then you must *edit* your prose to fix the problem.

Identifying known errors. Read your paper slowly from start to finish but don't become immersed in the ideas. Instead, look carefully and deliberately at each paragraph, circling or marking any errors in grammar, punctuation, and sentence logic. If you can quickly correct an error along the way, do so. If you're not certain how to correct the error, wait until you've finished identifying problems; then refer to the appropriate sections in this handbook or ask a teacher or a knowledgeable peer for advice.

"Before" and "after" passages from Jim Tollefson's newsletter article on the Endangered Species Act for his local conservancy group show his circled errors (labeled in the margins) and his edited version.

DRAFT WITH ERRORS IDENTIFIED

caps/fragment/
apostrophe
Who?/comma
splice

Critics of the endangered species act think it is too broad. Because some specie's may be less vital to environmental balance than others. They want to protect species selectively, however, scientists still do not know which species are more important.

EDITED

Critics of the Endangered Species Act think it is too broad because some species may be less vital to environmental balance than others. These critics want to protect species selectively. However, scientists still do not know which species are more important.

SERIOUS MISTAKE

Serious mistakes. Here is a list of the ten mistakes many instructors are likely to consider quite serious because they confuse or irritate readers. Refer to the section of the text listed in parentheses for more information on identifying or correcting the mistake. (See also Chapter 34.)

SERIOUS
MISTAKE

TEN SERIOUS MISTAKES

1. **Fragment** (34a and 40a)
   The heavy rain turned the parking lot to mud. **And stranded thousands of cars.**

2. **Fused Sentence** (34b and 41b)
   The promoters called **the insurance company they discovered** their coverage for accidents was limited.

3. **Unclear Pronoun Reference** (34c and 42a-b)
   After talking with the groundskeeper, the security chief said **he** would not be responsible for the safety of the crowd.

4. **Lack of Subject-Verb Agreement** (34d and 38a-b)
   Away from the microphone, the mayor said, "I hope the security chief or the promoters **has** a plan to help everyone leave safely."

5. **Dangling Modifier** (34e and 42b)
   After announcing the cancellation from the stage, the crowd began complaining to the promoters.

6. **Shift** (34f and 44a)
   If **people** left the arena quickly, **you** could get to **your** car without standing in the rain.

7. **Misused or Missing Apostrophe** (34g and 55a)
   Even the **promoters promise** to reschedule and honor tickets did little to stop the crowd's complaints.

8. **Unnecessary Commas** (34h and 51j)
   Although, the muddy lot caused problems, all the cars and **people, began** to leave.

9. **Missing or Misused Quotation Marks** (34i and Chapter 54)
   "The grounds are **slippery, the** mayor repeated, "so please walk carefully."

10. **Double Negative** (34j and 39d)
    The authorities were relieved because they **hadn't scarcely** enough resources to cope.

Identifying suspected errors. You may suspect that you've made an error but aren't sure. *Don't take a risk.* Check the rule or convention, and edit accordingly.

STRATEGY   Create an editing checklist

Create an editing checklist of problems or errors that you often encounter in your writing. Apply the checklist to each paper you write. Begin by analyzing your own papers and by giving samples of your writing to a teacher or expert writer. Ask that person to identify *patterns* of errors in your writing, and also look for them on your own. Using this handbook, study the errors and try to identify their causes. Then create your own strategies for recognizing the errors, and turn them into a personalized editing checklist for your papers and other writing.

After editing her paper on the effects of loud music, Carrie Brehe added three items to her editing checklist.

1. A lot—sounds like one word but is actually two. Think of an entire "lot" full of whatever. Think of the opposite of a little. Search for all cases of alot.

2. Their vs. there. Sound the same. I usually write "there" for "their" when I make this mistake, but not the reverse. "Their" is possessive only, and "there" is location. Search for all cases of there/their.

3. If they would have known. I say this a lot (ha!). I'm still not sure what the subjunctive means, but this problem shows up when I write "if." Correct to "if they had" or "if they were." Search for all cases of "if + would."

Identifying unknown errors. A final category of mistakes consists of those you have no idea you're making.

Read your writing, preferably aloud. Sometimes this will help you to locate problems intuitively. Or you may recognize them because you encounter difficulty reading a passage. Circle everything you question; then use the Strategy on page 47 to check suspected errors. Add *all* previously unknown errors to your editing checklist (see above).

Ask someone to read your paper and to mark or circle any problems he or she encounters. Your reader doesn't need to be a grammarian to call attention to problems with sentences, usage, and the like. Because they're not as close to the text as you are, these readers may find problems you overlooked.

5f Collaborative editing

When you edit collaboratively, you identify and talk about specific problems in a paper with one or more consulting readers, usually friends or peers. Your goal is not just to rid your paper of errors but to learn to identify and correct errors on your own.

Exercise 6

On the day your teacher returns drafts or finished papers with comments, look for any errors he or she has noted. Working in groups of three or four, read each other's papers, looking for patterns of error. Compare these patterns and, as a group, try to write "rules" explaining how to fix them. In creating the rules, feel free to use your own terms and ways of explaining. Add any new items to your editing checklist.

COLLABORATIVE EDITING GUIDELINES

GUIDELINES FOR WRITERS

- Revise content and organization first to prepare your draft for editing. (Or ask your reader for feedback on larger revisions instead. See 5a.)
- Supply a clean draft; don't waste your reader's time on sloppiness.
- Share your requirements or writing concerns with your reader.

GUIDELINES FOR READERS

- Use familiar labels and symbols for comments. (The terms in this handbook are generally accepted in academic, public, and work communities. See the list of symbols on the inside back cover.)
- Just note possible errors. Let the writer use a dictionary, a style guide, or this handbook to identify and repair each problem.
- Be specific; *awkward* or *unclear* may not tell the writer exactly what's wrong. Briefly tell why something does or doesn't work.
- Identify outright errors, but don't "take over" the draft. Rewriting sentences and paragraphs is the writer's job.
- Look for patterns of error, noting repetition of the same mistakes.

5g Editing on the computer

Editing has its share of "quick fix" remedies. Among the most attractive are computer programs that "read" a piece of prose and then tell you how to correct or improve it. Before using or buying such a program, learn something about what it can and can't do.

1 What computer editors can do

When examining an editing program, see whether it will meet your specific needs. Use the following questions as a guide.

- Does the program identify errors in spelling, punctuation, capitalization, and usage? Does it identify incorrect sentence structure? How reliable are the identifications?
- Will the program alert you to unclear sentences, problems with subject-verb agreement or modifiers, sexist or discriminatory language, and vague expressions?
- Is it linked to a spell checker, thesaurus, dictionary, synonym finder, or other utility? Will it identify clichéd or vague expressions and commonly misused words?
- Does it allow you to design and add your own rules, tailoring the program to your editorial needs and to meet the conventions of use within your writing community? Does it reflect the expectations of a particular community, such as business readers and writers?

2 What computer editors can't do

Although they may claim to answer most of your writing problems, computerized editing programs are no match for human readers and editors. Most programs will alert you to a potential problem but leave you to identify and repair it yourself. The programs provide few options for different kinds of writing or for audiences that differ in sophistication and background knowledge. Beware, therefore, of blanket pronouncements from the program. They may be inappropriate for your writing situation.

5h Proofreading

After you've made as many conscious decisions about your writing as possible and you are ready to submit it, it's time for **proofreading,** looking for errors you may have missed during the editing process. No writer produces an absolutely flawless document every single time. As the slips accumulate, however, your credibility diminishes, and that can ruin the effectiveness of your ideas and lead to a poor assessment of your work.

When proofreading, you submit a piece of writing to a meticulous reading. Focus consciously on every word of your document. Don't let your eyes blur; move from word to word, fixing your eyes on each word to be sure it doesn't contain transposed letters, typographical errors, and the like. Use a spell checker. Or try reading your writing out loud. Every error you identify is a prize catch that increases your credibility.

When working in public settings, it also helps to have several people proofread separately to catch as many errors as possible.

Exercise 7

Two versions of a paragraph follow—one in an unedited form, the other partly edited. Without looking at the edited version, read the unedited draft as an editor would. Scrutinize the passage ruthlessly, making any corrections you wish and explaining them in a notebook. Then compare your editing with the changes made in the second paragraph. What differences do you find between your editing and the writer's editing?

UNEDITED DRAFT

At the start of her career, historian Barbara Smithey, felt forced to choose between a life of: public service vs. research. As curator of the Westville Museum of New England culture in Westville, Ct, she was passionately devoted to preserving or restoring old houses in disrepair and seeing to it that they were entered if they qualified into the National Register of Historical Places. At the same time, she had a kean interest in research on the town of Westville which had been settled in the early 17th-Century. She manfully seized control of all public documents on the area, that were not already protected and got them housed in the local historical archives. These included, some early notes about the Indian savages that the White men encountered when they settled the land. Also some personal diaries lady settlers kept.

EDITED DRAFT

At the start of her career, ~~h~~*the* historian Barbara Smithey, felt forced to

choose between a life of public service ~~vs.~~ *and* research. As curator of the

Westville Museum of New England Culture in Westville, ~~Ct~~ *Connecticut,* she was

passionat~~l~~*e*ly devoted to preserving or resto~~r~~*re*ing old houses in disrepair

and seeing to it that they were entered (if they qualified) into the

National Register of Historical Places. At the same time, she had a

ke~~e~~*e*n interest in research on the town of Westville , which had been

settled in the early ~~17th-Century~~ *seventeenth century.* She ~~manfully~~ seized control of all

public documents on the area , that were not already protected and ~~got~~ *had*

them ~~housed~~ *placed* in the local historical archives. These included , some

early *settlers'* notes about ~~the Indian savages that the White men encountered~~ *local Native Americans, as well as*

~~when they settled the land. Also~~ some personal diaries , *of women settlers.* ~~lady settlers kept.~~

---

mycomplab

Visit mycomplab.com for more resources and exercises on revising, editing, and proofreading.

Paragraphs

Every time you begin a new **paragraph,** you send a signal to readers: you tell them to watch for a shift in topic, a different perspective, or a special emphasis. Whether you're writing an essay for a history class, a memo at work, or a letter to the editor, you need to create paragraphs with a clear *focus* (*unity*), *coherence* among sentences, and adequate *development* of ideas and content. If you fail to do these things, your readers may have trouble deciding what a paragraph is about and following your reasoning from sentence to sentence, as in this example.

> The caffeine in popular beverages comes from natural sources: coffee beans (coffee), tea leaves (tea), evergreen leaves (maté), and kola nuts (colas). Tea comes from the leaves of bushes native to Asia. Maté comes from a South American shrub similar to holly. More caffeine is found in coffee or tea than in maté. Tea and maté are made in similar ways except that the water for maté is heated in a gourd. People often drink the beverage through a straw stuck into the gourd. In Paraguay, Argentina, Chile, and the southern regions of Brazil, many people find refreshment in a maté-filled gourd.
>
> READER'S REACTION: What is the topic of this paragraph: tea and coffee? caffeine? caffeinated beverages? maté? Every time one sentence focuses on a topic, the next sentence suddenly changes direction.

By making the relationship among and within paragraphs clear, you can help readers keep track of a line of argument or the logic of an explanation.

6a Focused paragraphs

By making a paragraph's topic, main idea, or perspective clear to your reader, and by maintaining this focus throughout, you can create a paragraph that is focused or unified. A **focused paragraph** doesn't confuse or mislead readers by straying into unrelated details. In a **unified paragraph,** all the sentences are clearly and directly related to the main idea.

STRATEGY Revise unfocused paragraphs

Use the following questions to identify and revise any unfocused paragraphs in your draft.

- What is my main point (or topic) in this paragraph?
- How many different topics does this paragraph cover?

- Have I announced my focus to readers? Where? How?
- Do statements in the paragraph elaborate on the main idea? Do details fit within the topic?

6b Creating paragraph focus

To bring focus to a paragraph, you need to decide what you want the paragraph to do for readers. Do you want it to announce and explain your conclusion or recommendation? Do you want it to explain a concept or process? Do you want it to support your arguments on an issue?

One way to keep a paragraph focused as you write, and to help readers recognize that focus, is to state your topic and your main idea or perspective in a single sentence, a **topic sentence.** As you write, you can use a topic sentence as the focal point for the other sentences in a paragraph. When you revise, you can often easily improve an unfocused paragraph by adding a topic sentence, placing it in an effective position in the paragraph.

PARAGRAPHING STRATEGIES FOR THREE COMMUNITIES

ACADEMIC SETTINGS	PUBLIC SETTINGS	WORK SETTINGS
Use introductory paragraphs to announce a thesis, to indicate the method of discussing and supporting the thesis, and to summarize prior research.	Use introductory paragraphs to highlight a situation requiring action or to introduce a need for information or changes in policy. Use concluding paragraphs to summarize recommendations or to call for action.	Use introductory paragraphs to outline a problem or to describe a situation requiring response from members of an organization.
Use paragraphing to indicate stages in the chain of reasoning and different kinds of supporting evidence, and use clear topic sentences and transitional expressions to announce steps in reasoning and to highlight evidence.	Develop paragraphs with examples, narratives, and causes or effects that appeal to values and emotions while providing clear support for a thesis or necessary information.	Use concluding paragraphs to restate the importance and implications of the proposed actions or policies.
Develop relatively long paragraphs, presenting and discussing detailed evidence and integrating supporting or competing points of view through quotation, paraphrase, or summary.		Develop problem-solution or question-and-answer paragraphs to focus readers' attention on tasks and goals

1 Topic sentence at the beginning

When you want readers to grasp the point of a paragraph right away, state it in a topic sentence at the beginning.

Topic sentence

Supporting example

When writing jokes, it's a good idea to avoid vague generalizations. Don't just talk about "fruit" when you can talk about "an apple." Strong writing creates a single image for everyone in the crowd, each person imagining the same thing. But when you say "fruit," people are either imagining several different kinds of fruit or they aren't really thinking of anything in particular, and both things can significantly reduce their emotional investment in the joke. But when you say "an apple," everyone has a clear picture, and thus a feeling.

—JAY SANKEY, "Zen and the Art of Stand-up Comedy"

2 Topic sentence plus a limiting or clarifying sentence

If you're covering a broad topic or offering much detailed information, you can create a **limiting** or **clarifying sentence** (or two) following the topic sentence, to tell readers which specific aspects of the topic you will discuss or to clarify your point of view.

Topic sentence

Clarifying sentence

In the Marine Corps appearance counts mightily, today as always. The corps insists that "no eccentricities of dress will be permitted" even in civilian clothes, and of course "the wearing of earrings by male Marines, under any circumstances, is prohibited." Likewise, when in uniform or out of it, Marines must obey certain specific rules about personal grooming. "No eccentricities in the manner of wearing head, facial, or body hair will be permitted." And there's official advice presumably aimed at female Marines, but nice to contemplate if aimed at all: "If worn, wigs will comply with grooming regulations."

—PAUL FUSSELL, *Uniforms*

3 Topic sentence at the end

A topic sentence at the end of a paragraph can summarize or draw conclusions from the information that comes before. This strategy can show how your perspective grows logically from the evidence, and it can tie together details with a forceful generalization.

Album after album was littered with rap songs referring to Black women as bitches, gold diggers, hos, hoodrats, chickenheads, pigeons, and so on. Music videos with rump shaking, scantily clad young Black women as stage props for rap artists soon became synonymous with rap music. Though dominated by what feminist critic bell hooks called "sexist, misogynist, patriarchal ways of thinking and believing" (*Z Magazine*, February 1994), rap lyrics simultaneously addressed every gender issue imaginable from dating, gender equality, and domestic violence to rape and sexual harassment. Due to its role in shaping a whole generation's worldview, including our ideas about sex, love, friendship, dating, and marriage, rap music is critical to any understanding of the hip-hop generation's gen-

Topic sentence der crisis. **More importantly, rap music is one of the few existing arenas where the full range of gender issues facing young Black men is documented in the voices of Black youth themselves.**

—BAKARI KITWANA, *The Hip-Hop Generation*

ESL ADVICE: ADJUSTING TO PARAGRAPH CONVENTIONS

In English, readers expect paragraphs to have a specific focus and often look to a topic sentence for guidance. In other languages, however, paragraph conventions can take quite different forms. For example, Hindi paragraphs need not focus on a sharply defined topic, do not require a clear topic sentence, and often contain discussion of loosely related ideas or information. Paragraphs in other languages, such as Thai, also differ from English paragraphs. Consequently, become familiar with paragraph conventions as you learn to write in a second language.

—ROBERT BICKNER and PATCHARIN PEYASANTIWONG, "Cultural Variation in Reflective Writing," and YAMUNA KACHRU, "Writers in Hindi and English," *Writing Across Languages and Cultures*, ed. Alan C. Purves (Newbury Park: Sage, 1988) 160–74, 109–37.

4 Topic sentence implied rather than stated

At times, the main point is so clear that you can rely on readers to recognize it without a topic statement. Omitting a topic statement is useful when you don't want to state a very obvious point or when an explicit statement might distract from examples and details. This strategy is also helpful when a topic clearly continues for more than one paragraph.

Whenever we went to my grandfather's house, he would lead the three of us to the closet stocked with toys, saying "I bought these especially for you" as his crystal blue eyes twinkled. I can remember playing with the toys outside on the lawn and running through the sprinkler he set up for me and my brothers on sunny days. Just when we started getting tired and hot, he would call us in for a lunch of hot dogs or tuna sandwiches with plenty of potato chips and soda pop. And there were always popsicles for dessert.

—CAREY BRAUN, College Student

READER'S REACTION: Your grandfather seems like a person who understands children and knows how to make them feel cared for and loved.

Exercise 1

Identify any topic sentence and clarifying or limiting sentence in the following paragraph. Analyze how the paragraph makes use of these sentences to create focus and emphasis.

Kids are in the mall not only in the passive role of shoppers—they also work there, especially as fast-food outlets infiltrate the mall's enclosure. There they learn how to hold a job and take responsibility, but still within the same value context. When *CBS Reports* went to Oak Park Mall in suburban Kansas City, Kansas, to tape part of the hour-long consideration of the mall, "After the Dream Comes True," they interviewed a teenaged girl who worked in a fast-food outlet there. In a sequence that didn't make the final program, she described the major goal of her present life, which was to perfect the curl on top of the ice-cream cones that were her store's specialty. If she could do that, she would be moved from the lowly soft-drink dispenser to the more prestigious ice-cream division, the curl on top of the status ladder at her restaurant. These are the achievements that are important at the mall.

—William Severini Kowinski, "Kids in the Mall:
Growing Up Controlled"

6c Paragraph coherence

When your readers can move from sentence to sentence within a paragraph without any trouble following your train of thought or explanation, the paragraph displays **coherence.** Lack of coherence comes from abrupt changes in your topic from sentence to sentence, or from a lack of transitions or other devices to guide readers from statement to statement.

LACKS COHERENCE

Captain James Cook discovered the island of Hawaii in 1779. Mauna Kea, on Hawaii, is the tallest mountain in the Pacific. Cook might have noticed the many mountains on the island as he sailed into Kealakekua Bay. The island also has five major volcanoes. Mauna Loa, another mountain on the island, is a dormant volcano that last erupted in 1984. Kilauea is the most active volcano on earth. It continues to enlarge the land that makes up this largest island in the Hawaiian chain. The volcano sends forth lava continuously.

READER'S REACTION: This paragraph jumps from sentence to sentence without saying much about the way the ideas and details fit together.

STRATEGY   Test paragraphs for coherence

- Does the paragraph highlight the topic and the main points?
- Do transition words alert readers to relationships between sentences?
- Do parallel words and structures highlight similar or related ideas?
- Do sentence beginnings identify a topic and stick to it?

6d Creating paragraph coherence

1 Repeating words and phrases

By repeating words and phrases that refer to your topic and main point, you keep readers aware of a paragraph's focus and you link one sentence to another. Synonyms and related words can also be part of a pattern of effective repetition.

2 Supplying transitions

You can use **transitional expressions,** statements, and paragraphs to alert readers to relationships among sentences and paragraphs and to highlight a paragraph's design and purpose.

Note how the use of transitions makes this paragraph easy to read, while repeated words and phrases (underlined) clarify the focus.

> Many people still consider the choice of college the most important career decision you can make. **These days, however,** graduate school is the most important choice **because** the competition for all kinds of jobs has gotten fiercer. **For example,** business positions at the entry level often go to people with MBAs and law degrees. **In addition,** many good jobs require advanced training and skills. **Moreover,** employers pay attention **not only** to the presence of an advanced degree on your résumé **but also** to the program of study **and** the quality of the school. **Therefore,** think about going to graduate school, **and** choose your school carefully.

To help present detailed reasoning or information, consider opening paragraphs with a **boundary statement**—a sentence at the start of a paragraph that acts as a bridge from the paragraph before. A boundary statement begins with a reminder of material covered in the preceding paragraph (or paragraphs). It then presents the topic sentence of the paragraph to come. For example, in the following sentence the writer briefly mentions the subject he has just finished discussing and then highlights the main point of the paragraph itself.

> **The rise of the Sunbelt** in recent years has been accompanied by **the decline of rural America.**
> —BRAD EDMONDSON, "Making Yourself at Home"

In short essays, simple transitions or boundary statements generally provide adequate guidance for readers. In longer essays or complicated discussions, you may need to give readers extra guidance with one- or two-sentence transition paragraphs.

TRANSITIONAL EXPRESSIONS

TIME AND SEQUENCE	next, later, after, while, meanwhile, immediately, somewhat earlier, first, second, third, shortly, thereafter, in the future, over the next two days, concurrently, subsequently, as long as, soon, since, finally, last, at that time, as soon as
COMPARISON	likewise, similarly, also, again, in the same manner, in comparison
CONTRAST	in contrast, on one hand . . . on the other hand, however, although, even though, still, yet, but, nevertheless, conversely, at the same time, regardless, despite
EXAMPLES	for example, for instance, such as, specifically, thus, to illustrate, namely
CAUSE AND EFFECT	as a result, consequently, since, accordingly, if . . . then, is due to this, for this reason, as a consequence of
PLACE	next to, above, behind, beyond, near, across from, to the right, here, there, in the foreground, in the background, in between, opposite
ADDITION	and, too, moreover, in addition, besides, furthermore, next, also, finally
CONCESSION	of course, naturally, it may be the case that, granted, it is true that, certainly
CONCLUSION	in conclusion, in short, as a result, as I have demonstrated, as the data show
REPETITION	to repeat, in other words, once again, as I said earlier
SUMMARY	on the whole, to sum up, in short, to summarize, therefore

3 Using parallel structure

You can link elements within a paragraph by using **parallelism**—repeating the same grammatical structures to highlight similar or related ideas (see also 46b). Note how the parallel words and phrases in the following paragraph create coherence.

I have a place on the West Coast **where** my relatives still farm, **where I heard** the stories of feuds and backbiting, and **where I saw** that people **survived and flourished** because fundamentally they **trusted and relied** upon one another. **A death in the family** is not just **a death in a family;** it is a **death in the community. I saw people** help each other with money, materials, labor, attention, and time. **I saw men** gather once a year, without fail, to clean the grounds of a ninety-year-old woman who had helped the community **before, during,** and **after** the war. **I saw her** remembering them with birthday cards sent to each of their children.

—KESAYA E. NODA, "Growing Up Asian in America"

Exercise 2

A. In the following paragraph, increase coherence and readability by repeating words, adding transitions, using parallel structures, and making any other changes necessary.

Heart attacks have many causes. Some heart attacks occur because a blood clot closes a coronary artery. Sometimes a mass of fatty substances (plaque) has the same effect. Heart attacks with these causes are the most frequent. A spasm in an artery may also close it and prevent blood from reaching the heart. Smoking, hypertension, and diabetes can create conditions that keep blood from reaching the heart. The blood-starved tissue may die. This will cause permanent damage to the heart's ability to pump blood. A dead portion of the heart is called a myocardial infarction.

B. Copy a paragraph from one of your own essays, scrambling the order of the sentences, and then exchange scrambled paragraphs with a fellow student. Rewrite and strengthen your partner's paragraph by putting the sentences in the most effective order and revising to increase coherence among sentences.

6e Developed paragraphs

Paragraph development provides the examples, facts, concrete details, explanatory statements, or supporting arguments that make a paragraph informative and supportive of your ideas and opinions.

Suppose you encountered the following paragraph at a public Web site on choosing a pet. How would you react?

Dogs and cats make wonderful pets, but certainly not trendy ones. Exotic animals of all kinds, including Vietnamese pot-bellied pigs and llamas, have begun appearing in living rooms and backyards.

READER'S REACTION: The paragraph has a clear main point and a potentially interesting example but seems skimpy and uninteresting. Without supporting details, the paragraph is neither informative nor convincing.

1 Developing paragraphs with details

Fully developed paragraphs give readers an in-depth picture of a subject when this is necessary for the purpose and context of the writing. Your readers will usually expect two kinds of statements in a paragraph: those presenting ideas (including your own conclusions) and those presenting information. Beyond this, however, you have many choices, depending on what you want a paragraph to do.

CHECKLIST FOR DEVELOPING PARAGRAPH CONTENT

- **Examples.** Use brief, specific examples or an extended, detailed example.
- **Concrete details.** Recreate sights, sounds, tastes, smells, movements, and sensations of touch.
- **Facts and statistics.** Offer precise data from your own field research or from authoritative sources, perhaps in numerical form. Summarize the results or quote your sources. Facts and statistics are the kinds of evidence many readers consider convincing proof of generalizations and opinions. They also help readers understand complicated social and natural phenomena.
- **Summaries.** Summarize other people's opinions, conclusions, or explanations (21l). Tell how they agree with and support your conclusions. Or point out their omissions and weaknesses as a way of arguing for your own conclusions or insights.
- **Quotations.** Use statements you have gathered from field, electronic, or library research (27e) to support your conclusions or to make your discussion more dramatic and memorable.

Rely on examples. Whether brief or extended, examples are effective strategies for paragraph development because they help you clarify difficult concepts, provide good reasons for readers to agree with your opinion, or show how widespread a phenomenon is. Extended examples can draw readers into an event and connect with their emotions. Brief examples can play important roles, especially in work and public settings where readers have little patience for long explanations but still expect you to justify your opinions and recommendations. Brief examples can be particularly effective when blended with facts and statistics.

Interpret for your readers. When you use examples, details, facts, and statistics to develop a paragraph, you can make them more persuasive and easier to understand by providing interpretive statements of your own to link them to the paragraph's main point.

> Breakfast cereals can differ radically in serving size even though most cereal boxes define a single serving in the same way, as a one-ounce portion. A one-ounce serving of Cheerios is $1^1/_4$ cup, for example, while a one-ounce serving of Quaker 100% Natural Cereal is $^1/_4$ cup. Weight measurements can disguise the differences between products; measurement by volume reveals the contrasts. For dieters, volume

Interpretive statement

can be as important a measure as the number of calories per serving because the volume indicates how much cereal you will have to appease your appetite: two bites or a bowlful.

—SARA BRILLIANT, College Student

Exercise 3

First, examine the paragraph in Exercise 2A and identify the various strategies of development used by the writer. Which seem particularly effective, and why? Which, if any, seem ineffective?

Next, for each of the following topic sentences, explain which kind or kinds of supporting information (examples, concrete details, facts and statistics, or supporting statements) you believe would help to create the most effective paragraph.

1. The fall promotional campaign increased sales of our October and November issues.
2. Upgrading our computer software would result in more efficient handling of our customer accounts.
3. Increased funding would enable us to extend our after-school basketball program for preteen boys and girls.
4. Should our budget surplus be used to fund additional hours at the senior center or to assist meal-delivery programs?

2 Creating paragraph structures

How will you arrange the content of your paragraphs? **General patterns of development** such as narration, comparison, and cause and effect offer you ways to develop a paragraph's content as well as its arrangement.

PATTERNS FOR PARAGRAPH DEVELOPMENT

TASK	DEVELOPMENT STRATEGY
Tell a story; recreate events; present an anecdote	Narrating
Provide detail of a scene or object; portray someone's character; evoke a feeling	Describing
Explore similarities or differences; evaluate alternatives	Comparing and contrasting
Provide directions; explain the operation of a mechanism, procedure, or natural process	Explaining a process
Separate a subject into parts; explore the relationships among parts	Dividing

(continued)

PATTERNS FOR PARAGRAPH DEVELOPMENT *(continued)*	
Sort things or people into groups; explain the relationships among the groups	Classifying
Explain the meaning of a term or concept; explore and illustrate the meaning of a complicated concept or phenomenon	Defining
Consider why something happened or might happen; explore possible causes and consequences	Analyzing causes and effects

Narrating. Turn to **narration** to recount past or present events, recreate an experience, tell an anecdote, or envision the future.

Describing. You can create images of a place, an object, or a feeling or sketch a person's character through **description,** emphasizing emotional impact (**subjective description**) or physical details (**objective description**).

Comparing and contrasting. Paragraphs that **compare** and **contrast** can evaluate alternative policies or products, examine pros and cons, or compare qualities and explanations. A **point-by-point organization** examines each comparable feature for first one subject and then the next.

Topic sentence   But biology has a funny way of confounding expectations. Rather than disappear, the evidence for innate sexual
Feature 1   differences only began to mount. In medicine, researchers
documented that heart disease strikes men at a younger
Feature 2   age than it does women and that women have a more mod-
Feature 3   erate physiological response to stress. Researchers found
subtle neurological differences between the sexes both in
Feature 4   the brain's structure and in its functioning. In addition, another generation of parents discovered that, despite their
best efforts to give baseballs to their daughters and sewing
kits to their sons, girls still flocked to dollhouses while boys
clambered into tree forts. Perhaps nature is more important
than nurture after all.

—CHRISTINE GORMAN, "Sizing Up the Sexes"

A **subject-by-subject organization** considers each subject in its entirety, within a paragraph or a series of paragraphs.

Topic sentence   For everyone, home is a place to be offstage. But the
Subject 1   comfort of home can have opposite and incompatible meanings for women and men. For many men, the comfort of
home means freedom from having to prove themselves and
impress through verbal display. At last, they are in a situation

where talk is not required. They are free to remain silent. But
Subject 2 for women, home is a place where they are free to talk, and
where they feel the greatest need for talk, with those they are
closest to. For them, the comfort of home means the freedom
to talk without worrying about how their talk will be judged.
—DEBORAH TANNEN, "Put Down That Paper and Talk to Me!"

Explaining a process. To give directions, show how a mechanism or procedure works, or explain other processes, label the steps or stages clearly. Arrange them logically, usually chronologically. Devote a paragraph to each part of the process if you wish to emphasize its stages.

Dividing and classifying. When you divide a subject, you split it into parts, explaining it and the relationships of its parts. To classify, you sort several subjects into groups, exploring similarities *within* groups and differences and relationships *between* groups.

CLASSIFICATION

Men all have different styles of chopping wood, all of which are deemed by their practitioners as the only proper method. Often when I'm chopping wood in my own inept style, a neighbor will come over and "offer help." He'll bust up a few logs in his own manner, advising me as to the proper swing and means of analyzing the grain of the wood. There are "over the head" types and "swing from the shoulder" types, and guys who lay the logs down horizontally on the ground and still others who balance them on end, atop of stumps. I have one neighbor who uses what he calls "vector analysis." Using the right vectors, he says, the wood will practically *split itself.*
—JENNIFER FINNEY BOYLAN, "The Bean Curd Method"

Defining. When you introduce a term or concept to your readers, you may need to stipulate the meaning it will carry in your writing or want to contrast its definition with others.

You can eat lunch at a food court, as in any other restaurant, but a food court has some special traits. Go to a food court to see but not be heard. The open space jammed with tables will give you a chance to see and be seen, yet the clatter and bustle will make real conversation impossible. Food courts are world tours—Thai, Mexican, Chinese, and Italian with a side of sushi—where you can buy hot dogs, nuggets, and chocolate chip cookies. The quality beats a fast-food outlet but not a good restaurant. For two dollars more than a burger and fries and seven dollars less than a tablecloth and a waiter, food courts deliver a meal that comes somewhere in between.
—BIPIN ROY, College Student

Analyzing causes and effects. You may explain why something has occurred (causes), explore consequences (effects), or combine both.

Television used to depress me with forecasts of stormy weather, losers on game shows, and dramas of failed love. Then I learned to control the future. What caused me to acquire this skill? One day, upset with my favorite team's losing ways, I turned the television off and sat on the couch imagining a great comeback. Now when people ask me why I turn off the set before the end of a show, I tell them that this way my imagination can reunite long-separated lovers, help contestants with prize-winning answers, and create an upcoming week of warm, sunny days without a drop of rain.

—Dazhane Robinson, College Student

Exercise 4

A. Choose one of the following pairs of topics. Drawing on your own knowledge, develop each topic into a paragraph, using the pattern of development indicated in brackets.

1. A paragraph about finding a part-time or summer job [process] and a paragraph on a memorable person [description or narration]
2. A paragraph exploring different outlooks on the relationships of parents and children [comparison-contrast] and a paragraph providing advice about dealing with a difficulty in parent-child relationships [question and answer]
3. A paragraph identifying the differences between educational requirements, expected income, and working conditions for two jobs (such as restaurant manager and doctor, or teacher and chemical engineer) [comparison-contrast] and a paragraph exploring a common work or college problem and offering possible solutions [problem-solution]
4. A paragraph identifying the reasons some students do well (or poorly) on tests [cause-effect] and a paragraph describing a good way to study for tests [process]
5. A paragraph exploring views people hold about taking buses and driving cars [subject-by-subject comparison] and a paragraph identifying differences between educational requirements, expected income, and working conditions for two jobs [point-by-point comparison]

B. Working in a group, identify the patterns of development in the following paragraph. There may be a single dominant pattern or more than one. Explain how each pattern or combination is used.

None of the foreign geologists had ever encountered anything quite like the disaster at Lake Nyos. Our earliest hypotheses seemed to be almost as numerous as the scientific teams present. Some workers, impressed by the accounts of survivors who reported smelling rotten eggs or gunpowder and hearing explosions, were convinced that a volcanic eruption beneath the lake had released sulfurous gases. Others, including me, suspected that the gas had come from within the sediments on the lake bed. Eventually, though, geological and chemical investigations made it obvious that the lake had released carbon dioxide from within its own waters—independent apparently of any other process. Like an enormous bottle of soda water, it belched and fizzed gas from its depths.

—SAMUEL J. PREETH, "Incident at Lake Nyos"

6f
¶ dev

6f Introductory and concluding paragraphs

The paragraphing strategies you use to divide the body of an essay or report into parts don't work for beginnings or conclusions. For them you need special-purpose paragraphs.

1 Creating introductory paragraphs

In the opening paragraphs of an essay, report, or public document, you create a relationship with your readers, inviting them to learn about a subject, explore ideas, address a problem, or examine a line of argument.

TWELVE WAYS TO DEVELOP AN EFFECTIVE INTRODUCTORY PARAGRAPH

PROVIDE BACKGROUND
Provide background information on a topic or problem; present an issue in context; give the history of the subject.

TELL A STORY
Open with a brief anecdote or story.

OUTLINE A PROBLEM
Outline a problem, danger, or challenge.

EXPLAIN AN ISSUE
Present all sides of an issue, along with any particularly well-known or controversial events relevant to the topic.

PRESENT A SITUATION
Describe a situation, a set of relationships, or recent events that require some response from readers or an organization to which they belong.

OFFER A DEFINITION
Define an important concept or term that will recur throughout the piece.

(continued)

> ## TWELVE WAYS TO DEVELOP AN EFFECTIVE INTRODUCTORY PARAGRAPH *(continued)*
>
> ### ASK A QUESTION
> Present provocative questions or opinions that require further discussion.
>
> ### USE AN EXTENDED EXAMPLE
> Start with an extended example related to the topic and main idea.
>
> ### PRESENT A QUOTATION
> Quote from an authority or from someone whose opinion leads into the topic or highlights key ideas.
>
> ### MAKE A COMPARISON
> Highlight the importance of a topic or issue by comparing it to another situation, historical period, subject, or issue; offer an intriguing analogy.
>
> ### PROVIDE STATISTICS
> Supply facts and statistics that introduce the topic or that help define an important issue or problem.
>
> ### DESCRIBE A MYSTERY
> Present a mysterious or interesting phenomenon worth exploring or explaining.

ANECDOTE   It was advertised as the biggest non-nuclear explosion in Nevada history. On October 27, 1993, Steve Wynn, the State's official "god of hospitality," flashed his trademark smile and pushed the detonator button. As 200,000 Las Vegans cheered, the 18-story Dunes sign, once the tallest neon structure in the world, crumbled to the desert floor.

—MIKE DAVIS, "House of Cards"

Davis introduces the environmental threat posed by Las Vegas culture.

2 Creating concluding paragraphs

Paragraphs that conclude essays should generally remind readers of key ideas and encourage them to think about information or proposals you have presented. The following paragraph illustrates one strategy used in concluding paragraphs.

SUMMARY OF MAIN POINTS

So if it's any consolation to those of us who just don't manage to fit enough sleep into our packed days, being chronically tired probably won't do us any permanent harm. And if things get desperate enough, we just might have to schedule a nap somewhere on our busy calendars.

—DANIEL GOLEMAN, "Too Little, Too Late"

EIGHT WAYS TO DEVELOP AN EFFECTIVE CONCLUDING PARAGRAPH

SUMMARIZE MAIN POINTS

Review the main points briefly; a detailed summary will seem repetitive.

RESTATE THE THESIS

Put the thesis in different words to drive home the essay's main point.

RECOMMEND ACTIONS OR SOLUTIONS

Repeat, for emphasis, the specific solutions, policies, recommendations, or actions proposed in the text, perhaps summarizing them in a list.

PREDICT FUTURE EVENTS OR SPECULATE

Look at relatively clear consequences, not those requiring explanation; keep speculations interesting but not so provocative that they require extensive discussion.

PROVIDE A QUOTATION

Use a quotation that makes key ideas memorable or supports your conclusions.

OFFER A STRIKING EXAMPLE, ANECDOTE, OR IMAGE

Supply a mental picture or brief narrative to reinforce an essay's message.

ECHO THE INTRODUCTION

Use this echo to create a sense of completion.

RESTATE IMPLICATIONS

Review the implications of actions or policies discussed in the text.

Exercise 5

A. Revise the following concluding paragraph to make it more effective.

I probably have left out some of the arguments for and against gun control, though I think I have covered the main ones. The point I really want to stress most is that gun control is a difficult question. Simple proposals such as banning all handguns or getting rid of all regulations won't work. We need new ideas that balance the rights of gun owners with the right to be free from violence and crime. Though I have not explained it in detail, we probably need a program like the national registration and education system that has been recently proposed. And we certainly need to do something about the many handguns readily available to teenagers.

B. Have each of the members of a writing group bring in a popular magazine containing relatively long articles. As a group, examine the articles and choose three openings and three conclusions that you consider successful. Identify the strategies used in each.

Visit mycomplab.com for more resources and exercises on developing paragraphs.

CHAPTER 7

Sentences

Effective sentences are generally clear, direct, and emphatic. You can achieve these qualities in a variety of ways.

7a Clear sentences

Generally, the clearest sentences answer the question "Who does what (to whom)?"

	subject	verb	object

CLEAR   The research team investigated seizure disorders in infants.
               Who?   does what?   to whom?

CLEAR   The seizures often become harmful.
               Who?   does what?

SENTENCE STRATEGIES FOR THREE COMMUNITIES OF READERS

ACADEMIC SETTINGS	PUBLIC SETTINGS	WORK SETTINGS
Use direct, clear sentences for statement of thesis or conclusions and for summaries of others' research.	Use direct, clear sentences to present key ideas, recommendations, information, or proposed actions.	Use direct sentences with significant subjects and specific verbs, especially when discussing problems, solutions, or key ideas.
Use emphatic sentence patterns to highlight relationships among ideas and supporting information.	Use clear and specific verbs.	Consider using *I, we,* and *you* frequently to establish direct contact with readers.
Consider using *I* or *we.*	Prefer active to passive voice.	Prefer active to passive voice.
Avoid excessive nominalization and use of passive voice.	Limit use of nominalizations.	Limit use of nominalizations, noun strings, and expletive structures.
Use summative and resumptive modifiers.	Use sentence variety and emphasis to keep an audience attentive and involved.	

Many well-written sentences are more complicated than those that move directly from subject to verb (to object), yet they are still clear when they help readers to answer the question "Who does what (to whom)?"

1 Use significant subjects

Sentences with subjects that name important ideas, people, topics, things, or events are generally easy for readers to understand. To create sentences with significant subjects, ask "What (or whom) am I talking about in this sentence?" and "Is this the subject I want to emphasize?" Consider this sentence from an essay titled "Should You Try to Get a Tan?"

UNFOCUSED
The greatest risk comes from exposure to a tanning machine as well as the sun because both of them can damage the skin.

READER'S REACTION: I thought this essay was about the dangers posed by sunbathing and tanning salons. Why are these subjects buried in the middle of the sentence?

POSSIBLE
REVISION
Either **the sun or a tanning machine** can damage the skin, and the greatest risk comes from exposure to **both** of them.

2 Avoid unnecessary nominalizations

When you create a noun from another kind of word, the result is a **nominalization.** A verb like *complete* can become a noun like *completion;* an adjective like *happy* turns into a noun like *happiness.* Some nominalizations play important roles in effective sentences, often naming ideas and issues essential to a discussion; others act as stumbling blocks for readers.

USEFUL
NOMINALIZATION
Distractions like television and lights (for reading) keep us up at night, robbing us of the hours of sleep previous generations enjoyed.
Distractions, a nominalization, comes from *distract,* a verb.

VAGUE
Dissatisfaction among employees often leads to shoddiness in products.
Nominalizations created from adjectives may lead to vague statements, as is the case here with *dissatisfaction* and *shoddiness.*

REVISED
Dissatisfied employees often make shoddy products.
The new verb, *make,* specifies the action more clearly.

STRATEGY Revise nominalization problems

As you write or review a draft, pay attention to nominalizations that

- Draw readers' attention away from a sentence's proper focus
- Lead to vague sentence subjects or objects
- Cause you to leave important information out of a sentence

Replace inappropriate nominalizations with words indicating a clear and significant subject (or object), and name the sentence's action (did what?) in the verb.

COMMON NOMINALIZATIONS

Spotting nominalizations can be difficult at first, but you can quickly turn this search into a useful habit. Words ending in -*tion*, -*ence*, -*ance*, -*ing*, and -*ness* are often nominalizations. Here is a list of common nominalizations.

NOUN	VERB	ADJECTIVE
analysis	analyze	
appropriateness		appropriate
beginning	begin	
calculation	calculate	
comparison	compare	
convenience		convenient
delivery	deliver	
denial	deny	
guidance	guide	
investigation	investigate	
opening	open	
openness		open
preference	prefer	
solution	solve	
suggestion	suggest	

3 Use *I*, *we*, and *you* as subjects

Although *I*, *we*, and *you* are often inappropriate in academic and professional writing, there are many settings in which these pronouns can act as clear subjects in effective sentences.

Using *I*. When you are the subject of an essay, when you are speaking directly to readers, or when you are reporting on your own investigations or conclusions, *I* is an appropriate subject.

> In designing the survey, **I** avoided questions likely to embarrass respondents.

Adding statements like *I think* and *I feel* when you are already clearly stating your point of view, however, makes your writing more wordy but not more effective.

Using *we*. *We* is appropriate when you use it to report the actions of a group or to discuss experiences you as a writer share with most readers.

> **We** [North Americans] consume a large portion of the world's resources.

Using *you*. *You* is appropriate when used to mean "you, the reader." Consider using *people, individuals*, or a similar word if your reader will incorrectly assume you are referring to him or her and not to people in general.

APPROPRIATE   Before asking people to complete the survey, **you** should test it on a few individuals to identify any flaw in the design.

INAPPROPRIATE   According to an article in *Rolling Stone*, **you** were less drawn to the 1960s British rock invasion if **you** lived in the Midwest than if **you** lived on the East or West Coast.

READER'S REACTION: I was born in 1990. Is the author writing to my parents?

REVISED   According to an article in *Rolling Stone*, **people** were less drawn to the 1960s British rock invasion if **they** lived in the Midwest than if **they** lived on the East or West Coast.

4 Be careful with strings of nouns

In a **noun string,** one noun modifies another. Or nouns plus adjectives modify other nouns.

ADJECTIVE	NOUN	NOUN	NOUN
	computer	network	server
triple	bypass	heart	surgery

Familiar noun strings can help you create concise yet clear sentences. Unfamiliar noun strings, however, can make sentences hard to understand. Readers may have trouble deciding which noun represents the focal point.

CONFUSING   The team did a ceramic valve lining design flaw analysis.

READER'S REACTION: Did the team analyze flaws or use a special procedure called flaw analysis? Did they study ceramic valves or valve linings made of ceramic material?

One solution is to turn the key word in a string (usually the last noun) into a verb. Then form the other nouns into prepositional phrases.

REVISED   The team **analyzed** flaws **in** the lining design **for** ceramic valves.

Another strategy involves turning one noun into the subject.

REVISED   **Flaws** in the lining design for ceramic valves were analyzed by the team.

This version highlights the subject being analyzed.

Exercise 1

Revise the following sentences to create clear subjects and make the sentences easier to understand.

EXAMPLE

We expect   to
~~Our expectation is that~~ athletic shoes will look good as well as feel comfortable.

1. Our expectation is that our elected officials will look like the populations of people they represent.
2. Fifty years ago, election of only one gender of people, male, and of only one race, white, was possible.
3. Today, politicians boast of every level of our government's racial and gender diversity.
4. Choice between candidates is on the basis of their stand on the issues, their media savvy, and their ability to communicate.
5. Choice of candidate is not always based on race, in other words.

5 Use clear and specific verbs

Clear, specific verbs can make sentences forceful and easy to understand. Overuse of the verb *be* (*is, are, was, were, will be*) can lead to weak sentences. Always consider replacing forms of *be* with more forceful verbs.

WEAK   Our agency is responsible for all aspects of disaster relief.

STRONGER   Our agency **plans, funds,** and **delivers** disaster relief.

Look for predicate nouns (nominalizations) you can turn into clear, specific verbs (see 7a-2). Eliminate general verbs (*do, give, have, get, provide, shape, make*) linked to nouns by turning the nouns into verbs.

WEAK   Our company **has done a study** of the new design project and **will provide funding** for it.

STRONGER   Our company **has studied** the new design project and **will fund** it.

6 Keep subjects and verbs clearly related

Clear subjects and verbs play key roles in effective sentences. When key sentence elements are separated by long phrases, readers may find the sentence difficult to understand.

The veterinary association / in response to concern about the costly facilities required by new guidelines for animal care and disposal of medical waste / has created a low-cost loan program for its members.

7b Direct sentences

A direct sentence structure moves from subject to verb (to object). An indirect sentence structure uses an **expletive construction** (*there is*, *there are*, or *it is*) to control the arrangement of the words. Much of the time, expletive constructions make your sentences wordy and hard to understand.

EXPLETIVE   It is important for us to increase community awareness.

REVISED   We should increase community awareness.

An expletive construction may also enable you to withhold information about the "doer," the person or thing responsible for an action. You need to decide whether this is appropriate, given your context and purpose, or whether you are omitting details important to your readers.

DOER NOT
NAMED   There was considerable debate over whether to build
                 a new library or renovate the old one.

DOER NAMED   Members of the fund-raising committee debated whether to
                 build a new library or renovate the old one.

You can sometimes use expletive constructions to good effect. By waiting until late in a sentence to name the subject, you can create suspense and surprise. And you can use expletives to introduce topics that will be taken up in following sentences. (See 7d-3.) A sentence with an expletive construction may also be the clearest and most precise way to make a statement.

Historians used to believe that a sudden invasion by shepherding tribes caused major changes in the region's culture. Now, however, **there is** new archaeological evidence that the "invasion" was actually a gradual resettling that took about a century.

ESL ADVICE: THERE IS AND THERE ARE

Academic writing in English often contains sentences beginning *there is* or *there are*. Sometimes the strategy is appropriate; often, however, the sentences are hard to write and read. Whenever you can, avoid opening sentences with these words so that your sentences are easier to write and read.

Exercise 2

A. Rewrite the following sentences, using clear verbs to make them easy to understand.

EXAMPLE

induces stress
Negotiating ~~is a stress-inducing experience~~ for many people in business.

1. Negotiating, regarded by many experts as an important element in successful business careers, especially on the executive level, is not offered as a course at many colleges.
2. Included among the programs offered by our company is a course in professional negotiation. It is considered to be very useful.
3. We also give demonstrations of how to prepare effective proposals, counter-offers, and other negotiation-related documents.
4. Our consultants can, if a company wishes, provide training for both small and large groups.
5. It is generally agreed that the training program is a confidence builder for many people.

B. Work with several other writers to turn the sentences in Exercise 2A into a clear, forceful paragraph that a consulting company might include in a pamphlet advertising its services. Add material if necessary to produce an effective paragraph, and combine or rearrange sentences as appropriate.

7c Emphatic sentences

You want your readers to notice the most important ideas and information in a sentence. In drafting and revising, you can highlight this material by placing it at the beginning or end of a sentence, by presenting it in a special sentence pattern, or by using the passive voice in a careful manner.

1 Use sentence beginnings and endings

A reader's attention gravitates toward sentence beginnings and endings. Shift material you wish to emphasize to a sentence's opening or closing.

UNEMPHATIC   Gases produced during the cheese-making process by the "eye former," a bacterium, create the holes in Swiss cheese.

REVISED   **The "eyes,"** or the holes in Swiss cheese, are created during the cheese-making process by gases produced by a bacterium, **the "eye former."**
Words at the beginning and end emphasize the unusual names. The verb shifts from active to passive voice (see 7c-3).

2 Create emphatic sentence patterns

Inverted sentence order, climactic order, periodic sentences, and cumulative sentences—which you've seen many times in your reading—all offer ways to create emphasis.

Inversion. By inverting the normal subject-verb-object/complement word order, you can shift the focus of a sentence. **Inverted sentence order** often calls attention to the element you have moved to the initial position.

INVERTED   **From the darkness near the rear of the auditorium thundered the director's voice** with criticisms of our acting.

NORMAL   **The director's voice thundered** from the darkness near the rear of the auditorium with criticisms of our acting.

Because inversion creates emphasis in part by disrupting a reader's expectations for sentence order, overuse of it or other exotic sentence arrangements will confuse or irritate readers.

Climactic order. Using **climactic sentence order**—in which elements build to a climax—can create powerful emphasis, especially on the last item.

What every truly modern home has, she said, is a dishwasher, a gas grill, a Jacuzzi, **and a divorce.**

Periodic sentences. A **periodic sentence** piles up phrases, clauses, and words at the beginning, delaying the main clause of the sentence. The suspense casts a spotlight on the main clause.

Because she knows that inspired designs often spring from hard work, because she loves perfection yet fears failure, and because she believes that risk-taking does not eliminate attention to detail, Jennifer is working eighteen hours a day on her fall clothing collection.

The risk, of course, lies in delaying so long that the reader loses track of the meaning.

Cumulative sentences. To build a **cumulative sentence,** you start with the main clause, then add details and statements in the form of modifying phrases, clauses, and words. The main clause provides a firm base to which you can add details and ideas, bit by bit.

A cumulative sentence allows you to build a detailed picture, an intricate explanation, or a cluster of ideas and information.

Main clause	Varna stumbled down the stairs,
Details	the flowerpot falling from her grip,

**7c
sent**

Details   spilling dirt into the air,
Details   shattering on the linoleum floor just seconds before she landed
                 among the shards of pottery and fragments of geranium,
Details   the loud thud bringing everyone in the house to attention.

3 Use the passive voice with care

When a sentence's verb is in the active voice (see 36e), the doer (or agent) is also the subject of the sentence.

> doer   action   goal
> The outfielder caught the towering fly ball.
> subject   verb   object

When you choose the **passive voice** for the verb form, you turn the sentence's goal into the subject and make naming the doer optional.

> goal   action   doer
> The towering fly ball was caught [by the outfielder].
> subject   verb   prepositional phrase

Using the passive voice, you de-emphasize the doer by placing it in a prepositional phrase or by dropping it altogether (see 36e). In addition, you create sentences that are generally wordier than corresponding versions in the active voice.

If you wish to emphasize the *doer*, use the active voice. If you wish to draw readers' attention to the goal or outcome of an action rather than its doer, consider using the passive voice.

ACTIVE   **Poorly trained contract workers** caused the explosion and fire at the refinery.
                Subject emphasizes cause.

PASSIVE   **The explosion and fire** at the refinery were caused by poorly trained contract workers.
                Subject emphasizes result.

You can also use the passive voice to highlight significant elements in a discussion.

Refineries are potentially dangerous workplaces. **Most accidents** can be prevented, however, by careful training of workers.
Passive voice in the second sentence keeps attention on the dangers.

You can choose whether or not to name the doer in a sentence written in the passive voice. When the doer is unknown, unimportant, or obvious, you can omit it.

Federal income tax forms will be mailed on January 1.
By the IRS, of course.

Exercise 3

A. Revise the following sentences to eliminate passive voice.

EXAMPLE

Grocery stores sell many

~~Many~~ different kinds of ice cream ~~are sold by grocery stores.~~

1. The superpremium ice cream brands are chosen by many people.
2. More butterfat and less air is contained in superpremium ice cream than in regular ice cream.
3. The high fat content ought to be considered before the ice cream is purchased.
4. The rich, tasty ice creams are being challenged by the new frozen dessert products.
5. Frozen yogurts with candy and nuts mixed in have been heavily promoted.

B. Examine the following passage carefully and identify the strategies the author uses to create emphasis. Then share your responses.

Moral decisions are a unique kind of decision. When you're picking out products in the grocery store, searching for the best possible strawberry jam, you are trying to maximize your own enjoyment. You are the only person that matters; it is your sense of pleasure that you are trying to please. In this case, selfishness is the ideal strategy. You should listen to those twitchy cells in the orbitofrontal cortex that tell you what you really want.

However, when you are making a moral decision, this egocentric strategy backfires. Moral decisions require taking other people into account. You can't act like a greedy brute or let your anger get out of control; that's a recipe for depravity and jail time. Doing the right thing means thinking about everybody else, using the emotional brain to mirror the emotions of strangers. Selfishness needs to be balanced by some selflessness.

—JONAH LEHRER, How We Decide

7d Revising for variety

Too many sentences of similar length, type, and structure can create unemphatic writing that bores readers. Variety helps. Many of the strategies that create emphasis (see 7c) can also create variety, and the two qualities often go together.

1 Vary sentence length

Revision is a good opportunity to pay attention to varying the length of sentences. Use short sentences for dramatic contrast and for emphasis.

Create longer sentences to explore relationships among ideas and to add rhythmic effects to your prose. Use middle-length sentences as workhorses, carrying the burden of explanation and description.

Note how variety in sentence length helps make this explanation easy to read and interesting.

> The real country ham may or may not be smoked after curing. Smithfield, Virginia, hams are smoked over hardwood or hardwood sawdust. Unscrupulous producers use smoke flavoring. But Mac Pierce, who runs the country's largest retail pork market, Nahunta Pork Center in Pikeville, North Carolina, says less than 1 percent of his hams are smoked, and most of those are bought by northerners. "Smoke masks a good ham's flavor," says Mac.
>
> —BILL NEAL, "How to Cure a Pig"

The sentences contain twelve, ten, five, thirty-six, and eight words, respectively.

2 Vary sentence types

It's easy to get into the habit of using only **declarative sentences,** sentences that make statements (see 35d for sentence types). An occasional exclamation (**exclamatory sentence**), a mild order (**imperative sentence**), or a question (**interrogative sentence**) can vary the pace of your prose effectively, making it more lively and memorable.

VARIED

Some of the less familiar sports offer good opportunities for entertainment and exercise. <u>Are you looking for fast-paced, thrilling events?</u> Go see a soccer game, a lacrosse match, or a bicycle race. <u>Do you want strenuous exercise and vigorous competition?</u> Sign up for a rugby team, a badminton class, or a squash league. To benefit from these activities you need only take a simple step: Get involved!

A **rhetorical question** (underlined in the example) is one that requires no answer or that you plan to answer yourself in the course of an essay.

ESL ADVICE: SENTENCE VARIETY

You may be tempted to use and re-use sentence patterns with which you are comfortable. Readers are likely to consider overuse of a limited number of patterns monotonous, however. As you write, and especially as you revise, analyze the sentence patterns you use regularly. Then consider introducing more variety to add emphasis and interest to your writing.

3 Vary sentence structures and patterns

You can create variety by blending sentence structures in your writing (use simple, compound, and complex sentences; see 35d) and by varying the kinds of coordination and subordination you employ (see Chapter 47). You can also create variety by using periodic and cumulative sentence patterns and inversion (see 7c-2). By trying different sentence openings (see 7c-1), you can make sure your sentences vary in arrangement.

EXPLETIVE | Then there was the time we painted our house.

PHRASE | **Looking for a bargain,** we bought paint at a discount store.

PHRASE | **The paint having been cheaply made,** the house began peeling within a year and a half.

DEPENDENT CLAUSE | **If you want to be happy with a paint job,** spend the money for quality materials.

TRANSITIONAL EXPRESSION | **In addition,** choose the color carefully.

Exercise 4

Rewrite the following passage to add variety. You may wish to re-arrange the order of statements, to cut or add words, or to combine some sentences and divide others.

Psychologists have been studying what events people remember. People from middle age on remember events from their early years more clearly than they remember more recent events. People in their seventies have clear memories of their thirties but less clear memories of their fifties. Most of us remember very little about child-hood. Almost no one remembers events from before four years old. Researchers think that we tend to remember events that are new or exciting to us and to forget routine events. Memorable events are most likely to occur early in life. Infants probably have not developed the mental abilities necessary to create memories, however.

4 Create surprise

Good writing often employs strategies that intrigue readers. **Summative modifiers, resumptive modifiers,** and **antithesis,** which change—or seem to change—the direction of a sentence, are particularly effective at creating surprise and interest.

A **summative modifier** summarizes the preceding part of a sentence and then sends it off in a new direction.

To protect your vegetables against harmful insects, you can use soap sprays, scatter insect-repelling plants among the beds, or introduce "friendly" insects like ladybugs and praying mantises—**three techniques** that will not leave a chemical residue on the food you grow.

A **resumptive modifier** extends a sentence that appears to have ended, adding new information or twists of thought.

People who are careful about what they eat may lead healthier lives—**healthier,** though not necessarily longer.

Antithesis—the use of parallelism to emphasize contrast—can be witty, dramatic, cynical, ironic, or memorable.

Can an honest politician be smart, or a smart politician honest?

Exercise 5

A. Browse through some current magazines, looking for one that contains relatively long essays with varied and often surprising writing style. You might look at *Vogue, The New Yorker, Rolling Stone, Business Week, GQ, Vanity Fair, Advertising Age, Utne Reader, Commentary, Tikkun, Scientific American,* or *Details.* Choose two paragraphs whose style you admire, and identify any of the sentence strategies discussed in this chapter. Be ready to discuss why the sentences can be considered effective in communicating the author's ideas.

B. Although correct and carefully crafted sentences are important for writing in most communities, sometimes complex sentences are unnecessary or even distracting. Make a list of types of writing that don't require complete sentences (for example, classified ads). Then speculate about when sophisticated or complex sentences are necessary and appropriate and when they are not.

Visit mycomplab.com for more resources and exercises on creating effective sentences.

CHAPTER 8

Assessing Writing

You look over your draft essay or report, and you ask yourself, "Should I revise this more?" and "How will my instructor or other people react to it?" These important questions represent just two of the roles assessing (evaluating) plays.

- **Assessing your own writing.** Should I revise or not? What should I change, add, cut, or retain?
- **Assessing others' writing.** What do I like? What do I want to see changed? How can I provide honest and useful feedback?
- **Understanding how others assess your writing.** What do readers notice? How do they evaluate and respond?
- **Selecting and assessing your portfolio.** Do these selections represent my best work? What changes should I make before presenting them in the portfolio? How can I explain my choices and my revisions?

8a Assessing your own writing

To assess your own writing, you need to place yourself outside the text. Self-assessment can be difficult because you bring more information to what you have written than your readers do: you are the insider. When you write "my house" in a paper, the world of your house with all its details comes to your mind, but not to your readers' minds. The fact that readers do not automatically share your understanding of details (and ideas) may not always be apparent to you.

1 Saying what you want to say

Writers often start out with a clear goal and then lose their way. Interesting and detailed sentences, effective examples and evidence, intriguing ideas—paying careful attention to these elements may require that you step back to remind yourself of what you want to say.

STRATEGY   Say it or write it briefly

After completing a draft, put it aside and try *saying aloud* what you want to say. Or try writing, *without looking at your draft*, a brief paragraph describing what you think you've been saying. Then reread the draft against what you just said or wrote.

- Are the two versions of your thinking the same?
- Does your draft address what you want to say directly, or does it drift around your point or purpose?

Prepare a plan for making your writing say what you want, from the beginning to the end.

2 Sharing what you want to share

Self-assessment requires honesty: Is this what you believe? Is this what happened? Does this reflect who you are? Have you represented the feelings and values you intended to share?

STRATEGY   Share feelings and values

Name your feelings, and put them in a numbered list. Include your feelings toward the subject and the feelings you hope readers will share. Start with a list of five. Then go to ten if you can.

In addition, name the values or beliefs you want to convey or that you hope readers will share. Put them in another list.

Finally, look over your draft and put a number corresponding to the lists at each place you communicate a feeling or value. Use this process to decide how effectively you have shared each feeling or value.

Here is the opening of a draft research paper in which Liv Dolphin wanted to share her worry that the uneven sleep schedules of college students could have serious negative effects.

> In my experience, college students stay up later than any other age range. Also, college students have been known to have different sleep schedules each week, weekend, or even daily. This can disrupt the circadian rhythm, a person's twenty-four-hour, day-night cycle that influences quantity and quality of sleep.

As she looked the passage over, Liv realized she had not communicated her feelings very effectively. Her revised passage makes her worry clearer to readers by asking them to pay attention to what she discusses in the paper.

> "I'm always tired."
> "I'm wide awake in the middle of the night, but I often sleep through classes."

Quotations are dramatic and realistic; they encourage read to pay attention

College students often make complaints like these about sleep and sleep patterns. It may be tempting to treat the complaints as routine college talk, but we need to take them as something more serious. They are often signs that an individual's twenty-four-hour, day-night cycle (called the *circadian rhythm*) has been disrupted, influencing the quantity and quality of sleep.

Highlighted words and phrases emphasize her worries.

3 Being honest about what doesn't work

Only you can know the choices you made as you drafted: where you cut corners or the sections that need more work. Being honest with yourself leads to an accurate assessment and appropriate revision.

STRATEGY Tackle the weak spots

Reread your draft and be honest with yourself. Wherever you see you took a shortcut, wrote too quickly, researched too minimally, or spent too little time reworking the material, place an asterisk. You can then work on each asterisked section in manageable chunks of time.

4 Recognizing what you don't understand

In writing based on external sources, you risk including information in which you don't have full confidence. Assess the reliability and authority of your writing by evaluating the accuracy of quotations, paraphrases, summaries, and factual material. In doing this, you may realize you have made claims that are too broad or that won't stand up to careful examination.

As she assessed her draft paper on depression, Katie Bohan began questioning some of the claims and details she included.

Most people do not view depression as a life-threatening disease because it often doesn't have the same kinds of physical symptoms that other diseases do. What people don't realize is that depression is one of the more dangerous diseases because it can affect absolutely anyone. Depression doesn't discriminate, and it can happen to the happiest person you know. Fifteen percent of people who are depressed will commit suicide, and studies show that by 2020 depression will be the second largest killer behind heart disease.

I think I saw this in several sources. Did I get the numbers right? I probably should document the source in a citation. Maybe the details would be more convincing if I used a citation or explained the information a bit more.

5 Deciding on a revision plan

After reading a draft, you should have a good sense of what you need to do to improve it. You may also get feedback from other readers. In either case, you will need to plan your revision.

| STRATEGY | Set priorities for revision |

- Write two or three sentences summing up the *global changes* you need to make. These are the large-scale additions or deletions of material, the reorganization of major chunks of the work, and the "ripple effect" changes such as altering the tone or voice of your writing throughout (see 5a).
- Make these global changes first. There is no sense in working on smaller concerns until you get the main text right.
- Then, working on the revised draft, begin *editing* by looking for paragraph coherence and stylistic problems (see 5b). Identify areas that need improvement and come back to them later.

8b Assessing someone else's writing

Are you in a peer response group in class? Are you reviewing a report for a friend or co-worker? Are you looking over a paper being prepared by a community or work group to which you belong? In situations like these, the ability to assess someone else's writing and respond helpfully will also help you learn to revise your own work.

1 Deciding what makes a difference for you as a reader

Because most people are wary of criticizing others, they may say that someone's writing is "OK" or "good," which is not a helpful response. Starting with positive observations is fine, but they alone won't improve your partner's paper. By far the best information you can give a writer is your honest reaction as a reader. Both you and your revision partner will feel much more comfortable if you don't alternate playing teacher or expert. Instead, give direct feedback as a reader.

| STRATEGY | Be a reader, not a critic |

- Come up with images of your experience: "I felt like you were beating me over the head with your point on this page" or "Most of us know this basic information, so I felt a little condescended to here." It's up to the writer to figure out how to solve these problems.
- Place check marks in the margin where the writing works especially well for you, and use some other mark (such as an asterisk) where the writing seems choppy, unorganized, or confusing.
- Place exclamation marks next to information that interests or engages you, and add a downward arrow wherever you lose focus or become bored.
- Compliment the writer on effective expression: clear phrases and sentences; well-designed paragraphs; helpful headings, examples, or visuals.

2 Believing and doubting

A well-known writing expert, Peter Elbow, has used the terms *believing game* and *doubting game* to refer to our attitudes as readers. When we play the believing game, we look for reasons to endorse what the writer is saying or we go along with the narrative, explanation, or argument. When we play the doubting game, we constantly look for reasons not to trust the writer.

STRATEGY   **Believe and doubt**

Start with the believing game. Read a text, commenting positively in the left-hand margin where you agree with what the writer is saying or sharing. Do so even when these positive comments are only small spaces in a thicket of disagreement. Point out what works: clear statements, powerful wording, well-developed paragraphs, compelling examples, enlightening visuals.

Move to the doubting game. In the right-hand margin of the same text, raise questions or points of disagreement you feel the writer ought to address. Ask for further information or explanation. Point out where the writing is hard to follow and where extensive revision may help.

BELIEVE		DOUBT
Neat idea!	Big museums may be interesting, but the small ones are the most fun. A big museum contains paintings and sculptures you have heard about and many you ought to know about. A small museum can't afford famous paintings, but it may contain funny sketches that a well-known artist made for fun. A small museum may concentrate on offbeat collections like teapots or musical instruments or sporting equipment. A large institution may keep these intriguing objects in a back room or storage facility.	I'd like an example here.
		This doesn't work because I can't think of any artists like this.

—ELLE ARIAN

3 Prompting change

Although you may be tempted to cover a paper with marks and corrections, writers will revise most effectively when they get just a few *meaningful* comments that prompt effective, major revisions. Meaningful comments can take two forms. Technical comments use the language of writing assessment common in academic settings; such terms are appropriate when you and the writer both know what they mean: *coherence, organization, paragraph structure, purpose statement, thesis, awareness of audience, appeal to logic, stance.* Big issue comments present the most important feedback concerning large-scale problems rather than small revisions.

STRATEGY   Look first for big issues, not details

- As you read a peer's writing, list the three most important concerns that could lead to improvement. For example, if the writer has assumed a tone that is too clinical or too removed from the subject, offer a comment about the overall tone, perhaps citing a specific example.
- If you notice a problem with a smaller detail such as the use of commas, resist marking every case. Mark one and respond to it with a readerly comment: "This comma tricks me into thinking that the second part of the sentence is related to the first, but it's not." Then note that this happens in other places in the writing, too.

4 Working with others

If you are working with a peer group or work group, remember that you are all collaborating, that your goal is to improve each other's work or the project you are working on together. You need to develop a common sense of direction, not one that simply suits you.

STRATEGY   Work productively with your group

- Participate responsibly. If you need to circulate drafts by a certain date, do your part. Don't miss a meeting: your peers or co-workers are counting on you. Prepare adequately; don't read papers only at the last minute. Be sure to write responses on the drafts or separately to remind you of issues you want to discuss.
- Keep apologies to a minimum. Don't bog down the meeting by spending time trying to save face.
- As a responder, strike a good tone. Be helpful and diplomatic, and avoid sarcasm, ridicule, and excessive criticism. As an author, accept criticism gratefully. Don't counter every concern with an explanation or become defensive. Listen to and write down your readers' responses, but make the final decision yourself.
- Don't dominate, either with your comments or in the amount of time spent on your paper. Divide the time evenly, and stick to the time allotted for each paper.

8c How others assess your writing

The more you anticipate how others will read and respond to your writing, the more effectively you can write in the first place. Your peers can be good trial readers for you. But you also need to develop a kind of internal sense for what readers like or dislike in what they read.

1 Where readers start evaluating

Typically, readers begin evaluating from the first line of your text—and sometimes even before, when they see a page that is poorly designed. You need to make a good impression, so pay attention to your introduction. If your first paragraph is garbled, too general, or filled with errors, readers may not want to keep going.

2 How readers move through your writing

Although some readers may skip around or skim as they read, most of the time they will try to move through your prose from beginning to end. However, they need clues about where they're going. For long papers, *headings* can help. For short papers, topic sentences and effective transitions are essential (Chapter 6).

3 How readers decide on evaluation standards

As soon as a reader recognizes the kind of writing and its audience or context, certain standards or expectations come to the reader's mind. When you read an account of an event on the front page of a newspaper, for example, you expect *accuracy, sufficient detail, lack of bias, reasonable brevity, journalistic style,* and an *organization* that moves from essential information first to more detail later. Or if you read a brief travelogue describing a vacation spot, your criteria will include at least some *evaluation* of the locale. In the same way, your readers will expect specific things from your writing, and when you are aware of these expectations, you can more effectively write or revise to match them.

STRATEGY Meet expectations

- Make a list of the three most important expectations your readers will have of the particular genre, or type of writing, you are creating. Think of these expectations as criteria for assessment.
- Look over your draft once for each expectation or criterion, judging how effectively you achieve it. If the kind of writing calls for lots of visual detail, ask yourself just how detailed your writing is, and jot comments in the margin indicating where you can deepen the detail.

8d Assembling and assessing your portfolio

Portfolios are collections of your writing, assembled so people can read, understand, evaluate, and enjoy what you have to say. Your portfolio may be a collection of all the writing you have produced in a course (or on the job), or it may be a presentation of your writing at its best, carefully chosen, revised, and introduced. The rest of this section looks at the role of assessment in creating the latter kind of portfolio.

1 Choosing the best

You need to choose selections that represent you as a writer *at your best*. But what is your best? Your best may vary from one kind of writing to another. For a portfolio, you need to start with writing that may not represent your best *right now* but will do so after you have finished revising it. In short, you must assess the possibilities: what your writing can become.

To assess your writing, you need to choose criteria, or standards, for judging what your writing is or can be.

> **STRATEGY**   Show your strengths
>
> Assemble the pieces of writing from which you plan to choose selections for your portfolio. For each, choose up to five terms you think could appropriately fill in the blank in this question:
>
> If I revised this selection, it could represent my writing at its _____.
>
> | best | most informative | most convincing |
> |------|------------------|-----------------|
> | clearest | most imaginative | most surprising |
> | freshest | most improved | most innovative |
> | funniest | most detailed | most fully developed |

2 Choosing and assessing for variety

A successful portfolio will also represent the range of your ability as a writer. For your portfolio, then, choose selections that differ in subject, strategy, and technique or in the demands and opportunities they present to readers.

> **STRATEGY**   Show your range
>
> Use the following qualities or categories to identify the kinds of writing to include in a portfolio. Look for selections that differ in these qualities:
>
> | purpose | arrangement | complexity |
> |---------|-------------|------------|
> | style | feelings | use of sources |
> | values | subject matter | amount of detail |

3 Introducing and explaining your selections

You introduce a portfolio with a brief essay that explains your choices, highlights the qualities of your writing, and helps readers approach the selections in ways that aid understanding and appreciation.

> **STRATEGY**   Introduce yourself and your writing
>
> Freewrite on topics like the following, thinking about how your introduction can best help readers understand you as a writer with particular

goals or aspirations and how your introduction can help readers appreciate the most important features of your writing.

Contrasts among the selections in your portfolio	Features you think are worth noticing
Ways the selections document your growth as a writer	Ways the selections try to alter or shape readers' perspectives
Choices you made in revising	Choices you considered but rejected
Things you learned about writing as you revised	Things you hope readers will remember from your portfolio
Information or ideas you added	Information or ideas you cut
Reasons you included the selections	Reasons you excluded some selections

Here is an introduction that Monica Noble provided for her portfolio. In it she explains her choices, her revision strategies, and some of her specific revisions. She also indicates the purpose of each selection, hoping to help readers understand her goals for writing and her goals for revision.

Your words are the windows to your soul, so how can you make sure the panes are clear? How can you invite someone into your home if you don't know the word for "welcome"? I kept these thoughts in mind as I chose three assignments that best reflected my abilities as a writer—that is, my abilities as a writer and a reviser.

This portfolio presents my best work from the course, but why are these selections the best? What have I learned from the course? We focused on research writing, and I learned how to inform without boring, how to document sources, and how to take information and present it in different ways. To demonstrate what I have learned, I chose my annotated bibliography, my documented profile, and my informative Web site. I revised each one, and I present them in this portfolio.

Researching and writing my annotated bibliography proved to be a cornerstone for my writing in the course. As I revised the bibliography, I added additional worthwhile entries that I discovered during the course and dropped some that I discovered were less useful or relevant. In adding or revising annotations, I made sure I indicated why each source was useful for understanding my topic. In particular, the Jason Beghe interview, which I found while researching for my Web site, provided important new information. I thought I followed the APA format accurately when I first submitted the annotated bibliography; I discovered otherwise when I revised the entries.

8d
assess

In researching and writing my profile for the original assignment, I found my understanding of the subject, L. Ron Hubbard, deepening and my desire to share my insights with readers growing stronger. This process went even further during my revision. I am particularly proud of the section titled "Impact" in the revision. In it I try to show that L. Ron Hubbard's ideas have spread all over the globe but not always for the best results. Through example and citation, I show that while Hubbard's ideas may have originally been harmless or even helpful, in the long run their effects have been negative. In this way, I hope to have increased the value of the profile for readers.

The last selection I am including is my advocacy Web site. I have made informative Web sites for school before, but not advocacy Web sites. I understood that the differences in purpose might lead to differences between the kinds of sites, but I didn't really know what the difference might be. An advocacy site is designed to persuade as well as to inform, but I began the project by writing primarily to share information. Information is important because without accurate information and citations, readers are not going to take an advocacy site seriously. In the revision, I added a new section on Jason Beghe's experiences by citing his interview, yet I also tried to be fair with my opposition while strengthening my criticism of it through added sources like the interview. I also tried to document my sources better, while trying to keep the citations from disrupting the flow of the discussion so that the text reads like a Web site and not a technical paper.

Visit mycomplab.com **for more resources and exercises on assessing writing.**

PART 2

Critical Thinking and Argument

CHAPTER **9**

Thinking Critically and Reading Critically

What convinces people to accept your conclusions about a subject, to share your views, to follow your recommendations, or to trust the explanations you offer? Many things do, and perhaps the most important of them is the quality of your reasoning: the kind of careful, logical, insightful thinking your writing embodies. Thinking that displays these qualities is called **critical thinking** (sometimes called **critical reasoning**). An important aspect of critical thinking, **critical reading** also helps you to evaluate the ideas and information you encounter and to develop alternative points of view and interpretations. Reading critically puts your mind to work on a text and gives you new ideas by helping you link what you read to your own experience, to other texts of all kinds, to issues and information, or to a problem or a responsibility. Your own writing then *adds* to the discussion of a topic by incorporating insights you've gained from your critical reading.

9a　What is critical thinking?

Critical thinking is any process of reasoning, inquiring, or explaining that displays the following qualities.

- Attention to the logic or reasonableness of conclusions, and to the evidence supporting them.
- Willingness to question one's own assumptions and consider different outlooks.
- Concern for precise information and clearly defined ideas.
- Desire to go beyond superficial explanations and opinions to reach fresh insights.

Consider the following two letters to the editor about a controversial proposal to build a greenway between two parks, one of which is in Coolidge (an economically depressed neighborhood) and the other in Lake Stearns (a wealthy, stable neighborhood).

92

LETTER 1 (LACKS CRITICAL THINKING)
City planners must be out of their minds to cook up this crazy idea. Drug pushers and thieves will have a field day preying on the people who use Lake Stearns Park, and soon the whole neighborhood will be destroyed by crime. We must stop these public officials before they totally destroy our lives with their senseless fantasies.

READER'S REACTION: This is just a collection of assertions with no evidence offered in support. The writer doesn't try to explain why the assertions are valid but feels free to dismiss other perspectives as unreasonable and illogical.

9b
reason

LETTER 2 (DISPLAYS CRITICAL THINKING)
The proposal to create a greenway between Coolidge and Lake Stearns Parks appears to bridge the gap between these two different communities. But the greenway will not solve the existing problems in Coolidge Park. Residents near Lake Stearns are unlikely to ride their bikes or jog into Coolidge, and the presence of Coolidge residents in Stearns will only create a feeling, unjustified though it may be, of defensiveness. City funds could better be used to improve Coolidge Park by adding lighting, a basketball court, and an updated community center.

READER'S REACTION: The problem isn't simple, and the writer gives it a careful, balanced treatment. The reasons both for objecting to the proposal and for an alternative solution are supported by specific details.

The lack of critical thinking displayed in Letter 1 undermines its persuasiveness, except perhaps for those readers who already agree with its conclusions. In Letter 2, the depth of critical thinking invites readers to take the writer's reasoning seriously and form their own opinions, agreeing or disagreeing in response.

9b Building a chain of reasoning

Critical thinking works toward creating a **chain of reasoning,** the path you take in linking ideas, conclusions, evidence, and alternative perspectives in order to convince your audience. Some links in a chain may consist of *information:* examples, facts, evidence, details, and scientific or scholarly data. Other links may offer *ideas:* reasons, analysis, logical argument, citations from authorities, and different points of view. It is crucial to be able to turn your thinking into a chain of critical reasoning that will give shape to your writing.

CRITICAL THINKING STRATEGIES FOR THREE COMMUNITIES

	ACADEMIC	PUBLIC	WORK
GOAL	Analysis of text, phenomenon, or creative work to interpret, explain, or offer insights	Participation in democratic processes to contribute, inform, or persuade	Analysis of problems to supply information and propose solutions
REASONING PROCESS	Detailed reasoning, often explained at length, with tight logic leading to conclusions	Accurate analysis of problem or need, with clear explanation of solution	Plausible reasoning, not ranting, focused on supporting a point of view
SPECIAL INTERESTS	Crucial citations of others as well as insights beyond common knowledge	Shared values and goals, often local, that support a cause or policy	Sharp focus on task, problem, or goal that promotes organization
EVIDENCE	Specific references to detailed evidence, gathered and presented to support conclusions	Relevant evidence, often local or interest-oriented, to support claims and substantiate probabilities	Sufficient evidence to show the importance of the problem and to justify a solution
VIEWPOINT	Balanced treatment recognizing and explaining other views	Fair recognition of other views, interests, and goals	Awareness of alternatives and likely results of actions
EXAMPLE	Analyzing byproducts of carbon emission reduction process	Debating the value of extremely low emissions, if possible only at considerable cost	Exploring ways to reduce carbon emission without increasing costs

ESL ADVICE: CRITICAL THINKING IN ACADEMIC CONTEXTS

Academic writing in English generally follows a pattern of generalization and support in both reasoning and expression. Readers will generally expect you to state a conclusion first, then offer evidence and reasons to support it. Academic traditions in some cultures follow a different approach: data and evidence first, then conclusions that emerge logically. Follow the conventions your particular audience expects, even when, for example, putting your conclusions first seems unnatural or uncomfortable.

1 Focus on conclusions

The links in your chain of reasoning may include supporting conclusions and related (though nonessential) observations, interpretations, or recommendations. The end point of the chain—the **main conclusion**—is the most important. In some cases, you may offer more than one conclusion.

STRATEGY	Focus on conclusions to strengthen your chain of reasoning

- **List** all your conclusions (interpretations, opinions, and so on), both major and minor. Decide which ones make up your main area of focus, and which ones offer support as part of the chain of reasoning. Create two more lists, one for main and one for secondary conclusions.
- **Review** your two lists of conclusions. Do any more come to mind? Are any important assertions missing? If so, do you need to develop them?
- **Consider** the lists as readers might. Will they see any assertions as interpretations or judgments? Will they expect your conclusions?

9b
reason

2 Include information and inferences

A chain of reasoning needs both information and inferences. **Information** includes facts of all kinds—examples, data, details, quotations—that you present as reliable, confirmable, or generally undisputed. **Inferences** or **generalizations** are conclusions you reach based on and supported by information. Information turns into **evidence** when it's used to persuade a reader that an idea or a proposition is reasonable.

STRATEGY	Distinguish between information and inference

- **List the key facts** related to your subject. Which facts will readers regard as undisputed? Which ones can you confirm with observations, details, or a reliable source? If facts are in dispute, what are the reasons for accepting them as you present them?
- **List your inferences.** What do the facts imply? Which inferences reflect your understanding of the subject? What *might* happen or be true as a result of the facts?

3 Assess evidence and reasoning

Readers expect you to select evidence carefully and to link it reasonably with assertions—that is, to proceed logically. Use these questions to evaluate evidence as you read and write.

- How *abundant* is the evidence? Is it *sufficient* to support the claim?
- Does it *directly* support the claim?
- How *relevant, accurate,* and *well documented* is the evidence?

Proceeding logically becomes complicated when evidence that would persuade one group of readers would not convince another group. Consider, for example, how two citizens' groups might respond to the proposal to build a greenway between the park in Coolidge (an economically depressed neighborhood) and the park in Lake Stearns (a wealthy, stable neighborhood of fine older homes). Starting from the assumption that the generally law-abiding residents of Coolidge are deprived of shopping and services that have left the area because of a high crime rate, the Coolidge Citizens' Consortium logically supports the greenway because it will give residents access to recreation and shopping in Lake Stearns. In contrast, starting from the assumption that the balance of a peaceful low-crime neighborhood can easily be upset, another group, Preserve Lake Stearns, argues logically that though most Coolidge residents are law-abiding, the greenway will draw some habitual criminals who will undermine the quality of life in both neighborhoods. Each side reasons logically, but each starts with different assumptions and arrives at different conclusions. (See also Chapters 10–11.)

STRATEGY   **Ask questions to evaluate your assumptions**

- How do I view the groups of people on each side of this issue?
- What will my readers want in a plan that addresses this problem?
- What do specialists in this field see as questions worth investigating?

4 Consider your readers' assumptions

Some values and assumptions are easy to identify, but others are unspoken. After hearing a lot of talk at work about efficiency, you might think that your co-workers and readers want only to cut costs. But preserving jobs and offering a quality product are also shared goals. The success of your reasoning may depend on how closely your assumptions correspond to those of your audience.

STRATEGY   **Focus on assertions to anticipate readers' reactions**

- List your assertions that identify cause-effect links, classify or compare, connect generalizations and examples, or define. Delete or rethink any that are weak or may be illogical (see 11a–b).
- To spot weak reasoning, imagine a skeptical reader's reaction to each assertion.

Violence in schools is rising because of increased violence in movies and on TV.

READER'S REACTION: Is this true? My kids watch a lot of TV, but they aren't more violent than I was as a kid, when TV was far less violent.

Exercise 1

Locate a document whose success or failure depends on the quality of its reasoning: a proposal, a position paper, an editorial, an academic article, or a memo on an important issue. Read it carefully, and identify its conclusions and the main kinds of evidence it presents. Next, try to identify any assumptions the writer makes that differ considerably from yours or those of another possible audience. Finally, use the questions posed in 9b-3 to assess the quality of the evidence.

9c Persuasive reasoning

How you represent your reasoning in writing or speaking is crucial to the acceptance of your information and ideas. Look again at how the writers of two letters to the editor represent themselves in arguing about the Coolidge–Lake Stearns greenway project (9a). Both letters argue the same point: the greenway proposal is shortsighted. But think about the ways in which these two writers present themselves.

9c
reason

WRITER 1	WRITER 2
Attacks proposers and Coolidge residents	Focuses on the proposal
Uses emotionally charged words (*insane, crazy*)	Uses balanced language
Comes up with vague ideas	Offers specific alternatives
Stereotypes Coolidge residents	Suggests enhancing quality of life in Coolidge
Seems impulsive, shallow, uninformed	Seems balanced and thoughtful

Clearly, the representation created by the first writer is unlikely to lend credibility to what the writer has to say, and it may discourage readers from agreeing with the writer's point of view. What can you do to avoid representing yourself in such a negative manner? What can you do to create a representation that encourages an audience to respect and trust what you have to say?

1 Be well informed

Information, issues, and ideas are embedded in the social, occupational, historical, or disciplinary contexts that surround a topic. Explore what you know, and draw on the insights and perspectives of others. List what you know about your topic and what surrounds it. Identify the most important areas, given your purpose, and try to define what's still unclear and where you might find material to fill the gaps.

2 Acknowledge other perspectives and anticipate readers' reactions

If you fail to acknowledge other views, contrary arguments, conflicting evidence, or alternative solutions to an issue, your readers may find your presentation one-sided and question your credibility. By anticipating such reactions, you can complete your chain of reasoning and build readers' confidence in you and your conclusions.

3 Be balanced and reasonable

Emotional language may be appropriate when you're urging a public audience to act on the basis of a shared belief. The same language would probably irritate, even offend, co-workers or academic readers, who generally expect a critical analysis of information. As you select the words and the tone to represent your thinking, you create an image of yourself whose qualities may shape readers' responses. Your image can make your reader trust and respect you, distrust and dislike you, or find you imbalanced and your conclusions ridiculous or unconsidered.

9c
reason

> The greenway will just transport the Coolidge low-lifes into Lake Stearns Park and destroy its peace and quiet.
>
> READER 1: What's a "low-life"? Is this term based on race? or class? Is everyone in Coolidge a "low-life"?
>
> READER 2: Why—and how—would people from Coolidge destroy the "peace and quiet" of Lake Stearns?

4 Assess the appropriateness of strong bias

To write effectively, you must know when to be cool and logical and when to show an emotional commitment. At work, bias is expected when you represent an organization, but you'll need to write objective internal memos and reports. In public, your devotion to a cause will generally be accepted as such. Your academic writing, however, should lean toward unimpassioned, reasoned assessments.

Exercise 2

A. Locate an essay, article, or report on a controversial topic or issue, and analyze the ways in which the writer succeeds or fails to represent his or her thinking convincingly. Begin by deciding what community or communities of readers the author is addressing. Base your judgments on the presentation's appropriateness for particular readers, and on its purpose. Use the following questions to guide your analysis.

1. Does the writer appear well informed?
2. Does the writer acknowledge other perspectives?
3. Does the writer seem to respect his or her audience?
4. Is the presentation balanced and reasonable?
5. Does the writer anticipate readers' reactions?
6. Is the writer's bias appropriate for the occasion?

B. Locate a site where two or more people discuss the same topic in writing or speaking, preferably directly addressing each other's reasoning: an online discussion, a newspaper opinion page with contrasting editorials, a magazine article or interview, or records of a debate. Briefly summarize the position of each participant, and then discuss how each addresses or criticizes flaws or gaps in the reasoning of the other, either directly or by implication.

C. Working with a group in class or online, begin a discussion by briefly stating your conclusions on an issue and giving the most important evidence for them. Pass this statement on, asking the next person to add further conclusions, evidence, objections, and counterarguments. Have the last person summarize the conclusions, evidence, and objections and circulate the original document and the summary to the rest of the group. Discuss how your group's reasoning was changed by the serial dialogue.

9e
read

9d What is critical reading?

Critical reading is the kind of reading that leads to writing. It begins with your understanding what you have read; it moves on to response, evaluation, and even argument; and it ends with the development of your own ideas and insights.

9e Read to understand

If you are like most people, you begin reading on the first page and then read on, sentence by sentence, paragraph by paragraph. By "starting cold," however, you may have too much to do at once: to understand the details in the text, to grasp the writer's conclusions, and to develop your critical responses. Instead, you need to "warm up" by previewing the text and developing a reading plan.

1 Prereading strategies

What "big" features of reading that shape a text's meaning, its ideas, or its relationship to readers are you likely to miss if you jump right into reading? You may fail to recognize the text's overall design, the specific situation (academic, public, or work) that it addresses, or the writer's particular purposes. Fortunately, you can use prereading strategies to develop an understanding of these features before you begin your careful reading.

Preview the organization. For books and long articles or reports, skim the table of contents to see how a work is organized. For a Web site, look for a site map. In articles or reports without tables of contents, look for headings and subheadings; they are road maps that tell you where the reading will take you and help you to plan your time.

Examine the context. Consider the social setting in which the text was produced and the audience or community it seems to address. What is the author's background? Does the text address a specific community? Did the text originally appear in a publication associated with a particular point of view, industry, or political organization? When was the text published, and how current are its information and ideas?

Sample the content. Sample the content to bring to mind what you already know about the topic, the writer's outlook, or the issues being addressed.

Sample key words and specialized terms. If you notice unfamiliar terms, look for patterns of related terms, or consult a dictionary or online glossary.

Read the visuals. Examine graphs, charts, diagrams, and other illustrations; analyze what they say and how they relate to the written text.

Make predictions. Sample some paragraphs, sentences, or visuals, and try to predict what the text is about and where it will take you. Do your samples imply a particular direction, focus, or purpose? Jot your predictions down and later note which ones were confirmed as you read.

CRITICAL READING STRATEGIES FOR THREE COMMUNITIES

ACADEMIC SETTINGS	PUBLIC SETTINGS	WORK SETTINGS
Critical reading in academic settings calls for attention to reasoning and evidence as well as the claims (thesis) a writer advances. Check that interpretations and conclusions are each supported by evidence that is accurate, specific, and convincing. See that alternative scholarly perspectives have been taken into account. Verify that the theory or method used to analyze and interpret the subject is applied correctly and consistently.	Critical reading in public settings calls for special attention to the clarity of the writer's recommendations or judgments as well as evaluation of supporting evidence. Note how effectively the writer deals with alternative policies or value judgments. Evaluate the writer's position according to what you know about the context and about alternative points of view. Take note of any objections or reservations that come to mind.	Critical reading in work settings focuses on how accurately the writer analyzes problems or challenges. It pays particular attention to proposed solutions, policies, and other actions, especially to their practicality, efficiency, and likelihood of success. It also evaluates the ethical dimensions of any proposed action or policy.

Exercise 3

Locate a short article, a short electronic document, or a portion of a longer text that has no obvious structure—no headings, section divisions, or other organizational signals. Then skim (preread) the material and create headings or divisions for the main parts of the reading.

2 Reading strategies during and after

You've probably had the experience of reaching the end of a passage (or the end of a work) only to realize that you haven't even the vaguest sense of what you've been reading. To avoid this problem, try the following strategies.

9e
read

Pause and assess. When you reach a place at which you can stop reading without interrupting a line of reasoning or a crucial narrative, put the reading aside for a moment. Where are you? What have you learned so far? What do you think? What still confuses you? Jot down answers to these questions in your journal or on a piece of paper. Then go back and skim what you've read.

Highlight important information. If you're an avid highlighter *while* you read, try to change your style. Don't spend a lot of time attending to tiny details the first time through your reading. Instead, read to capture the essential points of the piece. This will let you see the bigger picture, the organizational or argumentative structure(s), without getting lost in the details.

STRATEGY Highlight only what's important

Do most of your highlighting *after* your first reading. Go back and write notes in the margins of your reading to identify important points and details, or use your highlighter to identify what's *truly* important.

Identify generalizations. General statements of all sorts help to organize information and ideas and help readers to understand the insights and line of reasoning a writer is offering. Identifying those statements helps you understand and remember an essay or an article's main points, line of reasoning, and overall organization. Look for generalizations near the beginning of a selection (including a thesis statement), at the beginning of each section of the text (including any headings and subheads), at the beginning or end of paragraphs, and in special paragraphs that summarize main ideas and the organizational plan (see 3c–d, 6b and f).

Annotate. If you own the book or document you're reading, go ahead and annotate it, using whatever white space is on the page. If you don't own it, consider making a photocopy of relevant material. If you're reading a Web page or other electronic document, consider downloading or printing it so you can make annotations.

STRATEGY   **Annotate while you read**

- **Interpretations.** What does the writer mean?
- **Confusions.** At what points am I puzzled, and why?
- **Questions.** What more do I need to know?
- **Disagreements.** What disagreements does the writer seem to anticipate (or fail to anticipate)? Where and why do I disagree?
- **Evaluative responses.** What do I like or dislike about the text as a whole or about specific parts of it?
- **Restatements.** How might I restate the text's key ideas in my own words?
- **Communities.** What will different communities of readers perceive as the most important ideas and information in the text? Why might people in different settings respond in different ways?
- **Memories.** What experiences, memories, or related issues or problems come to mind as I read?
- **Retentions.** Which details, insights, or opinions in the text are most likely to stick in readers' minds after they have finished, and why?

Clint Graff made responsive annotations to a passage from a document about the information provided to consumers on food labels.

What were they asked? And do people really read the info?

How does this study lead to this conclusion?

Points to tension between consumer desire for info & fear that it's just hype. I'm skeptical too. But aren't there ways to get trustworthy information to consumers? Write about this?

A recent review on communication of food, nutrition, and health messages did not include dietary supplement labeling specifically but did address consumer understanding of nutrient content and health claims on food labels (80). In an appendix to this report, Levy (83) indicates that <u>consumers in focus groups were interested in having information</u> about the relationship between diet and disease. Some commissioners interpret this study as <u>suggesting that consumer research has not yet</u> established a "mandate" for having health information on food labels as opposed to obtaining such information from health care providers, books, or the print and telecommunications media. Moreover, considering that food labels are viewed by consumers as reflective of the manufacturer's interest in selling the product, <u>consumers are skeptical about the veracity of health messages on food labels.</u>

Read with your audience and purpose in mind. Often we read in order to write: we gather information and ideas or we develop insights and solutions that we plan to share with readers. When this is your goal, highlight or make notes on those sections of a text that are relevant either to the community of readers you plan to address or to your specific purposes for reading.

Reread and review. If you're learning sophisticated concepts, studying complicated issues and problems, or working through difficult arguments, you may need to read material more than once. Each time you read something again, you'll find more information or new ideas.

Exercise 4

Find a relatively challenging article, electronic document, or book chapter, or choose one that you've begun to read for a specific purpose, perhaps as a course assignment or in preparation for a report or some other writing task. Then try several of the reading strategies outlined in this section, taking note of which one best aids your understanding and which one seems most likely to be useful to you as a writer.

9f
read

9f Read to respond and evaluate

What is the central idea a writer is trying to convey? Do you have a better or a different idea of your own? What new insights does a piece of writing offer you? What insights of your own come to mind as you read? Can you describe the writer's opinions, generalizations, and attitudes toward the subject matter? Do you agree with them? Has the writer missed important points? What are your opinions? How might you state your own perspective for readers?

When you read for response and evaluation, these are some of the questions you will try to answer. They link an understanding of the text to an evaluation of its content and then to the development of your own perspective. Clearly, this kind of reading is *active* and *engaged*. It is also *responsive*—you respond to the content and strategies of a text by evaluating them according to your purposes for reading and the situation to which the text is addressed (academic, public, or work). You respond by developing your own ideas and interests and by beginning to think about the kinds of writing you might produce as a consequence of your reading.

1 Note responses while reading

When you read carefully, you respond to the content and evaluate it according to your purposes and the standards of the community of readers and writers to which a text is addressed.

Make responsive annotations. As you read and reread, it's important for you to keep track of your questions, thoughts, reactions, agreements, and disagreements. You can do this in the margin, on a separate sheet of paper, or on your computer.

Note repetition and emphasis. Words, phrases, ideas, and details that appear repeatedly in a text may shape its meaning and its effect. Devices for creating emphasis—headings, thesis statements, topic sentences—also highlight and create meaning and focus a text's purpose.

Summarize in chunks. Most texts have natural resting points, often marked with road signs like headings and subheadings or shifts in focus. These are good places to take stock of what you've learned and how you are reacting to the reading. This process can help you to monitor your comprehension and begin interpreting the piece.

2 Share interpretations and insights

Go public with the conversation you're having internally with a piece of writing. If other people have read the same piece, their responses can help you to formulate and test your own interpretation.

9f
read

3 Respond in writing

A journal or reading log provides an especially effective method for reading critically (see 2b). If you're keeping a journal, jot down your conclusions about the writer's purpose(s) and key ideas. Be ready to reread the text to check your perceptions and understandings. By struggling to put the text's ideas into your own language, you are already developing your interpretation— and working toward ideas you might develop later in your own writing.

Exercise 5

A. Obtain a copy of the minutes from a recent city council or other public meeting (they may be available online). Read the minutes carefully, making responsive annotations as you read; then summarize the document for a partner. Once you have done this, speculate about how different communities might read this document. Is there specialized terminology that might be confusing to some audiences? Did any one issue seem like an ongoing problem or controversy? If so, were solutions proposed? Can you tell, from the minutes, who the most influential or powerful participants were?

B. Compare the interpretive reading of an academic text to that of a workplace document. Select a challenging excerpt from your course reading, and locate a text from a workplace context. (You might use a document from a current or former job, ask individuals you know in the working world to share a text with you, or locate a relevant document from a work- or profession-related Web site.) Use interpretive reading strategies (making responsive annotations, noting repetition and emphasis, summarizing in chunks, sharing interpretations, and responding in writing) as you actively read the two pieces. Then reflect, in writing, on the differences between your interpretive readings of the two texts: Does one lend itself to this kind of reading more easily? Which strategies were most useful with each text? Which text elicited the strongest response?

Visit mycomplab.com for more resources and exercises on thinking and reading critically.

CHAPTER 10

Constructing an Argument

Argumentative writing has specific qualities that set it apart from writing that aims to explain, inform, or interpret.

- **Argument deals with issues and opinions, not certainties.** It addresses situations in which more than one opinion, interpretation, or course of action is possible.
- **Argument is evaluative.** It takes a stand, presenting and endorsing an outlook, a judgment, or an opinion.
- **Argument aims at persuasion.** It focuses on the reasons, evidence, and values most likely to encourage readers (or listeners) to share an opinion or undertake an action.
- **Argument interacts.** It engages an audience's attitudes and values as well as alternative points of view, pro or con.

10a Occasions for argument

If you think about the kinds of writing you may have occasion to do in academic, public, or work settings, you will recognize that much of it is **argumentative,** designed to persuade readers to share your opinion or perspective rather than another point of view.

ARGUMENTS IN THREE COMMUNITIES

ACADEMIC SETTINGS	PUBLIC SETTINGS	WORK SETTINGS
Anyone advancing a new interpretation, perspective, or conclusion may need to argue why it is superior to other points of view. Prior research often provides unresolved issues and problems as a focus for arguments.	Proposals for new policies, projects, or procedures often take argumentative form in order to gather public support or to demonstrate why they are preferable to the alternatives. Even suggestions for adopting noncontroversial practices or presentations of useful information may need to take argumentative form. Controversial practices and information generally require argumentative presentation.	Discussions of problems and solutions generally take argumentative form to create agreement in understanding a problem and to encourage group action in solving it. Arguments also build support for policies or programs and lead to agreement on goals and values.

At the heart of most occasions that call for argument is an **issue,** a topic about which people may hold sharply different points of view.

1 Existing issues

10a
arg

Many arguments you construct will address existing issues. An existing issue is a matter of ongoing disagreement or a continuing struggle to find a satisfactory solution. Issues of this sort come to you partially formed: others have already identified the dimensions of disagreement, gathered supporting ideas and information, and taken stances pro and con. Some issues, such as gun control or responses to global warming, will have broad relevance; others, such as a proposal for a new campus drinking policy, will be of concern only to a specific audience. Issues of limited or local concern may provide a clearer focus and draw more interest than overly broad issues, even those of global concern.

	ACADEMIC	PUBLIC	WORK
GENERAL	Affirmative action in college admissions	Violence and sex on television	Child care at work
LOCAL	Housing regulations at Nontanko River State University	A community crusade against a television series	Discipline policies at Abtech's Child-Care Center

---

STRATEGY   List the issues and get involved

- **List current issues.** Make a list of the disagreements you encounter in various settings—academic, public, work—to help you focus your own response to the issues. Listing can help you spot the disagreements or problems that define or divide communities and it can help you develop your own responses to the issues.
- **Talk to yourself.** In a journal, on a piece of paper, or on a screen, talk to yourself about problems, controversies, trends, or ideas that concern you or influence how we live. For each issue, write a one- or two-sentence summary of at least two different opinions on the subject. To identify and explore separate opinions, try imagining yourself as someone with a very different outlook from your own.
- **Interview.** Talk with people about questions and problems that concern them and inspire strong opinions. Keep a record of their responses, and add your own ideas to them.
- **Read and listen.** Leaf through news and opinion magazines such as *The Nation* and *National Review*, or editorials in local and national newspapers, or listen to issue-oriented discussion shows on television and radio. Consult online discussion groups or issue-oriented electronic publications such as *Salon*. List the issues that interest you, and write down opposing opinions and important information or ideas.

Exercise 1

A. Using the strategies described above, prepare a list of issues or controversies that interest you. Choose one issue or controversy, summarize it in a sentence or two, and then summarize the main conflicting opinions, pro and con, each in one sentence.

B. Working in a group, share your lists of issues. Choose an issue on someone else's list (other than the issue that person expanded) and develop it in the same manner, by summarizing the issue and the main conflicting opinions.

10a
arg

2 Potential issues

When you focus on a problem no one has yet identified, offer an opinion or evaluation likely to be controversial, or propose a change in a long-agreed-upon policy, you address a potential issue. Though a potential issue is not yet a focus of argument, you can probably anticipate some members of your audience responding with opposing opinions and contrary proposals that will turn the potential issue into an actual issue.

STRATEGY Recognize potential issues

- **Review the consequences.** A policy, program, or organization often starts out with specific goals. Evaluate the likely consequences of policies or actions to see if they will actually meet the goals as a way of uncovering issues worth discussing.
- **Question the taken-for-granted.** The opinions or activity that people take for granted may mask important disagreements and issues. Make a list of things you think most people take for granted (for example, that economic prosperity is good) or that a particular group assumes (for example, environmentalists believing that prosperity increases pollution). Then look for contradictions within and among your lists: *economic prosperity is good* vs. *prosperity increases pollution*. Or raise questions about an assumption: Has prosperity ever decreased pollution?
- **Question definitions and categories.** Use questions to probe definitions and classifications. People frequently talk and write about "chick flicks," that is, films that appeal to women (but not men) by focusing on relationships rather than action. Do men really dislike such films? Do women actually prefer such films?
- **Question evaluations.** An evaluation or a judgment is an opinion—subject to challenge—and therefore always a potential issue. Raising questions about an evaluation or a judgment can help you probe the reasoning behind conclusions and decisions and turn potential issues into real ones. Popular opinion holds that early

decision programs benefit college applicants. But what about people who need to choose among financial packages? Aren't regular applicants disadvantaged when a large percentage of the spaces in an incoming class have already been filled by the time they apply?

- **Question silence by developing contrasts.** Try focusing on an organization, a community, or a policy. Identify a loosely similar one and use contrasts to identify potential issues. A seemingly issue-free college athletic administration can appear as a source of potential controversy when viewed in contrast with a differently structured, perhaps more successful, program.

- **Offer an evaluation.** When you state a judgment about the quality of a performance, policy, program, or anything else that can be legitimately evaluated, you create an issue to the extent that you intend others to share your opinion. (A simple expression of personal taste is not a subject for debate.)

Exercise 2

A. Use two of the strategies described above for identifying potential issues. Identify at least five potential issues, making sure you employ both techniques at least twice. Then summarize each issue in a sentence or two, and summarize any potentially conflicting opinions about it in a sentence each.

B. Choose one of the potential issues from your list and explain briefly why you think an audience should be concerned about it.

3 Identify arguable issues

To have an argument in a formal sense, you must begin with an arguable **issue,** a subject about which your audience can recognize two (or more) clearly differing, reasonable opinions. Drunk driving, for example, is not an issue. No one would be willing to argue that driving while intoxicated is a good thing; anyone who tried to advance this opinion would be considered foolish at best. However, reasonable people will disagree about which policies are most likely to discourage people from driving while intoxicated—strict laws? harsh punishments? roadblocks? advertising campaigns? For most people this question is an arguable issue, and most people would probably listen to various opinions in hopes of discovering the best way to deal with the problem.

Use the following questions to determine whether you have chosen an issue worth arguing about.

1. ***Is the issue clearly debatable?*** A fact is something about which there can be no debate ("Mice are rodents"). The only facts that can be debated are those that might be reasonably challenged *as* facts. For

example, it was widely held as "fact" that peptic ulcers were caused by excess acidity in the diet. New evidence, however, now supports a theory that ulcers are caused by a bacterium. In light of this information, the question "Are peptic ulcers caused by diet?" is a debatable issue.

2. ***Can you explore the issue with something more than pure speculation?*** Claims that cannot be verified often make for interesting philosophical discussion, but they don't lend themselves fully to argument. The question "Where do we go when we die?" is impossible to answer conclusively and therefore hard to develop into an arguable issue. Statements for which there is only tentative supporting evidence ("There may be life on other planets") also make difficult choices for argument.

3. ***Is the issue more than a matter of pure taste or preference?*** An author's own values and beliefs need to be supported in argument with sound reasoning or evidence. Statements such as "I hate anything with tomatoes in it" can't be supported with anything more than circular reasoning ("because I hate tomatoes"). However, evaluative statements based on comparisons or analyses, such as those found in reviews, can become reasonable supporting evidence for a broader assertion ("The food at Alfredo's Restaurant is highly overrated").

4. ***Does the issue avoid assumptions that are so deeply or universally held that they cannot be argued?*** Arguments about topics such as the right to die and capital punishment may invoke systems of belief, including religious beliefs, that cannot be logically debated. Debates between nonreligious students and their fundamentalist peers rarely end in resolution or change, interesting or confrontational though the discussions may be. When you choose a topic, ask yourself whether and how it can be explored through the use of sound reasoning and evidence.

Exercise 3

A. Examine the following issue statements. Decide which of the issues could be developed into argumentative papers and which would not lend themselves to such development. Explain why.

1. Banning campus visits by environmentally insensitive firms
2. The taste of fresh orange juice
3. The sale of pharmaceuticals (aspirin, sunscreen, condoms, tampons) in campus vending machines
4. Belief in the sacredness of cows
5. The reinstitution of chain gangs (prisoners shackled together at the legs) to do highway work

B. In a small group, compare your analyses of the issue statements. Collectively choose two issue statements that would make good argumentative papers.

10b Developing your stance

You construct an argument to help persuade people to accept your opinion. To argue effectively, therefore, you first need a clear idea of your own opinion and of the reasons why you hold it. Even at this early stage, however, thinking about how readers (or listeners) will respond to your reasoning is important. Argument is an interactive process: to persuade others to accept your perspective, you need to engage their opinions, values, and likely objections.

It is often easy to voice opinions in a lively discussion among friends. If another person disagrees, you can promptly defend or clarify what you have said or you can challenge the person with another point. In written argument, however, you don't have this immediacy. When readers can't respond to you "live," you need to anticipate their reactions and counterarguments.

To develop your argumentative stance, you need to do two things:

1. *Articulate* your opinion, along with supporting reasons and information, to yourself.
2. *Clarify* your ideas and supporting evidence through an interchange with competing perspectives.

It is crucial that you do these things *in writing* because the act of writing pushes your thinking and reasoning.

1 Articulate your stance

Begin by exploring your stance on paper as a way of focusing your ideas, values, and feelings.

- **Write informally** (perhaps in your journal) about your intuitive reactions to your chosen issue. Does the issue make you feel scornful, pitying, fearful, outraged? If the issue angers you, exactly what about it makes you angry?
- **List the specific elements of the issue** to which you have responded emotionally, and briefly summarize your responses. Add to this list other points that you may not react to emotionally but that, on an intellectual level, support your first reaction.
- **Identify facts, examples, and ideas** that support your opinions. Also begin thinking about objections to your point of view. If you need to go outside your experience to provide support or to deal with opposing opinions, make a preliminary research plan identifying the kinds of information and ideas you may need to gather.

2 Clarify your ideas

Clarify your ideas through interaction with competing perspectives.

- **Read** about the subject, focusing on how others have defined the issue: their opinions, the kinds of support they cite, and the potentially useful information they present.
- **Talk** with people about the issue, gathering their opinions and feelings into an understanding of how perspectives on the subject differ.
- **Listen** to debates in person, on television, or on the radio, and record the various opinions, supporting ideas, evidence, and counterarguments.
- **Visit** an online discussion group to observe and take note of the varied points of view on an issue and how participants respond to and counter each other's arguments.

10c
arg

10c Developing a thesis

As you begin identifying your point of view, try to limit the scope of your argument. If your issue is too broad, you will have a hard time covering it in a reasonable space and time and an equally difficult time persuading audiences to agree with you. Most of all, you need to develop a clear statement of your own opinion—the point of view with which you want readers to agree. Your opinion (your **thesis** or **argumentative claim**) will become a major focus as you develop your argument in writing. The ideas, supporting information, and organization you choose should all help further your thesis or claim.

1 Focus on an argumentative claim

One good way to focus your effort is to ask yourself what kind of **argumentative claim** you plan to make and argue for.

- *Do you want to argue that an activity, belief, arrangement, or performance is good or bad (effective or ineffective, healthful or harmful, desirable or undesirable)?* If so, you are asking readers (or listeners) to agree with a **value judgment.**
- *Do you want to persuade your audience that a particular course of action ought to be undertaken or avoided?* If so, you are asking for agreement on a **policy.**
- *Do you want people to agree that a particular explanation is correct or incorrect?* If so, you are asking them to endorse or reject an **interpretation.**

Put your claim in writing so you can share it with others and analyze it carefully yourself. Your claim needs to be relatively specific; after all, when you ask people to agree with you, they will be unlikely to do so unless you can indicate your opinion and purpose clearly and specifically.

10c
arg

STRATEGY   **Put your purpose and your goals in writing**

Make sure you agree with yourself on the purpose and goals of your argument. Write a memo to yourself explaining your goals. Use the memo as an opportunity to think out loud and clarify your purpose as you write.

To: Self

From: Me

I find using roadblocks as a way of catching drunk drivers really disturbing. I know it is important to keep drunk drivers off the road, of course. I think this remedy is extreme. I guess what I really want to do is to get my audience to agree that the roadblocks are a violation of civil liberties and should be banned.

A memo to yourself that takes into account fresh evidence, new ideas, or counterarguments you have encountered can be a good place to revise and redirect your opinion and the direction of your argument.

Be ready to revise your claim. As you construct your argument, bringing together your ideas and the evidence to support them, you may decide to modify your argumentative **claim,** that is, the opinion, judgment, or course of action you want your audience to adopt.

To: Self

From: Me

Subject: Roadblocks are effective

Roadblocks violate civil liberties, but the three studies I found online through NorthernLight.com say that the roadblocks take a lot of drunk drivers off the road and may reduce accidents. Self, you've got to deal with this evidence and the arguments *for* roadblocks it suggests. Perhaps you can propose an effective alternative that does not violate civil liberties.

2 Create a thesis statement

An explicit **thesis statement** makes your argumentative claim clear and helps your audience follow your reasoning and evidence.

Prepare a tentative thesis statement as you plan and draft your argument, and expect to revise it as you refine your ideas and evidence. Make sure your thesis statement is not just a general statement of your point of view but an **argumentative thesis** specifying your opinion on an issue. An effective thesis does these things:

1. Identifies a specific issue and your opinion on it
2. Provides a clear and logical statement of your argumentative claim
3. Suggests a general direction for your argument
4. Indicates related claims or opinions

Arguments are often complex and can involve several closely related claims. Pay special attention to making such relationships clear. Imagine that you are drafting a thesis statement for your essay arguing that because stopping all cars on a highway to search for drunk drivers is a violation of civil liberties, roadblocks should be replaced with another technique for keeping intoxicated people from driving. You need to recognize that this claim commits you to arguing both a value judgment (roadblocks violate civil liberties) and a policy (another technique for enforcing laws against drunk driving); if you understand this, you can make sure your thesis (and your essay as a whole) does not blur these points and the evidence you use to support them.

**10c
arg**

3 Revise your thesis statement

In a sentence (or at most two sentences) state your thesis (your opinion or proposal) and indicate the general kind of reasoning you will offer to support it. Try using a sentence pattern like "*X* should be altered/banned/etc. because . . ." or "I propose the following plan/policy/actions/etc. because . . ." or "*Y* is inappropriate/ineffective/harmful/etc. because. . . ."

Next, check whether your tentative thesis blurs your specific purposes for arguing or is illogical.

Police should stop conducting unconstitutional roadblocks and substitute more frequent visual checks of erratic driving to identify people who are driving while intoxicated.

The value judgment and policy proposal are blurred in this thesis statement. In addition, the thesis is potentially illogical because the writer seems to assume that the roadblocks are unconstitutional and does not acknowledge that this value judgment needs to be argued (see "Begging the Question," p. 128).

Make sure that your thesis either focuses on a single claim or identifies two related claims you will argue in an appropriate order.

SINGLE
PROPOSITIONS

Roadblocks used to identify drunk drivers are unconstitutional.

Police should make more frequent visual checks of erratic driving to identify people who are driving while intoxicated.

RELATED
PROPOSITIONS

The current practice of using roadblocks to identify drunk drivers is unconstitutional; therefore, police should use an alternative procedure such as instituting more frequent visual checks of erratic driving behavior.

10c
arg

Exercise 4

Consider the following propositions as possible thesis statements for argumentative essays. Decide whether each example provides an adequate thesis, and explain your judgments.

1. The United States should deregulate all mail service in order to increase competition and improve the quality of service.
2. Rap music, which is violent, vulgar, and sexist, should be banned from public consumption, and fines should be imposed on anyone listening to it in public places.
3. The demands for "computer literacy" (knowledge of how to use computers on the job, at home, and in all aspects of public life) will keep increasing with each generation; therefore, public schools should be required to have courses in computer literacy for all students.
4. All Americans select and wear their attire on the basis of a discriminatory class system which, in the schools, distracts students from their education; therefore, we should pass a federal law requiring all students in public schools to wear identical uniforms.
5. Arson is not a crime; it is a mental disease and should be treated as such.
6. If children read when they are growing up, they will become literate.
7. Orange juice tastes better than cranberry juice.
8. Recirculating the hot air from your clothes dryer into your basement during the cold winter months can significantly reduce your heating costs.
9. Humanity's woes began when Eve tasted the forbidden fruit in the Garden of Eden.
10. The telephone resulted in a society less prone to writing, but email will likely lead us right back to the written word as a primary form of communication.

mycomplab

Visit mycomplab.com for more resources and exercises on constructing an argument.

Developing, Supporting, and Documenting an Argument

To encourage readers to agree with your argumentative claim—your opinion, interpretation, or proposal—you need to give them good reasons in the form of ideas and evidence that support your proposition.

11a Developing reasons that support your claim

When you consider your argument from your audience's point of view, you realize that the reasoning you use to support your claim is as important as the claim itself. Viewed from this perspective, an argument is a series of reasons that help audience members convince themselves that your point of view is preferable to competing ones.

Envision your argument as a claim linked to a series of reasons. One good way to create a link between your claim (opinion) and the reasons supporting it is to draft a working thesis statement centered on the word *because* (or *since, therefore, consequently*) followed by the supporting reasons.

CLAIM (IN THE FORM OF A WORKING OR PRELIMINARY THESIS STATEMENT)
Coursework for teacher certification should continue after people have started working as classroom teachers *because* this approach will be more effective and efficient, *because* it will help increase the number of new teachers, and *because* it will help others decide more quickly whether teaching is the right career for them.

REASON 1
We learn about a professional skill or activity best while we are doing it.
[Evidence: compare to examples of medical internships and residencies; examples and charts drawn from research on innovative teacher training programs]

REASON 2
Practicing teachers are often more motivated learners than are pre-service teachers.
[Evidence: information from scholarly article comparing responses of participants in pre-service and in-service courses]

REASON 3
Reducing the amount of time people have to spend before they begin teaching will help increase the number of new teachers available in a time of teacher shortages.
[Evidence: interviews with fellow students; statistics and examples from news reports and online discussion groups]

115

REASON 4 (COUNTERARGUMENT)

New teachers will still be capable of doing good work in their first teaching jobs, especially if they are adequately supervised and supported by the schools that hire them.

[Evidence: newspaper reports, interviews with two school superintendents]

1 Think of your argument as reasons *plus* evidence

Reasons alone are seldom enough to convince an audience. Reasons need to be developed with evidence (see the example above) that does these things:

- Provides logical justification for the writer's (speaker's) opinions and reasoning
- Encourages an audience to trust the writer's conclusions and proposals
- Enables an audience to understand the reasoning in depth and perhaps draw links between it and their own experiences
- Points out similarities among the values and attitudes underlying the writer's claims or proposals and the values and beliefs of the audience
- Helps readers (listeners) envision a proposed course of action or a new policy and regard it as plausible or desirable

11b Using varied kinds of evidence

As you work on your reasoning, consider the potential sources of support discussed below. Choose those that are most relevant to the reasons supporting your claim and that address most directly your audience's concerns as well as any opposing argument. Try to achieve a balance of facts and statistics, quotations from experts, examples, and personal knowledge.

1 Use examples

Examples drawn from your own or others' experiences can be among the most persuasive kinds of evidence. Events, people, ideas, objects, feelings, stories, images, and texts can be turned into brief or extended examples to support a claim and encourage readers to share your point of view.

In choosing examples to support an argument, you need to keep in mind both the readiness of readers to be persuaded by examples and the likelihood that they will approach examples critically. Remember, too, that the power of examples to persuade often rests in the detail a writer provides. Detail serves to illustrate and strengthen the point being made. Supply both clear explanation to make your point and sufficient detail to give it power.

> The era of the modern family system had come to an end, and few could feel sanguine about the postmodern family condition that had succeeded it. Unaccustomed to a state of normative instability and definitional crisis, the populace split its behavior from its beliefs.

Many who contributed actively to such postmodern family statistics as divorce, remarriage, blended families, single parenthood, joint custody, abortion, domestic partnership, two-career households, and the like still yearned nostalgically for the *Father Knows Best* world they had lost.

—JUDITH STACEY, "The Family Values Fable"

2 Use quotations and ideas from authorities

11b
arg

By turning to the words or ideas of a recognized authority on a subject, you can add to the reasons for readers to agree with your point of view. Most readers are likely to maintain an intelligently critical attitude toward your use of ideas and quotations from experts. They will expect you to cite well-known authorities or to indicate why the person you are citing should be viewed as an authority. They may also reject the perspective of someone whose biases suggest a lack of fairness or balance, particularly if those biases differ from their own. As a result, you may need to present the words or ideas you are citing in ways that make clear that your source is both fair and authoritative.

Do not expect an authority to do all the work. After all, you cite an authority only to add weight to your own thesis and perspective. You encourage readers to agree with you by pointing out that someone whose opinion carries weight already agrees with you. For this process to be effective, you need to make sure that your words appear along with those of your source. No matter how well written your source, readers will ultimately be persuaded by your words, not by selected statements from someone else. In the following paragraph, for example, the writer uses the final sentence to make sure readers see how the information he cites fits his own argument.

Accompanying this modern view of the nuclear family were the sentiments that enlivened it. The first of these was the sentiment, as described by Edward Shorter in *The Making of the Modern Family*, of *romantic love*. Beginning with nineteenth-century individualism, the belief arose that for each of us there is one other individual who was created as our perfect mate. Once we encountered that person, we would know it instantly and proceed to spend the rest of our lives forever "happily-ever-aftering." An essential condition of this romantic ideal was that a young woman would "save" herself for her fated partner. In this romantic context, [her] virginity was a valuable commodity that could be exchanged for a lifelong commitment to the relationship. Romantic love worked to keep couples together even when they were unhappy. **While this ideal was unfortunate for parents in unrewarding relationships, it often benefited children because parents stayed together and usually did not blame the children for the failure of the marriage.**

—DAVID ELKIND, "The Family in the Postmodern World"

3 Use factual information

The range of facts available to you on most issues is wide; it includes statistics, technical information, the results of surveys and interviews, background information, and historical data. Which of these sources you choose and the role each plays in your writing will depend on the issue you are addressing, your point of view, and the views or knowledge of your intended readers. Be alert to the varieties of factual information as you think about an issue and undertake research, and consider how you might use facts to support your argument. Here is an example of factual information gathered to support an author's thesis.

11b
arg

> Meanwhile, young people find it harder and harder to form or sustain families. According to an Associated Press report of April 25, 1995, the median income of men aged twenty-five to thirty-four fell by 26 percent between 1972 and 1994, while the proportion of such men with earnings below the poverty level for a family of four more than doubled to 32 percent. The figures are even worse for African American and Latino men. Poor individuals are twice as likely to divorce as more affluent ones, three to four times less likely to marry in the first place, and five to seven times more likely to have a child out of wedlock.
>
> —STEPHANIE COONTZ, "The Way We Weren't"

4 Use comparisons

One important way to arrive at a judgment is to compare an issue or a problem about which you are uncertain to one about which you are more certain. Comparisons can be particularly useful when you are arguing for a policy; your readers will be concerned about the consequences of the policy and its likelihood for success or failure. In trying to decide whether to expand a local recycling program, for example, you might reasonably look at the success of similar programs. A comparison can help to persuade because it points to the probability of certain outcomes.

At the same time, you should expect readers to approach comparisons critically. Instead of asking a comparison to stand on its own, take care to point out its applicability and to answer possible objections to it. The author of the following passage uses comparison to argue for two-parent, child-centered families even though he acknowledges that one-parent families can raise children successfully.

> Infants and children need, at minimum, one adult to care for them. Yet, given the complexities of the task, childrearing in all societies until recent years has been shared by many adults. The institutional bond of marriage between biological parents, with the essential function of tying the father to the mother and child, is found in virtually every society. Marriage is the most universal social institution known; in no society has nonmarital childbirth, or the single parent,

been the cultural norm. In all societies the biological father is identi-fied where possible, and in almost all societies he plays an important role in his children's upbringing, even though his primary task is of-ten that of protector and breadwinner.

—DAVID POPENOE, "The American Family Crisis"

STRATEGY **Find support for your proposition**

11c
arg

Develop a list of questions that can guide your search for facts, ideas, and experiences to support your proposition. Here are possible questions.

- What might be the good or the bad consequences of this policy?
- What do experts say about solutions to the problem?
- What religious or moral values support my position on this issue?
- What comparisons could be made to help readers understand my perspective?

Answering these questions can help you decide whether your own knowledge is enough to support an assertion or whether you need additional information.

11c Incorporating counterarguments

Traditional argumentation is like debate: you imagine an adversary, someone who doesn't go along with your ideas, and try to undermine that ad-versary's points or **counterarguments.** Yet most contemporary approaches to argument aren't quite so battle-like. Your goal should be not so much to win as to acknowledge other people's perspectives and still convince them of the validity of your views. With any kind of argument, however, you need to anticipate your readers' reactions.

STRATEGY **Develop counterarguments**

Use lists and columns to help develop counterarguments. Divide a sheet of paper into three columns. On the left, list the main points supporting your opinion. Write opposing points (counterarguments) in the middle column, making the strongest case for the other point of view. In the right column, list the possible defenses to each counterargument in the middle column.

If you have difficulty imagining a point of view other than your own, take your thesis or position to a more public forum. Put the idea forward tentatively—ask "What do you think about this issue?" or "Do you think that we ought to do X to solve Y?"—and listen carefully and take note of the responses. You might gently extend others' reasoning by raising a subsidiary issue or coun-terargument: "But what about the fact that . . . ?" Again, listen to the responses.

Exercise 1

A. Using the strategy described in 10c, develop a working thesis statement. List at least three items of supporting evidence or arguments for your assertion.

B. In a small group, use the Strategy in 11c to create a list of counter-arguments for each member's main supporting arguments. In a discussion of each thesis statement, respond collectively to the counter-arguments in ways that weaken the objections to the original arguments.

11d Logical strategies (Logos)

When you employ **logical strategies** for argument, you arrange your ideas and evidence in ways that correspond with patterns of thought that most people accept as reasonable and convincing. You do not have to provide absolute proof for your opinion; if you could, there would be no need to argue. After all, arguments are made to resolve disagreements precisely because an absolutely correct position cannot be identified. An argument helps readers choose among reasonable alternatives.

Here are four of the most commonly used logical strategies.

- **Reasoning from consequences.** You argue for or against an action, outlook, or interpretation, basing your argument on its real or likely consequences, good or bad.
- **Reasoning from comparison.** You argue for or against a policy or point of view, basing your argument on similar situations, problems, or actions.
- **Reasoning from authority and testimony.** You draw ideas and evidence to support your outlook from recognized experts or from people whose experience makes them trustworthy witnesses.
- **Reasoning from example and statistics.** You draw on events, situations, and problems presented as illustrations (examples) or in summarized, numerical form (statistics) to support your point of view.

Inductive and deductive arguments. Induction and deduction are other commonly used logical strategies. A **deductive argument** begins with an explicitly stated **premise** (or assertion or claim) and then goes on to support that premise. It uses **syllogistic reasoning** as its basic logical format. A **syllogism** includes a **major premise,** a **minor premise,** and a **conclusion.** Here is a simple truthful syllogism.

MAJOR PREMISE	All landowners in Clarksville must pay taxes.
MINOR PREMISE	Fred Hammil owns land in Clarksville.
CONCLUSION	Therefore, Fred Hammil must pay taxes.

Faulty syllogistic reasoning is easily illustrated in a flawed syllogism.

MAJOR PREMISE	All Ferraris are fast.
MINOR PREMISE	That car is fast.
CONCLUSION	Therefore, that car is a Ferrari.

11d
arg

In a complex deductive argument these kinds of reasoning are much more elaborate, but this basic syllogistic pattern can be used to shape each paragraph as well as to frame the paper as a whole.

An **inductive argument** does not explicitly state a premise; rather, it leads readers through an accumulation of evidence until they conclude what the writer wants them to. Such arguments usually begin with a **hypothesis,** which differs from an assertion in being a tentative idea that the writer wants to consider but has not yet reached a hard-and-fast conclusion about. Of course, in a finished written argument, this hypothesis is somewhat disingenuous because the writer *does* have a conclusion but withholds it until readers are convinced by the supporting points.

This form of argument can be effective when you take a controversial stand on an issue. If you were to assert your stand explicitly at the beginning of the paper, you might put many readers on the defensive, ready to reject whatever you say. However, if you hold off your assertion, readers may also hold off their judgment.

Exercise 2

Compose a simple proposition or thesis, and then try to support it with each of the four logical strategies described in 11d (reasoning from consequences, reasoning from comparison, reasoning from authority and testimony, and reasoning from example and statistics). Invent authoritative statements or statistics if you wish.

EXAMPLE

Simple proposition: The student senate's proposal to allow alcoholic beverages to be served in the student union should not be passed.

Reasoning from consequences: The consumption of alcohol will increase crime on campus, especially personal assaults, drunk driving, and rape.

Reasoning from comparison: Easy availability of alcohol deters
students from their academic work; when a bar opened briefly
three years ago near fraternity row, every fraternity experienced a
drop in average grades.

Reasoning from authority and testimony: Having alcohol so easily
available on campus may subvert our college's mission by
contributing not to students' growth but to their deterioration.
According to research conducted by Legman and Witherall, a large
percentage of alcoholics over the age of thirty reported that their
college binge drinking set a strong pattern for their later addiction.

Reasoning from example and statistics: Bars on campus draw students
away from more beneficial activities. Two years after Carmon College
opened a wine and beer hall on campus, participation in lectures
and special events had dropped by 26 percent; attendance at the
film series declined by 18 percent; and weekend library usage
between 5 p.m. and midnight dropped by 43 percent.

11e Emotional strategies (Pathos)

In drawing on **emotional strategies,** you focus on the values, attitudes, belief systems, and feelings that guide people's lives and that are central to any decision-making process.

Values and beliefs. You may present examples, ideas, or
statements that confirm or contradict your readers' probable
values.

Emotions and attitudes. You may present examples or use language that draws emotional responses, positive or negative,
from your readers: "The consequence of this policy will be an
increase in the already horrifying flood of bruised, battered,
undernourished two- and three-year-olds brought into emergency rooms by parents who deny even the most obvious
evidence of abuse."

Be aware that readers often see emotional strategies as weaker support for a point than reason or logic. In an argument against the use of animals for research, for example, an emotional appeal to end cruelty to animals could be countered by an emotional appeal to continue research to cure terrible diseases. A general emotional appeal about animal suffering would not be as strong as specific, verifiable accounts of animals being subjected to unbearable pain in the name of research. Often the most powerful emotional appeals will be those directly linked to other forms of logical support.

EMOTIONAL STRATEGIES IN THREE COMMUNITIES

	ACADEMIC	PUBLIC	WORK
GOALS	Argue for one meaning of a concept or value (e.g., democracy, capitalism, literacy). Argue that a specific kind of analysis or technique is preferable because of the values it embodies (e.g., humanistic sociology, minimally invasive surgery).	Persuade an audience that a policy or program is consistent with its values. Use emotions to encourage actions consistent with an audience's beliefs.	Argue that a particular solution or policy is consistent with the organization's values or will reinforce the work community.
STRATEGIES	Argue for definition of beliefs and values. Endorse sets of values. Apply values to evaluate actions, institutions, or policies.	Define beliefs and values; endorse them through appeal to emotions and values (e.g., patriotism, caring, service, group unity). Use beliefs and emotional commitments to encourage people to act or to support a policy.	Refer to shared values and argue that a particular policy embodies those values. Point out likely effects on feelings of those in the work community.
EXAMPLE	Counseling techniques that go beyond what patients are readily willing to share are invasive and show a gross lack of respect.	The proposal to create a Safe Sports program is consistent with the city council's "Raising Healthy Children" initiative and will reflect the feelings and values of the many young families that have moved to Watertown in the last decade.	Adopting healthy workplace activities will be consistent with the concept of a workplace community and will create feelings of well-being among employees.

11f
arg

11f Data-warrant-claim (Toulmin) reasoning

In *The Uses of Argument* (1964), Stephen Toulmin proposes **data-warrant-claim reasoning,** which draws on the kinds of statements reasonable people usually make when they argue: statements of data, claims, and warrants. A statement of *data* corresponds to your evidence and *claim* to your conclusion. *Warrant*, however, is a more complex term: it refers to the mental process by which a reader connects the data to the claim. It answers the question "How?" Another way to understand this is to think of data as the indisputable facts and the warrant as the probable facts and assertions.

For instance, your data might be the results of a factual study of the likelihood of injury in each of the models of cars currently on the market. You could make a number of interpretive statements about the data (warrants) and point out the patterns you see (probable facts: warrants) in order to offer reasoning that links the data to your claim: for the average consumer, buying a large car is a good way to reduce the likelihood of being injured in an accident.

To argue effectively, you need to show your readers *how* the data and the claim are connected. To warrant such a claim, you could say that there are small, medium, and large cars in the ratings and extend this warrant by pointing out that the large cars have a higher safety rating. To back up this warrant, you point out that although some of the smaller cars on each list are quite safe, in general, the large cars are the safest. You could extend the argument by citing further statistics (data) about safety along with arguments and reasoning from other sources (warrants).

11f
arg

DATA

Ratings of each car model according to likelihood of injury to driver and passenger (scale: 1 = low to 10 = high)

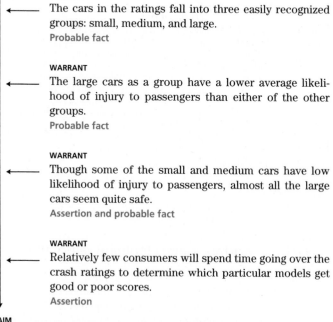

WARRANT

The cars in the ratings fall into three easily recognized groups: small, medium, and large.
Probable fact

WARRANT

The large cars as a group have a lower average likelihood of injury to passengers than either of the other groups.
Probable fact

WARRANT

Though some of the small and medium cars have low likelihood of injury to passengers, almost all the large cars seem quite safe.
Assertion and probable fact

WARRANT

Relatively few consumers will spend time going over the crash ratings to determine which particular models get good or poor scores.
Assertion

CLAIM

For the average consumer, buying a large car is a good way to reduce the likelihood of being injured in an accident.

11g Audience and purpose (Rogerian argument)

Remember that you won't write an effective argument if all you do is stridently voice your opinion on an issue. An argument is effective only when it's part of a relationship between you and your audience. Determining who your audience members are, how you want them to perceive you, and what you want to convince them of is the essential first step to constructing an argument (see Chapter 3).

Rogerian argument, based on the theories of the psychologist and group therapist Carl Rogers, provides a useful perspective for considering the responses of your audience. Rogers argued that people's minds can more easily be changed when their opponent seems like an ally instead of an enemy. A highly combative or adversarial approach immediately puts a reader on the defensive, thereby setting up a barrier to your ideas. The reader's psychological reaction is "Oh yeah? Well, let me tell you something, Buster!" rather than "Hmmm, that's an interesting point worth considering."

Identifying alternative views. To practice a Rogerian strategy, imagine for a moment that you share the views of someone who is opposed to your own position or solution. What is your opponent's frame of reference? What assumptions might have led him or her to those views? What validity can you see in anything your opponent might say? Rogers found that a good way to understand someone's point of view is to try to restate it rather than counter it. Statements of reflection and repetition—"What I hear you saying is . . ." and "It sounds to me like you're trying to . . ." —allow not only for a mutual understanding of each other's points but for a mutual respect for differences of opinion once those points are clearly articulated.

Making a concession. When you understand your opponent's ideas, you may be prepared to work a **concession** into your argument. You make a concession when you acknowledge or consider a view opposed to the one you are arguing. A concession does not have to be so strong that it undermines your entire argument. But placed strategically, it can show your effort to be fair and help persuade a reader to listen. Signal such a concession with *although* or *of course.*

In a letter to the editor bemoaning the extinction of family-run hardware stores in the shadow of warehouse-sized lumber centers, Angie Krastaat made an extended concession—that consumers may be attracted by lower prices and the large selection at the lumber centers—but then countered it with an anecdote that led to a generalization.

> Of course, the lumber centers do have their draws: paint in every color, discounted power tools, and items too large to fit into most small stores. But what they gain in selection and pricing they sorely lack in their robot-like relationship with their customers. Where else can you get a

single nut, bolt, or nail—just one—than a local hardware store? What large lumber center will replace that torn screen or broken window while you wait? Where can you find someone at Mega-Hardware who will work with you in the store to repair something, using ingenuity and bins full of single items?

| **STRATEGY** | **Limit your audience** |

To make your argument on "hot" issues more effective, try limiting your audience. Focus on a particular group of people concerned about the issue—on abortion, for example, focus on reaching sexually active teens, unmarried mothers, or the people who protest at abortion clinics. Also consider your image as an arguer. How do you want your readers to perceive you? Do you want to be perceived as erudite, rational, and coolly objective? as passionate and moving? as outraged? as reflective and forgiving?

11h Misleading and illogical reasoning

A **fallacy** is a flaw in the reasoning of any persuasive work, whether it's an argumentative essay, a report, a review, or an advertisement. An ad for beer that shows attractive, bikini-clad women and muscular, handsome men romping on a California beach implies (illogically) that drinking the beer will get you that lifestyle. This example of faulty cause-effect reasoning implies that *because* you drink the beer, you'll be like the people in the ad. The same fallacy may appear in academic and professional writing as well, but it may not be so obvious. For instance, if you read an article that says legalizing marijuana will result in a dangerous increase in cocaine use, you ought to question how the writer demonstrates that cause-effect relationship and ask what evidence links marijuana use to cocaine use.

Faulty cause-effect relationship. This problem is also called *post hoc, ergo propter hoc* (Latin for "after this, therefore because of this") or simply a **post hoc fallacy.** This flawed reasoning attempts to persuade you that because one event happens after the other, the first event causes the second.

FAULTY CAUSE-EFFECT The increase in explicit violence on television is making the crime rate soar.
READER'S REACTION: This *may* be true, but no evidence is presented here linking the two situations.

False analogy. Analogies are comparisons between two things, often on the basis of shared characteristics. In a false analogy, the things may at first seem to be comparable but are not. (See the discussion of the red herring and *ad populum* fallacies in this section.)

FALSE ANALOGY Raising the national speed limit is like offering free cocktails at a meeting of recovering alcoholics.

> READER'S REACTION: I don't see the connection. Most drivers aren't recovering from an addiction to high-speed driving, and a legal limit is not the same thing as self-restraint.

Misleading language/misleading evidence. This fallacy is also called **equivocation** and **slanted statistics**. A writer can use misleading language by beginning with one definition of a term (usually one that everyone agrees with) and then shifting to another sense of the word, one that supports the writer's argument but that not all readers may agree with.

11h
arg

MISLEADING
LANGUAGE
Everyone has the right of free speech, so censoring films by rating them Triple X is against one's constitutional rights.

> READER'S REACTION: This tries to pass off the *rating* of films as censorship (which it is not) and assumes that *free speech* and *censorship* are directly opposite terms (which they are not necessarily).

Misleading evidence includes statistics, survey results, and expert opinion stacked in favor of one side of an argument. For instance, someone who used an opinion poll to argue for the preservation of the spotted owl but polled only people at an environmental rally would have overwhelmingly favorable but misleading evidence.

Red herring. Similar to misleading evidence is the red herring fallacy. A *red herring* is something that distracts readers from the real argument.

RED HERRING Gun control laws need to be passed as soon as possible to decrease the rate of domestic violence and home firearms accidents. The people who think guns should not be controlled are probably criminals themselves.

> READER'S REACTION: The second sentence doesn't logically follow from the first; it just attacks the people who would oppose the writer's argument instead of supporting the initial assertion.

Ad populum. *Ad populum* means "to the people" and refers to an argument that appeals to the audience's biases instead of offering rational support.

AD POPULUM All doctors should be tested for AIDS and should not be allowed to practice if they test HIV-positive, so they don't spread the disease to their patients. Do you want to be one of those patients?

> READER'S REACTION: This writer is obviously trying to invoke my fear of getting AIDS. The claim that HIV-positive doctors will pass on the disease to patients is not founded on valid research.

Ad hominem. Another faulty argument based on audience biases is the *ad hominem* fallacy, which means "to the man." This is a personal attack on an opponent rather than a debate on the issue.

AD HOMINEM   Of course Walt Smith would support a bill to provide financial assistance to farmers—he owns several large farms in
the Midwest. Besides, how can he be a good senator after
cheating on his wife?

READER'S REACTION: I'd like to hear reactions to Walt Smith's ideas,
please. I don't really care whether he had an affair fifteen years ago.

Bandwagon. This fallacy is also called *consensus gentium*, "consensus of
the people." A **bandwagon argument** is one that tries to convince you that
because everyone else agrees with the idea already, you ought to join in.

BANDWAGON   Each year an increasing number of people are quitting
smoking, so you ought to quit, too.

READER'S REACTION: This writer is trying to convince me to quit by
saying that other people are doing it. Even though the assertion
may be valid, the support is not.

Begging the question. This fallacy is also called **overgeneralization** or
hasty generalization. An argument begs the question when it presents assumptions as if they were facts, sometimes using the words and phrases
obviously, certainly, clearly, people always/never, and even the seemingly
innocuous *some people say.*

BEGGING   Most people these days are trying to be more physically fit;
THE QUESTION   obviously, they are afraid of getting old.

READER'S REACTION: No evidence is presented for either the claim
that most people are trying to be more fit or the claim that they
are afraid of getting old. On what basis are these stated as
facts?

Either/or. An **either/or strategy** oversimplifies an issue, making it seem as
if it has only two sides.

EITHER/OR   On the matter of abortion, there are two positions: either
we support a human's right to life, or we allow women to
have complete control over their bodies.

READER'S REACTION: Why can't someone endorse protecting life
while also supporting the right to choose what happens to one's
body?

Circular reasoning. *Circular reasoning,* also called **tautology,** is an attempt to support an assertion with the assertion itself.

CIRCULAR   The university should increase funding of intramural sports
REASONING   because it has a responsibility to back its sports programs
financially.

READER'S REACTION: All this says is that the university should fund
sports because it should fund sports.

Exercise 2

A. Choose a controversial topic you know something about—gun control, abortion, the death penalty, the right to die. Now choose any three of the fallacies described in 11h and write one example of each fallacy to make claims about your topic. (Don't identify the names of the fallacies in your response.)

B. In a small group, exchange copies of your fallacious arguments. Discuss each set of fallacies and try to identify the logical problems. Then suggest revisions or identify the specific kinds of support that may be needed.

11i Documented argument or position paper

A **position** paper or **documented argument** is a sharply focused form of argumentative writing that draws heavily on research to take a stand on a question of action or policy, generally an issue of considerable concern in academic, public, or work communities. A position paper defines its issue, considers its audience, and draws on evidence and logical strategies to make its point.

1 Sample position paper

In the following paper, note how the writer frames his argument with an opening reference to fast-food chains and the growing problem of obesity in America. As you read, consider who the writer's audience is, what the main argument is, and how he constructs the support for the argument. What are the counterarguments, and how does he address them? What kind of support, if any, is missing? What fallacies, if any, do you detect?

Pusateri 1

Paul Pusateri

Dr. Drept

WRT 101

15 October 2008

Running Uphill

1   Who is at fault? Is it the fast-food chains for putting

such fattening items in front of consumers with endless

promotions and marketing schemes? Or is it the consumer's

Defines the
issue

Pusateri 2

fault for eating the unhealthy meals knowing full well the

negative consequences? Suing a fast-food chain for causing

**Mentions
authorities**

your own obesity, as some people have done (Cohen), may be

extreme. As one report puts it, "Fast-food litigation has been

greeted coolly so far because it appears to run up against a

**11i
arg**

core American value: personal responsibility" (Cohen A24). At

the same time, this does not mean that the fast-food chains

are free from significant blame for the rise of obesity and

similar health problems that affect many people today (Surgeon

General). The truth is that most people know fast food may not

be good for them; they simply don't realize just how unhealthy

it is. For example, how many of us know that a "quick lunch" at

McDonald's, including a Big Mac, fries, and a Coke, has 62

grams of fat and 1,500 calories? (Barrett 74). Even though the

chains are starting to make their menus healthier, they are still

**Argumentative
proposition**

to blame. Their pricing policies, overall menus, and marketing

techniques lead people to eat fast food no matter how much

fat it contains or how many calories it provides.

2   How are we to know what is good for us and not so good

in the food we eat? What standard can we use to judge the

**Standards for
evaluating
audience**

meals offered by fast-food restaurants? To maintain a desirable,

healthy weight, men need about 2,700 calories per day, and

women need about 2,000. The American Heart Association

recommends less than three hundred milligrams of cholesterol

and fifty to eighty grams of fat per day, while the National

Academy of Sciences recommends 1,100 to 3,300 milligrams of

salt per day (Minnesota Attorney General). In each case, the

national average intake is higher (Minnesota Attorney General),

driven in part, perhaps, by the amount of fast food we eat.

3   Not all fast food contains excessive salt, cholesterol, and calories, of course, but the items that dominate the menus at a Wendy's, Burger King, McDonald's, and other fast-food restaurants and that appear frequently in advertising generally do. For example, a report by the Minnesota Attorney General gives these nutrition facts for two staples of fast-food menus, a cheeseburger dinner and a pizza dinner.

11i
arg

1. Quarter-Pound Cheeseburger, large fries, 16 oz. soda (McDonald's)

Supporting evidence

This meal:	Recommended daily intake:
1,166 calories	2,000–2,700 calories
51 g fat	No more than 50–80 g
95 mg cholesterol	No more than 300 mg
1,450 mg sodium	No more than 1,100–3,300 mg

2. Four slices sausage and mushroom pizza, 16 oz. soda (Domino's)

This meal:	Recommended daily intake:
1,000 calories	2,000–2,700 calories
28 g fat	No more than 50–80 g
62 mg cholesterol	No more than 300 mg
2,302 mg sodium	No more than 1,100–3,300 mg

4   The information in these charts is probably astonishing to most of us. Even though restaurants make nutrition facts available to customers and publish them online—for example, at a McDonald's Web site (McDonald's USA)—the "need for speed" and convenience that makes us turn to fast-food restaurants in the first place means that most of us do not consult the lists of nutritional facts. Instead, we order foods prominently displayed on menus or we order by price, from a

Brief concession followed by supporting arguments

11i
arg

Pusateri 4

value menu or a promotional special, both of which in my experience feature familiar and relatively unhealthful choices. In so doing, we often pass by the better choices, the small fries rather than the large, for example. At McDonald's, instead of a quarter-pound cheeseburger and large fries, we might choose a hamburger and small fries with 481 calories and 19 grams of fat, a healthier solution (Minnesota Attorney General).

Concession

5   Admittedly, fast-food chains have been adding healthier options to their menus. Arby's Light Roast Chicken has 276 calories and only seven grams of fat; Wendy's has a healthy chili with 210 calories and seven grams of fat. Burger King and McDonald's offer a vanilla shake with five grams of fat and a chicken salad with only four grams of fat, respectively (Minnesota Attorney General).

Menu
placement

6   These items often do not receive adequate emphasis in advertising or menu placement, however. In addition, the lack of adequate emphasis frequently means that customers end up thinking that some kinds of food are healthy when they are not. As Kelly Frey points out in "Salad Not Always Healthiest Fast-Food Choice," a Crispy Chicken Salad with ranch dressing at McDonald's has eight more calories and nineteen more grams of fat than a Big Mac. Salads from Wendy's and Burger King may also have more fat and calories than the burgers. Even a Cobb Salad with low-fat dressing at McDonald's would take a 150-pound person sixty minutes to walk off all 320 calories it contains (Barrett 74).

Advertising
and
marketing

7   Even television ads that pass certain tests for truthfulness can be misleading. The ads for Subway, for example, leave the impression that the chain's sandwiches are healthful. Some are, yet many are not. Subway's advertising is factually true. The specific sandwiches advertised as healthful

Pusateri 5

actually are; it is the others that are not, but they tend to fall within the general impression of healthfulness created by the advertising. At Subway, a six-inch BMT Italian sandwich has thirty-nine grams of fat, the same as a Big Mac from McDonald's and a Bacon Double Cheeseburger from Burger King (Diet Riot). A Quarter Pounder or a Whopper Jr. would be a better choice for me than the Cold Cut Trio I commonly eat at Subway.

11i
arg

8   The blame may lie with the fast-food chains, but the responsibility for making healthier choices is ours as well. There are ways we can do this, but even the available healthy choices are outside the range of those usually marketed by the chains. Nonetheless, an article like Jo Lichten's "Healthiest Fast Food for Busy Travelers" can be a guide. From it I learned that Burger King's Mustard Whopper Jr., which replaces mayonnaise with mustard, decreases calories by eighty. I thought that Mexican fast food could not taste good and be healthy; I found that a Bean Burrito from Taco Bell can be a complete meal with only 370 calories and twelve grams of fat (Lichten). It's like running uphill, but it is possible to begin reversing the unhealthy practices for which fast-food chains are still to blame.

Modifies
argumentative
proposition

Proposes
course of
action

Pusateri 6

Works Cited

Barrett, Jennifer. "Fast Food Need Not Be Fat Food." *Newsweek*
    13 Oct. 2003: 73-74. Academic First Search. *EBSCO*. Web.
    21 Oct. 2008.

Cohen, Adam. "The McNugget of Truth in the Fast-Food Lawsuits."
    New York Times 3 Feb. 2003, late ed.: A24. Print.

Pusateri 7

"Diet Riot." *DietRiot.com* 14 Oct. 2003. Web. 19 Oct. 2008.

Frey, Kelly. "Salad Not Always Healthiest Fast-Food Choice." *The Pittsburgh Channel.com* 15 May 2003. Web. 19 Oct. 2008.

Lichten, Jo. "Healthiest Fast Food for Busy Travelers." *American Woman Road and Travel.* 2003. Web. 5 Oct. 2008.

McDonald's USA. "McDonald's USA Nutrition Information." 21 Oct. 2003. Web. 31 Oct. 2008.

Minnesota Attorney General. *Fast Food Facts*. Web. 19 Oct. 2008.

Surgeon General of the United States. *The Surgeon General's Call to Action: Prevent and Decrease Overweight and Obesity.* Washington: GPO, 2003. Print.

2 Comment on Paul Pusateri's Paper

Pusateri's argumentative thesis is clear, if a bit complicated. He does a good job of supporting it with a variety of evidence. Some readers are likely to agree with his outlook, at least in part. As he admits, however, many are likely to prefer to put the responsibility elsewhere: on the people who choose the food they eat, not on the restaurants that serve it. Whether or not they are persuaded, however, most readers are likely to agree that he has made a sound case for his point of view.

Visit mycomplab.com for more resources and exercises on developing, supporting, and documenting an argument.

CHAPTER 12

Creating a Visual Argument

Visuals can be an important and even critical component of argument. They can help explain an issue or problem. They can clarify supporting evidence. They can draw on emotions and values to make your argument especially persuasive. However, visuals can't do all the work of argument and shouldn't be expected to substitute for careful reasoning and factual supporting evidence.

12a Presenting the argument

The issues and information you present in an argument can be complex and detailed, yet you need to discuss them clearly and concisely if you expect readers to understand your point of view and follow your reasoning. Visuals can both simplify and clarify your presentation: they can emphasize the importance of an issue while providing details that can be quickly seen and understood.

1 Calling attention to an issue

A picture or a chart can illustrate or document a problem in ways that explain it briefly and help readers understand why it is worth arguing about. Here are the opening sentences of a paper arguing against the strip mining of coal as a way to solve future energy needs. They are supported by two visuals, Figures 12.1 and 12.2.

> Cold winters and hot summers remind us that we need to develop new sources of energy and turn from a reliance on foreign oil to abundant domestic sources like coal. But are new sources like ethanol much better for the environment than oil?
>
> Can ethanol production from sources like soybeans actually aid deforestation?
>
> Do coal mining's effects on the environment outweigh its availability and relatively low cost? How about the ravages of strip mining for coal or new sources such as shale or tar sands?

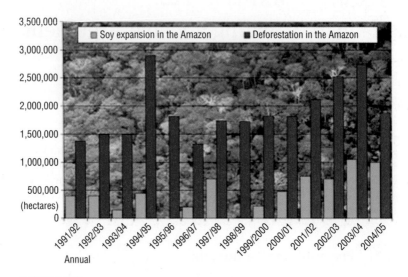

FIGURE 12.1 Soy expansion and deforestation in the Brazilian Amazon, 1990–2005
Source: <http://rainforests.mongabay.com/amazon/deforestationcalculation>.

FIGURE 12.2 This image of a strip mine in Texas reminds us of U.S. coal mining destruction

BEING CRITICAL

A visual that calls attention to an issue can do so with such emotional power that it goes beyond explaining to arguing. As a reader, be alert to the power of visuals and ask critical questions of them. Is the information accurate? Does it tell the whole story? Are other interpretations possible?

Of the two visuals above (Figures 12.1 and 12.2), you might ask, "Is ethanol from soybeans likely to play much of a role in the United States?" and "Are all landscapes going to be as difficult to restore as the one in the picture?" Because some people might answer yes to both questions, a responsible writer would use the visuals to call attention to the issue but suggest that reasonable people might have different opinions.

12a
arg

2 Explaining an issue or a problem

When an issue or a problem needs to be understood in terms of numbers, statistics, or relationships among facts, a table (p. 139), a graph (p. 140), or a chart (Figure 12.3) can substitute for sentences filled with potentially confusing detail.

COMPLICATED   A recent survey showed considerable support for noise reduction efforts in the town. Of the respondents, 45 percent strongly supported the efforts; 20 percent gave moderate support; 15 percent gave mild support; and 20 percent offered no support.

CLEAR AT A
GLANCE

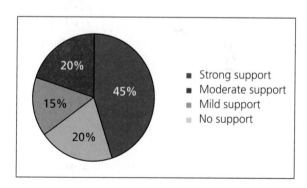

FIGURE 12.3 Survey results: Support for noise-reduction laws

Pictures can help readers understand complicated physical settings or problems such as dorms that pose a fire hazard or neighborhoods that need to be revitalized. They can present social relationships or issues, including

Omar is 13 years old and has experienced the violent uprooting of his family and extreme personal loss. He has missed out on most of his education and his sense of security and stability has been shattered. Save the Children opened a children's center at the camp where Omar and his siblings live and now he spends every day there.

"I come to the centre because I like to learn new things"

Omar's Story ➤

Fifty-five thousand children have already attended these centers, which have been established in eleven different locations around West Darfur. The child-friendly spaces provide a secure location for children like Omar who have become, through conflict, part of a new and transient community facing special risks. Some are neglected, most miss out on adult attention and guidance, and they are at risk of abuse if left unsupervised. Families can make use of the centers for temporary child care as an alternative to leaving their children alone. At the same time they can learn basic literacy, numeracy, hygiene practices and social skills.

FIGURE 12.4   Omar's story: Save the Children
Source: <http://www.savethechildren.org/campaigns/rewrite-the-future/omars-story.html>.

those that involve values or emotions. The organization Save the Children, for example, uses photographs integrated with text to emphasize the poverty and need of the children it serves as well as the urgency of the problem (see Figure 12.4). The photos also support the agency's attempts to persuade readers to contribute to the organization.

12b Providing evidence

Visuals can add depth and detail to the reasoning and evidence you present in words, or they can stand more or less on their own, relying on verbal commentary in the visuals themselves. Visual evidence is of two kinds: (1) facts and statistics presented in the form of graphs, tables, or charts, and (2) photographs or drawings that are evidence in themselves. Facts and statistics presented as columns of figures (tables) or in graphs and charts can simplify the presentation of complex evidence. They can also highlight key points. They make evidence easier to understand and more persuasive. For

Country	Overall Pace of Life	Walking Speeds	Postal Times	Clock Accuracy
THE PACE OF LIFE IN 31 COUNTRIES				
Switzerland	1	3	2	1
Ireland	2	1	3	11
Germany	3	5	1	8
Japan	4	7	4	6
Italy	5	10	12	2
England	6	4	9	13
Sweden	7	13	5	7
Austria	8	23	8	3
Netherlands	9	2	14	25
Hong Kong	10	14	6	14
France	11	8	18	10
Poland	12	12	15	8
Costa Rica	13	16	10	15
Taiwan	14	18	7	21
Singapore	15	25	11	4
USA	16	6	23	20
Canada	17	11	21	22
S. Korea	18	20	20	16
Hungary	19	19	19	18
Czech Republic	20	21	17	23
Greece	21	14	13	29
Kenya	22	9	30	24
China	23	24	25	12
Bulgaria	24	27	22	17
Romania	25	30	29	5
Jordan	26	28	27	19
Syria	27	29	28	27
El Salvador	28	22	16	31
Brazil	29	31	24	28
Indonesia	30	26	26	30
Mexico	31	17	31	26

12b
arg

FIGURE 12.5 The pace of life in thirty-one countries
Source: Levine, Robert. "The Pace of Life in 31 Countries." *American Demographics,* 19 (1997): 20–29.

example, comparative data about the relative pace of life in thirty-one countries is efficiently summarized in the table above (Figure 12.5).

Visual presentations can also appeal to values and emotions, as does the map on page 140 (Figure 12.6), in which the color red indicates states with what the author considers fewer or inadequate gun control laws. (Note: Using such strategies to add emphasis to weak or questionable evidence is unethical.)

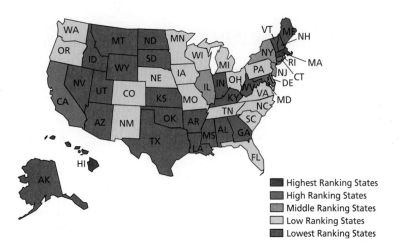

■ Highest Ranking States
■ High Ranking States
■ Middle Ranking States
□ Low Ranking States
■ Lowest Ranking States

FIGURE 12.6   A comparative survey of state firearm laws: highest refers to adequate gun control laws, lowest refers to inadequate gun control laws.
Source: <http://www.soros.org/initiaves/justice/articles_publications/publications/gun_report_2000401/GunReport_Chart1.pdf>.

Photographs and artwork (including line drawings) can highlight appeals to values and emotions and create vivid representatives of a larger group of examples.

Visuals can also help explain complicated reasoning; the graph below (Figure 12.7) highlights the consequences of failing to decrease birth rates in less-developed countries.

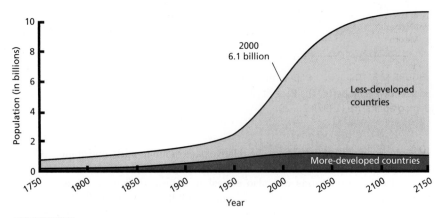

FIGURE 12.7   World population growth, 1750–2150
Source: <http://www.prb.org/PrintTemplate.cfm?Section=Population_Growth&template=/ContentManagement/HTMLDisplay.cfm&ContentID=5602>.

> **BEING CRITICAL**
>
> Visuals may seem to support a writer's argument, but they are always open to interpretation. As a reader, you'll want to ask these questions of visuals:
>
> - Does the writer offer an interpretation of the visual that takes into account other ways of interpreting it?
> - Is the interpretation convincing?
> - Does the visual provide complete information and evidence, or does it leave gaps?
> - Does incomplete information suggest that other interpretations are possible?
> - Even if the evidence is complete, are there other reasonable interpretations that need to be dealt with?

12d
arg

12c Reading images critically

As both a writer and a reader, you need to approach images with a critical eye and to analyze them carefully, both in terms of content and for their contribution to an argument. Keep this checklist in mind.

- **Information.** Look at the evidence a visual presents, and check it for accuracy. Writers may provide a discussion of the content of a visual in order to support its accuracy by citing additional sources.
- **Interpretation.** See if interpretations in the visual or in the accompanying text are well-reasoned, taking into account competing interpretations. Writers need to provide reasonable interpretations of the visuals they offer, as images can often be viewed in more than one way.
- **Beliefs, values, and feelings.** See if the feelings created by a visual are justified by the evidence presented in the argument. (Or are they excessive or loosely related to the argumentative proposition and evidence?) Writers should make clear the specific values and feelings to which they are appealing—telling why such appeals are justified.
- **Look for distortions.** Gaps in the information, excessive emotional appeals, and visuals that support an argument from which the writer personally benefits are suspect. Writers should provide as much relevant information as they can, limit the emotional dimensions of a visual, and be open about the fact that they might benefit. Readers should always ask, "Who benefits?"

12d Multimodal materials

There are several multimodal options that contemporary presentations can employ: audio with or without video; *PowerPoint* slides that provide music and spoken texts along with images; podcasts; and video clips inserted in a word-processed text. A text-based document can now incorporate multi-modal elements. Generally, its overall structure remains similar to that of a written argument text with added elements that offer variety, complexity, and depth. The added materials can make it more persuasive for many readers.

Other multimodal documents are likely to have a less strict beginning, middle, and end organization. A persuasive Web page, for example, is more likely to be a set of materials through which readers can choose their own path. Such a document (or similar ones such as a *PowerPoint* slide) should have a clear proposition and a sense that each element is related to this proposition by providing evidence or reinforcing key points. The order of the elements may be chosen by the writer, of course, but it is just as likely to be chosen by the reader.

12d arg

The Web site *PetFinder*, for instance, has a clear proposition: You (the reader) should adopt a pet—or at least consider seriously adopting a pet from a shelter or a similar institution (see Figure 12.8). To encourage this action, the site offers arguments and evidence in several modes: written text on the home page; pictures on the home page and on linked pages; links to a video with sound; interactive surveys and guides; places to share experiences with other readers; and a search engine for finding available pets.

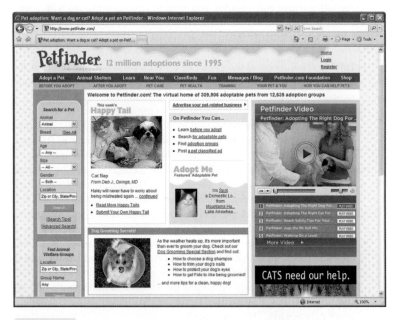

FIGURE 12.8 Petfinder Web site
Source: <http://www.petfinder.com/>.

Visit mycomplab.com for more resources and exercises on creating a visual argument.

PART 3

Presenting Your Work

Designing Documents

With all the resources available today electronically—pictures, graphs, color, type fonts, even streaming video—it's obvious that writing is far more than words alone. Writing now means producing an entire document, not just the words, and the final product can take many forms: paper, electronic, and multimedia. You can combine these elements in many ways, making choices appropriate for the community of readers you are addressing, the information you are presenting, the ideas you are exploring, and your purposes for writing.

13a Goals of document design

The choices you must make in designing a document fall into five categories: *goals, format, content and style, layout,* and *medium.* The goals you set for document design ought to shape all your other choices.

A well-designed document can achieve many goals.

- It alerts readers to your purpose(s).
- It emphasizes key points or ideas.
- It helps readers locate information.
- It explains relationships or supports arguments.
- It helps readers visualize information and heightens the effect of your words.
- It makes your writing more persuasive.

13b Format choice

Designing effective documents requires planning. There is no substitute for taking the time to consider your writing task and audience before you determine what format, layout, and visual aids (if any) you will use to support and enhance your presentation.

1 Consider your rhetorical situation and readers' needs

Your document design choices are affected by the same concerns that define your writing task: audience, purpose, and context. Readers need different things from different documents. The same reader approaches an essay about air pollution quite differently from a set of instructions for the operation of a chain saw. Equally true is the fact that two people might approach the same document in different ways. An engineer for a chemical plant that seeks to comply with EPA guidelines will read an essay about pollution with concerns very different from those of a homeowner who lives downwind from the plant.

2 Determine the form and shape of your document

As you begin considering document design, start with the big picture— the entire document and its overall shape—and then move to the important details of how you will integrate the various design elements.

- What format or document type will you use? How will you lay out the pages?
- What highlighting devices will you use to make your organization readily visible?
- What kind of font, typeface, and type size will you use?
- Will you use visual aids? If so, which ones?
- If you will use aids such as photographs or drawings, are there copyright issues or legal concerns you must address first?

13c
design

After you answer these questions, you should create a mock-up version of your document—a sketch that will help with planning. A sketched version of a document enables you to visualize how the various design elements addressed in Sections 13c–e will work together.

13c Layout

Layout is the arrangement of words, paragraphs, lists, tables, graphs, and pictures on a page or computer screen. Laying out your document effectively involves presenting information in a way that is easy to read, access, understand, and use.

1 Use visual cues

To increase the readability of your document, use visual cues such as boldface text and color. These devices will simplify your readers' task and influence their attitudes. But be careful to avoid overwhelming your text with visuals. Simplicity—a few well-chosen visual cues—often works best.

Use highlighting to direct the reader's eye and create emphasis. Typographic devices (see 13d) such as **boldface,** *italics*, shading, underlining, and boxes signal distinctions among items in a text, create impact by emphasizing a specific section, and help the reader locate main sections.

STRATEGY **Use highlighting to create emphasis**

- Use italics for emphasis or when irony or humor is intended. (See Chapter 58 for more on using italics.)
- When you want to emphasize something, consider using **boldface type.**
- Use capital letters for emphasis only, and use them infrequently. The use of all capital letters in a text's body becomes monotonous and hard to read. (See Chapter 57 for more on using capital letters.)
- Don't overuse exclamation marks. Be **angry,** or perhaps *angry,* but not angry!!! (For more on exclamation points, see 55c.)
- Don't use underlining on Web pages. Underlining on Web pages can cause confusion because hypertext links are almost always underlined. (For more on underlining, see 58b.)

Use color to create order. Using color effectively can help readers identify recurring themes (titles and subtitles), can reveal patterns and relationships (charts and graphs), and can speed searches. Be aware, however, that colors have different connotations among professional audiences (as shown below) and that color is not appropriate or necessary in all contexts.

COLOR	ENGINEERING	MEDICINE	FINANCE
blue	cold/water	death	reliable/corporate
red	danger	healthy/oxygenated	loss
green	safe/environmental	infection	profit

STRATEGY **Use color effectively**

- Use color to accomplish specific goals (to warn or caution, for instance), not just to decorate.
- Use color to prioritize information. Readers will go to bright colors first.
- Use color to symbolize. Draw on your knowledge of your readers.
- Use color to identify a theme that recurs or to sequence information.
- Use color to code symbols or sections and make searching for information easier.

---

2 Arrange information effectively

Effective document design enables users to locate important information quickly.

Use white space. *White space* is the term for open space not filled by design elements. It can be the spaces between letters, words, lines within a paragraph, or paragraphs. It also includes the margins and the space surrounding graphics. Used effectively, white space can guide the reader's eye from one point to another. Crowded pages are never crowd pleasers; always be sure there is adequate white space on every page of your document.

Use informative headings. Headings, concise phrases that forecast or announce content in upcoming sections, are usually larger and darker than the basic text of a document. Headings move readers along, helping them to see the organization of a document (the big picture) and to find the specific information they seek.

Notice how this handbook makes use of headings. You are reading at this point in the chapter:

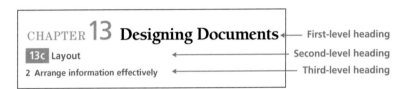

CHAPTER 13 **Designing Documents** ◄─── First-level heading

13c Layout ◄─────────────── Second-level heading

2 Arrange information effectively ◄───── Third-level heading

13c
design

STRATEGY   **Create appropriate headings**

- Use consistent type size and style for headings.
- Use different size type to indicate different levels of headings.
- Make your headings stand out—use boldface type and/or white space between headings and text.
- Position your headings consistently (for example, if you center first-level headings, do so throughout your document).
- Make headings content-specific and task- or reader-oriented (*"Deducting Student Loan Interest"* rather than *"Student Loan Interest"*).
- Make headings parallel in structure (see Chapter 46).
- Use only the headings you need; avoid clutter.

Use lists. Lists are an effective way to present information, making it easy for readers to grasp your major points. They break up dense text and make your document look more pleasing. Consider highlighting list items with cues such as bullets or numbers.

Rely on visual conventions. Just as our language has grammatical conventions, there are conventions for document design. Depending on the community you're in and the document you're writing, readers will expect to find certain features. Letters, memos, reports, and brochures all require their own formatting conventions. Your history teacher will expect to see a report that follows certain conventions while your prospective employer will look for others in your résumé.

13d Typeface choices

In preparing your document, you can take advantage of the large variety of typefaces and type sizes available with today's computers and software. But do so judiciously. Most readers would rather see no more than two or three different fonts in a single document. In addition, always select a typeface or font that addresses your audience and purpose in a tone that best reflects the subject matter without sacrificing readability.

- **Use a proper type size and weight to influence readers and help them read quickly and easily.** Type size affects legibility. Standard type size is 10, 11, or 12 point.

<table>
<tr><td>12 point</td><td>10 point</td></tr>
<tr><td>A New Deal.</td><td>A New Deal.</td></tr>
</table>

Because some fonts have thicker or wider letters, you can use type weight to highlight messages without relying on the use of boldface, italics, or shading.

- **Make reading easier by using serif and sans serif typefaces appropriately.** Serif typefaces have the "feet" or small strokes at the end of each letterform. Sans serif fonts lack them.

<table>
<tr><td>Serif</td><td>Sans serif</td></tr>
<tr><td>N</td><td>N</td></tr>
</table>

Readers tend to find serif typefaces easier on their eyes. Sans serif fonts are harder to read in long documents but work well in titles, headings, and labels. They also work well for material that will be presented on a computer screen. (Notice how serif and sans serif fonts are used in this handbook, for example.) Serif typefaces include Times New Roman, Courier, Garamond, and Century Schoolbook. Sans serif faces include Arial, **Impact**, and Tahoma.

- **Add interesting flourishes with display or decorative fonts.** Some documents, such as brochures, invitations, and posters, can use decorative fonts such as *Mistral*, Sand, **Cooper Black**, or Harrington to add special touches to catch readers' attention or sway their emotions. However, because these fonts are intended to be more ornamental than informative, they should be used with discretion.
- **Add emphasis or direct attention with symbols.** Used carefully, symbol fonts (such as those you find in Zapf Dingbats, Monotype Sorts, and Wingdings) can direct a reader's attention, emphasize a point, and add simple graphic flourishes to your documents. There are many of these special characters, and you should find them listed under

"symbols" in a pull-down menu in a word-processing program or in a list of fonts. You may find ornamental symbols and icons like these in your font menu.

ϑ ☐ Ξ ↔ ✎ ♪ 3̄ ♥

13e Visuals

Albert Einstein once said, "I rarely think in words at all." He thought in symbols and pictures; he envisioned concepts and information. Sometimes words aren't sufficient or aren't as efficient as tables, graphs, charts, photographs, maps, and drawings are in making a point. These visual aids, or graphics, are effective in bringing information to life.

- Graphics communicate what words cannot.
- Visuals are understood more quickly than words.
- Tables, charts, and other visuals help readers learn and retain information.
- Graphics entice readers, especially in public settings, where attention-getting is at a premium.

13e
design

VISUALS IN THREE COMMUNITIES

ACADEMIC SETTINGS	PUBLIC SETTINGS	WORK SETTINGS
Summarize and clarify complex relationships.	Emphasize appeals to emotions and values.	Outline features of a problem.
Present complicated data.	Highlight elements of a policy or proposed action.	Summarize goals.
Highlight conclusions.	Summarize key information.	Highlight recommendations or solutions.
In an academic report on sleep deprivation, you might use graphs and tables to supplement and extend your written discussion.	In a newspaper article on student sleeplessness, you might use a photograph of students sleeping in the library to grab the attention of your readers and remind them of their own experiences.	Enumerate procedures or elements of an agreement. In creating a Web site on sleep deprivation for a mattress company, you might use charts to show the numbers of sufferers— the potential market for your new product.

1 Tables organize information

Tables are useful when you need to present factual information— usually words or numbers in columns and rows—in a relatively small space. They also help in displaying complex information. Tables (see Table 13.1) are labeled as such and are numbered and titled, as in the example; all other graphics are **figures.**

	PUBLIC UNIVERSITY	**PRIVATE UNIVERSITY**	**PUBLIC 4-YR. COLLEGE**	**PRIVATE 4-YR. COLLEGE**	**COMMUNITY COLLEGE**
Undergraduate application	99	90	95	96	96
ePortfolio	32	27	37	28	10
Journals & reference	92	96	92	94	84
Course reserves	78	81	66	67	35
Course registration	97	94	97	80	97
Online course	95	67	88	54	94
E-Commerce capacity	92	81	87	57	85

Table 1 Web Site Services, 2005 (percentages, by sector)

Source: "The Campus Computing Project," www.campuscomputing.net

13e
design

TABLE 13.1   Usage rates of Web site services among colleges

2 Graphs and charts represent relationships among data

If you want to emphasize trends, add credibility, interest the reader in data, or forecast future values, graphs or charts will be very useful. Graphs, like Figure 13.1, rely on two labeled axes (vertical and horizontal) to show relationships between two variables. Charts display relationships

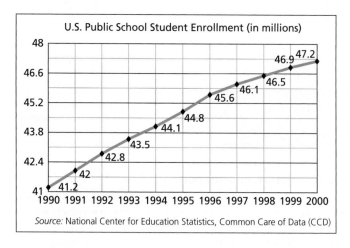

FIGURE 13.1   Number of students enrolled in public schools
Source: <http://nces.ed.gov>.

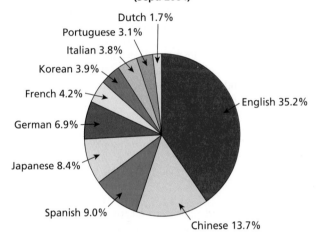

**Online Language Populations
Total: 801.4 Million
(Sept. 2004)**

Dutch 1.7%
Portuguese 3.1%
Italian 3.8%
Korean 3.9%
French 4.2%
German 6.9%
Japanese 8.4%
Spanish 9.0%
Chinese 13.7%
English 35.2%

FIGURE 13.2 Online population by language group
Source: GlobalReach, <http://global-reach.biz/globstats/index.php3>.

**13e
design**

in other ways. Some, such as pie charts (Figure 13.2), show percentages of a whole; others, such as bar charts, compare items or show correlations. Graphs and charts need to be labeled with a figure number and a brief caption.

3 Other visual devices serve varied purposes

Use drawings and diagrams to present physical appearances, to show connections among parts, and to illustrate spatial relationships so that readers *see* what to do or how something works. You can use photographs and illustrations to record reality, to define and provide examples, just as newspapers and magazines do. You can also use "clip art"—simple drawings that are easily pasted into your document to enhance a point or draw a reader's attention. Clip art and stock photography are available through some word-processing programs, at many Web sites, and for purchase on CD-ROMs.

In all cases, keep in mind the need to credit borrowed sources and the appropriateness of using visual devices in various contexts without overusing them. You must be sure that your use of images complies with copyright rules. Most disks, publications, and Web sites of clip art and photographs include information on copyright; if you aren't certain, and no contact information is given, you should look for an alternative image.

| STRATEGY | Use visuals effectively |

- Choose an appropriate visual aid.
- Use the visual to illustrate one point, and make sure it supports that point. Don't use graphics as decoration or filler.
- Keep graphics as simple as possible to achieve your end.
- Set graphics off with white space. Don't crowd them.
- Use textual cues to guide the reader: label the graphics consistently, number them, and provide accurate, concise captions that explain the relationship of the graphic to the text.
- Help readers make sense of your graphics by positioning them as close to their text references as possible.
- Be sure to credit sources for borrowed graphics.

13f Web pages

Whether you have had experience creating Web pages or you're just a frequent Web surfer, you know that well-designed Web pages are attractive and easy to navigate. They represent their company, organization, or creator well, while those that are poorly designed are hard to use and leave an unfavorable impression.

1 Establishing a purpose and a persona

The most common type of Web page is the **personal home page,** an individual author's effort to create a place for herself online. You will also find many commercial sites (including corporate pages, sites sponsored by nonprofit organizations, and online shopping opportunities), educational sites (including school and university pages, scholarly journals, and free informational presentations), and news and entertainment sites (including newspapers, magazines, and other media).

| DOMAIN NAMES AND TYPES |

A **domain name** locates an organization or other entity on the Internet. A number of suffixes used by American Web sites can tell you a great deal about what you are reading.

.com	commercial site
.edu	educational site
.gov	government site
.net	network site
.org	nonprofit organization

If you're building a personal home page on the Web, consider first its general format. Are you preparing a class project on coral reef preservation, to be designed as a resource for those with similar interests? Are you setting up a résumé, with factual information about your professional interests and abilities? Or are you producing a kind of autobiography, so your friends and family can see what you're up to?

You need to determine who your audience will be and what aspects of yourself you want to present to the online community. Will you be surprised or annoyed if someone you do not want to hear from or have never met sends you email about your site? If you intend your autobiographical page to show off your keen sarcastic wit and your political views, will you be comfortable knowing that a potential employer may find that site by using a search engine?

STRATEGY Study sites with similar purposes

Before building any Web site, spend time studying sites with similar purposes. Make lists of what you do and do not like about those sites. Consider contacting the authors and designers of those pages to ask for advice before you start, or for feedback after you have begun. And, just as you would ask for peer feedback on a paper in progress, ask fellow students, colleagues, or friends for comments and suggestions.

Be careful how you name your site. Search engines will index it based on the words that appear in the title and in the text of the site. Select your words carefully, and when you're ready to publish, visit the major search engine sites to learn the process of registering and indexing your site. When writing for the Web, effective search engine registration is almost as important as making sure the information in your site is accurate.

13g
models

2 Considering your audience

Getting feedback from your intended Web audience is the best way to user-test your site and find out how others feel about its layout. Keep a few simple rules in mind when constructing and maintaining a site.

- **Content is key.** Most Web users are looking for information, not "cool" design and graphics. Make sure any graphics reinforce your topic rather than just take up space.
- **Allow ample white space.**
- **Test your Web pages on various platforms and browsers.**
- **Always include contact information,** preferably in the form of an automatic email link. However, *never* put your full name, address, and phone number (or other vital information) in this space.

13g Model documents

The following model documents show how the principles of document design outlined in this chapter work in action.

13g
models

(1) Daisy Garcia
Professor L. Miles
HPR 101
17 December 2003

Rebuilding

September 11, 2001, marks a day when your feelings of shock
and loss of direction matched with others across the country no
matter where you were or what you were doing when the twin
towers of the World Trade Center collapsed. Deciding what, if
anything, to build on the site has been a process of differing
emotions, perceptions, and plans. The various proposals have
been ambitious, breathtaking, moving, and, above all, quite
different in perspective and style.

·   ·   ·

Freedom Tower is designed to stand as the tallest building
in the world in its completion at a symbolic height as a 1,776-
foot spire. The antenna structure will be the home of various
channels in the NY area and have a
representational design relating
(2) to the Statue of Liberty. David M.
Childs is collaborating with
Libeskind as the design architect.
It will contain a vertical garden
known as "Gardens of the World,"
observation decks, and programs
for recreational commercial use.
The commercial buildings are going
to be designed by the other three
architects chosen by Silverstein.

There are about 10 million square feet of office space in five
towers and 880,000 square feet of retail space. The Wedge of Light
is an area designed and aligned with the heavens so that on
September 11th of each year, it is lit.

Sample page from student paper on the World Trade Center memorial

(1) MLA opener
(2) Integration of photograph

Phillips Park

ZOOLENNIUM
Fall Festival

Sunday, September 28th from 11 a.m. to 3 p.m.

The Friends of Phillips Park and the City of Aurora invite you to take in the park's beautiful array of fall colors while you enjoy a day filled with activities, attractions, and fun for the whole family.

FREE Pony Rides

Pumpkin Painting

Petting Zoo

Hay Rides

Super Slide

Jumping Castle

Face Painting

Scratch Art & Sand Art

LIVE ENTERTAINMENT......

11 am Buttons The Clown
12 pm The Aurora Suzuki Violins
1pm Dave Rudolf
2 pm The Truly Remarkable Loon

VISIT THE PUMPKIN PATCH

Stop and shop for your Halloween Pumpkins and fall decorations from A-1 Farms large on-site selection.

Be among the first 1,200 youngsters to visit the Pumpkin Painting Tent and you'll receive a free pumpkin to paint and take home with you. In the display area you'll find fire trucks, emergency vehicles, D.A.R.E.-Mobiles and K-9 Units, along with special appearances by "McGruff" the crime fighting police dog, "Ozzie" the Kane County Cougar's mascot, and "Ollie" the Phillips Park Zoo mascot. If you relish food with an Oktoberfest flair, bratwurst, sauerkraut, hot dogs and pork chop sandwiches - will be served up hot off the grill, along with hot apple cider, fresh donuts, and hot pretzels.

Be sure to visit the Phillips Park Zoo, where you'll find bald eagles, wolves, foxes, otters, elk, goats, pot-bellied pigs, llamas, swans, reptiles, and peacocks. Located on more than 325 acres, attractions at Phillips Park include the Visitors Center & Mastodon Gallery, the Sunken Garden, the Phillips Park Golf Course, the Aquatic Center, Mastodon Lake-a twenty-eight acre fishing lake with a 1-mile jogging/bike path and island exhibits, the waterfall, World War I cannons, and several veteran related monuments. Among the amenities you'll find a large state-of-the-art playground, softball fields, picnic pavilions, sand volleyball courts, tennis courts, horseshoe courts, and more.

Parking lots are located along Moses and Wyeth Drives and at the Aquatic Center. Additional parking is available along Smith Boulevard. For more information visit the City of Aurora Web site at *www.aurora-il.org* and go to Parks & Recreation, or call (630) 898-7228.

Details are subject to change.

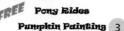

Flyer from a community-based organization
Source: <http://www.aurora-il.org/Parks%20Operation/zoolenium fallfest2003.html>.

13g
models

1. Unique font draws attention to headline
2. Date and time of the event prominently placed
3. Activities separated into scheduled (right side) and constant (left side)
4. Color and artwork add visual interest
5. Details provided in carefully organized paragraphs and legible font

This first page of a newsletter from an organization dedicated to informing the public about mountain lions entices the reader with both photos and buttons leading to additional pages of information and a video.

1 Picture highlights beauty of animal and calls attention to the site

2 Buttons provide map of information in site and access to each category of information

3 White background makes text easy to read. Ghosted profile of mountain lion emphasizes elusive nature of the animal

Visit mycomplab.com for more resources and exercises on designing documents.

CHAPTER 14

Multimodal Presentations

Sandra Tsing Loh proposes a subject for her program on National Public Radio, *The Loh Down on Science*. With her producer and the rest of her team in agreement on the project, she drafts a script, drawing on research and personal knowledge. Sound engineers and other technicians ensure that the segment, "Thinking Rats," is broadcast. They also make it available as a podcast recording accessible as an MP3 file or as a computer file. Anyone interested can download it at <http://podcasts.scpr.org/loh_down>.

Working as an intern for her college's office of student affairs and as a student in a composition course, Lara Jureviscius prepares an advertisement for a campus substance abuse prevention program. She proposes the project to her instructor and her boss through a memo. She integrates visuals and text in a flyer and adds audio plus electronic links for the Web version. For her instructor, she writes a reflection that tells how her advertisement met assignment goals and explains the process she followed.

What do these activities have in common? They are both **multimodal** compositions, meaning that they both combine and appear in a variety of media—written, oral, visual, electronic.

14a Multimodal compositions

Multimodal compositions use a range of resources to communicate: written texts, photographs, oral presentation, video, music, artwork, electronic resources. Multimodal composition, like a written text, can inform, persuade, and entertain, but it can often do so with greater depth and variety than can written text alone. For readers or listeners, the result may be more interesting, more compelling, or more suggestive than written text alone.

1 Photographs

Photographs (or other artworks, such as drawings), either fully integrated with written text or standing on their own in a photo essay, do not simply illustrate points made elsewhere (see p. 138). They convey ideas and information on their own. (For photo essays and other works consisting substantially of visuals, most instructors will require a written proposal and a reflective discussion of the final project.)

A photo essay has a clear plan or theme to which each picture contributes information and ideas, much as the paragraphs in an essay contribute to the whole. In a photo essay on aging, for example, you might provide a series of facial photographs showing the development of wrinkles, age spots, and changes in facial expression over years, suggesting both physical decline and emotional growth.

Photos fully integrated with written text can take the place of writing and add new ideas and perspectives. In his book *Farewell, My Subaru: An Epic Adventure in Local Living,* Doug Fine uses a quotation and a photograph to suggest that nonpolluting solutions such as biodiesel have been available for many years but have become fashionable only in the past few years.

14a
multi-
modal

PART THREE

<hr>

CONVERTED

*The use of vegetable oils for engine fuels
may seem insignificant today, but such
oils may become in the course of time as
important as petroleum and the coal tar
products of the present time.*

—RUDOLPH DIESEL, died 1913

2 Advertisements

Advertisements in print combine visuals (photographs or other artworks) with written text. Video and electronic advertisements may add sound and motion. Ads generally need to communicate a clear purpose: buy this product, support this cause, contribute to this organization. At the same time, ads generally need to be subtle and complex: every physical detail, color choice, text element, and placement on the page or screen should contribute to the purpose.

In preparing an advertisement for the Museum of Rock Climbing, Leticia Meza-Zimering uses color and shape to split the ad into sections. She uses the central sections to convey the main messages about the activity of rock climbing and the museum itself, and she has the smaller sections describe elements related to the museum and the activity (see p. 160).

3 Videos

Documentaries, demonstrations, tours, reenactments, and personal narratives can all deliver information and ideas. Filmed with a video camera or captured digitally, a video needs to be presented on screen through a DVD or through software that enables computers to show a video or string together a set of digital slides (as does *PowerPoint*).

A recorded voice (that of a narrator or a participant) or an on-screen text should provide commentary and information to emphasize the presentation's main idea or theme, to provide factual information, and to indicate how the visual elements work together for a purpose. (Many instructors will ask for a written proposal and a reflective commentary explaining the selection and arrangement of visual elements.)

Editing software such as *Adobe Premier Pro* can help you to arrange, splice, and revise a presentation and to add spoken or written text. A tour of a historic site or building and an examination of an architecturally important structure are among the many appropriate subjects for videos. Complicated medical or scientific instruments often need video explanation or instructions. Explanations of natural, mechanical, or electronic processes also benefit from multimodal presentations. (A YouTube video produced by make-up artist Queen of Blending provides a detailed explanation of artistic ways to apply make-up; see 14b-2.)

14a
multi-
modal

4 Oral presentations

An oral presentation such as a podcast, a digital recording, or a recorded tour of a museum or exhibit needs to be precise in expression, filled with relevant facts, and clear in purpose and content. Though presented orally, such multimodal performances are almost always scripted, rehearsed carefully, and revised before being recorded.

To create a recorded tour of a shoe museum, Kate Stone decided on the shoes she felt would most benefit from an introduction and gave her writing instructor a proposal outlining the kinds of information her audio tour would provide and the order of presentation. She researched the designs, drafted the introductions in a script, and recorded the presentation. She then

June 10, 2009 4:00 p.m.-10:00 p.m.
Museum Opening
111 Main Street
Providence, RI

Museum of Rock Climbing
Ascend New Heights

Explore   Discover   Climb

Museum Opening Events   Special Guests Lynn Hill and Dean Potter
Gear Giveaways sponsored by The Northface
Discovery Rock Climbing – Stand Alone Film Premier

Rock Climbing   Rock Climbing   Climbing
    Films   History   Wall

Photo Credits: National Park Service and NASA

14a
multi-
modal

listened to the recording and revised her script for clarity, focus, and ease of presentation. Finally, she rehearsed the presentation and made several recordings, choosing the best segments and splicing them together for the final product. In the following script excerpt, note the sound effects directions Stone supplies at the end.

Pumps & Struts Lounge

Audio Tour Commentary:

Exhibit [8] Christian Louboutin Very Privie Graffiti Pumps

Narrator: Christian Louboutin draws inspiration from everywhere, ranging from the showgirls of Paris' scorching nightclub scene, to the classic art of the local museums, to the city's long-reaching, graffiti-splattered bridges—the specific inspiration for this sky-high heel. While the vibrant, street-like patterning of the Very Privie was drawn from the street of France's capital, it was actually a museum that drove Louboutin to design such terrifyingly tall, sharp stilettos.

At a young age, Christian Louboutin visited the Atlantic Museum of Oceanic Art and was particularly plagued by a small sign on display. The sign forbade the entrance of women sporting sharp high heels, for fear the stilettos would damage the museum's fine wood flooring. Louboutin has been quoted, saying he "wanted to defy that," he "wanted to create something that broke rules and made women feel confident and empowered."

The edgy juxtaposition of 4-inch spike and urban, illegal art achieves Louboutin's goal in this canvas open-toe shoe. The Very Privie is a part of the larger Graffiti Collection, and is yet another tribute to the idea that art imitates life—even if that life is an unexpected form of art, that you stroll by daily on your way to work, having origins in a spray paint can.

If nothing else, the Very Privie Graffiti Pump encourages women to strut across a hardwood floor, aware that an undeniable sense of confidence is worth more than classic flooring any day.

[The audio commentary of this exhibit closes
with the sound of pumps walking across a hardwood floor.]

14b multi- modal

14b Analyzing multimodal presentations

What should you look for in a multimodal presentation as a member of the audience or as a composer considering the likely effects of your work?

1 Purpose and focus

The audience for a multimodal presentation should be able to understand readily both its purpose and its focus or topic. As you analyze, look for direct statements, oral or written; for repeated words or phrases; for repeated kinds of examples or for repeated visual images. These strategies should highlight purpose, topic, and thesis or theme.

2 Detail and explanation

Facts, figures, descriptions, narratives, pictures, quotations, and explanations are at the heart of successful informative and argumentative presentation. Without them, a presentation can neither inform nor persuade. They may come in the form of direct statements or of images an audience needs to respond to or interpret. As you look for and analyze these elements, ask if their meaning is clear, if audience members are likely to find them trustworthy or persuasive, and if their relation to the main theme or idea is made apparent.

The following presentation by Christina Pereira uses text to provide details that explain the subject and the photograph; the photograph provides details that the text cannot present as effectively. When viewed electronically, viewers could click on the image to see make-up artist Queen of Blending discuss the artistic uses of MAC make-up. These elements work together to create an effective multimodal presentation.

14b
multi-modal

MAC Cosmetics Used as Art

Make-up Artists
Monica Suy
Lauren Diaz
Ashley Wood
Heather Blair
Hanna Lee
Monica Saysone

MAC Cosmetics, Inc. (Make-up Art Cosmetics) was started in Canada by Frank Toskan and Frank Angelo in 1984. Angelo was the original founder. Toskan was a make-up artist and photographer, and Angelo was the owner of a chain of hair salons. They were both involved in fashion photography and quickly recognized the need for more durable, versatile, and creative cosmetic products that could handle the demands of professional photo shoots. Not only is MAC used for photo shoots and regular make-up, but it is also used as a form of art that has influenced people all over the world to think about make-up as more than just a way to "make people pretty" or "to be used just for movies." Now it has become a form of art in the view of many.

Always on the cutting edge with their engagement of celebrity endorsements, awareness of social and cultural diversity, and involvement in charitable social initiatives, MAC Cosmetics has now grown to become one of the most popular and influential cosmetics companies in the world.

Sponsors
Amica
PCU
Citizens
Dunkin Donuts
MAC

3 Design

The arrangement of elements on a screen or pages; the size of the text and the images; the placement of pictures, symbols, and text in the background and foreground; the choice of color; the pacing of episodes and explanations—all these factors contribute to a multimodal presentation's effectiveness.

Erica Courtmanche prepared the advertising flyer on page 164 by presenting the text in different fonts at different places on the page, by varying the colors and pictures, and by dividing the whole into sections that related in effective ways to each other and to the overall message.

14c Composing multimodal presentations

Multimodal presentations call for many skills: writing, speaking, document design, video or photographic know-how, and others. Computer programs can help add to your abilities, and working in a group can bring together many talents.

1 Developing your craft

Before you consider a multimodal presentation, take an inventory of your skills and the skills needed for a project.

- What kinds of writing and speaking are you particularly good at?
- Can you draw, design a Web page, or add color and illustrations to a text?
- Are you skilled at creating videos or photographs?
- Can you blend sound or music with a text file?
- What other talents do you have—or think you can develop?

In the course of this inventory, revise your conception of a project if your skills suggest additional directions you might take.

- What kinds of writing or speaking will this presentation require?
- What kinds of artwork, illustrations, or design features do you envision for the project?
- Will all or part of this presentation be in video? What kind of video?
- What kinds of sound or music will the presentation require?

Look over your inventory of needed skills to see if you already possess them or will need help from computer software or other members of the team.

2 Computer software

Using computer software to present or create may already be part of your talents, or you may need to expand your skills. New software appears constantly, with helpful instruction books and online tutorials. Decide what

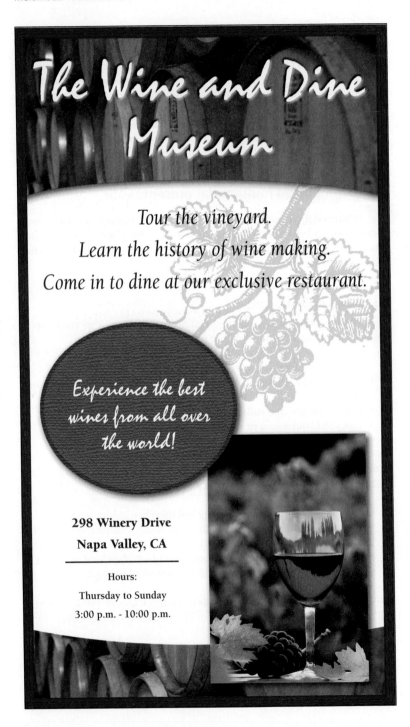

you want to do, then search online or in stores for appropriate help. You may want to start with one of these popular resources.

- **Presentation aids.** Use *PowerPoint* slides to create electronic or print slides that integrate text, photographs, audio, and video with design elements. Create your own multimedia presentation using online tutorials or a book like *Cutting Edge PowerPoint for Dummies.*
- **Podcasts and videocasts.** To create a podcast, consider software like Apple Podcast Producer or QuickTime Pro (Apple or Windows). These and other programs provide tutorials. Videocasting software is also available.
- **Images.** You can edit and create images using programs like Photoshop for photographs and other images, Flash for animations, Word for photographs and clip art, and Excel for graphs.
- **Blogs and Wikis.** Blogs (Chapter 15) can incorporate various modes of presentation, as can wikis (Chapter 15), created and edited by a group. Books and online instructions for these applications can give you both specific help and a sense of the possibilities for your presentation.
- **Web sites.** When creating a Web site, some knowledge of basic HTML (hypertext markup language) can be helpful, but many word-processing programs will convert your document to HTML for you. For more advanced work, consider programs such as Microsoft FrontPage or Dreamweaver. Many services (such as Google and Yahoo!) will host your site for free. It is especially important when creating a Web site to focus on the organization and design. A flashy site with disorganized content will not impress readers.

14d
multi-
modal

14d Evaluating multimodal presentations

Who needs to evaluate multimodal presentations? Audiences need to evaluate multimodal presentations as part of the process of understanding and responding to the ideas and information being presented. Writers need to evaluate their own multimodal presentations in order to decide what and how to revise. Anyone assembling a portfolio of work (Chapter 8) needs to evaluate presentations to decide what to include in the portfolio, what to revise, and what to say in a critical introduction to the portfolio.

Look at each of the following areas as you evaluate.

- **Purpose and focus.** An effective multimodal presentation makes clear its specific intent and does not try to cover too many topics. For example, an ad's goal may be to encourage readers to visit a museum. But if the ad also provides details of the museum's contents, it may either confuse readers or give them so much information that its overall purpose will be lost.
- **Detail.** An effective multimodal presentation gives its audience enough detail to serve its purpose—but not too much. A presentation that aims

to persuade needs to provide facts and arguments (Chapters 10–11), but it should avoid extensive informative detail that detracts from the focus on persuading. An informative presentation, on the other hand, should provide both the facts an audience needs and other details that audience members might enjoy or employ in another context.

- **Design.** A successful multimodal presentation, whether to persuade or to inform, avoids distracting an audience with unrelated elements or features. It draws on many aspects of design to deliver its message: visuals (size, resolution, quality, clarity, clearness of purpose, placement); layout (placement of text and videos on a page and in relation to each other), color (appropriateness, clarity, variety, relation of colors to subject and to each other); order of visuals; relationship of visuals to text; pacing of sound or visuals; special effects for visuals and sound.

Visit mycomplab.com for more resources and exercises on creating multimodal presentations.

CHAPTER **15**

Writing Online

Some online environments are like libraries: you go there and retrieve information, opening Web sites and downloading documents. But many other online environments involve more than the passive receipt of information: they involve interactive *exchange.* Whenever you participate in an online course, chat with friends through an instant messenger (IM) service, email a question or a comment to a nonprofit organization, read and write on a Web-based forum, or post a response to a blog, you are participating in an **online community.** Each of these communities has certain expectations and follows certain standards for people's membership in the group.

15a Online writing

Whether you are writing an email message to classmates about a collaborative project, building a personal Web site to supplement your résumé, or participating in an online discussion about a local environmental issue, you're writing in a *context:* you need to consider the specific needs of your online audience, your purpose for writing, how you want to represent yourself to others, and what "rules" govern the way you can participate.

1 Understanding your online audience and your purpose

Online writers must tailor their messages to specific audiences to communicate effectively. People often join online communities because they're interested in a particular topic. Fans of the Dallas Cowboys can chat daily about the latest trade rumor or game story. Opponents of a bill in Congress can use email to gather electronic signatures on petitions to their legislative representatives.

If you're not sure about the audience expectations for an online community, try a brief period of lurking (reading without participating). Lurking can help you to see who else participates, learn the rules of participation, and pick up the terms or ideas commonly used by the participants. If you send a response to a discussion without taking the time to see what messages have already been sent, you may seem to be "out of the loop" and lose credibility. Recipients have more time to study your message than during oral interchanges. Briefly considering your message and planning its wording can help avoid embarrassment or misunderstanding by making your meaning clear.

> **STRATEGY**   **Think before you send**
>
> - What's the context of your message? How does your information extend, amplify, or clarify prior information?
> - Why will readers find your information helpful or interesting?
> - What do you want readers to *do* with the information or ideas: respond? take action? think more deeply about the issue?

2 Creating an online persona

When you participate in an online community, your **persona,** or how you define yourself to others, can be developed in depth because you can make repeated contributions in response to what others say. Still, this aspect of online communication differs from face-to-face communication in important ways.

- You can often remain anonymous.
- You can identify or conceal your gender or ethnicity.
- You can choose to be a silent type and contribute rarely, or you can contribute often.
- You can represent yourself in different styles or voices.
- You can use your real name or choose a made-up name or even an online personality (an "avatar").

Many blog writers create strong, easily identifiable, though partly fictional personas. This may at times be an important element of blogging, but it can be a problem if some readers, potential employers, for example, assume that your persona is an accurate representation of your traits or a literal record of your behavior. When you blog, always consider the possible effects of the online record you are leaving behind.

Tailor your persona to suit your purpose. If you're contributing your knowledge and expertise, for example, present yourself as helpful and concerned, not as a know-it-all. If you're contributing to an online peer review of a classmate's paper or presentation, you'll want to be supportive and friendly—neither too casual nor too harshly critical.

3 Netiquette

Online communities vary widely in the kinds of language and behavior they tolerate and expect from members. It's your responsibility to familiarize yourself with commonsense guidelines (known as **netiquette**) that apply across nearly all Internet communities and to learn the standards of the specific group you want to address.

- **Think before you click.** You can't take back a sent email. Avoid putting anything in an email message you wouldn't want your mother or a future employer to read.

- **Learn before you send.** Lurk and learn the norms of the community. If a discussion group has a searchable archive, see if a previous discussion provides the information that can help you to answer a question.
- **Consider off-list responses.** If you post a question that you think most of a discussion list's members will not be interested in, ask respondents to write to you "off list" (using your email address, not the list address).
- **Act, don't react.** Avoid posting "flames" (personal attacks) to contributors you disagree with.
- **Don't use ALL CAPS.** Like shouting, this practice is considered rude.
- **Attend to grammar.** Even if online messages seem informal, bad grammar, spelling mistakes, and poor word usage still convey a feeling of sloppiness or a lack of concern for readers. (When sending IMs or texting, however, use abbreviation conventions to save space—but don't carry them over to email or printed documents, where they will seem out of place and careless.)
- **Cut the fat.** Include only *relevant* information from previous messages to which you are replying.
- **The Golden Rule of netiquette.** Don't forget that real people are behind every computer that receives your email or downloads your Web site.

15b
online

15b Avoiding plagiarism and acting ethically online

Online environments now offer you access to almost limitless texts, images, music, and streaming video. Because digital technology allows you to download this material to your own computer, it's tempting to see all of it as yours, free for the taking. But it's not. Worse, it's not always obvious whether something on the Internet is copyrighted, which makes it unclear whether you're doing anything wrong when you copy or distribute something. Downloading a song from your favorite band or printing and circulating a story or cartoon may violate federal copyright laws, resulting in a fine (or worse) if you're caught. When working online, avoid practices that are illegal or unethical, and avoid those that can create suspicion or investigation. When in doubt, err on the side of caution. (See also Chapter 27.)

1 Always document or credit borrowed information

It's so easy to forward electronic mail, download software programs and images, create Web pages, and copy material published online that governments worldwide are being forced to reconsider the concept of intellectual property. Who owns the rights to words, images, or ideas? How can those rights be protected without prohibiting the free flow of information that the Internet makes possible? These issues make it important for you to document every online source you use in developing your writing.

Remember too that your credibility depends on the credibility of the community resource you choose to rely on. If you're writing a paper about diabetes, citing sources from American Diabetes Association Web pages and a moderated discussion group for endocrinologists is far more effective than citing email from a local bulletin board about a new home remedy. For all information from online sources you wish to cite, ask yourself "Where did it come from?" If you are not confident about your answer, your instructor might be able to help you evaluate the credibility of a source. You should also be prepared to find an alternative site. (Remember to acknowledge and document your sources; see Chapters 29–33.)

> **STRATEGY**   **Avoid plagiarism online**
>
> - Always write down the address of any Web site you are using, and clearly label the text you copy from that site. Print the first page of each Web site you're using for easy reference in case your later drafts require further documentation. The printout should include the site's URL so you can return to it for reference and for citation purposes.
> - Always note the date you found the information. Web sites can be updated at any time, and your cited information may disappear. In addition, you will need to provide the access date in your citation if you use the information in your final document. (For more on citation issues, see Chapters 29–33.)
> - If you're citing an email, listserv, or Web forum message that has not been posted to a publicly accessible location, ask the author's permission before quoting. It's a good idea to do this even if the posting is public.
> - Corroborate your sources. Follow the journalist's rule: If you can't find information in at least two credible places on the Internet, don't use the material.

15b
online

2 Do your own work

Never buy or download a paper and claim that it is your own work. Consider the moral implications and the consequences of borrowing Internet resources and presenting them as your own. Remember that your instructor has access to those same sources; a common practice among teachers who suspect plagiarism is to input suspect phrases from student papers into a search engine to see whether those phrases appear anywhere on the Web. Plagiarism detection services do much the same thing. (See Chapter 27.)

3 Know the rules

When you're using an email account provided by a college or university or by a business or public organization—even when you access it away from the institution—you are responsible for adhering to the institution's policies and regulations. If you access the Internet through a service provider, you're obligated to abide by the client rights and responsibilities outlined in your contract. Policies on computer use can be extensive, and you should thoroughly review them.

15c Email choices

Email is a popular means of communication primarily because it's *fast*. But its speed shouldn't be an excuse to avoid writing carefully and thoughtfully before your message speeds through cyberspace to its destination(s).

1 Elements of email

Every email message has elements that convey a specific kind of information and help you effectively communicate your purpose. While you are probably familiar with the basic components of email, it helps to consider how certain choices create an online persona.

15c
email

From. While some email programs show a sender's address in the "from" section, others display a chosen **screen name,** a self-identifier the user chooses for herself. A screen name like *BradFan* might entertain your friends, but it won't make a positive impression on a potential employer.

Sent. This line displays the date and time your email is sent. Because recipients may need this information, make sure your computer's time and date settings are correct.

To. It's good practice to check the "to" line every time before sending your email—just to be sure it's going to the right place. Two other lines—"cc:" (carbon copy) and "bcc:" (blind carbon copy)—enable you to send email to people who are not part of the primary audience but who might be interested in the subject matter. With a blind carbon copy, you can send copies without the main recipient's knowing because the addresses for the copies will not appear in the text sent to the main recipient.

Subject. Use this line to draw readers into reading the actual message. Short and clear subject lines are best.

Message body. Be concise. Long messages are more likely to be deleted, left unread, or read only in part.

Signature or sig file. Sign your email. If you have a mail program that allows you to attach a signature file automatically, write out your full name and some contact information. Many people include clever quotations, song lyrics, and jokes in their signature files; be aware of how such additions affect your online persona.

2 Email appearance

Most email systems produce "primitive" text, without the formatting options that you have in word-processing programs. For the purposes of a vast number of daily email messages, it doesn't much matter what your text looks like. Yet a few considerations can make your communications more efficient and show your sensitivity to the needs of your audience.

- Don't let email do the work of full-length documents. If you need to send a paper, report, or other substantive text to someone, send it as an attached document.
- Break your messages into paragraphs. People become tired and frustrated when they must read long blocks of email text.
- Use emoticons and acronyms appropriately, based on your audience. **Emoticons** *(emotion + icon)* are a kind of shorthand code that allows writers to add a jolt of feeling to their text. Emoticons (such as smiling or frowning faces) can be drawn with keyboard characters; increasingly, many email programs now convert typed emoticons into graphic representations. Internet **acronyms** (FYI, BTW) are abbreviations of common phrases, used to speed up communication.

15d
online

Emoticons and acronyms are generally considered to be appropriate for casual communication but not for professional or academic writing.

3 Using the functions of email

Just as each email message has certain elements (see 15c-1), every email program has buttons or commands that allow you to manage your correspondence in a variety of ways.

Reply and **Reply-all.** Remember that when you use the *Reply-all* function, your message will go to all the other people who received the original communication. Be careful that you don't accidentally send a response to unintended recipients.

Forward. Before forwarding other people's messages, consider whether the original author would want his or her message forwarded to someone else. When in doubt, urge the original author to send the message to the person(s) you have in mind.

Attach. If you attach files (such as word-processed files, spreadsheets, and pictures), remember that some recipients may not be able to read your document. Give the recipient time to open the attachment or write back to you if there's a problem, and be ready with alternative formats or ways to send the information.

15d Participating in online communities

The three most common formats for online communities are discussion lists; Web forums (blogs); and real-time writing, including IMing and texting. Each format plays host to communities engaged in writing on a variety of topics.

1 Discussion lists

To join or subscribe to a **discussion list,** you send an email message to the service that hosts the list. You then automatically receive all the messages from the list at your email address. When you post a message, usually it's first reviewed by the list moderator (some lists are not moderated). If it passes the moderator's standards, he or she sends it to the personal addresses of all the people subscribed. It's important, then, to adapt to the community's standards, or your messages will never be made available to your peers.

You can access **newsgroups** without having email messages sent to your personal address. You can scan the topics and threads for a subject that interests you and choose the individual posts you wish to read. Newsgroups are usually not moderated, so the message you send to a newsgroup is immediately posted and available for reading by anyone.

2 Web-based forums and blogs

Web-based forums allow users to easily access sites where they can participate in conversations with others who share interests, from current events to entertainment. Some forums are moderated and may ask you to set up a user name with a password; and a few charge fees.

Writing in Web-based forums makes frequent use of informal language, emoticons and abbreviations, and the citing of previously written material to provide context.

Blogs, short for Web logs, are interactive Web sites where the blog owner posts information, reflections, news stories, and the like; those who visit the blog can then post responses. A few bloggers have achieved such prominence that they are cited frequently by other writers or television commentators; some have books collecting and reprinting their daily musings.

15d
online

3 Real-time writing

The Internet now supports a variety of ways for people to participate in real-time electronic discussions and communities. **Real time** means that the discussion takes place without delay: your words appear on the screen of every user involved in the discussion as soon as they are typed.

One popular real-time community in current use is the **chat room** hosted by a private Internet service or available via the Internet relay chat (IRC) network. Chat rooms are usually quite informal. Chats open to the public, such as interviews with celebrities and "town hall" meetings, are almost always moderated, so your writing will be controlled by an editor who decides whether you may post your questions or comments.

An **IM** (Instant Messaging) service allows you to chat in real time with a limited number of people, often one to one. IMing allows for the spontaneity and directness of conversation, but because most people type more slowly than they talk, IMing makes frequent use of radical abbreviations (RU OK?) in order to keep the exchange going at a comfortable pace. This style of communication is highly informal, making it clearly inappropriate for most other means of formal communication.

Texting is a type of short message service (SMS) that is available on most cell phones, pagers, and hand-held devices. Texting is similar to IMing; compressed, IM-like messages are sent to a mobile device.

15e Participating in virtual classrooms

Many teachers across the college curriculum are now using digital technologies to enhance or supplement their classroom instruction. If you enroll in a course with an online component, your virtual persona will be crucial to your success, just as it would be in the classroom. Opting out of participation, being disruptive, dominating the conversation, using inappropriate diction—these and other unacceptable aspects of face-to-face communication also count against you in the online environment.

1 Using electronic courseware

Most courseware that supplements classroom instruction can be easily navigated, having plenty of help screens in case you're not familiar with some elements. *WebCT*™, *Blackboard*, *Sakai*, and other commercial courseware systems commonly include a home page where you can get assignments and schedules, information about your grades or your progress, and links to other Internet sources on the subject of your course. In addition, such systems often provide a course chat room, a discussion board, and an internal email system. Electronic conversations may be recorded so your instructor can assess your contributions. Bulletin boards, where you post information asynchronously, are usually organized by topic; be sure you choose the correct topic when you post a message.

It helps to explore such systems before your course and its assignments begin, so that you will be familiar at the outset with how they work. Explore the site fully, taking note of how it works and what you're required to do. Many teachers also post ground rules for participation, and these rules may stipulate the kinds and amount of your interaction.

2 Taking courses online

Many universities now offer courses that you can take entirely online. In such courses, you'll continue to do much of your work independently, but almost all interaction will take place online instead of in a classroom. Although each online course will be unique, some general strategies are helpful for working in this environment.

STRATEGY Suggestions for success online

- Read everything. You may be so used to surfing and skimming the Internet that online courses trigger a similar process when you first enter or log on to a course site. Slow down. Read the screens carefully, and take notes or print out the most important information.

- Know the rules. Just as in regular courses, Internet courses will have tardy and absence policies, ground rules for participation, and due dates.
- Think community. Although sitting at a computer may make you feel that there is no social accountability in your course, just the reverse is true. To work well, Internet courses require full participation from all members. Learn the names or avatars of the other students, try referring to their ideas, and generally make yourself a member of the virtual community.

Exercise 1

Reflect in writing on your experiences with electronically enhanced learning. How did it work? What was your role? Can you think of instructive stories or anecdotes?

Visit mycomplab.com **for more resources and exercises on writing online.**

15e
virtual

CHAPTER 16

Speaking Effectively

Surveys show that people are more afraid of public speaking than almost anything else they can imagine, including being fired from a job—but why? Fear often comes from too little preparation. Good speakers use planning, practice, and experience to turn anxiety into a kind of energy that helps them to present their ideas clearly and enthusiastically.

You can greatly improve your performance if you break the presentation down into four stages: *planning*, *practice*, *delivery*, and *reflection*.

16a Effective oral presentations

It's Shaun Sullivan's turn. He makes his way awkwardly to the front of the room, saying, "OK, I'm gonna talk about, um, my project is, let's see, what I want to tell you about is what I, what my project, the real story of the *Exxon Valdez* oil spill ten, fifteen, after, um, you know, like what biologists found and stuff when they, like what the data says about it all." Twenty-three faces are staring at him. He fumbles for the notes he had jotted down the night before, spilling the pages from the folder onto the floor. The seconds tick by, an eternity of silence. "Um, let's see," he continues, still sorting the pages. He avoids eye contact with his audience, desperately trying to collect his thoughts.

Startled awake by his alarm, Sullivan is relieved to find that his clumsy presentation was just a bad dream. Luckily, he has several more days to prepare for the real thing. Careful planning and rehearsal will eliminate all but the most unforeseen problem.

1 Planning your presentation

Before beginning to draft and practice your presentation, you'll need a plan.

Analyze your situation. To plan effectively, begin by writing down everything you know about your speaking situation.

- What's the occasion?
- How many people will be there?
- How long is the entire gathering, and how long will you speak?
- What sort of place or space will you speak in? Where will you speak from?
- How will you know when to speak?

A clear understanding of your speaking situation can help you to plan the content and delivery of your remarks. For example, knowing how much time you have to speak will help you determine how much detail to provide, how many points to cover, and what materials to prepare. It's always helpful to go to the place where you'll be speaking when it's empty and scope out the room, noting its size, lighting, and seating arrangement.

Focus on your purpose and your audience. Knowing something about the people you will address helps you make important decisions about your presentation. You wouldn't say the same things about your science project to a group of middle-school kids as you would to a group of judges at a college science fair. What do you know about your audience? What might they already know about your subject? What do they expect to find out from your remarks? (See also Chapter 3.)

You'll also want to ask yourself what *you* hope your presentation will accomplish. Are you trying to persuade people to take action or to vote a certain way on an issue? Are you giving them information they can use in their own work or activities? Do you want them to learn something new and come away from your remarks feeling enlightened and interested in a subject? (See also Chapter 3.)

16a
speak

Research your topic. Unless you're an expert on the topic of your presentation, you'll need to consult external sources to plan your remarks, just as you would in a documented paper. (See Chapters 22–28.) Remember, live audiences have even less tolerance than readers for abstract information presented in dull, lifeless language. Choose information that makes your presentation come alive without leaving out essential facts or details.

Organize your content. Instead of trying to write your talk like a paper, begin by creating an outline. Usually your talk will consist of three parts.

- **Introductory remarks,** in which you introduce yourself and give your audience a preview of what you'll say.
- **Content or substance of the presentation,** which consists of your main ideas, illustrations, and material.
- **Conclusion,** which sums up and restates your purpose.

Create talking points. Talking points are key phrases, words, visual cues, or other reminders that guide you through your speech. They include not only your main points, but signals to help you coordinate your talk: "check time," "change overhead," "circulate handout." Most of the time, talking points will be words or short phrases, but you should write out all of your introductory remarks and your conclusion. Doing so will help lead you into your presentation smoothly and allow you to wrap it up cleanly and dramatically. Use typical transitional phrases, such as "next," "now let's consider," "in conclusion," "finally," or "to sum up" (see the chart on p. 58).

Your talking points should include transitions that link one part to the next. These transitions, which you should write out as phrases or full sentences, are important guideposts for your audience. In one of Sullivan's transitions, he moved from the immediate impact of the oil spill to the main part of his presentation: "As we've seen, the *Valdez* oil spill had a devastating short-term effect on the Alaskan shoreline and its ecosystem. I want to turn now to some of the research that has been conducted to assess the long-term environmental impact of the spill."

Plan your timing. If your presentation can be no longer than, say, fifteen minutes, begin by estimating the time for each of the components, and then divide the middle part into more specific chunks of time.

As Sullivan planned his presentation, he created the following outline.

> <u>Introduction</u> (2 minutes): "Have any of you been to Alaska or seen it in films?" (wait . . .) "Someone describe the land for me." (Get 2-3 brief responses.) Unfortunately, all that beauty you describe is seriously threatened by pollution, oil exploration, and development. A case in point is the infamous Exxon Valdez oil spill of 1989. In March of that year, (explain). My purpose is to give a status report, based on secondary research, of the environmental impact of the Exxon Valdez oil spill fifteen years later, and to reach a conclusion about the total impact of the spill and whether Exxon met its obligations to restore the environment.
> <u>Substance</u>:
>> <u>Background</u> (3 minutes): (Put up Overhead #1.) Remind audience of the original situation and promised restitution. (Pause for effect and check time.)
>> —What I did (2 minutes): (Put up Overhead #2.) Explain how I gathered information and from which sources. Special focus on Valdez Oil Spill Trustee Council. (Check time.)
>> —Major findings (6 minutes): (Put up Overhead #3.) Summary of the most important findings, divided into three categories of assessment (soil/beach, wildlife, long-term ecology). (Be sure to cover statistics.)
>> <u>Conclusion</u> (2 minutes): "In summary. . . ." Explain results of the study and answer question it asked. "As illustrated by this presentation and the evidence I have provided, we must use whatever means—through new legislation, public protest, and private foundations—to safeguard our pristine Alaskan wilderness and shoreline so that we never experience another Exxon Valdez. All of us, no matter what our political leanings, have a fundamental responsibility to protect our environment."

Use note cards. After sketching out your talking points, creating an outline, and working out a time plan, transfer your material to note cards. Number the cards so you'll always know where you are in your presentation.

Exercise 1

Choose a subject that you know something about and that would make a good informative presentation. First describe a purpose for conveying this information and an audience that might find it useful. Create an outline for a ten-minute oral presentation on this subject to this audience; then sketch out a series of talking points, following the advice in 16a-1, including transitions between points and an estimate of the time for each part of the presentation.

2 Rehearsing your presentation

As you plan your presentation, don't assume you have to "get it right" before you can begin rehearsing. Hearing yourself talking out what you've written down will give you new ideas that, in turn, will alter your plans.

Stand and deliver. If you recline in a comfortable chair to rehearse your presentation, you won't be building the confidence you need to speak to your audience. Standing up will match the physical and spatial conditions of your talk. Your body, your breathing, the placement of your feet, your eye movements will all be affected by where you're positioned during your rehearsals.

16a
speak

Rehearse alone, then with an audience. If possible, the first few times you rehearse your presentation, do it alone. As you build confidence and iron out the wrinkles in your talk, it helps to give a dry run of your talk to one or more trusted listeners. Work through the entire presentation at once, then ask them for their suggestions.

Try videotaping or recording your presentation. If you have access to video equipment, tape your presentation and then watch it several times to see if you can discern problems, distracting habits, inappropriate pace, poor transitions, or unclear statements.

Rehearse with your visual aids. Be sure to include any visual aids in your rehearsal so you can practice your timing and transitions. If possible, set up the visual-aid equipment that you will use. This step will allow you to find out where to stand so you don't block the screen, how to coordinate your visual aids with your remarks, and how to operate the equipment effectively.

Practice. Keep rehearsing until you know every part of your presentation— its transitions, dramatic pauses, reminders to look at your audience, and so on.

3 Giving your presentation

The following suggestions can help you develop the skills you need to connect with your audience and present information in a lively, engaging manner.

Avoid reading verbatim. Most audiences prefer speakers to *present* their ideas instead of *reading* them. This kind of speaking is called **extemporaneous speaking** or **conversational speaking,** a mode of delivery that emphasizes greater interaction among speaker, audience, and ideas. In this kind of speaking, you prepare a set of ideas, not a verbatim text, and you speak from and about those ideas. This is not to say that you don't craft the words for your presentation in advance; you just recall what you want to say from memory and from your note cards rather than read long sentences out loud.

Speak loudly and clearly. It's important for you to be heard, and speaking up will also affect your confidence. Articulate your words clearly, and monitor your speech rate, being careful not to race through your talk. Vary the pitch and cadence of your voice to accentuate certain points you're making, but don't exaggerate your emotions.

Use purposeful, natural gestures. Standing stock-still may not give your presentation variety, but be careful not to get carried away with wild gestures or movements. Move around if you wish but don't pace or make repeated motions. Avoid distracting movements (drumming the lectern, jingling change in your pocket, twisting your hair, or shifting your weight). Instead, subtly accentuate your remarks with gestures and facial expressions.

16a
speak

Maintain eye contact. As you begin your remarks, look at your audience. Look directly at individuals in the audience, but don't do so for more than two or three seconds unless you are in a question-and-answer mode, and don't keep returning to the same person. Vary your eye movement so that you don't favor one part of the room or one group of people. If it helps, work in a pattern, such as front-left, front-right, center-left, center-right, rear-left, rear-right. If you're using visual aids, glance at them from time to time but keep your focus mainly on your audience.

Use visuals effectively. If you will be using a chalkboard or a flip chart to call attention to certain ideas, prepare everything ahead of time. Audiences become impatient if they must wait for a speaker to write something down during a presentation. A more effective way to present information visually is to use an overhead transparency and project it on a screen. If you use transparencies, make sure that everything you project is readable from anywhere in the audience.

Certain software programs, such as *PowerPoint*, allow you to create stunning slides that include words, pictures, and other media. If you use such programs, be sure to follow the suggestions that accompany them; learn and practice with the technology before using it. Always bring backup overhead transparencies with you in case of equipment failure. Be careful not to make your visual presentation so gimmicky that your ideas are lost in the glitz.

16a
speak

FIGURE 16.1 Six *PowerPoint* slides from a presentation on an oil spill in Alaskan waters.

Avoid reading every word on your slides: the audience is capable of doing that themselves. Instead, paraphrase or call attention to the material on the slides, or let bullet points summarize points you are making in more detail.

Shaun Sullivan projected the *PowerPoint* slides shown in Figure 16.1 as part of his presentation.

Don't panic. If something goes wrong during your presentation—the projector won't turn on, a microphone isn't working, or you lose your place in your talking notes—remain calm. It's better to focus on the source of the problem for a few seconds, even if this is a distraction, than to allow yourself to lose your thoughts or become confused about what to do next. Audiences are more forgiving than you think. If the problem can't be fixed, such as a broken bulb in a projector, move on without it.

4 Assessing the results

Don't be satisfied to step down and put your presentation behind you; actively seek further information so you can develop your abilities.

Ask a confidante to be in the audience. If possible, ask someone you trust and respect to attend your presentation, and ask that person to look for specific areas you're concerned about, such as your body movements or the rate of your speech.

Carefully study any scoring guides or remarks you may receive from a teacher. Teachers often use sets of criteria to judge the quality of a presentation. If you're doing more than one presentation, work on the weakest categories in the assessment of the first one.

Do a self-assessment. Although you can't see or know everything about your presentation, you'll probably have some immediate impressions. Write them down as soon as possible. After identifying areas of concern, spend some time thinking of strategies to overcome the problems.

Exercise 2

Write down what you consider your two primary delivery difficulties (nervous gestures, filler words, or voice projection). For each, describe (1) when the difficulty usually happens (for example, during transitions or when you look at notes) and (2) something you can do to resolve this difficulty (such as pausing instead of using filler words or placing your hands on the table instead of in your pocket).

16b Managing speech anxiety

No one is entirely immune to the apprehension of public speaking, yet some people handle the pressure reasonably well, whereas others have intense emotional responses. To help overcome your anxiety, try these strategies.

1 Analyze the causes of your anxiety

Write down what makes you most anxious about public speaking. Does it have to do with the audience? the subject? your preparation? what you will look like? what people will think? Compartmentalize your fears, then work through each one, finding productive, personal strategies for overcoming them.

2 Control your breathing and calm your body

The fact that your palms sweat before you speak, or your neck flushes, or your stomach gets butterflies doesn't predict anything about the quality of your presentation; all it means is that you're like most other people, even highly effective speakers. If you let these physical responses control your presentation, they will. You need to control them instead.

Start with your breathing. Discreetly taking long, deep breaths before you talk will help to slow your heart rate, calm your nerves, and provide oxygen to your brain. Think about your entire body from top to bottom, and find the places where you're most tense. Then deliberately relax those tense spots, continuing to breathe slowly and deeply. Keep your focus on your ideas, not on yourself, how you look, or what your audience will think about you. When it's your turn to speak, focus first on getting to your speaking position. Move deliberately and carefully; you don't need to rush. Don't begin to speak until you're facing your audience; you can even take a second or two to organize yourself if you have notes or if you need to adjust a microphone.

STRATEGY Respond effectively to audience questions

16c
speak

- Anticipate the kinds of questions you may be asked; where necessary, prepare brief answers ahead of time that you can recall during your presentation.
- Ask for clarification if you don't understand a question.
- Respond directly, not evasively. If you don't know the answer, admit it. Perhaps say that the question suggests a fruitful area for further study or investigation.
- Don't indulge hostile questioners. Answer them briefly and diplomatically, with a yes or no, or "I'm not sure," and move to the next questioner.

Exercise 3 ————————————————

List and describe your greatest fears about public speaking. Are you afraid you will lose your place? forget your material? say something wrong? Are you fearful that your voice will shake or your hands tremble? For each fear, consider what you can do ahead of time to reduce your anxiety.

16c Group presentations and other public forums

Public speaking includes occasions when one person or a small team addresses people in a public or group setting. The need to be articulate and focused is just as great in these settings as it is in a traditional speech. A few strategies can help you present yourself effectively.

1 Effective group presentations

Split up the responsibility for researching your presentation, then come back together to create joint talking points. It's essential that all members of your team participate; don't allow one member to sketch out his or her remarks briefly and tell you it will all work out. Everyone should have a copy of all the talking points for the group.

Behave as a team. During your presentation, an initial lead presenter should introduce the other speaker(s) on the team. Each presenter should create a transition to the next presenter, but these transitions should, whenever possible, be oriented toward your content, not the fact that you're changing speakers. Instead of saying, "Now Ephraim will talk," try something like "The underlying social causes of this phenomenon, to which Ephraim will now turn, help to explain why it became popular in the 1960s."

Speak to a common theme. Even if members of your team have come up with different information and ideas, don't place yourselves in opposition to each other. Instead, create a single presentation that allows you to reveal differences in your subject matter: "Ephraim has described one way of interpreting this social phenomenon; now I'd like to explain it from another perspective."

16c
speak

Divide your time and stick to the plan. Audiences are aware of imbalances in the time each presenter takes. Divide your time evenly among your team. Monitor your own time carefully so that you don't take away from the time of presenters who follow you.

2 Effective speaking in public forums

Every day in your community, people gather to share ideas and opinions about local concerns. You can speak effectively in these settings by using simple but powerful strategies.

Become informed before voicing an opinion. Don't rush to a meeting of your city council armed with opposition to a proposal until you're well informed. Better still, if you don't know enough about an issue to speak to it, attend the meeting in order to learn.

Bring information. If you feel confident enough about an issue to voice an opinion, bring information and evidence that support your points (see Chapter 11 on supporting evidence). Opinion alone will help decision makers to know how a community feels, but it may not persuade them as powerfully as facts will.

Plan your remarks. In many public forums, you'll have only a minute or two to speak. Nevertheless, plan and rehearse your remarks. Don't alienate those who might disagree with you; instead, try to strike a balanced, reasonable posture while making your own position clear.

Assess the progress of the meeting. Wait until the focus of the discussion aligns with what you want to say, then try to make your comments when they will have the most impact. If possible, tie your remarks to the discussion by referring to something someone else has said.

Make your comments clear and persuasive. Fear and nervousness also tend to affect people's demeanor in public settings, causing them to speak angrily, make accusations, or even cry. If you prepare for a tense public meeting by thinking through your ideas carefully and framing a clear, logical argument for your position, you won't fall prey to your emotions, and your audience will be more likely to think about your ideas and modify their positions on an issue.

Exercise 4

Watch a brief oral presentation. If you can't find a nonprofessional example and decide to use television, don't choose a news broadcast or other journalistic presentation, but look for a presentation that is given to a live audience, such as a speech in Congress. Local and cable-access stations may broadcast town council meetings, school board meetings, and the like. Choose one that lasts at least five minutes. As you watch, jot down notes about topics discussed in this chapter: the method of delivery, eye contact, the use of notes, body and facial movements, pauses, distracting features, and so on. Write a brief analysis and evaluation of what you saw.

16c
speak

Visit mycomplab.com **for more resources and exercises on speaking effectively.**

PART 4

Writing for Specific Communities

CHAPTER 17

Academic Writing: General Education

The kinds of academic writing you do in college will vary with the type and level of courses you take. **General academic writing** is common in introductory courses that are not designed for majors or specialists (often referred to as general education courses). Many of these courses require similar ways of thinking and working with information and texts. In such courses, you might be asked to weigh two sides of an issue, analyze why something happens, or summarize the main ideas in an article. In more advanced courses, you will do more **discipline-based writing.** This kind of writing draws on forms, styles, structures, and other characteristics shaped by the community of people who work within a field. It's still academic writing, but it shares features with the writing of professionals in the field. Different types of academic writing also call for different kinds of intellectual activities, sources of information, styles, structures, and formats.

17a Analyzing assignments

College writing begins with an assignment, and assignments are usually announced in a course syllabus, at least in general form. (More specific information may come from the instructor later, when you begin working on the task.)

1 Syllabus assignments

Begin by looking through a course syllabus for general statements about the nature and purpose of writing in that course. Then take the following steps.

- Note titles and due dates of writing assignments.
- Make a separate list of all the writing assignments. Next to each assignment, jot down any information that explains its nature, purpose, or complexity.
- Note whether the assignments appear to be *sequenced* in some way. Do they build on previous assignments? Does the *type* of writing change in any way? Note patterns in the assignments, such as three "short analyses" (one due every five weeks) and a long term paper at the end.
- Look for relationships between and among the assignments and the overall coverage of course material.

TYPES OF ACADEMIC WRITING

	CHARACTERISTIC ACTIVITIES	COMMON FORMS
REFLECTING	Responding, reacting, speculating, exploring, inquiring	Reading journals, logs (data observations and insights), personal essays, reaction papers, autobiographies, reflexive writing (self-observing and self-critical)
DRAWING ON SOURCES	Summarizing, paraphrasing, synthesizing, analyzing, comparing, compiling, evaluating	Summaries and abstracts, reviews and syntheses (research, ideas, or information), book reviews and reports, annotated bibliographies, informative research papers, poster presentations, analyses of issues or controversies
INTERPRETING	Analyzing, defining key ideas and meanings, identifying causes and effects, describing patterns, applying a theory, drawing a conclusion, taking a stand on an issue	Interpretations of a text or work of art (documented or not), analyses of phenomena (historical, social, or cultural), "thesis" papers taking a stand on scholarly issues, documented arguments drawing on research
OBSERVING, EXPERIMENTING	Making observations; designing surveys and experiments; collecting, synthesizing, and analyzing data; recognizing patterns	Scientific reports and articles, logs of observations and experiments, lab reports, field research reports, project evaluations
ARGUING	Expressing and supporting an opinion or claim, changing readers' perspectives, providing new evidence for a point of view	Argumentative or persuasive papers, position papers, reports with recommendations
DEMONSTRATING	Explaining, supporting, defining, presenting information and ideas, offering conclusions	Essay tests, take-home exams, tests requiring sentence- or paragraph-length answers, written responses to readings

17a
gen ed

2 Detailed assignments

Instructors' assignment styles vary greatly. Some like to hand out brief descriptions, others like to clarify the assignment in class, and still others create Web pages with lengthy explanations and links to resources. Whatever its form, you need to spend time analyzing an assignment carefully, noting specific or unusual expectations. Pay attention to four key elements.

1. **How formal?** Usually, the longer an assignment, the more formal it is. Your instructor will assume that you won't spend a lot of time on an overnight response paper of one page, but, for a fifteen-page term paper, will assume multiple drafts, careful revision and editing, and flawless grammar and documentation.

2. **How open?** Some assignments will allow you freedom to explore a topic, while others will limit you to specific readings or information.

3. **For what purpose(s)?** An assignment may be designed to give you practice, help you learn something, convince someone of a point of view, share new information, or reveal a new understanding about a text, phenomenon, object, or process. Purposes are usually revealed by the specific nouns and verbs in an assignment (see 3a).

4. **For which audience(s)?** The default audience for most assignments is the instructor, but instructors often push aside their own tastes and opinions to play the role of a wider, educated college audience when they read your work. Sometimes instructors will ask you to address a specific audience, such as the people opposed to your solution to a problem or the members of a professional group. You may also be asked to share your writing with your peers in the classroom (see 5c).

STRATEGY   Analyze your assignments

- Examine the description of the assignment carefully.
- Take notes: What is the task called? Is its name unfamiliar? If so, does it seem to be a name that's shared within the field of study, or is it a name that the instructor has created for classroom purposes?
- Describe its level of formality, its freedom versus constraint in subject matter, its purpose(s), and its audience(s).
- If an assignment includes longer descriptions, "assignment guides," suggestions for completion, or grading scales, circle key words and identify verbs that signal what you need to do. Look for clues about the structure, style or voice, and content of the task.
- Figure out whether you are supposed to report impartially or take a position and argue a point (see 10a).

17a
gen ed

3 Assignment goals

Most assignments have three broad goals:

- *Learning goals* help you gain knowledge or practice a skill (such as researching a topic or summarizing information).
- *Rhetorical goals* present information or argue a point.
- *Assessment goals* show your instructor how well you've accomplished the learning and/or rhetorical goals of the assignment.

To understand a writing assignment, identify the goals involved. Sometimes the goals are clearly specified, as in this excerpt from an assignment in an introductory psychology course:

There are two main goals for this assignment: first, to give you practice summarizing the main points of articles that report original psychological research; second, to help you to critique research by asking questions about its design and conclusions.

In other cases, the learning goals won't be so clear. You may need to look at an assignment's **grading criteria** to figure out what the instructor is emphasizing in the task.

Academic assignments can also be divided into those that ask you to report information objectively (**information-driven;** see 17b) and those in which you make a case for your own interpretation or evaluation (argumentative or **point-driven;** see 17h).

17b Common information-driven assignments

Some college writing assignments ask you to gather information and present it objectively to others. In such writing, you don't try to support your opinion or your critical insights. Instead, you adopt the stance of a reporter, carefully gathering, analyzing, and synthesizing information. Rather than thinking of your readers as people who need to be sold something, imagine that they are your clients, and that they want you to supply information thoroughly, objectively, and clearly, in a way that is new, interesting, or useful to them.

STRATEGY   Use grouping and outlining to find the internal logic

Informative writing relies on an internal logic that helps readers to process and understand information (see also Chapter 2).

17b
gen ed

- **Chunks.** List the main areas, or chunks, your paper will cover. All the information you have gathered should fit into these chunks. If something doesn't fit, reconsider your list; perhaps you should create additional categories.
- **Patterns.** Look for patterns in your information. For example, if you are **comparing** or **contrasting** two phenomena, your work will involve dividing your paper into two large sections or into a number of subtopics, each of which covers part of the two main topics. If you use **classification,** you will organize information in terms of groups, categories, or parts, each presented in its own section. (See also 6e on patterns in paragraphs.)
- **Sequence.** Consider presenting information in a **sequential order,** perhaps in a *spatial sequence* (describing physical features in relationship with each other), a *chronological sequence* (describing events in a series to explain a history or the stages in a process), or a *hierarchical sequence* (describing relationships and the relative importance of a subject's features or parts).

17c Summaries

A **summary** is a general term for a piece of writing in which you present concisely the key information in a longer text (or an event), without extraneous detail or embellishment. In an **objective summary,** your job is to present in compressed form the substance of a text, using your own words, without evaluation or commentary. In an **evaluative summary,** you add a consideration of the coverage, accuracy, or usefulness of your source. (See 22l-1 for more on summary.)

Before you can write a summary, you need to be very familiar with the work you are summarizing. Reread the text, underlining key passages and taking notes. If the work is not a text but an event such as a lecture, presentation, or class discussion, take good notes during the event. Identify the main points in the text or the most important elements you included in your notes about an event, and state them in a sentence or two. Then create an outline of subpoints, either chronologically as presented in the text, or from most to least important. Because it's easy to include too much when summarizing, ask yourself whether you are providing more detail than is needed to understand the author's key points and how he or she arrived at them. You can begin your summary with the main point (usually an extensive introduction is not necessary) and then explain the subpoints in order.

Here are the opening sentences of a summary Jen Halliday wrote for her introductory sociology course, in which she summarizes an article reporting changes in students' racial attitudes. Notice how she provides the central point of the reading first, then begins moving into the substance.

> In this article, the authors report on a study of change in the racial attitudes of a sample of White college students when they had increased contact with African American students and were exposed to increased information about racial issues. To conduct their research, the authors first randomly selected a group of ten White college students between the ages of 18 and 23 at a midsized Midwestern university. To gauge these subjects' existing attitudes and feelings toward African Americans, they used a combination of surveys and interviews. . . .

An **abstract** is a special form of summary that often accompanies a lab report, a detailed study, or a research paper. Instructors may ask you to submit an abstract with a paper; you may also encounter abstracts in research databases and on Internet sites (see Chapters 24–25).

Abstracts are entirely objective, restating the content of a paper without extraneous commentary. By reading an abstract, someone not familiar with a paper should be able to understand its general contents, methods, stance (theory or opinion), and conclusions.

17d Annotated bibliographies

An **annotated bibliography** is a bibliography (see Chapters 29–33) in which each entry also includes a description of the aim, purpose, or content of the work cited. Annotated bibliographies help readers survey what has been written on a topic and suggest specific works to consult for their own research. Instructors often assign annotated bibliographies to help you survey and report on a body of scholarship or to help you prepare for an extended research paper.

Annotated bibliographies usually begin with a brief introduction to the topic, perhaps highlighting the kinds of works covered in the bibliography. Next, they present the citations of the works, each one followed by an annotation of at most a paragraph or two in length.

The example below comes from student Ian Preston's annotated bibliography, which consisted of an introduction to the topic followed by sixteen entries. He prepared his bibliography for a project focusing on bilingualism in the United States.

17d
gen ed

Glazer, Nathan. "Where Is Multiculturalism Leading Us?"*Phi Delta Kappan*

75 (1993): 319-24. Print.

This article describes the Center for the Study of Books in Spanish for

Children and Adolescents, an organization that promotes the positive

aspects of bilingualism. Unlike other organizations that portray their

ethnic groups as victims, the Center, Glazer argues, ought to be

followed as a model of a bilingual program.

Notice how Preston writes objectively (impartially) even as he *represents* the argument of the author.

STRATEGY   **Write an effective annotated bibliography**

- In the introduction, orient readers to the topic.
- Use a consistent documentation style for the references (Chapters 29–33).
- In each annotation, provide a brief summary of the work, accurately representing its contents and perspective but without unnecessary detail.
- Arrange the entries in alphabetical order by authors' last names. You can separate long or complex bibliographies into sections, sometimes chronologically ("Nineteenth-Century Studies," "Twentieth-Century Studies"), sometimes by general topic or focus ("Critical Studies: General Satire," "Critical Studies: Individual Satirists").

17e Literature reviews

A **literature review,** sometimes called a *survey paper* or a *review of the literature,* is usually one section of a longer paper, yet instructors sometimes assign it on its own. A literature review synthesizes the existing research on a topic—describing the content, similarities, and disagreements among research efforts. It provides a backdrop for the study or analysis that follows or a justification for your own research. Literature reviews can be totally objective or they can evaluate previous work. For example, two or more studies may reveal major disagreements in a field, but the review might document those disagreements without judging the studies themselves. In contrast, an author of a medical research article may present the findings of previous studies while criticizing their methods. Such a review tends to be more point-driven because the writer is laying the groundwork for a claim that his or her own methods are superior.

In most college courses requiring a literature review, however, you will be asked to summarize the literature, not criticize it. Your reviews will be informative, aiming at the summary (22l-1) and the synthesis (22l-3) of knowledge. The research papers in Chapters 18 and 19 of this text provide examples of literature reviews used to begin longer papers. Note how the writers use the reviews to explain and justify the goals of their studies and to provide background for readers.

**17e
gen ed**

STRATEGY   **Write an effective literature review**

- Remember that your goal is to summarize the results of prior research accurately and concisely.
- Without providing extraneous detail, synthesize the information and the conclusions, noting overlaps but giving credit to individual researchers.

- When relevant, note major disagreements among the studies you're reviewing.
- If your review sets the stage for your own study or research paper, be sure that it justifies and creates a framework for what will follow.

17f Essay exams (information-driven)

In many classes, instructors give **essay exams** to evaluate your skills as a synthesizer of information and as a critical thinker, skills that can't be demonstrated in true/false or multiple-choice tests. In informative essay exams you provide objective information in essay form. (For essays that defend and explore a claim or point, see 17k.)

To begin the exam, *read the question(s) carefully.* You will need to write quickly and concisely in a limited time, yet you will also need to answer the question(s) specifically, giving as much support as possible. Understanding what kind of answer the instructor expects is crucial; your planning before you write, though brief, needs to address the question directly.

To write an organized, clear, and detailed essay exam, spend a few minutes at the start developing a simple outline. Separating your answer into three to five sections or paragraphs—more, if appropriate—can help you organize information into easy-to-understand chunks so that your reader can see from point to point that your essay embodies adequate knowledge of the subject. Writing as much as you can without a specific focus, hoping to hit the right points, will not impress your instructor.

1 Sample information-driven essay exam response

On an exam in an introductory biology course, Nicholas Branahan responded to the question "Define the concept of natural selection, being sure to explain its main features and how it affects behavior." The question required Branahan to provide a succinct response that demonstrated his knowledge of the basic principles he had studied. Here is his response, preceded by his preliminary outline.

> Introduction: Basic definition of Natural Selection
> 1. How heredity effects reproduction (use example to explain how a species becomes dominant, define phenotype)
> 2. Two conditions necessary for natural selection
>   1. genetically inheritable trait (example)
>   2. trait needs to be linked to survival and reproduction (example)
> Conclusion: example from textbook > moths during England's industrial revolution to demonstrate entire process
>
> Natural selection, a term coined by Charles Darwin, is a process in which the characteristics of an organism that best promote its ability to reproduce are selected and the characteristics that hinder it are weeded out. As random gene mutations form new characteristics, natural selection will select those that enhance the

organism's ability to reproduce. Ability to reproduce depends on adaptability to the weather, ability to find food, avoidance of predators, and other aspects necessary for survival.

Natural selection is linked to evolutionary processes through the genetics of heredity. For example, if brown and green beetles are found on trees in the same area and the green beetle is more easily identified by birds, its numbers will decrease more rapidly than the brown beetles, who will be able to reproduce to a higher potential. The genetic characteristics of the brown beetle will be favored as they reproduce, and eventually they will become dominant. The phenotype (the outward characteristics of an organism) manifest the genotype, or genetically inherited basis for the phenotype. As organisms adapt to specific environmental and ecological conditions, a new species can emerge, demonstrating the process of evolution.

Two conditions are essential for the process of natural selection to occur. First, there needs to be some genetically inheritable trait present in the organism, such as color, claw size, ability to climb trees, or speed if chased. Second, that trait needs to be linked to survival and reproduction. If one or the other condition is not met, natural selection can't occur. For example, if some rodents are faster than other rodents, but a raptor is so much faster that the rodents' speed doesn't matter, then no evolutionary process will select for speed in the rodents.

One of the most famous examples of natural selection is the change in color of a moth indigenous to England. At the start of the industrial revolution, the moth typically had a light color; dark colored varieties were rare. As soot and other industrial factors caused tree bark to darken, the moths became vulnerable to birds because they stood out. Over time, darker moths survived better, passing on their genetic characteristics while the lighter-colored moths died off. Eventually the entire species of moth had become a dark color, with rare, light-colored moths found only in areas far from cities.

2 Commentary on the information-driven essay exam

Branahan began by taking a minute to sort his thoughts and outline his response. In the essay itself, Branahan does a good job of first defining the concept briefly (as requested) and then explaining its main features. In two subsequent paragraphs he explains how natural selection affects behavior and what happens to an organism when its environment changes. He provides a general example (green and brown beetles) to show that he understands how certain traits are selected because of environmental conditions; then he offers an extended example, presumably from his readings or a lecture, of natural selection in a species of moth. Although he could have been even more specific (by saying more about the second condition of natural selection in paragraph 3, or naming the exact species of moth in paragraph 5), his answer demonstrates that he understands the basic theory of natural selection and can analyze specific cases to judge how natural selection might apply to them.

Write a successful informative essay exam

- Address the exam question directly, without adding loosely related information.
- Take a minute or two to organize your answer clearly and logically so that each paragraph focuses on a different section of the topic.
- Include brief examples, cases, and references.

17g Short documented paper

The techniques useful for an extended research project (see Parts 5 and 6) apply as well to short documented papers in a more focused form. Typically, a short informative paper does not provide a detailed examination of a topic or answer a complicated research question; instead it offers an overview of an issue, phenomenon, or event by drawing on a few sources. Such papers are designed to *inform* readers, not to analyze a topic or issue exhaustively.

Jake Lloyd's paper focuses on the hotly debated question of whether playing video games has negative effects on players, especially young people. In his introduction, which follows, Lloyd first draws interest in his topic by describing the worldwide growth of video games, which creates a sense of *exigence* in his readers—if the games are harmful, their astronomical growth is cause for alarm.

Video Games Do WHAT?

Jake Lloyd

17g
gen ed

One of today's most popular and profitable ventures is the world of video games. Over the past few years, video games have become "a multibillion dollar business" (Videogames, 39) that is consuming countries throughout the world. Major corporations have made fortunes designing and marketing newer, more realistic "virtual realities." However, many people believe that video games are a negative influence on today's society. Recently, there has been much debate in the research community about what effects video games can have on humans. Can playing a certain video game really change the way a person thinks? Do children behave more aggressively after playing an aggressive video game? Can video games trigger seizures, hallucinations, and other health problems? These and many other questions have arisen because of the spread and increased use of video games.

It is important to understand first that video games cannot solely be blamed for changes in human behavior, given that violent movies and television shows are just as numerous and popular in present society. That is not to say that video games do not have any influence on traits like aggression and violence, but these theories need to be supported with more conclusive evidence. Furthermore, recent trends in research have shown that video games may have as many beneficial effects as harmful effects. The more important question is whether the benefits of video games outweigh the possible dangers. As popular as video games are, it is important for the scientific community to reach a consensus concerning the consequences of video game play. Although more and more research is being done to accurately determine the true effects of video games, studies so far are inconclusive in presenting concrete evidence that significantly characterizes video games as a danger to humanity.

STRATEGY   **Write a successful short documented paper**

- Remember that your goal is to summarize or synthesize the views, research results, or positions of other writers concisely and accurately.
- Although you are not providing an exhaustive analysis or review of existing research, your conclusions should be based on a reasoned consideration of the works you examine. That should allow readers to decide on the significance of your conclusions for policies, beliefs, and possible action.
- Your paper should be clearly organized around its main issues, questions, or themes.

17i
gen ed

17h Common point-driven assignments

When you write point-driven papers, you comment on or evaluate a text or an idea. Your writing conveys and supports your point in a commentary, opinion, analysis, or argument. Such writing usually requires you to *begin* in the role of reporter by collecting information, opinions, or data (see 11b). When you draw on this material for a paper, your role becomes that of arbitrator, jurist, or judge as you weigh the issues, evidence, and opinions. This kind of writing requires *critical analysis* and care in representing yourself and your reasoning (see 9b).

17i Critiques

A formal **critique** summarizes a text and offers a critical reaction to it. The summary should objectively condense the work yet include all its main ideas. The critical response is a subjective reaction to the work, but no opinion should be expressed without evidence to support it. A good critique tries to explain *how* and *why* a work is written as well as *how well*. In a critique, you make a point about a body of knowledge and opinion, thereby helping readers to see it from a fresh perspective.

College student Reid Nelson's critique begins with an objective summary.

> In the speech "Some Concerns Central to the Writing of Indian History," Alfonso Ortiz addresses the inadequacies created when non-Native American historians write Native American histories. Ortiz feels there is a need for historians to develop "greater sensitivity toward, and respect for, tribal traditions, and . . . learning Indian languages" (20).

The summary continues for five more paragraphs. Nelson then shifts to critique.

> Ortiz's simple and straightforward argument uses neither complex theorizing nor bewildering terminology. He clearly spells out the negative consequences that occur when academics are not confronted with responses from the groups they are writing about. In this case, the consequences are the continued misunderstanding of Native Americans and poor relations between the two groups. The point is strengthened through Ortiz's use of repetition. Of course, the reception of his ideas will depend on whether historians agree that there is a problem in the way they write history, and whether they agree that Ortiz's proposals will benefit non-Native Americans' understanding of Indian history.

Notice how Nelson moves from description to evaluation in this paragraph, interpreting what Ortiz has done (and how successfully he has done it) and analyzing how historians might accept his ideas. The paper continues in this direction and ends with a full reference to the printed source for the speech.

17i
gen ed

| **STRATEGY** | Write a successful critique |

- Differentiate between objective summary and subjective opinion. A good critique provides sufficient objective detail to allow the reader to understand the elements of the text or event and to trust in the writer's analysis.
- Summarize all of the text's main ideas and important questions.
- Express any critical opinion of the text or event fairly, stressing how and why it works and balancing positive and negative points.
- Give the reader a clear picture of the text's content, its writer's stance, and the strengths and weaknesses of its argument.

17j Reviews

A **review** is a critical appraisal of an event, an object, or a phenomenon, such as an art show, a concert, a book, or a restaurant. Reviews help people make decisions or test their judgment against that of another person. In a review, you describe, analyze, and evaluate your subject from an informed perspective that may range from fairly objective to strongly judgmental.

Some reviews use a simple two-part structure: a description followed by an evaluation. Others begin with an evaluative point in a kind of thesis statement: *Subject X is a success (or failure), good in some areas but poor in others.* Whatever the format, good reviews don't just state an opinion; they support it with specific information and detail. In addition, good reviews are informed by knowledge of the subject and form. In writing your own review, therefore, it may help to read a professional review of the same work or event and note the style, structure, and choice of language.

Amy Singh, a student in an introductory linguistics course, introduces the subject of the book she is reviewing before she moves on to the review itself.

> The preservation of a language, though the community that uses it may be small, is crucial. Language is not just a communicative amenity—it is a reflection of (and an influence on) a specific culture. Not only does a language allow a culture to flourish, but it allows the people within that culture to flourish. In some cases, a language is particularly well suited to a specific culture because it is all that allows its users to function in society. To allow or force a language so tailored to die is to leave the culture with no effective means of communication, only whatever its people have managed to acquire, usually by bare necessity, of the surrounding, dominant language.
>
> Cathryn Carroll's *Laurent Clerc: The Story of His Early Years* (Washington, DC: Kendall Green Publications, 1991) gives the reader a broader platform on which to base these convictions. Set in the early nineteenth century, Clerc examines the beliefs, stereotypes, and attitudes surrounding the deaf and their language. . . .

Singh's paper continues for another five paragraphs, detailing the contents of the book and commenting on the importance of its points. Although she doesn't spend much time evaluating the book, the way she describes its content implies that she thinks the book is successful and worth reading. She makes this clear in her conclusion:

> Carroll's fascinating book illustrates the folly of expecting one mode of communication—one language—to suffice for every member of society. Her book portrays the struggle of the deaf to gain equal standing in a greater society that had so much trouble accepting them. . . .

STRATEGY **Write a successful review**

- Describe the subject of the review at the start, providing all the information a reader needs to understand it.
- Offer a reasoned, supported evaluation of the subject's main elements.
- Demonstrate your knowledge of the subject so that readers are more likely to respect the conclusions you present.
- Support your conclusions so that readers have reason to respect them even when they do not agree with them.

17k Essay exams (point-driven)

A **point-driven essay** responds to an exam question that asks you to present a position or argue for your own interpretation of a work, a phenomenon, or an event. In such an essay, listing data without discussing their significance or making connections is not acceptable. You will need to offer a conclusion or an interpretation—a thesis—for which you provide supporting evidence and reasoning (see Chapter 3).

First, *read the exam question(s) carefully.* Because you will need to write quickly and concisely, answering the question with as much support as possible, it's crucial to understand what kind of answer the instructor expects and to plan your essay briefly before you begin writing. Decide what position you want to take or what point you will make. This will become your working thesis or proposition—a perspective or interpretation that you will support with evidence. Try creating a rough outline for your answer, listing just a few ideas or items on the facing page of the test booklet or an extra sheet of paper. Working from an outline will help make your paper more focused, point-driven, and clearly organized. Avoid going off on tangents, and keep from making very complicated arguments (unless you have time to revise).

The following sample begins an exam essay in which student Ted Wolfe answers a question asking him to identify and discuss a major theme from a survey course in American literature, drawing examples from two stories. (Students could use their books to find quotations.) Note how Wolfe focuses on one theme, the conflict between good and evil, and draws on elements of a story to illustrate it.

17k
gen ed

Hawthorne's "Young Goodman Brown" explores the conflict between good and evil. Young Goodman Brown has his religious faith tested during a journey into the woods. In what may or may not have been a dream, the devil shows him that everyone he believed to be good is evil. . . . When the devil is about to baptize him, Brown calls out for faith, his wife, telling her to resist temptation. He is really calling out for faith, as in faith in God. When he does this, the hellish vision passes, and he is alone in the woods. From this, we can conclude that Hawthorne believes people should try to resist temptation and lead moral lives.

Goodman Brown is never the same after the experience, be it a dream or reality. He becomes "a stern, a sad, a darkly meditative, if not a desperate man."

As Wolfe continues his answer, he argues that Hawthorne is not just offering a pious message but suggesting that "one should not get so caught up in trying to be morally perfect that it ruins one's life. People must learn to 'find the perfect future in the present.'" Wolfe explores the theme effectively, offering evidence and quotations from the text.

> **STRATEGY** Write a successful point-driven essay exam
>
> - Be sure to address the exam question directly, taking into account all parts of the question.
> - Use references—quotations, facts, other information—to support your conclusion, but don't overload the essay with detail.
> - Try to synthesize material, make connections among references, interpret the evidence and discuss its significance; don't merely list information.

17l Position papers

When you write a position paper, you take a stand on an issue or a controversy and then support your position. Your position paper may be documented, using sources to support your points, or it may be argued using internal logic, personal experience, or anecdote, as appropriate. Position papers must focus on an actual controversy, one that others have expressed different opinions on. Topics that are not arguable include your personal likes and dislikes, matters of indisputable fact, and beliefs based on conviction rather than empirical evidence (which includes most religious beliefs). In a position paper you advocate a specific perspective, interpretation, or solution; therefore, your paper will follow conventions of argumentative writing (see Chapters 10–11). For an example of a position paper, see 11i.

17l
gen ed

> **STRATEGY** Write a successful position paper
>
> - State clearly your position on an arguable issue.
> - Use factual knowledge, statistics, logical reasoning, or carefully selected, relevant anecdotes to support your opinion or interpretation.
> - Show that your reasoning is careful and thorough by including alternative points of view, even if you don't agree with them (see 11c).
> - Explain the issue in a thesis or position statement and follow it with paragraphs that provide appropriate supporting evidence.

Visit mycomplab.com for more resources and exercises on writing for academic audiences.

CHAPTER **18**

Writing in the Arts and Humanities

The arts and humanities include literature, philosophy, history, art history, music, languages, classical studies, the performing arts, studio arts, cultural studies, and related fields. When you take courses in these fields, you will interpret texts, performances, and artworks, examining the relationship of various elements, looking for underlying meaning or significance, and analyzing the techniques of their creators or performers. Writing in the arts and humanities develops theories to help us understand our lives and our cultures; it analyzes patterns of meaning in past events and projections of the future; and it evaluates (or reviews) texts, performances, ideas, and interpretations.

As you move from general education courses to upper-level courses in the arts and humanities, the writing tasks you encounter will differ in complexity and subject matter. Some kinds of writing may be similar to the general assignments you encountered earlier, such as summaries and short documented papers, yet they will require more sophisticated analysis and interpretation. In addition, common assignments will emphasize different rhetorical goals, different forms of evidence, and different writing styles, depending on the discipline.

18a Writing about texts

Research in literature, film, cultural studies, languages, music, and similar fields focuses on verbal, aural, or visual **texts**—a term that often refers to any artifact of thought (book, film, picture, etc.). This research pays attention to the actions of people represented in the text, the techniques used to create the text, its visual images and patterns, and the ideas it conveys. Researchers try to interpret the relationships of these elements and what the elements of the text and its content convey (intentionally or not) about ideas, culture, society, or history. Writing about texts, therefore, often takes the form of **analysis** (understanding the elements of a work) and **interpretation** (understanding the relationship of the elements and the overall meaning, either of the work itself or of the culture or society it embodies).

In analyzing works of imaginative literature (fiction, poetry, drama, screenplays), a writer calls attention to the techniques of presentation, such as characterization, plot, symbolism, and figurative uses of language. Imaginative literature often conveys its meanings through a fictional representation of some setting or human activity: the events of a story, a confrontation between characters, a monologue revealing thoughts and emotions, or a scene where events take place.

DISCIPLINARY COMMUNITIES IN THE HUMANITIES

	LITERATURE	VISUAL ARTS
GOALS	To analyze and interpret literary texts and their contexts, both from a thematic or meaning-based perspective and from the perspective of art or craft, and to reflect on their philosophical significance for understanding the human condition.	To render expressions or interpretations of the human condition, human emotion, or ideas about artistic expression themselves through aesthetic means such as painting, sculpture, or multimedia.
EVIDENCE	Specific elements of a text, such as language or style, plot, characterization, time, and setting.	Specific visual elements such as brushstroke, texture, light and shade, color, choice of media, and composition.
SAMPLE RESEARCH QUESTIONS	What role does communication (speaking or letter-writing) vs. remaining silent play in the underlying thematic interpretation of *King Lear*?	What influences of African art from Henry Moore's exposure to the collection of Sir Michael Sadler can we discern in his later work, and how did those elements blend with other influences?
COMMON ASSIGNMENTS	"Close reading" (meticulous analysis of text); interpretive essay; research essay (based on what scholars have said about a text); analysis based on historical information or information about an author.	Interpretive analysis of a work of art; historical or biographical essay; analysis of artistic technique.

18b
lit

In analyzing works of art, writers focus on visual elements in place of language: composition and design, light and shadow, the position of objects in a scene. To understand the meaning of such texts, you need to read them with a different kind of attention than you give to written texts. Likewise, to present in writing your interpretation of and responses to visual texts, you need to use appropriate strategies of explanation and support.

18b Reading literary and artistic texts

When you read a novel, short story, poem, or graphic novel, or see a play or a film, you need to pay attention to both meaning and artistic technique. But remember that there are many strategies for reading and interpreting such works, and your choice of strategy can determine how you interpret a work's meaning and how you respond to a writer's forms of expression. Your goal as a reader and a writer is to develop and present interpretations that your readers will find insightful and convincing.

1 Reading for meaning

For many critics and students of literature, to read for meaning is to read for theme. You can view **theme** as an idea, a perspective, an insight, or

PHILOSOPHY	HISTORY
To explore (using systematic, logical reasoning) questions of human existence, knowledge, language, justice, truth, ethics, beauty, rationality, law, and mind or consciousness in order to come to a better understanding of what it means to be human, and to reflect on the difference between human constructions of ideas and universal principles.	To study the past in order to understand how sequences of events are causally related, or to analyze records of the past in order to come to a clearer understanding of the truth about particular events and what caused them.
Evidence will vary (there is much debate about the nature of evidence, "truth," what can be known from the senses, and what leads to logical conclusions).	Primary documents (written accounts, maps and charts, pictures, oral narratives); secondary historical accounts and interpretations.
If the practice of philosophy is correlated with the material conditions or wealth of societies, what forms does "philosophy" take in undeveloped societies?	How did residents of German-speaking towns in Minnesota reconcile their resistance to the imposition of English instruction with statehood and adherence to federal policies?
Reconstruction of an argument; "thought experiment"; responses to ideas and theories; application of an idea or theory to a specific case; original argument.	Historical research papers (primary or secondary); historiographical essays; response papers; book reviews.

18b
lit

a cluster of feelings that a work conveys or that permeates a work, organizing the relationships among its parts. Or you can view theme as the responses and insights readers are likely to take from reading a work. In reading for meaning, therefore, you need to pay attention to theme both as it is developed *in* a work and as it develops in your *responses* to the work.

STRATEGY Read for meaning

As you read, write down any ideas, perspectives, insights, or feelings the work seems to focus on. Pay attention to the techniques writers employ for conveying meaning (see 18b-2): characterization and dialogue, events and conflicts, descriptions or scenes, and discussions of ideas and emotions (by the characters, the speaker, or the writer addressing readers). Write down potentially important ideas or themes in the margins (if you own the book), on a sheet of paper, or in a journal you keep while you read. You don't need to explore potential themes in depth; for a first reading at least, an informal list can be valuable. Look especially for repetition and contrast as a key to importance. Repeated words and ideas, contrasting characters or events, and patterns of images can signal themes worth noticing.

2 Reading for technique

When you read for meaning, you inevitably read for technique. A writer can't create events, portray characters, represent scenes, or elicit a reader's reactions without using techniques of characterization, plot, setting, and imaginative language. Because these techniques are an important feature of every literary text, you may want to focus on them as you read, either to understand a writer's artistry or to cite the writer's use of the techniques as evidence in your discussion of a work's meaning.

Pay attention to the following elements of a novel, short story, poem, or drama and to the techniques the writer uses in creating these elements.

Character. Identify the major and minor characters and their personality traits. Are they represented in depth with a variety of traits, even contradictions, or are they one-dimensional? Observe how the characters change and develop—or fail to change—in response to events. Note how self-aware the characters are. Which ones are presented positively, which negatively? Which characters, if any, represent values that the work seems to endorse?

Plot. Identify the order of events. Is it chronological, or have events been rearranged in some way? Decide what role conflict plays in developing the plot. Ask whether the events spring from the characters' personalities or serve primarily to reveal character traits. Is there a main conflict, a chain of conflicts, or a climax to which the work builds? Weigh the possibility that not all events are to be taken at face value. Watch for subplots alongside the main plot. Is the meaning of events clear to characters (and readers) from the start or only later? Pay attention to techniques of foreshadowing and suspense.

Setting. Note the time and place of events. Does the setting help explain the characters' actions or reactions? Does it convey a mood that shapes the reader's reactions or the work's meaning? If the work is from an earlier period, check for elements in the setting that require historical explanation.

Point of view. For novels and stories, decide who is telling the story. Stories can be narrated in the first person (*I*) either by a character in the narrative or by a narrative voice that may or may not represent the author. They can also be told in the third person by an "invisible" narrator who speaks of the characters as *he* and *she* but doesn't identify himself or herself as *I*. Narrators may be limited in what they know, or they may be omniscient (knowing and seeing things the characters cannot), or they can be both (perhaps knowing everything about just one of the characters). Narrators may be reliable and truthful, unreliable and deceptive, or a mix of these and other traits. The speaker in a poem may be a character or a persona, a voice that speaks for the poet.

Language. Look for special uses of language: similes, metaphors, understatement, paradox, ironic comment. Pay attention to language that creates vivid scenes and images. Look for unusual word choice and striking arrangements of words. Be alert for rhythms in the wording and for patterns of sound and rhyme.

Genre. Pay attention to **genre**—the specific form or kind of work: novel, short story, poem, drama, film. Be alert to the techniques and conventions characteristic of each form, and note how writers use the conventions to convey meanings and shape readers' reactions. Note instances in which the writer varies or alters the conventions, perhaps by undermining them or developing them in unusual directions.

T. J. Corini's marginal notes on the opening paragraph of John Edgar Wideman's novel *Philadelphia Fire* identify techniques and link them to meaning in a way that points toward a paper he might write.

What's going on?

first character—a hero? an outlaw?

On a day like this the big toe of Zivanias had failed him. Zivanias named for the moonshine his grandfather cooked, best white lightning on the island. Cudjoe had listened to the story of the name many times. Was slightly envious. He would like to be named for something his father or grandfather had done well. A name celebrating a deed. A name to stamp him, guide him. They'd shared a meal once. Zivanias crunching fried fish like Rice Krispies. Laughing at Cudjoe. Pointing to Cudjoe's heap of cast-off crust and bones, his own clean platter. Zivanias had lived up to his name. Deserted a flock of goats, a wife and three sons up in the hills, scavenged work on the waterfront till he talked himself onto one of the launches jitneying tourists around the island. A captain soon. Then captain of captains. Best pilot, lover, drinker, dancer, storyteller of them all. He said so. No one said different. On a day like this when nobody else dared leave port, he drove a boatload of bootleg whiskey to the bottom of the ocean. Never a trace. Not a bottle or bone.

2nd character Cudjoe uncertain of his manliness? Admires Z?

The bones symbolize the contrast

His actions make him seem verbal, self-assured

2. self-sufficient? Sure of himself? Characterization— 2.'s actions and attitudes contrast w/C.'s contrast

Repetition and parallelism help emphasize his growing legend

Contrast

Whole ¶ presents contrasts of character, attitude, perspective, and detail

**18c
lit**

18c Writing about literary and artistic texts

When you write about a literary or other artistic text, you interpret and analyze an author's words and techniques. To do so, you must arrive at conclusions—by making observations and judgments—and then convince your readers that your conclusions are both reasonable and well founded. You can generally do this by offering evidence from the text or from secondary sources.

1 Writing about meaning

In writing about the meaning of a literary work, you may explain and support your conclusions about its theme. Or you may focus on the insights you develop by applying a particular perspective to the work (a historical perspective, for example, or a feminist perspective).

Developing a thesis. When you are writing about a work's theme, make sure readers can easily identify your statement of the theme. Presenting your conclusion about the theme in a thesis statement early in your paper is an effective strategy. In addition, if you develop a working thesis early in your drafting, you can revise it and use it to help focus your supporting paragraphs.

Selecting evidence. Suppose you developed this working thesis:

> In "Young Goodman Brown," Hawthorne focuses on dangers to human relationships and community posed by excessive concern with the self.

For supporting evidence, you can turn to passages in the text, either those that seem to state this theme or those you can analyze and explain in ways that support your conclusion. Simply quoting passages from the work is not enough; you need to discuss and analyze them closely to show readers why the passages support your interpretation. You can also cite or summarize the events, characters, and symbols of a work, analyzing them to show that the text and the techniques it employs are consistent with your interpretation. Finally, you can cite the writings of critics and scholars to support your thesis.

18c
lit

Organizing. Because a paper about meaning focuses on your view of a text's theme or on your interpretation of the work, you need to organize the paper to explain and defend your perspective. There are two general ways to do this (and each has many variations). One way is to break your thesis into parts and take up each one in a different section of your paper. In writing about Hawthorne's "Young Goodman Brown," you might first demonstrate that the story deals with a character obsessed with the self, then look at what the story says about the consequences of this behavior. The other way to organize your paper is to divide it into parts that correspond to segments of the work (beginning, middle, end) or to its elements (characters, language, symbols), showing in each section of your paper how a particular part or element supports your thesis.

2 Writing about technique

In writing about technique, you explain the choices the author has made in creating a work of fiction, poetry, or drama, and you draw conclusions about how the chosen techniques shape the work's meaning and the likely responses of readers.

Developing a thesis. Your thesis statement should reflect your dual emphasis on describing one or more techniques and then relating them to meaning. In writing about "Young Goodman Brown," you might say, "Hawthorne uses ambiguity in setting, symbolism, and characterization to suggest how excessive concern with the self can alter one's perception of everyday events."

Selecting evidence. The primary evidence in a paper about technique is the text itself. Using quotations, paraphrase, or summary, you need to discuss the evidence, explaining the particular ways in which a technique is used and pointing out how this use supports your conclusions about the text's meaning. (The work of critics and scholars can also provide supporting evidence.)

Organizing. If you are examining a single technique, consider dividing your essay into parts that correspond to sections of the work, and explain how the technique is employed in each section and for what purpose. (For a short work such as a poem, you might examine the work line by line or sentence by sentence, creating an **explication.**) If you examine more than one technique, you can divide your paper into parts, each concerned with a different technique. Or you can take up each section of a work in turn, looking at the various techniques used therein.

STRATEGY   Follow conventions for writing about literature

- Use the present tense when summarizing the action or content of literary texts: "In the next section of the play, Falstaff *acts* in a manner that calls into question the kind of morality he *represents*."
- Use the present tense for discussing what a writer does in a work or works: "Dickens *uses* descriptive passages in *Bleak House* to develop symbols that *comment* on the action and the characters."
- Use the past tense for discussing a work in a historical context: "During the Vietnam War, Levertov's poetry *took on* a distinctly political tone."

18d
lit

18d The text analysis

A **text analysis** is a frequent assignment in many courses in the arts and humanities. The first of the three examples here focuses on meaning in a short story.

1 Sample literary text analysis

As you read, notice how the writer backs up her interpretation with quotations from the story but does not let the quotations dominate the paper. If you have read this short story, consider other ways it could be interpreted; if you have not read the story, consider other ways the quotations used in this sample could be interpreted.

Images of Self in "The Yellow Wallpaper"

by Jennifer O'Berry

1   During the 1800s the idea of the "new woman" was appearing. Women began to realize that they were seen only as their husbands' and society's "property." They began to pursue their independence and create their own identities. In Charlotte Perkins Gilman's short story "The Yellow Wallpaper," a nameless woman is searching for her personal identity and freedom from the oppressive childlike treatment inflicted on her by her doctor/husband. Gilman presents an elaborate metaphor about the images seen by the woman within the wallpaper found in her nursery/bedroom. This metaphor and the images the woman finds in the wallpaper play a significant role in the woman's achievement of finding her true self. Her state of insanity at the end of the story serves as a safe mask for her newly found freedom from alienation and oppression.

2   Gilman presents the woman in her story as a somewhat unstable character who believes that she is sick, although John, her doctor/husband, believes that she is only suffering from a "slight hysterical tendency" (416). This characterization seems intentional on the part of Gilman because it makes the reader see clearly that the woman's ideas are oppressed, even from the beginning, by her husband. John thinks that all his wife needs is a strict rest schedule in which she is "absolutely forbidden to 'work'" (416) until she is "well" again. Gilman seems to suggest, by putting *work* in quotes, that the duties of the woman, and all women at that time, were not truly considered work. She was forbidden to write and to have visitors. Early in the story, when the "rules" for her recovery are stated, the woman begins to comment on her disagreement with her husband, but she stops abruptly, as if she does not dare to have such thoughts. She believes that she would more quickly recover if, instead of being quarantined and forbidden from such pleasures as her writing, she "had less opposition and more society and stimulus" (416).

3   The woman tells the reader that "Mary is so good with the baby" (417), implying that she herself does not want to spend time with the baby. The child is also never mentioned by the woman as being with her or spending time with her. This seems to suggest that she may actually be experiencing a type of postpartum depression, causing her to want to abandon her child. The thoughts that lead her

to feel that she may be ill may actually be due to her desire to abandon her role of wife and mother which was so rigidly demanded by society at that time. She gets "unreasonably angry" (416) about the condition of things sometimes, but she blames this anger on her "nervous condition" (416). She tries to dismiss these thoughts because she feels that they are not proper. Therefore, she feels that she must be ill.

4   Gilman uses many images to enlighten the reader about the childlike treatment of the woman by her husband. The woman is directed by her husband to rest in a bedroom that used to serve as a nursery. Gilman chooses this room to show how John thinks of his wife. When referring to his wife, John commonly chooses names such as "blessed little goose" (418), "blessed child" (420), and "little girl" (421). This shows that he does not see his wife as an equal but rather as a helpless child who is solely dependent on him. As the woman begins to realize that she has been a subject of this type of oppression, she begins to be "a little afraid of John" (422) and to "wish he would take another room" (424), which exhibits her awareness of this treatment and the desire to be free from it, and from him.

5   Because of her rigid rest schedule, the woman is forced to spend most of her time in her nursery/bedroom, where she begins to explore the "worst [wall]paper" (417) she has ever seen in her life. Since she is not allowed to do much else, she commits herself to "follow that pointless pattern to some sort of conclusion" (419). She finds many images in the pattern, all of which aid in her "improvement" (423) "because of the wallpaper" (423) out of her mother/wife roles. She describes the pattern as images that will "plunge off at outrageous angles, [and] destroy themselves in unheard-of contradiction" (417). These "contradictions" seem to be referring to the contradictory treatment of her by her husband and society's contradictory expectations of her to be the perfect wife and mother. She becomes entranced by the wallpaper and "follows the pattern about by the hour" (419). With each second, the images become more numerous and complex. She begins to see "a broken neck and two bulbous eyes" (418), a woman behind the pattern in the wallpaper. This woman "is all the time trying to climb through . . . but nobody could climb through . . . it strangles so" (424). She begins to identify with the woman and decides that she will stop at nothing until the woman is released from her entrapment.

18d
lit

6   At the end of the story, the woman is simultaneously on the brink of self-identity and insanity. On the last night she is to stay in the house, she is left alone in the room where she finally frees the woman in the wallpaper. When the woman in the wallpaper begins to "crawl and shake the pattern" (425), the main character "[runs] to help her" (425). Through the night, the two women pull and shake the bars and are able to "peel off yards of that paper" (425). She breaks down some of these cultural bars with the help from the woman in the wallpaper. When morning arrives, there is only one woman—the two have merged, and the woman's true identity has been found. In the remaining wallpaper are "many of those creeping women" (426). This symbolically represents the great number of women who also desire to be freed from the bars put up by society. She wonders if those women will ever "come out of the wallpaper as [she] did" (426). This shows her symbolic escape and her desire for other women to experience this personal freedom.

7   John returns at the end of the story to discover his wife in a state of insanity. When he sees her as the woman in the wallpaper, creeping around the room, he faints. She "had to creep over him" (426) because he was blocking her path. This strongly symbolizes the conquering of her husband because of her dominant position over him. She tells him that he cannot "put [her] back" (426) because she is finally free. Her creeping, which is like that of an infant, seems to represent a birth of her new self. At the same time, she has become completely insane. It is rather ironic that she must move into this state in order to be free from oppression. This seems to represent society's view of a liberated and self-identified woman. John believes that his wife is not ill before she begins her pursuit of self-discovery. When this discovery is complete, he sees her as insane. The opposite is true for the woman herself. She sees herself as ill before her process of identification and fully healthy afterward.

8   The woman in Gilman's short story uses the yellow wallpaper as a tool to find her true self. The color of the wallpaper itself seems to represent the brightness and hope of a new horizon, yet at the same time, it is a reminder of the "old, foul, bad yellow things" (423), like a fungus that grows and decays. This is representative of the woman's life. She can never truly be free because society's views and ideas will never acknowledge that a liberated woman can achieve her own identity.

18d
lit

2 Commentary on the literary text analysis

Jennifer O'Berry uses quotations from the text well; she seems to have an intuitive sense of what is significant about them and how they relate to each other. She could improve the paper by discussing these quotations in more depth, explaining why they are significant in understanding how this story illustrates the ways women were oppressed. In the paper, the significance of the quotations is a bit unclear, mainly because Jennifer does not define the terms *self-identity, true self, insanity, oppression*) that she uses to explain that significance. Defining these terms would help strengthen the connection between the quotations and the discussion.

STRATEGY Write a successful text analysis

- Present a unified interpretation intended to convince readers that there is one specific way of reading the text.
- Account for every idea, argument, image, or allusion; don't overlook elements that don't fit your interpretation.
- Don't hide behind a facade of objectivity by presenting opinions as absolute truths or suggesting that "one person's opinion is just as valid as another's"; use the text to support *your* claims.
- Avoid repeating what has already been written about the text; you're not writing a summary of others' ideas but proposing a *new* way of reading the text.

18e Analyzing and interpreting visual texts

Visual texts such as films, paintings, videos, photographs, architecture, sculpture, and digital compositions call for a different analytical approach than you would apply to novels, poetry, drama, and other written works. In part, the difference is one of technique: films and videos draw on the technical resources of photography and animation. The difference is also a matter of space and time: photographs, paintings, sculpture, and architecture occupy space but don't unfold in time as novels or films do.

An analysis of visual texts pays close attention to particular features and qualities.

18e
hum

- **Arrangement.** How are the elements placed with regard to each other? Where are the figures in a picture, the objects in a photograph, or the parts of a building situated with respect to other elements?
- **Color.** What color scheme dominates (pastels? sepia? shades of gray?), and what patterns in the use of color are apparent?
- **White space.** How much of the work has visual content and how much is left empty or "white"? For example, is a central figure surrounded by white or neutral space, or is the entire frame of the painting, photograph, or film scene filled with people, objects, and background material?

- **Cinematography and photographic style.** What film or video techniques (fades, quick cuts, slow motion) does the work employ? What use of lenses (long distance, graininess, sharp or blurred focus) or recording material (film, tape, digital) characterize the work?
- **Realism vs. abstraction.** Are the representations of people, objects, or settings presented in realistic detail (a still life of fruit), or are they abstracted to a greater or lesser extent (an abstract representation of a human figure, nonrepresentational masses of color and form)?
- **Sound.** Does the work include spoken words and other sounds (most movies and videos), or does it consist entirely of form, shape, and volume occupying space (paintings, sculptures, architecture, photographs)?
- **Eye movement.** Do your eyes move around a visual based on ways people (or animals) in the film, cartoon, or picture look at or relate to each other (**gaze movement**)? Or do your eyes move around the visual according to geometrical, structural, or similar relationships among the objects and colors (**structural movement**)?

Understanding how these elements relate to one another and to the work as a whole is the key concern in analyzing visual texts. This task is also an essential part of interpreting the ideas a visual text conveys and the psychological, cultural, social, or philosophical insights and meanings it embodies.

The elements of Figure 18.1, a Web page, are organized to attract viewers to enter the site. As the page opens, pieces of the collage float into the screen and position themselves while orchestral strings play a few notes. Once the collage is assembled, mousing across the screen highlights certain

FIGURE 18.1   Screenshot <okaydave.com>

groups of collage elements that match the links below. The links take the viewer to projects created by the site's author, a student of design at The Portfolio Center. Notice how the multiple images at the site encourage viewers to take an interest in what it contains.

1 Sample visual analysis

In her analysis of a Tropicana juice advertisement, Olivia Garabedian considers each element of the ad in turn, showing how it uses specific appeals to create an image in the mind of the viewer that helps to sell the product.

Tropicana: A Squeeze of Love

1   From the moment Americans wake up, they are bombarded with advertisements and marketing schemes. From turning on the television to watching the traffic and weather report to getting into their cars and listening to the radio while driving past billboards, advertisements are simply inescapable. But what are these ads *really* trying to sell? A Tropicana orange juice advertisement in the March 2, 2009, issue of *People* magazine sells orange juice along with feelings of comfort and love to women, specifically mothers. The ad effectively uses a strong emotional appeal (pathos), color contrast, and subtle linear framing.

2   The full-page ad features the slogan "squeeze, it's a natural" above a black and white photo of a mother and daughter hugging and laughing. The pair are clothed in white and are reclining on white bedding. Across the top of the advertisement the word "squeeze" is printed in a large font, easily four times the size of all other writing in the advertisement. The bright red font gradually fades to bright orange as you read the text from left to right. The second half of the slogan, "it's a natural," appears aligned right below the word "squeeze"—just above the faces of the mother and daughter. More writing appears across the bottom of the advertisement in a much smaller font. It says "Tropicana, 100% orange, pure and natural, squeezed from fresh oranges." Finally, the lower right-hand corner of the ad features a carton of Tropicana orange juice.

3   Upon first glance, the audience's eyes are drawn to the two people in the middle of the ad: a mother and daughter hugging, laughing, and enjoying their time together. *People* magazine's readers are mostly women ages 16 to 50, a bulk of these women being mothers with an age range of 25 to 45. The mother in the ad

18e
hum

appears to be in her early thirties and her daughter looks to be about 7 or 8 years old. Considering this, the ad effectively appeals to its target audience. Tropicana is trying to correlate its product, orange juice, with a feeling of love and family.

4   One way it succeeds at this is by having the word "squeeze" and the phrase "it's a natural" at the top of the ad. The words are in boldface and written in a large font in comparison to the rest of the ad. This means that the marketers wanted this part of the ad to be one of the most attention grabbing. Squeezing is exactly what the mother and daughter are doing; they are hugging tightly as a way of expressing their love for each other. As for its meaning related to Tropicana's product, the orange juice is squeezed from fresh oranges. The phrase "it's a natural" is used to mean that a mother's love for her daughter is "natural," as is their relationship. Hence, the love shown is natural, and so is the orange juice Tropicana is selling.

5   The bottom of the ad features words as well; however, these words are much smaller and less notable. It is the last element the audience notices when reviewing the ad. The words "pure and natural" once again link the mother and daughter to the product. Here, however, the words are explicitly describing the orange juice. The text at the top was more directed toward the picture and less descriptive about the product.

6   It can also be said that Tropicana is trying to associate its product with a feeling of home. Thus, it can remind other readers of *People* magazine, such as female college students who may be away from home, that drinking Tropicana orange juice can take them back to a place they love and cherish, without even being there.

7   The colors of the ad strongly contrast with each other, which is another way the marketers of Tropicana try to catch the attention of the audience. The main colors featured in the ad are black, white, red, and orange. The picture of the mother and daughter is in black and white, while the text is in red and orange. The use of such different colors creates a stark contrast. Because of this contrast, the reader is drawn first to the mother and daughter and then to the letters at the top. The third element they notice is the Tropicana orange juice carton, which is ultimately what is being sold.

8   The choice of the advertisers to use these colors has reasoning behind it. Orange is used for the obvious reason that the product they are selling is *orange*

juice. The red, however, can have a deeper meaning. The color red is traditionally associated with love and rarely used in the marketing of orange juice. Therefore, the red is used to support the theme of love found in the ad. The black and white photo of the mother and daughter is used to create the aforementioned contrast.

9   The color green has a small part in the ad. It is used for the Tropicana logo on the bottom left of the ad and on the juice carton. Green is often used to promote a feeling of freshness and health, and its role in this ad is no exception.

10   The final appeal used in this ad is that of framing. Although the juice carton is the third element of the ad that the audience notices, it is carefully framed by subtle linear lines. The little girl's arm creates a linear frame with the juice carton. The frame starts at the top of her elbow and continues all the way down to her shoulder. This angle almost naturally points straight down to the Tropicana carton.

11   The juice carton is also framed by the pillows and sheets. The daughter's head and body create a curve in the pillow. The orange juice is thoughtfully placed in the middle of this curve, as if it were a perfect fit.

12   With the use of rhetorical and visual appeals, the Tropicana orange juice ad in *People* effectively catches the attention of its target audience: mothers. The feelings of love and comfort are part of the strong emotional appeal of the ad. Everyone wants to experience those feelings as much as possible, and by drinking Tropicana orange juice, you may just be one step closer. The colors provide a strong contrast while also possessing a deeper meaning. Finally, the subtle linear framing of the ad directs the reader's attention to the carton of Tropicana juice. More important, the ad leaves you with a happy feeling, something that Tropicana is sure to benefit from.

**18e
hum**

Work Cited

Tropicana Orange Juice. Advertisement. *People* 2 Mar. 2009: 27.
        Print.

2 Commentary on the visual analysis

Olivia Garabedian knew that she had to show how the Tropicana ad deliberately used certain visual devices to persuade readers of *People* to buy the product. She effectively breaks the advertisement down into its component parts, focusing on each in a separate paragraph. Notice how she sums up her analysis in her concluding paragraph. Although there is no broader point to the essay other than that the ad is effective, it represents a successful application of the skills of careful, systematic observation and rhetorical analysis. To improve her paper, Olivia could have used some simple features of her word-processing program to splice in parts of the advertisement, thus allowing her readers not only to read her description and analysis of the ad's components, but to consider those visually in turn.

> **STRATEGY** Write a successful visual analysis
>
> - Begin with background on the context, creator, and/or history of the work. If it is an advertisement, tell where it appears.
> - Consider the organization of your analysis: do you want to structure it spatially, thematically, or from most to least important features?
> - Use terminology to describe the work that is appropriate to its context.
> - Provide specific examples and details from the work to support your observations about it.

18f Reviews and critical analyses (critiques) in the arts and humanities

In many arts and humanities courses, instructors will ask you to analyze, evaluate, and respond to what someone else has had to say about a text or a performance, about events or social patterns. Writing in the fields of history, art history, and music history focuses on events and social or artistic developments. Writing in the fields of literature, cultural studies, music, languages, the performing arts, and classical studies usually focuses on texts and performances.

A **review** is a critical appraisal of a text, a performance, an artwork, or an event. Reviews evaluate using specific standards (or criteria) drawn from a field of study. Academic reviews aim at conveying a judgment about achievements and weaknesses based on the standards of the field and comparisons with similar works. They may also incorporate more personal judgments. The goal of an academic review is to convey an opinion about a work's value to other people working and researching in the field. (For a discussion of reviews, see 17j.)

A **critical analysis** or **critique** is similar to a review, yet it has a stronger emphasis on the analysis of the parts of a work and on their implications for further research and theory or for the field as a whole. While it is possible to critique performances, artworks, and musical pieces, critiques are more likely to focus on written texts, either literary or scholarly and theoretical texts. In a history course, an instructor might ask you to critique a recent work of historical analysis focusing on the late seventeenth century or to critique a representative text from the same period. In a music course, an instructor might ask you to critique an account of the origins and social roles of hip hop or an account of Mozart's role in musical and social history.

Critiques typically begin with background information on the work being examined, along with an overview of the standards (or criteria) the writer will use to evaluate the work. Following this, a critique usually offers a brief summary of the work and an analysis of its major elements, ideas, key information, and presentation techniques. *Analysis* in this context means the identification of the most important information, ideas, and strategies in the work and a judgment about their success or failure relative to the standards of the field, to general standards for scholarly or informative writing, or to the achievements of similar works. The last section of a critique typically offers the writer's judgment of the overall value of the work—its ideas, the policies it proposes, and the interpretations it offers. This judgment relates the work to knowledge and research within the field, to current social and political developments, or to the writer's own perspective.

1 Sample critical analysis of a film

Notice how the student Jason Fester organizes his paper and uses details from the film to illustrate and support his points.

Realism and Visual Effect in *Educating Rita*

by Jason Fester

1   *Educating Rita* is a realistic film. It depicts an older woman hairdresser who returns to college to become educated. As a realistic film it presents itself very conventionally with authentic sets, vernacular dialogue, and routine eye-level shots with conversations consisting of medium two-shots and close-ups. Since the film concentrates on language and the interaction of characters, the other elements of cinematic technique seem secondary, and as a realistic film, this seems appropriate. "Realists . . . try to preserve the illusion that their film world is unmanipulated; an objective mirror of the actual world" (Giannetti 3). But the director inconspicuously uses color to parallel character development and contribute to the theme of his movie.

2   When Rita is first seen, she is light-skinned and has bleached blond hair. She wears red lipstick, a thin white shirt, high heels, and a tight hot-pink skirt. The next time she is seen, she wears a white shirt, a bright red skirt, high heels, dangling silver earrings, and this time pink highlights adorn her hair. Rita is a vivacious, vivid woman, and the colors of her wardrobe reflect this. Her appearance presents her as sexual and corporeal.

3   The university, however, is a dull, colorless place. The building's walls are dirty white and gray stone. Frank's office is a dungeon of brown curtains, olive walls, and a drab red carpet, all bordered by a montage of tan, matte yellow,

18f
hum

earth brown, and olive drab books. Everything associated with the university is plain, colorless, and somber. Frank's house continues the decorum of his office with brown curtains, muted yellow, and olive drab wallpaper. Frank wears suits exclusively in varying tones of tan; his friend exists in the same gray suit throughout the movie, and even Julia limits her wardrobe to red-browns. There is no vividness to any of these places or people. Everything, except Frank, is sober.

4   This is the world to which Rita commits herself, regardless of Frank's warning that she will have to "suppress, perhaps even abandon altogether, [her] uniqueness." Thus it is appropriate that at the stage of her development when she has chosen to commit to her education, saying "I want to change," she is wearing a tan jacket with a brown skirt.

5   With the advent of spring comes the next phase of Rita's transformation: summer school. Here her apparel consists of the light blues and greens of the fertile season, suggesting that Rita herself is flourishing and growing. Upon her return to Cambridge, she responds to a compliment on her appearance with "I got a whole new wardrobe." Her appearance is now quite different from when she was first introduced. Her hair is now her natural brown; she is unadorned with jewelry or makeup; and she is clothed in a blue blazer, loose-fitting white pants, and a long white scarf. These neutral, asexual colors and styles continue throughout this period of her activities: light blues, greens, and soft grays cause her to blend with the garments of her student peers and the lusterlessness of the college.

6   Exceptions to this pattern are the retrogressive Roaring Twenties outfits Rita wears for the bistro. They consist of hot pinks, turquoise, pink and blue leopard skins, and lime greens arrayed in clashing ensembles. But these serve to mock her original style, for when she jokingly displays one outfit to Frank, he humourlessly replies, "Why can't you just be yourself?"

7   The end of the movie presents a Rita vastly different from the one introduced at the beginning. Rita is now merely Susan, a confused, unfulfilled woman. She is dressed in blue jeans, common and ordinary. She wears no makeup. Her long brown hair hangs limply on her shoulders. As she walks along, her blue clothes merge with the dreary blues and grays of the wet rained-on streets. She doesn't know where she's going; she doesn't know what she wants to do.

8   The director uses the colors of Rita's clothes contrasted against the colors
of her environment to further express the character changes she undergoes. Even
though this is a realistic film, the director surreptitiously manipulates one
technique, color, in a way that affects the emotions and responses of the viewer.

Work Cited

Giannetti, Louis D. *Understanding Movies.* 10th ed. Englewood Cliffs:

Prentice, 2004. Print.

2 Commentary on the critical analysis of a film

Jason Fester assumes that readers will be familiar with the film he is
analyzing, and as a result he does not adequately identify all of the characters, scenes, and relationships he discusses. At the same time, however, his
discussion of Rita's appearance and its relationship to her character is especially clear. He organizes his discussion so that it follows the chronology of
the film. This is particularly appropriate not only because the organization
aids him in demonstrating the pattern in Rita's changing dress but also because it allows him to draw parallels with Rita's changes in character and the
themes developed through these changes. He also presents evidence about
the film's techniques that is detailed enough to convincingly support his interpretations of the director's work.

STRATEGY   Write a successful critical analysis

- Don't assume that your readers are familiar with the work; always
  provide a concise summary to prepare them for your analysis.
- Describe the standards or criteria you will use to evaluate a work,
  and indicate the relevance of those standards to the goals of the particular field of study.
- Draw on specific examples and details from the work (or from similar works) to support your points and especially your evaluation of
  the work's success or limitations.

18f
hum

Visit mycomplab.com for more resources and exercises on writing in the arts
and humanities.

CHAPTER 19

Writing in the Social and Natural Sciences

As you move from general education courses to advanced courses, your writing tasks will change, along with the complexity of the subject matter you write about. The kinds of written documents you create will be similar to the kinds professionals create, but (in most cases) without the depth and level of detail typical of advanced research and scholarship. Some of your assignments, such as lab reports and reviews of the scholarly literature, will be part of coursework in many fields. Others will be unique to a specific field or practice, as in the case of nursing care plans, a form of writing characteristic of nursing and allied health sciences.

In this chapter we look at kinds of writing commonly assigned in the social sciences and in the natural sciences.

DISCIPLINARY COMMUNITIES IN THE SOCIAL SCIENCES

	POLITICAL SCIENCE	LINGUISTICS
GOALS	To understand and reflect on the role of politics, political processes, and the history and development of political systems in local, national, or international contexts.	In formal linguistics, to understand the nature and structure of human languages; in sociolinguistics, to understand the ways that human language varies as a function of its use in social contexts and communities.
EVIDENCE	Historical documents, political treatises, and theoretical works; documents emerging from politics and political activity; political and demographic data collected from surveys, interviews, or censuses.	In formal linguistics, units of spoken language; in sociolinguistics, language data as a function of use and context.
SAMPLE RESEARCH QUESTION	What political factors explain regime longevity in North Korea?	What is the nature, function, use, and variation of the word "dude" in casual American speech?
COMMON ASSIGNMENTS	Theoretical and interpretive papers; short documented papers; summaries; analyses of political data; debates; original studies based on data; "prescription" papers (how things should be changed).	Short research papers on specific topics; analyses of language data; original studies of language phenomena; summaries of books and articles; papers based on linguistic observation.

19a Research in the social sciences

The **social sciences** study human behavior and relationships, including both individual behavior and group characteristics and actions.

SOCIAL SCIENCE FIELDS

anthropology	folklore	political science
(cultural, social,	gender studies	psychology
linguistic)	geography	social policy
archaeology	history	social work
business	linguistics	sociology
communication	peace and conflict	urban studies
economics	studies	
education		

Typically, social scientists study data gathered from observing human behavior or by soliciting information from individuals or groups. Their studies may report on aspects of behavior over an extended period (**case studies**), or they may provide information about behaviors characteristic of a location (rural community, city neighborhood, manufacturing plant) or a group of people such as elementary school students, restaurant workers, or professional

PSYCHOLOGY	CULTURAL ANTHROPOLOGY
To study and explain human behavior and mental processes; *social psychology* focuses on the interaction of the individual in a social context or the behavior of groups of people.	To understand the ways that human societies or communities are organized and behave relative to their environments.
Data about human behavior collected by observation or from controlled experiments or clinical settings.	Artifacts of specific cultures, including behaviors and customs, tools, dress, domestic objects, etc., collected through observations, interviews, or immersion.
What psychological basis exists for the relationship, if any, between prayer and health?	How has logging affected the cultural, social, economic, and political life of the Dayak tribe of Sarawak, Borneo?
Literature reviews; lab reports; research proposals; short documented papers; term papers; reports of primary research.	Critical essays; ethnographic projects (including mini-ethnographies); observation reports; short documented papers; analyses of cultural artifacts.

19a
soc sci

athletes (**ethnographies**). The methods of study can include gathering opinions from a substantial number of people (**surveys**); focusing on the behaviors, attitudes, and ideas of individuals or small groups (**interviews, focus groups, observations**); and conducting **experiments** that compare the behaviors of groups acting in normal situations (**control groups**) with those acting in altered situations (**experimental groups**).

The box on pages 222–223 shows how, in four social science fields, typical writing assignments will emphasize different goals of inquiry, different forms of evidence, and different research questions.

All fields in the social and natural sciences have subfields that pose different questions, have different focuses, or use different (and sometimes competing) research methods. For example, one of the major social sciences is cultural anthropology, which studies remote communities of people or elements of advanced cultures such as our own. Another branch of anthropology, physical anthropology, studies human evolution and how communities or cultures have varied biologically. The objects of study for physical anthropologists will be the fossil remains of humans and other primates; their goal is to more fully understand human evolutionary processes. As such, physical anthropology is often included in the natural or hard sciences and subsumes other subfields such as paleoanthropology, paleoprimatology, comparative primate morphology, molecular anthropology, primate behavior and ecology, nutritional anthropology (the study of what early humans ate and the effects of their diet on their development, migration, and evolution), and forensic anthropology (the study of human bones, skeletal remains, bite marks, or blood types to help solve crimes or support expert witness testimony). These and other subfields may use different methods of data collection and analysis, and while they share the general language of the entire field, they will also have their own specialized vocabularies and may use somewhat different styles, structures, and reference systems.

Although academia maintains for convenience the divisions that organize the chapters in this section, be aware that many disciplines engage in a wide range of practices and methods, from interpretive and philosophical to empirical and rigorously scientific. As you explore particular fields, pay attention to how they make sense of the objects of their study and how they communicate their ideas and findings to others.

19b Common writing assignments in social science courses

Writing assignments in social science courses often ask for reviews of current research or opinion (see 19c), informative or interpretive reports on current issues or problems (see 19d), reports of original research (surveys, interviews, case studies; see 19e), policy proposals (a form of argumentative writing; see Chapters 10–11), and critiques or reports on articles and books (see 17i, 17j).

19c Reviews of research

An effective review of research reports the conclusions, the methods, and the strengths and weaknesses of current research on a topic of significant interest in its field. The writer selects the ideas and information for the review based on both the content of the research (conveying it accurately and concisely) and the purposes of the review.

Some reviews focus on a problem or a challenge, using current research to define and explain it. Other reviews examine current research to identify unanswered questions or possibilities for further research, often using the review to introduce and justify the writers' own research or to lead up to research questions they plan to explore (for a discussion of research questions, see 22d). In either case, writers need to be both accurate and selective, presenting the key ideas and facts of a source while putting greater focus on the details that help define a problem or a question.

1 Sample social science literature review

In a psychology course, Erica Abed became interested in exploring whether there is any truth to the myth that creative persons are more likely to suffer from depression and mood disorders. Her review of the literature on this topic unearthed a range of studies, some based on empirical research and others based on theory.

Mood Disorders and Creativity

Erica Abed

19c
soc sci

1   For centuries, artists, writers, and other creative persons have been viewed as strange, eccentric, troubled, and even crazy. Some have even believed that the mark of a great writer is loneliness and depression. Creative individuals such as Vincent Van Gogh, Ludwig van Beethoven, Michelangelo, Edgar Allan Poe, and Picasso all bring to mind such characteristics as erratic behavior, depression, mood swings, loneliness, eccentricity, and even madness. Over the centuries, many other individuals working in creative professions have likewise been labeled with these characteristics. Researchers have only recently begun to investigate the reasons behind this association. Is it because the presence of creativity leaves an individual prone to mood disorders (Kaufman, 2005; Runco, 1998; Thomas & Duke, 2007)? Is creativity simply a result of mood disorders and mental illness (Kohányi 2005)? Or is this supposed link in fact largely in our imaginations (Verhaeghen, Joormann, & Khan, 2005)?

2   Researchers have employed multiple methods of observation in order to further investigate this theory. Some have used quantitative methods—for example, studying data such as books and music created by depressed individuals compared to those of non-depressed individuals (Kaufman, 2005; Runco, 1998; Thomas & Duke, 2007). Other researchers have employed qualitative methods of research such as conducting interviews with individuals who are willing participants of a study (Verhaeghen, Joormann, & Khan, 2005). On the one hand, the results from the collection and comparison of data in the form of artistic pieces from known depressed and non-depressed professionals has the benefit of being easily controllable and difficult to influence. On the other hand, more qualitative methods that require interaction with creative individuals may prove to be more relevant in that the data collected is more recent (the artists are still living), thus not subject to change, as is a possibility in other studies. However, neither form of research methods has produced conclusive results. Although researchers have discovered a clear correlation between creativity and mood disorders, the details and significance of this connection are far less clear. While there is a great deal of evidence supporting this hypothesis, there is, as yet, none to solidly refute it.

Poets and Mood Disorders

19c
soc sci

3   In his article "The Door that Leads into Madness: Eastern European Poets and Mental Illness," Kaufman (2005) quotes the writer and poet Christopher Morley, who mused that the courage of the poet is to "keep ajar the door that leads into madness" (p. 1). Kaufman addresses the idea that creativity may lead to mood disorders. While he focuses mainly on Eastern European poets, he also mentions individuals in other creative professions, spending the bulk of the article discussing how poets differ from individuals working in the other observed professions in their personalities and their tendency toward mental illness and mood disorders. After studying 826 artistic individuals (251 fiction writers, 396 poets, 59 playwrights, and 120 nonfiction writers) living from 390 to 1957, Kaufman found that poets were the most likely to suffer from mental illness, and fiction writers were the least likely (p. 3). In "Suicide and

Creativity: The Case of Sylvia Plath," Runco (1998) reinforces this idea, additionally suggesting that "[Sylvia Plath's] depression [occurred] as a result of her writing" (p. 2). While Kaufman and Runco agree that the correlation between creativity and mood disorders is not necessarily limited to poets, their results dramatically support the hypothesis that poets are the most severely affected by depression (Kaufman, p. 3; Runco, p. 3) In fact, according to Ludwig (1995), 26% of poets attempt suicide—the highest rate of any creative profession. Additionally, 87% of the poets he sampled experienced emotional disorders, with fiction writers, musical artists, actors, and entertainers following closely at 68–77%. In contrast, the other non-artistic professions he observed produced a rate of emotional disorders starting at 27%, which is 41% lower than the artists he studied. Thomas and Duke (2007) achieved much the same results through the analysis and comparison of the works of 72 writers (36 depressed and 36 not depressed) living from the 1700s through the 1900s. After creating a system for measuring depression through these author's literary works, Thomas and Duke discovered through further evaluation that poets were indeed significantly more likely to be depressed (p. 10).

4   Verhaeghen, Joormann, and Khan (2005) take yet another approach to the theory of a link between creativity and mood disorders. After much evaluation of creative individuals known to be suffering from depression, they propose that depression in fact hinders creativity in most creative professions (pp. 1–2). However, they believe that there are two exceptions, namely poets and creative writers. Their reasoning for this hypothesis is that "self-reflective rumination" (essentially the contemplation of oneself) is a characteristic of depression, which is in fact used for introspective literature such as poetry (pp. 1–2). While Kohányi (2005) does not specifically argue against Verhaeghen, Joormann, and Khan's claim, he does argue that certain mood disorders (although not necessarily depression) may actually be conducive to the writing process. In particular, he states that certain types of mania may aid creative writers by giving them "abundant energy" and fast thinking processes, as well as enabling them to produce a large number of ideas and to work for an extended period of time (p. 3).

19c
soc sci

Explanations

5   Kaufman (2005) offers numerous explanations for his results. For example, he suggests that perhaps this phenomenon was most distinguished in the area of his study, namely Eastern Europe, reasoning that many American writers in particular have strong roots in Eastern Europe (p. 4). In addition, he proposes that poetry is used more often as a coping mechanism for those experiencing depression than are activities in the other professions he studied, arguing that depression leads to more contemplative thoughts, for which poetry is a desirable outlet (p. 4). Yet his final hypothesis takes a different turn, suggesting that poets do not reap the same health benefits as other creative writers. According to the research of Pennebaker and Seagal (1999), writers must "form a narrative" in order to benefit mentally and physically from the writing activity. However, they state that poets do not typically translate their thoughts in this fashion, possibly leaving many pent up frustrations that would be more easily expressed by other writers. Runco (1998) offers similar explanations, stating that creativity can be influenced by a number of different factors, including personal tragedy and socioeconomic status (p. 5). His main reason for believing in "investment" (wealth) as a factor is that individuals with more to lose (namely their financial wealth) would be less likely to risk losing those investments in pursuit of an artistic career (p. 5). Runco, as well as most other authors who write about the correlation between creativity and mood disorders, suggests that while it is certainly likely that mood disorders are the direct result of creativity, it is perhaps just as likely that the reverse is true. He adds, however, that the most likely explanation is that both are true, and each occurs just as often as the other (p. 9).

6   Another theory suggested by Rothenberg (1990) is the possibility that creative writing can lead to self-discovery, possibly leading to anxiety, which is closely followed by depression (pp. 196–197). Thomas and Duke (2007), while agreeing with many of the previous ideas, also propose a hypothesis of their own. Previous research discovered that poets tend to have an external locus control, meaning that they tend to attribute their success (or failure) to some power outside their body such as a muse, rather than to themselves (Kaufman & Baer, 2002).

19c
soc sci

Thomas and Duke take this finding to another level, suggesting that this external locus of control leads to a low self-efficacy, which is essentially one's belief in their ability to perform a task (p. 13). Naturally, a low sense of self-worth can easily lead to depression, as Thomas and Duke suggest is commonly the case in many poets.

Mood Disorders Leading to Creative Behavior

7   As Kohányi (2005) observes in his article, there is not only a correlation between creativity and mood disorders, but also between creative writing and unusual amounts of stress experienced during childhood (p. 1). In addition, he concludes that these two correlations are related; however, "atypical" childhood stress is not in itself a factor in determining if an individual will be either creative or depressed, much less both. Nonetheless, by realizing that this connection was important, he broadened his research and subsequently came up with four factors that, as the title of his article suggests, may possibly "Predict the Emergence of Creative Writing" (p. 1). These factors are (in addition to "atypical" stress in childhood), "growing up in an enriched and child-centered family (which can co-exist with stress), having high verbal ability, and having an unusually rich imaginative life" (p. 1). Although these are the four factors that his proposed model consists of, he also describes many other factors that could play a contributing role. At the end of his article, however, he says that not one of these factors is in itself enough to predict creativity, yet the four factors that he focuses on are together sufficient for determining creative behavior as a result of depressive qualities (pp. 9–10).

Other Opinions

8   Verhaeghen, Joormann, and Khan believe that creativity is hindered by depression (pp. 1–2). According to their data from research into the productivity of creative individuals when they were and were not in a stage of depression, individuals in the majority of creative professions (excluding poets and creative writers) were significantly less productive in periods of depression. In fact, the majority of their popular work was produced in the periods of their lives when they experienced no depression. They add that "mood stabilizers" actually assist

19c
soc sci

in the creative process rather than hindering it, and that the "depressive episode itself is indeed debilitating" (p. 1). In support of this argument, Slater and Meyer (1959) give the example of the composer Robert Schumann, who reportedly "wrote most of his works in a state of hypomania and remained silent during episodes of severe depression."

9   Interestingly, Lois Lowry, among other authors who have experienced personal tragedy, has found that writing can be an ideal outlet for grief. In the biography portion of her persona Web site, Lowry (2002) states that "I try, through writing, to convey my passionate awareness that we live intertwined on this planet and that our future depends upon our caring more for one another." As she has stated in many interviews, her purpose in writing is not to relieve herself of feelings of depression, nor do her creative pursuits cause her any depression. Instead, she writes in order to help individuals (particularly children) discover their purpose, and to create a unified community.

10   As the result of countless studies spanning centuries, it is clear that there is some link, however remote, between creativity and mood disorders, particularly depression. Therefore, in order to better understand such mood disorders that can be so destructive as to lead to suicide, it is necessary to study this link further in the hopes of better treating, and possibly even preventing, such harmful psychological disorders. If this link is better understood using psychological methods of research, then it could perhaps lead to further medical discoveries concerning depression, an ailment experienced by at least 16% of Americans ("Depression," 2009).

11   In order to produce results more constructive to the understanding of mood disorders, it is necessary to alter research methods. The one thing that current studies fail to take into account is the possible social factor that may play a crucial role in the influence on creative individuals. Perhaps creative individuals feel the need to conform to the general social belief that artists are, indeed, affected by mood disorders. It has also been speculated that genetic coding plays a role in both creativity and depression (Levinson, 2006; Dunbar & Petitto, 2008). Questions must also be asked about the reliability of individual

research studies without comparing them to studies by researchers of conflicting opinions. Are the results of these authors' research dependent on their research methods, or is it pure coincidence that all the authors who employ similar research methods seem to hold the same opinions about the theory of a link between creativity and mood disorders? If scientists from separate fields such as biology, sociology, and psychology were to combine their research findings, possibly in addition to collaborating in order to conduct further research, then perhaps a more definite conclusion can be made from the data that has already been discovered. Because depression affects such a large number of individuals, directly as well as indirectly, it is quickly becoming an issue that will be difficult to ignore.

[new page]

References

Depression. (2009). Who gets depression? Retrieved from http://www
.depression.com

Dunbar, K., & Petitto, L. (2008). Creativity may have genetic roots. Retrieved
from the University of Toronto Scarborough, Department of
Psychology Web site: http://www.utsc.utoronto.ca/~dunbarlab/

Kaufman, J. C., & Baer, J. (2002). I bask in dreams of suicide: Mental
illness, poetry, and women. *Review of General Psychology, 6,* 271–286.
doi:10.1037/1089-2680.6.3.271

Kaufman, J. C. (2005). The door that leads into madness: Eastern European
poets and mental illness. *Creativity Research Journal, 17*(1), 99–103.
doi:10.1207/s15326934crj1701_8

Kohányi, A. (2005). Four factors that may predict the emergence of
creative writing: A proposed model. *Creativity Research Journal,
17*(2&3), 195–205. doi:10.1207/s15326934crj1702&3_6

Levinson, D. F. (2006). The genetics of depression: A review. *Biological
Psychiatry, 60*(2). Retrieved from http://depressiongenetics.med
.upenn.edu/DLResearch/Levinson_GeneticsDepression.pdf

Lowry, L. (2002). *Biography.* Retrieved from http://www.loislowry.com/bio.html

Ludwig, A. M. (1995). *The price of greatness.* New York, NY: Guilford.

19c
soc sci

Pennebaker, J. W., & Seagal, J. D. (1999). Forming a story: The health benefits of narrative. *Journal of Clinical Psychology, 55,* 1243–1254. doi:10.1002/(SICI)1097-4679(199910)55:10<1243::AID-JCLP6> 3.0.CO;2-N

Rothenberg, A. (1990). Creativity, mental health, and alcohol. *Creativity Research Journal, 3,* 179–201.

Runco, M. A. (1998). Suicide and creativity: The case of Sylvia Plath. *Death Studies, 22*(7), 637–654. doi:10.1080/074811898201335

Slater, E., & Meyer, A. (1959). Contributions to a pathography of the musicians: 1. Robert Schumann. *Confinia Psychatrica, 2,* 65–94.

Thomas, K. M., & Duke, M. (2007). Depressed writing: Cognitive distortions in the works of depressed and nondepressed poets and writers. *Psychology of Aesthetics, Creativity, and the Arts, 1*(4), 204–218. doi:10.1037/1931-3896.1.4.204

Verhaeghen, P., Joorman, J., & Khan, R. (2005). Why we sing the blues: The relationship between self-reflective rumination, mood, and creativity. *Emotion 5*(2), 226–232. doi:10.1037/1528-3542.5.2.226

2 Commentary on the social science literature review

Abed has chosen a topic that will be of interest to many readers, particularly in psychology. Although her assignment did not call for an exhaustive coverage of the literature on depression and mood disorders, she has clearly been able to gather a number of important studies on the question of whether creative individuals, especially poets and writers, are more prone to such problems than others. Her introduction effectively draws the reader in by invoking several famous artists who suffered from depression, but, in keeping with the disciplinary focus of her review, she points out that this question has been studied in a number of ways. The second paragraph allows her to preview the research literature she will discuss by foregrounding its diversity of methodologies.

Abed carefully and logically organizes her review, starting with a section on poets, who are among the most often studied cohort in the relationship between profession or activity and mood disorder. In this section, Abed mainly reports the results of research studies, but she saves the explanation of those results for a separate section, perhaps in order to make it easier for the reader to understand the complex studies. Her third section broadens her focus to the concept of creativity more generally but from the perspective that perhaps the disorders precede the creativity. Her final section, "Other Opinions," draws on studies that do not fit neatly into the earlier clusters of research but do raise additional questions. Because the third and final sections (before the conclusion) are brief, they might have been combined. Abed concludes her review by suggesting avenues for further investigation from a multidisciplinary perspective.

> **STRATEGY** Write a successful literature review
>
> - Begin by identifying the specific topic, issue, or problem that is the focus of research.
> - Clearly identify each piece of research; summarize concisely what each one says about the topic.
> - Highlight the most important, most controversial, and most influential contributions of the researchers.
> - Summarize the current state of knowledge or opinion and suggest directions for future research and discussion.
> - Point out what each piece of research has contributed to the development of knowledge.

19d Informative reports

An informative report in the social sciences brings readers knowledge drawn from research. Readers of such reports may want practical information, or they may seek a greater understanding of social phenomena, or they may just be curious. Unlike a casual magazine article, an informative report reveals its sources of information: articles, books, newsletters, research databases. But in most cases it doesn't just survey its sources and the conclusions they offer, as would a review of research (see 19c). Instead, effective informative reports focus on the information readers need; the reports are arranged to cover relevant aspects of a topic and to highlight key points for readers. (See the suggestions for writing a short documented paper in 17g.)

In a sociology course focusing on current issues, Maha Krishnasami decided to explore the myth that marriage leads to instant happiness. In the introductory paragraph of her paper she describes the focus of her report. Notice how she first draws in her readers by appealing to universal beliefs about marriage and common memories of fairy-tale unions between princes and princesses. She then makes it clear that her discussion will be based on research and academic theory rather than opinion, anecdote, or personal speculation.

According to *Webster's Dictionary,* marriage is the legal union of a man and woman as husband and wife. However, people develop their views and values about marriage from a variety of sources, such as church, family, childhood, and their culture. Marriage is often perceived as a very revered event in a person's life—an event to look forward to. Young girls tend to be in the trance of the "happily ever after" spell. As we have all seen, in the Disney princesses' lives, a prince, or someone they deeply love, comes at the end to save each of them and eventually marry them and live *happily ever after*. No one has any idea what the couple goes through after marriage. Thus, as the audience, we see marriage as the underlying cause of happiness and satisfaction and the most appropriate solution to the problems that each princess faces. This assumption that marriage leads to eternal happiness has been a lingering question debated among sociologists and psychologists, and yet it has not yielded a clear answer. Does an individual's marital status significantly influence his or her level of happiness, or do other factors play a role in creating happiness?

STRATEGY   Write a successful informative report

- Identify a need for information and respond to it.
- Draw on reliable recent research for information.
- Provide clear explanations, including visuals, and present the information in ways that are accessible to readers.
- Follow an organization that highlights the important facets of the subject and the information most likely to be of use or interest to readers.

19e
soc sci

Reports of original research

A research report in the social sciences often follows the arrangement of a typical scientific paper: introduction and research question(s), materials and methods, results, and discussion (see 19f). This kind of paper reports on a tightly focused, controlled study that aims to answer a particular research question or questions, for example: "What elements of student loan procedures do college students find most confusing?" or "Are there psychological consequences for professional athletes who use steroids?" or "Do high school students retain language abilities gained in elementary school foreign language classes?"

Typically, successful research reports focus on questions developed from reading the current research and understanding the ongoing research "conversation." They identify a population to be studied, and they report the results of a method of inquiry (interview, observation, survey, experiment). Not all social research takes this form, however. Researchers conducting extended and detailed observations and interviews (case studies in psychology or education, for example) or long-term observations of activities (ethnographies of a social or cultural group in anthropology, for instance) may report their data and conclusions through extended narration and description accompanied by discussion and conclusions.

Nonetheless, understanding and using the standard elements of a research report can help you focus your research and share the results clearly and effectively.

- **Introduction.** A survey of prior research and a statement of the research question(s).
- **Methods.** Identification of the population studied and a description of the research method. (May include a copy of a survey or the interview questions.)
- **Results.** A detailed presentation of the results or data from the study.
- **Discussion.** Presentation of the conclusions about the results, including key observations and a discussion of the extent to which the data provide an answer to the research question(s).

In a course on American politics, Lee Colavito became interested in studies showing what citizens know about their democratic political system. Colavito decided to conduct his own research and prepared a survey that he administered to people of varying backgrounds and age groups. His paper, "Political Ignorance: Determined by Education and Economics?" begins by establishing the context for his study (an increase in citizen interest in voting and in political issues) and then citing recent research suggesting that typical Americans know very little about the democratic system that gives them the right to determine their own political destiny. He concludes his introduction with a clear statement of focus: "The purpose of this study is to isolate a few key variables of the American population . . . and to determine if these factors are related to a citizen's knowledge of American politics." Here is the opening of Colavito's first main section, "Hypothesis."

19e
soc sci

According to Abraham Lincoln's 1863 Gettysburg Address, our government officials are elected "of the people, by the people, and for the people." Yet in recent years those we have elected to government office are experiencing progressively plummeting approval ratings. Citizens with vastly different levels of education and economic standing are voting for officials about whom they know very little, if anything. In addition, statistics show that the voter demographic is expanding its numbers to include those who are not considered to be "educated and economically stable" and who do not actively follow politics. Their newly found involvement might be attributed to the "political hype" built up by the media surrounding elections like the United States national election of 2008, or a desire to feel that they are a part of their system of government. In order to explore these possibilities, the following study hypothesizes that officials are elected by an ignorant voting public, and that this ignorance is not affected by educational or economic status.

Colavito's research study, based primarily on orally administered surveys, confirms his hypothesis by concluding that regardless of age, socioeconomic status, race, and other demographic factors, voting citizens in his city know very little about the elected officials in their state and local governments. His report effectively interests us in his survey of political knowledge by reminding us that our system of government is established by and for the people, and then it cites previous research that calls into question how much we know about that system. This leads to his hypothesis, that citizens know little about their own elected officials or the processes by which they are governed. The rest of his paper is organized like an empirical study in the social sciences: first he describes his research methods and his subjects; then he provides his data analysis along with interpretations of the results; finally, he offers a conclusion based on what he found out from his survey. (He also includes several tables that display his survey data.)

19e
soc sci

STRATEGY Write a successful research report

- Review the prior research briefly and explain the reasons for conducting the study.
- Identify a clear research question or set of questions.
- Identify the group of people (population) being studied.
- Specify the method of investigation and provide details about the interview questions, surveys, or other instruments.
- Give an account of the process of investigation and describe any problems or noteworthy events.
- Specify the data gathered, providing examples or tables and charts when appropriate.
- Discuss the extent to which the data provide answers to the research question(s) and the extent to which the study is consistent with prior research or identifies new directions for investigation.

19f Research in the natural and applied sciences

The subjects of research in the natural and applied sciences are familiar to most of us: the natural world (rocks, weather, oceans, stars, planets, chemicals, atoms); organisms of all kinds; plants and animals, including humans. We are all familiar with the methods of inquiry, both from studying them in natural science courses and from portraits of scientific research in films and novels and on television: detailed observations in the field, microscopic examination in a laboratory, and experiments in laboratories, hospitals, and special facilities like wind tunnels and cyclotrons. The natural sciences are sometimes included in the "hard" sciences, which also include the formal sciences (mathematics, systems science, computer science) and applied sciences such as civil engineering and military science. Again, fields will overlap and sometimes defy easy categorization: architecture is, from one perspective, an applied science, but from another perspective it shares features with the arts. Entire colleges devoted to one field (textiles, for example) can include programs and courses that range from applied sciences such as textiles chemistry to arts such as apparel design and to social sciences such as marketing.

NATURAL SCIENCE FIELDS

anatomy	engineering (and	meteorology
astronomy	subfields)	oceanography
biology	genetics	paleontology
chemistry	geology	pharmacy
environmental	kinesiology	physical anthropology
science	medicine	physics

19f
nat sci

Typically, natural scientists gather data through careful observation and collection techniques, often employing sophisticated equipment to measure phenomena not apparent to the human senses, such as electrical waves or atomic and subatomic particles. They use recording techniques to observe and collect data that change slowly over time (the growth of an organism) or that are dangerous to sample (fumes from a volcano). Measurements of change or of the physical dimensions and components of a subject are key techniques for natural scientists. Looking for relationships among events, materials, or matter and energy are focal points for scientific research, especially in the search for mathematical correlations or cause-effect relationships. The sheer volume of inquiry in the natural sciences means that a researcher needs to be aware that any topic may be the subject of many research articles and reports. In addition, the complexity of the phenomena studied by natural scientists means that individual research projects tend to focus on only one small part of a phenomenon.

The box on pages 238–239 shows how the goals, evidence, research questions, and common assignments can differ in four general areas in the natural sciences.

DISCIPLINARY COMMUNITIES IN THE SCIENCES

	ASTRONOMY	PHYSICS
GOALS	To understand the nature, history, and composition of celestial objects (stars, planets, asteroids, galaxies) and other phenomena in space, such as radio waves, black holes, quarks, and supernovas. It also focuses on the origins and formation of the entire universe.	To understand the physical properties and phenomena of the earth and universe, including matter, energy, force and motion. Its goal is to know how the universe "works"—how it behaves and what it's made up of.
EVIDENCE	Observational (from telescopes, satellites, receivers, and space probes); theoretical and empirical (from simulations on earth); physical (from material collected from the moon or planets); textual (from historical records of celestial events).	Observational; experimental (e.g., using nuclear reactors or cyclotrons); theoretical (reasoning from mathematical formulas).
SAMPLE RESEARCH QUESTIONS	If, as theorized, black holes emit "Hawking radiation," how would we explain the eventual disappearance of what's inside given their gravitational pull?	In accelerator studies of antimatter, why do some interactions between antiparticles look slightly different than the same interactions between the corresponding particles?
COMMON ASSIGNMENTS	Lab reports; observational reports; research proposals; topical reviews; critiques; articles for general audiences (popular magazines such as *Astronomy*).	Lab reports; explanations of reasoning from problem sets; short documented papers; literature reviews; cases and brief narrative problems; analyses of data (charts, graphs).

19g Common writing assignments in natural and applied science courses

Writing assignments in natural and applied science courses often ask for reports of students' laboratory work (lab reports; see 19h), informative or interpretive reports on current issues or problems (see 19j), abstracts (see 19i), reviews of current research (19c), or reports of original research (observations, experiments, innovative practices; see 19k).

19h Lab reports

A **lab report** concisely and objectively summarizes an experiment or series of observations conducted for the purpose of testing, measuring, or analyzing some object, phenomenon, organism, or process. When most people think of a lab report, they imagine an experiment conducted in a laboratory with liquids, beakers, and Bunsen burners. But many lab reports use as their lab the natural world (a river or stream where water samples are collected,

BIOLOGY	GEOLOGY
To understand the nature, functions, structures, origins, adaptation, and evolution of all living organisms and to classify them and map their distribution.	To understand the nature, history, and current and future status of the solid and liquid elements that make up the earth, including how these elements came to be, how they move or change, and how they interact with each other.
Data collection (observations of natural habitats or in labs by controlled experiment), which can range from macro-level (species) to micro- or molecular level (gene mutations).	Data collection and analysis (observations or lab experiments), including all the elements of the earth (rocks, minerals, volcanic emissions, soil, sediment).
Since most cold and flu viruses stay in the upper respiratory system, why does SARS penetrate deep into the lungs, where it can cause alveolar damage that can kill its host?	Are iridium spikes sufficient evidence to support a theory of meteorologically caused extinction of species in the Triassic-Jurassic period?
Lab reports; observation reports; scenarios or puzzles; analyses of data; explanations of a concept.	Lab reports; field research; summaries of research; identification papers (e.g., the components of rock); article summaries.

19h
nat sci

for example). Instructors assign lab reports in order to read (quickly) what you did in an experiment or collected through a series of observations or analyses, so you will need to make your report as concise and clear as possible.

Lab reports follow formats determined by the field of study and even the requirements of individual instructors. However, a typical structure begins with an overview or *abstract* of the experiment that states its focus or goal (why it was done). The abstract is followed by an *introduction* to the problem or the principles involved (what it shows), a description of the *methods* used (how it was done), an explanation of the *results* (what happened), a *discussion* of the outcomes (what the results mean), and a *conclusion* (what the experiment shows).

1 Sample lab report

As part of an assignment in introductory plant biology, Evan Brisson conducted a research study involving the careful observation of a plant species in its natural environment. As you read Brisson's study, notice how certain elements of style, organization, and language choice place his paper in the genre of a scientific study.

Observations of *Nandina domestica* and

Its Interactions with Its Surrounding Environment

Evan Brisson

Abstract

1   An investigation was conducted during midwinter at Pullen Park located in Raleigh, North Carolina. Over the course of three days, a growth of *Nandina domestica*, or "Heavenly Bamboo," was observed and monitored for possible signs of interactions with its surrounding environment. In this case, the primary indicator of change was the total number of berries present on a certain stem of the plant. The test was performed with the goal of understanding whether the plant served as a source of food for contiguous species of birds, insects, or other animals such as small mammals and, consequently, if its reproductive cycle was assisted by these creatures. Due to the plant's copious yield of berries, compared to the other species in the area, it was reasoned that it did serve as a source of food for animals and insects. After three days of observation, the plant was identified to be a resource for surrounding species, most likely birds and insects. While other land animals such as small mammals were deemed less likely to consume the berries, the possibility was not ruled out.

Introduction

19h
nat sci

2   *Nandina domestica* is a flowering plant that is native to Asia. Though it is not truly a bamboo species, its strong skinny stalk and rigid appearance have earned it the nickname "Heavenly Bamboo." Nandina is a resilient species that can adapt reasonably well to many diverse climates (1). Because it grows best in low to medium elevations, it can be found in states along the southern border of the U.S. The species averages 1.5 to 2.5 meters in height. Nandina grows year round and forms white flowers in the spring. The most notable trait of the plant is the persistence of its fruit during winter. The plant forms berries in the early fall and is able to hold on to these berries well throughout the colder months (2).

3   The purpose of this experiment was to examine a growth of the Nandina and observe how the plant interacts with and responds to its biotic and abiotic surroundings in order to understand how its reproductive process might be stimulated by animals. The goal was to figure out what species of animals, if any,

consumed the plant's fruit. Because the growth of Nandina appeared to be one of the only living plants in the vicinity, it was hypothesized that the plant played a dynamic role in the diet of surrounding animal species, including birds, ducks, insects, and small mammals, and therefore relied on these species for assistance in its reproduction cycle.

Methods

4   The plant was observed during midwinter in Pullen Park in the temperate deciduous climate of Raleigh, North Carolina. It was monitored for approximately ten minutes each day from 12:00 PM to 12:10 PM over the course of three days. On day one, static observations were recorded to serve as the constant for monitoring any possible changes.

5   A single branch from the plant was arbitrarily selected as a test site for berry count. A five centimeter strand of bright yellow plastic was wrapped around the base of this branch for identification purposes. An initial berry count was taken on day one and subsequent berry counts were taken on the next two days of observations. During each ten minute encounter, the plant's appearance as well as any other obvious natural aspects in association with the plant were observed and recorded, including changes in temperature and humidity, changes in the activity of surrounding animals, and changes in the plant itself.

Results

19h
nat sci

6   Static Observations. The plant reached roughly 1.5 meters at its highest bough while the entire growth spanned a width of about three meters. The growth was comprised of three rigid main shoots which were straight and had diameters of roughly one centimeter. From these main shoots, several stems branched out into numerous subdivisions, each with three leaf clusters of leaves with lengths of between five and ten centimeters. The leaves were dark green, fading to deep amethyst on certain tips. Roughly one fourth of the stems contained groups of bright red berries ranging in number from ten to one hundred joining to the ends of their twigs. These berries measured between 1 and 1.5 centimeters in diameter.

7   Dynamic Observations. The growth was found atop a thirty degree sloped embankment, roughly fifty meters from an artificial lake which lay below. From

the opposite direction, the plant measured approximately seventy-five meters away from a busy road. Around the perimeter of the plant was a lower bush containing sharp, glossy, dark green leaves. This plant was roughly one half the height and two times the width of the plant being investigated. Additionally, a wooden railing roughly .5 meters high extended around the perimeter plant on the side of the plant adjacent to the road.

8   Systemic Observations. On day one, thirty-two berries were counted on the test branch of the plant. No berries were found on the ground in the vicinity of the plant. The temperature was approximately fifty-five degrees Fahrenheit and the air was relatively dry. Approximately fifteen ducks and other waterfowl were observed in and around the artificial lake. Two pedestrians were observed circling the lake and birds were heard vocalizing in nearby trees. The trees in the vicinity appeared to be void of leaves. Birds' nests were noticed in these trees.

9   On day two the berry count on the marked branch totaled thirty. No berries were found on the ground in the vicinity of the plant. The temperature had dropped significantly since day one to around forty-two degrees Fahrenheit and the air was relatively dry. No waterfowl were spotted in the lake and approximately thirty cars were observed traveling on the nearby road.

10   By day three the temperature had increased significantly to approximately seventy degrees Fahrenheit and the air was relatively humid. Twenty-five berries were counted on the test site and no berries were discovered on the ground in the vicinity of the plant. On this day gnats appeared to be hovering above the plant's berry sites in dense clouds. Three species of waterfowl were seen splashing in the lake while approximately twelve pedestrians walked around the perimeter of the lake. Freshly discarded human trash was observed in the vicinity of the plant. Bird droppings were noticeable on the wooden railing of the fence and five berries on the test site contained dark patches and partially missing or ripped coatings. The thin red coatings contained a soft white inside and a dense tawny colored seed rested at each berry's core.

Discussion

11   Analysis of the plant's leaves, stems, and berries positively identified it as the flowering plant *Nandina domestica*. Because the berry count steadily declined

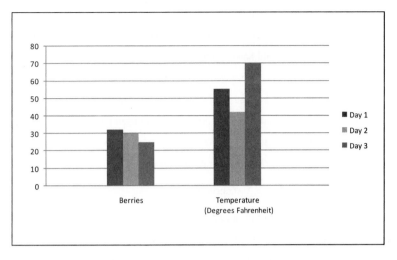

Fig. 1 Changes in Berry Count and Temperature over Three Days

over the course of three days and no berries were found on the ground that could have fallen off the plant due to abiotic factors such as wind, the loss of berries was attributed to their being a source of food for animals. Furthermore, as seen in Figure 1, the relationship between temperature and berries did not seem to reflect any obvious trend or correlation.

12   Because of the obstructed position of the plant due to the surrounding wooden fence as well as its precarious location atop a steep slope and its proximity to a busy road, it was assumed that land animals would not have easy access to the berries and therefore did not regularly consume them. Furthermore, the bird droppings on the railing surrounding the plant, along with sightings of ducks, birds, and birds' nests in the area, suggested that there were birds present in the vicinity and that these birds could have been responsible for the recorded decline in berries.

13   Another observation related the increase of activity to the berry count as the temperature rose on the final day of observation. On this day, the largest deficit of berries was recorded. Because the temperature was characteristic of an early spring, it is possible that birds were more able or willing to consume or collect berries on that day. The analogous increase in human activity and the accompanying trash could possibly have attracted small mammals such as

19h
nat sci

opossums or rodents to the area. However, there is no evidence that these land animals would not have faced the same topographical and manmade impediments on this day that they would have on the previous days.

14 Furthermore, the gnats that were observed circling the berries on the final day of observation may have had something to do with the dark spots evident on some of the berries on that day. The berries may have been partially consumed by these insects. Another possibility is that the thin skins of the berries were damaged by the relatively high temperatures that day.

Conclusion

15 The results and uncertainties of this experiment introduce many new inquiries. Questions raised by the outcome of this experiment include "What species of birds or insects consume the plant's berries?" and "Would land animals be more likely to consume the berries if the plant was not obstructed by a fence, a steep slope, and a busy road?" The question, "How would the trend of berries counted have ended up after the final day of observation which brought higher temperatures, increased humidity and increased human activity?" could bring a more definitive answer to the uncertainty of what species were consuming the berries. And finally, further observation on the effects of heat and humidity on the plant's berries may help to prove whether or not abiotic factors affected the plant and its berries in any significant way.

16 In order to positively determine what was consuming the fruit, a more sufficient knowledge of the surrounding animal species would have been necessary. And because there is no way to tell for sure what animals consume the berries unless they are witnessed doing so, the plant would have to be monitored extensively at different times of the day and even nocturnally in order to answer these questions with any certainty. Furthermore, in order to realize what animal species are involved with Nandina year round, observation of the plant would need to be conducted over the course of four seasons. Further steps to ensure accuracy would be to observe growths of *Nandina domestica* that occur deeper into the park or in other locations. Additionally, in order to accurately identify the plants' reproductive tendencies, Nandina would need to be studied over the course of a few generations.

19h
nat sci

[new page]

References

1. Nandina (Heavenly Bamboo). University of Hawaii at Manoa.

   1998 Sept. Available from: http://scholarspace.manoa.hawaii.edu/

   bitstream/10125/2886/1/OF-26.pdf.

2. Gilman E. *Nandina Domestica*. University of Florida Cooperative

   Extension Services Institute of Food and Agricultural Sciences.

   1999 Oct. Available from: http://hort.ifas.ufl.edu/shrubs/nandoma.pdf.

2 Commentary on the lab report

This assignment was designed to give students practice in close scientific observation and data collection and in the writing of scientific research reports, not to contribute new findings to the field of plant biology. Brisson does an excellent job of concisely providing the background for his study, including the object and purpose of his analysis. He structures the report to follow the typical scientific scheme of introducing the subject, explaining the methods, reporting the results, and then discussing their implications. He further breaks the results section into kinds of data (static, dynamic, and systemic) so that he can organize them relevant to the plant itself as well as its interaction with its surrounding environment. Brisson's style is clear, precise, and objective. Rather than make himself the object of attention ("I enjoyed observing this plant," or "It was a cold day, and I hunched further into my winter jacket"), he focuses on the plant and its environment and thereby creates in his readers a trust that he carefully and objectively gathered and analyzed his data. His conclusion describes the limitations of his study and suggests other avenues for investigation.

**19i
nat sci**

STRATEGY Write a successful lab report

- Follow the lab report format required by the instructor.
- Do not digress into unnecessary commentary on the experiment.
- Use specific terminology and unambiguous language.
- Present data and results accurately, without distortion.

19i Abstracts

Lab reports, informative reports, and reports of original research in the natural sciences often begin with an **abstract,** and many instructors require abstracts along with the papers they assign. An abstract is a concise summary of a paper. It is entirely objective, restating the content of the paper without extraneous commentary. An abstract for a scientific study must include, at a minimum, a summary of the hypothesis, the method, the results, and the discussion sections of the paper. An abstract of the review of literature might be needed as well. The reader of an abstract, having no familiarity with the paper, should be able to understand not only the gist of the paper but also its method, stance (theory or opinion), and conclusions. (See the abstract that introduces the report in 19h on p. 240.)

> **STRATEGY** Write a successful abstract
> - Summarize all the important sections of a paper.
> - Define key terms and words used in unique or unusual ways.
> - Present information concisely, eliminating unnecessary words and phrases

19j Informative reports

Findings made in the natural sciences are important and interesting yet complex. Consequently, informative reports that present and interpret scientific knowledge play important roles: they can identify problems, offer practical solutions, or suggest policies. In the course of exploring recent developments or outlining problems and policies, reports often provide reviews of current research. (For reviews of research in the social sciences, see 19c).

For courses in the natural sciences, students are often asked to write informative reports as a way of developing an understanding of topics or problems that call for further research. For a course in ecology, Katherine Buck wrote an informative report on the degrading habitat of the arctic polar bear. Her paper was based on a single but very comprehensive article that also provided a synthesis of research on polar bear habitat. Buck's paper, "Polar Bears Face Arctic Meltdown," uses the Greek rhetorical concept of *kairos*, "a propitious moment"—in this case, the urgency of global warming's effects on the polar ice cap—to draw in her readers.

19j
nat sci

Although more research is needed, many experts agree that climate warming will significantly damage the polar bear population as a direct effect of the polar bear's specialized nature and dependence on sea ice. Polar bears use the sea ice as a means to hunt and to travel. These are two very important elements to ensure their survival. Not only does the sea ice allow them to hunt and eat, but they also use it as a means to socialize with other bears (1). This leads to reproduction and allows them to sustain their numbers. This dependence on the sea ice is why the polar bears are facing a new and potentially fatal problem from their constantly warming climate.

The continuous warming of the Arctic climate has already begun to show its effects on the sea ice. The vital characteristics of the ice have begun to alter. It is not as thick as the ice has been in years past, and therefore it is more susceptible to fractures and cracking. Not only is the ice thinning, but it is also forming later in the year and melting sooner (1). These two factors combined cause the polar bears to have to go for long periods of time without food and isolate themselves from their fellow bears.

Buck continues her report by working through the somewhat mixed results of other research in an attempt to arrive at an informed conclusion about the fate of polar bears.

STRATEGY   **Write a successful informative report**

- Provide accurate summaries of research.
- Clearly identify problems, solutions, or policies.
- Give details of the ideas and research conclusions relevant to a problem, solution, or policy and identify the sources of the information and ideas.
- Use pictures, tables, graphs, or other visuals to explain complicated information.

19k Popular science

The complexity of much academic research today puts it out of reach for the millions of people who don't share the specialized knowledge and terminology that would allow them to read research reports and scientific articles. Yet it is important for the average citizen to know about the results of research in many areas that will affect his or her life. For this reason, an increasingly common assignment asks you to take the specialized information you are learning in your course work and "translate" it—render it accessible and interesting—for lay audiences. Such assignments give you practice writing for multiple audiences (a skill that you will use whatever your chosen profession) and virtually guarantee that you understand what you are writing about because you can't rely on the language of the original text to write your summary, analysis, synthesis, or interpretation.

To write a successful popular science article, you will need not only to render the material in a language and a style that most nonspecialized audiences can understand, but you may also need to structure your paper in a way that doesn't follow the typical organization of scientific research. Instead of beginning with an abstract, an introduction, and a literature review, for example, you might start with an anecdote or a specific example of the issue at hand. The rest of your text could mix references to scientific research with human interest stories, or you could create a kind of narrative out of the progress of the research.

In a course in astronomy, Tyson Mao created a popular science article about how planets are determined and classified.

19k
nat sci

1 Sample popular science article

The Planet Debate

Tyson Mao

Though elementary school mnemonics have been frequently used as study aids for young children, they also provide insight to societal norms and accepted practices. Mathematicians use "Please Excuse My Dear Aunt Sally" for the order of operations. Biologists have "King Philip Came Over From Greater Spain" for the order of taxonomy. As a nine-year-old elementary school student, I remember "My Very Earnest Mother Just Served Us Nine Pickles" being used to identify the order of the planets. However, that was 1992 and it would be another seven years until that mnemonic was accurate again. Due to their orbits, from January 21, 1979, to February 11, 1999, Pluto was actually closer to the Sun than Neptune. Accepted standards and doctrines are never concrete; instead, they are updated as we learn more about the universe.

On July 29, 2005, a team of astronomers consisting of Michael E. Brown (Caltech), Chadwick A. Trujillo (Gemini Observatory), and David Rabinowitz (Yale University) discovered a Kuiper belt object. Tentatively called 2003 UB_{313}, the icy body has an orbital period of 560 years, and curiously, is larger than Pluto. If Pluto is a planet, then what is 2003 UB_{313}? Furthermore, how does one classify other Kuiper belt objects such as Quaoar and Sedna, and what are we to do when sky surveys find more and more objects, some perhaps even larger than 2003 UB_{313}? In other words, did my very earnest mother just serve us nine pickles? Perhaps my very earnest mother just served us nine pickled Sedated Quails, Understand?

Unlike the discovery of the first seven planets, the discovery of Neptune was not the result of a chance observation. The orbit of Uranus was perturbed from calculated expectations and astronomers proposed that another body farther from the Sun was responsible for the irregularities of the orbit. Calculations predicted Neptune's location in the sky, and on September 23, 1846, Neptune was discovered.

But, the planet search was still incomplete. Neptune's mass and orbital parameters did not sufficiently explain the irregularity of Uranus' orbit.

Common Perspective of the Solar System
Source: <http://starchild.gsfc.nasa.gov/docs/StarChild/
solar_system_level1/solar_system.html>.

Furthermore, Neptune's orbit itself was perturbed at a moderate inclination so astronomers searched for yet another massive body that could explain this aberration. In 1911 the Indian astronomer, Venkatesh Ketakar produced calculations predicting the location of Pluto. In 1930, Clyde Tombaugh made the discovery at the Lowell Observatory in Arizona. Significantly smaller than the other gas giants, Pluto is composed mostly of methane ice. Even though Pluto's composition was uncharacteristic of the gas giants discovered beyond the asteroid belt, it was a round object that orbited the Sun and was immediately called a planet.

For the popular masses, Pluto was consistent with the other planets. Planets were bodies that orbited the Sun. With the exception of Mercury and Venus, planets had satellites orbiting around them. Furthermore, they were spherically shaped as opposed to irregularly shaped like the less massive asteroids and the moons of Mars. Culturally, it was very satisfying to know that our solar system had planets and planets were objects that orbited the Sun. Scientifically, after the discovery of Pluto, the term "planet" was now under scrutiny.

19k
nat sci

Clearly, Pluto had formed under different circumstances than Jupiter, Saturn, Uranus, and Neptune. The smallest of the four gas giants, Neptune, is easily many times larger than the combined mass of all of the inner planets. Pluto, on the other hand, is only one sixth of the mass of Earth's moon. It was an open question. What was Pluto? How did it form? Why was it different from the other planets?

Furthermore, Pluto still did not provide an explanation to Neptune's perturbed orbit and so the search for a larger planet was underway. However, nothing was discovered, and Pluto became cemented in both scientific and popular terminology as "a planet" while astronomers dodged the obvious abnormality in the gas giant pattern. Through years of Kuiper Belt Object searching, most objects were significantly smaller than Pluto, which caused hesitation among scientists to classify Pluto as a KBO instead of a planet.

In 2002, astronomers Michael E. Brown and Chad Trujillo announced the discovery of 50000 Quaoar. Through spectroscopic analysis, they found Quaoar to be very similar to Pluto in composition and size. However, in many respects, Quaoar is more characteristic of a planet than Pluto. Unlike Pluto's high inclination at 17° and high eccentricity at 0.25, Quaoar orbits at 8° with an eccentricity of 0.034. However, with a diameter two-thirds the size of Pluto's, Quaoar was considered too small to be a planet and instead was classified as a trans-Neptunian object. Approximately one year later, Brown, Trujillo, and David Rabinowitz of Yale University found Sedna on November 14, 2003. Sedna has an eccentricity of 0.855 and a diameter between 1180 and 1800 km. Pluto's diameter is 2300 km, so again, no object larger than Pluto was known in the solar system. Are these objects not considered planets simply on the basis of size? Quaoar is 1250 km in diameter. Some other similar objects such as Varuna and 2002 AW197 are 900 km in diameter. What is it about Pluto that sets the planet standard at 2300 km objects?

Through spectroscopic analysis, we have seen that the composition and physical structure of these trans-Neptunian objects were very similar to Pluto's composition and structure. Pluto and these small KBOs are icy bodies composed primarily of water and methane ice. Defining a planet by comparing the body to the physical parameters of Pluto was simply a means of preserving the historical value of Pluto. With nothing discovered in the 70-year gap between Pluto and Quaoar, Pluto was accepted into the ranks of planet-hood. The prospect of

19k
nat sci

including Quaoar, Sedna, and other objects as planets was disagreeable—popular culture has glorified the idea of planets. Planets are bodies that orbit stars, and Earth is a planet. Planets are likely the key to finding extra-solar life in the future. Including smaller trans-Neptunian objects would dilute the integrity of the class of objects known as planets.

But what happens if astronomers discover scores of objects larger than Pluto? The addition of many Pluto-sized rocks into the group of planets would surely change the concept of our solar system. Of course, the discovery of scores of objects begins with the discovery of a single object, and in 2005, Brown and his team announced the discovery of 2003 UB_{313}. This object was precisely the catalyst to reopen the planet debate. Through albedo predictions, spectroscopy analysis, and reflected light calculations, the object has a diameter of 2400 km and is larger than Pluto.

If Pluto is a planet, then 2003 UB_{313} is a planet as well. Similarly, any future objects found orbiting the sun to be larger than Pluto would also be called planets. However, this classification criterion is not scientifically viable. Under what scientific justification would an object slightly smaller than Pluto, if only by a few kilometers in diameter, not be considered a planet?

The ambiguity could only be resolved slightly by considering the term planet in both popular and scientific context. According to history and society, planets are large round objects that orbit the Sun in a roughly circular orbit. Without regard to their methods of formation or physical characteristics, this definition relies on the definition of the word *large*. However, for scientists, classification suggests some physical parameters, either in formation or structural composition. Type Ia supernovas, for example, are formed specifically when white dwarf stars accrete enough mass to exceed the Chandrasekhar limit. Neutron stars are composed of neutrons and form as a result of stellar deaths. Scientifically, classifying Pluto and 2003 UB_{313} as planets creates an inconsistency between the formation methods of the inner eight planets and trans-Neptunian objects.

The IAU met in August 2006 and defined the term planet for the first time. Planets must orbit the sun, be large enough to hold their spherical shape by their own gravitational force, and have cleared the areas adjacent to their orbits. Pluto, which fails to meet the third criterion, was re-categorized as a "dwarf

19k
nat sci

planet," a decision that has been contested by some in the scientific community and many in popular society. Science is an evolving entity, and simply said language itself evolves over time as well. How we define what is a planet is merely a reflection on our understanding of the classified objects. The next time an elementary school child returns home reciting mnemonics, one must always consider the relevance to the current times. As of today, it seems that my very earnest mother just served us nothing?

2 Commentary on the translation of scientific research

Conforming to the expectations of readers of popular scientific journals such as *Scientific American*, Mao offers a readable and engaging account of how astronomers determine the planets and their order. He begins by connecting to most readers' experiences using elementary school mnemonics, devices used to help us remember sequences of numbers or objects. This immediately establishes his authorial persona as someone who will help us to understand complex scientific research without a lot of overly technical jargon or concepts. He reveals for us how astronomers debate the definition of planets and helps us to see that the field is in a constant state of development. Notice also how he splices in an image to help our understanding and provide visual appeal, and how he incorporates sources into his paper instead of creating academic-looking reference lists. Mao's original paper was structured like a typical article in a popular science magazine, with two columns and text that wrapped around the image.

19k
nat sci

STRATEGY   Write a successful popular science article

- Draw readers in with an interesting, engaging introduction.
- Use language that non-specialist readers can understand, avoiding excessive field-specific jargon or sophisticated terminology.
- Give readers a story to follow about the research, making it relevant to their interests.
- Avoid pandering or "talking down"; assume at least some knowledge of the subject.
- Provide an objective account that offers all sides of any controversies or disagreements in the scientific community.
- Use appealing and informative visuals when possible.

Visit mycomplab.com for more resources and exercises on writing in the social and natural sciences.

CHAPTER **20**

Public Writing

In every public and civic context, people write to convey information, express their views, organize collective efforts, and challenge injustice. Such writing not only improves your skills and your flexibility but also helps you to become a better-informed citizen.

20a Goals of public writing

When you address a public audience, you're likely to think of yourself as a volunteer, an activist, or a committee member, not a writer. Your primary concern may be to organize a beach cleanup or elect a mayor. You'll write to achieve your civic goals: to motivate others to support your cause, to influence policy decisions, and to promote democratic processes.

20b Analyzing public audiences

When you prepare a meeting reminder for your book club or a newsletter for your neighbors, you address readers you know personally. They expect clear information, and they may appreciate motivation, but often they will already agree about issues or activities. But when you begin to draft publicity for the tennis club's pasta dinner—its big fund-raiser—you'll need to address a wider circle that includes readers you don't know personally and who won't support the dinner unless you can persuade them that your cause is worthwhile.

Connect readers and goals. Use the following questions to frame your writing with a strong relationship to your audience's values and expectations.

- Why are you writing? What do you hope to accomplish?
- Who are your readers? What do they value? How much do they know or care about your project or issue?
- Do you primarily want to inform or to motivate them? Do you want readers to agree with you or to take action—to go to a meeting, contribute time or money, vote yes or no, call an official, or join your group?
- To persuade your readers to do what you want, what might appeal to their anger, passion, or fear—your sincerity, testimonials from others, information, or connections to their own interests or community values?

- How might you approach these readers? Will they respond best to impassioned appeals, logical analyses, or combined strategies? Will they expect a neighborly letter, a flyer, or a polished brochure?
- How can you contact prospective readers—through flyers at a meeting, appeals by mail or email, or letters in the newspaper?

STRATEGY Ask questions to focus your public writing

- What is your task? Who will do what as you work on it?
- What's your deadline? How soon will recipients need information? How much time should you allow for printing, mailing, or other steps?
- What type of material should you prepare? What is the usual format? Do you have models or samples of past materials?
- Does your material require approval from anyone?
- Do you need to reserve a meeting room, coordinate with another group, or make other arrangements before you can finish your text?
- How will you distribute your material? Do you need to arrange duplication, mailing, or volunteers to deliver or post materials?

20c Types of public writing

Many types of public writing—letters, flyers, pamphlets, newsletters—are flexible documents. They can be directed to a variety of readers, such as group members, newspaper readers, officials, and local residents. They can address one or more goals by providing information, building support, motivating action, or supporting participatory democracy.

20d
public

20d Flyers

A common form of public writing is the flyer informing people about a meeting, an activity, or an event. Flyers also supply directions, advice, and information to residents, citizens, and other groups. Sometimes they are prepared as companions to posters—which may supply similar information as they promote events.

STRATEGY Write a successful public flyer

- Open with a topic ("Hostetler Annual Reunion"), a general appeal ("Light a candle for peace!"), or a greeting ("Dear Choir Members").
- Give the essentials information needed to attend or participate: date, time, place, directions, plans, equipment or supplies, contact and emergency telephone numbers, rain date.

- Stick to essentials and omit long explanations or background.
- Use headings, graphics, and white space to highlight crucial information. (See 13c–e.)
- Be formal or informal, depending on the audience and the topic.

TYPES OF PUBLIC WRITING		
	CHARACTERISTIC ACTIVITIES	COMMON FORMS
PROVIDING INFORMATION	Gathering information, exploring issues, examining other views and alternative solutions, comparing, summarizing, synthesizing, and presenting material	Flyer, newsletter, fact sheet, informative report or article, pamphlet, poster, letter (to supporters, interested parties, officials, residents, or the community)
BUILDING SUPPORT	Reaching consensus within a group, articulating a stance, defining a problem, proposing a solution, appealing to others with similar or different values, presenting evidence, finding shared values, advocating, persuading	Position paper, policy guidelines, statement of principles, letter (to prospective supporters, officials, newspaper, or others concerned or involved)
MOTIVATING TO ACTION	Defining action, orchestrating participation, supplying information about involvement, motivating participants	Action proposal, grant proposal, flyer, letter, call to action in newsletter or other publication
PARTICIPATING IN DEMOCRATIC PROCESSES	Attending public meetings, meeting with officials, understanding legislative processes and timing, advocating civic involvement, distributing information on public or civic actions	Meeting minutes, committee report, legislative update, letter to officials, letter to group members, call to participate in newsletters or other publications, summary or analysis of public actions, petitions

**20d
public**

The following flyer announces a group's special event: a meeting to collect signed petitions for presentation to the school board.

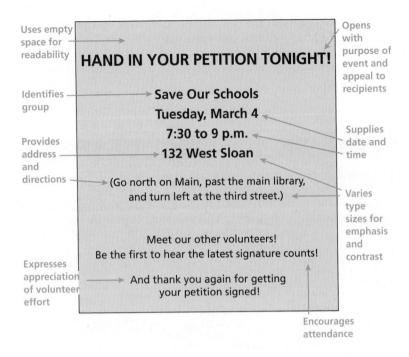

Uses empty space for readability

HAND IN YOUR PETITION TONIGHT!

Opens with purpose of event and appeal to recipients

Identifies group

Save Our Schools
Tuesday, March 4
7:30 to 9 p.m.
132 West Sloan

Supplies date and time

Provides address and directions

(Go north on Main, past the main library, and turn left at the third street.)

Varies type sizes for emphasis and contrast

Meet our other volunteers!
Be the first to hear the latest signature counts!

Expresses appreciation of volunteer effort

And thank you again for getting your petition signed!

Encourages attendance

20e Letters to the editor

Both partisans and interested citizens submit letters to the editor in order to comment on current issues or engage in topical debate. Check the opinion section of your local or campus paper, either in print or online, to read the current letters selected for publication and to locate directions for submitting your own letter.

STRATEGY Write an effective letter to the editor

- Respect the length limit established by the newspaper or other publication.
- Clearly identify your topic and point of view or proposal.
- Give reasons or evidence to persuade readers to consider or agree with your point of view. (See Chapter 11.)
- Treat other views and other writers respectfully, even those who disagree with your opinions.

Two letters to the editor appear below and on page 258: the first defending a group criticized by the writer of an earlier letter; the second primarily informative.

Letter to the Editor
April 16, 2009
Greeks Wrong in Punishing Critics

I am writing in response to the recent letter from Jillian Soares (April 14, 2009). As president of the Pan-Hellenic Council, she claims that the Council has the right to fine a fraternity or sorority if any of its members "speak publicly in ways that undermine the integrity or reputation of the Greek societies at Central Range State University." She uses this passage from the Pan-Hellenic Council's bylaws to justify fining Nina Campbell's sorority for statements she made in a recent Snowcap Advocate column. In it, Campbell criticized lack of fraternity and sorority support for the University's "All Campus Diversity Initiative."

As a sorority member myself, I think Campbell's criticisms were inaccurate and overstated. Certainly the Greeks can do a better job of promoting diversity—but then everybody can. After all, would a "Diversity Initiative" be necessary if everyone were doing a good job? But I think the Greeks have done more than most others on campus and that Campbell simply ignores all sorts of positive evidence. Campbell's opinions aren't the real problem, however. The proposed punishment is, along with the policy that makes it possible.

In her letter, Soares claims that the issue isn't a question of free speech because no one is trying to prevent Campbell from stating her opinion. She says that Campbell can avoid the fine for her sorority by resigning from the organization. She also states that the Council is not trying to prevent any Pan-Hellenic members from criticizing fraternity or sorority activities—the policy is only for statements that "distort the facts" or that are "needlessly insulting." But who is to determine the "facts"? When people don't like what they are hearing, they often claim that critics have "got the facts wrong."

The biggest problem with the policy is that it might discourage people from speaking out about actions that are truly discriminatory, unjust, or illegal. Soares says that anyone who wishes to speak out without violating the policy can resign from the fraternity or sorority. The policy might not prevent people from making reasonable criticisms, but it would certainly discourage them. Even when a person knows she is right to criticize, she might not want to cause trouble or expense for her "sisters."

Do we really want to force people to resign when they are speaking from the heart about things they believe are wrong—even if we disagree with them or even if they see the "facts" differently? Isn't this discriminatory?

Rebecca Fala

Sorority Circle

20f
speak

20f Speaking in public settings

People gather daily to exchange opinions about local concerns. Citizens lobby officials for actions; campus forums draw students, faculty, and administrators to discuss policies; interest groups engage members and visitors. Careful preparation and a good knowledge of the issue are the key factors for speaking successfully in public.

Letter to the Editor
February 18, 2009
"Balanced Education" Limits Diversity in Ideas

Last week at the South Valley School Board meeting, Concerned Citizens for a Balanced Education made a proposal that ought to be voted down at the next meeting. Concerned Citizens is critical of student government at South Valley High for sponsoring a talk by Malcom Zindt, who disapproves of the current president and many of his policies. They want to ban any speakers who "do not offer students a balanced perspective on issues or current events" in order to guarantee that "a South Valley education is a balanced education."

I believe that there are three important reasons for voting against this proposal.

(1) The proposal requires that any speakers present a "balanced" view. Speakers worth listening to generally present their own views, however. We want to listen to them because they offer special insights or because they are strong representatives of a point of view. Speakers who offer balanced perspectives are often less interesting—even boring. As a result, fewer students will attend their presentations and fewer will have a chance to encounter challenging ideas.

(2) By requiring that each speaker provide a balance of ideas, the proposal will eliminate the possibility of a set of lectures that create balance by presenting speakers with very different points of view. The student government has already set up a talk by Rose Azavone, a well-known critic of Zindt's and a supporter of current government policies. Concerned Citizens opposes this proposal because it would "require spending extra money for a job that one speaker could do." I believe Concerned Citizens is less interested in balance than in making sure students do not get to hear ideas the Citizens don't like!

(3) Concerned Citizens makes it clear that its idea of "balance" is pro versus con, left versus right. They seem to think that each issue has only two sides. This view is too simple. As a college student, I have come to realize that there are usually more than two ways of looking at an issue.

I hope the Concerned Citizens proposal will be defeated. I would like students at my former high school to get a chance to hear many voices and then make their own conclusions.

Ken Park, S.V.H.S., Class of 2006

20f
speak

STRATEGY **Speak effectively in public settings**

- Attend meetings, listen, and read to be informed about issues.
- Plan and rehearse (see 16c), even when you will speak for only a minute or two.
- Be reasonable; don't alienate those who are undecided or disagree.
- Use facts and other evidence, not emotion, for support.
- Stay calm at a tense meeting so that fear and nervousness don't lead you to speak angrily, make accusations, or even cry.

Visit mycomplab.com for more resources and exercises on writing for public audiences.

CHAPTER 21

Workplace Writing

Enhanced by new technologies, communication between individuals and groups is a critical factor in virtually all workplace tasks. A complete discussion of workplace communication would take a book in itself. This chapter has more modest goals: to introduce you to proven strategies that will help you achieve success in workplace writing, and to acquaint you with standard styles and practices.

21a Goals of workplace writing

Business writing is reader centered: you're writing to persuade, inform, or meet the needs and expectations of your audience. However, your audience's expectations are less likely to reflect individual outlooks than general goals and conventions for workplace writing. In many settings, moreover, conventions may be relatively specific and even rigid, while in others they may be more open to negotiation and innovation.

1 Plan according to your readers' needs

Your main focus in planning workplace writing will be the relationship between your information and your audience. Sometimes your audience will be made up of people working in different positions (for example, someone in the marketing department and someone who handles shipments in the warehouse). Be sensitive to the needs and perspectives of all your intended readers.

Because your readers are likely to be busy and impatient, you need to be especially careful in organizing your information. Workplace documents should have a friendly design and layout. Is there enough white space in your document to keep it from looking cluttered? Are your margins sufficiently wide? Are sections squeezed together, or have you left enough space to show blocks of information? Remember that a readable document is attractive and inviting, not tight and cluttered.

> **STRATEGY** Analyze your audience
>
> Using the audience continuum in 3e, spend a few minutes making notes about your intended readers. What do they know about the topic? How will they use the document? What do you know about their technical background, their level of education, their interest in the topic, and their need for what you have to offer?

259

TYPES OF WORKPLACE WRITING		
	CHARACTERISTIC ACTIVITIES	COMMON FORMS
PROVIDING INFORMATION	Gathering information; exploring issues; comparing competing products or services; tracing background information; summarizing, synthesizing, compiling, and presenting information	Report, study, agenda, minutes, instructions, manual, policy guides, memo, email message, summary, technical description, organizational chart, brochure, letter (of transmittal, response, adjustment, acknowledgment, good or bad news, application), position description, résumé, visuals
REQUESTING INFORMATION OR ACTION	Identifying an issue or a problem, identifying objectives or operational goals, identifying gaps in data or other information, identifying and evaluating potential sources and resources	Memo, email message, directive, letter (of request, inquiry, commitment, or complaint), sales letter, marketing material, advertisements, order form, letter of application, contract
IDENTIFYING ALTERNATIVES OR RECOMMENDING SOLUTIONS	Analyzing, evaluating, or selecting alternatives; comparing and contrasting; organizing supporting evidence; clarifying implications; advocating	Proposal, report, study, analysis, letter, email message, memo, summary, abstract, projection, evaluation, recommendation

21a
work

2 Draft as clearly as possible

As you draft, remember to emphasize clarity. Effective workplace writing is easy to read—unambiguous, uncluttered, and direct.

STRATEGY Focus on clarity

Instead of drafting with an eye to style, try to write the essential information as clearly and directly as you can. As you write, concentrate on exactly what you need to say. You can revise for a smoother and more appealing style after you've presented the main information directly.

3 Revise and edit

In some workplace settings you may be under pressure to write a document quickly, even more quickly than a paper due in two days for your composition class. Under these circumstances it's easy to skip the editing and revising process. Be especially careful not to fall into this trap; reread *all* your documents. Plan your schedule so you have at least some time for revising and editing. Even a single badly chosen word, one garbled sentence, or a lone instance of misinformation can be embarrassing.

21b Workplace writing process

As a new employee, one of your best resources is the fresh set of eyes you bring to the workplace. While observing the writing process in your organization, look for answers to the following questions, which will accelerate your understanding of the ways in which the writing process is organized locally.

1 How are writing projects assigned?

Are assignments made by email, by memo, or by word of mouth? If your supervisor assigns projects orally, be sure to take careful notes. However the assignment is made, check and double check that you have followed instructions exactly. If you have questions about the assignment, ask the supervisor, but don't pepper the boss with questions unless you have learned that she or he welcomes frequent discussions about work-in-progress.

2 Is most writing done individually or in work groups?

If writing is done collaboratively, how is it done? Are individuals assigned to write sections of a project which are then assembled into a document, or do writers brainstorm and draft the document as a team, working around a conference table? Does collaboration occur electronically? Your co-workers are a good source of information about how your company approaches the invention and drafting process.

3 Does the company have a formal editing process?

Some companies have established formal levels of editing that will be assigned based on the type of document being produced. For example, an internal company memo might require only light editing for usage and clarity, but a proposal to win a competitive contract will probably require a heavy edit, which includes the elements of a light edit plus checking for style, organizational soundness, tone, coherence, and other more global issues.

Regardless of the kind of editing process used by your company, it is important that you learn the expectations of your supervisor. Some supervisors want to see a draft quickly and care little about usage, mechanics, and style. Other supervisors want to see complete, well-edited drafts, regardless of the time constraints. Until you learn the needs and desires of your supervisor, careful self-editing is a must. Part 9 of this handbook will be an invaluable aid to you in this process.

4 Does the company have a formal set of writing models?

Many companies have a set of document templates they expect writers to use. Other companies just direct their writers to a model document to follow. Some very large businesses and governmental organizations have

21b
work

created their own style guides. Again, your fellow writers can be a helpful source for this kind of information.

5 How are revisions to manufacturing documents controlled?

Documents that are used to create a product, or that define the materials that go into a product, require careful control. It is important that companies have procedures to ensure that products are built to the specifications agreed upon with their customers. Many manufacturing firms have a technical library or a document control office that oversees the revision of critical documents. If you are assigned to write this type of document for the first time, talk to the personnel who administer the system to ensure that you meet stylistic and administrative expectations.

Exercise 1

A. Interview a supervisor or a writer at a local company. Ask the person to describe how the editing and revision process is controlled in the company. Also ask which type of errors are most troubling. Prepare a short presentation to share what you learned about this local business community with the class or your collaborative group.

B. In a small group, compare your findings from the interview. Find common processes and themes, and note where interviewees differed. Prepare a short presentation to share what you learned with the class.

21c Business letters

**21c
work**

Good business letters follow standard practices and established formats. The first sample letter included here is a sales solicitation (see p. 263); the second is a job application (see p. 266). Follow these guidelines for business correspondence:

- **Stationery.** The best is 25 percent or 50 percent white cotton bond paper of standard business weight (20 pound). Résumés and letters of application are often printed on a more durable paper (24 pound). Avoid colors and fancy paper styles.
- **Print quality and style.** Check that your printer and word processor are in good repair. Avoid nonstandard or stylized fonts—they can be difficult to read and are often associated by readers with personal or nonprofessional correspondence.
- **Format.** Most business letters are written using **block format** on company letterhead. In block format, often used for short letters, all paragraphs (including the greeting and signature) are flush at the left margin (see p. 263). Some longer business letters and many letters not printed on letterhead use a **modified block format** in which the return address and the closing and signature are aligned at the center of the page, but paragraphs are not indented from the left margin (see p. 266).

Acme Technical Products

3515 Lansing Road/Jackson, Michigan 49203
(517) 783-6651
www.acme.com

February 15, 2009

Ms. Janet Anderson
Purchasing Agent
Everett Batteries
15 Johnstown Boulevard
Westerly, RI 02891

Dear Ms. Anderson,

Thank you for using Acme products in your lithium-ion battery research and development program. Acme is ready to support you with your future needs as you transition from this developmental battery into a manufacturable consumer product. We are ready to provide you with volume discounts and to work with you to develop a "just-in-time" inventory control, which will save you inventory and storage costs.

We also would like to provide you with information on our new separator materials designed specifically for lithium-ion battery development. The enclosed catalog provides you with pricing and technical data on a number of different separator products designed for a variety of battery needs.

I look forward to working with you in the future.

Sincerely,

Steve Adams

Steve Adams
Sales Associate

Enclosure (1)

SA: rd
cc: Sales Manager

21c
work

- **Salutations.** Use the first name of your recipient only if you are already on a first name basis. Use the full name if you don't know the person's gender. Avoid gender-specific salutations such as "Dear Sir"; they are not appropriate. If you do not know the name of the person to whom you are writing, use a general salutation and title such as "Dear Accounts Department" or "Dear Credit Manager."
- **Notations following the signature.** Place any notations flush left, including initials for the writer and typist (RL: gw), *Enc.* or *Enclosure,* or *cc: Nancy Harris* (the person being sent a copy).
- **Longer letters.** Use letterhead stationery only for the first page. For all other pages, use plain paper of the same weight and color as the first page.
- **Envelope.** Envelope paper should be the same color and weight as the letter, and the font should match that of the letter.

21d Memos

Most companies use a corporate memo template or one of the standard memo templates found in word-processing programs. The organization's name and logo, or letterhead, may appear at the top of the memo, but no address information is needed because memos are internal company documents.

The words *To, From, Date,* and *Subject* appear on all memos, often in the order shown on the memo below. Spacing, notations for enclosures, additional pages, and copies all follow the same pattern as in a business letter.

Everett Batteries: Internal Memo

TO: Bob Rogers, Director of Battery Research and Development

FROM: Janet Anderson, Purchasing Agent

DATE: October 11, 2009

SUBJECT: Evaluation of Future Separator Needs

I recently received correspondence from Acme Technical Products with pricing information on their battery separator, as well as a catalog of new separator products. I am in the process of developing a purchasing plan detailing our separator needs for the next twelve months. Could you please provide me with a forecast of your department's projected use of Acme separator material on a month-by-month basis? I need this information by November 12 in order to meet MRP system deadlines.

I have enclosed a copy of the new catalog which contains technical specifications and pricing information for your use.

jck
Attachment

21e Email

The email message is replacing the memo as the preferred genre for internal communication within many organizations. Because the use of email is now commonplace in business and personal communication, people have developed the habit of writing email more casually. Yet a poorly composed email can damage a writer's credibility with readers in the same way a poorly composed letter or memo does. Developing the following habits when using electronic communication will help you avoid this pitfall.

- **Choose your addressees carefully.** Organizational lore is full of stories of persons who inadvertently sent a personal response to a message from an electronic mailing list or to a group of recipients. In some cases, such a response might insult a reader within the electronic community.
- **Proofread your message.** Don't use abbreviations, acronyms, or jargon unless you are certain all recipients will understand them. Don't use all capital letters within an electronic message unless you intend to strongly emphasize a point. (Typing a message in all-capital letters is equivalent to shouting.)
- **Use a subject line.** A clear subject line will help recipients to screen and identify those messages they need or wish to read immediately, and to delete unimportant messages.

21f Résumés and application letters

21f
work

Résumés and their accompanying cover letters are among the most important sales documents you will write; the product is, after all, you and your accomplishments. There are countless "right" ways to prepare these documents, but their goal is always to convey the necessary information and to make you appear professional and organized.

Your letter of application should be closely related to your résumé. Letters of application offer you the chance to discuss or highlight skills or experiences mentioned in your résumé or to add information not in your résumé. These letters function best when the writer tailors the cover letter to relate to the résumé, the skills and educational requirements found in the job advertisement or the description of the position. (See the sample job application letter on page 266.)

The purpose of the résumé package (résumé and application letter) is to get an interview, not a job. Employers favor job candidates who know how to start and finish a project independently and who are self-motivated, capable, and willing to face challenges confidently. You can't simply state these things; your résumé package must demonstrate these traits. Describe your experiences not only in terms of what you have done, but in terms of what you have learned from the experiences and how they will help you in

½" margin at top above
writer's complete address

1" margin
on each
side

Recipient's
complete
address

Salutation
with colon

Identifies
job
sought

Highlights
recent
training

Single-
spaced
text with
double-
spaced ¶s

Identifies
special
skills that
supplement
résumé

Explains
benefits of
experience

Supplies
contact
information

Notes
enclosure
(résumé)

550 Sundown Ct.
Dayton, OH 45420
June 12, 2009

Jennifer Low, Director of Personnel
Marshall School
232 Willow Way
Huber Heights, OH 45424

Dear Ms. Low:

I am seeking employment in elementary education, grades one through eight, and Jan Blake informed me of your junior high opening. During the past year as a student teacher, I have met many people at Marshall School, and I would love the opportunity to work with such a wonderful teaching staff.

My recent schooling at Wright State University has equipped me with many strategies that I am excited about implementing into my teaching. One strategy I am ready to try is the use of procedures. If students know what is expected of them, I believe that they can and will live up to those expectations.

My greatest strengths as a teacher are my creativity and time management skills. Both are assets when planning my lessons and keeping students interested while using class time wisely. During one past teaching experience, my task seemed impossible until I designed learning centers to combat time constraints.

I firmly believe in inquiry teaching, a technique that always worked well during my student teaching. One of the joys of working with children has been seeing their eyes light up when they begin to understand new information.

I feel that I would be an asset to Marshall School and hope to start my career in your district next fall. I can be reached at 453-555-5555 and look forward to an interview with you.

Sincerely,
Tammy Helton
Tammy Helton

Enclosure

the future. Many employers receive hundreds of résumé packages for every job position posted, so you need to concentrate on highlighting your skills and achievements objectively and clearly—and be sure to proofread.

STRATEGY   Prepare a résumé checklist

Write informally in response to the following questions. Jot down your ideas and as many examples from your background as you can remember. Later you can select the best ideas and examples for your purposes.

1. What kind of work do you want to do? What kind of job do you want?
2. What are your career goals?
3. What jobs have you held?
4. What volunteer positions have you held?
5. What are your skills, abilities, or interests? (Include items even where you have not had formal training.)
6. What are the main features of your educational background?
   a. College major, minor, and concentrations
   b. Special projects or research
   c. Honors and awards
   d. Memberships and offices in organizations
   e. Volunteer positions
   f. Special skills
   g. Grade-point average (overall, and within major field)
7. What other awards or special honors have you received (from work, volunteer efforts, or community organizations)?
8. Who might make a good reference for you? Try to identify at least one former or current professor, one former job supervisor or employer, and one personal reference.
9. What makes you different from other applicants? Why should a prospective employer interview you rather than someone else?

21f
work

1 Use categories to construct your résumé

After you've collected the information for your résumé, your task is one of construction: placing the information into appropriate categories, phrasing it concisely, and arranging it in a visually appealing way that stresses your strongest traits first, as in the sample résumé on page 268.

Career objective. When you state your career objective, be specific! Avoid empty phrases like *position of responsibility in a fast-growing firm*. Consider tailoring your objective to each type of position for which you apply.

Job experience. Make a list of all the duties you had, then choose the ones that are most similar to those of the job you want. If you have held many jobs, list those jobs that you held the longest, the ones that most resemble

---

Carol E. Westermeyer

College Address:	Home Address:
Apt. 22 College Park	7562 Galsworth Road
Greenville, Virginia 20205	Squires, Texas 30303
(804) 555-3345	(512) 555-7912
cwesr@school.edu	

Objective   Entry-level position as an electrical engineer

Education

• **B.S. Electrical Engineering, May 2009**
   Virginia Polytechnic Institute, Blacksburg, Virginia 24060
   G.P.A. 3.18/4.0 Minor: Economics

Experience

• **Technician/Assembler, May 2003–September 2005**
   Communication Technology, Inc., Fairview, Virginia 24059
   -Developed cost analysis and designed prototype wireless communication products for Masters Mountain Laboratories.
   -Built and tested various AF and RF products: transmitters, receivers, headsets, amplifiers, and antenna networks.
   -Served as company representative to demonstrate a new generation of wireless radios at Atlanta National Radio Conference.

• **Interoffice Administrator (part time), 2005–present**
   Bergland Technology Associates, Lakeview, Virginia 24051
   -Updated and reorganized shop inventory control using Microsoft Office software.

Project

• **Member, Design Team for Electric Vehicle**
   Department of Electrical Engineering, Virginia Polytechnic Institute, Blacksburg, Virginia 24060
   -Controller group duties included design and programming of a constant velocity transmission (CVT) controller.

Skills   Experienced with a variety of computer software programs, including Microsoft Office, Autocad, and Statistica.

Activities   Vice President, Student Senate, Virginia Polytechnic Institute

---

21f
work

---

the job for which you are applying, or the ones that demonstrate your most employable characteristics. If you think you have little specific experience that relates to the job you seek, highlight other job skills such as the ability to work as part of a team, to handle responsibility, to supervise others, and to work with little or no supervision. When possible, don't simply state these skills; provide examples from your experience.

Volunteer experience. If you've held volunteer or unpaid internship positions that may be attractive to an employer, list them. Note that the position was voluntary, but handle the rest of the information as you would for any other job experience.

Sequence of experience. Typically, jobs are listed in reverse chronological order (with your most recent job first). If your most important job experience is not your most recent, however, list that one first, and then list the remaining jobs in reverse chronological order.

References. Unless the employer has specifically asked for references, use the general statement *References available upon request.* Few employers will want to look at your references unless they plan to interview you. You should bring with you to the interview a separate page listing the names, addresses, and phone numbers or email addresses of three or four references. (Always ask permission of someone *before* you use him or her as a reference.)

2 Submitting your résumé

Some companies may prefer that you submit your résumé electronically. If so, be sure to follow any instructions they may provide for formatting the electronic file. Frequently the résumé file will be attached to an email that will function as your letter of application. Another way of getting your résumé to a number of potential employers is to submit your electronic résumé to an Internet job service.

Many people now create their résumés on the Web. Some advantages of Web-based résumés include the ability to "nest" information on subsequent pages without cluttering the main résumé page. For example, you might include links from the positions you have held to pages that describe those positions and your accomplishments in them. If you choose to develop a Web-based résumé, however, be sure to pay special attention to issues of layout and design and make navigation of the site user-friendly. Like paper résumés, Web-based résumés need to present you and your work elegantly and error-free.

21f
work

Visit mycomplab.com for more resources and exercises on writing for workplace audiences.

PART 5

Researching
and Writing

CHAPTER 22

Getting Started:
Researching and Writing

Research is systematic inquiry into a subject through written sources (print or electronic), fieldwork (interviews, surveys, ethnographic observation), or even a systematic examination of your own experience. You can use the depth of information, ideas, and insights you develop through research for many purposes.

22a Choosing a topic

Your research can grow from a personal interest, an assignment, a strong feeling or point of view, a pressing issue or problem, a desire for understanding, or the interests and needs of potential readers. Remember,

AUDIENCE EXPECTATIONS FOR RESEARCH WRITING		
	ACADEMIC	**PUBLIC**	**WORK**
GOALS	Explain or prove, offer well-supported interpretations or conclusions, analyze or synthesize information for use in other settings	Support arguments for policy or course of action; inform or advise for the public good	Document problems, propose a project or course of action, compare information, improve performance
TYPICAL QUESTIONS	What does it mean? What happened? How does it occur? How might it be modified?	How can this policy be made better? What do people need or want to know?	What is the problem? How can we solve it? What course of action will help us achieve our goals?
TYPICAL FORMS	Interpretive (thesis) paper, informative paper, research report, grant report	Position paper, editorial, proposal, informative article, pamphlet, guidelines	Proposal, report, feasibility study, memorandum
AUDIENCE EXPECTA-TIONS	Detailed evidence from varied sources including quotations, paraphrases, and summaries; documented sources that acknowledge scholarship	Accessible, fair, and persuasive information with evidence; informal documentation	Clear, direct, and precise information; appropriate detail; less formal documentation

however, that your choice of focus for your research needs to be guided by the space, time, and resources available to you.

1 Respond to your assignment

Read your assignment carefully, underlining key terms. Then respond to the assignment in the following ways.

- If a word or phrase immediately suggests a topic, write it down, and add a list of synonyms or alternative terms.
- If you can't identify a topic at first, take key words and phrases, write them down, and brainstorm related words and phrases along with the topics they suggest.
- Consider asking whoever made the assignment for thoughts on a potential topic—and for further topic suggestions. Consider asking potential readers for their reactions.

In an intermediate composition course, Summer Arrigo-Nelson and Jennifer Figliozzi received an assignment that asked them to "investigate the psychological or social dimensions of a local or campus problem." They underlined the words *psychological or social dimensions* and *campus problem,* then made a list of campus problems.

low class attendance	new majors	date rape
inadequate library	role of sports	student alcohol use
living conditions	canceled classes	student fees
parking	drugs	crime

They chose "student alcohol use" as a focus; the topic interested them. They also thought that they could easily find research sources and that doing field research of their own wouldn't be too difficult. Some initial reading and brainstorming led them to wonder about the role of parents in determining the drinking habits of college students, and they decided to address this question in their research.

2 Recognize your interests

Perhaps you have an interest, a passion, a job you like (or hate), a curiosity, or some other part of your life that might be intriguing to readers—if you can bring together what you already know with what you discover through research.

A strong feeling, general awareness of a problem, or curiosity will help you identify specific issues or subjects worth further study. Here is how several students turned their feelings, interests, general awareness of issues, and curiosity into research projects.

22a
resrch

INTEREST	TITLE OF FINAL PAPER
Curiosity: Why do so many workers in fast-food restaurants seem to be recent immigrants?	Easy to Hire, Easy to Fire: Recent Immigrants and the Fast-Food Industry
Job: I have been working as an EMT, but I'll bet most people don't know anything about the job.	You Won't Meet Us Until You Need Us: What EMTs Do
Strong Feeling: I like my SUV, and I'm sick of hearing people criticize SUVs and their owners.	What's *Good* About SUVs
General Awareness: I've seen a lot more deer grazing beside highways lately, and I've been hearing about many deer-related car accidents.	Keeping Deer and Cars Apart: A Proposal

3 Browse for an issue or a problem

You can recognize "big" issues easily enough: "Global Warming: Real or Not?" "Does Television Violence Lead to Violent Behavior?" So much has been written about "big" topics that they easily exceed the scope of even the most ambitious research paper. However, a bit of browsing can lead you to more focused issues, problems, and topics. Search one or two issues of a magazine or newspaper; scan the entries in a database; consult informational Web sites. Look for words, phrases, and titles that suggest topics, especially questions that remain unanswered and issues that (for most people) have not been resolved.

Exercise 1

Start a research project in one of three ways.

1. Create a journal entry in which you explore your experiences and interests, looking for incidents, interests, or questions that suggest a subject for research and writing.
2. Look through magazines, newspapers, or Web sites for discussions and topics that interest you as a subject for research; take notes on the areas of interest you encounter.
3. Underline key words in your assignment, then create a paragraph explaining your understanding of the assignment and naming one or more subjects you consider appropriate to it.

CREATING A RESEARCH FILE

A **research file** is a place where you record and store systematically your activities throughout the research and writing process—ready to be recalled for later use. These activities include:

- Probing ideas through discovery techniques (3a)
- Identifying a *specific topic* (22a) and developing a *research question* (22d) or *tentative thesis* (22e)
- Creating a *search strategy* (22g), listing *resources* (22g-1), and assembling a list of sources or a *working bibliography* (22g-4)
- *Note taking*—making a record of relevant ideas and information from sources, including summaries, paraphrases, and quotations; copying (or recording) passages (or images) for possible inclusion in your writing
- *Documenting sources* (Chapters 29–33)
- *Drafting* and *revising* (Chapter 28), including integrating your insights with ideas and information from your sources (Chapter 27)

You can keep a research file in a notebook, in a folder, on note cards, or in a computer file. Your file should contain sections corresponding to each of the main stages of your research and writing, along with a timeline for completing your work.

Exercise 2

Choose a format for a research file: folder, electronic file, notebook, word-processing document, or whatever form you find comfortable and useful. Make sure it can be divided into parts for your various research and writing activities. Create some initial entries, perhaps from the activities described in Exercise 1, to see if the format you have chosen is accessible and useful. Then, take the file with you wherever you plan to do research—at the library, online, or in field research such as an interview—and add information to the entries you have already created. If the format you have chosen seems cumbersome, revise it before you move further into the research process.

22b Narrowing a topic

Perhaps you have already identified a subject, an issue, or a problem. You aren't quite ready to begin, however. First you need to focus or narrow your topic so you can do the necessary research in a reasonable amount of time and cover the important elements in detail in a paper that isn't overly long.

1 Broad subject to limited topic

Think of a subject as a broad field filled with clusters of information, ideas, and written interchanges—clusters that are often only loosely related to each other even though they fall within the same subject field. A **topic** is a single cluster of ideas and information within a broader subject, usually the *topic* of an ongoing *conversation* involving writers and readers.

2 Surveying potential topics

By limiting your attention to a particular topic or conversation (or to some element within the conversation—a *subtopic*), you take an important step toward making your research project manageable. But how can you identify the various conversations in a subject field in ways that help you narrow the topic for your own research and writing? You can survey briefly some of the same kinds of resources you will revisit later as you plan and execute your *search strategy* (22g): databases, indexes of articles, electronic search engines, magazines and journals, library catalogs, and printed books. At this stage, however, limit yourself to a sampling of potential resources.

Here are notes Tou Yang made in his research file (p. 275) from his survey of the database *Academic Search Premier* on the subject *athletic dietary supplements*, along with his comments on two potential topics the notes helped him identify.

> "Eat Powder? Build Muscle! Burn Calories!"—creatine monohydrate, lots of athletes swear by it, claim it has only good effects
> "Creatine Monohydrate Supplementation Enhances High-Intensity Exercise Performance in Males and Females"—controversy over whether creatine works or not; they claim it does
> "From Ephedra to Creatine: Using Theory to Respond to Dietary Supplement Use in Young Athletes"—understanding why athletes use dietary supplements even though they are probably not effective

> Some disagreement over whether creatine works or at least over how well it works—take a position on this? Or explain how it works and what it seems to add to sports performance?

Exercise 3

Create an entry for your research file in which you record the steps you have taken to narrow your topic. List the options you have for narrowing your topic and the advantages or disadvantages of each one. Then create a statement identifying the focused topic you have chosen and your reasons for choosing it.

22c
resrch

22c Aims of research writing

No matter what subject you set out to investigate, your research will be heavily influenced by your answer to this question: Will I use my research to *inform* or to *persuade*? The answer you give early in a research project is important because it helps shape your decisions, yet it is not final. Be ready to modify your purpose (or change it altogether) as you research and write.

1 Informative research project

Informative research writing focuses on the *subject* you are planning to explore and explain. You therefore focus your research and writing on discovering information and ideas about your subject and sharing them with readers: your efforts will be *subject-driven*.

Taking this approach does not mean your writing will be an unoriginal reciting of facts and statements from sources. On the contrary, successful informative research writing draws ideas and information from sources, then organizes them to aid readers' understanding or to answer potential questions, and finally offers (and supports) insights or conclusions about the topic.

In an early entry in her research file (see the box on p. 275 for guidelines), Jenny Latimer recorded a recent experience and the questions it brought to mind. In doing so, she came to recognize her informative purpose.

> After I had stuffed a couple of red licorice sticks into my mouth in front of my co-worker Julie, she picked up the wrapper and said, "I didn't realize they had hydrogenated oils in them. I'll never eat them again!" I started wondering about a number of things. What are hydrogenated oils, and why do they seem to be in everything we eat? When did this start? Is there a proposal to get them out of foods? What do they do to you? Do we really need to worry?

2 Persuasive research project

Persuasive research writing focuses on your **thesis** or **conclusion.** Your research and writing will concentrate on evidence and explanatory details, chosen for their logical support of your point of view, their persuasiveness for readers, and their usefulness in explaining issues or problems. (See Chapters 9–12 for a discussion of argumentative writing.)

Your research should focus on more than just the evidence and ideas that support your conclusions, however. An argument will not be likely to persuade readers to agree with your thesis unless it offers detailed information about the issues or problem you are addressing.

Your research will help you explain a particular issue or problem on which you wish to take a stand or a subject you wish to analyze and interpret. It will also help you develop, refine, and support your thesis, your proposal, or your interpretation.

22d
resrch

22d Research questions

Research writing, especially informative writing, aims to answer questions, both those raised in the conversation among members of a research community addressing a subject and those likely to be raised by readers. By developing a **research question**—formulating a few simple questions about your subject early in the research process—you can set limits on the scope of your topic and focus on the most important ideas and information you gather through research.

Research questions can take several forms, depending on your own preferences and your purposes for writing. Some writers prefer questions that focus on factual or informational matters: *who, what, where, when, why,* and *how.* Other writers prefer questions that suggest both a purpose and an eventual organizational pattern for writing. Jennifer Latimer arrived at her research questions in this way:

> I looked at the licorice package, the sour candy package, the snack crackers box, even the pudding pack—all contained hydrogenated oils. I did some preliminary research and developed two questions for my research and my readers:
>> What effects do hydrogenated oils have on us?
>> Should I (and we) ever again eat delicious treats containing them?

STRATEGY   Develop your research question

The following question patterns may be helpful to you in developing your research question.

- How did X come about? What are its consequences?
- What are some new developments? What benefits or dangers do they involve?
- What is X and into what categories does it fall?
- Why is X a problem? What can we do in response to it?
- What unusual (intriguing, surprising) features does X have? Why are they important to us?
- What choices does X pose?
- Is X as important (dangerous, valuable, unusual) as many people claim?
- Who is affected by X? What should they know about it or do about it?

22e Preliminary thesis

Almost all research essays, reports, documents—even Web sites—use a **thesis statement** (3c–d) to guide readers' attention and state the writer's key idea or theme. The form and scope of a thesis statement will vary according to your purpose for writing. In persuasive writing, a thesis statement plays a special role by presenting the argumentative proposition (10c), proposal, or interpretation your writing supports.

By creating a thesis statement early in the research and writing process, you can narrow your topic and shape your search strategy (22g) accordingly. Later you will modify your thesis in response to what you have learned. Thesis statements that guide research often follow one of four patterns.

- **Issue.** What is the issue, and what is my stand on it?
- **Problem.** What is the problem, and what solution am I offering?
- **Public question.** What is the situation we are facing, and how should we respond?
- **Academic question.** What is the phenomenon, and what is my analysis and interpretation?

Revise your thesis statement regularly, perhaps devoting a section of your research file to this effort. Use the opportunity to consider changes in direction or emphasis triggered by what you learned through research and to begin envisioning the strategies you will use in writing your paper.

Exercise 4

Create a preliminary thesis statement to narrow your focus to a specific issue or problem. You might use more than one sentence at this point in the process, one stating the issue, problem, question, or phenomenon you are addressing, another offering your (tentative) opinion or conclusion.

22f Audience inventory

As you identify the conversations that writers are having about your topic and as you begin your own research, remember that various communities of readers may expect different things from a report or paper. Academic readers look for detailed evidence from a variety of sources and expect carefully documented sources and quotations. Readers in a work setting expect a clear and direct presentation, accurate information, and detail appropriate to the subject and the audience's expertise, along with less formal documentation. And readers in public communities expect information and supporting evidence that is accurate, clear, accessible, and persuasive, without quite as much attention to documentation.

22f
resrch

STRATEGY Create an audience inventory

- What problems or issues has the audience been facing?
- What new discoveries or information might interest the audience or be useful to it?
- What policies or programs are causing your readers difficulty or might be helpful to them?

Arrigo-Nelson and Figliozzi prepared an audience inventory to help plan their paper on the effects of alcohol consumption among college students. One item in their inventory focused on the audience of their own campus community.

AUDIENCE INVENTORY QUESTION *What new discoveries or information about student alcohol use might benefit the campus community?*

WRITER'S RESPONSE *Our conclusion about the relationship between student drinking behavior in college and parental permissiveness for drinking in the home could be important for a campus program aiming to reduce student alcohol use.*

Exercise 5

Develop a set of potential questions to help understand your audience's interests, needs, and expectations. Then use these questions to develop an audience inventory.

22g Developing a search strategy

A **search strategy** is a plan for locating the resources you need to answer your research question and support your thesis. It will help you to consult a variety of sources providing different kinds of information and points of view. A search strategy has five elements: resources; search tools; keywording; working bibliography; and a timeline.

1 Resources

Your search strategy should begin with a list of the kinds of resources you plan to use—printed books, scholarly journals, newspapers, databases, Web sites, interviews, and surveys, for example. Draw on your preliminary research (22b) to create your initial resource list, and update it as you discover further potential resources. If you have specific titles, Web sites, or people in mind as sources, list them.

2 Search tools

Obvious search tools come readily to mind when you begin researching: your library's online catalog and Web search engines like *Google*. They are adequate starting points but not always the best or most precise means of locating resources, particularly when your research moves beyond information and ideas that are generally known. See Chapters 23–26 for the discussion of specialized research tools.

3 Keywording

Indexes, databases, library catalogs (23b), and many other reference sources are arranged (or searched) by **keywords.** If you identify the keywords or phrases for printed or electronic indexes, you can usually locate all the resources you need. If you don't, you may waste time following the wrong paths and locating useless sources.

Of course, you may not know which are the preferred terms and phrases until you begin your search, and there may be some necessary trial and error in your work. Sometimes it helps to have in mind two or three alternative keywords or phrases. If a particular database or other resource yields little under one keyword, you can try others before moving to another resource.

Exercise 6

As part of your developing search strategy, make a list of possible sources you have discovered and a list of keywords and phrases that may help guide your research.

4 Working bibliography

Your search strategy should make provision for recording information that will help you or your readers locate a source. A list of sources you have examined and may decide to draw on as you write is called a **working bibliography.** In a working bibliography, you should record the types of information you will need to provide in your final paper in a list of works cited, a references list, a list of works consulted, or footnotes (see Chapters 29–33).

INFORMATION FOR A WORKING BIBLIOGRAPHY

When you examine a source, record the following kinds of information in your working bibliography, ready to be used in compiling the list of sources for your final paper.

PRINTED BOOKS

- Author(s) or editor(s)
- Title
- Publication information: place of publication, name of publisher, date of publication
- Volume or edition numbers, if any
- Call number (to locate the book in library stacks)

PRINTED ARTICLES

- Author(s) or editor(s)
- Title
- Name of journal, magazine, newspaper, or collection of articles
- Publication information
  - Article in a periodical: volume number, issue number, month or day of publication, page numbers of article (inclusive)
  - Article in a collection: title of collection and editor's name, place of publication, name of publisher, date of publication, page numbers of article (inclusive)

(continued)

22g
resrch

> ### INFORMATION FOR A WORKING BIBLIOGRAPHY (*continued*)
>
> #### ELECTRONIC OR ONLINE WORK
>
> - Author(s), editor(s), or group(s) responsible for the document
> - Title or name of Web site
> - Information about any corresponding print publication (as above)
> - Electronic publication information: date of electronic publication or latest update, date you accessed document, and complete URL; (for an online journal) volume and issue number, publication date; (for a database or CD-ROM) document access number or version number; (for email or post to a discussion list) name of sender, subject line, date of posting, name of list, date of access.

Organizing your working bibliography. You can organize the entries in a working bibliography in several ways.

- **Alphabetically,** as they will eventually appear in a list of works cited or a references page. This strategy can save time and effort when you prepare your final text.
- In **categories** reflecting the parts of your subject or the kinds of evidence they provide for your argument. This strategy can help you identify at a glance areas for your work and those needing further investigation.
- **According to the plan** for your paper. This strategy can help you gather your resources efficiently as you write.

Annotating. Some writers add comments, evaluations, or brief summaries to the references in their working bibliographies (for a discussion of annotated bibliographies, see 17d). The annotated bibliographies they create in this manner can be papers in their own right or part of a longer research project.

Exercise 7

Assemble the notes you have taken for your working bibliography. Use them to create a working bibliography as part of your research file. Organize the entries in a manner appropriate to your purposes for researching and writing. If possible, link the entries electronically to notes you have taken on the sources.

22h
resrch

22h Timeline

Planning involves dividing up your work and sticking to a schedule. By being methodical in the process of your research, you'll make the most efficient use of your time.

Answer the following questions to help create a timeline for your work.

1. **How much time do I have?** When should my report or document be in final form? Do I have to produce intermediate assignments, such as a progress report, drafts, or notes?
2. **What kind of report or document will I be creating, and for whom?** What form will my work take? What resources will I have to gather or develop in order to produce such work? What audience or community of readers will I be addressing? What will I need to learn about them and their expectations? Will I need to share or discuss the project with them while I'm researching and writing?
3. **What kind of research must I do?** Will I be doing research in printed sources (articles, books), electronic sources (databases, Web sites), or field sources (interviews, surveys, observations)?

WHAT TO INCLUDE IN A TIMELINE OR CALENDAR

When you create a calendar for your research, include the following tasks, allowing four days to a week for each.

1. Choose a subject. Do the preliminary research necessary to identify a specific topic.
2. Narrow your topic so that it is realistic in the time you have available for research and writing. Begin identifying possible resources.
3. Develop a research question or tentative thesis. Create an audience inventory. Develop a search strategy. Begin a working bibliography.
4. Begin research. Identify possible resources, read and evaluate them, and take notes. Record bibliographical information for sources.
5. Review your research notes. Begin looking for patterns in the information and ideas you consider appropriate for your project. Begin summarizing key ideas or information; begin drafting those sections of your project you see as important parts of the final document. Identify areas needing further investigation and continue your research. Revise your research question or tentative thesis in a form close to the version that will appear in the final paper.
6. Start writing your first draft. Develop a plan for your paper and begin drafting. Include preliminary in-text references or endnotes. Maintain a working list of sources cited as you draft. Check for missing bibliographical information.
7. Finish drafting. Review your draft for areas needing further research; share it with others who can give you honest, practical responses and advice. Revise your paper and prepare documentation in final form.
8. Polish and proofread the final draft; share it with someone who can help spot problems, omissions, or errors you did not notice. Submit your work.

22h
resrch

Put your plans into calendar form so you can envision the process as a whole and evaluate your plan. Be ready to revise your calendar to accommodate the realities of research and writing and to reflect changes in the direction of your work.

You can maintain your calendar in handwritten form on a paper calendar or in a dated list of activities. Or you can use the calendar and planning programs in your computer. In choosing a format for your calendar, make sure you can include it in your research file.

STRATEGY   Work backward

Create a research and writing plan by working backward from the due date for a project. Even if you don't follow the plan precisely, a calendar, list of dates, electronic project planning graph, or chart of activities can help you get started on a project and give you a sense of direction.

Exercise 8

Develop a timeline for your research and writing project. Put it in the form of a calendar, a project graph, or a chart of activities. Work backward from your due date and estimate the amount of time you will need to allot to each activity.

22i   Assessing sources

Your search strategy (22g) should provide you with a list of possible sources for your writing. When you examine specific sources, you should do so critically, using the techniques described in 23c, 24f, and 25d to evaluate the quality of information and ideas in printed sources, database documents, and Web pages, respectively. Before you get to this point, however, you need to decide which possible sources are worth consulting. Most likely, you will have this information about a source available as you decide: title, author's name, abstract or summary, source publication, and others' statements about the source.

- **Title.** Start with those sources whose titles seem to best fit your topic and those whose titles suggest fresh ideas or perspectives that will add to or modify the outlook with which you are beginning.
- **Author.** Look at sources written by authorities in the field, by well-known writers, or by people cited in other sources.
- **Abstract or summary.** If your search engine or an annotated bibliography gives you either a brief description or an abstract of a source, you should use it to assess whether a potential source is relevant to your topic and likely to provide useful information and ideas.
- **Source publication.** Some publications, such as encyclopedias, will give you general information rather than the details and specific ideas you need. Others, such as scholarly journal articles, books, and Web sites sponsored by professional organizations, are likely to offer reputable, detailed, and current material. Take the kind of source publication and the reputation of those responsible for it into account as you assess potential resources. (For *Wikipedia*, see page 286.)
- **Others' statements.** When other writers cite a source or a writer frequently, or offer positive evaluations, you should consider consulting it.

22i
resrch

USING INFORMATION FROM *WIKIPEDIA*

Wikipedia, an online encyclopedia, covers many topics, including definitions of terms, explanations of concepts, background material, and related elements of a topic. Unlike print or electronic encyclopedias created by experts, *Wikipedia* is constantly updated by its users, some of whom are experts, some not. Like other encyclopedias, it can be a good place to start learning about a topic, but as a source, it has two serious limitations.

1. *Wikipedia* presents what is generally known, not original research. If you use it as a source, you'll repeat, not add to, what readers know.

2. *Wikipedia* users can edit the entries. Some of them are experts, but many are not, so the quality can be uneven and sometimes wrong.

22j Reading sources critically

To read critically, you must be able to do four things: (1) *identify* in your sources the unanswered questions (academic), unresolved issues (public), or unsolved problems (work) that you can make the focus of your research and writing; (2) *synthesize* different perspectives among sources; (3) *interpret* your sources; (4) *evaluate* your sources.

1 Identifying questions

As you read and reflect on your topic, record and explore unanswered questions, unsolved problems, and unresolved issues. Try stating them as concisely as you can in a *question paragraph* (or a *problem* or *issue paragraph*). Such a paragraph can suggest ways for you to develop your paper or report, and you may even include all or part of it in the finished product. Here are critical notes student Lily Germaine made for a paper about bodybuilding.

22j
resrch

> Tucker, Larry A. "Effect of Weight Training on Self-Concept: A Profile of Those Influenced Most." *Research Quarterly for Exercise and Sport*, Introduction, pp. 389-91.

> Tucker uses the word "although" at least four times when summarizing other studies, and he tends to use phrases such as "only a few studies have shown. . . ." He's being nice on the surface but is setting his readers up to find fault with the other studies. That basic fault is their lack of objective methodology, which he seems to plan on rectifying by using mathematical measurements and rigid definitions of terms. A glance through the rest of the article reveals lots of equations and two tables of statistics. He seems to think he can be completely objective in determining such a slippery thing as "self-concept." I really have to question this assumption.

Germaine's question paragraph begins with insights and wording from her notes.

> Does bodybuilding affect self-concept? Before we can answer this question, we need to ask if we can accurately measure such a slippery thing as "self-concept." Some researchers, like Tucker, believe that self-concept can be accurately gauged using mathematical measurements and rigid definitions of terms. For several reasons, however, this assumption is questionable. . . .

22k Taking notes

The research notes you take as you review sources can be informational, critical, or both. **Informational notes** record facts, details, concepts, interpretations, and quotations from your sources. These notes help you focus on material relevant to your research question(s). They also help you retrieve material easily as you write, revise, and document sources. **Critical notes** include comments, interpretations, or evaluations of a source. They also indicate the relationship of the source to your research question(s) and include the necessary information for documentation. Most often, your comments will accompany information from your sources, though you may wish to devote some notes entirely to your critical observations.

Many writers keep their notes in an electronic file. Others use a research file, and still others use note cards. Whatever form you choose, make sure you *write down the complete source information* for later use. Include the page numbers to which the notes refer, especially for any quoted material. Include also an annotation that tells how the material is related to your topic and your research questions so you'll have an easier time following your thread of research and drawing on the material as you draft and revise.

1 Cards

You can use a word-processing file as a set of note cards (one page = one note card). Or you can use index cards, either $4'' \times 6''$ or $5'' \times 7''$. At the top of each page or card write the topic, and restrict each page or card to one kind of note taking (quotation, summary of facts and ideas, paraphrase). As you plan or write a paper, you can arrange and rearrange pages or cards in related groups. Some computer programs are specially designed for note taking and make all these steps easy.

2 Research journal

If you use a research journal (electronic or a paper notebook), you'll have space to record information, reflect on new knowledge, and begin assembling the parts of a paper or a report. Use an entry's heading or make marginal comments to show what's covered in the notes. These annotations

22k
resrch

will help you organize your notes later. If your research journal is a notebook with pockets or a folder, you can also use it to store photocopies of print materials or downloaded copies of electronic sources. Write the source and topic at the top of the copy (if the source title is printed on the page, circle it).

> **STRATEGY**   Check your quotations
>
> Check your quotations carefully. Sometimes you'll need to work with original sources—printed books and journals, not electronic publications or photocopies. In such situations, be very careful when you include quotations in your notes. You should be *absolutely certain* that you've copied them word for word and that you've recorded the exact page numbers where each quotation appears. Having to return to your source later, especially when you are writing, will use valuable time.

22l Summarizing, paraphrasing, and synthesizing

You can't identify and use research sources without reading them. A research project calls for two types of reading: reading for understanding and critical reading. Reading for understanding leads to the summaries, paraphrases, syntheses, quotations, and details you will draw on as you write. Critical reading leads to many of the insights you will offer to readers.

In a **summary,** you present the essential information in a text without interpreting it. A summary is shorter than the original, *compressing* the information and presenting only the key ideas and support. In a **paraphrase,** you restate an author's ideas in your own words, retaining the content and sense of the original but providing your own expression. A **synthesis** brings together summaries of several sources and points out the relationships among the ideas and information.

1 Summarizing

You create summaries as a concise way of presenting ideas and information from a source in your own writing. In an **objective summary,** you focus on presenting the content of the source in compressed form and avoid speculating on the source's line of reasoning. In an **evaluative summary,** you add your opinions, evaluating or commenting on the original passage.

In a summary you can present the key ideas from a source without including unnecessary detail that might distract readers. Arrigo-Nelson and Figliozzi used two one-sentence summaries of research to help introduce one of the questions for their academic research paper.

First, research has shown that adolescents who have open and close relationships with their parents use alcohol less often than do those with conflictual relationships (Sieving 1996). For example, a survey given to students in seventh through twelfth grades reported that *approximately 35 percent of adolescent drinkers were under parental supervision while drinking (Dept. of Education 1993). Based on this research, we are interested in determining if students who were given permission to drink while living with their parents would possess different drinking patterns, upon reaching college, than those who did not previously have permission to drink.*

STRATEGY   Prepare a summary

- **Read** the selection, looking for the most important ideas, evidence, and information. Underline, highlight, or make note of key points and information that you think should be mentioned in your summary.
- **Scan** (reread quickly) the selection to decide which of the ideas and bits of information you noted during your first reading are the *most* important. Try also to decide on the writer's main purpose in the selection and to identify the major sections of the discussion.
- **Summarize** *each section* of the source (each step in the argument, each stage in the explanation) in a *single sentence* that mentions the key ideas and information.
- **Encapsulate** the *entire passage* in a *single sentence* that captures its main point or conclusion.
- **Combine** your section summaries with your encapsulation (above) to produce a draft summary of the main point, other important points, and the most important information.
- **Revise** to make sure your summary is logical and easy to read. Check against the source for accuracy.
- **Document** clearly the source of your summary using a standard style of documentation (see Chapters 29–33).

2 Paraphrasing

A good paraphrase doesn't add to or detract from the original but often helps you understand a difficult work. When you want to incorporate the detailed ideas and information from a passage into your own writing but don't want to quote your source because the wording is too dense or confusing, then a **paraphrase** can be the answer.

22l
resrch

As part of her research for an editorial supporting a new alcohol abuse program on her campus, Figliozzi encountered the following passage in a report on current programs at various schools.

> The university also now notifies parents when their sons or daughters violate the alcohol policy or any other aspect of the student code of conduct. "We were hoping that the support of parents would help change students' behavior, and we believe it has," says Timothy F. Brooks, an assistant vice-president and the dean of students at the University of Delaware.

Because she wanted to avoid long quotations and instead integrate the information smoothly into her discussion, she paraphrased part of the passage.

Officials at the University of Delaware thought that letting parents know when students violate regulations on alcohol use would change students' drinking habits, and one administrator now says, "We believe it has" (Reisberg 42).

STRATEGY   Prepare a paraphrase

To paraphrase part of a source, put the information in your own words, retaining the content and ideas of the original as well as the sequence of presentation. (Many paraphrases contain sentences that correspond with the original except for changes in wording and sentence structure.)

- **Read** the selection carefully so that you understand the wording as well as the content.
- **Write** a draft of your paraphrase, using your own words and phrases in place of the original. Rely on synonyms and equivalent expressions. You can retain names, proper nouns, and the like from the original, of course.
- **Revise** for smooth reading and clarity. Change sentence structures and phrasing to make sure your version is easier to understand than your source.
- **Document** clearly the source of your paraphrase using a standard style of documentation (see Chapters 29–33).

Exercise 9

Choose an article that interests you in a magazine such as *Natural History* or *Scientific American*. Paraphrase the first paragraph or two or any passage of a few lines or more. Do as Figliozzi has done above, and try to integrate the passage into an imaginary research report, putting much or most of the passage into your own words.

221
resrch

3 Synthesizing

By bringing together summaries of several sources and pointing out their relationships in a **synthesis,** you can use your sources in special ways: to provide background information, to explore causes and effects, to look at contrasting explanations or arguments, and to bring together ideas and information in support of a thesis.

> **STRATEGY**   Prepare a synthesis
>
> - **Identify** the role a synthesis would play in your explanation or argument as well as the kind of information and ideas you wish to share with readers.
> - **Gather** the sources you plan to synthesize.
> - **Read** your sources, and prepare to summarize them.
> - **Focus** on the purpose of your synthesis, and draft a sentence summing up your conclusion about the relationships of the sources.
> - **Arrange** the order in which you will present your sources in the synthesis.
> - **Write** a draft of your synthesis, presenting summaries of your sources and offering your conclusion about the relationship(s).
> - **Revise** so that your synthesis is easy to read. Make sure readers can identify the sources of the ideas and information.
> - **Document** clearly the sources for your synthesis using a standard style of documentation.

Many papers use a **critical synthesis** to provide readers with a unified discussion reflecting the writer's understanding of various perspectives. A critical synthesis also pays special attention to highlighting and summarizing differences and to presenting conclusions about the sources.

> **STRATEGY**   Synthesize perspectives
>
> - Be true to the ideas and information in your sources.
> - Suggest relationships (among conclusions, opinions, ideas, and facts) that go beyond those relationships discussed in your sources.
> - In a thesis statement (3c) or a statement of the central idea of the synthesis, summarize the relationships you observe.
> - Be selective. Focus on material that relates directly to your central idea.
> - Be balanced. Acknowledge facts, opinions, and alternative perspectives that contradict the central idea of your synthesis.
> - Base your synthesis on your own thinking as well as material from your sources.

22l
resrch

Here is the critical synthesis Kimlee Cunningham wrote to introduce the thesis of her academic paper on three Disney animated feature films.

It is probably an exaggeration to say that a character like Belle in *Beauty and the Beast* is a lot like a contemporary feminist. As one critic suggests, "She wants adventure and he wants commitment; he holds a mirror and she hugs a book" (Showalter). However, we should not simply ignore an interpretation like this by claiming "that it takes a classic fairy tale, and turns it around and analyzes it from a modern feminist view" (Hoffman). Even if many people view a film like *Beauty and the Beast* (or *Aladdin*) as "just a love story" (Hoffman), the films nonetheless grow out of the complicated values and roles that shape relationships today. Disney's contemporary portrayal of women characters shows a willingness to change with the times but also a reluctance to abandon traditional values and stereotypes.

4 Interpreting sources

Most research papers or reports should present a point of view about their topic: a conclusion about its meaning or causes, a commitment to a particular course of action, or a stand on an issue. At the same time, you need to share with your readers the various outlooks embodied in your sources, and to indicate why readers should accept your interpretation. Here are basic questions concerning the outlook (or bias) of your sources.

1. Does the source display a balanced perspective in its conclusions?
2. Does the source advocate strongly, though fairly, for a particular point of view?
3. Does the source display one-sided bias, including misrepresentation of facts and distortions of others' positions?

In an **interpretation,** you build on synthesis (see 22l-3) by explicitly including your opinions and giving priority to your own ideas and points of view. Interpreting involves **generalizing** (coming to broad conclusions about what your research has to say about your topic) and **extending** (going beyond this to connect your source's ideas to your own).

> **STRATEGY**   **Prepare an interpretation**
>
> Begin an interpretation by stating the point of view of your source(s) as accurately as possible. Add your own ideas and conclusions. Take into account any strong advocacy (or questionable bias) in the source(s).
>
> 1. Present material from your sources accurately. Select material most relevant to the point you want to make, but do not suppress contradictory, biased, or partisan material.
> 2. Present your point of view and provide supporting evidence, perhaps comparing the perspective of one source to that of another and to your own.
> 3. Add interpretations and conclusions of your own not present in the sources, or present in a different form.

Visit mycomplab.com for more resources and exercises on researching and writing.

CHAPTER 23

Library Resources

Libraries give you access to books, periodicals, recordings, government documents, microforms, historical archives, collections, and, through computer terminals, CD-ROMs and online resources (see Chapter 24). As research locations, libraries have distinct advantages and disadvantages.

Advantages

- Books, microforms, and other publications may not be available online.
- Reference librarians can provide considerable help and advice—and are eager to do so.
- Internet access at a library allows you to follow a strand of research at *one* location, whether it takes you to printed sources, databases, or the Web.

Disadvantages

- Library research may require a considerable block of time, and library hours may not correspond with your schedule.
- Library resources may be difficult to navigate, especially when you are not familiar with the organization of research libraries.

23a From general to specific resources

Your research will usually move from general, less detailed sources to specific, more detailed ones as you narrow your topic and begin adding depth of detail and evidence to your writing. The distinction between general and specific treatment of a topic holds true for online and field resources also, but it is especially sharp for library resources.

General resources

You can use general resources to gain a broad overview of a topic, including background information, and a sense of relationships to other subjects. General references can also provide names, keywords, and phrases useful for tracing a topic, as well as bibliographies of potential resources.

LIBRARY RESOURCES FOR THREE COMMUNITIES		
ACADEMIC SETTINGS	**PUBLIC SETTINGS**	**WORK SETTINGS**
Research libraries offer resources often unavailable in public libraries or through the Internet. Scholarly journals, specialized books, government documents, and limited circulation magazines offer access to current research and information about work in technical fields. Microforms and recordings provide records of unpublished papers, conference presentations, and artistic performances. Online catalogs often include the holdings of more than one library and enable access through interlibrary loans.	Research libraries generally subscribe to a wide range of national and international magazines, enabling researchers to identify public concerns and needs for information. Local, national, and international newspapers provide opportunities to note current issues and problems that concern either specific or general public audiences. Government documents provide access to important information for the public and to the services and actions of public agencies.	Research libraries subscribe to magazines, newsletters, and newspapers, often directed at business or professional audiences, enabling researchers to identify current challenges or recent developments of importance to their organizations. Government documents provide information about regulations, policies, and programs of interest to readers in the workplace. Research librarians can help locate information about companies, financial organizations, and international trade and governmental relations.

General encyclopedias, ready references, maps, and dictionaries.
These works provide very basic information on a wide range of topics. They are good places to find an overview of your topic, but they don't usually provide in-depth information.

> *New Encyclopaedia Britannica, Columbia Encyclopedia, Microsoft Encarta, World Almanac and Book of Facts, Canadian Almanac and Directory, Statistical Abstract of the United States, National Geographic Atlas of the World, The American Heritage Dictionary of the English Language, Oxford English Dictionary*

23a
source

Specialized encyclopedias and dictionaries. These volumes provide greater depth of coverage of a specific topic or area. Such works can be easily located in a library's catalog or by searching online.

> *Dictionary of the Social Sciences, Dictionary of American Biography, Current Biography, Who's Who in America, McGraw-Hill Encyclopedia of Science and Technology, Encyclopedia of World Art, International Encyclopedia of Business and Management, Encyclopedia of Advertising, International Encyclopedia of Film, International Television Almanac, Encyclopedia of Computer Science, Encyclopedia of Educational Research, Dictionary of Anthropology,*

Encyclopedia of Psychology, Encyclopedia of the Environment, New Grove Dictionary of Music and Musicians, Encyclopedia of Nursing Research, Encyclopedia of Religion, Encyclopedia of Sociology, Women's Studies Encyclopedia

Bibliographies. These works provide organized lists of books and articles on specific topics within a field of study or interest.

Bibliographic Index: A Cumulative Bibliography of Bibliographies, MLA Bibliography of Books and Articles on the Modern Languages and Literatures, International Bibliography of the Social Sciences, Foreign Affairs Bibliography, Film Research: A Critical Bibliography with Annotations and Essays

23b Kinds of library resources

In general, library resources fall into two categories, each with its own system for locating specific sources.

- Books, pamphlets, and miscellaneous resources including photographs, films, and recordings: Use **online catalogs.**
- Articles in magazines, scholarly journals, and other periodicals: Use **electronic and print indexes,** some of which may be accessed through a library's Web site.

1 Online catalogs

Library catalogs give you access to books and to many other resources, including periodicals, recordings, government documents, films, historical archives, and collections of photographs. Your library's catalog is most likely an **online catalog,** though **card catalogs** are still in use in some small libraries. You can search under the *author's name,* the *title of a work,* the *subject area,* the title of a *series or periodical containing the work,* and, in some libraries, *words in the title or in a work's description.*

Rachel Torres discovered that her library belonged to a group of college libraries when she began her search for resources on Afro-Cuban music. She began by typing her topic into the search screen, and the catalog returned a number of possible sources (see Figure 23.1 on page 296).

Torres chose item 4 from the list, and the next catalog screen provided detailed information about the book along with the location of an available copy at a cooperating library (see Figure 23.2 on page 297).

If none of the libraries had had the book in its collection, she would have been able to get a copy through a lending service called **interlibrary loan.** Many online catalogs even allow you to search the catalogs of other libraries within a consortium of libraries.

23b
source

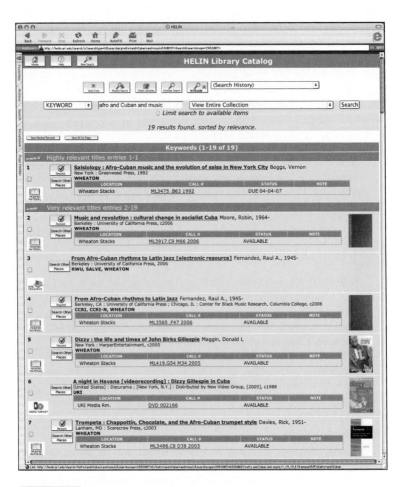

FIGURE 23.1   Search results for the keywords *Afro and Cuban* and *music*

2 Periodicals, print and electronic indexes, and government documents

Periodicals are publications containing articles by numerous authors. **General-interest magazines** appear once a month or weekly, with each issue paginated separately. **Scholarly journals** generally appear less frequently than magazines, perhaps four times a year, often with page numbers running continuously through the sequence of issues that make up an annual volume. **Newspapers** generally appear daily or weekly and frequently consist of separately numbered (or lettered) sections.

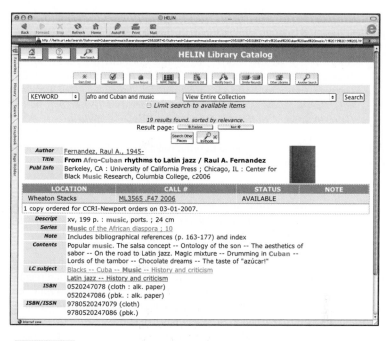

FIGURE 23.2 Detailed information for one entry under *Afro and Cuban and music*

Most scholarly journals are still available primarily in printed form, though many colleges and universities now subscribe to journals in electronic form, with current and back issues available online either through terminals in the library or through the library's Web site. Many general-interest magazines and newspapers are now available in electronic as well as printed form.

You can locate articles in print (and in electronic form) by consulting the many **indexes.** Many of these aids are quite specialized in coverage, providing lists or electronic links to related resources. They may also offer brief summaries (or **abstracts**) of the contents of articles and books.

23b
source

General and newspaper indexes. These indexes give you a way to search for topics in newspapers, magazines, and other periodicals intended for the general public as well as some intended for more specialized audiences.

Academic Index, Readers' Guide to Periodical Literature, Wall Street Journal Index, Washington Post Index, PAIS (Public Affairs Information Services), InfoTrac, Editorials on File, Hispanic American Periodicals Index, OCLC/World Catalog

Specialized indexes. Specialized indexes provide ways to search through publications that contain professional, technical, and academic resources.

> *Anthropological Literature, Art Index, Humanities Index, Music Index, BIZZ (Business Index), EconLit, Education Index, ERIC Current Index to Journals in Education, Index to Legal Periodicals, Social Sciences Index, Applied Science and Technology Index, General Science Index, Geobase, Index Medicus, Medline*

Abstracts. Collections of abstracts bring together brief summaries of articles in specialized fields.

> *Abstracts of English Studies, Biological Abstracts, Chemical Abstracts, Dissertation Abstracts International, Historical Abstracts, Language and Language Behavior Abstracts, Newspaper Abstracts, Psychological Abstracts, Sociological Abstracts*

Government documents are reports of information and research, records of hearings, pamphlets, public information publications, and regulations issued by Congress, federal agencies, and state and local governments. These documents, rich sources of information both general and technical, are sometimes housed in separate collections in a library.

To access government documents published after 1976, search the *Catalog of U.S. Government Publications.* Its Web site is <http://catalog.gpo.gov/>. Follow the directions on screen to locate the records for publications you want to consult. Copy information about the documents, including the SuDocs number, which many libraries use to identify documents on their shelves. (Note: Many government documents are available electronically.) For government documents published before 1976, consult the printed *Monthly Catalog of United States Government Publications.* Use its index to find information about the publications you need, including the SuDocs number.

In reading several magazine and newspaper articles about tornadoes, Michael Micchie noticed that some writers cited government documents and government-sponsored research as the source of their information. He decided to see what government publications he could find that addressed tornadoes and especially the problem of detecting them before they do harm. His search using the keyword *tornadoes* returned nineteen citations, each with a link to a full description of the document and a link to a list of libraries likely to have a copy of it. Figure 23.3 shows part of the response he received.

23b
source

Exercise 1

Make a list of the resources named in 23b–d that you are not familiar with but that might be appropriate for your research. Choose two and examine them briefly. List the potential sources about which they provide information.

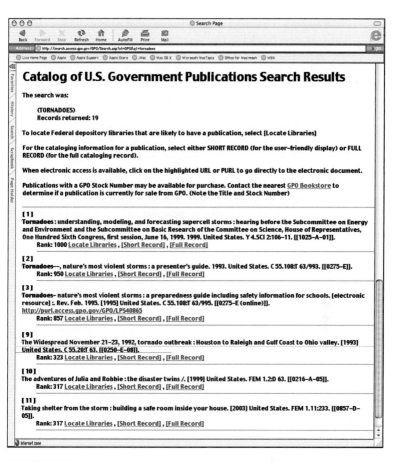

FIGURE 23.3 Search results for the keyword *tornadoes* in U.S. government publications

23c Evaluating library resources

Library sources—books from reputable publishers, articles from scholarly or well-known periodicals, government documents—often have been reviewed by experts and produced with editorial checks. Even so, once you locate these sources, you'll need to decide whether they are appropriate for your research community and your questions and whether they support or deepen your thesis.

Questions for evaluating library sources

- Does the publisher, journal, or sponsoring organization have a reputation for balance and accuracy? Is it an *advocate* whose views require caution?

- Is the author's reputation clear? What do other sources think of the author's fairness, reliability, and importance?
- How accurate is your source, especially if it presents facts as truth? Can you spot obvious errors? Which points are well documented?
- How does the author support generalizations? Do they go beyond the facts? Are they consistent with your knowledge?
- Are the ideas generally consistent with those in your other sources? If not, do they seem insightful or misleading and eccentric?
- Does the source meet the expectations of your research community?
- Does the source appropriately document information, quotations, and ideas or clearly attribute them to other authors?
- Has the source appeared without an editorial or review process? Does it apply only to a specific setting? Is its information outdated? Does it cite experts who have political or financial interests? Does it try to obscure its own bias? If so, consider it questionable; use it with caution.

Visit mycomplab.com **for more resources and exercises on using library** resources.

CHAPTER 24

Databases

Texts in electronic form have begun replacing printed articles, documents, and even books. College, university, and public libraries have greatly increased the number of online collections (or databases) of electronic documents they make available, and they will probably continue to do so. These electronic databases have clear advantages as well as some disadvantages.

Advantages

- The number of publications to which a library provides access is greatly increased by the number of electronic databases available.
- The texts available through databases are often identical in content and presentation to the printed versions.
- Many databases provide abstracts (summaries of content).
- Databases often provide search engines useful for locating a document as well as related publications.
- Databases are often available both through library terminals and on a library's Web site.

Disadvantages

- The most recent issues of publications are sometimes not available in database form.
- The range and number of texts available through databases are growing rapidly, yet not all publications are available through electronic databases.
- Some articles are available only in abstract form, not full-text form through databases.
- Most databases do not enable you to look at entire issues of a periodical, only at individual articles. As a result, you may not be aware of groupings of texts created by the editors of a journal or periodical.

24a Reference databases

Reference databases are simply files of information available through the Internet or the Web or, occasionally, on CD-ROMs. Most databases

RESEARCH DATABASE RESOURCES FOR THREE COMMUNITIES		
ACADEMIC SETTINGS	**PUBLIC SETTINGS**	**WORK SETTINGS**
Research libraries offer database resources and generally pay the subscription fees for users. (Large public libraries may also offer access to research databases.) The high cost of print subscriptions to scholarly publications means that libraries are often able to offer access to a wider range of online scholarly journals, specialized books, government documents, and limited circulation magazines than to their print equivalents. Specialized searching tools in databases help researchers identify technical and scholarly sources not accessible through Internet searches. Databases provide full texts of hard-to-locate sources.	Research and public libraries subscribe to databases providing access to articles in popular and specialized magazines, local and national newspapers, and professional or technical newsletters addressing topics of public interest. Databases contain current publications, and their search engines may allow users to highlight a specific set of dates, a locale, an issue, or a topic. Databases may provide collections of materials on a particular topic or issue.	Research and public libraries subscribe to databases providing information on profit-making and nonprofit organizations, including their operations, policies, management strategies, and financial condition. This information is sometimes not available in print form or it is available only after it is no longer current. Information on the latest regulations or developments often appears in online publications indexed and made accessible through databases.

focus on specialized or technical fields. Specialized databases are expensive to construct and maintain; they index hundreds of thousands of documents and must be updated continually to serve the needs of researchers who require access to the latest information, ideas, and results of experiment and inquiry. Consequently, most databases restrict access to paying customers, but access is allowed to students and faculty at most universities, their fees paid by the library making the database available.

Databases are of several kinds, varying according to the kinds of information they provide: *full-text databases*, *databases containing abstracts*, and *indexing* or *bibliographic databases*. Other kinds of databases include those providing research aids and those housing various kinds of information such as pictures or statistics. Databases also differ according to field of study or interest and in the number and range of resources they contain.

Databases are generally searchable by author, title, and keyword or by special categories that reflect the scope and emphasis of the particular materials included in a collection.

24b Full-text databases

Full-text databases list articles and other documents and provide brief summaries of the content of each item. In addition, they provide the entire texts of all or most of the items indexed. As a result, they can save you time and effort in locating the texts of potential sources. In their coverage, full-text databases range from extensive collections of scholarly or general interest articles like *Academic Search Premier* and *Academic Universe* to highly focused collections like *Health Reference Center Academic.*

Some of the most useful full-text databases are listed below.

- **General full-text databases**

Academic Search Premier (EBSCOhost)
Full texts of thousands of scholarly publications in such fields as social sciences, humanities, education, computer science, engineering, language and linguistics, arts and literature, medical sciences, and ethnic studies. Most entries are from the early 1990s to the present.

Academic Universe (LexisNexis)
News, law, and business information. Includes news from national and international newspapers and wire services; articles from hundreds of periodicals; and other reference sources.

National Newspapers
Indexing, abstracts, and full text of the *New York Times*, the *Wall Street Journal*, the *Washington Post*, and the *Christian Science Monitor*, beginning in the 1980s.

InfoTrac OneFile (InfoTrac)
News and periodical articles on topics such as business, computers, current events, economics, education, environmental issues, health care, hobbies, humanities, law, literature and art, politics, science, social science, sports, and technology.

- **Specialized full-text databases**

CQ Researcher
Weekly reports on topics such as social issues, environment, health, education, science, and technology. Each report focuses on one issue and includes pros and cons, charts and graphs, lengthy bibliographies, and discussions by a variety of researchers or experts.

National Environmental Publications Internet Site
More than 6,000 full-text EPA documents published since 1977.

**24b
source**

Health Reference Center—Academic (InfoTrac)
Provides articles from the last thirty years on subjects such as
fitness, pregnancy, medicine, nutrition, diseases, public health,
occupational health and safety, alcohol and drug abuse, HMOs,
and prescription drugs.

Jenny Latimer (see Chapter 22) was looking for factual information to
use in her paper about the presence of hydrogenated oils in snack foods, especially candy. She knew her research would involve technical information,
but she didn't know which field of study would be most likely to provide the
information she needed: food science and nutrition? health sciences? chemistry? biology? In addition, she was worried about finding herself limited to
sources that were too technical for her to understand or explain to readers.
As a result, she decided to consult a database that covered general-interest
as well as academic publications and to use one that provided both abstracts
and full texts.

First she entered her search terms into the query screen of the database, using the terms *hydrogenated oils* and *candy*. When the search engine
was unable to identify any sources using these terms, she broadened the
search by using the terms *hydrogenated oils* and *food* (using the Boolean operator AND; see 25b-2). This search identified sixteen sources, some of
which seemed promising (see Figure 24.1).

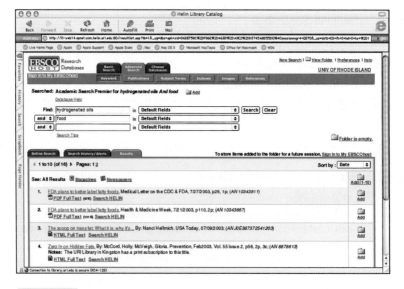

24b
source

FIGURE 24.1 Database search results for the terms *hydrogenated oils* and
food, using a Boolean operator

Latimer looked at the first four articles, both the abstract and the full text, and took notes on several. One of them provided specific examples she felt might be important for her paper (see Figure 24.2).

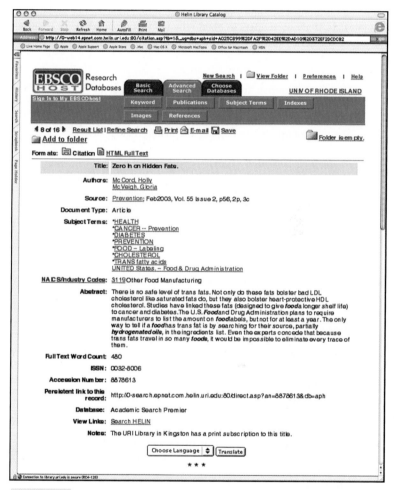

FIGURE 24.2 Detailed information for one entry under *hydrogenated oils* and *food*

After reading and taking notes, Latimer decided that the areas of study most likely to provide her with the kinds of information and insights she needed for her paper were nutrition studies and health sciences.

24c Databases containing abstracts

A large number of databases, especially those focusing on academic or technical fields, provide abstracts (brief summaries of a document's content) and sometimes full texts of selected items. A new feature of some of these databases is a link to a library's online subscription to academic and technical journals. It allows readers to obtain the full text of an article in a journal for which the library has an online subscription.

PsycINFO
Abstracts of journal articles and books in psychology.

CINAHL (OVID)
Abstracts of articles on nursing and health-related subjects.

Sociological Abstracts (CSA)
Abstracts and indexes of articles, books, dissertations, and conference papers in sociology and behavioral sciences.

Biological Abstracts
Abstracts of articles in journals in the life sciences.

America: History and Life (ABC-CLIO)
Abstracts of journal articles and other materials covering the history of the United States and Canada.

MLA Bibliography (FirstSearch)
Indexes and abstracts of journals, books, and other materials in language and literature.

ComAbstracts
Abstracts of articles in the field of communications.

MEDLINE (FirstSearch)
Indexes and provides abstracts of journals in medicine.

ERIC (FirstSearch)
Abstracts of journals and other materials in education.

Jenny Latimer's search for information on hydrogenated oils in foods led her to research in nutrition and health sciences and to the database *Health Reference Center—Academic*, which provides abstracts of scholarly articles and conference presentations. In this database she found an abstract that suggested that the dangers of hydrogenated oils are not as clear as many people claim (see Figure 24.3).

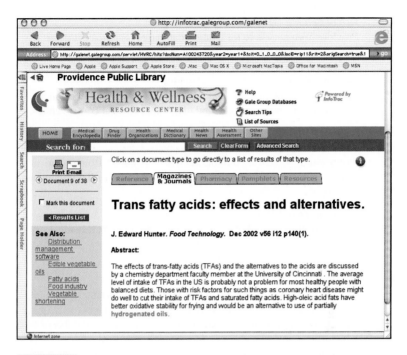

FIGURE 24.3 An abstract from the database *Health Reference Center—Academic*

24d Indexing or bibliographic databases

Many databases provide titles and publication (or access) information for articles and documents in a specialized field. They can be quite useful for identifying and locating potential sources. But you will generally need to locate the texts of these sources by other means, though some databases do provide a link to a library's online subscription to a scholarly journal.

Art Index (FirstSearch)
Indexes over 400 publications in the arts.

GEOBASE (FirstSearch)
Indexes over 2,000 journals on topics in geology, geography, and ecology.

24e Resource databases

Resource databases provide access to information, images, and documents arranged in the form of an electronic reference work, or they offer tools for researchers. Three databases may be helpful in conducting research and writing a research paper.

24e
source

Web of Science (ISI)
Provides Web access to ISI citation databases (*Science Citation Index, Social Sciences Citation Index,* and *Arts & Humanities Citation Index*). Citation indexes allow you to identify the sources used by researchers in their work and to track the strands of a research conversation. In doing so, you can trace influences on a researcher's or writer's work and identify issues and controversies.

RefWorks (CSA)
Web-based service that helps you to create reference lists or lists of works cited by drawing bibliographical information from online sources. Creates bibliographical entries in more than 100 documentation styles.

WorldCat (FirstSearch)
Catalog of library holdings and Internet resources worldwide.

STRATEGY Use reference databases effectively

- Use the databases described in this section only as a starting point. Watch for databases that are better suited to your needs.
- Most libraries prepare handouts describing the online databases to which they subscribe and provide detailed, practical advice. These handouts will provide you with up-to-date information on the availability and features of the library's databases.
- Move from general databases to more specialized ones.
- Keep detailed records of the databases you consult and the possible sources, abstracts, or full texts you have located. Download or print out copies.
- Pay attention to links and alternative search paths suggested by a database; they may lead you to unexpected and worthwhile resources.
- When the full text of an article is not available online, check your library's catalog to see if it is available.
- If a database provides only an abstract or a citation to an article, check if the database will email you the full text. Some databases charge for this service; others will provide texts for free.

24e
source

Exercise 1

Spend time searching electronic databases (general and specialized) for possible sources, and take notes on one or more full-text documents appropriate for your project. Then list briefly what you consider the advantages and disadvantages of databases as a resource.

24f Evaluating database resources

Database texts are often electronic versions of printed texts—books from reputable publishers, articles from scholarly or well-known periodicals, government documents—which have been reviewed by experts and produced with editorial checks. Even so, once you locate these sources, you'll need to decide whether they are appropriate for your research community and your questions and whether they support or deepen your thesis.

Other database texts appear only in electronic form, created by organizations, individual authors, or even database providers themselves. To evaluate both kinds of texts, the questions on pages 299–300 for evaluating library sources will be helpful. Additional questions for database sources follow.

> **STRATEGY**   Evaluate database sources
>
> - Does the database provider, the journal or periodical, or the sponsoring organization have a reputation for balance and accuracy? Is it an advocate whose views require caution?
> - Is an abstract or summary consistent with the title of the source (if the full text is not provided) or with other texts by the same author or from the same organization?
> - Is the electronic document complete, or has it been excerpted or otherwise altered from the print original? Are changes from the original indicated clearly? Are the changes consistent with the purpose and perspective of the original text?
> - Are the sources of documents clearly indicated in the electronic text?
> - Do the electronic documents cite sources in conventional ways?
> - Are the goals and coverage of a database indicated clearly?

Visit mycomplab.com for more resources and exercises on using database resources.

CHAPTER 25

Internet Resources

Many writers begin their research on the World Wide Web. They do so because of its accessibility, the vast number and wide range of resources available, and the currentness of much of the information and opinions that Web sites offer. But Web research has important limitations. The texts are often shorter, less detailed, and less fully developed in explanation or argument than print texts. The review and editorial processes to which print texts are often submitted are frequently missing from Web sites. And the absence of cataloging and indexing systems makes the use of search tools and a well-thought-out search strategy a necessity.

Critical evaluation, an important part of your research in printed sources, is even more important when you review Web sites (see 25d). As a consequence, you should generally make these sources only a part—not the whole—of the resources on which you draw.

INTERNET RESOURCES FOR THREE COMMUNITIES

ACADEMIC SETTINGS	PUBLIC SETTINGS	WORK SETTINGS
Some scholarly and technical resources are available online. Researchers need to evaluate the information and conclusions carefully, paying particular attention to the people or organizations responsible for a document and to the accuracy and level of bias in a text. Some Web search engines, such as <Google.scholar>, specialize in locating scholarly and technical Web resources. More general search engines may not identify such resources.	Web sites provide insights into public concerns and issues, along with detailed information. Discussion sites may provide an in-depth view of opinions, arguments, and counterarguments. Accuracy and bias are always concerns with Web and Internet documents, so researchers need to evaluate carefully the sources of documents and the information they contain as well as the purposes and biases of the people responsible for them.	The Web provides many up-to-date documents for organizations responding to internal or external challenges. Information on the Web may be copyrighted or proprietary, however, so borrowing or implementing material may require formal permission from those responsible for a Web site. Web sites may also provide the most current information on new developments or policies—information whose accuracy generally needs to be carefully evaluated.

25a Internet search strategy

Your search strategy for Internet resources should be part of your general search strategy, which also covers library and field resources. In creating your Internet search strategy, emphasize diversity.

The sheer volume of available resources and the lack of a standard catalog or classification system for Web and Internet documents mean you should know the available search tools, their strengths and their weaknesses, and you should include these tools in your search strategy.

STRATEGY   Create an Internet research checklist

Use the following list as a reminder to include a wide range of electronic resources in your research.

- Web sites
- Online versions of printed texts
- Online databases (see Chapter 24)
- Online collections of documents
- Discussion groups and newsgroups
- Visual and audio documents
- Synchronous devices
- Links

25b Search engines

To locate sites relevant to your research, use a **search engine,** an electronic search tool that identifies and gathers data about Web sites and organizes information about those sites for your use. The kinds of sites a search engine identifies, the kinds of information it gathers, and the ways it selects and organizes information depend on two things: (1) the principles on which the search engine operates and (2) the questions you ask of it.

1 General search engines

General search engines typically search for resources according to keywords or phrases you type into a field. Search engines do not index the entire Web; each one examines only a part of the potential sites on the Web, some more, some less. In addition, the Web site descriptions that search engines provide can vary considerably. Since these descriptions often shape your decision to consult or ignore a site, you need to read them carefully. It is worth your while, therefore, to use several search engines.

25b
source

GENERAL SEARCH ENGINES

Google	<http://www.google.com>
Bing	<http://www.bing.com>
AltaVista	<http://altavista.com>
Yahoo!	<http://www.yahoo.com>
Lycos	<http://www.lycos.com>
HotBot	<http://hotbot.com>

Rashelle Jackson was working on a project guided by this research question: "What techniques used in hip-hop performance make it different from other kinds of music?" She typed the words *hip hop techniques* into several search engines, and each responded with lists of resources that included a site with the title "The Phonograph Turntable and Performance Practice in Hip Hop Music." But the descriptions of the site provided by the first three search engines were uninformative, incomplete, even misleading. Only the fourth gave her a good idea of the site's contents and its relevance to her search.

SEARCH ENGINE RESULTS FOR *HIP HOP TECHNIQUES*

SEARCH ENGINE 1

The Phonograph Turntable and Performance Practice in **Hip Hop** . . .
. . . This transformation has been concurrent with the invention by the **Hip Hop** DJ of a . . . sliding lever which allows the performer to effect certain **techniques** on a . . .

SEARCH ENGINE 2

The **Phonograph Turntable** and Performance Practice in **Hip Hop** Music
The **Phonograph Turntable** and Performance Practice in **Hip Hop** Music Miles White . . . globalization of **Hip Hop** music and culture . . . invention by the **Hip Hop** DJ of a new technical . . . capabilities of . . .

SEARCH ENGINE 3

The **Phonograph Turntable** and Performance Practice in **Hip Hop** Music
White. Introduction . . .

SEARCH ENGINE 4

The **Phonograph Turntable** and Performance Practice in **Hip Hop** Music
The **Phonograph Turntable** and Performance Practice in **Hip Hop** Music Miles White . . . globalization of **Hip Hop** music and culture . . . invention by the **Hip Hop** DJ of a new technical . . . capabilities of the **phonograph,** a process which . . . Description: The popularization and globalization of **Hip Hop** music and culture over the past twenty or so years has provided new and refreshing areas of inquiry and research across a number of academic disciplines and critical approaches. The scholarly work . . .

STRATEGY Improve search results

Standard searches sometimes return disappointing or confusing results. The keywords or phrases you enter may not be the ones used by some sites, and the search engine passes them by. When that happens, try synonyms or related words and phrases. In searching for information on techniques employed in hip-hop performances, Rashelle Jackson employed a variety of terms: *hip-hop techniques, DJ techniques, scratching, cueing, beatboxing, crossfader technique, beat matching,* and other terms she drew from her own knowledge and the sources she consulted. Each term produced a slightly different list of sources, with some overlap.

Your query may be appropriate but the results disappointing because of a quirk in the search engine. For instance, in researching a paper on the singer Amy Grant, you might type in her name and get a few useful references and others that appear simply because they contain the two words of her name—in unconnected form: "List of recent graduates: . . . **Amy** Hollings, Rebecca Olivera, **Grant** Snyder. . . ."

2 Advanced searches

Many search engines offer advanced options (or screens) that enable you to specify and focus the conditions of a search (see Figure 25.1). To expand or limit your electronic search, use **Boolean logic** to link terms with

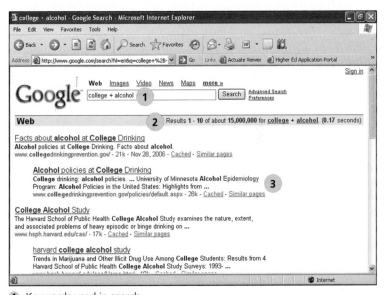

1 Keywords used in search
2 Results of search
3 One source with annotation

FIGURE 25.1 Results of a *Google* search using the keywords *college* and *alcohol*

25b
source

the operators OR, AND, and NOT. Consult the instructions on the main page of the search engine to see if this strategy will help.

OR (expands): X OR Y	Search for either term (documents referring to either X or Y)
AND (restricts): X AND Y	Search for both terms (documents referring to both X and Y, but not to either alone)
NOT (excludes): X NOT Y	Search for X unless X includes the term Y (documents referring to X, except those that also refer to Y)

DISCOVERING A SEARCH ENGINE'S CAPABILITIES

At the main page of your search engine, find the link to the page that explains the system ("search tips," "about this site," etc.). Find answers to as many of the following questions as possible.

- How is the system organized?
- What are the basic search procedures?
- Does the engine recognize Boolean operators? Which ones?
- Does the engine exclude "stop words" such as *where* and *how*, which slow down a search? If so, what command executes that exclusion?
- What are the advanced search features? What procedures can you use to conduct a search *within* preliminary results?
- Can you personalize the engine?
- How are results displayed? Can you vary the parameters of that display, such as increasing the number on each page while decreasing the length of the annotations, or vice versa?

---

3 Metasearch sites

A **metasearch** site enables you to conduct your search using several search engines simultaneously—and then to compare the results. Conducted early in your research, a metasearch can help you identify which search engines are most likely to be useful for your task. Metasearches can also suggest interesting new directions for your inquiry. Here are three useful sites.

25b
source

Dogpile	<http://dogpile.com>
Momma	<http://www.momma.com>
Metacrawler	<http://metacrawler.com>

4 Focused search sites and question-oriented sites

Some search sites focus on specific disciplines, fields of inquiry, or content areas. As you narrow your search, these focused search sites become more useful. Academic research papers (in sociology, art history, and literature, for example) can benefit especially from specialized sites such as *Google Scholar* at <http://scholar.google.com>.

Other search tools allow you to ask questions rather than use keywords: for example, *Ask* at <http://ask.com>. Or they may link keyword queries to what (sometimes) are related, relevant resources, as does *WebReference* at <http://webreference.com>.

25c Kinds of Web sites

To identify and use appropriate resources online, you should recognize some important kinds of sites, their content, purposes, and uses.

1 Individual Web sites

Individual Web sites are not necessarily *about* individual persons, though they may be, as is the case with *home pages* created by individuals to share events in their lives, their opinions, or their collections. Although many Web sites are so idiosyncratic or personal as to be of little use for research, others may prove to be good resources. Some home pages share accounts of experiences you can cite as examples: white-water rafting, service on a United Nations peacekeeping force, work on an oil rig in Northern Alaska.

Many people maintain Web sites about topics that fascinate them or about issues on which they have strong opinions (see 25c-3). Though some such sources are sloppy, out of date, inaccurate, or misleading, others are rich sources of information and ideas and may offer links to more valuable resources. Approach these resources critically, but with an awareness of their potential usefulness. At the very least, they may help you understand the attitudes at least some of your readers will have about your topic.

2 Sponsored Web sites

Organizations of all kinds sponsor Web sites: public, private, corporate, academic, governmental, religious, and social. The suffixes on the electronic addresses often indicate what kind of organization the sponsor is.

edu	educational institution
gov	government agency
org	nonprofit or service organization
com	business organization (commercial)
net	network organization

The usefulness and the integrity of a site generally depend on the character of the sponsoring organization and the resources devoted to creating and maintaining it. When examining sponsored Web sites, use the evaluation questions for online resources (25d) and draw information and ideas from the site with an awareness of its purpose and the bias of the sponsoring organization.

You may find two types of sponsored Web sites particularly helpful in your research: advocacy Web sites and informational Web sites.

Advocacy Web sites. Advocacy Web sites explain or defend an organization's actions and beliefs and argue for specific policies (see Figure 25.2). Although they are biased in favor of the organization's position, many are of high quality, explaining positions, answering critics, and providing *detailed* supporting evidence and documentation along with lists of readings on a topic or issue. Advocacy Web sites include public service Web sites that encourage responsible behavior or action for public health and safety. Unfortunately, good intentions do not guarantee the accuracy or currency of information, and you need to approach these sites as critically as you would any other.

FIGURE 25.2 Home page of an advocacy Web site

FIGURE 25.3 Home page for the American Psychological Association Web site

Informational Web sites. Informational Web sites may focus on a particular subject, such as sleep research, horror movies, or the poetry of the Beat Generation of the 1950s; on an activity such as an environmental project or a process for developing a healthy lifestyle; or on the sponsoring institution itself, providing information about its activities, ongoing research projects, and research results. Carefully organized informational Web sites provide tables of data, historical background, reports of research, answers to frequently asked questions (FAQs), links, and lists of references. Universities, research institutes, and professional organizations often maintain research-oriented Web sites, as does the American Psychological Association (see Figure 25.3). Web sites can also act as repositories, or archives, for collections of documents, images, data, and sound recordings.

Be aware, however, that many informational Web sites are poorly organized, unevenly developed, and even untrustworthy. Look on the Web site for information about the sponsoring organization, how information for the Web site is gathered and maintained, and the date of the last update. To investigate the usefulness and trustworthiness of a particular informational Web site, draw on the advice for evaluating online sources presented in 25d.

While looking for information for a paper on the techniques used in hip-hop performances, Rashelle Jackson reached the Web site shown in Figure 25.4. She identified it as a commercially sponsored Web site featuring hip-hop related products, but she saw that it also offered the kinds of information she wanted and links to a host of other potentially useful sites.

25c
source

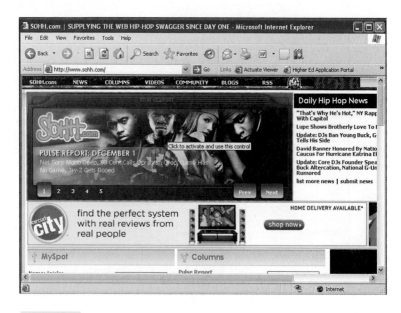

FIGURE 25.4   Commercially sponsored Web site SOHH.com devoted to hip hop

3 Blogs

Blogs are Web sites offering daily or weekly accounts of one person's activities and thoughts. The material available on blogs can be fascinating and useful, especially when they are maintained by people of power and influence, by authorities in a field, or by writers of special skill. Yet such blogs can be untrustworthy, especially those maintained by people about whom we readers know little or nothing. Before drawing on blogs or home pages for your research, find out as much as you can about the person(s) responsible for them, and evaluate their contents critically (see 25d).

4 Electronic versions of print publications

**25c
source**

Online magazines, newspapers, and scholarly journals are similar to print publications in many ways. Indeed, many appear in both online and print versions (see Figure 25.5).

Newsweek	<http://www.newsweek.com>
Business Week	<http://www.businessweek.com>
Weekly Standard	<http://www.weeklystandard.com>
The Nation	<http://www.thenation.com>
Dallas Star-Telegram	<http://www.dfw.com>

Many online sites go one step further and make back issues or selected articles available. Online publications often make use of the Web's ability to

FIGURE 25.5   Current events Web site with photos; such sites may also include audiovisuals

incorporate audio clips and streaming video or to display simultaneously different sections of text in contrasting formats or *frames* (see Figure 25.5 above).

Classic works of literature, major historical texts, biographies, and similar works that appeared first in print are now available in online libraries like *Berkeley Digital Library SunSite* at <http://sunsite.berkeley.edu> and *Gutenberg Project* at <www.gutenberg.org>. Some books now appear only online, though that trend is developing slowly.

5 Government publications sites

Government publications on an astonishing range of topics are available in print form in most college and university libraries (23b). In addition, many government agencies have spent considerable effort developing Web sites for access to their reports and documents. (See Figure 25.6.) Use the following sites to identify government publications relevant to your research.

25c
source

FirstGov   <http://www.firstgov.gov>
Catalog of U.S.   <http://www.access.gpo.gov/su_docs/locators/cgp>
  Government
  Publications
FedStats   <http://www.fedstats.gov/search.html>
FedWord   <http://www.fedworld.gov>

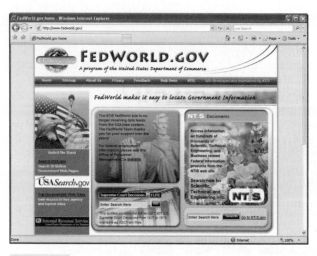

FIGURE 25.6   A Web site that incorporates audio clips and streaming video

6 Discussion groups and newsgroups

The Internet and the Web play host to many discussion groups, some focusing on highly specialized topics like beekeeping, small countries in Eastern Europe or Africa, and poetry slams. The postings to such lists vary in quality, from inquiries by novices to discussions and responses from nationally recognized experts. It can be difficult to judge the quality of contributions because the writers may identify themselves only by screen names. (See 25d for a discussion of ways to evaluate materials from such sources.)

A **discussion group** posts messages from members of a mailing list to all other members and gives them a chance to respond. **Newsgroups** or **bulletin boards** are open sites where you can post messages or questions of your own and read postings from other people. Many search engines will help you locate postings. Those in Figures 25.7 (facing page) and 25.8 (page 322) are from *Google*.

25c
source

25d Evaluating online resources

Online resources pose special problems for evaluation. Many Web sites are produced without the editorial checks and balances that make books from reputable publishers or articles in scholarly journals and some magazines relatively trustworthy sources. In addition, the wide circulation of

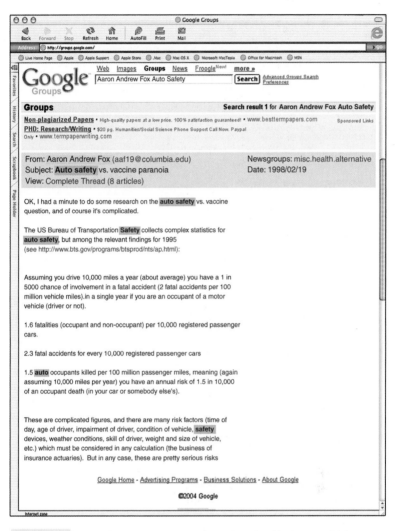

FIGURE 25.7 Discussion group message from *Google* with data on driving fatalities

Web pages means that many people employ them for political or social ends, sometimes without making their purposes clear. A Web site may also fail to announce clearly who is responsible for that site, making it harder to identify biases and evaluate the information and ideas presented.

Begin your work with online resources by asking three sets of questions to help identify the purposes and biases behind the seemingly neutral, factual, or public service approach some Web sites employ.

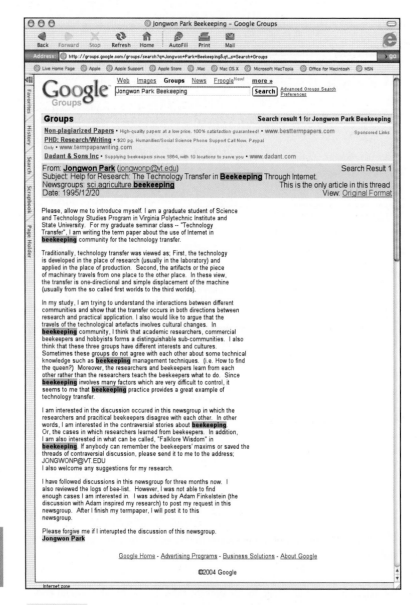

FIGURE 25.8 Discussion group message from *Google* requesting help with personal research

Who benefits? What difference does that make? A Web page on nutrition may be sponsored by a business organization that produces a food (a dairy or a meat producers cooperative) or by a group with a particular set of beliefs (a "slow food" or a "buy local" interest group). Those groups may believe in the importance of their purposes and their commitment to the public good; nonetheless, they benefit from a site, and that site may not give other perspectives as much attention as they deserve.

Who's talking? What difference does that make? The speaker responsible for the "facts" on a Web site may not be clearly identified. Knowing who is talking is an important part of judging the reliability of facts and ideas. Can readers trust the "facts" presented by a group that goes unnamed or whose name is unfamiliar? Perhaps; but giving readers a chance to do more research on the source and to make informed decisions is important.

What's missing? What difference does that make? No site can cover all relevant information and ideas—without being much longer that most readers will tolerate. But does the missing information make a difference? Has something important been left out, something that might contradict the points made in the site? Have the omissions been made for practical reasons, or do they attempt to hide something or thwart further inquiry?

STRATEGY   **Evaluating online resources**

- Does the person or organization responsible for the site or document have a reputation for balance and accuracy? Is it an advocate whose views require caution? Does it make any biases or special perspectives clear?
- Is the document complete, or has it been excerpted or otherwise altered from another document? Are changes from the original indicated clearly, and are they consistent with the purpose and perspective of the original text?
- Does the site provide sufficient, accurate, and verifiable information about the writer or organization responsible? Does it indicate clearly any biases or special perspectives?
- Is the information presented clear and complete? Are sources cited in conventional ways?
- Does the document seem to invite critical examination and questioning, or does it take a hostile perspective to readers who might inquire into the information and ideas it presents?

25d
source

Visit mycomplab.com for more resources and exercises on using internet resources.

CHAPTER 26

Field Resources and Fieldwork

Much of the research you've done in college has probably focused on published sources (books, articles, Web texts). Many researchers, however, also gather information firsthand, "in the field." When you conduct **field research,** you collect information directly from the observation of events, places, and phenomena, or from **informants,** people you interview or survey.

26a Field research

You may wonder what you can learn from people and events "out there," beyond a library or research lab. But if you picked up something to eat at the drive-through of a fast-food restaurant, the service and food you received were probably influenced by surveys other patrons had filled out for market-research companies. If you drank from a water fountain on your way to class, the source of that water is likely to be tested constantly, through field research, to assess its contents and safety.

In thousands of cases, research involves the firsthand collection and analysis of data. Yet fieldwork doesn't exclude information from published resources. In most cases, field researchers supplement their work with data gathered by other researchers and writers, or they refer to prior research in order to extend or refine it. Still, your own fieldwork will yield original results—that is, the material in your research paper or report will come from your work, not from somebody else's research, and the information and ideas you present are more likely to be fresh and original.

It's important that you begin your field research with a completely open mind or a neutral perspective on what you're investigating. If you launch your original field research too quickly, you might overlook important perspectives or miss the chance to think more carefully about your data-gathering process. Instead, do some background research before beginning a field research project. What have other people said or found out about your topic? What problems or unanswered questions arise from their work? Be sure to plan your fieldwork carefully so that you won't feel you've missed something important.

FIELD RESEARCH IN THREE COMMUNITIES		
ACADEMIC SETTINGS	**PUBLIC SETTINGS**	**WORK SETTINGS**
Field researchers in sociology, psychology, business, education, and urban planning may study people's behaviors or outlooks in order to identify patterns or causes and effects. Anthropologists study human and social behavior by immersing themselves as much as possible in a culture: they make observations, participate in events or rituals, take copious notes, and try to make sense of their experiences and records. When field research takes the form of scientific inquiry in chemistry, engineering, and pharmacy, it investigates how substances, organisms, objects, and machines work or can be constructed.	Field researchers in public settings often collect and interpret people's opinions, attitudes, and values in relation to policies, public programs, and institutions as well as to issues affecting society. Government-sponsored research in the public interest provides information that can have profound effects on laws and regulations. Researchers working for the Environmental Protection Agency collect samples of soil, water, and air from across the country to measure the levels of pollutants or contaminants.	Field researchers in businesses and other organizations look at how customers (or staff) act and interact, focusing on problems, programs, or future actions and choices. Industrial researchers may study a manufacturing plant to look for inefficiencies in production. Market researchers conduct extensive polls and surveys to gauge the public's interest in a product, and they may recruit people to take taste tests or engage in "focus groups" to provide information for improving a product or refining a marketing strategy.

Good field research also involves interpretation. Be prepared to give the data you collect the same kind of critical reading and analysis you give to print and electronic resources (see 23c, 24f, and 25d).

26b Surveys, polls, and questionnaires

Surveys, polls, and questionnaires can be administered orally (a researcher asks questions in a mall or on the phone), on paper (an informant fills out a satisfaction survey in a restaurant), and, increasingly, on computers. Regardless of the format you choose, you'll need to think through your questions carefully and test your instrument before you administer it.

26b
field

1 Surveys and polls

Surveys and **polls** collect short answers, often in *yes* or *no* form. They provide statistics you can present in charts and tables, measure against research findings, and use to support your opinions. Following are a few of the questions Shane Hand asked people about recycling. As they answered, he marked a tally sheet.

DO YOU . . .

use coffee mugs instead of polystyrene cups?	(Yes)	No
reuse plastic wrap, foil, and plastic bags?	Yes	(No)
recycle newspapers and/or magazines?	(Yes)	No

ARE YOU WILLING TO . . .

take your own bags to the store?	(Yes)	No
shop at a store that's harder to get to but carries biodegradable products?	Yes	(No)

2 Questionnaires

Questionnaires allow you to gather more in-depth information, sometimes from a large number of people. Because they're usually mailed or offered on the Internet, most questionnaires don't require the live contact time of interviews, but they need to be prepared carefully so they don't confuse or mislead respondents and ruin a project.

The University of Florida's Office of Financial Aid uses an opinion survey to gauge satisfaction with its services. After some factual, poll-like questions (status of the respondent, number of times he or she used the service), the questionnaire uses a combination of multiple-choice questions and open-ended questions (where respondents can type their thoughts inside boxes). Figure 26.1 shows each type of question. Notice especially the range of possible responses and the relationship between the multiple-choice question (which provides the surveyor with numerical data) and the open-ended question (which allows the respondent to explain his or her choices).

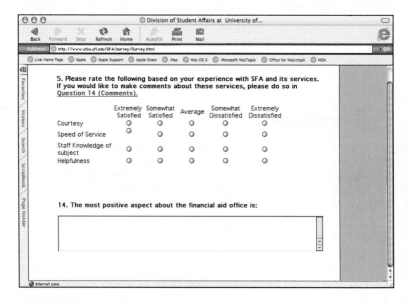

FIGURE 26.1 Sample multiple-choice and open-ended questions from an opinion survey at <http://www.ufsa.ufl.edu/SFA/survey/Survey.html>

STRATEGY   Plan your questionnaire

- *Consider your purpose.* Begin your survey, poll, or questionnaire with a clear sense of what you want to find out and why. Creating and refining a research question (see 22d) will help you to focus on relevant questions or data.
- *Consider your subjects,* the people you will question. Do you want to select them on the basis of gender, age, or occupation? If you are comparing the opinions of college students and parents about alcohol use, you will need a large enough sample from each group to enable you to generalize about the differences you find.
- *Consider what you're expecting.* If your questionnaire is long or complicated, will your respondents tire and toss it away? Consider providing a reward of some sort for answering lengthy surveys and questionnaires. If you're creating a Web-based questionnaire, give respondents a sense of its length before they begin, especially if they can't see all the screens at the start.
- *Consider what you're asking.* Will your respondents be uncomfortable? Will they be able to provide the information without becoming frustrated or finding that "it all depends"? Are your questions too subjective?
- *Consider your location or context.* Think carefully about where you'll conduct your survey or poll because the location you choose may determine what particular groups of people answer your questions. Polling people in a bar about their attitudes toward alcohol use will yield quite different results from conducting the same poll in the parking lot of a health food co-op.
- *Consider the form of your instrument.* Will you ask respondents to write out explanations, check boxes, or circle choices? Will you use a multiple-choice format or a rating scale?
- *Anticipate responses* and design questions accordingly. If you ask a yes or no question, will a yes or no answer give you enough information? If you ask an open-ended question (requiring a freeform written or oral response), how will you organize and make sense of the responses?
- *Draft a list of questions* that will yield the information you want. Scrutinize your wording carefully, and test your draft on at least two or three people. Ask them to describe points at which they were confused or needed more information.
- *Above all, test the instrument.* Ask class members or friends to take your survey, poll, or questionnaire, and to tell you when they were confused or frustrated, or felt something was oversimplified or too subjective. Take note of their problems.
- *Revise the instrument and prepare it for distribution.* You may need to test and revise your instrument several times to get it right. Remember that it's very difficult to readminister a survey or questionnaire if you find serious problems with it after gathering your data (which may be unusable). In your final version, fit your questions on one page (front and back) if possible, but leave room for longhand comments if you will have time to analyze them.

26b
field

26c Interviews

Field researchers use interviews to gather in-depth information from informants or subjects about their opinions or experiences. You can use interviews to supplement your research in print and electronic resources either by talking with experts or by contacting people whose experiences may help you test the validity of the conclusions offered in other sources. You can also decide to make interviews your main method of research.

Interviews can be highly planned or open-ended. As you plan your interview questions, think carefully about your goals and shape the interview protocol accordingly.

STRATEGY   Plan your interview

1. *List potential interviewees.* Begin by formulating questions you'd like to have answered; then list the people who might be able to answer them. Consider whether you'll need to do a thorough, lengthy interview or just collect short answers to a few questions.
2. *Write out questions you want to ask your interviewees.* Arrange your questions logically; avoid those that can be answered yes or no unless you plan follow-ups. If possible, rehearse questions with friends to discover those that are ineffective.
3. *Be courteous when you contact your interviewees.* Explain your project and ask permission to do the interview. (See 26d.)
4. *Use your list of questions, but don't be shackled by it.* Follow the train of new information and ideas as long as it serves your purpose.
5. *Consider recording your interview instead of writing everything down.* Using a tape recorder or other recording equipment will let you focus on the content of the interview. Always ask permission to record your interview, and bring along extra tapes.
6. *After the interview, send a thank-you note to each interviewee.* Not only is this polite procedure, but you may also need a follow-up interview.

Exercise 1

A. Imagine you're writing an interview paper describing someone's unusual occupation. Choose an occupation and draft a list of questions you might ask a person with that occupation during an interview.

B. In a small group, compare and discuss your list of questions. Concentrate on the form of the questions and the sorts of information they might elicit. Consider role-playing parts of your interviews to tease out potential problems in the phrasing of the questions and in the ways an interviewer might follow up on them during the interview.

26d Obtaining human subjects' consent and approval

Whenever you conduct research on human beings, even in administering a questionnaire, you need to abide by certain ethical and legal principles to avoid injuring your subjects. "Injury" doesn't just mean harming someone physically, such as having people test a product that might cause cancer. It can also refer to psychological injury, such as interviewing children about traumatic events in their lives. Furthermore, subjects are protected by privacy laws; although most people know when they become uncomfortable answering questions, they may not always be aware of how the law protects them. Consulting with a teacher or a human subjects board member on your campus will help ensure that your research meets the proper standards.

Most campuses have a committee, board, or administrative unit that provides information and advice on the involvement of human subjects in research. Such boards or committees are responsible for approving plans for research after considering the legal and ethical implications of those plans. Such boards also consider the kinds of information a researcher proposes to gather from subjects, and a board can approve or disapprove a proposal or send it back for revision.

Approval to conduct human subject research is usually required on most campuses—and it has the benefit of protecting the researcher as well as the subjects. Whether you need approval for field research involving human subjects will depend on various factors. In some cases, an entire class can receive general approval to conduct surveys, polls, or questionnaires; in other cases, no approval may be necessary. Be sure that you and your instructor know the practices on your campus, and follow the requirements accordingly.

STRATEGY   Design an ethical research plan

- Explain your research to your subjects. In some cases, you may need to keep the explanation general so that you don't influence their responses, but you should not conceal the purpose and nature of your study.
- Make clear to your subjects what will happen with the data you gather. Who will see the data? How long will it be kept? (Institutional Review Board—IRB—committees have requirements for the collection, use, storage, and disposal of data, and you should follow those requirements.)
- Explain that your subjects' anonymity will be preserved or that they will have the option of anonymity. If you need to use names, will you use pseudonyms?
- Give your subjects the option of seeing the results of your research.

26d
field

26e Ethnographies

You can use **ethnographic research** to interpret the practices, behaviors, language, and attitudes of particular groups that may be tied together by their interests or ways of understanding and acting in the world. Such cultural analyses are at the heart of much important research on human belief and ritual. *Ethnography* means the writing ("graphy") of culture ("ethno"); a written report of ethnographic research (an **ethnography**) aims to provide an in-depth understanding of its subject. For this reason, you may need to use several methods to gather pertinent information about your subject: the **observation** of people, events, and settings; **interviews** with **informants** (people who provide you with information about the group to which they belong); and the collection of **artifacts** (material objects characteristic of a group or culture).

Most full-scale ethnographies require months or even years of participation in a community. But a popular kind of paper in college courses draws on the general principles and methods of ethnography without meeting its requirements for sustained immersion in a context. Such studies are sometimes called micro-ethnographies, mini-ethnographies, or cultural analyses. Their aim is to introduce you to the methods of careful sociocultural analysis without demanding a huge investment of time. Such investigations may require you to choose a group or subculture with which you're unfamiliar, and then spend considerable time "on site," learning about its customs, beliefs, practices, behaviors, and norms. For example, you might spend a series of evenings at the local meeting place of an Alcoholics Anonymous group, or regular hours at the meetings and the convention of a Japanese anime club.

To understand your subject in depth, you'll have to focus your fieldwork on a specific setting, activity, person, or group of people to which you can devote enough time and energy to arrive at worthwhile conclusions. You'll conduct **structured observations** in which you carefully and objectively look at a situation, behavior, or relationship in order to understand its elements and processes. (For instance, in researching the ways preschoolers use language during play, you might arrange and plan in detail a series of structured observations at a day-care center.) You'll interview participants, trying not to make your interviews too formal or to put your subjects on guard. You'll talk to them about their activities and be as spontaneous as possible, writing down as much detail as you can about the physical location and the participants' actions and behaviors.

STRATEGY   Plan a structured observation

1. Choose the site and, if necessary, get permission to conduct your observation or participate in the group.
2. Decide how to situate yourself. Will you move around or remain inconspicuous? How will you explain your presence to the people you are observing?

3. Decide what information you want to gather and why. Consider how you will use it in your report.

4. Consider your means for recording information: tape recorder, camera, notepad, video camera. (The more intrusive your methods, the less likely you may be to get spontaneous data.)

5. Make a list of problems that might arise and develop strategies for dealing with them.

6. Between visits to your site, be sure to reread your notes and reflect on them, generating questions and hypotheses for your next visit.

7. Above all, don't think one visit to your site will suffice. Make multiple visits—the more, the better. People, rituals, agendas, activities can all change between visits, and you'll want as full a picture of your culture or community as you can create.

Visit mycomplab.com for more resources and exercises on conducting fieldwork and using field resources.

CHAPTER **27**

Avoiding Plagiarism and Integrating Sources

Plagiarism, which comes from a Latin word for "kidnapping," refers to the theft of another person's ideas or words. However, plagiarism is fundamentally a cultural concept, part of a system of beliefs and regulations that govern how we write and how we use other people's words.

AVOIDING PLAGIARISM AND INTEGRATING SOURCES IN THREE COMMUNITIES		
ACADEMIC SETTINGS	**PUBLIC SETTINGS**	**WORK SETTINGS**
College professors, researchers, and other professionals view documents and research results as intellectual property of considerable importance. They have high standards for the acknowledgment and documentation of material drawn from print, electronic, or field sources. They also expect conclusions to be supported by extensive use of quotations, ideas, conclusions, and data drawn from authoritative sources that are always carefully cited.	Failure to acknowledge sources of information or texts being summarized and paraphrased can undermine confidence in public documents and in the writers responsible for the documents. Careful acknowledgment (and documentation) of sources, especially for paraphrases and summaries, not just for quotations, is necessary for public writing. Quotations and data from sources are important in informative writing and in argumentative writing, though their use may sometimes be less extensive than in academic documents.	Many organizations are dedicated to producing business surveys, collections of information, and compilations of opinions. Using their work without acknowledgment (and, sometimes, without paying for permission to use it) is wrong. Quotations, graphs, tables, and summaries of information drawn from sources are persuasive and useful elements in much workplace writing, though the level of detail may sometimes be less than in technical and scholarly writing produced in academic settings.

27a Plagiarism in college

While plagiarism exists in all communities, the standards that apply to the acknowledgment of authors and the citation of sources vary from one context to another. In college, the rules on plagiarism are strict and apply to almost any kind of work done for a course. Not learning and following those rules can lead you to a failing grade for a paper or an entire course, a special plagiarism notation on your transcript, and even expulsion from your college or university. Very serious plagiarism, especially at higher levels of research and scholarship, can result in lawsuits and damage judgments that ruin a person's academic or professional career.

According to the Council of Writing Program Administrators (WPA), plagiarism in an academic setting "occurs when a writer deliberately uses someone else's language, ideas, or original (not common-knowledge) material without acknowledging its source" (<www.wpacouncil.org>). Thus, turning in someone else's paper as your own, taking someone's original idea or analysis from a book and passing it off as yours, and copying passages or even sentences from a source into your paper without saying where they came from—all represent plagiarism. Technically, turning in work that you had previously written isn't plagiarism, but by not producing something new, or a substantially reworked version of the original paper, you are violating certain requirements of your school and your courses and denying yourself the chance to learn.

27b The problem of intention

Figure 27.1 is a representation of plagiarism from the perspective of the writer and a reader or teacher. At the top of this figure, cases of plagiarism are conscious and deliberate: you know exactly what you're doing, you know it's wrong, and you take the risk. Toward the bottom of the figure, plagiarism becomes increasingly unconscious—these are cases in which the writer doesn't document sources well, perhaps because he or she has never learned all the elements of proper documentation or comes from a culture where such practices differ. For most honest writers, the problem of plagiarism begins somewhere near the bottom of the figure, as they try to acknowledge sources but do so clumsily or incorrectly.

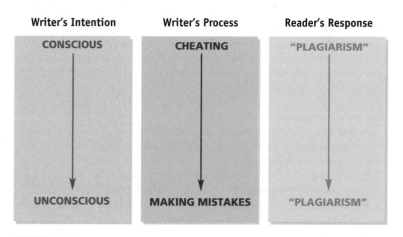

Writer's Intention	Writer's Process	Reader's Response
CONSCIOUS	CHEATING	"PLAGIARISM"
↓	↓	↓
UNCONSCIOUS	MAKING MISTAKES	"PLAGIARISM"

FIGURE 27.1 Plagiarism as seen by the writer and by the reader

27b
plag

Although plagiarism gradually loses its maliciousness and severity as you move from top to bottom of Figure 27.1, it's important for you to realize that *for many readers and teachers, your naiveté makes no difference at all,* as you can see from the right side of the figure. The result *looks* like plagiarism, and you are still likely to be found guilty of academic misconduct, whether you were conscious of it or not, ill-intentioned, or uninformed about how to cite sources.

Little can be said about cases toward the top of Figure 27.1. If you choose to plagiarize consciously and deceptively, your plagiarism will hurt everyone including you: it cheats you out of your learning opportunity, it robs your parents and the taxpayers who may be funding your education, it subverts and complicates the work of teachers who are trying to help you learn, it slows social progress by undermining the achievement of higher standards of education and work, and it assaults those who put the time and energy into producing the work you're stealing.

27c When to document sources

In general, you need to document the words, ideas, and information you draw from another person's work. Keep in mind the three most important reasons for documenting sources.

1. **Add support** to your conclusions and credibility to your explanations by showing that they are based on careful research.
2. **Give credit** to someone for their original work.
3. **Show your readers** where they can obtain the materials you cite (and from there, perhaps others).

Decisions on what needs documenting may vary from audience to audience. If you're writing for a general audience, readers may expect you to cite sources for your discussion of subatomic particles. If you're writing for a physics professor or an audience of physicists, you might fairly assume that such matters are common knowledge. However, in some college classrooms, your teacher may want to know all the works you have consulted in order to see the evidence of your explorations.

You must document
- Word-for-word (direct) quotations taken from someone else's work
- Paraphrases or summaries of someone else's work, whether published or presented informally in an interview or email message
- Ideas, opinions, and interpretations that others have developed and presented, even if they are based on common knowledge
- Facts or data that someone else has gathered or identified if the information is not widely enough known to be considered common knowledge
- Information that is not widely accepted or that is disputed

- Illustrations, charts, graphs, photographs, recordings, original software, performances, interviews, and the like

You do not document
- Ideas, opinions, and interpretations that are your own
- Widely known ideas and information—the sort you can locate in common reference works or that people writing or speaking on a topic usually present as common knowledge
- Commonly used quotations ("To be, or not to be")

27d Common knowledge

In every field, researchers share certain kinds of knowledge. Everyone in medicine, biology, and related sciences knows what a "double helix" is, and if you were to use the term in a research article, you would not have to cite a source for the term itself. Nor would you cite the statement that "it is legal, subject to prior background checks, for Americans to own handguns." Such information is called **common knowledge.**

When you're working in a topic area or discipline that is unfamiliar to you, however, you may not know what counts as common knowledge. Everything will seem equally specialized and worthy of citation. How will you know when to include a source for information you put in your paper and when it's appropriate to assume information is common knowledge?

The answer to this question depends on your intended audience and the community of writers and readers you're working in. Because this relationship can become tricky, you should pay attention to it as you write and revise your paper.

STRATEGY Identify and cite common knowledge

- For any information you have gathered from other sources (that is, whatever is not your own informational contribution), assess whether this information is widely shared by typical educated readers. If it's not, *cite the source.*
- Consider your instructor as a primary audience. Usually, instructors in writing courses and general education courses want to know that you have learned from your sources. From this perspective, it's better to include citations for what might be considered common knowledge in a specialized field.
- Before making a decision, ask others whether they know a piece of information about which you're uncertain whether to credit to a source.
- Use yourself as a litmus test: if you didn't know the information, cite the source.
- When in doubt, *cite.* It's much easier in the revision process to cut a reference than to have to find it again in your notes.

27e Quotations, summaries, facts, and visuals

You can integrate sources into your paper in several ways, as quotations or as summaries and paraphrases. (You may also want to include visuals such as charts, pictures, graphs, and screen shots.)

When you include quotations, paraphrases, and summaries in your writing, you *must* acknowledge their sources. If you don't, you're treating someone else's work as your own.

- Be sure you enclose someone else's exact words in quotation marks.
- Make sure that paraphrases and summaries are in your own words.
- Be sure to cite the source of any ideas or information that you quote, paraphrase, or summarize.

1 Quotations

Quoting someone's words means putting them into your paper or oral presentation in the *exact* way that they appeared in the original text (this is why it's so important that you be accurate in taking notes during your research). Avoid stringing quotations together or setting off many long quotations in blocks (it may look like padding). Instead, use direct quotations

- to show that you're accurately representing ideas that you want to challenge, modify, or extend;
- to preserve an especially stylish, persuasive, or concise way of saying something;
- to show vividly and dramatically what other people think;
- to provide a change of pace or a jumping-off point for your thoughts.

You can quote entire sentences from a source and let them stand on their own, with proper attribution.

> Yet alcohol awareness campaigns have seen only moderate success. "Although heavy drinking and monthly and daily alcohol use among high school seniors have declined since the 1980s, the decline is less among college-bound seniors, and binge drinking is a widespread problem on college campuses" (Bradley and Miller 1).

You can use an **embedded quotation** if it is less than a line or two.

> Yet a 1994 government investigation of the Roswell Incident "located no records at existing Air Force offices that indicated any 'cover-up' by the USAF or any indication of such a recovery" of alien debris (Weaver 1).

A **block quotation** is a long passage from a source, set off from your own prose because of its length (more than four sentences). Remember that readers expect you to *do* something with block quotations, not just insert them.

> Some psychologists believe that conspiracy theories have their origins in the public's trust in authority. If that "authority" is not fully credentialed but appears to be, the public may formulate beliefs that are not supported by evidence, a point made by Robyn M. Dawes in an analysis of why people believe in epidemic cases of child sexual abuse and the presence of satanic cults:
>
> > Asking people to doubt the conclusions concerning widespread childhood sexual abuse and satanic cults is asking them not only to reject the usual bases of authority and consensus for establishing reality, but in addition to accept principles that violate foundations of everyday functioning. Now in point of fact we do ask people to accept such principles, and they do. Few people, for example, believe that the world is flat, even though it appears to be, or believe that cigarettes and alcohol are good for them, even though both may have very pleasant effects. We return once more to the efficacy of authority. People who have no direct experience of the curvature of the earth believe that it is not flat, and even the greatest devotees of tobacco and alcohol believe that these drugs are harming them. We accept what we have been told by "reputable authorities." (We even accept what has been communicated by very minor authority figures, such as the person who draws a map that shows the Suez Canal to be longer than the Panama Canal.) (<http://www.fmsfonline.org/dawes.html>)

2 Summaries and paraphrases

To make your writing smoother and more sophisticated, be selective in using quotations. Usually you can summarize, even combining several sources, or paraphrase, putting a passage in your own words, rather than quote sources directly. (See 22l-1 on summarizing and 22l-2 on paraphrasing.)

The following paraphrase comes too close to repeating the original to be presented without quotation marks. It would be considered plagiarized, even if the writer had done it without knowing better.

27e
plag

ORIGINAL PASSAGE

Malnutrition was a widespread and increasingly severe problem throughout the least developed parts of the world in the 1970s, and would continue to be serious, occasionally reaching famine conditions, as the millennium approached. Among the cells of the human body most dependent upon a steady source of nutrients are those of the immune system, most of which live, even under ideal conditions, for only days at a time.

—LAURIE GARRETT, *The Coming Plague*

POORLY PARAPHRASED VERSION
Garrett points out that malnutrition can give microbes an advantage as they spread through the population. Malnutrition continues to be a severe problem throughout the least developed parts of the world. The human immune system contains cells that are dependent upon a steady source of nutrients. These cells may live, even under ideal conditions, for only days at a time.

The writer of the poorly paraphrased version made only minor changes in some phrases and lifted others verbatim. It's difficult, therefore, to tell which words or ideas are Garrett's and which are the writer's.

APPROPRIATE PARAPHRASE
Garrett points out that malnutrition can give microbes an advantage as they spread through the population. The human body contains immune cells that help to fight off various diseases. When the body is deprived of nutrients, these immune cells will weaken (Garrett 199).

Because this writer's paper focused on the general threat of global disease, he could have simply summarized the passage.

APPROPRIATE SUMMARY
It has been suggested that malnutrition can weaken the immune system and make people more susceptible to diseases they would otherwise fight off (Garrett 199).

> **STRATEGY**   Avoid unintentional plagiarism
>
> Whenever you paraphrase or summarize a source, be sure to look back at the source and compare your words with those in the source. If you find phrases or sentences are too close to the original, either quote the material directly and exactly (using quotation marks) or revise your summary or paraphrase so that you're not using the author's words as your own.

3 Facts, details, and statistics

You can build entire paragraphs around facts, details, and statistics drawn from sources as long as you indicate those sources clearly. You may retain some of the emphasis of a source in using it; more likely, you'll integrate the details into prose that reflects your own purposes.

4 Visuals

Visuals (drawings, photos, graphs, and the like) can sometimes present or emphasize data better than words can. If you copy a visual from a print source or download it from an electronic source, you'll need to cite the source, and you may need permission to use it. Whether you create a visual yourself or draw it from your research, make sure it adds to the written text and doesn't simply substitute for it. Visuals that add to or extend a text imaginatively can increase the credibility and effectiveness of your writing. (See Chapter 12 and 13e.)

STRATEGY   Use visuals effectively

- Place the visual as near the relevant text as you can without disrupting the flow of the text or distorting the visual.
- Don't interrupt the writing in ways that make it hard to read.
- Make sure your visuals are of good quality and are an appropriate size for the page.
- Ask one or more readers whether your visuals are easy to understand and whether they add to the text's ideas and effectiveness.
- Label each visual (*Figure 1, Figure 2; Table 1, Table 2*).

Exercise 1

Below is a paragraph from Sam Roles's research on the Roswell Incident; it comes from a Web site that shows problems with the Air Force's conclusion that the Roswell Incident was not the crash of an alien spacecraft. Consider Roles's lead-in to this information; then incorporate the material into the text by (1) quoting it directly; (2) summarizing it; and (3) paraphrasing it.

ROLES'S LEAD-IN

In keeping with the processes of building a conspiracy theory, detractors of the Air Force report about the incident try to poke holes in specific versions of the historical record. For example, the Air Force report indicates that the testimony of Frank Kaufman, who was stationed in Roswell, was ignored. Seizing on this omission, Mark Rodeghier, writing for the J. Allen Hynek Center for UFO Studies, argues that

27e
plag

PASSAGE TO INCORPORATE (EXACT WORDS FROM THE SOURCE)

Kaufman claims to have been involved with the recovery of the alien bodies, and he was in the military stationed at Roswell. His claims have never been convincingly refuted. His testimony should have been included in the report. It was, most likely, not included because it is impossible to suggest that Kaufman could be confused about events in which he participated and for which he took written notes. (<http://www.cufos.org/airforce.htm>)

CITING RESEARCH IN THREE COMMUNITIES		
ACADEMIC SETTINGS	**PUBLIC SETTINGS**	**WORK SETTINGS**
Draws on the work of previous scholars and researchers and always acknowledges it. Writer explains where he or she fits in the tradition of research on a topic and explains agreements and disagreements with others' work. Thorough and accurate presentation of data, evidence, and quotations to support interpretations and conclusions. Quotations often long to present complex ideas completely. Expects precise, formal documentation in appropriate style (see Chapters 29–33).	Expects accuracy in presentation of facts, evidence, and others' ideas. Looks for clarity, precision, and conciseness in citing others' ideas and opinions. Uses quotations accurately and responsibly but prefers short quotations. Cites varied opinions and ideas to identify broad agreements and specify disagreements and issues. Uses factual evidence to explain or convince, but avoids too much technicality because audience expertise varies. May cite sources in an informal fashion (names, titles, dates are important) to avoid documentation that overwhelms readers.	Expects brief treatment of ideas and information readers are familiar with. Expect accuracy in details and data, especially those used to formulate a policy or plan of action. Prefer information presented concisely, often in summaries, tables, graphs, or illustrations. Expect information to be verifiable through a recognizable citation system (see Chapters 29–33), often APA (see Chapter 31). Documentation should provide support in a concise manner that does not interfere with discussions or recommendations.

27f Integrating sources for specific purposes

Although your research paper is an original contribution to a subject area—something *you* create through your methodical search for information and your particular way of pulling information together and presenting it for others to learn from—it's also about *other people's* work. It's your way of representing what a community of scholars, researchers, and commentators has said about a topic or how this community has tried to answer a question.

Weaving other people's words and ideas into your paper can accomplish many specific purposes. How you integrate outside material into your writing often depends on what you're trying to do with the source. Being clear about the reasons for citing someone's work can help you to structure a more effective research paper.

27f
plag

STRATEGY   Work with sources

- As you gather and read source material, make notes about the purposes it might serve in your paper.
- As you write the paper (see Chapter 28), refer to your notes when you make strategic decisions about what to incorporate at different points in the paper.

- Avoid trying to force a quotation to fit a purpose it doesn't serve. If an author has cited or described a controversial position, it could misrepresent that author to imply that he or she holds that position as well.
- Be willing to scrap a source or citation if it serves no purpose in your paper.
- Avoid the "display for teacher" syndrome—putting in quotations and referencing sources just to show your instructor that you have collected some information. Research papers can't be developed by merely stringing together quantities of material.

1 Introducing a topic and providing background

At the beginning of your paper, you may want to use sources to establish a context, to introduce the general area of your topic, or to give a history of activity or thought on the subject. Be careful not to rely too much on sources in your introduction, however; you need to establish your own voice and to explain what you will do in the paper.

In a paper on conspiracy theories, Sam Roles decided to use sources to provide background on why conspiracy theories are so hard to refute. (Here and elsewhere in this chapter, material from Roles's paper follows MLA style in documenting sources; see Chapter 30.)

> Conspiracy theories arise, according to scholars, for a number of reasons: political fragmentation and suspicion of difference (Pipes); something to occupy the imagination of a bored subculture (Fenster); and fear of more powerful groups (Johnson). For example, in the 1950s and 1960s, communism provided a . . . .

2 Summarizing prior research

In some cases, your research paper may explore an area, a specific focus, or a relationship that many others have written about. Instead of providing lots of references, use some of your sources selectively to give a brief summary before moving into your specific focus.

Sam Roles found large amounts of information about conspiracy theory, and he wanted to acknowledge the scope of his topic before focusing on the Roswell Incident as a case study of the concept. Notice how he selects representative references in each category.

27f
plag

> Conspiracy theories are studied within several disciplines. Psychologists, for example, consider the relationship between conspiracy theories and disorders such as paranoia (Edmunds). Sociologists examine the formation and spread of conspiracy theories within a culture or group, and its underlying causes (Haskins). Political scientists focus on the way that political

ideologies can lead to the creation of beliefs about leaders' motives (Argyle). And experts in anthropology consider the cultural bases of myth creation, fear of persecution, or the construction of alternative realities (Lizaro). In my . . . .

3 Providing examples and cases

As you make general statements about your topic or question, you will want to provide specific examples or cases to illustrate your points. Sometimes you will summarize them (see 22l-1, 27e-2) because you don't want a long example to overwhelm your paper or divert you from your discussion. You could also refer briefly to several cases to show how your general statement is manifested.

In one paragraph of his paper on the Roswell Incident, Sam Roles illustrates his general statement (in red) with three examples (in blue). Notice how each example comes from a different source.

> Many conspiracy theories surround political figures or political events. The Apollo moon missions, for example, are now questioned by conspiracy theorists as having been staged by the government in a studio (Adams). For decades, it has been thought that Jack the Ripper was actually Prince Albert Victor Christian Edward ("Prince Eddy"), the Duke of Clarence (Evans and Skinner). And theories of who assassinated President John F. Kennedy abound (Posner).

4 Showing evidence or support

As you create specific points or make claims and arguments in your research paper, the words of experts can support your ideas.

To present both sides of the debate concerning the Roswell Incident, Sam Roles incorporated a quotation to begin laying out opposition to the alien theory.

> But were these sightings really UFOs? As Berlitz and Moore have pointed out, New Mexico in the late 1940s was "the site of the major portion of America's postwar defense efforts in atomic research, rocketry, aircraft and missile development, and radar-electronics experimentation" (18). Such activity, such as flashes of light in the sky, could have been mistaken for the presence of UFOs.

In his notes on his sources, Roles made the following annotation to remind himself that he has found a specific purpose for the material in his broader plan for his paper.

Use to begin showing disagreement with UFO claim.

5 Expanding an idea

As you develop an idea, you can use your sources to extend, refine, and elaborate on that idea. This approach is especially useful as you make transitions from one part of your paper to the next.

To move from his discussion of the Roswell Incident to the main focus of his paper (how the incident represents a case study of the concept of conspiracy theory), Sam needed to show that the argument about the truth or falseness of the alien accounts was not really the point, that it simply illustrates the social nature of conspiracy theories. He decided to use a block quotation (see 27e-1) to accomplish this purpose.

> Joltes points out how difficult it is to change the views of conspiracy theorists even when there is overwhelming evidence and rational explanation to account for a phenomenon:
>
>> Likewise, when the US Air Force discloses the existence of a weather balloon experiment that offers a rational explanation for the "Roswell incident" a conspiracy buff will claim that records were faked, witnesses bought off or silenced, or whatever was necessary to conceal evidence of alien contact. The aliens really do exist, but all the evidence has been suppressed, destroyed, or altered . . . therefore the conspiracy theorist has had to work diligently to reconstruct what really happened, often producing "evidence" that is obviously contrived and illogical. But this matters not as long as it fits the theory.

6 Taking issue with a claim

In your paper, you may want to argue against what someone else has said or what some group (of scholars or people) believes (see 11c). After clearly explaining and referencing the opinion or belief, you can use other references to refute or answer the original claim. In this way, a section of your paper becomes a kind of conversation among scholars or commentators. Your artful use of sources can show weaknesses in one line of reasoning, or it can advance your own theory or position as in the following example.

27f
plag

> In summarizing his report of a carefully coordinated 1994 investigation of the Roswell Incident, Col. Richard M. Weaver says "the Air Force research did not locate or develop any information that the 'Roswell Incident' was a UFO event." Records did indicate, however, that the government was engaged in a "top secret balloon project, designed to attempt to monitor Soviet nuclear tests, known as Project Mogul." Tests of these balloons are the only plausible explanation of numerous UFO sightings and of the desert debris assumed to be an alien spacecraft.

Exercise 2

Make a list of the sources you have collected for your research paper, leaving several lines after each source. For each source, think of one or more purposes it might serve in your paper. Consider the list of purposes discussed in this section. What could you use the source to *do*? (In some cases, you may not be ready to answer this question completely until your paper is further developed; yet even tentative notes at this point will help you to think about the potential role of your sources and help you to know their contexts more clearly.)

Visit mycomplab.com for more resources and exercises on avoiding plagiarism and integrating sources.

CHAPTER **28**

Writing, Revising, and Presenting Research

How do you know when to begin writing your informative or persuasive research paper? There's no set time; when you've gathered enough material to create a solid draft of your paper, you can begin writing. But instead of launching into the first word of the first line, think strategically about the nature and shape of your task.

PRESENTING RESEARCH IN THREE COMMUNITIES

ACADEMIC SETTINGS	PUBLIC SETTINGS	WORK SETTINGS
Academic audiences will expect you to present your interpretation, conclusion, argumentative proposition, or outlook (your thesis) clearly and to focus on developing and supporting it throughout your paper. They will expect clear and detailed support and explanation. They may expect you to present complicated information in tables or graphs.	Public audiences will look for a clear statement of your position on an issue or a direct statement of the need you are addressing in your presentation of information. They will look for sufficient support and reasoning to explain your position—support that takes into account the concerns of your audience. Visual presentations including *PowerPoint*, graphs, and illustrations can be particularly effective with public audiences.	Workplace audiences will expect you to address directly and concisely the problem or challenge you are discussing and to present solutions or proposed actions in specific but not excessive detail. This audience will appreciate visuals (including *PowerPoint*) that help them understand the situation you are addressing and that will help them remember and implement your proposals or solutions.

28a Planning

You started out with a goal for your paper. You also began with a plan, perhaps a formal outline, a set of notes, or a statement of goals for each section of your paper (see Chapter 2 for a discussion of planning). Now is the time to revisit early decisions and revise or refine them.

1 Think about your goal—again!

Think about your general goals (to inform, to persuade) as well as your specific goals (to get a committee to adopt a policy; to explain the possibilities created by a new technology). Now write out your goals so that you can consider them more thoroughly, critique them, and perhaps revise them. Ask yourself if your primary goal is informative, persuasive, or a combination of the two.

For most writing, you should expect some overlap in purpose. To persuade readers to adopt a particular policy on campus alcohol use, for example, you may need to explain the background of the issue and provide details of the actions you propose.

2 Review your research questions

The research questions you formulated to focus and guide your research (22d) should have evolved as you worked, reflecting your developing knowledge of your subject. Use the latest versions of your research questions and arrange them in a logical order. Ask yourself in what sequence you want to address the questions in your essay or report. Add any further questions that you now think you ought to address. Develop this list as a tentative guide for drafting. The sequence you create at this point may change as you become more deeply involved with the details of your writing.

STRATEGY Create a purpose structure

As you review your notes and research questions, create a purpose structure, a series of statements that describe briefly what you intend to do in each section of a paper. A purpose structure will help you visualize the finished product (3b-1).

DeLeo Covington created the following purpose structure for his paper on addressing the problem of sleep deficits among high school students.

BEGINNING	Explain what sleep deficits are and how studies show that most high school students' schoolwork suffers because they have sleep deficits. Argue that the solution to the problem is to begin the school day later.
FIRST MIDDLE	Explain the problem: High school students need more sleep than most people suppose; the early beginning of the high school day robs them of sleep they need.
SECOND MIDDLE	Explain that the high school day begins early because the buses have to be used by elementary, middle, and high school students; most districts can't afford more buses. Show that most school administrators believe it's ok for high school students to get up early in the morning.

THIRD MIDDLE   Argue that changing starting times is important despite the
difficulties. Tell how high schools that have moved to later
beginning times show improvement in student performance
linked to overcoming sleep deficits. Explain that they claim the
change has been worth the cost.

FOURTH MIDDLE   Outline the cost-effective strategies that districts having made
the change came up with. Argue that these strategies can be
adopted by almost all school districts and that they should do so
to help solve the problem.

END   Summarize the solution; encourage readers to take action within
their school districts.

Now is the time to revisit early decisions and revise or refine them.

3 Redevelop your thesis

If you began with a tentative thesis statement as a way of focusing
your research (22e), take this opportunity to restate it in view of what you
have learned in doing your research. Envision your paper as a means of
supporting your thesis and persuading readers. To use your thesis statement as an organizing strategy for drafting your paper, state your thesis,
break it into parts, and develop related supporting statements arranged in a
series that helps you focus on a persuasive purpose for each section of
your paper.

28b Drafting

The moment you begin your research, you're planning your project.
When you've collected most of the information you need, it's time to focus
more sharply on the organization and content of your paper.

28b
source

STRATEGY   Revise your plan and begin drafting

- **Create a working outline.** Make a working outline (2c-5) of the
  general sequence of information and the relationships between segments. This process will give you a clear sense of how the parts of
  your paper might fit together.
- **Cluster information.** Clustering or grouping your information
  (2c-1–2) is a useful tactic when you have many bits of information
  but no clear idea of how they can be related.

- **Cut and paste.** If you've been keeping a research journal to record and reflect on your research, you may already have the segments of your draft. Try rearranging those pieces you've already sketched to create a skeleton for your paper.
- **Focus on the introduction and conclusion.** Sometimes writing your introduction and conclusion first helps you envision a plan for the whole. In preparing the introduction and conclusion, you'll need to consider your readers' interests and their familiarity with your topic and to signal your paper's design and goals.

28c An informative research paper

It's true—but only part of the story—to say that an informative research paper follows the shape of its subject. The other parts of the story are (1) the need to take into account your readers' expectations, knowledge, and values, and (2) the need to make sure readers understand your insights and conclusions. Here are strategies that may be especially helpful for informative writing.

1 Consider readers

Readers may be interested in your topic for the same reasons you are—or maybe not. Perhaps you started your research paper in response to a *National Geographic* television special on the explorations in the Black Sea. You may have always been curious about this kind of exploration, but chances are many of your readers won't share that curiosity. Try to identify the reasons your readers might have for being interested in your topic. Or think of how you might convince them that your topic is worth their attention.

Exercise 1

To help bring your readers and your research together, write down five reasons why readers *might* or *ought to be* interested in your topic. Then try a bit harder and write down five more reasons. Next, identify those aspects of your topic you think are most likely to interest readers or to be of use to them. The aim of this activity is to help you see your topic from a reader's perspective as well as your own.

Draw on all three lists as you plan your paper and prepare an introduction designed to lead readers into your paper. Create an informal outline of the information and ideas you plan to discuss, arranging them in an order that reflects both your interests and those of your readers.

28c
source

2 Look for a pattern

The information and ideas in your research notes should suggest ways to organize your writing. Review your notes to see if they answer any of the following questions in depth and in detail. If so, make the answers a significant part of your writing.

QUESTIONS	PATTERN
What are the clusters or categories of ideas and information?	Classification
What are the differences or similarities among the concepts, activities, outlooks, situations, or subjects?	Comparison/Contrast
Are there surprising similarities between one subject and another, seemingly very different subject?	Analogy
How does it work? How can it be done?	Process
Why did it happen? What is likely to happen in the future?	Cause-Effect
What are the important concepts and how are they defined?	Definition
What are the features (physical, emotional, relational) of the subject?	Description
What happened? To whom? When? Where? Why? How?	Narration

3 Consider familiar plans

If you don't yet have an overall plan in mind, consider building your writing around one (or more) of these familiar informative plans.

- Describe a surprising or puzzling phenomenon, then provide an explanation.
- Outline a challenging task or goal, then suggest ways to accomplish it.
- Explain a common way of looking at events or situations, then suggest a new perspective.
- Focus on relationships, events, or objects that many people think are unimportant and explain why, to the contrary, they are very important.
- Compare the customs, values, or beliefs of one social or cultural group to those of another; or explain them to people unfamiliar or perhaps unsympathetic to those customs or beliefs.
- Start with a phenomenon about which people have offered many different, less than satisfactory explanations; then offer your own explanation, presenting it in detail and indicating why you think it a better one.

28c
source

28d A persuasive research paper

A persuasive research essay advances, supports, and defends a thesis. The thesis may be a stand on an issue (an argumentative proposition), a proposed policy or a solution to a problem, or an interpretation of a subject. What sets persuasive research writing apart is the presence of alternative opinions, policies, interpretations. Thus, your planning needs to account not only for the reasons and evidence that support your thesis but also for grounds for preferring it to the alternatives.

1 Key elements

To be successful, persuasive writing needs to do three things.

- Explain the issue, problem, or object of interpretation.
- Make clear your opinion (argumentative proposition), solution, or interpretation.
- Acknowledge and summarize other points of view and demonstrate why yours is preferable.

2 Plan your reasoning and support

Persuasive writing offers readers a chain of reasons (see 9b) that add up to a case in favor of the writer's thesis. Begin your planning by writing down all the major reasons you have for readers to agree with you, drawing on your research notes. Then arrange these statements in an order that you consider logical and likely to persuade. Remember to include alternative points of view.

Next, summarize the evidence and further reasons you can offer to persuade readers to agree with your line of reasoning. Write out your summaries under each of the corresponding major reasons from your earlier list, drawing on your research notes. The result will be an informal outline to guide your drafting.

3 Arrange statements and evidence in persuasive order

As you create your plan and begin writing, consider the procedures that many writers and readers have found effective in persuasion. Some of them are detailed in 11a–h; here are three more that are appropriate for persuasive research writing:

28d
source

- **Present alternatives.** Begin by discussing the issue or problem. Then discuss the alternatives in detail, indicating why each is lacking in whole or in part. End with an extensive presentation of your own perspective, which may incorporate parts of the alternatives. This strategy is useful when your research has identified extensive arguments in favor of other opinions or solutions.

- **Summarize the scholarship.** Begin with a detailed analysis of other interpretations (in academic writing) or other solutions and policies (in public writing). Indicate why that earlier work is flawed or inadequate, then offer your own solution or interpretation.
- **Take a middle ground.** Begin by outlining other opinions, interpretations, or solutions that take extreme positions, none of which is fully satisfactory. Then present your own perspective that takes a reasonable middle ground, avoiding the extremes of other outlooks.

28e Presentation strategies

Perhaps you see a research paper or report as the outcome of your efforts: a stack of neatly laid out pages emerging from your computer printer. But is this your *only* option or your *best* choice? Are there fresh ways of presenting and explaining information available to you? What kinds of documents other than standard essays or reports could you create?

Most alternative presentation strategies also enable you to create multimodal presentations (see also Chapter 14). Thus your research paper could be a presentation combining, for instance, sound, pictures, and a video that you create. Remember, however, that whatever the presentation strategy, you need to provide detailed and researched facts, ideas, and analysis.

1 Create a presentation

Software programs such as *PowerPoint* allow you to create slides that contain text, graphics, pictures, sound, and special effects (such as fade-to-black or text that appears line-by-line). The screens you produce (called "slides") can be projected, viewed on a computer screen, or printed. Presented in order, either manually or automatically, they make up a document called a slide show.

A slide show needs to be more than a series of visuals; it is a document that provides and develops information and ideas. Each slide is another page of the document. Create each page as a discrete element in your explanation and argument, and use the text and graphics to tell readers how they work together to form a coherent text. Use subheads and titles to let viewers know the parts of the presentation and the main ideas or most important information. Write detailed explanations and arguments as you would in a word-processed text and provide carefully researched details and documented sources as you would in a research paper. Remember, however, that long stretches of text in a small typeface are hard to read; you need to balance text with headings, graphics, and visuals, as in Figure 28.1.

28e
source

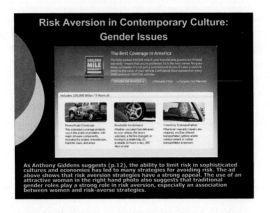

FIGURE 28.1 *PowerPoint* slide from "Cultural Responses to Advertising" by Christopher Ursinus

Use summary pages to organize an explanation or argument and to predict the next slides in a sequence (see Figure 28.2).

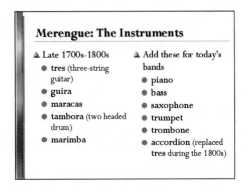

FIGURE 28.2 *PowerPoint* presentation within a document

2 Use photographs

A program like *Word* can incorporate photographs and illustrations. A photographic editing program like *Photoshop* can help you go beyond illustrating your text to presenting your ideas *through* photographs.

The Italian Renaissance painter Caravaggio often depicted saints and biblical characters as ordinary people with tattered clothes and dirty feet, unlike the painters before him, who presented more idealized figures. In an art history paper on Caravaggio, you might do research that indicates which paintings are the best examples of this trait. You could go online to get copies of the pictures, create a text discussing specific elements of the paintings, and finish your paper by using *Photoshop* to highlight those elements, even drawing lines from parts of the picture to your discussion. You might also enlarge and isolate elements of the painting for closer inspection and analysis in your text.

In contrast to the idealized portraits of religious subjects typical of pictures from artists working earlier in the Italian Renaissance, Caravaggio produced pictures with strong realistic details emphasizing the earthiness, even crudeness of his subjects. The dirty, calloused feet of the figures in the foreground of *Madonna of the Rosary* mark them as laborers or peasants. Their outstretched arms are directed at the priest, who acts as an intermediary by directing his gaze to Mary (and then to Jesus), who are in turn illuminated by light from the window—the light of the Divine.

Caravaggio, *Madonna of the Rosary*

28e
source

In a paper on game strategy, you might present a sequence of pictures to show how a sport follows one or more game strategies. You could integrate explanatory text with the illustrations, and focus or segment the photos for detailed analysis.

3 Create a film

A film of a process or an event can be a research paper when it contains commentary and analysis that draws on sources, when it provides researched text on the screen, or when it is accompanied by an explanatory text. If you want to discuss a new plastics injection process, you might prepare an explanatory script using authoritative sources. Then you would design a film, planning the scenes and the timings. A camcorder could film the scenes you plan, allowing several shots for each scene to make sure all the elements are included, with proper focus and the appropriate angle. A computer editing program will allow you to choose, edit, and splice the scenes and to add a spoken text from your script. Finally, an accompanying text might enhance the film by providing background, a statement of goals, analysis, and a list of works cited or an annotated bibliography.

4 Design a Web page

Web pages can include extended text discussions (as in a word-processed research paper), visuals, streaming audio, streaming video, and links to other sources or resources. A webbed document—a Web page or a file written in HTML or a similar language—allows readers to move around at will within it. It also includes links that readers can use to access related documents or source material. Thus, in a webbed document, readers control the sequence and content of a presentation according to their own interests and expectations—as long as the writer has included the necessary options (links, tables of contents and other navigational aids such as headings).

In an argument for a vegetarian lifestyle, Naomi Roth included links to vegetarian menus and recipes and to famous people who are committed vegetarians as a way of answering potential objections to her arguments.

Misperception #3 Nobody really important is a vegetarian.

On the contrary, famous people ranging from the actor Keenan Ivory Wayans to the actress Reese Witherspoon to the power lifter Pat Reeves to the late comedian Milton Berle (lived to 93) were either vegetarians or vegans. Want to learn about others? Try this link for famous vegetarians and vegans (with some biographies) and this link for vegetarians and vegans both past and present.

28e source

mycomplab

Visit mycomplab.com for more resources and exercises on writing, revising, and presenting research.

PART 6

Documenting Sources

CHAPTER **29**

Ten Serious Documentation Mistakes

What to document, where to place documentation, how to format documentation entries, whose name to put in a citation, which documentation system to use, and many similar questions face a writer who needs to document the sources of ideas, information, and quotations in an essay or a report. Ten particular documentation problems can arise as you work on providing clear and informative documentation. Being aware of the ways to resolve these serious problems is an important step in creating effective researched writing.

DOCUMENTATION NEEDS IN THREE COMMUNITIES

ACADEMIC SETTINGS	WORK SETTINGS	PUBLIC SETTINGS
Fresh ideas and research results are *intellectual property* whose sources must be acknowledged precisely and completely.	Precise data from reputable sources and data that can be verified are essential to making good decisions.	Documented sources provide reliable information about ideas, opinions, and data, and they identify the people or groups responsible. Documentation identifies possible sources for further information.
Scholars need to be able to locate data, ideas, and quotations to use in work of their own.	Patents, policies, regulations, products, and marketing all have legal dimensions calling for precise documentation.	
Precise documentation lends credibility to the writer and adds to the persuasiveness of evidence and arguments.	Concise documentation reduces clutter and gets to the point.	Concise documentation identifies sources without providing excessive detail.
Documentation places the writer's work in the context of other research.	Documentation shows how up to date sources are.	

TEN SERIOUS DOCUMENTATION MISTAKES

GENERAL PROBLEMS

1. Choosing the right documentation style (29a)
2. Deciding what to document (29b and 27d)
3. Understanding the importance of documentation (29c and 27c)
4. Following a publication's style (29d)

(continued)

TEN SERIOUS DOCUMENTATION MISTAKES (*continued*)

TEXT CITATIONS

5. Incorrect placement of a citation (29e)
6. Missing information in a citation (29f)
7. Wrong details in a citation (29g)

WORKS CITED OR REFERENCES LIST

8. Wrong kind of entry in a references list (29h)
9. Missing information in a references entry (29i)
10. Wrong details in a references entry (29j)

29a Choosing the right documentation style

Documentation styles specify how to indicate sources in the body of a document and how to provide detailed information about sources in a list of references or works cited. The major styles are quite different; a reader familiar with one style will know where to look for information where that style is used, but he or she may feel uncomfortable or confused looking for the same information where another style is used. Instructors may require the style used in their discipline, such as MLA for English, APA for the social sciences, CMS for history, or CSE for the natural sciences. Publications and organizations may require a particular style or use one of their own (see 29d). Or you may be left on your own to choose a style appropriate for your audience and your academic, public, or work situation. The following chart should help you make informed and careful choices.

DOCUMENTATION CHOICES IN THREE COMMUNITIES		
ACADEMIC SETTINGS	**PUBLIC SETTINGS**	**WORK SETTINGS**
MLA STYLE For humanities fields (English, foreign languages, art history, philosophy, or film, for example) when the instructor requires MLA style. When you are looking for a simple form of documentation. When a publication or organization requires MLA style.	When readers are not expecting a specific style but you feel they are best served by a simple, direct system that seldom uses footnotes. When other writers in the setting use either MLA style or a modified version of it.	When readers are not expecting a specific form of documentation and you feel they are best served by a simple, direct documentation style without footnotes or endnotes. (*continued*)

29a
doc
prob

DOCUMENTATION CHOICES IN THREE COMMUNITIES (*continued*)

	ACADEMIC SETTINGS	PUBLIC SETTINGS	WORK SETTINGS
APA STYLE	For social science fields such as psychology, sociology, business, economics, education, or political science. When an instructor requests a name-and-date style. When a publication or an organization requires APA style.	For readers whose professions or interests are linked to academic fields in the social sciences (social workers or school administrators, for example). When you are drawing heavily on social science research for information or support. When other writers addressing similar audiences use APA style or a modified version of it.	In business, because many business audiences prefer a name-and-date system, in part because it indicates how current the writer's sources are. In business, because many academic business programs use APA style.
CMS STYLE	For fields such as history and philosophy that ask for a footnote or endnote style. When writing for an instructor, organization, or publication that requests documentation using Turabian or *Chicago Manual* style or a footnote/endnote style.	When your readers expect footnotes or endnotes or when other writers addressing the same audience generally use footnotes or endnotes. When you do not wish to distract readers with names, page numbers, or dates in parentheses in the text—giving them instead a chance to consult only those notes they wish.	When you do not wish to distract readers by including author's names, page numbers, or dates throughout the text itself.
CSE STYLE	For natural science fields such as biology, physical anthropology, and physics. When writing for an instructor, organization, or publication that requests scientific documentation or CSE style. For a setting calling for the "number method" or the "name and year method."	When addressing scientific issues for an audience that is reasonably expert in the field and looks for current scientific knowledge.	When writing for professional groups or company divisions that expect the use of scientific documentation.

29b Deciding what to document

Some information and ideas do not need to be linked to specific sources because most educated readers will already know and understand them. In other cases, you will need to identify the sources of information, ideas, and specific words that are not your own. By doing this, you position your own work in relation to the work of others, you enable readers to consult and use the sources you found, and you avoid charges of plagiarism by identifying clearly the materials from elsewhere that you put to use in your own writing.

- **Document** word-for-word quotations, paraphrases, and summaries of someone else's work; data or facts that another person has collected or identified (if the information is not widely known); opinions and interpretations someone else has advanced; and illustrations, charts, graphs, photographs, recordings, original software, performances, and interviews.
- **Document** the sources of others' ideas or interpretations that you are synthesizing, contrasting, modifying, or using as a basis for your own ideas and interpretation.
- **Do not document** your own ideas, opinions, and interpretations or widely known ideas and information that is available in common reference works or usually regarded by educated people as *common knowledge:* $E = mc^2$; "To be, or not to be" (see 27d).

29c Understanding the importance of documentation

Some writers regard documentation only as protection—a way to avoid charges of plagiarism. But good writers develop a sense of when documentation is not only required but helpful. Consider adding source material and documentation at these places in an essay or a report:

- **When you want to assure readers of your accuracy and knowledge,** present or summarize details and specific information, then document the sources so that readers can check your work for accuracy and recognize the amount of research behind your statements.
- **When you want to show how your work fits with other research on the subject,** use documentation to identify related essays and reports or to indicate the sources for quotations and summaries presenting what others have to say about the topic.
- **When you want to add to the credibility and forcefulness of your writing,** draw memorable or effective statements from your sources and document them or use documentation as a way of supporting your own conclusions or insights.

Use documentation in your writing as a positive strategy, not simply as a way of avoiding negative consequences.

29c
doc
prob

29d Following a publication's style

Often an instructor or an organization will ask you to use a documentation style similar to that of some publication. To do this, you need to analyze the documentation style of the publication. Fortunately, many publications provide guidelines for authors preparing manuscripts for submission, generally with a title like "Information for Authors" or "Editorial policy and Manuscript Preparation Guidelines." This is especially true for research publications in science and engineering. The guidelines usually contain detailed advice about presenting citations and references, including examples, which you can supplement by finding examples in the publication itself.

Here is particularly detailed and helpful advice published in the *Journal of the Air & Waste Management Association.*

> References must be formatted according to the first reference style listed in the *ACS Style Guide* . . . ; that is, in consecutive order as they are cited within the text, using Arabic numeral superscripts (do not use the author-date format). Do not use an automatic footnoting or referencing function in word processing. Do not use "et al." in references unless there are more than 10 authors; rather, list all authors for each reference. At a minimum, all references should include author, title, publisher, place, year, volume and issue number, and page numbers. Examples of reference styles include the following:
>
> 1. Carson, M.A.; Atkinson, K.D.; Waechter, C.J. An Analysis of Leachate in Groundwater; *J. Biol. Chem.* **1982,** *257,* 8115-8121.
> 2. Bockris, J.O.; Reddy, A.K.N. *Modern Electrochemistry;* Plenum: New York, 1970; Vol. 2, p 132.
> 3. Geactinov, N.E. In *Polycyclic Hydrocarbons and Carcinogenesis;* Harvey, R.G., Ed.; ACS Symposium Series 283; American Chemical Society: Washington, DC, 1985; pp 12-45.
> 4. Kanter, H. Ph.D. Dissertation, University of Arizona, December 1984.
> 5. U.S. Environmental Protection Agency. *Quality Control for Pesticides and Related Compounds;* EPA-600/1-79/008; U.S. Government Printing Office: Washington, DC, 1979.
> 6. Roe, A.B. *J. Pharm. Sci.,* in press. [this means that the article has been accepted for publication but has not yet been published]
> 7. Roe, A.B. *J. Pharm. Sci.,* submitted for publication.
> 8. Urdal, K.; Fallon, J.D. Structure and Reactivity of Surfaces. In *Proceedings of the 80th Annual Meeting of the A&WMA,* Denver, CO, June 5-8, 1994; pp 173-204.
>
> Authors should look to previous issues of the *Journal,* as well as *The ACS Style Guide,* for reference styles not listed above.

For books, technical reports, and documents not providing guidelines, or for articles photocopied from a journal, consult the text itself for examples of citation and reference style. The following examples are from an article in *IEEE Transactions on Knowledge and Data Engineering* titled "Main Memory Database Systems: An Overview" by Hector Garcia-Molina and Kenneth Salem.

IMS, one of the earliest database systems, recognized these access differences, and has provided two systems in one for many years: Fast Path [9] for memory resident data, and conventional IMS for the rest. A recent paper by Stonebraker [25] also discusses some of the issues involved in multilevel database systems and data migration.

References

[9] D. Gawlick and D. Kinkade, "Varieties of concurrency control in IMS/VS Fast Path," *Data Eng. Bull.*, vol. 8, no. 2, pp. 3-10, June 1985.

[25] M. Stonebraker, "Managing persistent objects in a multi-level store," in *Proc. ACM SIGMOD Conf.*, Denver, CO, May 1991, pp. 2-11.

29e Incorrect placement of a citation

When you provide a source citation in the body of an essay or a report, make sure readers can readily identify the part of your text to which it refers. A confusing or ambiguous citation (either in the discussion itself or in parentheses) undermines the purpose of documentation and your hard work in locating sources.

Start by considering ways to use the writer's name or the name of the publication in the text itself, accompanied by added information in parentheses or a superscript number (for a footnote or endnote), according to the documentation style you are following (see Chapters 30–33). Names and titles in the text itself are often less disruptive than parenthetical citations or notes and give you more options for wording a passage.

Problem. Misplaced or ambiguous citations confuse readers and undermine your credibility as a writer.

Youth sports offer even more examples of adult expectations harming children (Quart 71). As Alyssa Quart points out, "The rise of golf for young players . . . has resulted in a growing number of children suffering head injuries."

Readers may wonder why this writer repeats Quart's name and whether the page number refers to Quart's overall discussion, the quotation, or both.

Solutions for misplaced in-text citations. Arrange your source information and citations so that they are clear to a reader.

29e
doc
prob

Strategy 1

Put a parenthetical citation *directly after* the specific words, information, opinion, or interpretation you are drawing from a source. If you name a source in the discussion, do so close to the words or information you are using, often right before the material you are citing.

> Youth sports offer even more examples of adult expectations harming
>
> children. As Alyssa Quart points out, "The rise of golf for young players . . .
>
> has resulted in a growing number of children suffering head injuries" (71).
> In this case, the author cites the source and page number in the second sentence; the first sentence contains her ideas, not Quart's. The name comes before the quoted material; the page number comes after it.

Strategy 2

Make sure readers can recognize the part of your text to which a general reference refers or the specific details drawn from a source. Don't simply name a general source (or group of sources) at the end of a paragraph or other section of your text, leaving readers to puzzle over the relationship of your text to the source(s).

CONFUSING REFERENCE Windmills may be a partial answer to both rising oil prices and global warming, but they aren't an instant answer. Outside a small Nebraska farm, thirty-six new wind turbines 230 feet high with huge blades provide power for the town. The wind in Nebraska and the willingness of the local power company helped make the project possible. Not all towns are going to be willing to spend the time and energy to complete such a project, however, and not all will have the sustained wind power to make a project successful (Barry).

CLEAR REFERENCE Windmills may be a partial answer to both rising oil prices and global warming, but they aren't an instant answer. Outside a small Nebraska farm, thirty-six new wind turbines 230 feet high with huge blades provide power for the town. In addition, the wind in Nebraska and the willingness of the local power company helped make the project possible (Barry A5). Not all towns are going to be willing to spend the time and energy to complete such a project, however, and not all will have the sustained wind power to make a project successful.

Strategy 3

When you summarize or synthesize sources, link each source clearly to the opinion, idea, or interpretation you are incorporating into your writing. Include more than one source in a citation *if* you are providing more than one source to support your ideas or offering readers several places to further their knowledge of the subject.

29e
doc
prob

For many psychologists and sports experts, the answer to overregulated children's sports is simple: Just let the kids play (Sutton-Smith; Bigelow, Moroney, and Hall). Other people point out that treating childhood as a time of play and unregulated activity is a relatively recent development in human society (Zelizer; Quart 71-73).

Put superscript numbers for footnotes and endnotes in the same places that you would put parenthetical citations.

29f Missing information in a citation

Documentation styles require specific kinds of information in in-text citations, depending on the details their users consider important. Make sure you do not leave important information out of your citations.

APA style places emphasis on the date of publication.

AS PART OF DISCUSSION	As early as 1989, JoAnne Yates documented the role of oral and written communication in the development of modern business.
PARENTHETICAL	Oral and written communication played a role in the development of modern business (Yates, 1989).

MLA style often documents discussions of particular passages.

AS PART OF DISCUSSION	Kerouac begins the novel abruptly, "I first met Dean not long after my wife and I split up" (1).
PARENTHETICAL	The novel begins abruptly, "I first met Dean not long after my wife and I split up" (Kerouac 1).

29g Wrong details in a citation

Sometimes writers provide too much information in parenthetical citations, adding unnecessary detail.

TOO MUCH INFORMATION	The human brain is a special type of computer that allows for partial, fuzzy, and value-directed decisions (R. Montague, *Why Choose This Book?* 27–29).
PRECISE	The human brain is a special type of computer that allows for partial, fuzzy, and value-directed decisions (Montague 27–29).

At other times writers add unnecessary detail, such as *pp.* (before the numerals in MLA citations) or a publication date (for MLA).

UNNECESSARY DETAIL

> According to Read Montague, "The style of computation used by the brain is very different from that of the computers inhabiting our cars, offices, and server rooms" (2006, p. 24).

Problem. In-text citations are meant to be brief, providing only enough detail to locate the source in a works cited list and to identify a specific location in the source (if appropriate). More information is distracting, not helpful.

Solutions for incorrect in-text citation format. Try these two options.

Strategy 1

Provide only a name (or title) to locate the source in a list of works cited, according to the requirements for a specific documentation style (see Chapters 30, 31, and 32).

Strategy 2

Avoid *p.* or *pp.* in MLA citations, but do include *fig.*, *par.*, or similar information if required by a specific kind of source.

CORRECT AND CONCISE

> According to Read Montague, "The style of computation used by the brain is very different from that of the computers inhabiting our cars, offices, and server rooms" (24).

29h Wrong kind of entry in a references list

Entries in a works cited list (MLA), a references list (APA, CSE), and a bibliography (CMS) take different forms and provide kinds of information depending on the kind of source: article, printed book, Web site, or video recording, for example.

Problem. If you choose the wrong format for an entry, you may fail to provide readers with the information they need, or you may mislead them about the kind of source you used.

MISLEADING FORMAT

> Useem, Andrea. "Women Only?" *Harvard Divinity Bulletin,* 36.2
> (2008): 13–15. Print.
>
> The use of a volume and issue number (36.2) suggests that this source is a scholarly journal and that the selection therefore reflects the writer's research or a review of the article by a panel of scholars. This is not the case, however. As the publication says about itself, *"Harvard Divinity Bulletin* is a magazine that includes articles, reviews, and opinion pieces. . . ."* The selection advances the writer's opinions and does not present the results of research, and the publication is a magazine.

CORRECT FORMAT

> Useem, Andrea. "Women Only?" *Harvard Divinity Bulletin* Spring
> 2008: 13-15. Print.
>
> This is the appropriate format for a magazine article (p. 384).

29h
doc
prob

Solution for the wrong kind of citation entry. MLA provides many different model formats for entries. To locate the correct format for a particular source, use the model entries and explanations (pp. 373–403) and the guide to them (pp. 371–373).

Step 1: Describe your source. Use these questions to help describe your source.

- **Article?** An article is a selection in a scholarly journal, magazine, newspaper, collection or anthology published in book form, or similar gathering of writings.
- **Book?** A book is a work or collection of materials issued on its own, including familiar hard covers, paperbacks, pamphlets, government documents and reports, and similar texts.
- **Periodical?** A periodical is a publication like a magazine, scholarly journal, or newspaper issued at more or less regular intervals with different contents each time it appears.
- **Nonperiodical?** A nonperiodical publication is issued once or irregularly, sometimes with variations or revisions of content or design.
- **Medium?**
  Printed document (Print)?
  Electronic document (Web)? Is it publicly available on the Internet or only through a subscription database?
  Data gathered through field research (survey, interview, observation)?
  Performance or lecture?
  Media resource (film or recording)?
  Electronic file (MP3 or Word file) or physical document (typescript or manuscript)?

SOURCE INFORMATION	Authors: Amy R. Wolfson and Mary A. Carskadon
	Title: "Sleep Schedules and Daytime Functioning in Adolescents"
	Publication information: Appeared in *Child Development*, a print publication. The volume number was 69, and the issue number was 4. It was published in August 1998. The page numbers were 875–87.
QUESTIONS ANSWERED	Article? Yes. It is one of a number of selections in the publication.
	Periodical? Yes. It has volume and issue numbers, indicating that it appears on a regular basis.
	Print? Yes. I found it in a printed copy of the publication.

Step 2: Locate the model format. Once you can describe a source in general terms, you should be able to locate the specific model format for it in the MLA chapter or the guide to it (pp. 371–373). Start with the general categories into which the model formats are arranged. Then identify the specific kind of entry that fits your source.

**29h
doc
prob**

> **GENERAL CATEGORIES FOR MLA WORKS CITED ENTRIES (pp. 371–373)**
>
> Articles from Print Periodicals and Selections from Books
> Books and Works Treated as Books
> Web Publications
> Online Database Resources
> Field Resources, Performances, and Media Resources

If you look over the information about Amy R. Wolfson and Mary A. Carskadon's "Sleep Schedules and Daytime Functioning in Adolescents" (see above), you will see it belongs in the general category "Articles from Print Periodicals and Selections from Books." If you look further at the kinds of model formats in this category (p. 371), you will see that the title, contents, and authorship suggest that the appropriate citation format is "Article in Scholarly Journal with Two or Three Authors."

CORRECT ENTRY   Wolfson, Amy R., and Mary A. Carskadon. "Sleep Schedules and

Daytime Functioning in Adolescents." *Child Development*

69.4 (1998): 875-87. Print.

29i   Missing information in a references entry

Here is an entry from an MLA works cited list in a student paper. It's a bit hard to understand because some information is missing

Is this the well-known writer Malcolm G.?   Magazine? Newspaper?

Gladwell. "In the Air: Who Says Big Ideas Are Rare?" *New Yorker,* May 2008.

Is this the date? Is it monthly? Weekly?

Pages? Print or electronic version?

COMPLETE ENTRY   Gladwell, Malcolm. "In the Air: Who Says Big Ideas Are Rare?"

New Yorker 12 May 2008: 50-60. Print.

Problem. If you fail to include enough information in a works cited entry, you leave readers with unanswered questions such as "Where exactly can I locate this information in the source?" or "How old (or new) is this source?"

Solutions for missing citation information. The solutions will depend on the reason you left information out of the entry.

1. You didn't know what kind of information to include.
2. You forgot to record necessary information while you were consulting the source.
3. You couldn't locate some of the needed information.

Strategy 1

Have your handbook at hand so you can readily *identify the information* you need to collect for each kind of source. *Or* use the general checklist (see pp. 281–282) to remind yourself what kind of information to include in your notes.

Strategy 2

Keep the checklist (pp. 281–282) at hand, perhaps making a copy for your notebook or folder. The checklist will remind you to *record the needed information. Or* reserve a special section of your research notebook or folder or a special electronic file for information about your sources. The existence of the file should remind you to record the necessary details.

Strategy 3

Put in a little extra effort trying to *locate the details* (and save a lot of time later because you won't have to retrace your steps). Consult the explanations and model entries for advice on *where to look and what to look for.*

Be sure to look at the copyright page in books (on the back of the title page) or at the bottom of the first page of an article in a scholarly journal. Both contain important information, and copying them can save you time and effort later. Remember to record inclusive page numbers for articles from those journals that do not include them on the first page. Also pay special attention to page numbers if they are not continuous, as is often the case with magazines and newspapers.

29j Wrong details in a references entry

Writers sometimes create works cited entries that seem correct because they look like entries they have seen in their sources. Often, the result is entries that are confusing or misleading because the details are wrong—details the writers failed to notice through inexperience or inattention.

WRONG DETAILS	Fem. and Polit. Theory. by C. Sunstein. UCP, 1990.
ACCURATE DETAILS	Sunstein, Cass R. *Feminism and Political Theory.* Chicago: U of Chicago P, 1990. Print.

29j doc prob

Knowledgeable readers come to a list of works cited or references with specific expectations for content, form, and details such as italics, commas, and colons. Because all these details convey important information, experienced readers may react quite negatively when the details are wrong.

Problem. Writers unfamiliar with documentation styles may fail to notice important details or treat them as silly or nitpicking issues.

Solution for wrong citation details. Learn the important details of formatting, arrangement, and punctuation, and apply them as you document sources. Use the following questions to examine model entries for the kinds of sources in your works cited list.

QUESTIONS TO IDENTIFY IMPORTANT DETAILS

Where should I use italics?
Where should I use quotation marks?
Where should I use commas, periods, and colons?
What dates do I need to include?
How do I abbreviate a date, a publisher's name, or another term?
Do I need to include volume and issue numbers?
What page numbers do I need to provide and in what form?
What do I need to capitalize?
What term do I use for the medium of a source?
What is the correct order for the elements of a particular source?
How much space do I need to provide between lines and between entries?
How much (and when) should I indent?

Visit mycomplab.com **for more resources and exercises on avoiding serious documentation mistakes.**

CHAPTER **30**

MLA Documentation

The documentation style of the Modern Language Association (MLA) offers a convenient system for acknowledging your sources for ideas, information, and quotations and for directing readers to those sources. It consists of an in-text citation (generally in parentheses) and a list of works cited (presented at the end of the text). (For advice on what to document and what not to document, see 29b.)

MLA style uses a citation in the text (generally an author's name) to identify a source that readers can locate in the list of works cited at the end of the paper. Many in-text citations also provide a page number to indicate exactly where in the source readers will find the particular information. Punctuation and abbreviations are kept to a minimum in MLA in-text parenthetical citations; no comma appears between an author's name and a page number, nor does *p.* or *pp.* appear before page numbers.

IN-TEXT CITATION

Most people link freedom of choice and overall happiness, yet having a wide range of choices for food, clothing, housing, and recreation can also lead to dissatisfaction and unhappiness. As one researcher puts it, "there comes a point at which opportunities become so numerous that we feel overwhelmed" (Schwartz 104).

—METILI SOVAN, College Student

ENTRY IN THE LIST OF WORKS CITED

Schwartz, Barry. *The Paradox of Choice: Why More Is Less.* New York:

Ecco-Harper, 2005. Print.

Citations may appear within parentheses or as part of the discussion (see Entries 1 and 2, pp. 373–374). They may refer to a work in general or to specific parts of a source (by including a page number; see Entries 4 and 5, pp. 374–375).

For details of the MLA documentation system, see the *MLA Handbook for Writers of Research Papers,* 7th ed. (New York: MLA, 2009) or the *MLA Style Manual and Guide to Scholarly Publishing,* 3rd ed. (New York: MLA, 2008) and recent changes online at <http://mla.org>.

MLA style classifies sources in two principal ways:

- **Medium** (print, Web, performance, recording, etc.)
- **Frequency of appearance** (**periodical**—appearing at regular, fixed intervals—such as a magazine, a newspaper, or a scholarly journal; **nonperiodical**—appearing only once or at irregular intervals—such as a book or a pamphlet)

To help you identify the kind of source you are working with, we have created a set of categories described in the box below. Use them to help remember what kind of information to record about a source you are consulting to help create a list of works cited. (See the list of model entries, pp. 371–373, and the model entries and explanations on pp. 373–403.)

MLA CATEGORIES FOR SOURCES

BOOKS AND OTHER NONPERIODICAL PRINT PUBLICATIONS

Books, pamphlets, collections of articles, graphic narratives, government publications, doctoral dissertations

ARTICLES FROM PRINT PERIODICALS AND SELECTIONS FROM BOOKS

Articles in scholarly journals, magazines, and newspapers; editorials and letters to the editor; selections in a collection of scholarly articles or in an anthology; chapters in a book or parts of a book

WEB PUBLICATIONS

Web sites; scholarly journals, magazines, or newspapers in electronic form; database documents; online postings; email; blogs; podcasts

FIELD RESOURCES, PERFORMANCES, AND MEDIA RESOURCES

Interviews, surveys, and observations; unpublished letters and memos; performances and lectures; maps and cartoons (including Web versions); advertisements (print and Web); films and television or radio programs (including Web versions); recordings (including Web versions); artworks (including Web versions)

MLA IN-TEXT (PARENTHETICAL) FORMATS

MLA WORKS CITED MODEL ENTRIES

**30
MLA**

30a In-text citation examples

In-text citations following MLA style will differ slightly depending on the number of authors, the number of volumes in a work, and the number of works being cited.

1. Author's name in parentheses

You can choose to provide the author's name in parentheses. For a quotation or for specific information, include the page number to indicate where the material appears in the source.

During World War II, government posters often portrayed homemakers as

"vital defenders of the nation's homes" (Honey 135).

30a
MLA

2. Author's name in discussion

You can make the author's name (or the title and other information as well) part of the discussion.

> According to Maureen Honey, government posters during World War II often
>
> portrayed homemakers as "vital defenders of the nation's homes" (135).

3. Placement of parenthetical citations

In general, put parenthetical citations close to the quotation, information, paraphrase, or summary you are documenting. Place the parenthetical citation either at the end of a sentence (before the final punctuation) or at a natural pause in the sentence.

> Wayland Hand reports on a folk belief that going to sleep on a rug made of
>
> bearskin can relieve backache (183).

If the citation applies to only part of the sentence, put it after the borrowed material at the point least likely to disrupt the sentence.

> The folk belief that "sleeping on a bear rug will cure backache" (Hand 183)
>
> is yet another example of a kind of magic in which external objects
>
> produce results inside the body.

4. General reference (citing an entire work)

A **general reference** enables you to refer to the main ideas in a source or to information presented throughout the work, not in a single place. You need not provide page numbers for a general reference.

PARENTHETICAL
> Many species of animals have developed complex systems of
>
> communication (Bright).

AUTHOR NAMED
IN DISCUSSION
> According to Michael Bright, many species of animals have
>
> developed complex systems of communication.

5. Specific reference to print source

A **specific reference** enables you to document words, ideas, or facts appearing in a particular place in a source, such as the page for a quotation or a summary.

QUOTATION
> People have trouble recognizing sound patterns dolphins use to
>
> communicate. Dolphins can perceive clicking sounds "made up of

30a
MLA

700 units of sound per second," yet "in the human ear the
sounds would fuse together in our minds at 20-30 clicks per
second" (Bright 52).

SUMMARY   According to Michael Bright, dolphins recognize patterns
consisting of seven hundred clicks each second, yet such
patterns begin to blur for people at around twenty or thirty
clicks each second (52).

6. Specific reference to electronic source

If the source does not contain numbered pages, paragraphs, or
screens, no number is needed. If available, give the page number; identify
numbered paragraphs (*par., pars.*) or screens (*screen*) as such.

WEB SITE (NO   Using alcohol to get to sleep often means awakening "halfway
NUMBERED
PAGES)   through the night" (Royal).

PDF FILE   *The Royal College of Psychiatrists* Web site says using alcohol
to get to sleep means awakening "halfway through the
night" (4).

WEB SITE   *Offspring.com* summarizes research on adolescents (Boynton
(NUMBERED
SCREENS)   screen 2).

7. Specific reference to other nonprint source

After identifying the author or title, add numbers for the page, paragraph (*par., pars.*), section (*sec.*), or screen (*screen*) if given. Otherwise, no
number is needed.

The heroine's mother in the film *Clueless* died as the result of an accident
during liposuction.

8. One author

Provide the author's last name in parentheses, or integrate either the
full name or the last name alone into the discussion.

According to Maureen Honey, government posters during World
War II often portrayed homemakers as "vital defenders of the nation's
homes" (135).

30a
MLA

> **STRATEGY**   Create in-text citations
>
> Use the following questions to help decide whether to make in-text citations general or specific and whether to make them parenthetical or part of the discussion.
>
> - Am I trying to weave broad concepts into my own explanation or argument (general), or am I looking for precise ideas and details to support my conclusions (specific)?
> - Will this part of my paper be clearer and more effective if I draw on the author's own words (specific) or if I merely point out that the author's text as a whole presents the concepts I am discussing (general)?
> - Do I wish to highlight the source by naming the author (part of discussion) or to emphasize the information itself (parenthetical)?
> - Will this passage be more concise, emphatic, or effective if I put the author's name in parentheses or if I work it into the discussion?
> - Do I wish to refer to more than one source without distracting readers (parenthetical), or do the several sources I am citing need individual attention (part of discussion)?

9. Two or three authors

Name all of the authors in parentheses or in the discussion.

By the time Elizabeth I died, Francis Bacon had amassed considerable debt

(Jardine and Stewart 275).

If the book had three authors, the citation would read (Jardine, Stewart, and Ringler 275).

10. Four or more authors

Supply the first author's name and the phrase *et al.* (meaning "and others") within parentheses. To introduce the citation as part of the discussion, use a phrase like "Chen and his colleagues point out. . . ." If you give all the authors' names rather than *et al.* in the works cited list (Entry 21, see p. 388), then give all the names in the in-text citation.

More funding would encourage creative research of complementary

medicine (Chen et al. 82).

11. Organization or group as author

If an organization or a government agency is named as the author, use its name in the citation; shorten a cumbersome name such as Project for Excellence in Journalism.

Concerns over the quality of local news programs led to a proposed system

of standards ("benchmarking") for raising the quality of journalism (Project

for Excellence 189–91).

12. More than one work by the same author

When the list of works cited includes more than one work by the same author, add the title in shortened form to your citation.

The members of some Protestant groups in the Appalachian region view the

"handling of serpents" during worship "as a supreme act of faith"

(Daugherty, "Serpent-Handling" 232).

13. Authors with the same last name

When the authors of different sources have the same last name, identify the specific author by giving the first initial (or the full first name, if necessary).

Medical errors remain a major problem (D. Adams 1); however, new

information systems may help reduce them (J. Adams 309).

14. No author given (citing by title)

When no author's name is given, use the title instead. Begin with the word used to alphabetize the work in the list of works cited, but shorten a long title, as in this version of *Baedeker's Czech/Slovak Republics.*

On January 1, 1993, the former state of Czechoslovakia split into two new

states, the Czech Republic and the Slovak Republic (*Baedeker's* 67).

15. "Quoted in" (indirect source)

When your source provides you with a quotation (or paraphrase) taken from yet another source, you need to include the phrase *qtd. in* (for "quoted in") to indicate the original source. Here, Feuch is the source for Vitz.

For Vitz, "art, especially great art, must engage all or almost all of the

major capacities of the nervous system" (qtd. in Feuch 65).

When referring to an indirect source, you should generally include in your discussion the name of the person from whom the quotation is taken. If the same information were presented in a parenthetical citation—(*Vitz, qtd. in Feuch 65*)—some readers might mistakenly look for Vitz rather than Feuch in the list of works cited.

16. Long quotation

The citation in parentheses comes at the end of a long quotation set off as a block (quotation not enclosed in quotation marks) (see pp. 336–337). Put the citation after the end punctuation, with a space before the parentheses.

> Cricket, as played in India, has taken a path of commercialization similar to that of American football and basketball.
>
> > Like other sports figures in the capitalist world, the best-known Indian cricket stars are now metacommodities, for sale themselves while fueling the circulation of other commodities. The sport is increasingly in the hands of advertisers, promoters, and entrepreneurs, with television, radio, and print media feeding the national passion for the sport and its stars. (Appadurai 106)

17. Short quotation

The citation in parentheses comes after the quotation marks that close the quotation. If the quotation ends with an exclamation point or question mark, put it inside the quotation marks. If the material you are quoting contains quotation marks, use double quotation marks to enclose the quotation as a whole and single quotation marks to enclose the interior quotation.

> According to Dubisch, "Being a 'healthfood person' involves more than simply changing one's diet or utilizing an alternative medical system" (61).

18. Two or more sources in a single citation

When you use a parenthetical citation to refer to more than one source, separate the sources with a semicolon.

> Differences in the ways people speak, especially differences in the ways men and women use language, can often be traced to who has power and who does not (Tannen 83–86; Tavris 297–301).

19. Selection in anthology or collection

If your source is a reprint of an essay, poem, short story, or other work appearing in an anthology, cite the work's author (not the anthology's editor), but refer to the page number(s) in the anthology.

> John Corry argues that pornographic material is not really available "with just the click of a button" (114).

20. Multivolume work

Give the volume number followed by a colon and a space, then the page number: (*Franklin 6: 434*). When referring to the volume as a whole, use a comma after the author's name and add *vol.* before the volume number: (*Franklin, vol. 6*).

> In 1888, Lewis Carroll let two students call their school paper *Jabberwock,* a made-up word from *Alice's Adventures in Wonderland* (Cohen 2: 695).

21. Literary work

When you refer to a literary work, consider including information that will help readers find the passage you are citing in any edition of the work. Begin by giving the page number of the particular edition followed by a semi-colon; then add the appropriate chapter, part, or section numbers.

> In *Huckleberry Finn*, Mark Twain ridicules the exaggerated histrionics of provincial actors through his portrayal of the King and the Duke as they rehearse Hamlet's famous soliloquy: "So [the duke] went to marching up and down, thinking, and frowning horrible every now and then; then he would hoist up his eyebrows; next he would squeeze his hand on his forehead and stagger back and kind of moan; next he would sigh, and next he'd let on to drop a tear" (178; ch. 21).

Note that there is a semicolon after the page number, followed by *ch.* (for "chapter"). If you also include a part number, use *pt.* followed by a comma and the chapter number, as in (*386; pt. 3, ch. 2*). For a play, note the act, scene, and line numbers, if needed, as in this reference to *Hamlet*: (*Ham. 1.2.76*). For poems, give line numbers (*55–57*) or, if there are part divisions, both part and line numbers (*4.220–23*).

22. Visual in text

In your discussion, refer to the visual as a *figure* (abbreviated *fig.*). Include citation information in the caption for the visual.

TEXT

> Satellite photos (fig. 2) give some idea of the damage flooding from Hurricane Katrina caused in New Orleans.

FIGURE CAPTION

> Fig. 2. Extent of flooding on September 8, 2005 (National Aeronautics and Space Administration).

23. Bible, Qur'an, or other religious text

Give book, chapter, and verse for the Bible, Qur'an, or other religious text. MLA style uses a period between the chapter and verse numbers (*Mark 2.3–4*). For parenthetical citations, use abbreviations for names of five or more letters, as in the case of Deuteronomy: (*Deut. 16.21–22*).

> God's instructions to Moses also cover issues of guilt, forgiveness, and
>
> restitution (Num. 5.5-8).

24. Email, interview, or personal communication

Direct readers to the information in your works cited list (pp. 400–401) by giving the name of the writer or the person being interviewed.

> One of the director's assistants recalls that staging the show for the first
>
> time was "an experiment in chaos and misunderstanding" (Shiels).

25. More than one reference to a source in a sentence or paragraph

If you refer to a source more than once in a passage, you may be able to combine references.

> Anthony Giddens views contemporary society as "a runaway world" in
>
> which belief in the powers of reason or rationality may be outmoded
>
> but "a world of multiple possibilities" is open to us (Bryant and Jary
>
> 263, 264).

or

> Anthony Giddens views contemporary society as "a runaway world" (Bryant
>
> and Jary 263). He argues that belief in the powers of reason or rationality
>
> may be outmoded but that a "world of multiple possibilities" is open to
>
> us (264).

26. Informative footnotes and endnotes

Use a note when you want to comment on a source or discuss a specific point at length and you recognize that doing so would disrupt the flow of the discussion and would be useful for only a few readers. Place a number (raised slightly above the line of the text) at a suitable point in your discussion. Then provide the note itself, labeled with a corresponding number at the bottom of a page (for a footnote) or at the end of the paper before the list of works cited on a page titled "Notes" (for an endnote).

30b Works Cited list

In an alphabetized list titled "Works Cited," placed on a new page that follows the last page of your paper or report, provide readers with detailed information about the sources you have cited in the text.

STRATEGY Format the works cited list

- **Page Format.** Use the heading "Works Cited" (or "Works Consulted," if you include all sources that you reviewed) centered one inch below the top edge of a new page. Double-space between the title and the first entry in the list. Continue the page numbering from the body of the paper.
- **Indentation.** Do not indent the first line of each entry. Indent all subsequent lines one-half inch or five spaces.
- **Spacing.** Double-space all lines, both within and between entries. Leave a single space (or two spaces, if you wish) after a period within an entry. Use consistent spacing throughout all entries.
- **Alphabetizing.** Alphabetize entries by last names of authors (if you have authors with the same last name, order them alphabetically by first name; if you have multiple works by the same author, order them alphabetically by title). For sources without an author, use the first word in the title (other than *a, an, the*).

---

1 Articles from print periodicals and selections from books

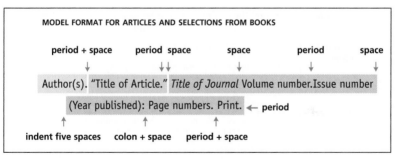

MODEL FORMAT FOR ARTICLES AND SELECTIONS FROM BOOKS

period + space   period space   space   period   space
↓   ↓↓   ↓   ↓   ↓
Author(s). "Title of Article." *Title of Journal* Volume number.Issue number

(Year published): Page numbers. Print. ← period
↑   ↑   ↑
indent five spaces   colon + space   period + space

- **Author(s).** Give the author's last name first, followed by the first name, any initial, and a period. If the work has more than one author, give subsequent names in regular order, separated by commas, with *and* preceding the final name.
- **Title of article.** Give the article's full title in quotation marks, concluding with a period unless the title ends with a question mark or an exclamation point.
- **Title of journal, periodical, or book.** Give the publication's title, italicized, but not including an opening *The, A,* or *An.* Do not end the title with a period.

- **Publication information.** Supply the volume number and the issue number, the year of publication (in parentheses), and the page numbers for the full article or selection. The volume number is always found on the publication's cover or title page; even if it is in Roman numerals, use Arabic numerals for your entry. For a scholarly journal, you don't need to include the month or season. For magazines and newspapers, identify the particular issue by date of publication. Introduce the page numbers with a colon. For page ranges, limit the second number to its two final numerals (14–21, 162–79 unless unclear 1498–1524).
- **Medium of publication.** After the publication information, give the medium of publication followed by a period: *Print.*

Article in print journal

Author's name →   Article title →

Arreola, Daniel D. "Forget the Alamo: The Border as Place in John Sayles'
Lone Star." *Journal of Cultural Geography* 23.1 (2005): 23–42.

Print. → Medium

Journal title   Volume number   Issue number   Year of publication   Pages

Year of publication

Journal title → *Journal of Cultural Geography Fall/Winter 2005* • 23(1):23–42 ← Volume, issue, page numbers

Article title → **Forget the Alamo: The Border as Place in John Sayles'** *Lone Star*

Author s name → **Daniel D. Arreola**

ABSTRACT. Mexicans have been pejorative in the American conception and mythologizing of the Mexican American borderland. Part of that vision has been shaped by popular cinema. John Sayles' *Lone Star* is examined as a critical case study that undermines many of these myths about Mexicans and portrays the border as an authentic place. Assessing these contours helps us see how the border moves from stereotyped space to authentic place in cinema, and demonstrates how film can capture the dynamic cultural geographic quality of this region and its people.

INTRODUCTION

In an early scene of Orson Welles' *Touch of Evil*, the American stereotype of the Mexican border comes alive. Descending a shadowy staircase in their honeymoon hotel in the fictitious seaside oil town of Los Robles—The Paris of the Border—Ramon Miguel "Mike" Vargas, a Mexican narcotics investigator played by a bronze-skinned and black mustached Charlton Heston, speaks to his newlywed wife, Susan, a platinum blond from Philadelphia who has never been to the border, played as the Hollywood sweater-girl archetype by Janet Leigh: "This isn't the real Mexico. You know that. All border towns bring out the worst in a country" (Comito 1995, 77).[1]

1. Article in scholarly journal

Look for the author's name at the beginning or end of the article. Look for publication information on the journal's cover, title page, or at the bottom of the first page. Then provide the journal's title, italicized (omitting an opening *A* or *The*); volume number, issue number (if available); year of publication (in parentheses); a colon; inclusive page numbers for the article; and a period. Next state the medium of publication you consulted, followed by a period. (For combined issues, hyphenate the issue number: *2-3*.)

ARTICLE IN JOURNAL WITH VOLUME AND ISSUE NUMBER

Fairfield, James. "Deadly Discourses: Examining the Roles of Language and

Silence in the Lynching of Emmett Till and Wright's *Native Son*."

Arizona Quarterly 63.4 (2007): 63-82. Print.

ARTICLE IN JOURNAL WITH VOLUME NUMBER ONLY

Eagleton, Terry. "Political Beckett?" *New Left Review* 40 (2006): 67-74.

Print.

2. Article in scholarly journal with two or three authors

Begin with the first author's last name. Add other names in regular order, separated by commas, with *and* before the final name.

Levin, C. Melinda, and Alicia Re Cruz. "Behind the Scenes of a Visual

Ethnography: A Dialogue between Anthropology and Film." *Journal of*

Film and Video 60.2 (2008): 59-68. Print.

3. Article in scholarly journal with four or more authors

After the first name, add *et al.* ("and others"). Or you may give all the names; if so, list them in the text citations, too (Entry 10, p. 376).

Heaton, Tim B., et al. "The Child Mortality Disadvantage among Indigenous

People in Mexico." *Population Review* 46.1 (2007): 1-11. Print.

Heaton, Tim, B., J. Lynn England, Myrna Garcia Bencomo, and Gerardo

Reyes Lopez. "The Child Mortality Disadvantage among Indigenous

People in Mexico." *Population Review* 46.1 (2007): 1-11. Print.

4. Article in weekly magazine

Put the day first, then the month (abbreviated except for May, June, and July), and then the year followed by a colon. Give inclusive page numbers. If the pages are not consecutive, give the first page with a plus sign (for

30b
MLA

example, *23*+). Treat biweekly or monthly magazines in a similar fashion, without listing the day.

> Conlin, Michelle. "Unmarried America." *Business Week* 20 Oct. 2003: 106+.
>
> > Print.

5. Article in monthly magazine

> Jacobson, Doranne. "Doing Lunch." *Natural History* Mar. 2000: 66-69. Print.

6. Unsigned article in magazine

Begin with the title (ignoring *A*, *An*, and *The* when alphabetizing).

> "The Obesity Industry." *Economist* 27 Sept. 2003: 64+. Print.

7. Article in newspaper

Treat a newspaper as a weekly magazine, including citation of pages (see Entry 4), but include the section number or letter with the page number. Omit *A*, *An*, or *The* at the beginning of a newspaper's name. For a local newspaper, give the city's name in brackets after the title unless the city is named in the title.

> Willis, Ellen. "Steal This Myth: Why We Still Try to Re-create the Rush of
>
> > the 60s." *New York Times* 20 Aug. 2000, late ed., sec. 2: AR1+. Print.

8. Editorial

Supply the title first for an unsigned editorial and the author's name first for a signed editorial. Identify with the word *editorial*.

> "A False Choice." Editorial. *Charlotte Observer* 16 Aug. 1998: 2C. Print.

9. Letter to the editor

Use the word *letter* to identify a letter to the editor.

> Hogner, Lindon. Letter. "Mandate Time Off for Fatigued Doctors."
>
> > *USA Today* 18 Dec. 2006: 20A. Print.

10. Interview—published

Treat the person interviewed, not the interviewer, as the author. For untitled interviews, include the word *Interview* (without underlining or quotation marks) in place of a title.

> Stewart, Martha. "'I Do Have a Brain.'" Interview with Kevin Kelly. *Wired*
>
> > Aug. 1998: 114. Print.

11. Review

Give the title after the name of the reviewer. Cite an unsigned review by its title.

Muñoz, José Esteban. "Citizens and Superheroes." Rev. of *The Queen of*
America Goes to Washington City, by Lauren Berlant. *American*
Quarterly 52.2 (2000): 397-404. Print.

For a review with no title, give the name of the reviewer followed by
Rev. of ("Review of"), the work's title, a comma, the word *by*, and the author
of the work.

Asante, Molefi Kete. Rev. of *Race and the Writing of History: Riddling the*
Sphinx, by Maghan Keita. *Journal of Black Studies* 31.5 (2001):
699-701. Print.

12. Article from encyclopedia or reference volume

Begin with the author's name or with the article's title if no author is
named. You need not include the publisher or place of publication for a common reference work or series; instead, note the edition and the date. If entries are arranged alphabetically, you need not note the volume or page(s).

Oliver, Paul, and Barry Kernfeld. "Blues." *The New Grove Dictionary of Jazz.*
Ed. Barry Kernfeld. New York: St. Martin's, 1994. Print.

"The History of Western Theatre." *The New Encyclopaedia Britannica:*
Macropaedia. 15th ed. 1987. Vol. 28. Print.

13. Chapter in edited book or selection in anthology

List the author of the chapter or selection and give the title in quotation marks (but italicize titles of novels, plays, and other works first published on their own). Next, provide the italicized title of the book containing
the selection or chapter. If the collection has an editor, follow with the abbreviation *Ed.* and the name(s) of the editor(s) in regular order. Conclude
with publication information and the selection's inclusive page numbers.

Atwood, Margaret. "Bluebeard's Egg." *Bluebeard's Egg and Other Stories.*
New York: Fawcett–Random, 1987. 131-64. Print.

After citing in full the original source for a selection reprinted in a collection, use the phrase *Rpt. in* ("Reprinted in") followed by information
about the source you consulted.

Atwood, Margaret. "Bluebeard's Egg." *Bluebeard's Egg and Other Stories.*
New York: Fawcett–Random, 1987. 131-64. Rpt. in *Don't Bet on the*
Prince: Contemporary Feminist Fairy Tales in North America and
England. Ed. Jack Zipes. New York: Methuen, 1989. 160-82. Print.

30b
MLA

14. More than one selection from collection or anthology (cross-reference)

Include one entry for the collection and provide a cross-reference for each individual selection.

> Hooper, Glenn, and Colin Graham, eds. *Irish and Postcolonial Writing:*
>
> *History, Theory, Practice.* London: Palgrave-Macmillian, 2002. Print.
>
> Innes, Lyn. "Orientalism and Celticism." Hooper and Graham 142-56. Print.
>
> Mustafa, Shakir. "Demythologizing Ireland: Revisionism and the Irish
>
> Colonial Experience." Hooper and Graham 66-86. Print.

15. Preface, foreword, introduction, or afterword

Identify the section as a preface, foreword, introduction, or afterword. Give the title of the work, then its author, preceded by the word *By.*

> Tomlin, Janice. Foreword. *The Complete Guide to Foreign Adoption.* By
>
> Barbara Brooke Bascom and Carole A. McKelvey. New York: Pocket,
>
> 1997. Print.

16. Letter—published

Treat the letter writer as the author. Indicate the date or the collection number of the letter if the information is available.

> Garland, Hamlin. "To Fred Lewis Pattee." 30 Dec. 1914. Letter 206 of
>
> *Selected Letters of Hamlin Garland.* Ed. Keith Newlin and Joseph B.
>
> McCullough. Lincoln: U of Nebraska P, 1998. Print.

17. Dissertation abstract

For an abstract of a dissertation published in *Dissertation Abstracts International* (*DAI*) or *Dissertation Abstracts* (*DA*), follow the author's name and the title with the abbreviation *Diss.* (for "Dissertation"), the institution's name, and the date of the degree. Conclude with publication information for the particular volume of abstracts.

> Hawkins, Joanne Berning. "Horror Cinema and the Avant–Garde." Diss. U of
>
> California, Berkeley, 1993. *DAI* 55 (1995): 1712A. Print.

18. Unpublished essay

Give the author's name, the title, the words *Unpublished essay,* and the date the essay was written. (Use TS for typescript and MS for manuscript.)

Solokov, Yvor. "From Theory to Practice in the Coming Century."

Unpublished essay, 2007. TS.

2 Books and works treated as books

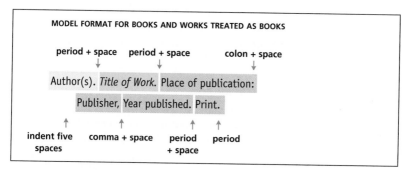

MODEL FORMAT FOR BOOKS AND WORKS TREATED AS BOOKS

period + space   period + space   colon + space

Author(s). *Title of Work.* Place of publication:

Publisher, Year published. Print.

indent five   comma + space   period   period
spaces   + space

- **Author(s).** Give the author's last name first, followed by the first name, any middle name or initial, and a period.
- **Title of work.** Give the title of the work, including any subtitle. Capitalize the main words, and end with a period unless the title ends with some other mark of punctuation. Italicize the title.
- **Publication information.** After the title, provide the city where the work was published, followed by a colon and a single space. If not obvious, add the country (abbreviated, as in *Dover, Eng.*). If more than one place of publication appears in the work, use only the first one in your citation. Then give the publisher's name in shortened form (U of Chicago P for University of Chicago Press or McGraw for McGraw-Hill, Inc.) followed by a comma and the year of publication, followed by a period. If any of the basic publication information is missing, use *n.p.* ("no place" or "no publisher") or *n.d.* ("no date").

19. Book with one author

Hockney, David. *Secret Knowledge: Recovering the Lost Techniques of the Old*

Masters. New York: Viking Studio, 2001. Print.

20. Book with two or three authors

Give the first author's name, starting with the last name, followed by the other names in regular order. Use commas to separate the names, and introduce the second of two names or the third name with *and.*

Kress, Gunther, and Theo van Leeuwen. *Reading Images: The Grammar of*

Graphic Design. London: Routledge, 1996. Print.

30b
MLA

21. Book with four or more authors

Use the first author's name and then the phrase *et al.* (meaning "and others"). You may choose to give all the names, but if you do, you must list all of them in any parenthetical citations (see Entry 10, p. 376).

> Bellah, Robert N., et al. *Habits of the Heart: Individualism and Commitment in American Life.* Berkeley: U of California P, 1985. Print.
>
> All authors listed: Bellah, Robert N., Richard Madsen, William M. Sullivan, Ann Swidler, and Steven M. Tipton.

22. Organization or group as author

Treat the corporation, organization, or government agency as the author, alphabetizing by the first main word of the organization's name. If the organization is also the publisher, repeat its name again, abbreviated if appropriate.

> United Nations Educational, Scientific, and Cultural Organization. *A Short Internet Guide.* New York: UNESCO, 2001. Print.

23. No author given

List the work alphabetically according to the first main word of its title.

> *Guide for Authors.* Oxford: Blackwell, 1985. Print.

24. More than one book by the same author

List multiple works by an author alphabetically by the first main word of the title. For the first entry, include the full name(s) of the author(s). For additional entries, use three hyphens in place of the name, followed by a period and a space, but only if the author or authors are *exactly* the same for each work. If the authorship differs in any way, include the name(s) in full.

> Tannen, Deborah. *The Argument Culture: Moving from Debate to Dialogue.* New York: Random, 1998. Print.
>
> ---. *You're Wearing That? Understanding Mothers and Daughters in Conversation.* New York: Random, 2006. Print.

25. One or more editors

Begin with the editor's name followed by a comma and the abbreviation *ed.* or *eds.*

> Achebe, Chinua, and C. L. Innes, eds. *African Short Stories.* London: Heinemann, 1985. Print.

26. Author and an editor

Begin with either the author's or the editor's name, depending on whether you are using the text itself or the editor's contributions.

> Leonardo da Vinci. *Leonardo on Painting*. Ed. Martin Kemp. New Haven: Yale
>
> > UP, 1989. Print.

27. Translator

Begin with the author unless you emphasize the translator's work. Abbreviate the translator's title as *Trans.*

> Baudrillard, Jean. *Cool Memories II: 1978-1990*. Trans. Chris Turner.
>
> > Durham: Duke UP, 1996. Print.

28. Edition other than the first

Note the edition (*3rd ed.*, *Rev. ed.*, *1998 ed.*) after the title.

> Coe, Michael D. *The Maya*. 7th ed. New York: Thames, 2005. Print.

29. Reprinted book

Supply the original publication date after the title. If pertinent, include the original publisher or place of publication. Then follow with the publication information from the work you are using.

> Kerouac, Jack. *On the Road*. 1957. New York: Viking, 1997. Print.

30. Multivolume work

Indicate the total number of volumes after the title (or after the editor's or translator's name).

> Tsao, Hsueh-chin. *The Story of the Stone*. Trans. David Hawkes. 5 vols.
>
> > Harmondsworth, Eng.: Penguin, 1983-86. Print.

If you are citing a particular volume instead of the whole work or several volumes from the whole work, supply only the particular volume number and publication information. Indicate the total number of volumes at the end of the entry.

> Tsao, Hsueh-chin. *The Story of the Stone*. Trans. David Hawkes. Vol. 1.
>
> > Harmondsworth, Eng.: Penguin, 1983. Print. 5 vols.

31. Work in a series

Give the series name and any item number at the end of the entry. Use abbreviations for familiar words in the name of the series (such as *ser.* for *series*).

Grover-Friedlander, Michal. *Vocal Apparitions: The Attraction of Cinema to Opera*. Princeton: Princeton UP, 2005. Print. Princeton Stud. in Opera.

32. Book published before 1900

Include the publisher's name only if it is relevant to your research. Use a comma rather than a colon after place of publication.

Darwin, Charles. *Descent of Man and Selection in Relation to Sex*. New York, 1896. Print.

33. Book with a publisher's imprint

Give the imprint name first, a hyphen and the publisher's name.

Sikes, Gini. *8 Ball Chicks: A Year in the Violent World of Girl Gangs*. New York: Anchor-Doubleday, 1997. Print.

34. Collection of articles or anthology

Supply the editor's name first, followed by *ed.*, and then the title of the collection. To cite a selection within an anthology or collection, see Entries 13 and 14 on pages 385–386.

Silver, Alain, and James Ursini, eds. *Horror Film Reader*. Pompton Plains, NJ: Limelight, 2001. Print.

35. Government document

Begin with the government or agency name(s) or the author, if any. Start with *United States* for a congressional document or a report from a federal agency; otherwise, begin with the name of the government and agency or the name of the independent agency. For congressional documents, write *Cong.* (for *Congress*), identify the branch (*Senate* or *House*), and give the number and session (for example, *101st Cong., 1st sess.*). Include the title of the specific document and the title of the book in which it is printed. Use *GPO* for *Government Printing Office.*

United States. Office of Juvenile Justice and Delinquency Prevention. *Promising Strategies to Reduce Gun Violence*. By David I. Sheppard and Shay Bilchik. Washington: GPO, 1999. Print.

United States. Cong. Senate. Committee on Commerce, Science, and Transportation. *Internet Filtering Systems*. 105th Cong., 2nd sess. Washington: GPO, 1998. Print.

36. Title within a title

When a book title contains another work's title, do not italicize the title of the second work. If the second title would normally be enclosed in quotation marks, add them and italicize the entire title.

Weick, Carl F. *Refiguring* Huckleberry Finn. Athens: U of Georgia P, 2000. Print.

37. Pamphlet

Use the same form for a pamphlet as for a book.

Vareika, William. *John La Farge: An American Master (1835-1910)*. Newport:

Gallery of American Art, 1989. Print.

38. Dissertation (published)

Treat a published doctoral dissertation as a book. Include the abbreviation *Diss.*, the school for which the dissertation was written, and the year the degree was awarded.

Said, Edward W. *Joseph Conrad and the Fiction of Autobiography*. Diss.

Harvard U, 1964. Cambridge: Harvard UP, 1966. Print.

39. Dissertation (unpublished)

Use quotation marks for the title; include the abbreviation *Diss.*, the school for which the dissertation was written, and the date of the degree.

Pennell, Michael. "English in the 'Hurricane Winds of Change': Labor Market

Intermediaries in Two Indiana Counties." Diss. Purdue U, 2005. Print.

40. Conference proceedings

Begin with the title unless an editor is named. Follow with details about the conference, including name and date.

Childhood Obesity: Causes and Prevention. Symposium Proc., 27 Oct. 1998.

Washington: Center for Nutrition Policy and Promotion, 1999. Print.

41. Sacred text

Identify the version, the editor or translator (if indicated), and the publication information.

Zondervan NIV Study Bible. Grand Rapids: Zondervan, 2006. Print.

42. Graphic novel or illustrated work

If author and illustrator are the same, use the following form.

Satrapi, Marjane. *Persepolis: The Story of a Childhood*. New York: Pantheon,

2004. Print.

30b
MLA

If you are focusing on the illustrator's work, as distinct from the author's, give the illustrator's name first, followed by a comma and *illus.* (for "illustrator"), a period, the title, a period, and the word *By* followed by the author's name.

3 Web publications

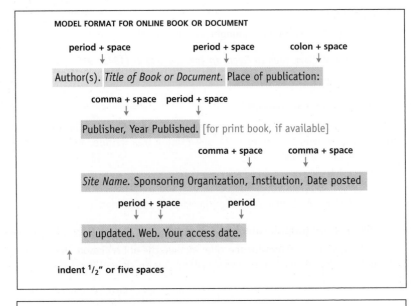

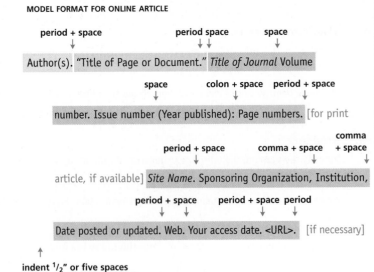

Article in scholarly Web journal

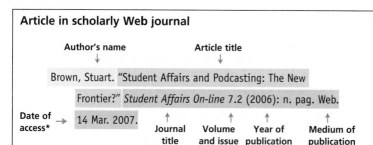

Author's name → Brown, Stuart. Article title → "Student Affairs and Podcasting: The New

Frontier?" *Student Affairs On-line* 7.2 (2006): n. pag. Web.

Date of access* → 14 Mar. 2007.

Journal title | Volume and issue numbers | Year of publication | Medium of publication

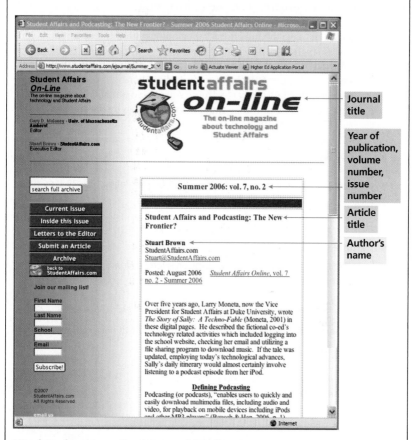

*For date of access, use the date you visited the source.

- **Author.** Name the author or person who is responsible for the site.
- **Title of work/site.** Name the work or document, italicizing if the document is independent or using quotation marks if it is part of a larger document. Follow with the Web site's name (italicized) if this differs from the title of the work or document.
- **Version.** Indicate the version or edition you used.
- **Publisher and date.** Name the sponsor or publisher (*N.p.* if not available). Indicate the day, month, and year of publication; use *n.d.* if the information is not available.
- **Medium and access date.** The medium is usually *Web*. Give the day, month, and year you accessed the site.
- **Uniform Resource Locator (URL).** Most citations do not need a URL. If such information is necessary for identifying and locating a document, give the full address, beginning with the access-mode identifier (*http, ftp, gopher, telnet*). Enclose the URL in angle brackets < > followed by a period. When a URL continues from one line to the next, break it only after a slash. Do not add a hyphen.
- **Page numbering.** Many electronic sources do not have pages. Include page, paragraph, or screen numbers when given by the source.

43. Web site

> *History of the American West, 1860–1920*. Denver Public Lib., 20 Mar. 2008.
>
> > Web. 19 Aug. 2008.

44. Home page

Give the creator, a title or description such as *Home page*, sponsor, and date (use *n.d.* for no date).

> Jobs, Steven. Home page. *Mac.com*. Apple, n.d. Web. 16 Apr. 2009.
>
> Baron, Dennis. Home page. Dept. of English, U of Illinois, n.d. Web.
>
> > 20 Apr. 2008.

45. Course home page

> Jolly, Jennifer. Arts in the Americas. Course home page. Art History Dept.,
>
> > Ithaca College, 23 Jan.-5 May 2008. Web. 17 Apr. 2008.

46. Article in scholarly Web journal

Include page or paragraph numbers, if available; if not, use *n. pag.* Finally, give the medium of publication (*Web*) and the date you accessed the site.

Dugdale, Timothy. "The Fan and (Auto)Biography: Writing the Self in the Start." *Journal of Mundane Behavior* 1.2 (2000): n. pag. Web. 14 July 2008.

47. Magazine article on Web

Wright, Laura. "My, What Big Eyes. . . ." *Discover.* Discover Magazine, 27 Oct. 2003. Web. 25 Apr. 2009.

48. Newspaper article on Web

Mulvihill, Kim. "Childhood Obesity." *San Francisco Chronicle.* San Francisco Chronicle, 12 July 2001. Web. 2 May 2009.

49. Government document on Web

Government documents may be difficult to locate without a URL.

United States. Dept. of Commerce. Bureau of the Census. *Census Brief: Disabilities Affect One-Fifth of All Americans.* Dec. 1997. Web. 5 Apr. 2009. <http://www.census.gov/prod/3/97pubs/cenbr975.pdf>.

50. Editorial on Web

"Mall Mania/A Measure of India's Success." Editorial. *startribune.com.* Minneapolis Star Tribune, 31 Oct. 2003. Web. 14 Nov. 2007.

51. Letter to editor on Web

Hadjiargyrou, Michael. "Stem Cells and Delicate Questions." Letter. *New York Times on the Web.* New York Times. 17 July 2001. Web. 23 Jan. 2009.

52. Interview on Web

Rikker, David. Interview with Victor Payan. *San Diego Latino Film Festival.* May 1999. Web. 10 Jan. 2008.

30b
MLA

53. Review on Web

> Chaudhury, Parama. Rev. of *Kandahar*, dir. Mohsen Makhmalbaf. *Film*
> *Monthly* 3.4 (2002): n. pag. Web. 6 Apr. 2008.

54. Abstract on Web

> Prelow, Hazel, and Charles A. Guarnaccia. "Ethnic and Racial Differences in
> Life Stress among High School Adolescents." Abstract. *Journal*
> *of Counseling and Development* 75.6 (1997): n. pag. Web.
> 6 Apr. 2008.

55. Posting

Aid readers (if you can) by citing an archived version.

> Brock, Stephen E. "School Crisis." Online posting. *Special Events Chat*
> *Transcripts*. Lycos Communities, 27 Apr. 2001. Web. 18 July 2001.

56. Email

Give the writer's name, message title (taken from the subject line), "Message to" with the recipient, and the date. Use *E-mail* as the medium of publication, and hyphenate it according to MLA style.

> Santos, Joel. "Developing Resources for Film Study." Message to the
> author. 12 July 2008. E-mail.

57. Blog

Give the name of the author, then the title of the posting or entry in quotation marks. Next provide the name of the blog (italicized), the date of the posting, *Web*, and the date of access.

> Ramsey, Doug. "Zoot, Red, Lorraine." *Rifftides*. 5 Mar. 2007. Web. 10 Mar.
> 2008.

58. Podcast

> Loh, Sandra Tsing. "You Are Getting Sleepy. . . ." *The Loh Down on Science*.
> KPCC, Natl. Public Radio, 15 Apr. 2008. MP3 file.

59. Web book also available in print

Include the author's name and the title; the name(s) of any editor, compiler, or translator (if relevant); information about print publication (if any); electronic publication information; the scholarly project containing the work (if any) and date of access.

> London, Jack. *The Iron Heel.* New York: Macmillan, 1908. *The*
>
>   *Jack London Collection.* Berkeley Digital Lib. SunSITE.
>
>   Web. 15 July 2009.

60. Selection from Web book

> Muir, John. "The City of the Saints." *Steep Trails.* Boston: Houghton Mifflin,
>
>   1918. Web. 17 Apr. 2007.

4 Online database resources

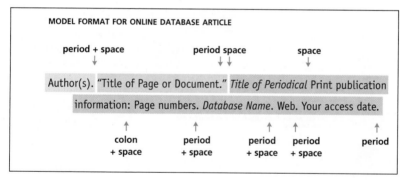

MODEL FORMAT FOR ONLINE DATABASE ARTICLE

period + space   period space   space

Author(s). "Title of Page or Document." *Title of Periodical* Print publication information: Page numbers. *Database Name.* Web. Your access date.

colon + space   period + space   period + space   period + space   period

- **Print publication information.** For sources available through on-line subscription databases provided by libraries (such as EBSCOhost, LexisNexis, Project Muse, or JSTOR), begin with information about print publication, if any, according to the kind of document (book, magazine article, or newspaper article, for example), but leave out the original medium of publication (*Print*).
- **Page numbers.** Include page numbers as you would for a print entry; if the service provides only the starting page of the printed text, give it followed by a period, for example: *147.*
- **Database name, medium, and access date.** Give the name of the database (italicized), the medium of publication (Web), and the date of access.

Journal article from a subscription database (HTML format)

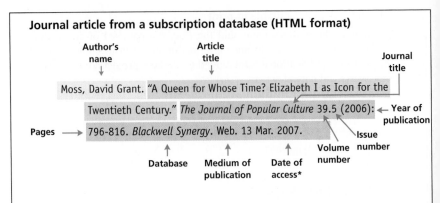

Author's name → Moss, David Grant.

Article title → "A Queen for Whose Time? Elizabeth I as Icon for the Twentieth Century."

Journal title → *The Journal of Popular Culture* 39.5 (2006):

Pages → 796-816. *Blackwell Synergy*. Web. 13 Mar. 2007.

Year of publication
Issue number
Volume number
Database
Medium of publication
Date of access*

Database

Journal title

Year of publication

Volume number, issue number, pages for print original (no page numbers in online HTML text)

Article title

Author's name

Database service

*For date of access, use the date you visited the source.

Journal article from a subscription database (PDF version)

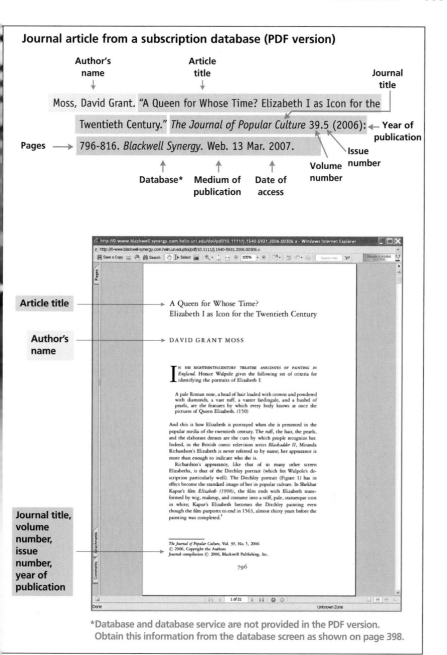

Author's name → Moss, David Grant.

Article title → "A Queen for Whose Time? Elizabeth I as Icon for the Twentieth Century."

Journal title → *The Journal of Popular Culture*

Year of publication → 39.5 (2006):

Pages → 796-816. *Blackwell Synergy*. Web. 13 Mar. 2007.

Database* — Medium of publication — Date of access

Volume number — Issue number

Article title → A Queen for Whose Time? Elizabeth I as Icon for the Twentieth Century

Author's name → DAVID GRANT MOSS

IN HIS EIGHTEENTH-CENTURY TREATISE *ANECDOTES OF PAINTING IN England*, Horace Walpole gives the following set of criteria for identifying the portraits of Elizabeth I:

A pale Roman nose, a head of hair loaded with crowns and powdered with diamonds, a vast ruff, a vaster fardingale, and a bushel of pearls, are the features by which every body knows at once the pictures of Queen Elizabeth. (150)

And this is how Elizabeth is portrayed when she is presented in the popular media of the twentieth century. The ruff, the hair, the pearls, and the elaborate dresses are the cues by which people recognize her. Indeed, in the British comic television series *Blackadder II*, Miranda Richardson's Elizabeth is never referred to by name; her appearance is more than enough to indicate who she is.

Richardson's appearance, like that of so many other screen Elizabeths, is that of the Ditchley portrait (which fits Walpole's description particularly well). The Ditchley portrait (Figure 1) has in effect become the standard image of her in popular culture. In Shekhar Kapur's film *Elizabeth (1998)*, the film ends with Elizabeth transformed by wig, makeup, and costume into a stiff, pale, statuesque icon in white; Kapur's Elizabeth becomes the Ditchley painting even though the film purports to end in 1563, almost thirty years before the painting was completed.[1]

Journal title, volume number, issue number, year of publication → *The Journal of Popular Culture*, Vol. 39, No. 5, 2006
© 2006, Copyright the Authors
Journal compilation © 2006, Blackwell Publishing, Inc.

796

*Database and database service are not provided in the PDF version.
Obtain this information from the database screen as shown on page 398.

61. Scholarly journal article from database

Use *n. pag.* if page numbers are not available.

FULL TEXT

Reger, Jo. "Where Are the Leaders? Music, Culture, and Contemporary Feminism." *American Behavioral Scientist* 50.10 (2007): 1350-69. *Electronic Journals Service.* Web. 19 June 2007.

ABSTRACT

Sofaer, Abraham D. "Presidential Power and National Security." Abstract. *Presidential Studies Quarterly* 37.1 (2007): 101+. *InfoTrac OneFile.* Web. 29 June 2007.

62. Magazine article from database

Barrett, Jennifer. "Fast Food Need Not Be Fat Food." *Newsweek* 13 Oct. 2003: 73-74. *Academic Search Premier.* Web. 31 Oct. 2007.

63. Newspaper article from database

Lee, R. "Class with the 'Ph.D. Diva.'" *New York Times* 18 Oct. 2003: B7. *InfoTrac OneFile.* Web. 31 Oct. 2008.

64. Summary of research from database

Holub, Tamara. "Early Decision Programs." ED470540.2002. *ERIC Digests.* Web. 7 Nov. 2009.

65. Collection of materials from database

"Combating Plagiarism." *CQ Researcher.* CQ P., 9 Sept. 2003. Web. 12 Nov. 2009.

5 Field resources, performances, and media resources

66. Interview (unpublished)

Give the name of the person interviewed. Indicate the type of interview: *Personal interview* (you did the interview in person), *Telephone interview* (done over the telephone), *Email interview* (done by email), or *Interview* (someone else conducted the interview, perhaps on a radio or television program). If a recorded or broadcast interview has a title, give it in place of the word *Interview*. Give the date of the interview.

Sedgwick, Kyra. Interview with James Lipton. *Inside the Actors Studio.* Bravo, 11 June 2007. Television.

67. Survey or questionnaire

MLA does not specify a form for these field resources. When citing your own field research, you may wish to use the following format. For medium of publication, use the medium in which the document or materials are preserved, for example, list the digital format followed by *file*.

> Arrigo-Nelson, Summer, and Jennifer Emily Figliozzi. Questionnaire on
>
> Student Alcohol Use and Parental Values. U of Rhode Island,
>
> Kingston, 15-20 Apr. 2004. *Microsoft Word* file.

68. Observations

MLA does not specify a form for this type of field research. You may wish to use the following form to cite your notes on field observations. Conclude with the name of the medium in which the materials are preserved.

> Ba, Ed. Ski Run Observation. Vail, CO, 26 Jun. 2006. JPEG file.

69. Letter or memo—unpublished

Give the author's name, a brief description (for example, *Letter to Jane Cote*), and the date of the document. For letters addressed to you, use the phrase *Letter to the author*; for letters between other people, give the name and location of any library holding the letter in its collection. Use *TS* to indicate a typescript or word-processed document; use *MS* to indicate a handwritten document.

> Hall, Donald. Letter to the author. 24 Jan. 1990. MS.

70. Performance

Following the title of the play, opera, dance, or other performance, supply the name of the composer, director, writer, theater or place of presentation, and city where the performance took place as well as the date (include actors when relevant).

> *The Producers*. By Mel Brooks and Thomas Meehan. Dir. Susan Stroman.
>
> St. James Theatre, New York. 8 July 2001. Performance.

71. Oral presentation or lecture

Identify speaker, title or type of presentation, and details of the meeting, sponsoring group, location, and date. Add a descriptive label according to the format of delivery: *address, lecture, keynote speech, reading*.

> Dunkelman, Martha. "Images of Salome in Italian Renaissance Art." The
>
> Renaissance Woman, II. Sixteenth Century Studies Conf., Adams Mark
>
> Hotel, St. Louis. 11 Dec. 1993. Address.

30b
MLA

72. Map or chart

Arkansas. Map. Comfort; TX: Gousha, 1996. Print.

73. Comic strip or cartoon

Provide the cartoonist's name and the title, if any. Include the word *Comic Strip* or *Cartoon* and publication information.

Cochran, Tony. "Agnes." Comic strip. *Denver Post* 18 Apr. 2007: 13F. Print.

74. Advertisement

Begin with the name of the subject of the advertisement (product, company, or organization).

Toyota. Advertisement. *GQ* July 2001: 8. Print.

75. Film or videotape

Alphabetize according to the title of the work. The director's name is almost always necessary; names of actors, producers, writers, musicians, or others are needed only if they are important to identification or to your discussion. Include the distributor, the date, and other relevant information. If the date of the original version is important, add this just before the description of the medium. Include the medium at the end of the entry: *Film, DVD*, and so on.

Super Size Me. Prod. Morgan Spurlock. Perf. Morgan Spurlock. Samuel

Goldwyn Films, 2004. Film.

76. Television or radio program

Begin with the episode title, and use it to alphabetize the entry. Give the program's name and, if they are pertinent to the discussion, include the names of the writer, director, actors, or others. Use abbreviations for their roles; for example, *Writ., Dir., Prod., Perf., Cond., Introd., Narr.*

"Love Comes to the Butcher." *All in the Family*. Dir. Paul Bogart. CBS.

15 Jan. 1978. Television.

77. Recording

Begin the entry with the title of the recording or with the name of the person whose role in the recording you wish to emphasize, for example, the performer, the composer, the conductor, or the speaker. Italicize the title of the compact disc, tape, or record. Put the name of a specific work in quotation marks unless the piece is identified by key, form, or number, such as *Symphony in A minor, no. 41*. Continue with performers or others involved, the manufacturer, and the year when the recording was issued. Indicate the medium; for example, *CD, audiocassette, LP*.

The Goo–Goo Dolls. *Dizzy Up the Girl*. Warner, 1998. CD.

Mozart, Wolfgang Amadeus. *Symphony no. 40 in G minor.* Vienna Philharmonic. Cond. Leonard Bernstein. Deutsche Grammophon, 1984. Audiocassette.

78. Artwork

Give the name of the artist, the title of the work, and the location of the work. Because many museum and gallery names are similar, indicate the city.

Uccello, Paolo. *Saint George and the Dragon*. N.d. Oil on canvas. National Gallery, London.

79. Film or video on Web

Coppola, Francis Ford, dir. *Apocalypse Now*. 1979. *Film.com*. Web. 17 July 2006.

80. Television or radio program on Web

Edwards, Bob. "Adoption: Redefining Family." *Morning Edition*. Natl. Public Radio. 28–29 June 2001. Web. 14 Nov. 2001.

81. Recording on Web

Malcolm X. "The Definition of Black Power." *Great Speeches*. 8 Mar. 1964. Web. 18 July 2006.

82. Artwork on Web

Elamite Goddess. 2100 BC(?). Louvre, Paris. Web. 8 Apr. 2007.

83. Map or chart on Web

"Beirut [Beyrout] 1912." Map. *Perry-Castaneda Library Map Collection*. University of Texas at Austin. 2008. Web. 16 July 2000.

84. Comic strip or cartoon on Web

Auth, Tony. "Spending Goals." Cartoon. *Slate.* 7 Sept. 2006. Web. 16 Oct. 2001.

85. Advertisement on Web

Mazda Miata. Advertisement. *Mazda*. Web. 16 July 2001. <http://www.mazdausa.com/miata/>.

30b
MLA

Exercise

A. Rewrite each item to include an MLA-style in-text citation.

1. The article concludes that "a 10-percent permanent increase in the price of cigarettes reduces current consumption by 4 percent in the short run and by 7.5 percent in the long run."

    The quotation is from page 397 of an article by Gary S. Becker, Michael Grossman, and Kevin M. Murphy. It appeared in *American Economic Review*. The volume number was 84, the year was 1994, and the article ran from page 396 to page 418.

2. The original release of Neil Young's concert film *Rust Never Sleeps* in 1979 was a major event in the history of rock and roll and popular music. According to one critic, the DVD release provides continued evidence of its importance.

    The reference is to a review by LC Smith in *Rolling Stone* magazine titled "My, My, Hey, Hey: A Neil Young Treasure Resurfaces." The date is 10/17/2002 and it appears on page 39. It was accessed on 14 November 2003 through Academic Search Premier, an EBSCO database, through the University of Rhode Island Library: http://0-web11.epnet.com.helin.uri.edu/citation.asp?tb=1&_ug=dbs+ 0+ln+en%2Dus+sid+D0695035%2D68B1%2D42F6%2DAABC%2D89 63F3EC6024%40sessionmgr3%2Dsessionmgr4+699B&_us=bs+San+ +Francisco++And+++sleep+db+0+ds+San++Francisco++And+++ sleep+dstb+ES+fh+0+hd+0+hs+0+or+Date+ri+KAAACBTB00365969 +sm+ES+ss+SO+302E&cf=1&fn=1&rn=6

3. In Samoa during the 1930s, girls separated socially from their siblings at about age seven and began to form close and lasting relationships with other girls their age.

    The reference is to Margaret Mead's Discussion in *Coming of Age in Samoa*, originally published in 1928 and reprinted in 1961 by Morrow Publishers in their Morrow Quill paperback series. It cites the general discussion in Chapter 5, "The Girl and Her Age Group," on pages 59 through 73 of the 1961 edition.

B. Create a list of works cited in MLA style that includes the following items.

1. A book by Peter Brazaitis titled *You Belong in a Zoo!* It was published in 2003 by Villard Books in New York.

2. A poem by Jorie Graham titled "Self-Portrait as Apollo and Daphne," available in her *The Dream of the Unified Field: Selected Poems, 1974–1994*. The book was published in 1995 by Ecco Press, and the poem appeared on pages 70–73.

3. A review in the online magazine *Salon.com*. The title of the review is "The Matrix Revolutions," and it was written by Andrew O'Hehir. It was accessed on November 5, 2003, at http://salon.com/ent/movies/ review/2003/11/5/matrix_revolutions/index_np.html. The date of publication is also November 5, 2003.

4. An abstract of an article titled "Understanding Sleep Disorders in a College Student Population." The article was written by Dallas R. Jensen. It appeared in the *Journal of College Counseling* in the Spring 2003 issue on pages 25–34. The abstract appeared in a research database, Academic Search Premier, created and maintained by EBSCO. It was accessed on November 15, 2003, through the University of Rhode Island Library at the URL http://0-search. epnet.com.helin.uri.edu:80/direct.asp?an=9744711&db=aph. It was first included in the database in 2003.

5. A book of 280 pages by Vera Rosenbluth titled *Keeping Family Stories Alive*. The subtitle is *A Creative Guide to Taping Your Family Life and Lore*. It was published in 1990 by Hartley and Marks, a publisher in Point Roberts, Washington.

STRATEGY   Format your paper in MLA style

- **Margins.** Use one-inch margins throughout your paper.
- **Spacing.** Double-space your *entire* paper.
- **Running head.** Your last name and the page number should appear about a half-inch from the upper right-hand corner of each page.
- **Works Cited.** Always begin your works cited list on a new page. (See page 381 for more on formatting the works cited page.)
- **First page.** Beginning at the upper left-hand margin, list the following elements, each on its own line: your name, instructor's name, course name, and date formatted in MLA style (i.e., 21 December 2009). Below this heading, center your title on its own line. Remember to double-space these elements as well as the body of your paper.
- **Optional Cover Page.** Although the *MLA Handbook* recommends beginning a research paper on the first page, many instructors require cover pages. If you decide to include a cover page, place the title one-third of the way down the page. Double-space twice, then provide your name. Double-spaced twice again, then supply your instructor's name and the course name, each on its own line, double-spaced. Finally, provide the date formatted in MLA style (i.e., 21 December 2009). Remember, center and double-space all lines, and double space twice between groups of lines.

30c Sample MLA paper

The following paper was written by a student using the MLA documentation style. The *MLA Handbook* recommends beginning a research paper with text on the first page, using the format shown on Kimlee Cunningham's page one.

30c
MLA

1" from top of page

↕ ½" from top

Cunningham 1

Kimlee Cunningham

Heading format without a title page

Professor N. Reynolds

Double-spaced heading and paper

1" margin on each side →

English 201

21 December 2009

Title reflects key ideas and catches readers' attention

Disney's Magic Mirror Reflects Traditions of Old

¶ indented 5 spaces

1   Since Disney Studio's first animated feature, *Snow White and the Seven Dwarfs* (1937), the portrayal of female characters

Introduces key ideas to be developed

has changed in some obvious ways but has also remained the same in some key respects. By contrasting *Snow White and the Seven Dwarfs* with the recent animated features *Beauty and the Beast* (1991) and *Aladdin* (1992), we can see the leading

Gives background

female characters becoming more independent and assertive. At the same time, a comparison of the three movies reveals the studio's continuing appeal to its audiences' sense of feminine physical beauty.

Synthesizes varied points of view

2   It is probably an exaggeration to say that a character like Belle in *Beauty and the Beast* is a lot like a contemporary feminist, as one critic suggests (Showalter). However, we

Omits page numbers for 1-page (Showalter) and electronic (Hoffman) sources

should not simply ignore an interpretation like this. Even if many people view a film like *Beauty and the Beast* (or *Aladdin*) as a simple love story (Hoffman), the films nonetheless grow out of the complicated values and roles that shape relationships today. Disney's contemporary portrayal of women characters shows a willingness to change with the times but also a reluctance to abandon traditional values and stereotypes.

3   Nearly sixty years separates *Snow White and the Seven Dwarfs* from *Beauty and the Beast* and *Aladdin*. During this

1" margin at bottom

Cunningham 2

time of great social change, the roles of women have expanded. The shift has been from American women as housewives to American women as workers, college students, and corporate executives. By contrasting the main female character in *Snow White* with those in *Beauty* and *Aladdin*, we can see that they reflect both their own times and the social changes separating the different time periods.

4   In *Snow White and the Seven Dwarfs*, Snow White is portrayed as a homemaker when she and her furry and feathered companions in the forest come upon the Dwarfs' cabin. Her first reaction upon seeing the inside of the cabin is "We'll clean the house and surprise them. Then maybe I can stay." Snow White also becomes a mother to the Dwarfs. Before dinner, she checks their hands and sends them out to wash. Later in the evening, she calls out, "Bedtime! Right upstairs to bed." Visually, Snow White looks like an adolescent girl with wide doe eyes, tiny mouth, and pure ivory skin (Allan 161) instead of looking like a woman.

5   Though Snow White is certainly not a feminist in contemporary terms, she is portrayed in ways that were probably viewed as at least partly progressive at the time the film was created. As Terri Martin Wright points out, "Disney's *Snow White* parallelled the popular heroines of the 1930s. . . . These women were resourceful individuals who not only survived but found a measure of freedom and independence in spite of their second-class status in a patriarchal society." Wright draws further parallels by pointing out that "Popular Hollywood films of the 1930s commonly included the motif of a

---

Repeats and develops key ideas while indicating method of analysis; refers to films listed in Works Cited

Supplies supporting evidence

Explains values implied in portrait of Snow White

Identifies details of appearance

Reaches conclusion

Electronic version cited here does not contain page numbers

30c
MLA

heroine taking refuge in the living quarters of men to avoid an unpalatable destiny arranged by others." Nonetheless, Snow White's way of speaking and her appearance certainly differ markedly from those of the later characters.

Introduces both *Beauty* and *Aladdin*

6   The facial features of both Belle in *Beauty and the Beast* and Jasmine in *Aladdin* are more realistic and womanly. Instead of looking like porcelain figurines, both Belle and Jasmine look like vigorous young women. Their skin has a realistic tone, their cheeks are not as artificially rounded as Snow White's, and their eyes are still wide but are not exaggerated. Their roles and personality traits are also very different from Snow White's.

Contrasts appearances of other characters

Supplies supporting detail

7   *Beauty and the Beast* is an unusual fairy tale in which the woman is the hero (McKenna A13). Belle's intelligence allows her to defeat her enemy, Gaston. Gaston, her would-be suitor, offers a masculine parallel to Belle's beauty but no equivalent to her intelligence. Gaston, the brawny, buff beefcake figure, is nothing short of brainless. Wisely, Belle cannot be wooed by looks alone, and Gaston's words would disappoint any intelligent woman. Gaston also manages to alienate Belle when he criticizes her zest for reading and books by saying, "It's not right for a woman to read. Soon she starts getting ideas and thinking."

Leads into discussion of contrasting values and characters

More on ¶ 3 discussion of Belle's personality, actions, and implied values

8   While Snow White has to wait passively for a man, her prince, to release her from her imprisonment in an unnatural sleep, Belle is an active agent in her fate. Belle's compassion is her father's salvation from death and the Beast's salvation from his curse. To release her father from the Beast's imprisonment, Belle offers her own eternal freedom in return for her father's.

Leads to start of next ¶

Cunningham 4

This action is also the first step toward the Beast's salvation from himself and the curse.

9   The curse that has been placed upon the Beast has severely altered his appearance, turning a handsome prince into a hairy creature mixing the features of a lion and a buffalo. In order for the spell to be broken, someone must be able to see past this appearance and love the Beast for his inner qualities before the last petal of an enchanted rose falls. It is Belle, through her compassion and understanding, who changes the spirit of the man who has been turned into a beast. He learns to control his temper and becomes kind and forbearing. Belle conquers adversity with her quick wit, compassion, understanding, and love. This is truly a refreshing contrast to the familiar "battle or conquest" approach of most heroes (McKenna A13).

> Summarizes preceding discussion

> Uses source to support conclusion

10   Jasmine of *Aladdin* has been acclaimed by some critics as the "most independent-minded Disney heroine yet" (Rosenberg). The rebellious spirit within causes her to do things that would be considered daring and bold for a princess. She escapes from her father's palace walls to assert her freedom by exploring the streets of Agrabah, but most significantly, she refuses to marry for politics or the tradition that the sultan's daughter must marry a prince. Jasmine rejects her princely suitors by saying that they lack character and that she does not love them. Jasmine's desire for true love is nothing new to Disney films; Snow White desires a true love as well, but in *Aladdin* the terms of love are dictated by the female character. She is someone to be wooed, but not a prize to be won. It is she who makes the real choice.

> Picks up theme that concludes ¶ 9

> Develops idea introduced in quotation

> Summarizes events

> Could have added quotations

30c
MLA

11 At the same time, by comparing *Snow White* with *Beauty and Aladdin*, we can see how Disney films still try to preserve some traditional attitudes. Although Snow White, Belle, and Jasmine may have different appearances, they all appeal to our culture's traditional sense of physical beauty. They are fragile and thin with perfect skin, hair, and teeth. Their figures are also proportioned in traditionally attractive ways. Snow White's looks draw a kiss from a prince; Belle's beauty (as the name itself implies) is part of her power to change the Beast; and Jasmine's looks are an essential part of her power, as illustrated by her ability to distract the evil vizier Jafar while Aladdin attempts to steal back the lamp.

12 None of the heroines is active or involved in any modern sense. Snow White cooks, cleans, and hums; Belle buries her nose in a book and takes care of her father; Jasmine sits in her father's palace and mopes, rejecting suitor after suitor. Their lives take a positive or active turn only when they are introduced to the men they will come to love. Regarding *Beauty and the Beast* as "a liberated love story for the '90s" (Showalter) seems to miss the film's balance of contemporary and traditional values.

13 Disney has frequently been criticized for its powerful ability to adapt reality to fit its own purposes (Baudrillard). But perhaps Disney's retention of stereotypes of feminine beauty and passivity reflects our culture's reluctance to let go of traditions. Many men and women are still trying to define their priorities in life, especially in terms of work and relationships. For many, this struggle becomes a battle between family and

---

Supplies transition to discussion of similarities

Might have developed key element of appearance in more detail

Mentions selected details from all three films

Reaches strong conclusion that seems to undermine earlier assertions of independence

Could discuss further, though interpretation is consistent with main idea

Broadens focus to look at films in culture

Cunningham 6

work. Like many people, Americans may need to focus on
traditional values when they believe that their culture and their
lives are undergoing painful change and potential disorder.

Returns to ideas introduced in opening ¶s

Could it be possible that *Beauty* and *Aladdin* reflect the need of
many in their audiences to retain certain traditional values and
behavior patterns while simultaneously endorsing new roles and
perspectives?

Raises question tentatively answered at end of paper

14   Despite the fact that *Snow White and the Seven Dwarfs*
was made roughly sixty years earlier than *Beauty and the
Beast* and *Aladdin*, many things in the movies remain the
same. There is a formula that Disney animators seem to follow
in creating the appearance of female characters, one of
conventional feminine beauty. The writers have also chosen
fairy tale patterns for the story lines with such familiar
features as the "happily-ever-after ending" and the image of a
woman swept away by a man's love. What is different is that
Beauty and the Beast and *Aladdin* weave themes of
independence, intelligence, and action into the stories,
centering them on the female characters. In contrast, the
character and actions of Snow White emphasize themes of
innocence, naiveté, and motherliness. While the continuing
popularity of *Snow White* reveals at the very least a nostalgia
for these themes, the shift to the more contemporary themes
of *Beauty* and *Aladdin* is probably a sign of Disney's accurate
perception of a society endorsing change yet looking for
reassurance.

Restates opening observations, then summarizes key points

Answers question raised in ¶ 13

30c
MLA

1" from top of page

½'' from top

Cunningham 7

Page num
continue

Works Cited | Heading centered

Sources from paper listed alphabetically

All lines double-spaced

First line of each entry not indented

Additional lines indented 5 spaces (½")

Aladdin. 1992. Walt Disney, 1993. Videocassette.

Allan, Robin. "Fifty Years of Snow White." *Journal of Popular*
Film and Television 24 (1988): 155-63. Print.

Baudrillard, Jean. "Disneyworld Company." Trans. Francois
Debrix. *CTHEORY* 27 Nov. 1996. Web. 6 Dec. 2009.

Beauty and the Beast. 1991. Walt Disney, 1991. Videocassette.

Hoffman, Loreen. "Feminism in a Disney Film." Online posting.
2 Feb. 1998. Web. 21 Nov. 2009. <wysiwyg://22/http://
faculty.ucr.edu/wcb/s . . . t/master/2/forums/forum2/
messages/7.htm>.

McKenna, M. A. J. "Film Provides 'Beauty'-ful Role Models."
Boston Herald 1 Dec. 1991: A13+. Print.

Rosenberg, Scott. "The Genie-us of Aladdin." *San Francisco*
Examiner 25 Nov. 1992: B2. Print.

Showalter, Elaine. "Beauty and the Beast: Disney Meets
Feminism in a Liberated Love Story for the '90s." *Premiere*
Oct. 1997: 66. Print.

Snow White and the Seven Dwarfs. 1937. Walt Disney, 1994.
Videocassette.

Wright, Terri Martin. "Romancing the Tale." *Journal of Popular*
Film and Television 25 (1997): 98-108. *Academic Search*
Premier. Web. 7 Dec. 2009.

PEARSON
mycomplab

Visit mycomplab.com for more resources and exercises on MLA documentation.

CHAPTER 31

APA Documentation

American Psychological Association (APA) documentation style calls for in-text (parenthetical) references and a reference list. This chapter discusses APA style and provides models for the most common kinds of entries you will use.

The in-text documentation style developed by the APA identifies the source of information, ideas, or quotations by providing the author's name and the date of publication for the source within parentheses. For this reason, APA style is often called a name-and-date style. The information in the parenthetical citation enables readers to locate more detailed information about the source in a **reference list** at the end of a paper or report.

APA style makes the year of publication part of an in-text citation, as in (*Kitwana, 2002*), and gives the date right after the author's name in a reference list to which the in-text citation refers.

Kitwana, B. (2002). *The hip hop generation: Young blacks and the crisis in*

African American culture. New York: Basic*Civitas*.

For more detailed discussion of this documentation style, consult the *Publication Manual of the American Psychological Association*, 6th ed. (2010). Updates appear online at <http://www.apastyle.org>.

31a In-text (parenthetical) citations

The APA system provides parenthetical citations for quotations, paraphrases, summaries, and other information in the text of a paper. For advice on what to document and what not to document, see 27d, 29b. For an APA in-text citation, include the author's name and the year of publication, separating these items with a comma. You may choose to name the author (and give the date) either within the parenthetical citation or within your text.

31a
APA

1. Author's name inside parentheses

Include the author's name and the year of publication inside parentheses, separating these items with a comma. When you are documenting the source of a quotation, paraphrase, or summary, follow the date with a comma, *p.* or *pp.*, and the page number or numbers on which the quoted material appears in the source.

> One recent study argues that "the fan's link to the star—or the team, the favorite composer, the game, the genre, the style—is emotional, visceral" (Gitlin, 2001, p. 129).

2. Author's name as part of discussion

When you make an author's name part of the discussion, give the date of the source in parentheses after the name. For quoted or paraphrased material, provide the page number in the source within parentheses following the quotation or paraphrase.

> As Gitlin (2001) argues, "the fan's link to the star—or the team, the favorite composer, the game, the genre, the style—is emotional, visceral" (p. 129).

3. Specific reference

Indicate what you are citing: *p.* ("page"), *pp.* ("pages"), *chapter, figure.* Spell potentially confusing words. For classic works, always indicate the part (*chapter 5*), not the page.

> Teenagers who survive suicide attempts experience distinct stages of
>
> recovery (Mauk & Weber, 1991, Table 1).

4. Specific reference to online source

Use what the document provides: page numbers, paragraph numbers (*para.*), or the section name and the number of the paragraph under it, as counted out.

> Bodybuilders sometimes suffer from muscle dysmorphia (Lee, 2006, What is
>
> dysmorphia? section, para. 4).

5. One author

Supply the author's last name and the date of the publication in parentheses, separated by a comma and a space. If the author's name appears in the text, give only the date in parentheses. If both the name and the date are included in the text, no other information need be cited.

> Mau's 2001 study of gender differences on the SAT, ACT, and college grades
> confirmed observations of test results made earlier (Arbeiter, 1985) as well
> as Young's (1994) study of gender differences in college grades.

6. Two authors

Include both names in citations. In a parenthetical reference, separate the names by an ampersand (&); in the text, use the word *and*.

> Given evidence that married men earn more than unmarried men (Chun & Lee, 2001), Nakosteen and Zimmer (2001) investigate how earnings affect spousal selection.

7. Three to five authors

Include all the authors' names, separated by commas, for the first citation. For parenthetical citations use an ampersand (&) rather than *and*. In the second and remaining citations, give only the first author's name followed by *et al.* and the date (for example, "Biber et al. (1998) present evidence that . . .").

8. Six or more authors

Give the name of the first author followed by *et al.* and the date in all citations: (*Berg et al., 2008*). Supply the names of the first seven authors in the reference list at the end of your report. For more than eight authors, list the first six, then add an ellipsis mark followed by the last author's name.

9. Organization or group author

Spell out the name of an association, corporation, or government agency each time it is referenced. If the organization name is well-known or cumbersome, spell out its name in the first citation, following with an abbreviation in brackets. You may use the abbreviation for later citations.

FIRST CITATION   Besides instilling fear, hate crimes limit where women live and work (National Organization of Women [NOW], 2001).

LATER CITATION   Pending legislation would strengthen the statutes on bias-motivated crimes (NOW, 2001).

10. No author given

Give the title or the first few words of a long title (*The Great Utopia: The Russian and Soviet Avant-Garde, 1915–1932* might appear in a citation as *Great Utopia*) and the year.

> Art and design in 1920s Russia mixed aesthetically startling images with political themes and an endorsement of social change (*Great Utopia*, 1992).

When the word *Anonymous* designates the author, use it in the citation: (*Anonymous, 2002*).

11. Work cited more than once

When you cite the same source more than once in a paragraph, repeat the source as necessary to clarify a specific page reference or to show which

31a
APA

information comes from one of several sources. If a second reference is clear, do not repeat the date.

> Personal debt has become a significant problem in the past decade. Much of the increase can be linked to the lack of restraint in spending people feel when using credit cards (Schor, 1998, p. 73). The problem is so widespread that "about one-third of the nation's population describe themselves as either heavily or moderately in financial debt" (Schor, p. 72).

12. Authors with the same last name

When your reference list contains works by two different authors with the same last name, provide each author's initials for each in-text citation.

> Scholars have looked in depth at the development of African American culture during slavery and reconstruction (E. Foner, 1988). The role of Frederick Douglass in this process has also been examined (P. Foner, 1950).

13. Two or more sources in a citation

If you are summarizing information found in more than one source, include all the sources—names and years—within the citation. Separate the authors and years with commas; separate the sources with semicolons. List sources alphabetically by author, then oldest to most recent for several sources by the same author, separating the dates with commas.

> Several researchers have investigated personal and organizational reasons for job satisfaction (Binghamr, Valenstein, Blow, & Alexander, 2002; Griffin, 2001, 2006).

14. Two or more works by the same author in the same year

If you use works published in the same year by the same author or author team, add letters after the year to distinguish the works.

> Gould (1987a, p. 73) makes a similar point.

15. Personal communications, including interviews and email

In your text, cite letters, memos, interviews, email, telephone conversations, and similar personal communications by giving the initials and last name of the person, the phrase *personal communication*, and the date. Readers probably will have no access to such sources, so you need not include them in your reference list.

AUTHOR NAMED IN TEXT   According to J. M. Hostos, the state has begun cutting funding for social services duplicated by county agencies (personal communication, October 7, 2009).

The state has begun cutting funding for social services duplicated by county agencies (J. M. Hostos, personal communication, October 7, 2009).

16. Work cited in another source

Include the phrase *as cited in* as part of a parenthetical citation for a source you did not use directly but drew from another source.

Writing in the late 1800s about Halloween customs, William Shepard Walsh lamented that "gangs of hoodlums throng the streets, ringing the door-bells or wrenching the handles from their sockets, and taking gates from off their hinges" (as cited in Skal, 2002, pp. 33–34).

17. Sacred text or classical text

Give the name or number of the book, section, or part along with the name of the particular version or translation you are citing, using standard abbreviations and part numbering. Cite the source in the body of your text only.

Aristotle argues that liberty is a fundamental element of democracy (Politics, VI.I.6).

18. Content footnotes

A **content footnote** allows you to expand on information presented in the text or discuss a point further without making the main text of your paper more complicated. Use such footnotes sparingly because too many footnotes or long footnotes can distract your readers.

Place a number slightly above the line of your text that relates to the footnote information. Make sure that you number the footnotes in your paper consecutively.

TEXT OF PAPER I tape-recorded all the interviews and later transcribed the relevant portions.[1]

On a separate page at the end of your paper, below the centered heading "Footnotes," present the notes in the order in which they appear in your text. Begin each note with its number, placed slightly above the line. Indent five to seven spaces, the same as a paragraph, for the first line only of each footnote, and double-space all notes.

FOOTNOTE [1]Sections of the recordings were hard to hear and understand because of problems with the tape recorder or background noises. These gaps did not substantially affect information needed for the study.

Your instructor may prefer that you type any footnote at the bottom of the page with the text reference.

31b References list

Immediately after the last page of your paper, you need to provide a list of references to enable readers to identify and consult the sources you have cited in your report.

> **STRATEGY** Format the APA reference list
>
> - **Page format.** One inch from the top margin of a separate page at the end of your report's text (before notes or appendixes), center the heading "References" without underlining or quotation marks.
> - **Alphabetizing.** List works cited in the report alphabetically by author or by the first main word of the title if there is no author. Arrange two or more works by the same author from the oldest to the most recent according to year of publication.
> - **Spacing.** Double-space all entries and between entries.
> - **Indentation.** Do not indent the first line, but indent five to seven spaces for the second and additional lines.

1 Books and works treated as books

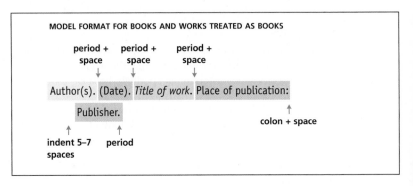

MODEL FORMAT FOR BOOKS AND WORKS TREATED AS BOOKS

- **Author(s).** Give the author's last name followed by a comma and the initials of the first and middle names. For a book with more than one author, use the same inverted order for each author. Separate the names with commas, using an ampersand before the final name.
- **Date.** Provide the year of publication (in parentheses) followed by a period.
- **Title of work.** Italicize the title and follow it with a period. Capitalize only the first word of the main title, the first word of any subtitle, and any proper nouns.
- **Publication information.** Name the city (and the country or the state's postal abbreviation) followed by a colon and a space; then supply the publisher's name, leaving out unnecessary words such as *Inc.* or *Publishers.*

1. One author

> Ortner, S. B. (2003). *New Jersey dreaming: Capital, culture, and the class of*
>> *'58.* Durham, NC: Duke University Press.

2. Two or more authors

List each author's last name first, followed by first and middle initials. For a book with eight or more authors, give the first six authors' names, then an ellipsis mark, followed by the last author's name.

> Biber, D., Conrad, S., & Reppen, R. (1998). *Corpus linguistics: Investigating*
>> *language structure and use.* Cambridge, England: Cambridge
>> University Press.

3. Organization or group author

Treat the organization or agency as an individual author, and alphabetize by the first main word. When author and publisher are the same, give the word *Author* following the place of publication instead of repeating the name.

> Amnesty International. (2003). *Annual Report 2003.* [Brochure]. London,
>> England: Author.

4. No author given

Give the title first, then the date. Use the first significant word of the title to alphabetize the entry. If the word *Anonymous* is used for the author, designate the author with it and alphabetize under *anonymous*.

> *Boas anniversary volume: Anthropological papers written in honor of Franz*
>> *Boas.* (1906). New York, NY: Stechert.

5. More than one work by the same author

List works in chronological order; give the author's name in each entry.

> Aronowitz, S. (1993). *Roll over Beethoven: The return of cultural strife.*
>> Hanover, NH: Wesleyan University Press.
> Aronowitz, S. (2000). *From the ashes of the old: American labor and*
>> *America's future.* New York, NY: Basic Books.

If the same lead author has works with different coauthors, alphabetize these entries based on the last names of the second authors.

6. More than one work by the same author in the same year

List in alphabetical order works appearing in the same year by the same author. Add lowercase letters after dates (e.g., *1992a, 1992b*). Alphabetize by the first main word in the title. For in-text citations, provide both the date and the letter (*Gould, 1987b*).

> Gould, S. J. (1987a). *Time's arrow, time's cycle: Myth and metaphor in the discovery of geological time.* Cambridge, MA: Harvard University Press.
>
> Gould, S. J. (1987b). *An urchin in the storm: Essays about books and ideas.* New York, NY: Norton.

7. One or more editors

Include (*Ed.*) or (*Eds.*) after the name(s) of the editors.

> Bowe, J., Bowe, M., & Streeter, S. C. (Eds.). (2001). *Gig: Americans talk about their jobs.* New York, NY: Three Rivers Press.

8. Translator

Include the translator's name, in normal order, followed by *Trans.*, in parentheses after the title.

> Bourdieu, P. (1990). *In other words: Essays towards a reflexive sociology* (M. Adamson, Trans.). Stanford, CA: Stanford University Press.

9. Edition other than the first

Include information about the specific edition in parentheses after the title (for example, *Rev. ed.* for "revised edition" or *3rd ed.* for "third edition").

> Groth–Marnat, G. (1996). *Handbook of psychological assessment* (3rd ed.). New York, NY: Wiley.

10. Reprint

> Butler, J. (1999). *Gender trouble.* New York, NY: Routledge. (Original work published 1990)

11. Multivolume work

Include the names of the editors or authors, making sure you indicate if they are editors. Then provide the inclusive years of publication. If the work is a revised edition or has a translator, give this information

Book with multiple editors

Editors' names
↓

Dye, T. R., Edwards, G. C., Fiorina, M. P., Greenberg, E. S., Light, P. C.,

Magleby, D. B., . . . Wattenberg, M. P. (Eds.). (2010). *Obama: Year*

one. New York, NY: Longman.

↑
Place of
publication,
publisher

↑ Date of
publication

↑ Book title

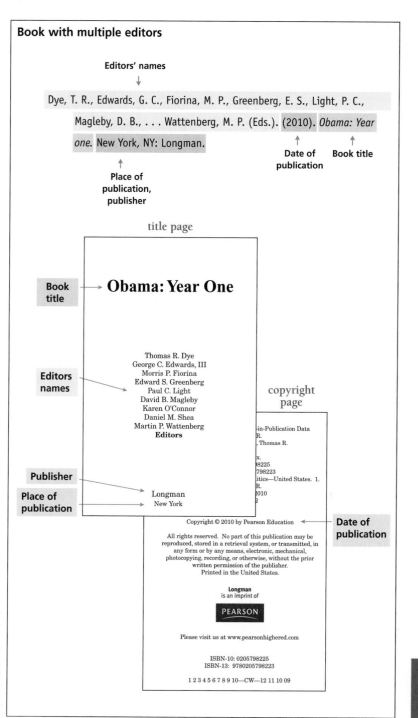

title page

Obama: Year One

Book
title →

Thomas R. Dye
George C. Edwards, III
Morris P. Fiorina
Edward S. Greenberg
Paul C. Light
David B. Magleby
Karen O'Connor
Daniel M. Shea
Martin P. Wattenberg
Editors

Editors
names

copyright
page

-in-Publication Data
R.
, Thomas R.

x.
8225
798223
itics—United States. 1.
R.
010
2

Publisher

Place of
publication

Longman
New York

Copyright © 2010 by Pearson Education ◄

Date of
publication

All rights reserved. No part of this publication may be
reproduced, stored in a retrieval system, or transmitted, in
any form or by any means, electronic, mechanical,
photocopying, recording, or otherwise, without the prior
written permission of the publisher.
Printed in the United States.

Longman
is an imprint of

PEARSON

Please visit us at www.pearsonhighered.com

ISBN-10: 0205798225
ISBN-13: 9780205798223

1 2 3 4 5 6 7 8 9 10—CW—12 11 10 09

after the title. Then identify in parentheses the volumes you are using for your paper.

> Strachey, J., Freud, A., Strachey, A., & Tyson, A. (Eds.). (1966–1974).
>
> *The standard edition of the complete psychological works of Sigmund*
>
> *Freud* (J. Strachey et al., Trans.) (Vols. 3–5). London, England:
>
> Hogarth Press and the Institute of Psycho–Analysis.

12. Collection of articles or anthology

Give the name of the editor(s) first, followed by the abbreviation *Ed.* or *Eds.* in parentheses.

> Appadurai, A. (Ed.). (2001). *Globalization*. Durham, NC: Duke University Press.
>
> Ghosh, A., & Ingene, C. A. (Eds.). (1991). *Spatial analysis in marketing:*
>
> *Theory, methods and applications*. Greenwich, CT: JAI.

13. *Diagnostic and Statistical Manual of Mental Disorders*

The *DSM-IV* is widely cited in fields such as psychology, social work, and psychiatry because its definitions and guidelines often have legal force and determine patterns of treatment. Following an initial full citation, you may use the standard abbreviations for this work: *DSM-III* (1980), *DSM-III-R* (1987), *DSM-IV* (1994), and *DSM-IV-TR* (2000).

> American Psychiatric Association. (1994). *Diagnostic and statistical manual*
>
> *of mental disorders* (4th ed.). Washington, DC: Author.

14. Encyclopedia or reference work

> Winn, P. (Ed.). (2001). *Dictionary of biological psychology*. London,
>
> England: Routledge.

15. Dissertation (unpublished)

> Gomes, C. S. (2001). *Selection and treatment effects in managed care*.
>
> Unpublished doctoral dissertation, Boston University, Boston, MA.

16. Government document

> Committee on Energy and Natural Resources. Senate. (2007). *Alaska water*
>
> *resources act of 2007* (Com. Rep. No. 110-020). Washington, DC:
>
> U.S. Government Printing Office.

Report

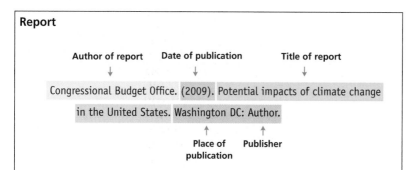

Author of report → Congressional Budget Office.

Date of publication → (2009).

Title of report → Potential impacts of climate change in the United States. Washington DC: Author.

↑ Place of publication

↑ Publisher

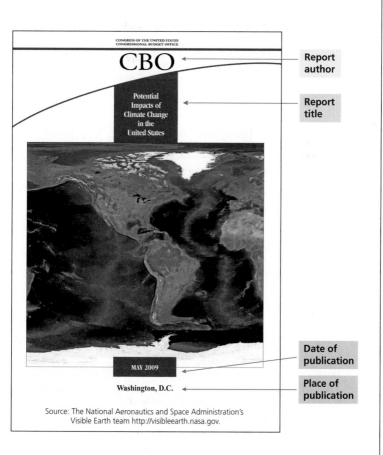

Report author

Report title

Date of publication

Place of publication

Source: The National Aeronautics and Space Administration's
Visible Earth team http://visibleearth.nasa.gov.

17. Report

Begin with the name of the author, whether an individual, a group, or a government agency. If the agency also publishes the report, use the word *Author* in the publication information instead of repeating the group's name.

> Advisory Commission to Study the Consumer Price Index. (1996). *Toward a*
>
> *more accurate measure of the cost of living.* Washington, DC: Senate
>
> Finance Committee.

If the report has a number, give it in parentheses after the title with no punctuation preceding it. When several numbers are listed in the report, choose the one most likely to help readers obtain the document.

> Dossey, J. A. (1988). *Mathematics: Are we measuring up?* (Report
>
> No. 17-M-02). Princeton, NJ: Educational Testing Service.
>
> (ERIC Document Reproduction Service No. ED3000207).

2 Articles and selections from books

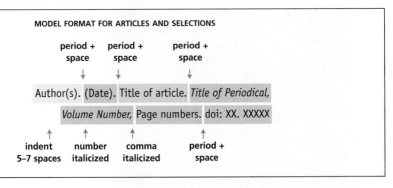

- **Author(s).** Give the author's last name and initials followed by a period and a space.
- **Date.** Supply the date in parentheses followed by a period and a space.
- **Title of article.** Give the article title, capitalizing only the first word (and the first word of any subtitle along with any proper names). Do not use quotation marks with the title. End with a period and a space.
- **Title of journal, periodical, or book.** Give the journal title in italics with all main words capitalized, the volume number (in italics), and the page numbers. Use commas to separate these.
- **DOI.** Include digital object identifier (DOI) number in reference if available. When a DOI is not shown on the first page of the article, APA recommends using *CrossRef* (http://www.crossref.org) to determine if a DOI for a print journal article exists.

Article in print journal*

Authors' names → Date of publication → Article title →

Riddle, K., Eyal, K., Mahood, C., & Potter, W. J. (2006). Judging the degree

of violence in media portrayals: A cross-genre comparison. *Journal of*

Journal title → *Broadcasting & Electronic Media,* 50(2), 270–286. doi: 10.1207/

s15506878jobem5000-6

↑ DOI

↑ Volume and issue numbers

↑ Pages

Journal of Broadcasting & Electronic Media/June 2006

Article title →

Judging the Degree of Violence in Media Portrayals: A Cross-Genre Comparison

Authors' names →

Karyn Riddle, Keren Eyal, Chad Mahood, and W. James Potter

This study tests the relative importance of different factors of television narratives in how they influence people's judgments of how violent those narratives are. After watching 1 of 3 videotapes of a violent narrative, 99 college students answered a series of questions about their interpretations of the violence. It was found that participants' judgments about the degree of violence in the narratives were more strongly associated with their perceptions of the graphicness of the violent acts and the harm to the victims than with other factors such as the number of violent acts or the seriousness of those acts. Thus, people's judgments of the degree of violence in television programs differs from researchers' conceptualization. Implications of these differences are discussed.

Ever since the rise in popularity of television in American households from the 1950s and continuing to today, the public has been complaining that there is too much violence in TV programming. In fact, the public has continually been putting pressure on Congress and the television industry to reduce the amount of violence (Potter, 2003; Rowland, 1983). During those five decades, social scientists have been conducting analyses of the violent content on television to document the amount of violence and to try to inform public debate about this issue. However, there is reason to believe that much of what social scientists carefully measure and report in their results is not what generates the complaints among the public. That is, there is a growing line of research indicating that the public perceives media violence in a different manner than do media researchers. The public's way of making interpretations about

Karyn Riddle (M.A., University of California, Santa Barbara) is a doctoral candidate in the Department of Communication at the University of California at Santa Barbara. Her research interests are long-term media effects.

Keren Eyal (Ph.D., University of California, Santa Barbara) is an Assistant Professor in the Department of Communication at the University of Arizona. Her research interests focus on media content and effects.

Chad Mahood (M.A., Pennsylvania State University) is a doctoral candidate in the Department of Communication at the University of California at Santa Barbara. His research interests include traditional media effects and video game effects.

W. James Potter (Ph.D., Indiana University) is a Professor in the Department of Communication at the University of California at Santa Barbara. His research interests are mass media effects, content, and literacy.

© 2006 Broadcast Education Association   *Journal of Broadcasting & Electronic Media 50(2), 2006, pp. 270–286.* ←

270

Journal title, volume and issue numbers, date of publication, pages

---

* When a DOI is not shown on the first page of the articles, APA recommends using *CrossRef* (http://www.crossref.org) to determine if a DOI for a print journal article exists.

31b
APA

18. Article in journal paginated by volume

If page numbers run continuously through the issues making up a volume, do not include an issue number.

Iran-Nejad, A., McKeachie, W. J., & Berliner, D. C. (1990). The multisource

nature of learning: An introduction. *Review of Educational Research,*

60, 509–515. doi: 10.1177/0002764203254621

Klein, R. D. (2003). Audience reactions to local TV news. *American*

Behavioral Scientist, 46, 1661–1672. doi: 10.1177/000276403254621

For references with up to seven authors, supply the names of all the authors in the reference list entry. For eight or more authors, list the first six authors' names, then an ellipsis mark followed by the last author's name.

All in-text citations for references having two authors should include both authors. For three to five authors, list all authors at the first citation; thereafter, give only the name of the first author followed by *et al.*, as in (*Albertini et al., 1986*). For six or more authors, cite the first author's surname followed by *et al.* and the date for all citations, including the first.

19. Article in journal paginated by issue

When each issue of a journal begins with page 1, include the issue number in parentheses immediately (with no space) after the volume number. Do not italicize the issue number.

Sadek, A., Raviv, A., & Gruber, R. (2000). Sleep patterns and sleep disruptions

in school-age children. *Developmental Psychology, 36*(3), 291–301. doi:

10.1037/0012-1649.36.3.291

20. Special issue of journal

Begin with the special issue's editor (if other than the regular editor); otherwise, place the title at the beginning, then the date. Indicate in brackets that it is a special issue. You need not include page numbers.

Balk, D. E. (Ed.). (1991). Death and adolescent bereavement [Special

issue]. *Journal of Adolescent Research, 6*(1).

21. Article in popular monthly magazine

Include the month and year of the magazine. Spell out months. Add the volume number (followed by the issue number in parentheses—not italicized—if available) and pages. If there is no author, put the title first, before the date.

Dold, C. (1998, September). Needles and nerves. *Discover, 19,* 59–62.

22. Article in popular weekly magazine

Supply the same information as you would for an article in a monthly magazine (see Entry 21), but add the specific date.

Kluger, J. (2007, June 11). The science of appetite. *Time, 169,* 48–52,

57–58, 61.

23. Article with no author given

Begin the entry with the article's title, and alphabetize using the first main word in the title.

Large TADS study hopes to determine best treatments for teenage

depression. (2001, February). *Brown University Child & Adolescent*

Psychopharmacology Update, 3(1),4–7.

24. Article in newspaper

Use *p.* or *pp.* to introduce the section and page numbers for newspaper articles. If no author is given, put the title first.

Murtaugh, P. (1998, August 10). Finding a brand's real essence. *Advertising*

Age, p. 12.

25. Letter to the editor or editorial

Treat a letter to the editor like another newspaper article (or formal article), but label it in brackets.

Ellis, S. (2001, September 7). Adults are problem with youth sports [Letter

to the editor]. *USA Today,* p. A14.

26. Interview—published

Although APA does not specify a form for published interviews, you may wish to employ the following form, which is similar to other APA references.

Dess, N. K. (2001). The new body–mind connection (John T. Cacioppo)

[Interview]. *Psychology Today, 34*(4), 30–31.

27. Review with a title

Following the title of the review, indicate in brackets the kind of work (*book, film, video program, television program,* and so on) and the title (italicized) of the work being reviewed.

Mack, A. (2007). Consumption nation [Review of the book *Sold American:*

Consumption and citizenship 1890–1945]. *Reviews in American*

History, 35, 253–259. doi: 10.1353/rah.2000.0034

28. Review without a title

Begin with the name of the reviewer. If the review article does not have a title, substitute a description in brackets consisting of the phrase *Review of the* followed by the type of material and the title of the book, motion picture, television show, or other topic of the review.

Verdery, K. (2002). [Review of the book *The politics of gender after*

socialism]. *American Anthropologist, 104,* 354–355. doi:

10.1525/aa.2002.104.1.354

29. Article from encyclopedia or reference work

If no author is identified, begin with the title of the article. Use *In* before the work's title, and follow it with the volume and page numbers.

Chernoff, H. (1978). Decision theory. In *International encyclopedia of*

statistics (Vol. 1, pp. 131–135). New York, NY: Free Press.

30. Chapter in edited book or selection in anthology

Begin with the author's name, the year the book was published, and the title of the selection. Following the word *In*, cite the editors, the title of the collection, and the page numbers.

Chisholm, J. S. (1999). Steps to an evolutionary ecology of mind.

In A. L. Hinton (Ed.), *Biocultural approaches to the emotions*

(pp. 117–150). Cambridge, England: Cambridge University Press.

31. Dissertation abstract

If you consult the dissertation on microfilm, give the University Microfilms number at the end of the entry in parentheses: (*UMI No. AAC–9004751*).

Yamada, H. (1989). American and Japanese topic management strategies in

business conversations. *Dissertation Abstracts International, 50*(09),

2982B.

3 Field and media resources

32. Unpublished raw data

When you use data from field research, including field observations or a survey, briefly describe its topic within brackets, and end with *Unpublished raw data*.

Molochevic, V. (2007). [Survey of response to proposed changes in Social

Security benefits]. Unpublished raw data.

33. Interview—unpublished

To refer to an interview you have conducted yourself, provide the information only as part of an in-text citation: (V. Friedman, personal communication, November 14, 2009). (See Entry 34.)

34. Personal communication (including email)

Letters, email, telephone conversations, and similar communications cannot be consulted by your readers, so do not include them in your reference list. Instead, cite them in text. (See p. 418–419 and Entry 33 for examples.)

35. Paper presented at a meeting

For an unpublished paper presented at a conference or symposium, include the month as well as the year, and list both the name and location of the meeting.

Nelson, J. S. (1993, August). *Political argument in political science: A*

meditation on the disappointment of political theory. Paper presented

at the annual meeting of the American Political Science Association,

Chicago, IL.

36. Videotape or film

Begin with the name or names of the people primarily responsible for the work, and indicate each person's role (for example, *Director* or *Producer*) in parentheses following the name. Italicize the title, then indicate the medium (for example, *Motion picture* or *Slides)* in brackets. At the end of the entry, within parentheses, indicate the location and name of the distributor (for example, *WGBH, Boston*). If the distributor is not well known, supply the address. For motion pictures, give the country of origin and the name of the studio.

31b
APA

Simon, T. (Producer), & LeBrun, N. (Writer). (1986). *Atocha:*

Quest for treasure [Motion picture]. United States: Columbia Tristar

Home Video.

Coen, E. (Producer), & Coen, J. (Director). (2000). *O brother,*

where art thou? [Motion picture]. United States: Universal

Pictures.

37. Television or radio program

Begin the entry for a series of programs with the name of the script writer, the producer, the director, or any other person whose role you wish to indicate. Give the title of the program or series (italicized) followed by *Television series* in brackets. Conclude with the location and name of the network or channel responsible for the broadcast.

Surnow, J., & Cochran, R. (Creators). (2001–2010). *24* [Television series].

Los Angeles, CA: Fox Broadcasting.

A specific episode in a series is treated much like an anthology. List the script's writer as you would an author, then the name of the director, with each of these followed by his or her function in parentheses. Follow the episode title with *Television series episode* in brackets, then indicate the producer in the editor position, before the italicized title of the series.

Moyers, B. A. (Writer), & Grubin, D. (Director). (1993). A life together

[Television series episode]. In D. Grubin (Producer), *Bill Moyers'*

journal. New York, NY: WNET.

38. Recording

Begin by giving the name of the writer and the date of copyright (in parentheses). Following the song title, supply the name of the recording artist in brackets, if this is someone other than the writer. Indicate the medium in brackets after the album title; include a number for the recording within the brackets if one is necessary for identifying the recording and obtaining a copy.

Give the location, followed by a colon and the name of the recording label. Include the recording date, if different from the copyright date, in parentheses, with no period after the final parenthesis.

Freeman, R. (1994). Porscha [Recorded by R. Freeman & The Rippingtons].

On *Sahara* [CD]. New York, NY: GRP Records.

4 Online and electronic resources

Journal article (online) (with DOI)

Authors' names | Date of Publication | Article title

Schnurr, P.P. & Lunney, C.A. (2008). Exploration of gender differences in how quality of life relates to posttraumatic stress disorder in male and female veterans. *Journal of Rehabilitation Research and Development*, 45(3) 383–394, doi: 10.1682/JRRD.2007.06.0099

— Journal title

Volume and issue numbers | Pages | DOI

Journal title

Article title

Authors' names

Volume, issue, date, pages

DOI

- As a general guide, adapt the nonelectronic pattern for a source as needed by replacing its print publication information with its online location unless you provide a DOI. When no DOI is available, supply a URL, and break if necessary *after* http:// but *before* other punctuation marks. Introduce the URL with "Retrieved from."
- For journal articles, include the issue number when the journal is paginated by issue.
- Give a DOI (Digital Object Identifier) rather than a URL when a publisher has assigned this permanent number to an article or text.

31b
APA

39. Web site

Include the information specified in Entry 42. APA does not provide a specific form for Web sites. Use the following form.

> Brown, D. K. (2001). *The children's literature Web guide*. Retrieved from
>
> http://www.ucalgary.ca/ndkbrown/

40. Online book or document

For texts lacking a publication date, use *n.d.* ("no date"). Include the DOI (Digital Object Identifier) if available; otherwise provide URL.

> Frary, R. B. (n.d.). *A brief guide to questionnaire development*. Retrieved from
>
> http://rov.wisc.edu/polisci/library/questionnaire.pdf

Following the title, include in brackets, information about specific electronic version if the information is available.

41. Selection from online book or document

> Lasswell, H. D. (1971). Professional training. In *A preview of*
>
> *policy sciences* (chapter 8). Retrieved from http://
>
> www.policysciences.org/classicworks.cfm

42. Online journal article with DOI

Some scholarly publishers provide a DOI (Digital Object Identifier) for an article or other text as a unique and permanent identification of the material. Cite the DOI when available, and do not provide the URL or other electronic address (which may change over time).

> Abrams, M. (2006). Why terrorism does not work. *International Security,*
>
> *3*(2), 42–78. doi: 10.1162/isec.2006.31.2.42

43. Online article without DOI

When a DOI is not available, cite the URL for the home page of the journal.

> Wynd, C. A. (2006). A proposed model for military disaster nursing. *OJIN:*
>
> *The Online Journal of Issues in Nursing, 11*(3). Retrieved from
>
> http://www.nursingworld.com/

44. Online newsletter article

Newsletters may be difficult to locate; URLs help in locating the text.

> Cashel, J. (2007, January 23). Community metrics. *Online Community*
>
> *Report*. Retrieved from http://www.onlinecommunityreport.com
>
> /134-community-metrics.html

45. Online newspaper or news service article

Give the URL of the homepage to avoid URLs for the article, which often do not work. Give the article URL if the homepage does not have a search function.

Dortch, D. T. (2007, April 19). Make a start in public service. *Washington Post Online*. Retrieved from http://www.washingtonpost.com

46. Online organization or agency document

Cherokee Nation. (2008). *Cherokee elder care: A community PACE program.* Retrieved from http://eldercare.cherokee.org

If the organization provides a number for the report, give it in parentheses after the title.

Vandell, D. L., & Wolfe, B. (2000). *Child care quality: Does it matter and does it need to be improved?* (Special Report No. 78). Available from University of Wisconsin, Institute for Research on Poverty Web site, http://www.ssc.wisc.edu

Use "Available from" rather than "Retrieved from" if the URL will take your reader to access information rather than the source itself.

47. Online government document

U.S. Department of Labor, Women's Bureau. (2001). *Women in the labor force in 2006*. Retrieved from http://www.dol.gove/wb/factsheets /Qf-laborforce-06.htm

48. Online document from academic site

Cultural Studies Program. (n.d.). Retrieved from Drake University, Cultural Studies website: http://www.multimedia.drake.edu/cs/

49. Online report

Amnesty International. (1998). *The death penalty in Texas: Lethal injustice.* Retrieved from http://www.web.amnesty.org/ai.nsf/index/AMR510101998

50. Online abstract

For an abstract, give the source of the original work and the location of the abstract.

Globus, G. (1995, August). Quantum consciousness is cybernetic. *PSYCHE, 2*(12). Abstract retrieved from http://psyche.cs.monash.edu.au /v2/psyche-2-12-curran.html

31b
APA

51. Abstract from online database

> Buboltz, W. C., Jr., Soper, B., Brown, F., & Jenkins, S. (2002). Treatment
> approaches for sleep difficulties in college students. *Counselling
> Psychology Quarterly, 15*(2), 229–237. Abstract retrieved from
> Academic Search Premier database.

52. Journal article from online database

Unless your source might be hard to find, you do not need to identify the database you used (here, InfoTrac Expanded Academic database).

> Piko, B. (2001). Gender differences and similarities in adolescents' ways of
> coping. *Psychological Record, 51*(2), 223–236. doi: 10.1016
> /j.adolescence.2004.08.004

53. Newspaper article from online database

> Sappenfield, M. (2002, June 24). New laws curb teen sports drugs. *The
> Christian Science Monitor.* Retrieved from http://www.csmonitor.com

54. Podcast

> Malakof, D. (Producer). (2007, April 30). Your questions: Carbon power.
> [Audio Podcast]. *Climate connections.* Retrieved from http://
> www.npr.org

55. Wiki

Because wikis are interactive and their content changes, include your date of access.

> Media ethics. (n.d.). Retrieved June 22, 2008, from *Wikipedia: The Free
> Encyclopedia:* http://en.wikipedia.org/wiki/media-ethics

56. Blog

> Baron, D. (2006, October 26). I found it on Wikipedia, the eBay for facts
> [Web log message] Retrieved from http://webtools.uiuc.edu
> /blog/view?blogId=25&topicId=298&count=&ACTION
> =TOPIC_ DIALOGS&skinId=286

57. Presentation from online conference

Wolfram, S. (2006, June 16). *The state of NKS in 2006* [Audio file].

Keynote address at the meeting of the NKS 2006 Wolfram Science

Conference. Retrieved from http://www.wolframscience.com

/conference/2006/presentations/

58. Email

Cite email only in your text. (See Entry 15 on pp. 418–419.)

59. Online posting

Treat online postings as personal communications (see Entry 15 on pp. 418–419) unless they are archived and accessible.

Lanbehn, K. (2001, May 9). Re: Effective rural outreach [online discussion

group comment]. Retrieved from http://www.acils.com/silc

Exercise

A. Turn to Exercise A in Chapter 30. Rewrite the sentences supplied there to add in-text citations in APA style.

B. Turn to Exercise B in Chapter 30. Rewrite the items supplied there to create a list of references in APA style.

C. Working with a partner or a small group, compare your answers to Exercises A and B above. Correct any errors in your answers, using your handbook or your instructor's advice to resolve any differences of opinion.

STRATEGY Format your paper in APA style

- **Cover Page.** Supply the title, your name, and the institution each on a new line. Center and double-space all lines. Ask your instructor if her or his name, the course name, and a date are necessary; if so, double-space twice before adding this information.
- **Running head.** An abbreviated title (50 characters maximum) should appear about a half-inch from the upper left-hand corner of each page. On the cover page, precede the title by the words "Running head" followed by a colon. Give the page number about a half-inch from the upper-hand corner of each page, including on the cover page.
- **Margins.** Use one-inch margins throughout your paper.
- **Spacing.** Double-space your *entire* paper. APA suggests putting two spaces at the end of each sentence; your instructor may prefer a single space.
- **References.** Always begin your references list on a new page. (See page 420 for more information on formatting the references page.)

31b
APA

31c Sample APA paper

Supply abbreviated title (50 characters maximum) for heading

Running head: BODY ESTEEM

Use running head and page number

1

Center title and all other lines

Supply name and institution

Body Esteem in Women and Men

Sharon Salamone

University of Rhode Island

Professor Robert Schwegler

Ask your instructor if instructor's name, course name, and date are necessary

Writing 233

Section 2

April 30, 2003

BODY ESTEEM | Use running head and page number | 2

Begin on new page

| Center heading | Abstract

Undergraduate students, male and female, were asked to complete a Body Esteem Scale survey to report attitudes toward their bodies (body images). Responses to the survey provided an answer to the question of whether the men or the women had a higher body esteem. The mean of the responses for women and men indicated a higher level of body esteem among men, with the difference in the means being statistically significant. Because the sample was limited to college undergraduates and displayed little variety in ethnicity (predominantly white), the conclusions of the study are somewhat limited. Prior research on ethnicity and body image suggests that a more ethnically varied sample might produce different results.

Summarize paper in one ¶, no more than 120 words

Double-space abstract and rest of paper

[Besides the abstract, typical sections in an APA paper are Introduction, Method, Results, and Discussion.]

31c
APA

Body Esteem in Women and Men

1   The concept of beauty has changed over the years in
Western society, especially for women. In past centuries the
ideal was a voluptuous and curved body; now it is a more
angular and thin shape (Monteath & McCabe, 1997). Lean,
muscular bodies are currently held up as ideals for men, too.
Ideals of physical appearance and attractiveness play an
important role in the lives of people. People considered
attractive are often preferred as working partners, as dating
partners, or as job candidates (Lennon, Lillethun, & Buckland,
1999). Media images endorse particular body ideals as well; for
example, "media in Western countries have portrayed a
steadily thinning female body ideal" (Monteath & McCabe,
1997, p. 711).

2   Most of us assume that women are quite concerned about
their weight and appearance—their body images—and that
they often lack positive body esteem, perhaps as a result of
media images and other cultural influences (Rodin, Silberstein,
& Striegel-Moore, 1984; Polivy & Herman, 1987; Wilcox & Laird,
2000). But what about men? Are they concerned as well? Is
their level of body esteem higher or lower than women's or
about the same? In this paper I report on a study I undertook
with a group of college undergraduates to compare the
attitudes of men and women toward their bodies. In particular,
I wanted to determine whether or not the men had a higher
body esteem than the women had.

Indent
¶s 1/2"

1"margin on
each side

Prior
research and
problem for
current
research

Multiple
sources in
one citation

Research
questions

1" margin at bottom

31c
APA

BODY ESTEEM   4

| Center boldface subhead | **Literature Review** |

3   Thinness is prized in contemporary society, especially for women. In our culture, thinness, a statistical deviation, has become the norm, leading millions of women to believe their bodies are abnormal. Therefore, it is reasonable for women to be concerned about their appearance and to compare themselves to others on the basis of what they believe to be the norm (Lennon et al., 1999). As Lennon et al. point out, "Comparison with such images may be related to negative outcomes such as low self-esteem (Freedman, 1984), dissatisfaction with appearance (Richens, 1991), eating disorders (Peterson, 1987; Stice et al., 1994), and negative body image (Freedman, 1984)."

Review of earlier studies

Citations part of passage being quoted

4   Body image is basically made up of two important components: one's perception and one's attitude toward body image. Social factors can play a large role in determining both components (Monteath & McCabe, 1997). Given the cultural pressures on women to be thin, we might expect many women to have somewhat negative body images. As Kathy Wilcox and James Laird (2000) put it, "To many observers, the media appear to be unwittingly engaged in a campaign to make women feel badly about themselves" (p. 279).

Body image defined for women

5   On the other hand, some researchers suggest that "men seem less obsessed with and disturbed by being or becoming fat: thus, the occurrence of pathogenic values related to eating and body size is extremely low among men" (Demarest & Allen, 2000, p. 465). Although there has been some research, "the

Male body image defined

31c
APA

literature on body image perception in men is far more limited"
than that on women (Pope, Gruber, Mangweth, Bureau, deCol,
Jouvent, & Hudson, 2000). Thus there are reasons to suspect
that men also suffer from distorted perceptions of body image.
This has been evident in two recent studies. First, men with
eating disorders believe that they are fatter than men of
normal weight are. Also, recent studies have shown that
athletes perceive themselves to be small and frail when they
are, in fact, large and muscular (Pope et al., 2000). Moreover,
in one particular study, men indicated that they would prefer to
have a body with twenty-seven pounds more muscle than they
actually have (Pope et al., 2000). Thus it seems reasonable to
ask whether men and women have clearly different levels of
body esteem.

Method

6   To measure differences between men's and women's levels
of body esteem, I administered a Body Esteem Scale (BES)
survey (Franzoi & Shields, 1984). Participants in my study were
a sample consisting of 174 undergraduate college students from
a state university. I approached them and asked them to
complete the BES. I asked each willing participant to read and
sign an informed consent form before participating. This form
states that the participant may stop at any point if he or she
feels uncomfortable answering a particular question or group of
questions and reassures each person that he or she will remain
anonymous.

7   The majority of the participants, between the ages of 18
and 59, were White, making up 81% of the sample. Blacks and

Describes methods for the study

Participants

31c
APA

BODY ESTEEM   6

African Americans made up 6.3%; Asian/Pacific Islanders
made up 3.4%; Latino/Latina, mixed race, and all others made
up 2.9% each; and Native Americans made up .6% of the
sample. The sample was equally divided between men and
women.

8   The Body Esteem Scale (BES) consists of general
questions (see Appendix) followed by three components (BES
1, BES 2, and BES 3). BES 1 makes up the Physical/Sexual
Attractiveness part of the scale, focusing primarily on
elements of the body; BES 3 consists of the Physical
Condition component of the scale, covering such matters as
stamina, physical condition, and strength. BES 1 and BES 3
have different forms and questions for women and men. For
BES 2, the women's questionnaire constitutes the Weight
Concern component of the scale while the men's
questionnaire constitutes the Upper Body Strength
component of the scale.

> Detailed discussion of questionnaire with cross-reference to appendix

Results and Discussion

9   I recorded the results from the questionnaires into an
Excel spreadsheet. In order to determine whether women or
men had higher levels of body esteem as measured by the BES,
I calculated the average score for each group (statistical
mean). The mean for women was lower than for men: for
women, $M = 3.2304$; for men, $M = 3.6514$. From this I arrived
at my preliminary conclusion that for this particular sample of
college students, the men had clearly higher body esteem than
did the women, by .4211, or approximately .4 on a scale
of 1–5.

> Results presented in detail

10   I realized, however, that results can occur by chance and that there are statistical procedures for determining the likelihood that chance was responsible for the difference between the two groups. To determine whether the results were statistically significant (not occurring by chance), I had the spreadsheet program calculate an ANOVA (univariate analysis of variance) to compare the two body esteem indexes. The results indicated that the differences were significant, $F(1.172) = 28.05$, $p < .05$.

Presents main conclusion

11   I conducted this study in order to determine whether men had higher, lower, or similar levels of body esteem than women had, at least for the group of people (university undergraduates) I was studying. For this group, it is clear that men had higher levels of body esteem.

Discusses limitations of the study and its conclusions

12   Comparing men's and women's body esteem is not as simple as this study might seem to suggest, however. The body esteem scales for men and women are certainly comparable, but they do not measure exactly the same things. According to Franzoi and Shields (1984), body esteem for women appears to consist of three primary components: sexual attractiveness, weight concern, and physical condition. The sexual attractiveness subscale consists of physical attributes that cannot generally be changed through exercise, but only through cosmetics. The physical appearance subscale includes body parts that can be altered through exercise or the control of food intake. The third subscale pertains to qualities such as stamina, agility, and strength. For men, the first subscale measures facial features and some aspects of the physique. The

BODY ESTEEM   8

second subscale is composed of upper body parts and functions that can be altered through exercising. The third subscale is similar to the woman's physical subscale, consisting of stamina, agility, and strength.

13   As social attitudes and values change, perhaps men's and women's versions of the BES may need to change too. As sports and physical strength become more important to women, parts of the BES may possibly need to be revised to be more parallel to the men's. Right now, however, the BES seems to provide some understanding of the different levels of bodily self-esteem held by women and men.

> Possibilities for future research

14   The great pressure on women in our society to be thin and physically attractive according to standards that do not represent a normal range of body types and sizes probably accounts for the difference between the women's and men's results. Franzoi and Shields (1984) make a comment that helps explain the higher body esteem of the males: "It appears that men associate these body parts and functions, not with how they and others assess them as static objects, but with how they will help or hinder physical activity."

> Analyzes findings in detail

15   My results are consistent with other research. For example, "In studies of body-shape perception, men typically have more positive body images than women do, regardless of their weight" (Demarest & Langer, 1996, p. 466). Overall, men are generally satisfied with their body size, although they misjudge what women think to be attractive (Demarest & Allen, 2000).

31c
APA

16   Gender is not the only factor that influences body image. Ethnicity is also very important, especially among women. In interviews conducted by Lopez, Blix, and Blix (1995) and by Rosen and Gross (1987), Black women seem to have more positive body images and less desire to be thin than White or Hispanic women (Demarest & Allen, 2000). When compared to Black women, White women showed greater body dissatisfaction at lower body weights (Demarest & Allen). It has also been found that Black men were less likely than White men to refuse a date with a woman because she was overweight. According to Demarest and Allen, among the female participants, Black women have a more accurate view of the perception of men, whereas White women have a more distorted perception.

17   In my study, the majority of the sample consisted of White participants. This may have affected my results and my conclusions. Because ethnicity is important in a study such as this, a more varied sample would lead to stronger conclusions.

References

Need a hanging indent

Demarest, J., & Allen, R. (2000). Body image: Gender, ethnic, and age differences. *Journal of Social Psychology, 140,* 465–471.

Demarest, J., & Langer, E. (1996). Perception of body shape by underweight, average-weight, and overweight men and women. *Perceptual and Motor Skills, 83,* 569–570.

Franzoi, S. L., & Shields, S. A. (1984). The body esteem scale: Multidimensional structure and sex differences in a college population. *Journal of Personality Assessment, 407,* 173–178.

Lennon, S. J., Lillethun, A., & Buckland, S. S. (1999). Attitudes toward social comparison as a function of self-esteem: Idealized appearance and body image. *Family & Consumer Science Research Journal, 27*(4), 379–406. doi: 10.1177/1077727X99274001

Lopez, E., Blix, G., & Blix, A. G. (1995). Body image of Latinas compared to body image of non-Latina white women. *Health Values, 19*(6), 3–10.

Monteath, S. A., & McCabe, M. P. (1997). The influence of societal factors on female body image. *Journal of Social Psychology, 137,* 708–727.

Polivy, J., & Herman, C. P. (1987). The diagnosis and treatment of abnormal eating. *Journal of Consulting Clinical Psychology, 55,* 635–644. Retrieved from http://www.cas.appstate.edu/vkms/classes/psy5150/Documents/PolivyHerman1987.pdf

Begin on new page

Sources listed alphabetically

All lines double-spaced

First line of each entry not indented; additional lines indented as you indent a ¶.

31c APA

BODY ESTEEM   11

Pope, H. G., Gruber, A. J., Mangweth, B., Bureau, B., deCol, C.,
        Jouvent, R., et al. (2000). Body image perception among
        men in three countries. *American Journal of Psychiatry*,
        157, 1297–1301. doi: 10.1176/appi.ajp.157.8.1297

Rodin, J., Silberstein, L., & Striegel-Moore, R. (1984). Women
        and weight: a normative discontent. In T. B. Sonderegger
        (Ed.), *Nebraska symposium on motivation: Psychology and
        gender.* Lincoln: University of Nebraska Press, 267–307.

Rosen, J. C., & Gross, J. (1987). Prevalence of weight reducing
        and weight gaining in adolescent boys and girls. *Health
        Psychology, 6*(2), 131–147.

Wilcox, K., & Laird, J. D. (2000). The impact of media images
        of super-slender women on women's self-esteem:
        Identification, social comparison, and self-perception.
        Journal of Research in Personality, 34, 278–286. doi:
        10.1006/jrpe.1999.2281

BODY ESTEEM   12

Begin on
new page

Appendix

Body Esteem Scale for Adolescents and Adults

General Questions

Instructions: Indicate how often you agree with the
following statements, ranging from "never" (0) to "always"
(4). Circle the appropriate number beside each statement

Never = 0; Seldom = 1; Sometimes = 2; Often = 3; Always = 4

31c
APA

BODY ESTEEM   13

1.   I like what I look like in pictures.   0 1 2 3 4

2.   Other people consider me good looking.   0 1 2 3 4

3.   I'm proud of my body.   0 1 2 3 4

4.   I am preoccupied with trying to change
     my body weight.   0 1 2 3 4

5.   I think my appearance would help me
     get a job.   0 1 2 3 4

6.   I like what I see when I look in the mirror.   0 1 2 3 4

7.   There are lots of things I'd change about
     my looks if I could.   0 1 2 3 4

8.   I am satisfied with my weight.   0 1 2 3 4

9.   I wish I looked better.   0 1 2 3 4

10. I really like what I weigh.   0 1 2 3 4

11. I wish I looked like someone else.   0 1 2 3 4

12. People my own age like my looks.   0 1 2 3 4

13. My looks upset me.   0 1 2 3 4

14. I'm as nice looking as most people.   0 1 2 3 4

15. I'm pretty happy about the way I look.   0 1 2 3 4

16. I feel I weigh the right amount for my height.   0 1 2 3 4

17. I feel ashamed of how I look.   0 1 2 3 4

18. Weighing myself depresses me.   0 1 2 3 4

19. My weight makes me unhappy.   0 1 2 3 4

20. My looks help me to get dates.   0 1 2 3 4

21. I worry about the way I look.   0 1 2 3 4

22. I think I have a good body.   0 1 2 3 4

23. I'm looking as nice as I'd like to.   0 1 2 3 4

Visit mycomplab.com for more resources and exercises on APA documentation.

31c
APA

CHAPTER 32

CMS Documentation

The Chicago Manual of Style (CMS) offers several methods of documentation, one of which calls for footnotes or endnotes and a bibliography. This chapter discusses CMS style and provides models for the most common kinds of entries you will use.

CMS BIBLIOGRAPHY FORMATS

CMS style, the documentation style outlined in *The Chicago Manual of Style*, 15th ed. (2003) and in Kate L. Turabian et al., *A Manual for Writers of Research Papers, Theses, and Dissertations*, 7th ed. (2007), provides references in the form of endnotes or footnotes. Endnotes or footnotes are signaled by a superscript numeral in the text (for example,[1]) and a correspondingly numbered reference note at the end of the paper (an endnote) or, less often, at the bottom of the page (a footnote). A bibliography at the end of the paper provides a list of all the sources in alphabetical order by author. Endnotes and footnotes are less compact than parenthetical references, yet they offer you a chance to cite a source in full and to include brief explanatory material. Readers especially interested in your sources will find themselves repeatedly turning away from the text itself to consult the notes, however.

32a Endnotes and footnotes

To indicate a reference in the body of your text, insert a number slightly above the line; number the references consecutively. At the end of the paper (in an endnote) or at the bottom of the page (in a footnote), provide detailed information about the source. To create notes, use the footnote/endnote generator in your word-processing program.

TEXT OF PAPER

To emphasize how isolated and impoverished his childhood neighborhood was, Wideman describes it as being not simply on "the wrong side of the tracks" but actually "under the tracks, if the truth be told—in a deep hollow between Penn and the abrupt rise of Bruston Hill."[1]

NOTE

1. John Edgar Wideman, *Brothers and Keepers* (New York: Penguin Books, 1984), 39.

1 Decide on endnotes or footnotes

When pages contain many footnotes or long footnotes, you may find it hard to place the notes on the same pages as the material to which they refer. Multiple or long notes at the bottom of a page can also draw readers' attention away from the text to the notes. For these reasons, even though it may be a bit easier for readers to look at the bottom of the page for a note than to turn to the end of the paper, you should generally employ endnotes. Most readers mark the page containing the endnotes so they can refer to notes with a minimum of disruption. Because readers may sometimes skip consulting a note unless they are particularly interested in your sources, you should make sure that you place all information necessary for understanding your argument or explanation in the body of your paper and not in the notes.

2 Content and explanatory notes

At times you may wish to supplement your text with material that may interest only a few readers. Notes are an appropriate place to do this, but don't make notes so detailed that they distract readers from the main text of the paper. You can also combine explanation with a source reference, though you need to make sure that a long and detailed discussion does not obscure the reference.

TEXT OF PAPER

Did some famous artists begin their paintings by tracing using a *camera obscura*? The answer is probably yes, and the process can be understood this way.

If a small hole is made in the wall of a darkened room, an image of the scene outside can be formed by light rays passing through the hole. The image may appear on a wall

opposite the hole, or can be observed on a sheet of paper
or other screen placed in front of the hole.[2]

NOTE   2. Philip Steadman, *Vermeer's Camera* (Oxford: Oxford
University Press, 2001), 4. In an electronic age, we often forget
that complex effects can be created by simple devices such as
the *camera obscura*.

32b Note examples

A typical note provides the author's name in regular order, the title of
the work being cited, publication information, and the page number(s).

Place endnotes at the end of a paper, after appendixes but before a
bibliography. Supply notes on a separate page with the centered heading
"Notes." Your word-processing footnote/endnote program should indent the
first line. If not, indent it one-half inch or five spaces. Start the note with the
number, followed by a period and a space. Do not indent the second line or
any others that follow. Double-space for ease of reading.

1 Books and works treated as books

```
MODEL FORMAT FOR BOOKS AND WORKS TREATED AS BOOKS

   number
   + period    comma
   + space     + space     space
      ↓           ↓          ↓
      1. Author(s), Title (Place of Publication: Publisher,

   Year), Page number(s).
      ↑
   comma + space
```

- **Author(s).** Give the name of the author(s) in regular order followed
  by a comma and a space.
- **Title.** Give the title of the work being cited. Italicize the title of a book
  and follow the title with a space. (See 57c on capitalization of titles.)
- **Publication information.** Give all publication information within
  parentheses. Start with the city of publication, followed by a comma
  and an abbreviation for the state or country if this information is necessary to avoid confusion between two cities with the same name or to
  identify little-known places. Add a colon and a space, then give the publisher's name followed by a comma, a space, and the date of publication.
  Place a comma followed by a space after the closing parenthesis mark.

32b
CMS

- **Page number(s).** Conclude with the specific page numbers containing the information being cited or the passage being quoted, paraphrased, or summarized.

1. One author

1. Bobby Bridger, *Buffalo Bill and Sitting Bull: Inventing the Wild West* (Austin: University of Texas Press, 2002), 297.

2. Two or three authors

Separate the names of two authors with *and*. Separate those of three authors with commas as well as *and* before the name of the third author.

2. Canter Brown Jr. and Barbara Gray Brown, *Family Records of the African American Pioneers of Tampa and Hillsborough County* (Tampa: University of Tampa Press, 2003), 129.

2. Michael Wood, Bruce Cole, and Adelheid Gealt, *Art of the Western World* (New York: Summit Books, 1989), 206–10.

3. Four or more authors

For works with more than three authors, give the name of the first author followed by *and others*. (Generally, all the names are supplied in the corresponding bibliography entry.)

3. Bernadette Casey and others, *Television Studies: The Key Concepts* (London: Routledge, 2002), 81.

4. Organization or group as author

4. National Restaurant Association Educational Foundation, *Food Production: Competency Guide* (Upper Saddle River: Pearson Prentice Hall, 2007), 48.

5. No author given

If the author is not known, begin the entry with the title.

5. *The Great Utopia: The Russian and Soviet Avant-Garde, 1915–1932* (New York: Guggenheim Museum, 1992), 661.

6. Editor

When a work has an editor, translator, or compiler (or some combination of them), give the name or names after the title preceded by a comma and the appropriate abbreviation, for example, *ed.*, *trans.*, or *comp.*

6. Mahatma Gandhi, *Gandhi in India: In His Own Words,* ed. Martin Green (Hanover, NH: University Press of New England, 1987), 261.

32b
CMS

If you wish to emphasize the role of the editor, translator, or compiler, give his or her name at the beginning of the entry. The word *by* with the author's name (*Harry S Truman*) would be appropriate following the title below, but it is not necessary because the author's name appears in the title.

> 6. Robert H. Ferrell, ed., *Dear Bess: The Letters from Harry to Bess Truman 1910–1959* (New York: W. W. Norton, 1983), 71–2.

7. Edition other than the first

Use an abbreviation following the title to indicate the particular edition, for example, *4th ed.* ("fourth edition") or *rev. and enl. ed.* ("revised and enlarged edition").

> 7. Thomas E. Skidmore and Peter H. Smith, *Modern Latin America,* 5th ed. (New York: Oxford University Press, 2001), 243.

For a work that has been reprinted or appears in a special paperback edition, give information about both the original publication and the reprint.

> 7. Henri Frankfort and others, *The Intellectual Adventure of Ancient Man* (1946; repr., Chicago: University of Chicago Press, 1977), 202–4. Citations are to the reprint edition.

8. Multivolume work

A multivolume work can consist of volumes all by a single author (sometimes with different titles for each) or of works by a variety of authors with an overall title. If you are referring to the whole multivolume work, include the number of volumes after the title. To indicate volume and page number for a specific volume, use volume and page numbers separated by a colon and no space. Give the volume number and name for separately titled volumes after the main title and omit the volume number in the page reference.

> 8. Sigmund Freud, *The Standard Edition of the Complete Psychological Works of Sigmund Freud,* trans. James Strachey (London: Hogarth Press, 1953), 11:180.

2 Articles and selections from books

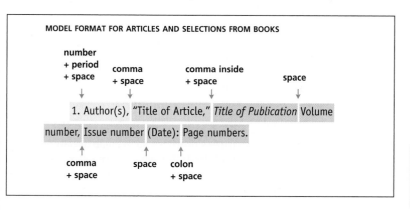

MODEL FORMAT FOR ARTICLES AND SELECTIONS FROM BOOKS

number + period + space ↓

comma + space ↓

comma inside + space ↓

space ↓

1. Author(s), "Title of Article," *Title of Publication* Volume number, Issue number (Date): Page numbers.

↑ comma + space

↑ space

↑ colon + space

- **Author(s).** Give the author's name in regular order.
- **Title.** Put the title of the article or selection in quotation marks. Put a comma inside the closing quotation mark, and leave a space after the quotation mark.
- **Publication information.** Next give the title of the journal or book, italicized, and leave a space after it with no punctuation. Supply the volume number, issue number, and then the date of publication in parentheses, varying the information and style for different types of publications. Place a colon after the final parenthesis, and leave a space.
- **Page number(s).** Supply the page numbers for the pertinent part of the article or selection.

9. Article in scholarly journal

Give the volume number and the issue number, but do not include the month or season of the individual issue containing the article. Give specific page numbers for the part of the article you are citing. If you wish to refer to the article as a whole, give inclusive page numbers for the entire article, for example, *98–114*. If a journal uses issue numbers only, put a comma after the title and follow it with the issue number.

9. Lily Zubaidah Rahim, "The Road Less Traveled: Islamic Militancy in Southeast Asia," *Critical Asian Studies* 35, no. 2 (2003): 224.

10. Article in popular magazine

Follow the name of the magazine with a comma and the date. Use this order for the date if it includes the day: *November 25, 1995*. Place a comma at the end of the date and then give a page number for the specific part of the article you are citing or inclusive page numbers for the entire article if you are referring to it as a whole.

10. Edward Hoagland, "The American Dissident: Individualism as a Matter of Conscience," *Harper's,* August 2003, 35.

11. Article in daily newspaper

Identify newspaper articles by date (rather than volume number) following the title of the article and the name of the newspaper. Present the date in this order: *February 4, 1996*. You may provide the section number or letter (before the issue date), and you may specify an edition (after the issue date). CMS style omits page numbers.

11. Mark Brennock, "55% of Young Know of Peer Suicide Attempts," *The Irish Times* (Dublin), September 20, 2003, sec. A.

When an American newspaper's title does not include the city's name, give it at the start of the title (italicized). For less-known newspapers, for those outside North America with the city not mentioned in the title, and for those from places easily confused with well-known cities, give the name of the state or country after the title or after the name of the city in the title: Westerly (RI) Sun; Times (*London*).

12. Chapter in book or selection from anthology

Give the name of the selection or chapter in quotation marks followed by *in* and the name of the book. If the book has an editor, follow the book's title with *ed.* and the editor's name.

CHAPTER IN A BOOK

12. Robert Glennon, "The Future of Water: Tourism and Grand Canyon National Park," in *Water Follies: Groundwater Pumping and the Fate of America's Fresh Waters* (Washington, DC: Island Press, 2002), 195.

SELECTION FROM AN EDITED COLLECTION OF ONE WRITER'S WORKS

12. W. E. B. Du Bois, "The Call of Kansas," in *W. E. B. Du Bois: A Reader,* ed. David Levering Lewis (New York: Henry Holt, 1995), 173.

SELECTION FROM AN EDITED COLLECTION OF ESSAYS

12. John Matviko, "Television Satire and the Presidency: The Case of *Saturday Night Live,*" in *Hollywood's White House: The American Presidency in Film and History,* ed. Peter C. Rollins and John E. O'Connor (Lexington: University of Kentucky Press, 2003), 341.

3 Field resources

13. Unpublished interview

For unpublished interviews done by someone else, begin with the name of the person interviewed followed by a comma; then give the phrase *interview by*, the name of the interviewer, the date (in this order: *May 2, 2001*), any file number, the medium (*tape recording* or *transcript*, for example), and the place where the interview is stored (such as *Erie County Historical Society, Buffalo, New York*). For interviews you conduct, provide the name of the person interviewed, the phrase *interview by author*, a description of the kind of interview, the medium, and the place and date of the interview.

13. LeJon Williams, interview by author, tape recording, San Diego, CA, October 11, 2009.

13. Lenelle Chu, telephone interview by author, transcript, Hinsdale, IL, June 5, 2009.

4 Media and electronic resources

14. Article in scholarly journal (online)

Use the form for *Article in scholarly journal* (Entry 9), but add the URL and the date of access. If you are referring to a particular section of the article, include the page (if available) or some other locator such as a heading.

> 14. Anthony B. Pinn, "DuBois' *Souls:* Thoughts on 'Veiled' Bodies and the Study of Black Religion," *The North Star: A Journal of African American Religious History* 6, no. 2 (2003), under "Music and the 'Style' of Life," http://northstar.vassar.edu/volume6/pinn.html (accessed October 7, 2006).

15. Magazine article (online)

Use the form for *Article in popular magazine* (Entry 10), but add the URL and the date of access.

> 15. Alexander Barnes Dryer, "Our Liberian Legacy," *The Atlantic Online,* July 30, 2003, http://www.theatlantic.com/unbound/flashbks/ liberia.htm (accessed October 24, 2008).

16. Newspaper article (online)

Use the form for *Article in daily newspaper* (Entry 11), but add the URL and the date of access.

> 16. Joshua Klein, "Scaring Up a Good Movie," *Chicago Tribune Online Edition,* October 28, 2003, http://www.chicagotribune.com/ (accessed October 28, 2009).

17. Article in database (online)

Follow the format for *Article in scholarly journal* (Entry 14). Include the URL (which also identifies the database) unless the URL is long and complicated and the selection is likely to be located with a simple search. Next, give the date accessed. Some URLs may be long; you may need to split them so they fit onto several lines.

> 17. Ann Brydon, "The Predicament of Nature: Keiko the Whale and the Cultural Politics of Whaling in Iceland," *Anthropological Quarterly* 79, no. 2 (2006). (Accessed April 16, 2009).

18. Book (online)

Include the kinds of information required in Entries 1–7. Indicate the URL and the date of access.

> 18. Sharon Marcus, *Apartment Stories: City and Home in Nineteenth-Century Paris and London* (Berkeley: University of California Press, 1999), http://ark.cdlib.org/ark:13030/ft0d5n99jz/ (accessed October 15, 2009).

For older works, use the following format.

> 18. Charles Darwin, *On the Origin of Species by Means of Natural Selection, or the Preservation of Favoured Races in the Struggle for Life*

(1859; Project Gutenberg 1998), ftp://sailor.gutenberg.org/pub/gutenberg/etext98/otoos10.txt (accessed November 1, 2009).

19. Web site

Provide the author of the content, the title of the site, the owner or group responsible for the site, the URL, and the date of access.

19. Smithsonian Center for Folklife and Cultural Heritage, "2002 Smithsonian Folklife Festival: The Silk Road," Smithsonian Institution, http://www.folklife.si.edu/CFCH/festival2002.htm (accessed October 27, 2008).

20. Post to electronic mailing list

Provide the name of the writer, an indication of the kind of document, the name of the list, date of the posting, URL, and date of access. You need not include this information in your bibliography.

20. Justin M. Sanders, e-mail to alt.war.civil.usa, February 15, 2002, http://groups.google.com/groups?q=civil+war&hl=en&lr=&ie=UTF-8&selm=civil-war-usa/faq/part2_1013770939%40rtfm.mit.edu&rnum=1 (accessed October 21, 2008).

21. Audio or video recording

Start with the title unless the recording features a particular individual. Give the names and roles (if appropriate) of performers or others. Add any recording number (audio) after the company name.

21. *James Baldwin*, VHS, directed by Karen Thorson (San Francisco: California Newsreel, 1990).

5 Multiple sources and sources cited in prior notes

22. Multiple sources

When you wish to cite more than one source in a note, separate the references with semicolons and give the entries in the order in which they were cited in the text.

22. See Greil Marcus, *Mystery Train: Images of America in Rock 'n Roll Music* (New York: E. P. Dutton, 1975), 119; Susan Orlean, "All Mixed Up," *New Yorker,* June 22, 1992, 90; and Cornel West, "Learning to Talk of Race," *New York Times Magazine,* August 2, 1992, 24.

23. Work cited more than once

The first time you provide a reference to a work, you need to list full information about the source in the note. In later notes you need to provide only the last name of the author(s), a shortened title, and the page(s). Separate these elements with commas.

> 23. Macklin, *Mortal,* 161.

> 23. Wood, Cole, and Gealt, *Art,* 207.

If a note refers to the same source as the note directly before, you can use a traditional scholarly abbreviation, *ibid.* (from the Latin for "in the same place"), for the second note. *Ibid.* means that the entire reference is identical, but if you add a new page reference, the addition shows that the specific page is different.

> 24. Tarr, "'A Man,'" 183.

> 25. Ibid.

> 26. Ibid., 186.

32c Bibliography

At the end of your paper you need to provide readers with an alphabetical list of the sources cited in your notes. CMS style calls for this list to be titled "Bibliography" or "Works Cited." If it includes all the works you consulted, you might call it "Works Consulted."

STRATEGY Format the bibliography

- Place your bibliography on a separate page at the end of your paper. Continue the page numbering used for your text.
- Center the title two inches below the upper edge.
- Double-space all entries for ease of reading. Do not indent the first line, but indent the second line and any subsequent lines five spaces.
- Alphabetize the entries according to the authors' last names or the first word of the title, excluding *A*, *An*, and *The*, if the author is unknown.

1 Books and works treated as books

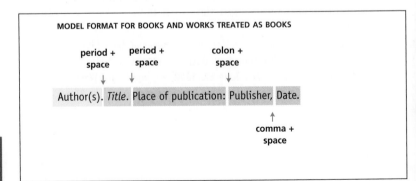

MODEL FORMAT FOR BOOKS AND WORKS TREATED AS BOOKS

period + space   period + space   colon + space

Author(s). *Title.* Place of publication: Publisher, Date.

comma + space

- **Author(s).** Give the author's last name followed by a comma, then the first and any middle names or initials followed by a period and a space.
- **Title.** Give the title of the work, italicized, ending with a period and a space. Capitalize the main words of the title and any subtitle. Do not capitalize *a, an, the,* coordinating conjunctions (such as *and, or,* and *but*), and prepositions. Always capitalize the first and last words of any title or subtitle.
- **Place of publication.** Give the city where the work was published, followed by a comma and an abbreviation for the state or country if necessary to avoid confusion between cities with the same name or to identify little-known places. End with a colon and a space.
- **Publisher.** Give the publisher's name followed by a comma and a single space.
- **Date.** Give the date of publication followed by a period.

1. One author

Bridger, Bobby. *Buffalo Bill and Sitting Bull: Inventing the Wild West.* Austin: University of Texas Press, 2002.

2. Two or three authors

Brown, Canter Jr., and Barbara Gray Brown. *Family Records of the African American Pioneers of Tampa and Hillsborough County.* Tampa: University of Tampa Press, 2003.

Wood, Michael, Bruce Cole, and Adelheid Gealt. *Art of the Western World.* New York: Summit Books, 1989.

3. Four or more authors

Casey, Bernadette, Neil Casey, Ben Calvert, Liam French, and Justin Lewis. *Television Studies: The Key Concepts.* London: Routledge, 2002.

4. Organization or group as author

National Restaurant Association Educational Foundation. *Food Production: Competency Guide.* Upper Saddle River: Pearson Prentice Hall, 2007.

5. No author given

The Great Utopia: The Russian and Soviet Avant-Garde, 1915–1932. New York: Guggenheim Museum, 1992.

6. Editor

Gandhi, Mahatma. *Gandhi in India: In His Own Words.* Edited by Martin Green. Hanover, NH: University Press of New England, 1987.

32c
CMS

Ferrell, Robert H., ed. *Dear Bess: The Letters from Harry to Bess Truman 1910–1959.* New York: W. W. Norton, 1983.

7. Edition other than the first

Skidmore, Thomas E., and Peter H. Smith. *Modern Latin America.* 5th ed. New York: Oxford University Press, 2001.

Frankfort, Henri, H. A. Frankfort, John A. Wilson, Thorkild Jacobsen, and William A. Irving. *The Intellectual Adventure of Ancient Man.* Chicago: University of Chicago Press, 1946. Reprint, Chicago: University of Chicago Press, 1977.

8. Multivolume work

Freud, Sigmund. *The Standard Edition of the Complete Psychological Works of Sigmund Freud.* Translated by James Strachey. Vol. 11. London: Hogarth Press, 1953.

2 Articles and selections from books

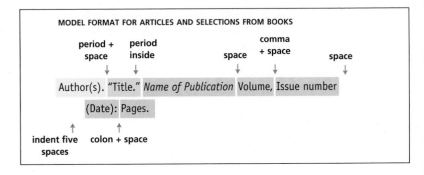

MODEL FORMAT FOR ARTICLES AND SELECTIONS FROM BOOKS

Author(s). "Title." *Name of Publication* Volume, Issue number (Date): Pages.

- **Author(s).** Give the author's last name followed by a comma, then the first and any middle names or initials followed by a period and a space.
- **Title.** Give the title of the article within quotation marks, and capitalize the main words of the title and of any subtitle. Do not capitalize *a, an, the,* coordinating conjunctions (such as *and* and *or*), and prepositions. Always capitalize the first and last words of any title or subtitle. If the article's title contains the title of a work that needs to be italicized, italicize it; if it contains a title that requires quotation marks, use single quotation marks to enclose the interior title.
- **Name of publication.** Give the title of the journal or magazine containing the article, and italicize it.

- **Volume.** Give the volume number of the periodical; separate it from the name of the publication by a space without a comma or any other punctuation. Include the issue number if available.
- **Date.** Provide the year in which the article was published (within parentheses), but indicate the month or season only for certain kinds of publications.
- **Pages.** Follow the parentheses containing the date with a colon and a space; then give the inclusive pages on which the article appears.

9. Article in scholarly journal

> Rahim, Lily Zubaidah. "The Road Less Traveled: Islamic Militancy in Southeast Asia." *Critical Asian Studies* 35, no. 2 (2003): 209–32.

10. Article in popular magazine

> Hoagland, Edward. "The American Dissident: Individualism as a Matter of Conscience." *Harper's,* August 2003, 33–41.

11. Article in daily newspaper

> Brennock, Mark. "55% of Young Know of Peer Suicide Attempts." *The Irish Times* (Dublin), September 20, 2003. sec. A.

Note: A newspaper article does not need to be included among works cited if it is documented in the text.

12. Chapter in book or selection from anthology

> Glennon, Robert. "The Future of Water: Tourism and Grand Canyon National Park." In *Water Follies: Groundwater Pumping and the Fate of America's Fresh Waters,* 195–207. Washington, DC: Island Press, 2002.

> Du Bois, W. E. B. "The Call of Kansas." In *W. E. B. Du Bois: A Reader,* edited by David Levering Lewis, 101–21. New York: Henry Holt, 1995.

> Matviko, John. "Television Satire and the Presidency: The Case of *Saturday Night Live.*" In *Hollywood's White House: The American Presidency in Film and History,* edited by Peter C. Rollins and John E. O'Connor, 341–60. Lexington: University of Kentucky Press, 2003.

3 Field resources

13. Unpublished interview

> Williams, LeJon. Interview by author. Tape recording. San Diego, CA, October 11, 2009.

32c
CMS

Chu, Lenelle. Telephone interview by author. Transcript. Hinsdale, IL, June 5, 2009.

4 Media and electronic resources

14. Article in scholarly journal (online)

Include the page range, if available.

Pinn, Anthony B. "DuBois' *Souls*: Thoughts on 'Veiled' Bodies and the Study of Black Religion." *The North Star: A Journal of African American Religious History* 6, no. 2 (2003). http://northstar.vassar.edu/volume6/pinn.html (accessed October 7, 2006).

15. Magazine article (online)

Dryer, Alexander Barnes. "Our Liberian Legacy." *The Atlantic Online,* July 30, 2003. http://www.theatlantic.com/unbound/flashbks/liberia.htm (accessed October 24, 2008).

16. Newspaper article (online)

Klein, Joshua. "Scaring Up a Good Movie." *Chicago Tribune Online Edition,* October 28, 2003. http://www.chicagotribune.com/ (accessed October 28, 2009).

17. Article in database (online)

See entry 17 on page 458 for advice on whether to include a URL.

Brydon, Ann. "The Predicament of Nature: Keiko the Whale and the Cultural Politics of Whaling in Iceland." *Anthropological Quarterly* 79, no. 2 (2006) (accessed April 16, 2009).

18. Book (online)

Marcus, Sharon. *Apartment Stories: City and Home in Nineteenth-Century Paris and London.* Berkeley: University of California Press, 1999. http://ark.cdlib.org/ark:13030/ft0d5n99jz/ (accessed October 15, 2009).

Darwin, Charles. *On the Origin of Species by Means of Natural Selection, or the Preservation of Favoured Races in the Struggle for Life.* 1859; Project Gutenberg 1998. ftp://sailor.gutenberg.org/pub/gutenberg/etext98/otoos10.txt (accessed November 1, 2009).

19. Web site

Smithsonian Center for Folklife and Cultural Heritage. "2002 Smithsonian Folklife Festival: The Silk Road." Smithsonian Institution. http://www.folklife.si.edu/CFCH/festival2002.htm (accessed October 27, 2009).

20. Audio or video recording

James Baldwin. VHS. Directed by Karen Thorson. San Francisco: California Newsreel, 1990.

5 Multiple sources

21. Multiple sources

When a note lists more than one source, list each one separately in your bibliography, integrating them in alphabetical order among your other sources.

Exercise

A. Turn to Exercise A in Chapter 30. Rewrite the sentences supplied there to add note numbers in CMS style. Then prepare the corresponding notes for these items.

B. Turn to Exercise B in Chapter 30. Rewrite the items supplied there to create a list of works cited in CMS style.

C. Working with a partner or a small group, compare your answers to Exercises A and B above. Correct any errors in your answers, using your handbook or your instructor's advice to resolve any differences of opinion.

STRATEGY Format your paper in CMS style

- **Cover Page.** Place your title one-third of the way down the page. In the bottom third of the page, give your name, instructor's name, course name, and date—each on a new line. Use all capital letters, center, and double-space all elements.
- **Page numbering.** The page number should appear about a half-inch from the upper right-hand corner of each page, excluding the cover page.
- **Margins.** Use one-inch margins throughout your paper.
- **Spacing.** Double-space your *entire* paper.
- **References.** Always begin your bibliography on a new page. (See page 460 for more information on formatting the bibliography.)

32c
CMS

32d Sample CMS Paper

Center title

Begin one-third of the way down the page

Study Drugs: The New Drug Craze Among College Students

Center and double-space all lines

Jenna Ianucilli

Dr. Schwegler

WRT 106

March 2, 2009

1

1   Have you ever had to stay up all night to cram for a big exam? Have you ever had to write three papers in one night because you put them all off until the last night? Ever felt like you could use something that could make you focus on your work during an all-night study session? Many people think they have found an effective strategy in the newest drug craze to sweep college campuses: drugs to increase academic performance.

2   The drugs they use are normally prescribed for attention deficit hyperactivity disorder (ADHD), with the most common drugs being Ritalin and Adderall. The drugs are usually prescribed to people suffering from ADHD to allow them to reach normal functioning level by stimulating the frontal lobes of the brain, areas that monitor task performance;[1] college students, however, often use the drugs as study aids. Dr. Eric Heiligenstein, a psychiatrist at the University of Wisconsin who studies substance abuse, points out that when taken by people with normal brain function, "The drugs can give healthy people an almost superhuman ability to focus for long periods."[2]

3   The drugs are stimulants, in the class of cocaine, caffeine, amphetamines, and methamphetamines, so the result in normal people is to feel like they are on "speed." They will have huge amounts of energy and will require less sleep. That can be a useful feeling when it is almost midnight and one has to cram in lots of studying for an organic chemistry exam at eight o'clock the next morning, yet side effects can include emotional and physical strains and anxiety and, in some cases, addiction or dependence.

¶ indented ½"

Double-space

Introduces topic

Superscript numbers refer to endnotes

Two ¶s provide background and explain the problem

Focus on danger

32d
CMS

2

4   In a survey of 13,500 college students conducted by the American College Health Association, 94 percent of respondents reported feeling overwhelmed by everything they had to do at school.[3] College life creates increased stress. Extracurricular activities that build résumés for graduate schools create strain. Students sleep less than normal. They worry more than ever about financial, social, and academic pressures.

5   In a survey I conducted, all the students believed that the competitiveness of college life might cause someone to choose to take drugs to improve academic performance.[4] The students also agreed that parents, peers, relatives, and teachers were other sources of pressure. Jobs are yet another cause of stress. Some college students work a substantial number of hours every week, not just for extra spending money but also to lighten some of the heavy debt load of student loans they will have once they graduate. For many, it is easier to pop a pill to aid concentration than to have to struggle to fit more sleep time into a full schedule of classes, extracurricular activities, parties, and work. Such students are at risk for misusing or abusing study drugs.

6   According to a 2002 Johns Hopkins University study, up to 20 percent of college-age students have regularly used drugs to enhance academic performance, and another study at the University of Wisconsin confirmed this.[5] Dr. Tim Wilens of Massachusetts General Hospital reports that a quarter of college-age students have tried stimulants such as Ritalin or Adderall without prescriptions.[6] These are staggering figures, which show the great lengths to which students will go to gain an edge.

Writer draws on own field research

CMS does not require note, but her instructor did

Article cited in footnote summarizes studies at Johns Hopkins and Wisconsin

Problem is widespread

32d
CMS

3

7   Where do the drugs come from, and how do they work? The drugs were developed to treat attention deficit hyperactivity disorder (ADHD), a condition that begins appearing in children in their preschool years. Between 30 and 70 percent of children with the disorder will continue to exhibit symptoms in their adult years. The principal characteristics of ADHD are inattention, hyperactivity, and impulsivity.[7]

8   Medications are one of the main treatments for ADHD. The most effective medications are stimulants such as Adderall and Ritalin. For many people afflicted with ADHD, the stimulants dramatically reduce hyperactivity and impulsivity and improve the ability to focus, work, and learn.[8]

How the drugs work

9   They have similar effects for college students, allowing them to work more efficiently while requiring less sleep. Adderall stimulates the central nervous system (the brain and nerves) by increasing the amount of certain chemicals, such as dopamine and norepinephrine, in the brain. These chemicals or neurotransmitters help the brain send signals between nerve cells. Adderall helps restore the balance of these neurotransmitters to the parts of the brain that control the ability to focus and pay attention.[9] "Think of a staticky radio signal," says Anthony Rostain, Professor of Psychiatry and Pediatrics at the University of Pennsylvania School of Medicine. "You turn the dial, and you get a better signal—the focusing and concentration are better."[10]

Discussion of Adderall

10   Ritalin is a mild stimulant to the central nervous system. The exact way that it works is unknown. The U.S. Drug

Discussion of Ritalin

32d
CMS

4

Enforcement Administration states that the medication produces the same effects as cocaine and amphetamines.[11] Adderall prescriptions have grown greatly, overtaking the once-popular medication Ritalin as the leader in treating ADHD. Adderall is the most common study drug as well.[12]

11   These seemingly innocuous academic-enhancing drugs can have serious and long-lasting side effects. For normal, healthy people who take them, the drugs can cause emotional and physical strain.[13] Side effects of Ritalin include insomnia, nervousness, drowsiness, dizziness, headache, blurred vision, tics, abdominal pain, nausea, vomiting, decreased appetite or weight loss, and slower weight gain. More serious side effects include irregular or fast heartbeat, confusion, and liver damage.[14] Side effects of Adderall include irregular heartbeat, very high blood pressure, hallucinations, abnormal behavior, and confusion. Other side effects include restlessness or tremor, anxiety or nervousness, headache, dizziness, insomnia, dryness of the mouth or unpleasant taste, diarrhea or constipation, and impotence or changes in sex drive.[15] Dr. John D. Hall, an addiction psychiatrist working in student mental health services at the University of Florida, says, "If you don't have ADHD, Adderall or Ritalin can cause significant anxiety."[16]

12   Users of study drugs are also at risk for dependence or addiction; users may become addicted to the energy the drug gives them.[17] With continued use of Adderall, a person can develop a tolerance and need for a higher dose to achieve the

Negative effects of the drugs

More negative effects

32d
CMS

5

same effects. Physical and psychological dependence can also occur. Ritalin can produce physical dependence as well.[18] There is also a risk of overdose, especially when the drug is obtained through a friend's prescription. Adderall or Ritalin dosage is carefully determined by height, weight, and symptoms. Another person's dosage can be dangerous, particularly if the person is bigger.[19]

13   In a society where the notion of popping a pill to solve problems is encouraged by advertisements suggesting that you "ask your doctor if Drug X is right for you," it seems logical for students to look for something that will help them stay alert longer and concentrate harder, especially if there are no obvious side effects. These seemingly innocuous and academically beneficial drugs can have serious side effects, however.

14   Though there have been no reported overdoses of study drugs, their use is still a serious problem, on a par with the use of performance-enhancing drugs in sports. The side effects of the drugs outweigh any academic advantage, and their use raises ethical questions as well in that it gives some students an unfair advantage. Dr. Hall, the addiction psychiatrist, offers simple advice: "Don't depend on a pill to get you through the pressures of exam week. The long-term solution is to plan ahead, do as well as you can in your exams, and take life as it comes."[20]

Final warning

32d
CMS

6

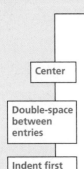

Center

Double-space between entries

Indent first line ½"

Endnotes listed in order in which they appear in the paper

Subsequent references to the same source include author's last name, shortened title, and page numbers

Ibid. is used for a subsequent reference to the same source when there are no intervening references

2"

Notes

1. Deborah Chun, "Abuse of Drugs for ADHD Up for Finals," *GainesvilleSun.com*, April 29, 2004, http://www.psychiatry.ufl.edu/Gainesvillesun_com2.htm (accessed January 20, 2009).

2. William Campbell Douglass, "College-Age Students Use ADHD Drugs to Make the Grade," *Real Health Breakthroughs*, January 14, 2005, http://www.healthiernews.com/dailydose/dd200501/dd20050114.html (accessed February 12, 2009).

3. Richard Kadison, "Getting an Edge—Use of Stimulants and Antidepressants in College," *New England Journal of Medicine* 353 (2005): 1089.

4. Jenna Ianucilli, Survey of Students' Attitudes on Academic-Enhancing Drugs, unpublished raw data, University of Rhode Island, 2009.

5. Kadison, "Getting an Edge," 1090.

6. New York University Health Center, "Health Promotion and Wellness—Study Drugs," New York University, http://www.nyu.edu/nyuhc/studydrugs (accessed January 31, 2009).

7. National Institute of Mental Health, *Attention Deficit Hyperactivity Disorder* (Baltimore: National Institute of Mental Health, 2003), 5.

8. Michael I. Reiff, *ADHD: A Complete and Authoritative Guide* (Chicago: American Academy of Pediatrics, 2004), 23.

9. Ibid., 15.

10. As quoted in Reiff, 24.

11. New York University Health Center, "Health Promotion and Wellness."

12. National Institute of Mental Health, *Attention Deficit Hyperactivity Disorder*, 7.

13. Kadison, "Getting an Edge," 1090.

14. New York University Health Center, "Health Promotion and Wellness."

15. Ibid.

32d
CMS

7

16. Chun, "Abuse of Drugs."

17. Kadison, "Getting an Edge," 1091.

18. New York University Health Center, "Health Promotion and Wellness."

19. Chun, "Abuse of Drugs."

20. Ibid.

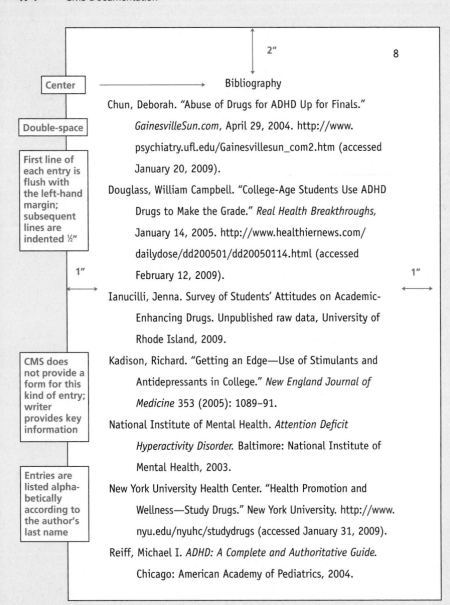

2"

8

Center ⟶ Bibliography

Chun, Deborah. "Abuse of Drugs for ADHD Up for Finals."

Double-space

GainesvilleSun.com, April 29, 2004. http://www.

psychiatry.ufl.edu/Gainesvillesun_com2.htm (accessed

First line of
each entry is
flush with
the left-hand
margin;
subsequent
lines are
indented ½"

January 20, 2009).

Douglass, William Campbell. "College-Age Students Use ADHD

Drugs to Make the Grade." Real Health Breakthroughs,

January 14, 2005. http://www.healthiernews.com/

dailydose/dd200501/dd20050114.html (accessed

1"

February 12, 2009).

1"

Ianucilli, Jenna. Survey of Students' Attitudes on Academic-

Enhancing Drugs. Unpublished raw data, University of

Rhode Island, 2009.

CMS does
not provide a
form for this
kind of entry;
writer
provides key
information

Kadison, Richard. "Getting an Edge—Use of Stimulants and

Antidepressants in College." New England Journal of

Medicine 353 (2005): 1089–91.

National Institute of Mental Health. Attention Deficit

Hyperactivity Disorder. Baltimore: National Institute of

Mental Health, 2003.

Entries are
listed alpha-
betically
according to
the author's
last name

New York University Health Center. "Health Promotion and

Wellness—Study Drugs." New York University. http://www.

nyu.edu/nyuhc/studydrugs (accessed January 31, 2009).

Reiff, Michael I. ADHD: A Complete and Authoritative Guide.

Chicago: American Academy of Pediatrics, 2004.

32d
CMS

CHAPTER **33**

CSE Documentation

The Council of Science Editors (CSE) endorses two styles for documentation, one that numbers each source and one that provides names and dates for each source. This chapter discusses both styles and provides models for in-text references and for a reference list.

CSE REFERENCES FORMATS

1. BOOKS AND WORKS TREATED AS BOOKS

You are preparing a paper in a course in engineering, the sciences, or a technical field, and you ask the instructor what documentation style you should use for references. The answer is likely to be "Use a scientific style; look at the professional journals you've been consulting and follow the style they recommend." (See 29d.) This means you will use the number method or the name-and-date method.

This guidance will be helpful if you can do three things.

1. Recognize situations calling for scientific or engineering documentation (see below).
2. Recognize the general elements of scientific and engineering style (see 33a).
3. Analyze and understand the documentation style used in a particular scientific, engineering, or technical publication (see 29d).

Students are not the only people who need these skills. Scientists, engineers, technicians, and technical writers also need to be able to choose a documentation style appropriate for a writing situation. Fortunately, some resources are available, though their influence is not as widespread or as uniform as that of the manuals outlining MLA and APA styles (see Chapters 30 and 31).

The manual published by the Council of Science Editors outlines a general scientific style known as CSE style: *Scientific Style and Format: The CSE Manual for Authors, Editors, and Publishers*, 7th ed. (2006). (See also the CSE Web site at <http://www.councilscienceeditors.org>.) The style endorsed by the American Chemical Society is used or adapted widely in engineering, technical, and scientific publications: *The ACS Style Guide: A Manual for Authors and Editors*, edited by Janet S. Dodd, 2nd ed. (1997). Two widely used engineering style guides are the following.

> *ASCE* [American Society of Civil Engineers] *Author's Guide to Journals, Books, and Reference Publications*
> "Information for IEEE Transactions and Journal Authors," <http://www.ieee.org/organizations/pubs/authors.html>

33a Elements of scientific and engineering styles

As is the case with other documentation styles, including MLA (Chapter 30) and APA (Chapter 31), scientific and engineering styles contain those kinds of information important for locating a source and identifying it in ways appropriate to a particular discipline or kind of publication.

1 In-text citations

In-text references in scientific and engineering writing take one of two forms. With the **number method,** numbers, either within parentheses (7) or as superscript figures raised above the line,[7] refer to numbered items in a reference list at the end of the text. The number method saves space (always at a premium in scientific and engineering publications, which are often expensive to publish). It does not disrupt reading, unless the reader decides to turn to the reference list to identify the source. It allows a writer to cite multiple sources (a common practice) in a brief space, for example, (1–3, 5, 7). Yet the number system does not enable readers to identify the author or currency (date) of a source without interrupting their reading.

With the **name-and-date method,** the name of the author or authors appears in the text along with the date of publication (both generally in parentheses, but not always. Without stopping to consult the reference list, therefore, readers can identify how recent the source is and may recognize the particular source from the author's name if they are familiar with work in the field. Name-and-date citations take more space, however, and they can disrupt reading, especially when a citation refers to several sources.

2 Reference list

Coming at the end of a text, a reference list provides information necessary to identify a source. This information generally includes the following.

- Author(s) name(s)
- Title of work or article
- Title of publication containing an article
- Publication information (for books—city, publisher, and date of publication; for articles—date, volume and issue number, and page numbers)
- Electronic address and date of access (for electronic sources)

Entries in a reference list are arranged either alphabetically (to correspond with name-and-date citations) or according to the order of citation in the text (to correspond with number citations).

The form and order of the elements in a reference list may vary slightly according to documentation style.

CSE

BOOK   Simpson HN. Invisible armies: the impact of disease on American history. Indianapolis (IN): Bobbs–Merrill; 1980.

ARTICLE   Yousef YA, Yu LL. Potential contamination of groundwater from Cu, Pb, and Zn in wet detention ponds receiving highway runoff. J Environ Sci Hlth 1992;27:1033–1044.

ACS

BOOK   Dresselhaus, M.S.; Dresselhaus, G.; Eklund, P.C. *Science of Fullerenes and Carbon Nanotubes;* Academic: New York, 1996; pp 126–141.

ARTICLE   Hill, M.; Fott, P. Kinetics of gasification of Czech brown coals. *Fuel* 1993, 72, 525–529.

33b Scientific in-text citations

This section and the next, covering a scientific reference list, provide examples in CSE style.

1 Using the name-and-date method

With this method, you include the name of the author or authors along with the publication date of the text. If you do not mention the author's name in the paper itself, include both the name and the year in parentheses; if you do mention the name, include only the year.

PARENTHETICAL REFERENCE
Decreases in the use of lead, cadmium, and zinc in industrial products have resulted in a "very large decrease in the large-scale pollution of the troposphere" (Boutron et al. 1991).

AUTHOR NAMED IN TEXT
Boutron et al. (1991) found that decreases in the use of lead, cadmium, and zinc in industrial products have resulted in a "very large decrease in the large-scale pollution of the troposphere."

If you cite several works by the same author, all of which appeared in a single year, use letters (*a*, *b*, and so forth) after the date to distinguish them.

ONE OF SEVERAL APPEARING IN THE SAME YEAR
Decreases in the use of lead, cadmium, and zinc in industrial products have resulted in a "very large decrease in the large-scale pollution of the troposphere" (Boutron et al. 1991a).

2 Using the number method

With this method, you use numbers instead of names of authors. The numbers can be placed in parentheses in the text or raised above the line as superscript figures. The numbers correspond to numbered works in your reference list. There are two ways to use the number method. In one style, you number your in-text citations consecutively as they appear in your paper and arrange them accordingly on the reference page.

Decreases in the use of lead, cadmium, and zinc in industrial products have reduced pollution in the troposphere (1).

In the second style, you alphabetize your references first, number them, and then refer to the corresponding number in your paper. Since only the number appears in your text, make sure you mention the author's name if it is important.

33c Scientific reference list

You may use "Cited References," "References," or "Bibliography" as the heading for your reference list. If your instructor asks you to supply references for all your sources, not just the ones cited in your text, prepare a second list called "Additional References" or "Additional Reading."

The order of the entries in your reference list should correspond to the method you use to cite them within your paper. If you use the name-and-date method, for example, alphabetize the references according to the last name of the main author and by date of publication for works by the same author(s).

If you use the consecutive number method, the reference list will not be alphabetical but will be arranged according to which work comes first in your paper, which second, and so forth. If you use the alphabetized number method, arrange your list alphabetically, and then number the entries.

The following examples show the most commonly used formats for entries. Refer to *Scientific Style and Format: The CSE Manual* for further examples of documentation.

1 Books and works treated as books

Formats for entries for the name-and-date method and the number method are the same except for the location of the year. The sample entries for a reference list follow the style for the number method, but model formats are shown for both methods.

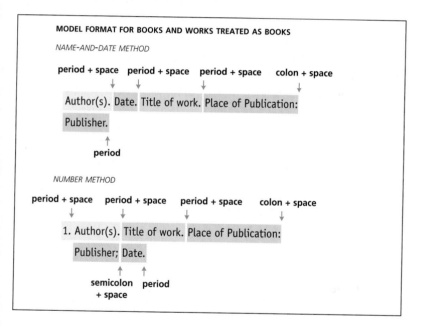

- **Author(s).** Give the author's name in inverted order, beginning with the last name and followed by *the initials only* (without periods or spaces) of the first and middle names, concluding with a period and a space. For more than one author, follow the same pattern for each author, and separate the names with a comma followed by a space. (Some scientific publications use full names for authors; check if this style is required for your paper.) If no author is given, begin with the word *Anonymous* in brackets.
- **Title of work.** Give the title followed by a period and a space. Do not underline the title, and capitalize only the first word and proper nouns or adjectives. Do not capitalize the subtitle following a colon.

33c
CSE

- **Publication information.** Indicate the city, publisher, and date of publication. Put a colon after the city and a semicolon after the publisher. Conclude with a period. To avoid confusion between two cities with the same name or to identify cities likely to be unfamiliar, leave a space after the city and include in parentheses the abbreviated name of the state or the country.
- **Spacing.** Double-space your entries. For the name-and-date method, do not indent any lines. For the number method, begin the second and any later lines underneath the beginning of the opening word in the first line. If your instructor gives you other spacing directions, follow them carefully.

1. One author

1. Kauffman, JM. Cases in emotional and behavioral disorders of children and youth. Upper Saddle River: Pearson Prentice Hall; 2009.

2. Two or more authors

List each author's last name first, and use commas to separate the authors.

2. Freeman JM, Kelly MT, Freeman JB. The epilepsy diet treatment: an introduction to the ketogenic diet. New York: Demo; 1994.

3. Organization or group author

Treat an organization or government agency responsible for a work as you would an individual author. If the author is also the publisher, include the name in both places. You can use an organization's acronym in place of the author's name if the acronym is well known.

3. Intergovernmental Panel on Climate Change. Climate change 1995: the science of climate change. Cambridge: Cambridge University Press; 1996.

4. Editor

Identify the editor(s) by including the word *editor(s)* (spelled out) after the name.

4. Bandy AR, editor. The chemistry of the atmosphere: oxidants and oxidation in the earth's atmosphere. Cambridge: Royal Society of Chemistry; 1995.

5. Translator

Give the translator's name after the title, followed by a comma and the word *translator.* If the work has an editor as well, place a semicolon after the word *translator* and then name the editor and conclude with the word *editor.* Give the original title at the end of the entry after the words *Translation of* and a colon.

5. Jacob F. The logic of life: a history of heredity. Spillmann BE, translator. New York: Pantheon Books; 1982. Translation of: Logique du vivant.

6. Conference proceedings

Begin with the name of the editor(s) and the title of the publication. Indicate the name, year, and location of the conference, using semicolons to separate the information. You need not name the conference if the title does so.

> 6. Witt I, editor. Protein C: biochemical and medical aspects. Proceedings of the International Workshop; 1984 Jul 9–11; Titisee, Germany. Berlin: De Gruyter; 1985.

7. Technical report

Treat a report as you would a book with an individual or corporate author, but include the total number of pages after the publication year. If the report is available through a particular agency—and it usually is—include the information a reader would need to order it. The report listed here can be obtained from the EPA department mentioned using the report number EPA/625/7-91/013. Enclose a widely accepted acronym for an agency in brackets following its name.

> 7. Environmental Protection Agency (US) [EPA]. Guides to pollution prevention: the automotive repair industry. Washington: US EPA; 1991; 46 p. Available from: EPA Office of Research and Development; EPA/625/7-91/013.

2 Articles and selections from books

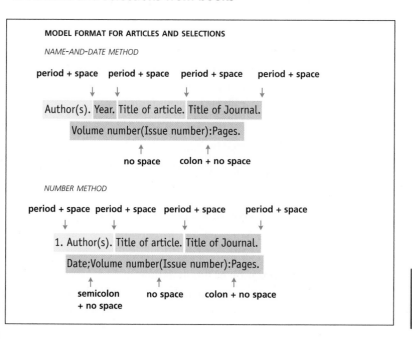

MODEL FORMAT FOR ARTICLES AND SELECTIONS

NAME-AND-DATE METHOD

period + space   period + space   period + space   period + space

Author(s). Year. Title of article. Title of Journal. Volume number(Issue number):Pages.

no space   colon + no space

NUMBER METHOD

period + space   period + space   period + space   period + space

1. Author(s). Title of article. Title of Journal. Date;Volume number(Issue number):Pages.

semicolon + no space   no space   colon + no space

33c
CSE

- **Author(s).** Give the author's name in inverted order, beginning with the last name and followed by the initials only (without periods or spaces) of the first and middle names, concluding with a period and a single space. For more than one author, follow the same pattern for each author, and separate the names with a comma followed by a space. If no author is given, begin with *Anonymous*, placed in brackets.
- **Title of article and publication information.** Give the article name, journal name, date, volume number and issue number (in parentheses), and page numbers. Do not enclose the article title in quotation marks or underline the journal title. Capitalize only the first word and any proper nouns in an article's title; do not capitalize the first word in a subtitle. For journal titles, follow regular capitalization rules, but use abbreviations standard in the field. Conclude the title of the article with a period and a space. Place a semicolon but no space between the date and the volume number. Do not include a space before or after the colon separating the volume number from the page numbers or between volume and issue numbers (issue number in parentheses).
- **Pages.** Include the specific pages of the article or chapter.
- **Journal title (abbreviated).** Always abbreviate a journal title unless it is a one-word title. To find out how to abbreviate titles, notice the abbreviations used in your sources and ask your instructor which book lists abbreviations for your field.
- **Spacing.** Double-space all entries. Do not indent the first line or any subsequent lines (name and year); align second and later lines under the beginning of the initial word of the first line.

8. Article in journal paginated by volume

8. Yousef YA, Yu LL. Potential contamination of groundwater from Cu, Pb, and Zn in wet detention ponds receiving highway runoff. J Environ Sci Hlth. 1992;27:1033–1044.

9. Article in journal paginated by issue

Give the issue number within parentheses immediately (with no space) after the volume number.

9. Boutron CF. Decrease in anthropogenic lead, cadmium and zinc in Greenland snows since the late 1960s. Nature. 1991;353(6340): 153–155, 160.

10. Article with organization or group author

Treat the corporate or group author as you would any author. If a person's name is part of the corporation, as in this example, do not transpose the first and last names. Alphabetize by the first main word in the corporation name, even if it is a first name.

> 10. Derek Sims Associates. Why and how of acoustic testing. Environ Eng. 1991;4(1):10–12.

11. Entire issue of journal

Include the title of the main editor or compiler of the specific issue because this person will often be a guest editor.

> 11. Savage A, editor. Proceedings of the workshop on the zoo–university connection: collaborative efforts in the conservation of endangered primates. Zoo Biol. 1989;1(Suppl).

12. Figure from article

Include the title of the figure (or table, chart, or diagram) and its number, as well as the page on which it appears. Use *p.* in this context.

> 12. Kanaori Y, Kawakami SI, Yairi K. Space–time distribution patterns of destructive earthquakes in the inner belt of central Japan. Engng Geol. 1991;31(3–4):209–230. Table 1, p. 216.

13. Selection in anthology or collection

The first name and title refer to the article; the second name and title refer to the book from which the article is taken. Include the page numbers of the article at the end of the citation.

> 13. Moro M. Supply and conservation efforts for nonhuman primates. In: Gengozian N, Deinhardt F, editors. Marmosets in experimental medicine. Basel: S. Karger AG; 1978. p. 37–40.

3 Electronic resources

14. Patent from database or information service

> 14. Collins FS, Drumm ML, Dawson DC, Wilkinson DJ, inventors; Method of testing potential cystic fibrosis treating compounds using cells in culture. United States patent 5,434,086. 1995 Jul 18. Available from: Lexis/Nexis/Lexpat library/ALL file.

15. Article (online)

> 15. Grolmusz V. On the weak mod m representation of Boolean functions. Chi J Theor Comp Sci [Internet]. 1995 [cited 1996 May 3];100–5. Available from: http://www.csuchicago.edu/ publication/cjtcs/articles/1995/2/contents.html

33c
CSE

16. Book (online)

16. Darwin C. On the origin of species by means of natural selection, or the preservation of favoured races in the struggle for life [Internet]. London: Down, Bromley, Kent; 1859. Available from: ftp://sailor.gutenberg.org/pub/gutenberg/etext98/otoos10.txt via the World Wide Web. Accessed 2009 Feb 12.

17. Abstract (online)

Use a form similar to that for journal articles, but give the word *abstract* in brackets following the title.

17. Smithies O, Maeda N. Gene targeting approaches to complex genetic diseases: atherosclerosis and essential hypertension [abstract]. Proc Natl Acad Sci USA [Internet]. 1995 [cited 1996 Jan 21]; 92(12):5266–5272. 1 screen. Available from: Lexis/Medline/ABST.

18. Web site

18. PandemicFlu.gov [Internet]. Washington (DC): Department of Health and Human Services (US); [updated 2009 May 5; cited 2009 May 22]. Available from: http://www.pandemicflu.gov/

Exercise

A. Turn to Exercise A in Chapter 30. Rewrite the sentences supplied there to add either form of in-text citations in CSE or ACS style. Prepare a corresponding list of references.

B. Turn to Exercise B in Chapter 30. Rewrite the items supplied there to create a list of references following either form used in CSE or ACS style.

C. Working with a partner or a small group, compare your answers to Exercises A and B above. Correct any errors in your answers, using your handbook or your instructor's advice to resolve any differences of opinion.

33d Sample CSE paper

Begin one-third of the way down the page

Center title

Predator Occurrence at Piping Plover Nesting Sites
in Rhode Island

Title indicates that paper will report on a scientific research project

Anne S. Bloomfield
University of Rhode Island

Center and double-space all lines

WRT 333
Professor Robert A. Schwegler
17 April 2006

33d
CSE

Abstract provides concise summary of content

Abstract

During the spring of 2006, I recorded predator occurrence based only on animal tracks on two beaches in Rhode Island. The main objective of the study was to predict the occurrence of potential predator species on piping plover (*Charadrius melodus*) nesting grounds in the area. I quantified the spatial distribution of predators at both beaches. Predators showed a preference for an area that was easily accessible to a salt pond from the barrier beach ($P < 0.05$ Table 1). Predator species present included gulls (*Laridae*), striped skunk (*Mephitis mephitis*), muskrat (*Ondatra zibethicus*) and red fox (*Vulpes vulpes*). This method was simple and low cost, but I found flaws in the experimental design that should be addressed in future studies.

Table 1. Chi-squared analysis showing preference of predators for a given area on a piping plover nesting site at Moonstone Beach, Rhode Island, spring 2006.

Actual Segment	Sign	No Sign
0–500	1	9
501–1000	1	9
1001–1500	1	9
1501–2000	11	7

Expected Segment	Sign	No Sign
0–500	2.917	1.458
501–1000	2.917	1.458
1001–1500	2.917	1.458
1501–2000	5.250	12.750

$p < 0.001$

1   In Rhode Island, the threatened piping plover (*Charadrius melodus*) prefers to breed on open beaches and sandflats.[1] Habitat destruction due to development of beaches and predation are contributing factors to the birds' decline.[2] For most ground-nesting bird species, the primary cause of nesting mortality is due to egg predation.[3] I investigated the spatial distribution and abundance of potential predators. This information, coupled with information on plover nesting success, could be used to better manage the species.

2   The main objectives of my research were to discover what types of predators occur at potential breeding sites and their spatial distribution along the beach. I was also interested in which species occurred most often. My data were collected solely based on mammalian and avian tracks on sites at the breeding grounds. Information on such studies has not been easily located in peer-reviewed literature. This approach was low cost, as the researcher only needs to visually search the beach for tracks. No restraint techniques or cameras were used to capture live predators physically or on film. A pen and paper were the only materials needed to collect data on site.

3   The results of my study will help wildlife biologists to implement the proper management strategies for predator control on the beaches. If the species predating the nests are better understood, then management strategies can be tailored to a specific species or a specific area.

Last name, one space, and page number

Focuses on specific topic and problem

Specific phenomenon being studied

Potential usefulness of research

States two closely related research questions

Literature review—little prior work on the subject

33d
CSE

Center headings if used

Study Area

4   I conducted fieldwork at Moonstone Beach at Trustom

Pond National Wildlife Refuge (NWR) and East Beach at

Describes location for the study

Ninigret NWR. The study was focused at Moonstone Beach,

but additional data were collected at Ninigret. These areas

are important seasonal nesting areas for the piping plover.

Both areas are barrier beaches with grassy dunes, bordering

large coastal salt ponds. Moonstone Beach had a particular

section which measured about 62 m that was free of

vegetation and dunes. This area of the beach supplied a

direct path from Trustom Pond to the beach area and coastal

waters. This type of habitat was not present at my study site

at Ninigret. These areas are managed by the U.S. Fish and

Wildlife Service (USFWS) for piping plovers. Moonstone Beach

is annually closed to the public, for this reason, beginning

on April 1. After April 1, I conducted fieldwork only at

Ninigret NWR.

Methods

5   During my research, I based the occurrence of predators

on the presence of their tracks in the sand. At Moonstone

Describes specific time, place, and technique (method) of study

Beach a 610 m stretch of beach was searched. This area was

searched on 24 March and 29 March for two hours each day. The

beach was marked in 30.5 m (100 ft) sections by PVC pole

markers on the foredune.

6   During each study period I recorded any factors on the

beach that would disrupt or bias data collection. This mainly

included human and domestic dog (*Canis familiaris*) tracks

on the beach. I searched for tracks in each 30.5 meter

33d
CSE

Bloomfield 3

section. When a track was located, the species was recorded.
In addition to the species, I recorded the quality of the track
on a 1-3 scale (1 being poorest). I also noted whether the
track was found in wet or dry sand. To limit identification
error, I always carried a tracking text with me which included
photographs, diagrams, and measurements. The same method
was used at Ninigret, with the exception of the 30.5 m
markers.

7   I used a chi-squared test to assess the spatial
distribution of predator tracks on the beach. This test was
only done for Moonstone Beach because the tracks and beach
quality at Ninigret were very poor during the study period.
Also, figures were constructed to show the frequency of track
occurrence, number of species per section, and number of
tracks per section at Moonstone Beach. The data from Ninigret
could only be used qualitatively to indicate which species were
present.

Results

8   The only predatory species present at Ninigret NWR was
gulls (*Laridae*). At Moonstone Beach, the spatial distribution of
predators was not uniform ($P < 0.001$), with more tracks
present on the section of beach extending from pole 15 to pole
20 (Table 1). The numbers of species per section and number of
tracks recorded were greatest in this area as well (Figures 1
and 2). This was particularly true in section 17, which was
located in the area with immediate access to the pond from the
beach. Red fox (*Vulpes vulpes*) covered the largest distance over
the study area, occurring in all 20 sections during both

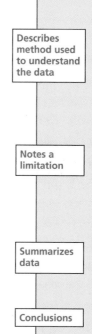

Describes
method used
to understand
the data

Notes a
limitation

Summarizes
data

Conclusions

33d
CSE

Bloomfield 4

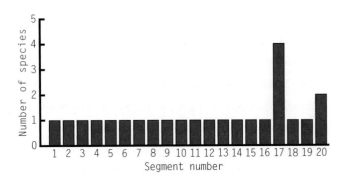

Figure 1. Number of species present at Moonstone Beach, Rhode Island, spring 2006, is highest in segment 17.

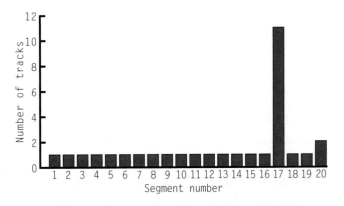

Figure 2. Sets of tracks were counted at Moonstone Beach, Rhode Island, spring 2006, and section 17 showed the greatest number of total tracks overall.

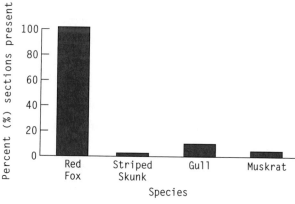

Figure 3. Occurrence of species across entire beach shows the red fox is present all along the shore of Moonstone Beach, Rhode Island, spring 2006.

study periods (Figure 3). The tracks always ran in a straight path parallel to the shore all the way across the study site and beyond.

Discussion

9   Using tracks to determine the presence of predators on the beach is a low-cost method which has the potential to yield promising results. Although this method was low-cost and a simple way to collect data, I found that there were many flaws in the experimental design that should be addressed in further studies. Public use and roping of the beaches were two of the greatest difficulties I encountered during my study.

10   The condition of East Beach at Ninigret NWR was so poor that the data had to be almost entirely discredited. Human and domestic dog tracks were so abundant at the site that detecting other tracks seemed almost impossible. Ninigret also lacked the

33d
CSE

Bloomfield 6

PVC poles to mark every 30.5 m. The quality of the data made them unusable for statistical and quantitative analysis. It is also important to note that one study suggested that in areas of beach open to domestic dogs, nests not protected by exclosures were all lost to dogs.[4] Keeping dogs off the beach or leashed is very important to the birds' survival.

11   The areas at Ninigret that were not overrun with human and dog tracks were roped off for the piping plovers. I tried to view tracks over the ropes with binoculars but decided this was not a very accurate technique. In the future, observers should be uniformed volunteers with USFWS so they can go behind roped areas. Letting the public know about the study would cut back on the amount of "clutter" to sort through on the beach.

Suggestions for future studies

12   Although ghost crabs (*Ocypode quadrata*) are more of a problem in southern areas, it is relatively unknown how large an impact they have on piping plover nest failure rates. Crab predation in Rhode Island is something my study did not address. Their tracks in the sand would have been impossible to find with all of the human disturbance. One study documented a ghost crab predating a piping plover chick. The research indicates that more studies must be done to determine if it was an isolated incident or if ghost crabs really are frequent predators of the piping plover.[5] Another study examined a beach with high piping plover mortality rates and abundant ghost crabs. The results showed a correlation, not necessarily a causation. Their data, at the same time, seemed to suggest that adult plovers would avoid bringing their chicks to forage in areas of abundant ghost crabs. They indicated that this could possibly indirectly lead to higher mortality rates of the chicks.[6]

More limitations

Prior research

33d
CSE

Bloomfield 7

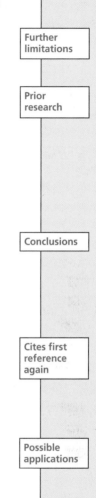

13 My research neglected to account for small mammal predation. Maier and DeGraff discovered, in 2000, that captive wild-caught white-footed mice (*Peromyscus leucopus*) were capable of consuming house sparrow eggs (*Passer domesticus*) in laboratory trials. They also noted that the effectiveness of the white-footed mouse as a significant predator of ground-nesting birds appears to be questionable.[7] While my study did not address crab or small mammal predation, it appears that the relevant literature does not show strong evidence for these animals as important nest predators.

Further limitations

Prior research

14 Based on the results (Table 1, Figures 1–3), I would expect the highest predation levels to be in segment 17 near the salt pond. More research must be done, though, because according to Golden and Regosin, plover broods with access to a salt pond habitat experienced higher fledgling success than broods limited to an ocean beachfront habitat.[1] Further research must be done to figure out how the birds can have higher fledgling success rates near salt ponds if predator occurrence also appears to be higher near salt ponds.

Conclusions

Cites first reference again

15 Predator exclosures are one way to reduce predation rates. A previous study[8] found that daily survival rates of pectoral sandpiper (*Calidris melanotos*) nests, behavioral responses to exclosures, and the fact that no protected nests were predated suggested that exclosure was effective at deterring predators. The authors suggest that this method may be used for other shorebirds as well. In addition, 9 out of 13 nests had attempted predation by Arctic fox (*Alopex lagopus*), but all of these nests remained successful. The exclosures had an effective anchoring system and mesh wire.

Possible applications

33d
CSE

Bloomfield 8

16   Some exclosures can actually cause the plovers to abandon their nests. Research was done to determine what conditions and types of exclosures resulted in nest abandonment. The data suggested that exclosure construction, size, shape, mesh size, and fence height were not significantly related to nest abandonment, but covered exclosures were.[9]

Applications set

17   My data could be useful to people interested in nest exclosures because if a biologist can predict what predators are in the area, an exclosure can be tailored to meet specific needs. Different designs could be implemented based on whether the predators are mainly diggers or mostly avian. My data could also be used to reduce nest abandonment related to exclosures. If biologists know where the predators are distributed along the beach, they can predict exactly where an exclosure is needed. If there is a low occurrence of predators in an area, then there is little or no need for an exclosure. In addition, knowing where predators occur could make it easier for biologists to trap predators in the area.

18   In summary, exclosures are a good way to protect nests if done correctly. Predator occurrence by tracking needs to be further researched to improve accuracy but appears to be a cost-effective way to sample for predators on beaches. This technique is only useful if the volunteer trackers are very skilled at tracking in sand. In addition, it was only efficient to collect data under ideal conditions when there was little or no human disturbance on the beaches. If the techniques are further developed and the problems addressed, this method has great potential to be a low-budget and easy way to determine presence of predators on piping plover nest sites.

Bloomfield 9

References

1. Goldin MR, Regosin JV. Chick behavior, habitat use, and reproductive success of piping plovers at Goosewing Beach, Rhode Island. J Field Ornith. 1998;69:228–234.

2. Haig SM. Piping plover. In: Poole A, Stettenheim PS, and Gill F, editors. The birds of North America. Washington (DC): American Ornithologists' Union; 1992. p. 1–18.

3. Skutch AF. A breeding bird census and nesting success in Central America. Ibis. 1996;108:1–16.

4. Nol E, Brooks RJ. Effects of predator exclosures on nesting success of killdeer. J Field Ornith. 1982;53:263–268.

5. Loegering JP, Fraser JD, Loegering LL. Ghost crab preys on piping plover chick. Wilson Bulletin. 1995;107:768–769.

6. Wolcott DL, Wolcott TG. High mortality of piping plovers on beaches with abundant ghost crabs: correlation, not causation. Wilson Bulletin. 1999;111:321–329.

7. Maier TJ, DeGraaf RM. Predation on Japanese quail vs. house sparrow eggs in artificial nests: small eggs reveal small predators. Condor. 2000;102:325–332.

8. Estelle VB, Mabee TJ, Farmer AH. Effectiveness of predator exclosures for pectoral sandpiper nests in Alaska. J Field Ornith. 1996;67:447–452.

9. Vaske JJ, Rimmer DW, Deblinger RD. The impact of different predator exclosures on piping plover nest abandonment. J Field Ornith. 1994;65:201–209.

Center heading

Indent references from number; no other indentation needed (number system)

Number sources (number method) or list references alphabetically (name & year system)

Visit mycomplab.com for more resources and exercises on CSE documentation.

33d
CSE

PART 7

Grammar

CHAPTER 34

Ten Serious Grammar Mistakes

What happens when readers encounter a serious error in grammar, punctuation, or expression? They may stop paying attention to what you have to say and start looking through the passage for information to resolve any confusion or distraction created by the error. They may feel irritated that your error has wasted their time and think of you as careless or worse.

To identify errors that readers consider most serious, we surveyed academics and professionals from varied fields. Here are ten errors they identified as likely to create strong negative reactions from readers.

SERIOUS
MISTAKE

Ten Serious Grammar Mistakes

1. **Fragment** (34a and 40a–b)
The heavy rain turned the parking lot to mud. **And stranded thousands of cars.**

2. **Fused Sentence** (34b and 41a–b)
The promoters called **the insurance company they discovered** their coverage for accidents was limited.

3. **Unclear Pronoun Reference** (34c and 42a)
After talking with the groundskeeper, the security chief said **he** would not be responsible for the safety of the crowd.

4. **Lack of Subject-Verb Agreement** (34d and 38a–b)
Away from the microphone, the mayor said, "I hope the security chief or the promoters **has** a plan to help everyone leave safely."

5. **Dangling Modifier** (34e and 43b)
After announcing the cancellation from the stage, the crowd began complaining to the promoters.

6. **Shift** (34f and 44a–d)
If **people** left the arena quickly, **you** could get to **your** car without standing in the rain.

7. **Misused or Missing Apostrophe** (34g and 53a–b)
Even the **promoters promise** to reschedule and honor **ticket's** did little to stop the crowd's complaints.

8. **Unnecessary Commas** (34h and 51j)
Although, the muddy lot caused problems, all the cars and **people, began** to leave.

9. **Missing or Misused Quotation Marks** (34i and 54a–c)
"The grounds are **slippery, the** mayor repeated, "so please walk carefully."

10. **Double Negative** (34j and 39d)
The authorities were relieved because they **hadn't scarcely** enough resources to cope.

34a Fragment

Recognize. Some fragments lack a subject or verb. They force readers to hunt for a likely subject or verb in the passage or to supply one (see 40a, including tests for fragments).

NO SUBJECT   Rewrote the zero-tolerance policy. (Who did?)

NO VERB   The school board. (Did or is what?)

Other fragments begin with a subordinating word such as *though, while,* or *that* (see 40a-2). These words introduce a subordinate clause and force readers to attach the clause to a nearby sentence.

FRAGMENT   Because tea is increasingly popular. (Then what?)

Revise. Either provide the missing subject or verb, or attach the subordinate clause to a sentence it modifies.

    The **school board rewrote** the zero-tolerance policy.

    Because tea is increasingly popular, **coffee shops offer it.**

RECOGNIZING A SENTENCE

    A **sentence**—also called **a main** (or **independent**) **clause**—is a word group that can stand alone. It has a subject and a predicate (a verb and any words that complete it).

SENTENCE   **Hungry bears** <u>were hunting</u> food in urban areas because spring snows <u>had damaged</u> many plants.

A **subordinate** (or **dependent**) **clause** has a subject and a predicate, yet it cannot stand on its own because it begins with a subordinating word such as *because, although, which,* or *that* (see 47c).

FRAGMENT   <u>Because</u> **spring snows** <u>had damaged</u> many plants

A **phrase** is a word group that lacks a subject, a predicate, or both, such as *were hunting, in urban areas,* or *the hungry bears.*

34b Fused sentence

Recognize. Two sentences joined without a punctuation mark or connecting word create a **fused sentence.** Look for a series of word groups that could stand alone as sentences but do not use words (*and, but, however,* or

**34c
gram
prob**

for example) or punctuation (a semicolon or colon; see 41b) to tell readers where one sentence ends and the next begins.

FUSED	Revenue will grow profits will not increase.
REVISED	Revenue will grow, **but** profits will not increase.

Revise. Choose one of the five strategies illustrated in 41b.

1. Divide into two sentences.
2. Join with a comma plus *and, but, or, for, nor, so,* or *yet.*
3. Connect with a semicolon.
4. Subordinate one part with a word like *though* or *that* (see 41b-5).
5. Connect with an expression such as *however, moreover, in contrast,* or *for example* (see 41b-4) plus a semicolon.

RECOGNIZING SENTENCE STRUCTURES

1. A **simple sentence** has one main (independent) clause and no subordinate (dependent) clauses.

   The mayor proposed an expansion of city hall.

2. A **compound sentence** has two or more main (independent) clauses and no subordinate (dependent) clauses (see 35d).

         main clause   main clause
   Most people praised the plan, yet **some found it dull.**

3. A **complex sentence** has one main (independent) clause and one or more subordinate (dependent) clauses (see 35d).

       subordinate clause   main clause
   Because people objected, **the architect revised the plans.**

34c Unclear pronoun reference

Recognize. A pronoun takes the place of a noun (or another pronoun) and makes sense to readers only if they can clearly recognize the word (**antecedent**) to which it refers.

           antecedent   pronoun
We installed **the tank,** but soon **it** started leaking.

Revise. Be sure that you state a pronoun's antecedent, place it nearby, and position it so that it is clear, not ambiguous (see 42b).

MISSING	After you turn on the fan, **it** will not be cool for an hour.
REVISED	After you turn on the fan, **the room** will not be cool for an hour.

AMBIGUOUS	Do not place the laptop near the router because **its** operation will be disrupted.
REVISED	Do not place the laptop near the router because **the laptop** will disrupt **its** operation.

34d Lack of subject-verb agreement

Recognize. Subjects and verbs should match (or agree), both singular or both plural. Mismatched parts distract readers or force them to re-read.

singular   singular

The **information** gathered by the team members **is** excellent.

Revise. Watch for a final -*s*, which often marks a plural subject but a singular verb. Look, too, for the *real* subject of a sentence (see 38b–c).

FAULTY	The cover [singular] resist [plural] dust.
REVISED	The cover **resists** dust.
FAULTY	The costs of an interactive program has grown.
REVISED	The **costs** of an interactive program **have** grown.

34e Dangling modifier

Recognize. Readers expect an initial modifying phrase to name the person, thing, or idea it modifies or to modify the subject of the sentence. If it does neither, readers will wonder why it seems to modify something else (see 43a).

DANGLING	Covered with grease, the boys could not climb the pole.

Revise. To revise a dangling modifier, add the word or words modified.

REVISED	Covered with grease, **the pole** was too slippery for the boys to climb.

34f Shift

Recognize. When a sentence shifts pronouns or time frame illogically, readers may be confused or irritated.

PRONOUN SHIFT	**People** [they] create businesses from something **you** like to do.
TENSE SHIFT	Even though I **added** [past] the catalyst, nothing **happens** [present].

Revise. Stick to a logical perspective (*I, we, you, they,* and *he, she,* or *it;* see 37 and 44a) or a logical presentation of shift in time (see 44b).

REVISED   **People** create businesses from something **they** like to do.

REVISED   Even though I **added** the catalyst, nothing **happened.**

34g Misused or missing apostrophe

Recognize. Writing *it's* (= *it is*) for the possessive *its* or *sport's* for *sports* (more than one) forces readers to decide the meaning by themselves. Even when they can easily do so, they may be irritated by stray or missing apostrophes (see 53a–b).

Revise. Proofread your apostrophes. Check words that sometimes, but not always, include them (*girls, girl's, girls'; its, it's*).

34h Unnecessary commas

Recognize. Commas appear often, but when too many fill a passage or too few join or set off sentence elements, readers may struggle to sort out ideas.

DISTRACTING   After, she had assembled the data, from her observations, Chris, reviewed the information, and decided, that she needed to do further research.

Revise. Instead of guessing where commas belong, learn the rules (see 51a–j) and edit with a reference like this handbook nearby.

REVISED   After she had assembled the data from her observations, Chris reviewed the information and decided that she needed to do further research.

34i Missing or misused quotation marks

Recognize. Quotation marks distinguish what the writer says and what another person or a source has said. Because they identify the actual words of a source, quotation marks when misused create inaccuracies and confuse readers.

MISUSED   "The novel, Stephen Rose claims," "Reflects the cultural conflicts caused by immigration, though this conclusion applies only to part of the work.

Revise. Quotation marks come in pairs (". . ."). Check for any that are missing (and thus don't acknowledge words from a source), that begin but don't end, or that enclose more than they should (see 54a–c).

REVISED   "The novel," Stephen Rose claims, "reflects the cultural conflicts caused by immigration," though this conclusion applies only to part of the work.

34j Double negative

Recognize. Informally, double negatives can be forceful: "I'm not going, no way, no how!" They have the opposite effect in formal writing, where readers may view them as inappropriate or uneducated expressions—a harsh but likely judgment.

Revise. Stick to one negative. Avoid pairing words such as *no, none, not, never, hardly, scarcely,* and *don't* (see 39d).

DOUBLE   I have **scarcely no** data to support my conclusions.

REVISED   I have **scarcely any** data to support my conclusions.

Exercise 1

The following exercise will help you develop the ability to recognize and then revise the ten serious grammar errors. For the sentences below, make only the changes needed to correct any error a sentence contains. No sentence contains more than one error. A few contain no errors at all. The first part of your task, therefore, is to identify the error (if any); the next part is to correct the error—or label the sentence "correct."

EXAMPLE   Tennis takes a long time to learn you can play it into your sixties or seventies.
            Is there an error? Yes, a fused sentence.

CORRECTED   Tennis takes a long time to learn, **but** you can play it into your sixties or seventies.

1. Young people can play some sports without spending much money. Soccer, for example.
2. People don't need hardly any equipment to play soccer.
3. A ball and shoes to run in is all a team needs to play soccer.
4. If someone wants to play football, you need to spend a lot more money on your equipment.
5. Basketball is inexpensive all you need to buy is a ball.

6. Most local parks or playgrounds have basketball courts you don't need to pay to play on them.
7. Many people say that tennis is a sport for someone with a lot of money.
8. The cost's for tennis equipment include shoes, balls, and a racket.
9. Public tennis courts, are widely available, so renting a court or joining a tennis club is not necessary.
10. Hockey is well known for it's high costs.
11. Hockey players' parents can expect to pay for ice time at a rink in addition to equipment.
12. One parent who was interviewed said, I bought used equipment, but it was still expensive.
13. Getting players to early-morning practices, hockey imposes another kind of cost on families.
14. Baseball can be either expensive or inexpensive for them.
15. Expensive if it involves new gloves and uniforms.
16. A ball, a bat, and gloves is all kids need to play baseball, however.
17. Requiring even less equipment, stickball is inexpensive and fun.
18. The popularity, of stickball, has been declining in recent, years, however.
19. I overheard one man telling his son that handball is the best game for him because it provides great exercise.
20. Another advantage of handball is that it required only a ball, a wall, hands, and (perhaps) a pair of gloves.

Visit mycomplab.com for more resources and exercises on avoiding serious grammar mistakes.

CHAPTER **35**

Sentence Elements and Patterns

To create a sentence, you do not need to name its parts. Most of the time, however, you do need a fundamental understanding of grammatical concepts and terms to spot difficulties in your writing, to correct them, or to find helpful information in a handbook.

35a Words

Sentences contain different types of words, the *parts of speech:* nouns, pronouns, verbs, adjectives, adverbs, prepositions, conjunctions, and interjections.

1 Recognizing nouns and articles

This familiar definition can help you: A **noun** is a word naming a person, place, idea, or thing.

Rosemary Wells employs **humor** in her **books** for **children.**

Nouns often require an **article:** *the, a,* or *an* (*a* before consonants, *an* before vowels).

A report proposes **an** administrative solution to **the** problem.

For more on nouns see 37a.

2 Recognizing pronouns

A **pronoun,** like *them, she, his,* or *it,* takes the place of a noun or pronoun, playing the same role in the sentence as the word to which it refers—the **antecedent.**

    antecedent   pronoun
    Jean presented **her** proposal to the committee.

Pronouns can also modify a noun or another pronoun.

pronoun noun   pronoun pronoun
    This <u>part</u> has been on order for a week, **that** <u>one</u> for twenty days.

35a
gram

Pronouns change form for the **number** (singular or plural) or **gender** (masculine, feminine, or neuter) of the noun to which they refer. They also change form according to their role in a sentence—subject, object, or possessive (see 37b).

PRONOUNS AND THEIR FUNCTIONS

Personal pronouns	Designate persons or things using a form reflecting the pronoun's role in a sentence (see 37b)
SINGULAR	*I, me, you, he, him, she, her, it*
PLURAL	*we, us, you, they, them*
Possessive pronouns	Show ownership (see 37b-4 on pronouns and 53a on apostrophes)
SINGULAR	*my, mine, your, yours, her, hers, his, its*
PLURAL	*our, ours, your, yours, their, theirs*
Relative pronouns	Introduce clauses that modify or add information to a main clause (see 35c and 47c on subordination)
	who, whom, whose, which, that
Interrogative pronouns	Introduce questions
	who, which
Reflexive and intensive pronouns	End in *-self* or *-selves*; enable the subject or doer also to be the receiver of and action (reflexive); add emphasis (intensive)
SINGULAR	*myself, yourself, herself, himself, itself*
PLURAL	*ourselves, yourselves, themselves*
Indefinite pronouns	Refer to people, things, and ideas in general rather than a specific antecedent (see 38c-2)
SINGULAR	*anybody, each, every, neither, none, something*
PLURAL	*both, few, fewer, many, others, several*
VARIABLE	*all, any, enough, more, most, some*
Demonstrative pronouns	Point out or highlight an antecedent; can refer to a noun or pronoun or sum up a phrase or clause
	this, that, these, those
Reciprocal pronouns	Refer to individual parts of a plural antecedent
	one another, each other

Exercise 1

A. Underline each noun *once* and each pronoun *twice*.

> Seconds later the Help Desk received a call from another user with the same problem. The switchboard lit up. There were callers from all over the company, all with the same complaint: their computers were making odd noises. It might be a tune, one of the callers added helpfully, coming from the computer's small internal speaker. The sixth caller recognized the melody. The computers were all playing tinny renditions of "Yankee Doodle."
>
> —PAUL MUNGO and BRYAN CLOUGH, "The Bulgarian Connection"

B. Exchange papers in progress with another writer, and identify all the nouns and pronouns in a relatively long paragraph of your partner's work. Then return the essay and point out where you agree or disagree with your partner's identification.

3 Recognizing verbs

Verbs express actions (*jump*, *build*), occurrences (*become*, *happen*), and states of being (*be*, *seem*). You change a verb's form to signal relationships in **tense** (time), **person,** and **number.**

TENSE	They **prepare** invoices.	They **prepared** invoices.
PERSON	He **restores** antique cars.	They **restore** antique cars.
NUMBER	The copier **makes** noise.	The copiers **make** noise.

Differences in **voice** (active or passive; see 36e) and **mood** (36g) also require changes in form.

You may employ a **main** verb on its own or with one or more **helping** (or **auxiliary**) **verbs,** including forms of *be*, *do*, and *have* (main verb + helping verb = **verb phrase**). You may use **modal auxiliary verbs** (*will/would*, *can/could*, *shall/should*, *may/might*, *must*, and *ought to*) as helping verbs, though never as main verbs. (See 36b.)

> helping main
>   verb verb
> The tourist agency **is planning** to make a video of the local attractions.

>   main
> modal verb
> They **might decide** to include the old courthouse.

A **verb phrase** consists of a main verb plus a helping verb.

> verb phrase   verb phrase
> I **am hoping** that the renovations **can be done** in time.

Exercise 2

A. Underline each main verb once and each helping verb twice.

EXAMPLE

The new construction in Maple Valley <u><u>has</u></u> <u>created</u> several problems.

1. The power company's engineers began studying a map of the area.
2. They had thought about using underground cables.
3. A field test revealed a large rock ledge, so the engineers decided that underground lines would be too expensive.
4. They proposed cutting a path through the woods for the power lines, but the contractor claimed that potential homebuyers might not like the effect on the scenery.
5. They strung the power lines on poles along the main road.

B. Exchange papers in progress with a fellow student. Choose a paragraph and underline all main verbs once and helping verbs twice.

4 Recognizing adjectives

Adjectives modify nouns, pronouns, or word groups acting as nouns. They answer questions like "How many?" "What kind?" and "Which one?"

HOW MANY?	The **three** meetings will last all day.
WHICH ONE?	Our report was the **longest** one.
WHAT KIND?	Their proposal was **unacceptable.**

Adjectives come in three degrees of comparison: *high, higher, highest; crooked, more crooked, most crooked* (see 39c).

ESL ADVICE: ADJECTIVE FORMS

Adjectives in English never use a plural form.

NOT APPROPRIATE	Santo Domingo is renowned for beautifuls beaches.
CORRECT	Santo Domingo is renowned for beautiful beaches.

5 Recognizing adverbs

Adverbs modify verbs, adjectives, other adverbs, and entire sentences. Use them to answer such questions as "When?" "Where?" "Why?" "How often?" "Which direction?" "What conditions?" and "What degree?"

WHEN?	Our committee met **yesterday.** [modifies verb *met*]
WHAT DEGREE?	We had a **very** long meeting. [modifies adjective *long*]
HOW OFTEN?	I attend school board meetings **quite frequently.** [modifies adverb *frequently*, which modifies verb *attend*]

Many adverbs consist of an adjective plus *-ly: quickly, blindly, frequently, efficiently*. Others do not take this form, including *very, too, tomorrow, not, never, sometimes, well,* and *so*. In addition, some adjectives end in *-ly,* including *neighborly, slovenly,* and *lovely*. The surest way to distinguish an adverb from an adjective, therefore, is to see whether the word modifies a noun or pronoun (it's an adjective) or a verb, adjective, or adverb (it's an adverb). By adding *more, less, most,* or *least* to many adverbs, you can describe three comparative levels: *quickly, more quickly, most quickly; clearly, less clearly, least clearly* (see 39c).

Conjunctive adverbs, such as *however, moreover, thus,* and *therefore,* indicate logical relationships. (See 41b-4.)

Exercise 3

A. Underline all adjectives once and all adverbs twice.

> Back in Chicago, Sereno's analysis of his new dinosaur's skeleton convinces him it is indeed more primitive than *Herrerasaurus*. It lacks a flexible jaw that let *Herrerasaurus* and later carnivores snag and trap struggling prey. Thus Sereno believes this new creature is the closest fossil we have to the first dinosaur.
>
> "I call it 'Eoraptor,'" he says. "Eos was the Greek goddess of dawn. Raptor means thief. It was a light-bodied little rascal. And it may have been a thief, dashing in to grasp scraps of someone else's kill."
>
> —Rick Gore, "Dinosaurs"

B. Expand the following sentences by adding details and information in the form of adjectives and adverbs.

EXAMPLE

generally *deep, extended*
The term *coma* refers to a state of unconsciousness.
         ^   ^

1. Accidents leave people in comas.
2. Comas are serious medical problems.
3. Newspapers contain reports of people awakening from comas.
4. Long comas are dangerous.
5. They cause irreversible damage.

6 Recognizing prepositions

A **preposition** is a word like *on*, *over*, *for*, or *with*. When followed by a noun or pronoun, it becomes a **prepositional phrase.** Prepositional phrases can add detailed and precise information to sentences.

A faint smell of grilled onions came through the window and
　　　　　　　adjective　　　　　　　adverb

mixed with the musty air of the dungeon.
　　　adverb　　　　　　adjective

—JIMMY BUFFETT, *Where Is Joe Merchant?*

COMMON PREPOSITIONS				
about	at	despite	near	to
above	before	down	of	toward
across	behind	during	off	under
after	below	except	on	until
against	beneath	for	out	up
along	between	from	outside	upon
among	beyond	in	over	with
around	by	into	past	within
as	concerning	like	through	without

Exercise 4

A. Underline all the prepositions in the following sentences. Circle all the prepositional phrases.

EXAMPLE

(At eighteen minutes) (after one o'clock,) the emergency number received a call (from Mrs. Serena Washington.)

1. From its station near city hall, the rescue truck drove to Briar Brook Avenue.
2. Along the way, it narrowly missed colliding with a bread truck that failed to pull to the side of the road.
3. Despite the near accident, the rescue team arrived at the Washingtons' home in less than five minutes.
4. Mr. Washington was complaining of pain in his chest and back and displaying other symptoms of a heart attack.
5. By its quick response to the emergency call, the rescue team may have saved a life.

B. For each of the following word groups, create two sentences, one using the words as a verb plus preposition, the other using the words as a phrasal verb (see 35a-3). Then rewrite the sentence that contains the phrasal verb, substituting another word or words for the phrasal verb.

EXAMPLE: TEAR OUT

Brian tore out the door.

Brian tore out the old shelving.

Brian removed the old shelving.

cut down	hang around	run up
fill in	put up with	call up

ESL ADVICE: PREPOSITIONS

PREPOSITIONS OF TIME

Use *at* for a specific time; *on* for days and dates; and *in* for nonspecific times during a day, month, season, or year.

Brandon was born **at** 11:11 a.m., **on** Monday, **in** the morning.

PREPOSITIONS OF PLACE

Use *at* for specific addresses, *on* for the names of streets, and *in* for large areas of land—counties, states, countries, and continents.

He works **at** 99 Tinker Street but lives **on** Chance Avenue, **in** Portland.

Follow this order: **prepositional phrase of place + prepositional phrase of time.**

place   time
The runners will be starting **in the park on Saturday.**

PREPOSITIONS OF PLACE: *IN, AT, ON,* AND NO PREPOSITION

IN	AT	ON	NO PREPOSITION
the bedroom	the bottom of the stairs	a bicycle	downstairs
the car	home	the ceiling	downtown
a mirror	the office	the floor	inside
the newspaper	a party	the horse	outside
a picture	school*	the plane	upstairs
school*	work	the train	uptown

*You may sometimes use different prepositions for these locations.

Going to a place. Use the preposition *to*.

I am going **to** work; she is going **to** the office.

Use no preposition in the following cases.

I am going home. They are going downstairs (downtown, inside).

Time expressions. Use *for* with an amount of time (minutes, hours, days, months, and years); use *since* with a specific date or time.

The housing program has been in operation **for** many years.

The housing program has been in operation **since** 1974.

Combinations. Some nouns, verbs, and adjectives are typically associated with specific prepositions.

noun + preposition
He has an **understanding of** global politics.

verb + preposition
Vegetarians often **care about** animal rights.

adjective + preposition
Life in your country is **similar to** life in mine.

NOUN + PREPOSITION COMBINATIONS

approval of	fondness for	need for
awareness of	grasp of	participation in
belief in	hatred of	reason for
concern for	hope for	respect for
confusion about	interest in	success in
desire for	love of	understanding of

VERB + PREPOSITION COMBINATIONS

apologize for	jump into	step into
ask about	look at	study for
ask for	look for	talk about
belong to	look into	think about
care for	participate in	trust in
come out of	pay for	walk away from
go by	prepare for	work for
grow into	refer to	worry about

ADJECTIVE + PREPOSITION COMBINATIONS

afraid of	fond of	proud of
angry at	happy about	similar to
aware of	interested in	sorry for
capable of	jealous of	sure of
careless about	made of	tired of
familiar with	married to	worried about

7 Recognizing conjunctions

Conjunctions join words and word groups, signaling relationships. Use the **coordinating conjunctions** (*and, but, or, nor, for, yet,* and *so*) to link grammatically equal elements.

**35a
gram**

WORDS	analyze **and** discuss
PHRASES	determined to cut costs **yet** worried about quality of service
CLAUSES	They surveyed the wetland, **and** they prepared a positive report.

Use **subordinating conjunctions** such as *because, although, while, if,* or *since* to create a subordinate or modifying clause (see 35c-5; see 47c for a list of conjunctions). The clause created by a subordinating conjunction is a modifier, so it cannot stand on its own as a sentence; attach it to a **main** (or **independent**) **clause** that it qualifies or limits.

      main clause   subordinate clause
The equipment still works, **although** it needs routine maintenance.

Correlative conjunctions come in pairs, including *not only . . . but also, either . . . or, neither . . . nor, both . . . and, whether . . . or,* and similar combinations. Use them to join grammatically equal sentence elements. (See 46b on parallelism.)

8 Recognizing interjections

You can use an **interjection** to convey a strong reaction or emotion, such as surprise (*Hey!*) or disappointment (*Oh, no!*). Interjections often stand on their own or are loosely linked to the rest of a sentence.

Exercise 5

A. Underline all the conjunctions and indicate whether each is a coordinating, subordinating, or correlative conjunction.

Thirty-five years ago, E. R. Guthrie and G. P. Horton described an experiment in which cats were placed in a glass-fronted puzzle box and trained to find their way out by jostling a slender vertical rod at the front of the box, thereby causing a door to open. What interested these investigators was not so much that the cats could learn to bump into the vertical rod, but that before doing so each animal performed a long ritual of highly stereotyped movements, rubbing their heads and backs against the front of the box, turning in circles, and finally touching the rod. The experiment has ranked as something of a classic in experimental psychology, even raising in some minds the notion of a ceremony of superstition on the part of cats:

before the rod will open the door, it is necessary to go through a magical sequence of motions.

—LEWIS THOMAS, "Clever Animals"

B. Working with a group, rewrite the passage above by employing different conjunctions than those in the original. Try to retain the general sense of the original, but feel free to add your own emphasis or perspective in the revision. Reword as necessary.

35b Subjects and predicates

Sentences need a **subject,** naming the doer or thing talked about, and a **predicate,** indicating an action or a relationship, conditions, and consequences.

1 Creating sentence subjects

A **simple subject** consists of one or more nouns (or pronouns) naming the doer or the topic. A **complete subject** is the simple subject *plus* all its modifying words or phrases.

SIMPLE SUBJECT   **Cellophane** was originally made from wood fiber.

COMPLETE
SUBJECT   **Clear plastic wraps** are petroleum products.

A subject may be singular, plural, or compound (linked by *and* or *or*).

Subject-verb order. In most sentences, the subject comes before the verb.

     subject   verb
Homeless people camped in this area during the summer.

You can delay the subject until after the verb by beginning sentences with **expletive constructions** such as *there is* (*are*) or *here is* (*are*) (see 7b).

     verb   subject
There **were homeless people** camping in this area during the summer.

For emphasis, you can reverse (invert) the subject and verb order (see 7c).

     verb   subject
In this valley, eons ago, **grew plants** whose leaves are now fossils.

Questions often place the subject between the helping verb and the main verb (see 35a-3).

helping verb	subject	main verb	

Did dinosaurs live in this valley millions of years ago?

The subject *you* is generally implied, not stated, in an imperative sentence (a request or command): [*You*] slide the liner under the ledge.

2 Creating sentence predicates

A sentence **predicate** indicates the action or relationship expressed in the sentence and may also specify the consequences or conditions.

A **simple predicate** consists of a verb (*met*) or a verb phrase (*might meet*) (see 35a-3). The verb may be single (*slipped*) or compound (linked by *and* or *or*, e.g., *slipped* and *fell*).

A **complete predicate** consists of a verb or verb phrase *plus* any modifiers or other words that receive the action or complete the verb.

Object patterns. With a *transitive verb*, you can include in the predicate a **direct object** that tells *who* or *what* receives the action.

subject	predicate	
The bank officer	approved	the loan application.
	verb	direct object

The sentence can also include an **indirect object,** a noun or pronoun letting readers know *to whom* or *for whom* the action is undertaken.

subject	verb	indirect object	direct object
The Marine Corps Reserve	gives	needy children	toys.
		to whom?	

You can add information to a predicate with an **object complement,** a word (noun or adjective) that renames or describes the direct object.

ADJECTIVE Critics judged the movie **inferior.**

NOUN His co-workers elected Jim **project leader.**

Subject complement patterns. A sentence built around a linking verb, such as *is*, *seems*, or *feels* (see 35a-3), allows you to include a **subject complement,** completing the verb by describing the subject or renaming it.

subject	verb	subject complement		subject	verb	subject complement
The new store	seems	successful.		The plan	is	too complicated.

Intransitive verb patterns. An intransitive verb does not take either an object or a complement; the verb's meaning is complete without them, for example, Our team **lost;** Last week, the ferryboat **sank.**

FIVE BASIC PREDICATE STRUCTURES

1. **Subject + intransitive verb**
   The bus crashed.

2. **Subject + transitive verb + direct object**
   A quick-thinking passenger called the police.

3. **Subject + transitive verb + indirect object + direct object**
   The paramedic gave everyone blankets.

4. **Subject + transitive verb + direct object + object complement**
   Officials found the driver negligent.

5. **Subject + linking verb + subject complement**
   The quick-thinking passenger was a hero.

Exercise 6

A. In each sentence, circle the complete subject and draw a wavy line under the complete predicate.

EXAMPLE

(Stories about Mount Everest) often mention people known as Sherpas.

1. The Sherpas are well-known guides for mountain-climbing expeditions in the Himalayas.
2. They are a group of about 35,000 people who live in Nepal.
3. The Sherpas, who are primarily Buddhists, live in a country dominated by Hindus.
4. Before the early 1900s, most Sherpas did not attempt to scale the mountains in their homeland.
5. Early in the last century, however, Westerners planning to climb the mountains hired many Sherpas as guides and laborers.

B. Exchange papers in progress with another writer. Choose two paragraphs, and identify which of the five predicate patterns (listed in the chart above) the writer uses in each sentence. Then suggest revisions that vary the predicate patterns in order to provide appropriate emphasis and variety. When you finish, work together to identify those suggested revisions most likely to improve each paper.

35c Phrases and clauses

A **main clause** (also called an **independent clause**) is a word group that includes a subject and a verb and can act as a complete sentence (see 35b). A **phrase** is a word group that lacks one or more elements needed to make a complete sentence. (For example, the phrase *will be climbing* lacks a subject; *the man running across the field* lacks a predicate; and *under the sink* lacks both.) A **subordinate clause** contains both a subject and a predicate yet cannot stand on its own because it begins with a subordinating word such as *because, since, although, which,* or *that* (see 35a-7).

1 Recognizing prepositional phrases

A prepositional phrase has two parts: a **preposition** (a word like *at, for, in, to, according to,* or *under;* see 35a-6) and the **object of the preposition**—the noun, pronoun, or word group that follows the preposition.

You can use a prepositional phrase as an adjective, almost always following the noun or pronoun it modifies.

The coupons **in the newspaper** offer savings **on groceries.**

When you use a prepositional phrase as an adverb, place it next to the verb being modified or elsewhere in the sentence.

Her electronic wristwatch started beeping **during the meeting.**

During the meeting, her electronic wristwatch started beeping.

2 Recognizing absolute phrases

An **absolute phrase** includes (1) a noun, a pronoun, or a word group acting as a noun; (2) a present or past participle and any modifiers (*the deadline approaching quickly*). You can use an absolute phrase to modify a sentence as a whole or a word or element within the sentence.

Their lungs burning from the acrid smoke, the firefighters pressed ahead into the burning building.

3 Recognizing appositive phrases

An **appositive** renames a noun to add information to a sentence. An **appositive phrase** is an appositive (generally a noun) plus its modifiers.

Ken Choi, **my classmate,** won an award for packaging design.

He used "environmentally conscious" materials, **for example, recycled paper and soy-based ink.**

4 Recognizing verbal phrases

The verb parts called **verbals** (**infinitives, present** and **past participles,** and **gerunds**) act as nouns, adjectives, or adverbs, but cannot act alone as verbs. A verbal plus its modifiers, object, or complements is a **verbal phrase.**

Participial phrases. You build a **participial phrase** around the *-ing* (present participle) or *-ed/-en* (past participle) forms of a verbal. You can use it as an adjective to modify a noun or pronoun.

Everyone **watching the show** failed to notice the smoke.

The chef chose a cake **flavored with orange peel.**

Gerund phrases. You build a **gerund phrase** around the *-ing* form of a verbal, and you can use it as a noun in a subject, object, or subject complement.

sentence subject   object of preposition
Closing the landfill will keep it from **polluting the groundwater.**

Infinitive phrases. You can create an **infinitive phrase** using the *to* form of a verbal and use it as an adjective, adverb, or noun.

noun (sentence subject)
To live in the mountains of Montana was his goal.

adverb
He used several books on organic farming **to help plan his garden.**

Exercise 7

A. First, identify all the phrases in the following passage, and tell whether each is a prepositional, verbal, absolute, or appositive phrase.

Without electricity, we would perish. We could learn to do without the flow of electrons that power VCRs and food processors, but the currents inside our bodies are vital. The brain needs electricity to issue its commands from neuron to neuron. When these signals reach a muscle, they set up a wave of electrical excitation in the fibers, which in turn triggers the chemical reactions that make the fibers contract or relax. The most important muscle is the heart; it shudders under a wave of electricity about once each second.

—CARL ZIMMER, "The Body Electric"

Next, combine the following sentences to create a paragraph that might follow the one above. Try to create a variety of phrases.

The heart has an electric field. The field radiates into the chest cavity. The field sends clues. The clues are about the heart's function. The clues go toward the skin. Cardiologists can get a peek at the heart. They are taping electrodes. The electrodes are taped to a person's torso. Each electrode produces a familiar squiggle. The squiggles are on an electrocardiogram. The electrocardiogram shows how the voltage changes at that single point. The point is on the body. Cardiologists spend years learning. They learn to infer heart function from these signals. They learn to recognize the telltale signs. The signs are in EKG readings. The signs tell of dangerous heart conditions.

B. Share your revised paragraph with a group of fellow writers and decide which versions are the most effective.

ESL ADVICE: GERUNDS AND INFINITIVES

Gerunds (base form of verb + *-ing*) and infinitives (base form of verb + *to*) are verbals (see 35c-4).

VERBS FOLLOWED BY EITHER GERUNDS OR INFINITIVES

You can use a gerund or an infinitive after some verbs.

Developers <u>prefer</u> **working** [gerund] with local contractors.

Developers <u>prefer</u> **to work** [infinitive] with local contractors.

COMMON VERBS TAKING EITHER GERUNDS OR INFINITIVES

begin	intend	regret
can't stand	learn	remember
continue	like	start
forget	love	stop
hate	prefer	try

The meaning of some verbs (such as *remember, forget,* and *stop*) will change depending on whether you use a gerund or an infinitive.

GERUND	I **remembered** <u>meeting</u> your friend.
	I recall an event in the past.
INFINITIVE	I **remembered** <u>to meet</u> your friend.
	I did not forget to do something in the past.
GERUND	I never **forget** <u>visiting</u> the Statue of Liberty.
	I recall a past event.

INFINITIVE	I never **forget** to study for exams.
	I remember to do something.
GERUND	I **stopped** smoking.
	I do not smoke anymore.
INFINITIVE	I **stopped** to smoke.
	I paused to smoke.

VERBS FOLLOWED BY GERUNDS

After some verbs you can use only a gerund (and not an infinitive).

subject + verb + gerund
GERUND Children enjoy **reading** fairy tales.

COMMON VERBS TAKING GERUNDS		
admit	deny	mind
anticipate	discuss	miss
appreciate	dismiss	postpone
avoid	enjoy	practice
can't help	finish	quit
consider	imagine	recommend
delay	keep	suggest

You *must* use gerunds with some idiomatic expressions.

- After the word *go* (in any tense): I **go** shopping. I **went** hiking.
- After the expression *spend time*: Researchers **spend** a lot of **time** preparing reports.
- After the expression *have* + noun: Young children **have difficulty** following directions.
- After a preposition: Physicians' assistants are trained **in** treating routine cases.

In the following examples, the phrase beginning with *to* is not an infinitive. *To* acts like a preposition in each sentence and must be followed by a gerund ending in *-ing*.

I am looking **forward** to living abroad.

Managers are **accustomed** to receiving frequent updates.

Patrons are **used** to viewing complex exhibits.

VERBS FOLLOWED BY INFINITIVES

After some verbs, you must use an infinitive instead of another verb form.

INFINITIVE Some students need **to work** part time.

COMMON VERBS TAKING INFINITIVES		
agree	hope	pretend
ask	intend	promise
choose	manage	refuse
decide	need	seem
expect	offer	venture
fail	plan	want

You must use an object and then the infinitive to follow some verbs.

subject   +   verb   +   object + infinitive
Doctors often **advise** their patients to eat well.

COMMON VERBS TAKING AN OBJECT + AN INFINITIVE			
advise	convince	force	teach
allow	encourage	permit	tell
ask	expect	persuade	urge

When *make, let,* and *have* suggest "cause" or "forced," they follow a different model, using the infinitive without *to* (the base form).

subject   +   verb   +   object + base form
She   **made/let/had**   me   clean my room.

Use infinitives after certain adjectives.

I	**am**	delighted	to meet you.
The report	**is**	easy	to understand.
The volunteers	**are**	pleased	to help.

5 Recognizing subordinate clauses

A **main** clause (or **independent clause**) contains a subject and a verb; it can stand on its own as a complete sentence. A **subordinate clause** also contains both a subject and a verb, yet it cannot stand on its own as a complete sentence because it begins with a subordinating word. This word (usually a subordinating conjunction like *because, although,* or *if,* or a relative pronoun like *who, which,* or *that;* see 35a-2 and 35a-7) signals that the clause merely modifies the main clause to which it is attached. Subordinate clauses are sometimes called **dependent clauses.**

SUBORDINATE CLAUSE	**because** I was very busy
AS PART OF A SENTENCE	**Because I was very busy,** I forgot to call.

Subordinate clauses as modifiers. You can modify a noun or a pronoun with a subordinate clause. Use a **relative pronoun** (*who, which, that, whom, whose*) or a **relative adverb** (*when, where*) as the subordinating word.

> Many people **who live in Foxwood Estates** came to the meeting.

> They asked about the industrial park **that the county plans to create.**

You can also use subordinate clauses as adverbs. An adverb clause begins with a subordinating conjunction such as *because, although, since,* or *while* (see 35a-7) and modifies verbs, adjectives, or adverbs.

> **As the workshop proceeded,** many of Jeanelle's questions were answered.
> The clause is an adverb answering the question "When?"

Subordinate clauses as nouns. Noun clauses begin with *who, whom, whose, whoever, whomever, what, whatever, when, where, why, whether,* or *how.* They can play the same roles as nouns: subject, object, or complement.

SENTENCE SUBJECT   **Whoever is interested in accounting** ought to attend.

DIRECT OBJECT   You should pack **what you need for the weekend.**

Exercise 8

A. Underline all subordinate clauses in the following passage.

> Because the tax laws have gotten more complex recently, we have published a guide to tax preparation that highlights new features of the tax code. In addition, the guide provides step-by-step instruction for tax forms, which should be helpful even if a person has considerable experience filling out the forms. Anyone who plans to file taxes for a small business will be interested in the special section on business tax laws. Although many professionals and businesspeople rely on accountants when tax time arrives, they will nonetheless find that the guide provides money-saving advice.

B. Working with another writer, revise the same passage by combining ideas and word groups in different ways and by using different supporting words. Retain the general sense of the passage, but feel free to add your own ideas and perspective.

ESL ADVICE: ADJECTIVE, ADVERB, AND NOUN CLAUSES

ADJECTIVE CLAUSES

Place a relative clause as close as possible to the noun (the antecedent) that it modifies.

DRAFT	The <u>attorney</u> is excellent **who advises on product liability.**
REVISED	The <u>attorney</u> **who advises on product liability** is excellent.

You may choose to drop the relative pronoun if it is not the subject of the clause.

INCLUDED	The apartment **that** we rented was very lovely.
OMITTED	The apartment we rented was very lovely.

When a relative pronoun is the subject of an adjective clause, you can change the clause to an **adjective phrase.** To change a clause with a *be* verb, omit the relative pronoun and the *be* verb.

CLAUSE (WITH *BE*)	He is the man **who is studying German.**
PHRASE	He is the man **studying German.**

To change a clause with another verb to a phrase, omit the relative pronoun and change the verb to the present participle form (see 36b).

CLAUSE (WITHOUT *BE*)	He is the man **who wants to study German.**
PHRASE	He is the man **wanting to study German.**

ADVERB CLAUSES

Adverb clauses give information about time, reason, contrast, and condition, acting like adverbs to modify verbs.

TIME	**When** the season changes, clients want to see new colors.
REASON	Last year's clothes seem dated **because** the color palette has changed.
CONTRAST	**Although** many clients want the new colors, some choose the old palette.
CONDITION	We may have cost overruns **unless** we move the inventory.

WORDS TO INTRODUCE ADVERB CLAUSES

TIME		REASON	CONTRAST	CONDITION
while	when	because	although	if
before	whenever	since	though	even if
since	as soon as	as	even though	only if
until	after	now that	while	unless
once	as		whereas	provided that
				as long as

NOUN CLAUSES

Noun clauses work in the same way as nouns in a sentence: subject, object, object of preposition, and complement of an adjective.

SUBJECT · · · · · · · · · · **What she said** was interesting.

OBJECT · · · · · · · · · · · We don't know **where the ambassador is going.**

OBJECT
OF PREPOSITION · · · · · · His parents were concerned about **how safe the car was.**

COMPLEMENT
OF ADJECTIVE · · · · · · · · They are confident **that he will pass the test.**

WORDS TO INTRODUCE NOUN CLAUSES

who	where	however
whom	why	how much
whose	whether	how many
what	that	how long
when	which	how often

You may also use noun clauses to report information questions. Change to statement order when the question includes a form of *be* and a subject complement, a modal, or the auxiliary *do, does, have, has,* or *had.*

QUESTION · · · · · · · · · Who **are** your friends?

NOUN CLAUSE · · · · · · · I wonder who your friends **are.**

QUESTION · · · · · · · · · How **can** I meet them?

NOUN CLAUSE · · · · · · · Please tell me how I **can** meet them.

QUESTION · · · · · · · · · When **do** you plan to introduce us?

NOUN CLAUSE · · · · · · · Let me know when you [do] plan to introduce us.

QUESTION · · · · · · · · · How **have** you met so many people?

NOUN CLAUSE · · · · · · · I'm interested in how you **have** met so many people.

Sometimes the word order remains the same as in the original question.

QUESTION	Who discovered the fire?
NOUN CLAUSE	Do you know **who discovered the fire?**

35d Sentence types

Sentences vary in structure according to the kind and number of clauses they include.

1 Recognizing sentence structures

A **simple sentence** is a sentence with one main (independent) clause and no subordinate (dependent) clauses.

The community development program sponsors construction projects.

A **compound sentence** is a sentence with two or more main (independent) clauses and no subordinate (dependent) clauses.

main clause   main clause
Most people liked the plans, yet some wanted more detail.

A **complex sentence** is a sentence with one main (independent) clause and one or more subordinate (dependent) clauses.

subordinate clause   main clause
Because people complained, the architect revised the plans.

A **compound-complex sentence** has two or more main (independent) clauses and one or more subordinate (dependent) clauses.

subordinate clause   subordinate clause
Because he wanted to make sure that work on the extension did not

main clause
damage the existing building, the architect asked the contractor to

main clause
test the soil for stability, and he then proceeded with the plans.

2 Recognizing sentence purposes

You can create various kinds of sentences according to the relationship you want to establish with readers. A **declarative sentence** makes a statement. An **interrogative sentence** poses a question. An **imperative**

35d
gram

sentence makes a request or command. An **exclamatory sentence** makes an exclamation.

DECLARATIVE   The motor is making a rattling noise.

INTERROGATIVE   Have you checked it for overheating?

IMPERATIVE   Check it again.

EXCLAMATORY   It's on fire!

> Visit mycomplab.com for more resources and exercises on sentence elements and patterns.

CHAPTER 36

Verbs

Readers may forgive a spelling mistake or two, but as soon as you write "The Dolphins done real good in the playoffs," readers are likely to lose confidence in your ideas. Editing verb problems in your writing is therefore an important skill.

36a Simple present and past tense

You can put a verb into the **present tense** for action occurring now or the **past tense** for action that has already occurred. Most verbs form their past tense by adding *-ed* to the present tense form, also called the **base form.** You need no special ending to mark the present tense *except* in the third person singular form (with *he, she,* or *it* or a singular noun).

The trucks **wait** in line until the border crossing **opens**.

1 Watch for irregular verbs

About sixty or seventy common English verbs are exceptions to the "add *-ed*" rule for past tense. Most of these irregular verbs change an internal vowel in the simple past tense, such as *run* (present) and *ran* (past).

COMMON IRREGULAR VERBS

PRESENT	PAST	PAST PARTICIPLE
am/is/are	was/were	been
begin	began	begun
break	broke	broken
bring	brought	brought
buy	bought	bought
catch	caught	caught
choose	chose	chosen
come	came	come
do	did	done
draw	drew	drawn
drink	drank	drunk
drive	drove	driven
eat	ate	eaten
fight	fought	fought

(continued)

COMMON IRREGULAR VERBS (*continued*)

PRESENT	PAST	PAST PARTICIPLE
forget	forgot	forgotten
get	got	got/gotten
give	gave	given
go	went	gone
grow	grew	grown
hang (object)	hung (object)	hung (object)
hang (person)	hanged/hung (person)	hanged/hung (person)
know	knew	known
lay	laid	laid
lead	led	led
lie	lay	lain
lose	lost	lost
prove	proved	proved/proven
ride	rode	ridden
rise	rose	risen
run	ran	run
see	saw	seen
set	set	set
sing	sang/sung	sung
sink	sank/sunk	sunk
sit	sat	sat
speak	spoke	spoken
spring	sprang	sprung
swim	swam	swum
swing	swung	swung
take	took	taken
tear	tore	torn
wear	wore	worn

2 Using present and past tense in academic settings

Academic readers may expect you to use the present and past tenses in special ways. When discussing a work of literature, a film, an essay, a painting, or a similar creative production, treat events, ideas, characters, or statements within such works as if they exist in an ongoing present tense.

In Louise Erdrich's *Love Medicine*, Albertine **returns** to the reservation.

In the social and natural sciences, use the present tense to discuss the results and implications of a current study or experiment, but use the past tense to review the findings of earlier researchers.

Although Maxwell (1991) **identified** three crucial classroom interactions, the current survey **suggests** two others as well.

36b Participles: Recognizing and editing

When you provide the main verb in a sentence with a **helping,** or **auxiliary, verb** (such as *is* or *has*) and also change the form of the main verb, you create complex verb forms that convey important aspects of past, present, or future time, as in the following sentences.

> After **having eaten** up all the cake, little Jennifer **would have begun** to feel guilty **had it not been** for her father's unexpected treat—a box of delicious parfaits for the family.

The form a verb takes when it's linked to a helping verb is called a **participle,** which itself can take two forms: **past participle** and **present participle.**

To form the present participle, add *-ing* to the base form of the verb (the form with no endings or markers).

HELPING VERB	PARTICIPLE (MAIN VERB)
He will be	loading the truck.

To form the past participle of most verbs, just use the simple past tense.

HELPING VERB	PAST PARTICIPLE (MAIN VERB)
Mike has	loaded the truck.

Some participial forms are irregular, however, involving an internal vowel change or an *-en* ending. (See the list of common irregular verbs on pp. 527–528.)

INCORRECT	Louise lost the pie eating contest because earlier she **had drank** three glasses of lemonade.
EDITED	Louise lost the pie eating contest because earlier she **had drunk** three glasses of lemonade.

ESL ADVICE: VERB FORMS

THIRD PERSON *-S* OR *-ES* ENDING

Be sure to add *-s* or *-es* to verbs that are third person singular.

SUBJECT	VERB	SUBJECT	VERB + *-S*
I/you/we/they	write	he/she/it (animal, thing, concept)	**writes**

SIMPLE PRESENT AND SIMPLE PAST

These two tenses add no helping verbs to form the verb, except for the negative and interrogative forms. No other verb forms can stand alone!

SIMPLE PRESENT	They **live** in the dormitory this semester.
SIMPLE PAST	They **lived** in an apartment last semester.

PRINCIPAL PARTS OF REGULAR VERBS IN ENGLISH			
BASE FORM	PAST	PRESENT PARTICIPLE	PAST PARTICIPLE
live	lived	living	lived
want	wanted	wanting	wanted

HELPING VERBS

Most verbs combine one or more helping verbs with a main verb to form a **verb phrase.** Helping verbs include *am, is, are, will, would, can, could, have, has, had, was, were, should, might, may, must, do, does,* and *did.* Sometimes these words work in combination, as in *have been, has been, had been, will be, will have,* and *will have been.*

Exercise 1

A. In each sentence, a correct or incorrect irregular verb form appears in parentheses. Edit each sentence to make it correct, or indicate that it's already correct.

EXAMPLE

The rain (~~had falled~~) all night.
had fallen

1. Jeremy (*had chose*) to work along the levee as part of the volunteer corps.
2. The floodwater (*had rised*) rapidly during the night.
3. The team (*had heaved*) sandbags for almost twenty-four hours.
4. Jim O'Connor (*had hung*) plastic sheeting up to plug a leak.
5. By eight o'clock in the morning, people (*had woke*) up to find that the river (*had fell*) by six inches and the town was safe.

B. Review the list of irregular verbs on pp. 527–528. Compose five sentences in which you correctly or incorrectly use the past or past participle form of an irregular verb. In a small group, exchange lists and edit your sentences. Discuss the changes you made or did not make.

36c Progressive and perfect tenses: Editing

The **present, past,** and **future progressive** tenses show an action in progress at some point in time. In the **progressive tense,** the main verb must take the *-ing* ending. In the future tense, the progressive must include *be.*

PRESENT PROGRESSIVE Sales **are increasing** this quarter.

PAST PROGRESSIVE At this time last year, we **were working** for improvement.

FUTURE PROGRESSIVE I **will be discussing** the results at the meeting.

Note that irregular main verbs are not affected in any unique way by the progressive tense; all consist of the base form plus *-ing.*

The **perfect tenses** are used to show the order in which events take place. The **past perfect tense** allows you to indicate that something had already happened before something else happened. The form consists of *had* plus the past participle (see 36b for participle forms).

> The general practitioner **had treated** the patient for six months before the specialist took over the case.

The **present perfect tense** works much like the past perfect, but the action is something that has recurred or that the writer insists has already occurred.

> I **have reported** the burglary already.

The present perfect also presents something begun in the past and continuing into the present. It differs from the simple past, which indicates an action already completed or specified in time.

PRESENT PERFECT   I **have lived** in St. Louis for three weeks.

SIMPLE PAST   I **lived** in St. Louis in 2001.

The **future perfect tense** shows that something will have happened by the time something else will be happening. This form consists of the helping verb *will* plus *have* plus the past participle of the main verb.

> The technician **will have finished** by the time the dentist is ready.

1 Check the helping verb in progressive tenses

Most errors in progressive tense occur when you either use the wrong form of the helping verb or omit part of it (as is common in some dialects).

DRAFT   The interview **starting** five minutes late.

EDITED   The interview is **starting** five minutes late.

DRAFT   The employees **was running** for the elevator.

EDITED   The employees **were running** for the elevator.

2 Check the form of the past participle in the past perfect tense

Writers sometimes set out to use the past perfect tense but mistakenly substitute a simple past tense form for the past participle.

DRAFT   Pierre **had rode** for six years before he was injured in a rodeo.

EDITED   Pierre **had ridden** for six years before he was injured in a rodeo.

ESL ADVICE: SIMPLE PRESENT AND PRESENT PROGRESSIVE TENSES

Use the **simple present** tense to describe factual or habitual activities. These activities occur in the present, but they are not necessarily in progress.

subject + verb (with -s if third person singular)

SHOWS FACT The planets **revolve** around the sun.

SHOWS HABIT The museum **offers** summer programs for children.

COMMON TIME EXPRESSIONS FOR PRESENT TENSE HABITUAL ACTIVITIES

all the time	every holiday	every year	rarely
always	every month	frequently	sometimes
every class	every semester	most of the time	usually
every day	every week	often	never

Use the **present progressive** tense to describe activities in progress.

subject + *am/is/are* + present participle
Santiago **is testing** the revised formula.

Santiago **is testing** the revised formula **this month.**

COMMON PROGRESSIVE TIME EXPRESSIONS FOR ACTIVITIES IN PROGRESS

at the moment	this afternoon	this month	this year
right now	this evening	this morning	today

CHOOSING BETWEEN SIMPLE PRESENT AND PRESENT PROGRESSIVE

When you choose between the simple present and present progressive tenses, think about which time expression best describes the activity. Is it happening only at the moment (present progressive) or all the time as a fact or habit (simple present)?

NOT APPROPRIATE All people are communicating in some language.

CORRECT All people communicate in some language.
This is a fact, so the correct tense must be simple present tense.

NOT APPROPRIATE The students are speaking their own languages in class.

CORRECT The students speak their own languages in class.
This is a habitual activity that occurs all the time, so the correct tense is simple present.

VERBS THAT CAN BE TROUBLESOME IN PROGRESSIVE TENSES

VERB	EXAMPLE	OTHER USAGES AND MEANINGS
SENSES		
see	I **see** the beauty.	Also: I **am seeing** the consultant. (meeting with, visiting, dating)
hear	I **hear** the birds.	Also: I **have been hearing** about the problem for a while. (receiving information)
smell	The flowers **smell** strong.	Also: I **am smelling** the flowers. (action in progress)
taste	The food **tastes** good.	Also: The cook **is tasting** the soup. (action in progress)
POSSESSION		
have	We **have** many friends.	Also: We **are having** a lot of fun. (experiencing)
own	They **own** many dogs.	
possess	She **possesses** much knowledge.	
belong	The book **belongs** to me.	
STATES OF MIND		
be	I **am** tired.	
know	I **know** the city well.	
STATES OF MIND		
believe	She **believes** in God.	
think	LaShonda **thinks** it is true. (knows, believes)	Also: LaShonda **is thinking** about relocating. (having thoughts about)
recognize	His dog always **recognizes** him. (knows)	
understand	The social worker **understands** the problem.	
mean	I **don't mean** to pry. (don't want)	Also: I **have been meaning** to visit you. (planning, intending)
WISH OR ATTITUDE		
want	We **want** peace.	
desire	He **desires** his freedom.	
need	We **need** rain.	
love	Children **love** snow.	Also: I **have been loving** this book. (enjoying)

(continued)

VERBS THAT CAN BE TROUBLESOME IN PROGRESSIVE TENSES (*continued*)		
VERB	EXAMPLE	OTHER USAGES AND MEANINGS
hate	Cats **hate** getting wet.	
like	He **likes** skiing.	
dislike	Patients **dislike** waiting.	
seem	The office **seems** efficient.	
appear	He **appears** tired. (seems to be)	Also: He **is appearing** at the theater. (acting, performing)
look	He **looks** tired. (seems to be)	Also: We **are looking** at the revised maps. (action of using eyes)
		I **am looking** it up in a dictionary. (consulting, investigating)

36d Troublesome verbs (*lie, lay, sit, set*)

Even for experienced writers, a few verbs can be tricky. Here are the verbs most often confused.

VERB	PRESENT	PAST	PARTICIPLE
lie (oneself)	lie	lay	lain
lay (an object)	lay	laid	laid
sit (oneself)	sit	sat	sat
set (an object)	set	set	set

DRAFT   I **laid** down yesterday afternoon for a nap. I **have laid** down at around 2 p.m. each day for over a year now.

EDITED   I **lay** down yesterday afternoon for a nap. I **have lain** down at around 2 p.m. each day for over a year now.

DRAFT   Dr. Parsons **lay** the cadaver on the table and began the autopsy.

EDITED   Dr. Parsons **laid** the cadaver on the table and began the autopsy.

DRAFT   First Erica and Steve **sat** the projector down on the table. Then they **set** down and listened to the chairperson's speech.

EDITED   First Erica and Steve **set** the projector down on the table. Then they **sat** down and listened to the chairperson's speech.

Exercise 2

A. For each sentence, circle the appropriate verb from the choices within parentheses.

EXAMPLE

A fire last Saturday (*lead*, (*led*)) to Sandy's first big assignment as a reporter.

1. Sandy (*laid/lay*) the article for the newspaper on her editor's desk.
2. To get information for the article, she (*sat/set*) in the waiting room of the fire commissioner's office for three days.
3. During the interview, she (*layed/lay/laid*) on his desk a copy of the report criticizing the fire department's performance during the Brocklin Warehouse fire.
4. The commissioner looked the report over and then (*sat/set*) it next to the other report, which praised the department's performance.
5. After she had (*lead/led*) the three-hour discussion with the commissioner, Sandy was convinced that the department had done an adequate job at the fire.

B. Write four or five sentences in which you use *incorrect* forms of *sit*, *set*, *lie*, and *lay*. Exchange your sentences in a small group, edit them, and then discuss your changes.

EXAMPLE

Mrs. Jones sat the tuna dangerously close to Puff, her Siamese cat.

36e Active and passive voice

Verbs in the **active voice** appear in sentences in which the doer of an action is the subject of the sentence.

	DOER (SUBJECT)	ACTION (VERB)	GOAL (OBJECT)
ACTIVE	The car	hit	the lamppost.
ACTIVE	Dana	distributed	the fliers.

To rewrite an active sentence in the **passive voice,** add a form of *be* as a helping verb and use the participial form of the verb. Place the subject (or doer) into the object position after the word *by*. (A prepositional phrase states the doer and is optional.)

	GOAL (SUBJECT)	ACTION (VERB)	[DOER] [PREPOSITIONAL PHRASE]
PASSIVE	The lamppost	**was hit**	[by the car].
PASSIVE	The fliers	**were distributed**	[by Dana].

The active voice and passive voice versions of a sentence create different kinds of emphasis. In addition, a passive sentence can eliminate any mention of the doer.

ACTIVE VOICE   The city council banned smoking in restaurants.

PASSIVE VOICE   Smoking in restaurants was banned by the city council.

AGENT ELIMINATED   Smoking in restaurants was banned.

(For a discussion of use and misuse of the passive voice, see 7c-3.)

ESL ADVICE: THE PASSIVE VOICE

All transitive verbs in English may be written in the passive voice *except* the progressive forms of the present perfect, past perfect, future, and future perfect. The verb *make* in the passive voice, unlike in the active voice, is followed by the infinitive.

ACTIVE VOICE   The council member made us **wait.**

PASSIVE VOICE   We were made **to wait** by the council member.

Exercise 3

A. Edit the following passage by rewriting unnecessary uses of the passive voice into the active voice. In rewriting passive voice sentences that do not indicate an agent (doer), fill in the names of the person(s) or thing(s) you consider responsible for the action.

Having cash registers full of change was found to increase the likelihood of a late-night robbery. In one example, a store clerk was held up at gunpoint. It was decided by management that requiring full payment for gasoline in advance of a purchase would minimize the risk of further holdups. This course of action had been voted on by the board of directors prior to implementation. The decision was posted at each location. Following implementation, it was discovered that holdups were not minimized unless large signs indicating the clerk's lack of available cash were placed in plain view. Once this was done, fewer holdups were experienced, and the turnover of late-night personnel was decreased.

B. Compare your rewritten version of the passage with those produced by other students. Be sure you explain why you have decided to let any sentences remain in the passive voice. Working with several other students, produce one version of the passage reflecting group agreement on the best way to rewrite the sentences.

36f Clear tense sequence

In conversation, we often shift from verb tense to verb tense indiscriminately, sometimes moving from past to present and back again with little warning or planning. In writing, however, such tense shifts can be annoying to readers who expect consistency. You need to maintain a clear **tense sequence** in your writing, indicating the time relationships of events and ideas.

When changes in tense do not reflect clear relationships in time or do so inconsistently, your readers may become confused.

INCONSISTENT The author **begins** by giving a factual account of the storm. He **said** that if people had heeded the warnings, many lives would have been saved.

EDITED The author **begins** by giving a factual account of the storm. He **says** that if people had heeded the warnings, many lives would have been saved.

You can shift tenses inside a sentence without creating confusion as long as you make the tense sequence logical.

LOGICAL
past   present
Although my parents both **loved** cats, I **dislike** them.

LOGICAL
present   past
People **forget** that four serious candidates **ran** in the 1948 presidential election.

LOGICAL
future   present
I **will accept** your recommendations; they **seem** reasonable.

LOGICAL
past
The accountant **destroyed** evidence because the police
past perfect
had forgotten to warn him of the files' importance.

LOGICAL
past perfect
None of the expedition's crew **had recognized** that food stored
present
in cans sealed with lead solder **is** poisonous.
Putting *is poisonous* in the present tense is appropriate because the phrase is a generally true (or widely applicable) statement.

36g Subjunctive mood

Sentences can be classified according to **mood,** a term that highlights the speaker's or writer's attitude as reflected in the statement. Most of your sentences will be in the **indicative mood** (characterizing statements intended as truthful or factual, like "You need to watch out") or the **imperative mood** (characterizing statements which function as commands, like "Watch out!").

The **subjunctive** mood is used to express uncertainty—supposition, prediction, or possibility. The subjunctive mood has faded from most casual speech, but it is still used on occasion, particularly in formal writing.

Were the deadline today, our proposal would not be ready.

Whenever you create sentences that express desires or wishes, whether positive or negative, the subjunctive may be required.

DRAFT   Jacqueline wished the news **was** not true.

EDITED   Jacqueline wished the news **were** not true.
(SUBJUNCTIVE)

Many **conditional statements,** expressing the improbable or hypothetical and often beginning with *if,* require the subjunctive.

DRAFT   If Sandy **was** a person who always wore a helmet, his family
                     would be much less worried about his riding motorcycles.

EDITED   If Sandy **were** a person who always wore a helmet, his family
(SUBJUNCTIVE)   would be much less worried about his riding motorcycles.

When you write conditional sentences (with *if*), be careful not to add the auxiliary *would* to the *had + verb* structure in the conditional clause. This error is common, in part because the clause after the conditional often does correctly contain that structure.

DRAFT   If Sandy **would have worn** his helmet on the night of the
                     party, he **would have hurt** himself less seriously.

EDITED   If Sandy **had worn** his helmet on the night of the party, he
                     would have hurt himself less seriously.

Finally, some clauses with *that* require a subjunctive verb when they follow certain verbs that make demands or requests. In such cases the main verb should be the same as the past participle (see 36c-2).

DRAFT   Parents desire that their child **shows** respect.

EDITED   Parents desire that their child **show** respect.

Exercise 4

A. Decide whether the complex verb forms highlighted in the following sentences are correct. Edit those that are not; explain why you left any as they appear.

36g
verb

EXAMPLE

The team leader **is planning** to ask for reports just after the produc-

tion meeting **will begin.** ^*begins.*^

1. Kamal **is finished** testing the circuit board by the time the production meeting **had started.**
2. The team members **will ask** Kamal if he **was planning** to test the
   remainder of the circuit boards.
3. As I prepare this report on the project, Michelle **is assembling** the
   prototype using the circuit boards.
4. The other people **will assemble** the extra machines as soon as the
   delivery van **arrived.**
5. If our customers **will be able** to recognize the advantages of our
   product, they **would order** more of the machines.

B. Compose five sentences with correct and incorrect subjunctive
mood or tense shifts. Edit each other's sentences in a small group;
then discuss the changes you made.

Exercise 5

A. Rewrite each of the following sentences in the tense or mood indicated in brackets by substituting appropriate main verb forms and any
necessary helping verbs for the verb in parentheses.

EXAMPLE

The airplane assembly plant (*fail*) for several years. [present perfect
progressive] ^*has been failing*^

1. First, the recession (*hurt*) the market for small airplanes. [past
   perfect]
2. Then a new management team announced, "We (*close*) the plant
   unless productivity increases." [future]
3. At the same time, the company (*lose*) a product liability lawsuit.
   [past progressive]
4. This week, the company president (*announce*), "Unless we get
   some new orders in a few days, we (*declare*) bankruptcy." [simple
   past; future progressive]
5. If the plant (*be*) closed, three hundred workers would lose their
   jobs. [past subjunctive]

B. Write five sentences of your own, three using different complex
tenses and two employing the subjunctive mood. Exchange sentences
with a fellow writer and check that your partner has used the tenses
and the subjunctive mood correctly.

ESL ADVICE: CONDITIONALS

Conditional statements may be (1) *true* in the present, *true* in the future, or possibly *true* in the future; (2) *untrue* or contrary to fact in the present; or (3) *untrue* or contrary to fact in the past. Each includes an *if* clause and a result clause that combine different verb tenses.

TYPE I: TRUE IN THE PRESENT

IF CLAUSE

RESULT CLAUSE

• Generally true as a habit or as a fact

if + subject + present tense verb
If Rafi **drives** to school every day,

subject + present tense verb
he gets to class on time.

• True in the future as a one-time event

if + subject + present tense verb
If Rafi **drives** to school today,

subject + future tense verb
he will get to class on time.

• Possibly true in the future as a one-time event

if + subject + present tense verb
If Rafi **drives** to school today,

subject + modal + base form verb
he may/might/could/should get to class on time.

TYPE II: UNTRUE IN THE PRESENT

IF CLAUSE

RESULT CLAUSE

if + subject + past tense verb
If Rafi **drove** to school,

subject + *would/could/might* + simple form of verb
he would/could/might arrive on time.

With Type II statements, the form of *be* in the *if* clause is always *were:* If she *were* president, she would reform tax laws.

TYPE III: UNTRUE IN THE PAST

IF CLAUSE

RESULT CLAUSE

if + subject + past perfect tense
If Rafi **had driven** to school,

subject + *would/could/might* + have + past participle
he would not have been late.

mycomplab

Visit mycomplab.com for more resources and exercises on verbs.

CHAPTER **37**

Nouns and Pronouns

Sentences need **nouns** (persons, places, ideas, or things) and **pronouns** (words that stand for nouns). Both nouns and pronouns take many forms and play many roles. Guiding your readers by choosing the appropriate forms is essential to helping them understand your meaning.

37a Noun forms

Nouns name persons, places, ideas, or things. Nouns often require an article: *the*, *a*, or *an* (*a* before consonants, *an* before vowels).

> noun   noun   noun   noun
> **Amberly** volunteers with **children** at **a hospital** on **weekends**.
>   article

Most nouns add *-s* to the singular form to make the plural: *cow* + *s* = *cows*. Some nouns ending with *s*-like sounds (*s*, *z*, *j*, *x*, *ch*, *sh*) add *-es* for the plural: *gas* + *es* = *gases*; base (silent *e*) + *es* = *bases*; *fax* + *es* = *faxes*. Some nouns have irregular plurals: child/children, deer/deer, goose/geese, mouse/mice, ox/oxen.

TYPES OF NOUNS	
Count noun	Names individual items that can be counted: *four cups*, *a hundred beans*
Noncount noun (mass noun)	Names material or abstractions that cannot be counted: *flour*, *water*, *steel*
Collective noun	Names a unit composed of more than one individual or thing (see 38b-2 on agreement): *group*, *board of directors*, *flock*
Proper noun	Names specific people, places, titles, or things (see 57b on capitalizing): *Miss America*; *Tuscaloosa, Alabama*; *Microsoft Corporation*
Common noun	Names nonspecific people, places, or things (see 57b on capitalizing): *children*, *winner*, *town*, *mountain*, *company*, *bike*

ESL ADVICE: THE ARTICLES *A*, *AN*, AND *THE*

Articles can be **indefinite** (*a* and *an*) or **definite** (*the*). Remember: you will still communicate your sentence's basic meaning even if you choose the wrong article or forget to use one.

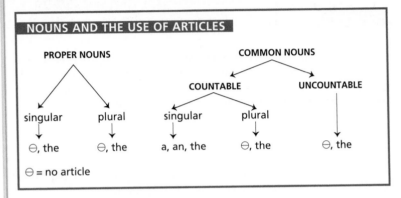

NOUNS AND THE USE OF ARTICLES

PROPER NOUNS   COMMON NOUNS

                                COUNTABLE   UNCOUNTABLE

singular   plural   singular   plural

⊖, the   ⊖, the   a, an, the   ⊖, the   ⊖, the

⊖ = no article

- **Singular proper nouns** generally use no article, and **plural proper nouns** usually use *the*.

    SINGULAR   **Rosa Parks** was important to the civil rights movement.

    PLURAL   **The Everglades** have abundant wildlife and tropical plants.

- Singular **count nouns** use *a*, *an*, or *the*. They cannot stand alone.

    The pig is an intelligent <u>animal</u>.

- **Plural count nouns** use either no article (to present a generalization) or *the* (to refer to something specific).

    Books are the best teachers. (generalization)

    The books on his desk are from the library. (specific)

- **Noncount (mass) nouns** use either no article or *the*, but never use *a* or *an*. **General noncount (mass) nouns** sometimes stand alone. **Specific noncount (mass) nouns** use *the*.

    INCORRECT   A laughter is good medicine.

    CORRECT   **Laughter** is good medicine. (general)

    CORRECT   **The laughter** of children is good medicine. (specific)

- Use *a* or *an* when you are not talking about a specific person or thing (a nonspecific, singular count noun).

    You need **an identification card** to cash a check.
    [nonspecific, *any* identification card]

- Use *the* when talking about a specific, singular noun, meaning you know the exact person or thing.

  You need **the university identification card** to borrow books.
  [a specific, known card]

- Use no article with plural nouns because most plural and mass nouns do not require one.

  COUNT   **Airline tickets** to Florida are at half price.

  MASS   **Information** about flights to Florida is available.

- Use *the* when a plural noun is followed by a modifier because plural count and mass nouns are specific when followed by modifiers.

  COUNT   **The** airline tickets that you bought are at half price.

  MASS   **The** information that you received has changed.

          The modifying clause makes the noun specific.

37b Pronoun forms

Because a pronoun's form can signal its role in a sentence, you need to choose those forms that accurately reflect your meaning.

1 Recognizing pronoun case

Pronouns acting as subjects take subjective form (**subjective case**). Those acting as objects take objective form (**objective case**). Those indicating possession or ownership take possessive form (**possessive case**).

SUBJECTIVE CASE   **He** designs furniture for Herman Miller Company.

OBJECTIVE CASE   The modular furniture we are using was designed by **him.**

POSSESSIVE CASE   **His** design team created the work spaces in the sales office.

FORMS OF PRONOUNS

PERSONAL PRONOUNS

	SUBJECTIVE		OBJECTIVE		POSSESSIVE	
	SINGULAR	PLURAL	SINGULAR	PLURAL	SINGULAR	PLURAL
FIRST PERSON	I	we	me	us	my mine	our ours
SECOND PERSON	you	you	you	you	your yours	your yours
THIRD PERSON	he/she/it	they	him/her/it	them	his/her/ hers/its	their/ theirs

(continued)

FORMS OF PRONOUNS (*continued*)

RELATIVE AND INTERROGATIVE PRONOUNS

SUBJECTIVE	OBJECTIVE	POSSESSIVE
who	whom	whose
whoever	whomever	whosever
which	which	
that	that	
what	what	

INDEFINITE PRONOUNS

SUBJECTIVE	OBJECTIVE	POSSESSIVE
anybody	anybody	anybody's
everyone	everyone	everyone's

---

2 Choosing subjective pronoun forms

Choose a subjective form when a pronoun acts as the subject of all or part of a sentence or it renames or restates a subject.

She attends class more regularly than **he.**

STRATEGY   Choose subjective pronoun forms

As you edit, check whether a pronoun is acting as a subject within its part of a sentence. Check also whether it renames or restates a subject. If it plays either role, use the subjective form.

subject of subordinate clause
Because **they** were unable to get a loan, the business failed.

subject of relative clause
Atco Manufacturers will be hiring people **who** are willing to work the night shift.

subject of implied verb
I attend class more regularly than **he** [does].

complement renames subject
The new auditor is **he,** the person at Sandi's desk.

appositives rename subject
Two people in the group, **she** and **I,** have experience with desktop publishing.

3 Choosing objective pronoun forms

When you make a pronoun the direct (or indirect) object of an entire sentence, use the objective form.

indirect object   direct object
The company bought **her an antivirus program.**

STRATEGY   Choose objective pronoun forms

As you edit, check whether a pronoun is acting as an object within its part of a sentence. Check also whether it renames or restates an object. If it plays either role, choose the objective form.

object of preposition
The rest of **them** had to wait several months for the software.

object in relative clause
An accountant **whom** the firm hired helped her out.

object in gerund phrase
Mr. Pederson's research for the report included interviewing **them.**

object in participial phrase
Having interviewed **us,** too, Mr. Pederson had a lot of material to summarize.

The report contained interviews with the two dissatisfied workers,
appositive renames object
her and him.

Pronouns used with infinitive phrases can be tricky, so keep the following example in mind.

Mr. Pederson asked **us** to read the summaries of the interviews.

You might be tempted to treat *us* as the subject of the phrase *to read the summaries of the interviews.* *Us* is the direct object of the sentence, however (*Mr. Pederson asked* us), and the objective form is correct.

4 Choosing possessive pronoun forms

When you use a pronoun to show possession, choose the possessive case. The form you choose depends on whether you use the pronoun *before a noun* or *in place of a noun.*

BEFORE NOUN   The Topeka office requested a copy of **her** report.

IN PLACE OF NOUN   **Hers** was the most thorough and up-to-date study available.

ESL

37b
pron

When you use the *-ing* form of a verb as a noun (a *gerund*, see 35c-4), use the possessive for a noun or pronoun that comes before it as a modifier.

gerund

Their requesting a copy of the report pleased the project supervisor.

CHOOSING POSSESSIVE FORMS

BEFORE A NOUN		IN PLACE OF A NOUN
my problem	=	mine
your problem	=	yours
her problem	=	hers
their problem	=	theirs
our problem	=	ours
BUT		
his problem	=	his
its problem	=	its

ESL ADVICE: APOSTROPHES AND POSSESSIVE PRONOUNS

Do not use an apostrophe with a possessive pronoun. (See 53a.) Use *it's* only as a contraction meaning *it is*.

INCORRECT   your's, her's, it's, their's

CORRECT   yours, hers, its, theirs

Form possessive nouns with an apostrophe: *Luis's, cat's, government's.* (See 53a.)

Exercise 1

A. In each sentence, choose the correct pronoun from the pair within parentheses. Then name the case of the pronoun you have chosen.

EXAMPLE

Ruth and (*I/me*) are planning to open a children's clothing store.
subjective

1. The design for the new store was prepared by (*she/her*).
2. The city requires (*we/us*) to submit plans for remodeling the store.
3. Having interviewed Ruth and (*I/me*) about our marketing plan, the bank's officer approved our loan.
4. The person who will choose the stock for our store is (*she/her*).
5. I will supervise the salespeople (*who/whom*) we hire.

B. Next, revise the following sentences by correcting any errors in pronoun case.

EXAMPLE

her

The foundation sent copies of the grant proposal to ~~she~~ and me.

1. Her and three other people worked for three weeks preparing the grant proposal.
2. The grant-writing team included two other people, Kristen and she.
3. Because I spent more time working on the grant, I think I ought to get more credit for its success than him.
4. It is me who will have to supervise work done under the grant.
5. Responsibility for budgeting the grant money is your's.

C. Working with a group of writers, choose a draft paper one of the group has written and examine two paragraphs carefully. Identify all pronouns in the subjective, objective, and possessive cases, and check to see that they are used correctly. Then suggest revisions for the paragraphs, drawing on the sentence and pronoun patterns illustrated in 37a–b.

37c Common problems with pronouns

Many problems with pronoun forms occur at predictable places in a sentence. Pay attention to the following troublesome sentence constructions.

1 Pay attention to compound subjects and objects

When you use a compound such as *the committee and I* or *Jim and me*, the rule is simple: Use the same case for pronouns in compounds that you would use for single pronouns playing the same role.

COMPOUND SUBJECT	Denise or (*he/him*) should create the database.
USE SUBJECTIVE CASE	Denise or **he** should create the database.
COMPOUND OBJECT	The coach selected (*she and him/her and him*) as team representatives.
USE OBJECTIVE CASE	The coach selected **her and him** as team representatives.

STRATEGY Use the focus-imagine-choose strategy

- **Focus** on the pronoun whose form you need to choose.

    UNEDITED   Anne-Marie and **me** will develop the videotapes.
    I or *me*?

- **Imagine** each choice for the pronoun as the complete subject (or object).

  Me will develop the videotapes.

  I will develop the videotapes.

- **Choose** the correct form, and use it in the compound subject (or object). If the correct form is not immediately apparent to you, refer to the chart on pages 543–544. (Choosing the form that "sounds right" can be a misleading strategy with compounds.)

  EDITED   Anne-Marie and **I** will develop the videotapes.

2 Watch for *we* or *us* with a noun

When you pair *we*, *us*, or other pronouns with nouns, make sure the pronoun form—*we, they* (subjective) or *us, them* (objective)—matches the role played by the noun (subject or object).

CORRECT   **We taxpayers** ought to demand that the city fill the potholes.

CORRECT   If a customer returns to our store because of the quality of the service, the credit belongs to **us salespeople.**

STRATEGY   Test the alternatives

Check for a correct match of pronoun and noun by imagining a sentence in alternative versions without the noun.

SENTENCE   The teaching evaluation should be conducted by (*us? we?*) students, not by the faculty or administration.

VERSION 1
(INCORRECT)   The teaching evaluation should be conducted by **we** . . .

VERSION 2
(CORRECT)   The teaching evaluation should be conducted by **us** . . .

EDITED   The teaching evaluation should be conducted by **us** students, not by the faculty or administration.

              Us is the object of a preposition and takes the objective form (see 37b-1).

3 Be alert for subject complements

When you follow a form of the verb *be* (*is, am, are, was, were*) with a pronoun renaming the subject, you create a **subject complement** (see 35b-2). You choose the subjective form because you are restating the subject.

CORRECT   The last graduates to get jobs were Rebecca and **I.**

In speaking, the objective form is often acceptable. Moreover, in writing, the correct form may seem stilted and call for rewriting.

CONVERSATION   The new traffic reporter is **him.**

STILTED   The new traffic reporter is **he.**

REWRITTEN   **He** is the new traffic reporter.

4 Check appositives

When you rename a preceding noun or pronoun in an appositive phrase (see 35c-3), match the case of the word being renamed.

CORRECT   The two sisters, **she** and her twin, bought a small chain of dry cleaners as an investment.

STRATEGY   Test the alternatives

Imagine alternative versions in which you leave out the noun (or pronoun) that was renamed in the original sentence.

SENTENCE   The two children's book illustrators on the panel, (*she? her?*) and (*I? me?*), discussed all the questions asked by the audience.

VERSION 1
(INCORRECT)   **Her and me** discussed all the audience's questions.

VERSION 1
(CORRECT)   **She and I** discussed all the audience's questions.

EDITED   The two children's book illustrators on the panel, **she and I,** discussed all the questions asked by the audience.
The pronouns rename the subject, so the subjective forms are correct.

---

5 Be careful with comparisons using *than* or *as*

When using *than* or *as* followed by a pronoun, make sure the pronoun form you choose accurately signals the information left out. A pronoun in the subjective case acts as the subject of the implied statement; a pronoun in the objective case acts as the object.

SUBJECTIVE   Josie located the resources more quickly than **he** [did].

OBJECTIVE   Josie located the resources more quickly than [she located] **him.**

Even when your sentences employ correct pronouns, if your readers might find them ambiguous or confusing, rewrite.

POTENTIALLY
AMBIGUOUS

I like working with Aisha better than she.

READER'S REACTION: Does this mean you prefer to work with Aisha? Or that you like to work with Aisha better than someone else does?

REWRITTEN   She doesn't like working with Aisha as much as I do.

6 Be cautious when using *myself* and other reflexive pronouns

People sometimes use *myself, yourself,* and other **reflexive pronouns** (see 35a-2) inappropriately as sentence subjects or objects.

INCORRECT   The Nucor project led to some major disagreements between Stan and myself.

CORRECT   The Nucor project led to some major disagreements between Stan and **me.**

Exercise 2

A. Correct any errors in pronoun case.

EXAMPLE

     she

Denise and her joined the Disney film group in our class.
     ∧

1. The rest of us team members decided we should use recent animated movies as the subject of our project.
2. Because their parents own a video store, her brother and her brought in tapes of the movies we planned to study.
3. Bill and I decided to take notes on *Aladdin;* Pat and her chose to study *Beauty and the Beast.*
4. I thought the notes we took were more detailed and better than they.
5. Writing the final paper led to an argument between the other members and myself.

B. Working with a group, create a brief story involving three or four characters. Use at least five of the troublesome pronoun case patterns discussed in 37c, avoiding problems in their use.

37d *Who* and *whom*

Choose *who* and *whoever* when you use the pronouns as subjects; choose *whom* and *whomever* when you use them as objects (see 37b-1–3).

SUBJECT   The artist **who creates a painting or sculpture** ought to benefit from its sale.

OBJECT   The proceeds benefit **whomever** the artist designates.

You need to choose the appropriate form according to the role the pronoun plays *within the relative clause* (see 35c-5). Ignore the role the clause plays *within the sentence.*

INCORRECT   The fine must be paid by **whomever** holds the deed.
Although the whole clause is the object of the preposition *by,* within the clause the pronoun acts as a subject, not an object.

EDITED   The fine must be paid by **whoever** holds the deed.

If you are in doubt about either the use of *whom* or its appropriateness, try rewording to avoid making the choice.

EDITED   The person with the deed must pay the fine.

Use *who* at the beginning of a question when the pronoun is the sentence subject; use *whom* when the pronoun is an object. (See 37b-2–3.)

SUBJECT   **Who** has the reader's sympathy, Huck or Jim?

OBJECT   **Whom** can Cordelia trust for counsel about her dilemma?

CASE OF *WHO* AND *WHOEVER*

	SUBJECTIVE	OBJECTIVE	POSSESSIVE
FIRST, SECOND, AND THIRD PERSON	who whoever	whom whomever	whose whosever

---

Exercise 3

A. Correct any errors in pronoun case.

EXAMPLE

Whoever
~~Whomever~~ has taken an IQ test probably remembers the score.
            ∧

1. In the past, psychologists assumed that whomever scored well on IQ tests was likely to succeed at school and work.
2. Recent studies of IQ tests have produced evidence of them being unable to predict success.
3. A test of constructive thinking skill may tell more about your or mine ability to meet challenges.

4. Reporting on research conducted by he and two of his colleagues, Sternberg points out the importance of practical intelligence.
5. Others claim that qualities like self-confidence and optimism may by theirselves have as much to do with our mental abilities as IQ does.

B. Working with fellow writers, identify the pronouns in the following passage and correct any mistakes in case. Keep a record of those identifications and corrections you found most difficult, and be ready to explain why you found them difficult.

For we humans, yawning is a familiar activity. You and me probably yawn when we stretch, though not always. Boredom is also a likely cause for us yawning. People often think that no one yawns as much as them, but this is seldom true. We all yawn frequently during a day. We may even start yawning ourselves when we notice someone else whom is yawning.

Visit mycomplab.com for more resources and exercises on nouns and pronouns.

CHAPTER **38**

Agreement

What's wrong with the following sentence?

INCORRECT The Citizenship Institute and the Civic Program focuses on social justice.

> READER'S REACTION: I assumed the sentence was about two things—the Citizenship Institute and the Civic Program—until I came to the word *focuses*. I know *focuses* is *singular* in form, so it can't refer to more than one thing.

EDITED The Citizenship Institute and the Civic Program **focus** on social justice.

Readers expect you to help them understand how ideas in a sentence relate by making the parts of a sentence work grammatically—by showing **agreement** in number, person, and gender.

38a Subject-verb agreement (simple)

Within a sentence, a subject and a verb should agree in **number** (singular or plural) and **person** (first, second, or third). Keeping your sentences aligned helps convey consistent, clear meaning.

SINGULAR The **worker** tears down the platform.

PLURAL The **workers** tear down the platform.

FIRST PERSON **I** operate the air compressor.

We operate the air compressor.

SECOND PERSON **You** operate the air compressor.

THIRD PERSON **He** (**she**, **it**) operates the air compressor.

They operate the air compressor.

Check subjects, then verbs. To identify (and edit) **subject-verb agreement,** look for a subject, identify its *number* (singular or plural) and *person* (first, second, or third), then make sure the verb agrees with it in grammatical form. (For help in identifying number and person, see pages 564–565.)

553

INCORRECT	The clients is impatient.
CORRECT	The **clients** <u>are</u> impatient.
CORRECT	The **client** <u>is</u> impatient.

Subjects plural in both form and meaning need plural verbs, but choosing the right verb forms can be tricky.

Exercise 1

A. Fill in the blanks with verbs that agree in number and person with their subject.

EXAMPLE

Every day I ___*Walk*___ past the Valois Cafeteria.

1. The retired men in the neighborhood _____ lunch at the cafeteria.
2. The cafeteria's motto, "See What You Eat," _____ on the sign above the entrance.
3. The restaurant _____ run down.
4. Nonetheless, it _____ a clean and safe place.
5. A sociologist has studied the ways people of different races and cultures _____ with each other at the cafeteria.

B. Copy a paragraph from one of your papers or a book, but replace the verbs with blanks (as above). Exchange paragraphs with a partner and fill in the blanks in that paragraph. Work together to check your answers.

ESL ADVICE: SUBJECT-VERB AGREEMENT WITH *BE*, *HAVE*, AND *DO*

Some troublesome verbs change form according to person or tense.

- ***Be* verbs** (present and past)

  I **am/was.**   He/She/It **is/was.**   You/We/They **are/were.**

- **Helping verb *be*** (present progressive and past progressive tenses)

I	**am** talking.	I/He/She/It	**was talking.**
You/We/They	**are** talking.	We/You/They	**were talking.**
He/She/It	**is** talking.		

- ***Have* verbs** (present)

  I/You/We/They **have** a new home.   He/She/It **has** a new home.

- **Helping verb *have*** (present perfect and present perfect progressive tenses)

I/You/We/They	**have** lived here for years.	**have** been living here since May.
He/She/It	**has** lived here for years.	**has** been living here since May.

- ***Do*** or ***does*** **to show emphasis**

   I/You/We/They **do** want the job.   He/She/It   **does** want it.

- ***Doesn't*** or ***don't*** **to show the negative**

   I/You/We/They **don't** exercise.   He/She/It   **doesn't** exercise.

38b Subject-verb agreement (complex)

Certain kinds of words and sentence structures pose special problems for writers seeking to match subject and verb forms. Keeping all the "rules" in mind as you write can be distracting. The best solution is to remember the kinds of words and structures likely to cause problems, and then be ready, if necessary, to look up strategies for editing the problems.

- Plural words with singular meanings (for example, *politics* and *statistics*)
- Collective nouns (for example, *audience, crew, herd*)
- Subjects linked by *and, or,* and *nor* (compound and alternative subjects), sometimes accompanied by the word *each*
- Word groups coming between subject and verb (often beginning *as well as* or *along with*)
- Unusual word order and sentences beginning *There is* or *There are*
- Words like *all, everybody, none, who, which, that, is,* and *seems*

1 Watch for plural forms with singular meanings

Subjects plural in form (*shoes, filters, children, we, they*) generally need a plural verb—but not always.

Nouns with plural forms and singular meanings. Words like *politics, statistics, mathematics, linguistics, news, physics, mumps,* and *athletics* have the *-s* ending of plural nouns but are singular in meaning—and need singular verbs.

   Mathematics is an increasingly popular field of study.

STRATEGY   Apply the pronoun test

Choose a pronoun that can accurately replace the subject: *he, she,* or *it* (singular); *they* (plural). Read the sentence with the replacement and edit the verb to agree.

DRAFT   The **news** about the job market _____ surprisingly good.

                 PRONOUN TEST: Replace "The news" with "it" to read "It is surprisingly good."

EDITED   The **news** about the job market **is** surprisingly good.

The pronoun test is especially useful for two special kinds of subjects.

- **Measurements or numbers**
  A measurement or figure (even one ending in *-s*) may still be singular if it names a quantity or unit as a whole. When it refers to individual elements, however, treat it as plural.

  Four years is the amount of time Dr. Santiago spent studying the effects of stress.
  PRONOUN TEST: "**It** is the amount of time Dr. Santiago spent. . . ."

  One-third of the job trainees **leave** the program after three weeks.
  PRONOUN TEST: **They** [plural] leave the program individually.

- **Titles and names**
  When the title of a work or a company's name is the subject, choose a singular verb even if the name or title is plural.

  New West Logistics **pays** high wages and **has** excellent benefits.
  PRONOUN TEST: "**It** [the company] pays high wages. . . ."

  The White Roses **is** second on the best-seller list this month.
  PRONOUN TEST: "**It** [the book] is second. . . ."

2 Be alert for collective nouns

A **collective noun** is singular in form yet identifies a group of individuals (*audience, crew, tribe*). When a group acts as a single unit, choose a singular verb; when its members act individually, choose a plural verb.

The **staff** is hardworking and well trained.

The **staff** have earned the respect of our clients.

If a plural verb makes a sentence awkward, rewrite using a plural subject.

AWKWARD   The congregation react to Reverend Cullen's sermons in different ways.

REWRITTEN   **Members** of the congregation react to Reverend Cullen's sermons in different ways.

3 Check subjects linked by *and, or,* and *nor*

And creates a **compound subject;** *or* and *nor* create **alternative subjects.** As you edit, look for subjects containing these words.

Compound subjects joined by *and*. Because *and* makes the subject plural even if one or all of the individual parts are singular, you generally need to choose a plural verb.

> **Aaron and the rest of the staff** <u>were</u> responsible for the display.

> **Both rain and condensation** <u>cause</u> damage to the frame.

However, if the parts should be taken as a unit or if the parts designate a single person, thing, or idea, you need to choose a singular verb.

UNIT (SINGULAR)   **Ham and eggs** <u>is</u> still my favorite breakfast.

TWO ELEMENTS (PLURAL)   **Ham and eggs** <u>are</u> the main ingredients in this casserole.

ONE PERSON   **My teacher and friend** also <u>has</u> paintings in the show.

TWO PEOPLE   **My teacher and my friend** also <u>have</u> paintings in the show.

Depending on where you place the words *each* or *every*, you can give a compound subject a singular or plural meaning.

EACH BEFORE COMPOUND SUBJECT

compound subject   singular verb

Each <u>shift manager and unit manager</u> **reviews** the progress logs daily.

EACH AFTER COMPOUND SUBJECT

compound subject   plural verb

The <u>shift managers and unit managers</u> **each review** the progress logs daily.

Alternative subjects joined by *or*. When you use *or* or *nor* (*either . . . or*, *neither . . . nor*) to link alternative elements of a subject, make the verb agree with the closer part. Putting the plural element closer to the verb generally makes a sentence less awkward.

PLURAL CLOSE TO VERB   The auditor or **the staff accountants** <u>review</u> each report.

SINGULAR CLOSE TO VERB   False records or **late reporting** <u>weakens</u> the review process.

When parts of a subject differ in person, make the verb agree with the part of the subject closer to it.

AWKWARD   Either the other new residents or **I** <u>am</u> going to file a complaint.

REWRITTEN   Either the other new **residents** <u>are</u> going to file a complaint or I <u>am</u>.

4 Pay attention to separated subjects and verbs

When you insert words or even a whole phrase between the subject and verb of a sentence, you may be tempted to make the verb agree with one of the intervening words rather than the actual subject.

FAULTY AGREEMENT The new trolley system, with its expanded routes and lower fares, are specially popular with senior citizens.

The words *routes* and *fares* are not the subject of the sentence.

EDITED The new trolley **system,** with its expanded routes and lower

fares, **is** especially popular with senior citizens.

To identify possible problems with subject-verb agreement, be alert for phrases like *as well as, in addition to, together with,* and *along with,* or any other clusters of words between a subject and a verb.

UNEDITED A regular tune-up, *along with* frequent oil **changes,** prolong the life of your car.

To recognize faulty agreement, identify the real subject by imagining the sentence without the intervening phrase, then check that the subject and verb agree.

FAULTY AGREEMENT A regular **tune-up** . . . prolong the life of your car.

EDITED A regular **tune-up,** along with frequent oil changes, prolongs the life of your car.

If you mean *and,* use the word itself.

REWRITTEN A regular tune-up **and** frequent oil charges prolong the life of your car.

Exercise 2

A. Choose the word in parentheses that creates subject-verb agreement.

EXAMPLE

The mayor, as well as members of the city council, (has/have) been searching for better ways to fund the zoo.

1. Several large lizards and an eight-foot python (*makes/make*) up the main attractions in the reptile building of the tiny zoo.
2. The displays as well as the building itself (*appears/appear*) well designed and well maintained.
3. The animals each (*displays/display*) good health and behavior.
4. Neither the zoo's overseers nor its director (*is/are*) satisfied with the reptile building and the number of animals on display.

5. Of the zoo's visitors, three-quarters (*says/say*) that the collection should be enlarged.
6. This year the Cajun and Bluegrass Festival (*features/feature*) several new bands.
7. The group *Beausoleil* (*appears/appear*) twice on the program.
8. The Cajun food, along with more familiar snacks, (*does/do*) draw many people to the refreshment tent.
9. The festival staff (*wears/wear*) buttons saying "Ask me for help."
10. Both the dancing lessons and the crafts display (*occupies/occupy*) the same tent.

B. Make up five sentences like those above on any topic of your choice. Give them to a partner to complete, and work on those your partner has created.

ESL ADVICE: PAIRED CONJUNCTIONS AND SEPARATED SUBJECTS AND VERBS

Both . . . and always needs a plural verb.

Both the president and her <u>advisor are</u> in Tokyo this week.

Both the president and her <u>advisors are</u> in Tokyo this week.

Either . . . or, neither . . . nor, and *not only . . . but also* may take either a singular or plural verb. The subject closer to the verb determines the verb's form.

Either the president **or** her <u>advisor is</u> in Tokyo.

Neither the president nor her <u>advisors are</u> in Tokyo.

Check agreement when phrases or clauses come between a subject and a verb.

PHRASES

NOT APPROPRIATE   A person <u>with sensitive eyes</u> have to wear sunglasses.

CORRECT   A **person** <u>with sensitive eyes</u> **has** to wear sunglasses.

CLAUSES

NOT APPROPRIATE   A person <u>whose eyes are sensitive</u> have to wear sunglasses.

CORRECT   A **person** <u>whose eyes are sensitive</u> **has** to wear sunglasses.

5 Recognize unusual word order

When you invert typical word order to create emphasis or ask a question, make sure the verb still agrees with the subject.

	verb	subject

QUESTION   Are **patient satisfaction and increased efficiency** possible at the New Rockville Medical Clinic?

EMPHASIS   Following landslide victories comes **overconfidence** for many politicians.

6 Watch for *there is, there are*

There is/are, it is/are, and *here is/are* help you reverse the usual subject-verb sentence order so you can present the subject *after* the verb. As a result, you need to make the verb agree with the subject *following* it.

	verb	subject

SINGULAR   There **is opportunity** for people starting service industries.

PLURAL   There **are** many new **opportunities** for service industries.

Although it is strictly grammatical to use *there are* with a compound subject, you may use *there is* if the first part of this subject is singular.

There is **a guard and an alarm system** protecting the warehouse.

7 Pay attention to *is, appears, feels,* and other linking verbs

When you build a sentence around *is, appears, feels,* or another linking verb (see 35a-3), make sure the verb agrees with the subject. You may be tempted to make it agree with the noun or pronoun renaming the subject (the complement—see 35b-2), but edit carefully to avoid this problem.

	subject	verb	complement

INCORRECT   The chief **obstacle** to change are the **mayor and her political allies.**

EDITED   The chief **obstacle** to change is the mayor and her political allies.

8 *All, everybody, none; who, which, that*—using special subjects

All, everybody, none (and other indefinite pronouns) do not refer to specific ideas, people, or things. Most have clearly singular meanings and require singular verbs.

Someone <u>is</u> preparing the pamphlet.

Everybody <u>has</u> the right to appeal a zoning decision.

STRATEGY   **Ask "Can it be counted?"**

- Does the pronoun refer to something that *cannot be counted*? Choose singular.

    SINGULAR   **All** of the food <u>is</u> for the elderly lunch program.

    all = singular noun
    food = food in general (not countable)

- Does the pronoun refer to two or more elements of something that *can be counted*? Choose plural.

    PLURAL   **All** of the food supplies <u>are</u> for the elderly lunch program.
    all = plural noun
    supplies = many kinds of supplies (countables) such as flour, meat, and canned vegetables

Who, which, and *that* (relative pronouns—see 35a-2) do not have singular and plural forms, yet the words to which they refer (antecedents) generally do have separate singular and plural forms. Choose a verb for *who, which,* or *that* so that it matches the number of the antecedent.

    SINGULAR   He prefers **a program** that <u>awards</u> grants to individuals.

    PLURAL   I support **programs** that <u>distribute</u> funds to community groups.

Make a habit of noticing the phrases *one of* and *the only one of.* They can create agreement problems when they come before *who, which,* or *that.*

Dr. Gotari is **one** of those professors who <u>help</u> students succeed.
Who refers to the plural *professors;* consequently the verb, *help,* is plural. There are other professors like Dr. Gotari.

Dr. Gotari is **the only one** of the professors who <u>helps</u> students succeed.
Who refers to the singular *Dr. Gotari;* consequently, the verb, *helps,* is singular. Dr. Gotari is the only supportive instructor.

9 Pay special attention to titles and names

When you use the title of a work or the name of a company as a sentence subject, choose a singular verb even when the name or title is plural.

New West Consultants **pays** high wages and **offers** excellent benefits.
Think to yourself: The company pays . . .

The White Roses **is** second on the best-seller list.
Think to yourself: The book is . . .

"Tall ships" **is** the name given to the largest sailing ships.

Exercise 3

A. Give the correct present tense form of the infinitive verb indicated in parentheses.

EXAMPLE

has

None of the department heads (*to have*) the same administrative style.
∧

1. Frieda O'Connor is one of those managers who (*to lead*) by example.
2. All the other department heads (*to respect*) her leadership ability.
3. She knows each of the employees who (*to work*) in her department.
4. Each year, Campos Design Associates (*to give*) a plaque and a bonus to the employee with the highest rating on a peer survey.
5. The award, both the plaque and the money, (*to be*) given to Frieda almost every other year.

B. Working with another student, correct the errors that have been introduced into the following passage from Thomas R. McDonough's "Is Anyone Out There?" Not all the sentences contain an error, and some may have more than one. If correcting an error results in an awkward sentence, rewrite, but do not do so simply to avoid dealing with an agreement problem. When finished, compare your corrections with those of another pair of students, and explain the differences.

Each of the scientists involved in the search are pretty sure something is out there. A lot of numbers, some high and some low, is thrown around to express the probability of intelligent life somewhere else in the universe. Here is some figures that are middle-of-the-road. There is an estimated four hundred billion stars in the Milky Way. Planets may be fairly common, so you can figure one out of every ten of these stars have planets, which equals forty billions stars with planets. But how many of these places seems suitable for life? Neither too hot nor too cold is the conditions needed for life forms similar to our own. An atmosphere along with some water are also necessary. In our solar system only Earth qualifies, though Mars and Venus each comes close. Let us be conservative and estimate that only one of each solar system's planets fit the pattern. That's still forty billion habitable planets.

ESL ADVICE: WORDS AFFECTING SUBJECT-VERB AGREEMENT

QUANTIFIERS

A quantifier—like *each, one,* or *many*—indicates the amount or quantity of a subject.

expressions followed by a plural noun	+	a singular verb
Each of/Every one of/One of/None of		the ESL **students** lives on campus.

expressions followed by a plural noun	+	a plural verb
Several of/Many of/Both of		the **students** live off campus.

In some cases, the noun after the expressions determines the verb form.

expressions followed by either
a singular or a plural verb   noncount noun + singular verb
Some of/Most of/All of/A lot of the **produce** is fresh.

plural noun + plural verb
Some of/Most of/A lot of/All of the **vegetables** are fresh.

MUCH AND MOST (NOT MUCH OF OR MOST OF) WITH NONCOUNT AND PLURAL NOUNS

NONCOUNT NOUN **Much traffic** occurs during rush hour.

PLURAL NOUN **Most Americans** live in the cities or suburbs.

OTHER, OTHERS, AND ANOTHER AS PRONOUNS OR ADJECTIVES

PRONOUNS

Others + **plural verb:** adds points about a topic; there may be more points.

I enjoy Paris for many reasons. Some reasons are the beautiful architecture and gardens; **others are** the wonderful people, culture, and language.

The others (plural) + **plural verb;** *the other* (singular) + **singular verb:** adds the last point or points about the topic; there are no more.

Some hikers favor Craig's plan; the **others want** to **follow Tina's.**

ADJECTIVES

Another + **singular noun:** adds an idea; there may be more ideas.
Other + **plural noun:** adds more ideas; there may be more ideas.

One strength of our engineering team is our knowledge of the problem. **Another strength** is our experience. **Other strengths** include our communication skills, our teamwork, and our energy.

The other + **singular or plural noun:** adds the final point or points to be discussed.

Of the two most important sights to see in Paris, one is the Louvre Museum and **the other** is the Cathedral of Notre Dame.

One of the major sights in Paris is the Louvre Museum. **The other** major sights are the Eiffel Tower, the Champs-Elysees, the Cathedral of Notre Dame, and the Arc de Triomphe.

38c Pronoun-antecedent agreement

A pronoun takes its meaning from another word to which it refers (its **antecedent**).

antecedent   pronoun
Campers should treat **their** tents with a mildew-preventing spray.

pronoun   antecedent
Its preference for damp fabric makes **mildew** a major problem.

Matching pronoun and antecedent (either a noun or another pronoun) in *gender, person,* and *number* helps link the two by creating pronoun-antecedent agreement. **Number** refers to singular or plural forms. **Person** refers to the speaker or the subject spoken to/about. **Gender** refers to masculine, feminine, or neuter qualities generally associated with a noun or pronoun.

NUMBER, PERSON, AND GENDER

NUMBER

Number shows whether words are singular or plural in meaning.

SINGULAR   This **community** needs its own recreation center.

PLURAL   Local **communities** need to share their facilities.

SINGULAR WORDS
1. Nouns naming individual people, animals, ideas, and things
2. *I, you, he, she, it* (personal pronouns referring to individuals)
3. *Each, someone* (indefinite pronouns) or *who, which, that* (relative pronouns) when they refer to singular nouns or pronouns
4. Verbs in their singular forms (I *am*, she *is*; I *analyze*, she *analyzes*)

PLURAL WORDS
1. Nouns naming more than one person, animal, idea, or thing
2. *We, you, they* (personal pronouns referring to more than one individual)
3. *All, none* (indefinite pronouns) or *who, which, that* (relative pronouns) when they refer to plural nouns or pronouns
4. Verbs in their plural forms (we *are*, they *are*; we *analyze*, they *analyze*)

PERSON

Person indicates the speaker or the subject being spoken to or about

First person (speaker): *I, we*

I operate the compressor.　　　**We** operate the compressor.

Second person (spoken to): *you*

You operate the forklift.

Third person (spoken about): *he, she, it, they;* nouns naming things, people, animals, ideas

He/she/it operates the drill.　　　**They** operate the drill.

GENDER

Gender refers to the masculine, feminine, or neuter character generally attributed to a noun or pronoun.

MASCULINE/FEMININE

While the father printed the document on **his** computer, his daughter completed the financial report on **hers.**

NEUTER

Despite **its** income from sales, the company has yet to show a profit.

Masculine wording: *he,* nouns indicating males, and pronouns (*everyone, somebody, who, which, that*) when they refer to males

Feminine wording: *she,* nouns indicating females, and pronouns (*everyone, somebody, who, which, that*) when they refer to females

Neuter wording: *it,* nouns indicating places, things, and ideas, and pronouns (*everything, something, which, that*) when they refer to places, things, and ideas

1 Recognize antecedents joined by *and, or,* and *nor*

When you wish to make a pronoun refer to several things (Luis *and* Jennifer, for example, or the other students *and* I), the pronoun form you choose should depend, to a great extent, on the word that links the elements of the antecedent: *and, or,* or *nor.*

Identify the antecedent and the word used to link its parts: *and, or* (*either . . . or*), or *nor* (*neither . . . nor*)

- **And** (compound antecedent)
  Choose a plural pronoun (such as *they*) even if one or more of the antecedent's parts are singular.

  Luis and Jennifer said that the tests they ran on the ground-water were conclusive.

The other students and I admit that the tests we ran were not conclusive.

Exception: A compound antecedent can refer to a single person, thing, or idea. When it does, use a singular pronoun.

My colleague and coauthor is someone skilled at analyzing soil samples.

You can place *each* and *every* before a compound antecedent to single out the individual elements. When you do, use a singular pronoun.

Each of the soil and water samples is brought to the lab in **its** own sterile container.

Every soil and water sample brought to the lab undergoes **its** own three tests.

- **Or** and **Nor** (alternative antecedent)
  Choose a pronoun that agrees with the part of the antecedent that is closer to **it.**

  Neither the project manager **nor** the engineers submitted their accident reports on time.

Editing advice: If one part of a subject is singular and the other part plural, consider putting the plural element second or rewriting to avoid an awkward or confusing sentence.

CONFUSING   Either Jamal and Alan or **Richard** will include the sales projections in his report.

READER'S REACTION: Does this mean that Jamal and Alan may be putting things in Richard's report? Or does it mean that there will be two reports, Richard's plus Jamal and Alan's, one of which will contain the projections?

EDITED   Either Richard or **Jamal** and **Alan** will include the sales projections in their report.

REWRITTEN   Either Richard will include the sales projections in his report, or Jamal and Alan will include the projections in theirs.

2 Pay attention to *everyone, any, something* (indefinite pronouns) as antecedents

Many words like *somebody* and *each* (indefinite pronouns) are singular. Make sure that the pronouns you use to refer to them are also singular.

Somebody left his or her confidential data disks in the lunchroom.

Each member of the women's basketball team has her own training regimen.

Sometimes you may use an indefinite pronoun to mean *many* or *all*. In formal writing or speaking, your audience may prefer a plural antecedent.

INFORMAL   Everyone on the research team handed in their sections of the report.

EDITED   **Members** of the research team handed in <u>their</u> sections of the report.

To avoid sexist language (see 50c), many publishers and communities of writers accept a plural pronoun with a singular antecedent; when in doubt, however, use *both* a plural pronoun and a plural antecedent.

SEXIST   Everybody should include charts and slides in his sales talk.

INFORMAL/
SOMETIMES
ACCEPTABLE   **Everybody** should include charts and slides in <u>their</u> sales **talks.**

SAFEST   **All presenters** should include charts and slides in <u>their</u> sales talks.

3 Watch for collective nouns as antecedents

A noun such as *team, group, clan, audience, army,* or *tribe* (a collective noun) can act as a singular or a plural antecedent, depending on whether it refers to the group as a whole or to the members acting separately.

SINGULAR   The **subcommittee** submitted its revised report.

PLURAL   The **subcommittee** brought their different suggestions for a revised report to the meeting for discussion.

ESL ADVICE: DEMONSTRATIVE ADJECTIVES OR PRONOUNS

In addition to subjects and verbs, other elements in a sentence must agree. **Demonstrative adjectives** or **pronouns** (*this, that, these,* and *those*) must be either singular or plural, depending on the noun being modified. (See also 35a-2.)

INAPPROPRIATE   This agencies conduct outreach programs in local schools.

APPROPRIATE   **These agencies** conduct outreach programs in local schools.

INAPPROPRIATE   Those agency conducts outreach programs in local schools.

APPROPRIATE   **That agency** conducts outreach programs in local schools.

Exercise 4

A. Correct any errors in pronoun-antecedent agreement. You may need to change other parts of a sentence besides the pronoun or the antecedent. Each sentence can be corrected in more than one way.

EXAMPLE

~~A~~ *People* ~~person~~ who ~~likes~~ *like* camping should no longer feel they are unusual.

1. In any circle of friends, several are likely to say that he or she enjoys camping.
2. Everyone who goes camping needs to attend to their equipment.
3. All hikers should select good shoes and socks to protect your feet.
4. A camper or a hiker needs to choose their clothing carefully, paying attention to comfort and protection as well as style.
5. Both regular campers and occasional campers should be willing to put his or her money into well-designed tents, sleeping bags, and cooking equipment.
6. Each store or chain of stores in the retail camping industry meets the needs of their customers in a different way.
7. A store catering to campers and the hiker usually offers him or her a wide choice of equipment at different prices.
8. Eddie Bauer or L.L. Bean provides mail-order service to his customers.
9. A camping supplies and athletic equipment store may provide a narrower range of choices to their customers because of the need to stock sporting goods as well as camping equipment.
10. Nonetheless, any of these businesses should be able to provide you and their other customers with good, safe camping equipment.

B. Working with a group of students, compare your corrections. Make note of any differences, and decide which version (if any) is preferable and why.

Visit mycomplab.com for more resources and exercises on agreement.

CHAPTER **39**

Adjectives and Adverbs

If you use adjectives and adverbs improperly, your readers will be likely to notice the errors.

39a What adjectives and adverbs do

Adjectives and adverbs **modify** other words, adding to, qualifying, focusing, limiting, or extending their meaning.

FEATURES OF ADJECTIVES AND ADVERBS

ADJECTIVES

- Modify nouns and pronouns
- Answer the questions "How many?" "What kind?" "Which one (or ones)?" and "What size, color, or shape?"
- Include words like *blue, complicated, good,* and *frightening*
- Include words created by adding endings like *-able, -ical, -less, -ful,* and *-ous* to nouns or verbs (such as *controllable, sociological, seamless, careful, nervous*)

ADVERBS

- Modify verbs, adjectives, and other adverbs
- Modify phrases (*almost* beyond the building), clauses (*soon after* I added the last ingredients), and sentences (*Remarkably,* the mechanism was not damaged)
- Answer questions such as "When?" "Where?" "How?" "How often?" "Which direction?" "What degree?"
- Consist mostly of words ending in *-ly,* like *quickly, carefully,* and *smoothly*
- Include some words that do not end in *-ly,* such as *fast, very, well, quite,* and *late*

39b Avoiding confusion between adjectives and adverbs

Much of the time you will have little trouble deciding whether to use the adjective or adverb form of a word. Nonetheless, some common sentence patterns need special attention.

1 Figure out what a modifier does in a sentence

If you can't tell which modifier to use, analyze what the word will do in your sentence. (See "Features of Adjectives and Adverbs," p. 569.)

DRAFT   Write **careful** so the directions are clear.
                    Write *how*? It answers an adverb question.

EDITED   Write **carefully** so the directions are clear.

STRATEGY   Draw an arrow to the modified word

If this word acts as a noun or pronoun, modify it with an adjective; if it acts as a verb, adjective, or adverb, modify it with an adverb.

DRAFT   The rubber insulation underwent **remarkable quick** deterioration.
                    CORRECTION: *Remarkable* modifies *quick* (and answers the adverb question "How quick?"). *Quick* in turn modifies *deterioration* and answers the adjective question "What kind of deterioration?"

EDITED   The rubber insulation experienced **remarkably quick** deterioration.

2 Be alert for verbs like *look*, *feel*, *prove*, and *is*

Verbs such as *look*, *feel*, and *prove* can show both states of being (**linking verbs**) and activities (**action verbs**). The verb *is* always acts as a linking verb. Choose an adjective for a state of being or an adverb for an activity. (The adjective following a linking verb is called a **complement**; see 35b-2.)

SUBJECT	LINKING VERB	COMPLEMENT (ADJECTIVE)
The room	smelled	musty.
The procedure	proved	unreliable.

ADJECTIVE   The movement <u>grew</u> **rapid.** [The motion became quick.]

ADVERB   The movement <u>grew</u> **rapidly.** [The group got bigger, and its ideas spread rapidly.]

3 Pay special attention to *real/really, sure/surely, bad/badly,* and *good/well*

Some common uses of words like *bad/badly*—especially *sure* for *surely*—may be acceptable in informal speech or writing, but not in other settings.

CHOOSING BETWEEN *BAD/BADLY, GOOD/WELL, REAL/REALLY*, AND *SURE/SURELY*

BAD/BADLY

Use *bad* (adjective) with linking verbs such as *is, seems*, or *appears*.

I feel **bad** that our group isn't working well together.

Use *badly* (adverb) with action verbs.

The expensive new breathing apparatus works **badly.**

GOOD/WELL

Use *good* (adjective) with linking verbs.

The chef's new oil and garlic dressing tastes **good.** (not *well*)

Use *well* (adverb) with action verbs, unless it refers to health.

The new pump works **well.**

REAL/REALLY

Use *really* (adverb) to modify an adverb like *fast, efficient*, or *hot*

Lu Ming is **really** efficient.

SURE/SURELY

Use *surely* (adverb) to modify adjectives like *misleading, outdated*, or *courageous*.

This drawing of the mechanism is **surely** misleading.

Exercise 1

A. Rewrite each sentence to eliminate any problems in adjective or adverb use.

EXAMPLE

I thought the band sounded ~~badly~~, though many of my friends enjoyed the music.
 (bad,)

1. Many scholars have begun studying some real surprising subjects such as rock music.
2. At first, they had trouble persuading many people to take their work serious.
3. Now they produce careful researched studies of musicians like the Beatles as well as biographies of influential figures like Sid Vicious, Joey Ramone, and Courtney Love.
4. Remember, just because a piece of rock music sounds well does not mean that it is worth careful study.
5. At a time when the careers of many rock musicians are going bad, rock is doing quite good on campus.

B. Working in a group, decide which piece of advice in sections 39a and b applies to the particular problem in adjective or adverb use illustrated by each of the following sentences. Make a note of each relevant section of the discussion, and rewrite the sentence to eliminate the problem.

EXAMPLE

> *surprisingly*
> Some dead rock musicians have ~~surprising~~ large and active fan clubs.
>   ^

1. Over the past year, the number of books devoted to rock groups or rock stars has grown remarkable.
2. The writer Greil Marcus has produced several high-regarded books that praise Elvis Presley as an artist and person.
3. The title of one of Marcus's books, *Dead Elvis: A Chronicle of a Cultural Obsession,* may suggest that he views Elvis "sightings" and memorabilia as humorously.
4. Some of the events he describes are undoubted weird.
5. Nonetheless, he feels surely that Elvis and his music really deserve respect.

ESL ADVICE: ADJECTIVES IN A SERIES

Place two or more adjectives in a series in correct order.

DETERMINER	QUALITY	PHYSICAL DESCRIPTION	NATIONALITY	MATERIAL	QUALIFYING NOUN	MAIN NOUN
that	expensive	smooth black	German	fiberglass	racing	car
our	friendly	big old	English		hunting	dog
four	little	round white		plastic	Ping-Pong	balls
several	beautiful	young red	Japanese		maple	trees

39c Comparatives and superlatives: Correct forms

You can use most adjectives and adverbs in three forms: positive, comparative, and superlative. Choose the form appropriate for your purpose.

POSITIVE   This is a **quick** route.

                    Rainha drove **quickly** through the circuit.

COMPARATIVE   This is a **quicker** route.

                    Rainha drove **more quickly** through the circuit.

SUPERLATIVE   This is the **quickest** route.

                    Rainha drove **most quickly** through the circuit.

IRREGULAR COMPARATIVES AND SUPERLATIVES		
POSITIVE	COMPARATIVE	SUPERLATIVE
ADJECTIVES		
bad	worse	worst
good	better	best
a little	less	least
many	more	most
much	more	most
some	more	most
ADVERBS		
badly	worse	worst
well (satisfactorily)	better	best

1 Watch out for illogical comparatives

Some adjectives and adverbs cannot logically take comparative or superlative form. These include *unique, impossible, pregnant, infinite, dead, gone, perfectly,* and *entirely.*

ILLOGICAL   Gottleib's *Nightscape* is a **most unique** painting.

         READER'S REACTION: *Unique* means "one of a kind." How can a thing be *more* or *most* if it is the only one?

LOGICAL   Gottleib's *Nightscape* is a **unique** painting.

2 Look for imprecise use of comparatives

In conversation, people often use comparative forms loosely, knowing listeners will still grasp the intended meaning of a phrase like "She is my oldest daughter" even though the speaker has only two daughters. In writing, you need to be more precise, especially if you are presenting facts and figures.

INACCURATE   The survey covered four age groups: 20–29, 30–44, 45–59, and 60+. The people in the older group smoked the least.

         READER'S REACTION: Did the people in the older *groups* smoke the least or did the people in the *oldest* group smoke the least?

PRECISE   The survey covered four age groups: 20–29, 30–44, 45–59, and 60+. The people in the **oldest group** smoked the least.

3 Check for double comparatives

Most readers will not accept double comparatives (*-er* form or *more*) or superlatives (*-est* form or *most*).

INCORRECT	Jorge is the **most agilest** athlete on the team.
EDITED	Jorge is the **most agile** athlete on the team.

39d Avoiding double negatives

Informal speech may combine negative words such as *no, none, not, never, neither, hardly, scarcely, barely* and words like *haven't* and *don't* (formed with *n't*, the abbreviation for *not*). In writing, however, when more than one appears in a sentence (a **double negative**), readers may view the negatives as canceling each other out.

DOUBLE NEGATIVE	The highway department hasn't done nothing about the dangerous exit ramp.
	READER'S REACTION: If the department hasn't done nothing, maybe it *has* done *something*.
EDITED	The highway department hasn't done anything about the dangerous exit ramp.

Exercise 2

A. Revise the following sentences to eliminate any incorrect use of adjectives or adverbs.

EXAMPLE

I think the real difference between Necco Wafers and Skittles is that
Necco Wafers last ~~longest~~. *longer*

1. Of the three candy bars, Snickers, Three Musketeers, and Baby Ruth, which is older?
2. Which of the two kinds of gummy bears is more sweeter?
3. Broccoli-flavored candy had even badder sales than chocolate-dipped carrots.
4. Trying to create a candy bar that pleases everyone's taste is a most impossible task.
5. Some people can't hardly bear the taste of sour-flavored candy.

B. Working in a group, create two different correct versions of each of the following sentences. Then decide as a group which version of each sentence you prefer and why.

1. Surveys of customers' preferences are the most costliest method of market research.

2. They are not unlikely to be a waste of money.
3. One survey showed that consumers find a blend of hazelnuts and raspberries a most tastier combination.
4. The company wanted a more unique combination, however.
5. By adding marshmallows to the blend, the company eventually turned the bar into a most complete marketing success.

39d
adj/adv

Visit mycomplab.com for more resources and exercises on adjectives and adverbs.

PART 8

Sentence Problems

CHAPTER **40**

Sentence Fragments

SERIOUS
MISTAKE

A cluster of words punctuated as a sentence but lacking a crucial element that enables it to stand alone as a sentence is called a **sentence fragment.** If you omit essential elements such as a subject and a verb, you may confuse readers by leaving out crucial information.

PARTS MISSING   The insurance company responsible for the costs.
                READER'S REACTION: What did the company do?

EDITED   The insurance company **became** responsible for the costs.

Fragments that confuse readers or make them do unnecessary work are serious errors. On occasion, an **intentional fragment** (also called a **partial sentence,** see 40c) may effectively create emphasis or a change of pace. For the most part, however, readers will judge a piece of writing (and its writer) harshly when they encounter a fragment.

SERIOUS
MISTAKE

40a Sentence fragments: Recognizing

Some sentence fragments are easy to recognize, others less so. Watch for word groups falling into one of three general categories.

- Word groups lacking a subject or a verb
- Modifying word groups detached from sentences
- Troublesome constructions, such as verbal phrases

1 Look for a subject and a verb

If a word group punctuated as a sentence lacks either a subject or a complete verb, expressed or implied, it is a fragment (see 35b).

| STRATEGY   Ask questions

- Ask *Who* (or *what*) *does?* or *Who* (or *what*) *is?* If a word group does not answer "Who?" or "What?" then it *lacks a subject.*

    FRAGMENT   Yet also needs to establish a family counseling program.
                READER'S REACTION: Who (or what) needs to establish the program?

    EDITED   Yet **Community Health Clinic** also needs to establish a family counseling program.

If a word group does not answer "Does?" or "Is?" then it lacks a verb.

FRAGMENT   The new policy to determine scholarship size on the basis of grades rather than on the basis of need.

READER'S REACTION: This doesn't indicate anything about what the new policy *does* or *is*.

EDITED   The new policy **determines** scholarship size on the basis of grades rather than on the basis of need.

In trying to identify the "Who" in a passage, remember that in commands, the subject *you* is understood: "[**You**] Use the spectrometer to test for the unknown chemical ingredient." Some familiar sentence patterns also use a clearly implied verb: "John went to Stanford, Regina [**went**] to UCLA."

40a
frag

* **Can a word group be turned into a question that can be answered *yes* or *no*?** If it can be, it is a sentence.

WORD GROUP   The company providing repairs for our computers.

QUESTION: Does the company providing repairs for our computers?

CAUTION: Do not begin the questions with *is/are* or *has/have*. In doing so you may unintentionally provide a verb for the word group you are testing.

CONCLUSION   The word *providing* cannot act as the verb in its present form. The word group is a fragment lacking a verb.

EDITED   The company **is** providing repairs for our computers.

In checking for fragments, be careful not to mistake a verbal for a verb. Verbals include words like *testing, tested* (participles), *to test* (infinitives), and *testing* (gerunds). A verbal alone cannot act as the verb in a sentence. (See 40a-3.)

Exercise 1

Indicate which of the following word groups are sentence fragments and which are complete sentences. Correct sentence fragments by supplying any information necessary to make complete sentences.

EXAMPLE

    is
Our job to find a new head for nursing services.
      ∧

1. Several people applying for the job.
2. The job description in the newspaper asks for someone who is a good administrator and also an innovator.

3. Is able to convince fellow workers to develop their own innovative staffing plan and present it to the hospital administration.
4. Julie Kim, the prior head of nursing services responsible for so much turmoil during her time in the job and also so many improvements in the way nurses interact with patients and physicians.
5. A study suggesting that nursing administrators develop in-service programs to create improved morale among the professional staff and also better patient care.

SERIOUS
MISTAKE

40a
frag

2 Look for *although, because, that, since,* and other subordinating words

Look for a word group beginning with a subordinating conjunction such as *after, although, if, because,* or *since* (see 47c) or with a relative pronoun (*that, what, which,* or *who*). Then check whether this word group is attached to a main clause (see 35c)—a cluster of words that can stand on its own as a sentence. If the word group is unattached, then it is a fragment.

FRAGMENT   Many experts think that the SAT and the ACT are somewhat biased. **Although they also consider most criticism of the tests overblown.**

EDITED   Many experts think that the SAT and the ACT are somewhat biased yet also consider most criticism of the tests overblown.

Exercise 2

Indicate which of the following word groups are sentence fragments and which are complete sentences. Correct all the sentence fragments by supplying any information necessary to make complete sentences or attaching a fragment to an adjacent main clause.

EXAMPLE
Although many people think that afternoon sleepiness is caused by a heavy lunch, Researchers say this is not true.

1. People such as interns and truck drivers often feel drowsy. Even though they are aware of a need to stay awake and alert.
2. Having an afternoon nap can greatly increase your alertness. Whether or not you got enough sleep the night before.
3. Almost accidentally, researchers started becoming aware of the importance of naps while they were mapping cycles of drowsiness and alertness we each go through during an entire day.

4. Almost everyone experiences sleepiness and a decline in mental alertness during the afternoon. Because our internal clocks tell us it is time to nap and get out of the sun's strongest rays.

5. Despite a widespread belief that siestas and naps are cultural customs. They actually have a biological base.

---

3 Look for troublesome constructions

Watch for structures often incorrectly treated as complete sentences: *for example* fragments, split predicates, and disconnected verbal phrases.

40a
frag

For example fragments. Word groups beginning with phrases like *for example, such as,* and *for instance* are sometimes disconnected from sentences and mistakenly made to stand on their own. You can identify such fragments by looking for one of the phrases at the beginning of a word group and then checking whether the word group is either (1) attached to a main clause or (2) contains all the elements needed to act as a complete sentence.

FRAGMENT   We are trying to hire a new staff member who has skills that none of us possess. **For example, knowledge of computer-aided design.**

EDITED
(SEPARATE
SENTENCE)   We are trying to hire a new staff member who has skills that none of us possess. For example, **we need someone with** knowledge of computer-aided design.

Split predicate. A sentence can contain two or more complete verbs (for example, "I *unfastened* the seat and *removed* it."). Writers sometimes mistakenly split off the second (or last) element as a separate sentence, perhaps unconsciously assuming that the subject in the opening section is still present in the later one. To recognize a fragment of this type, look for a word group whose verb comes near the beginning (often following a word like *and, yet,* or *but*) and whose subject is nearby—but in another sentence.

FRAGMENT   Beethoven's work as a composer began in a style similar to that of Mozart. **But soon took on its own unique style.**

CORRECTED
(SUBJECT ADDED)   Beethoven's work as a composer began in a style similar to that of Mozart. But **his work** soon took on its own unique style.

Disconnected verbal phrases. To identify a disconnected verbal phrase, you need to be aware of the difference between verbs and verbals. Verbals are similar in form to verbs, but play different roles: participles (*analyzing, analyzed*), infinitives (*to analyze*), and gerunds (*analyzing*). (See 35c-4.) When combined with a helping verb (such as *is, has, can,* or *should*—see 35a-3), a verbal can be part of a complete verb (*was analyzing, should analyze*). Often, verbal phrases (verbal plus object and modifiers) are detached from adjacent sentences or related to them as modifiers.

SERIOUS
MISTAKE

**40a
frag**

FRAGMENT (PARTICIPIAL PHRASE)	**Frustrated by the meager offerings in journalism.** She decided to transfer to another university.
EDITED (ATTACHED TO MAIN CLAUSE)	Frustrated by the meager offerings in journalism, she decided to transfer to another university.
FRAGMENT (INFINITIVE PHRASE)	Divorcing parents should seek advice from a counselor. **To help lessen emotional problems for their children.**
EDITED (ATTACHED TO MAIN CLAUSE)	Divorcing parents should seek advice from a counselor to help lessen emotional problems for their children.
FRAGMENT (GERUND PHRASE)	**Introducing competing varieties of crabs into the same tank.** He did this in order to study aggression.
EDITED (REWRITTEN)	He **introduced** competing varieties of crabs into the same tank in order to study aggression.

Exercise 3

Identify the fragments in the following word groups. Then combine word groups to form a paragraph consisting of complete sentences. Feel free to alter wording or add information necessary to make the paragraph interesting and clear.

1. One store chain asks people to provide an address when cashing a check. And uses the information to create a mailing list for its advertising.

2. As a result, people who buy two pairs of pants and a few blouses are going to be receiving something in the mail each week for the next few months. For instance, a colorful flyer about home furnishings or automobile accessories.

3. Some people resent this marketing strategy. And complain to the post office or the company itself.

4. Lots of people consider advertising brochures fun to read. And a way to make shopping easier.

5. I think they are one of the many small irritations we encounter every day. Such as free samples of useless products and computerized telephone calls.

40b Sentence fragments: Editing

You can correct sentence fragments in four ways.

Supply the missing sentence element.

FRAGMENT
(LACKS VERB)

Several arguments favor enabling adopted children to contact their birth parents. **Among the most important the need to find out about any hereditary diseases.**

EDITED

Several arguments favor enabling adopted children to contact their birth parents. Among the most important is the need to find out about any hereditary diseases.

**40b
frag**

Attach the fragment to a nearby main clause and rewrite if necessary.

FRAGMENT
(SUBORDINATE
CLAUSE)

Modern trauma centers are equipped to give prompt care to heart attack victims. **Because rapid treatment can minimize damage to heart muscles.**

EDITED

Modern trauma centers are equipped to give prompt care to heart attack victims because rapid treatment can minimize damage to heart muscles.

Drop a subordinating word so the subordinate clause can act as a complete sentence (main clause).

FRAGMENT

Although several people argued strenuously against the motion. It passed by a considerable majority nonetheless.

EDITED

Several people argued strenuously against the motion. It passed by a considerable majority nonetheless.

Rewrite a passage to eliminate the fragment.

FRAGMENT

Some sports attract large numbers of participants in their fifties, sixties, and even seventies. **For example, tennis and bowling.**

EDITED

Some sports, **such as tennis and bowling,** attract large numbers of participants in their fifties, sixties, and even seventies.

Exercise 4

Correct any fragments in the following passages in two different ways.

EXAMPLE

Living and working in another country creates many challenges for families. For example, arranging for children's schooling.

Living and working in another country creates many challenges for families. Arranging for children's schooling is one such challenge.

1. The armed forces run elementary and secondary schools around the world. To provide education for dependents.
2. Japanese executives working in North America worry about educating their children in the Japanese language. And worry about whether they will fit into Japanese culture when they are adults.
3. Americans and Canadians working outside North America often look for schools conducted in English. To make sure their children will be prepared to attend college when the families return home.
4. The modern world makes many demands on parents. Who must spend considerable time and energy educating their children.
5. Whoever grows up with knowledge of two different cultures. I think that person will have some distinct advantages.
6. Realizing that musical tastes are probably changing. Many record companies have decided to explore new and newly rediscovered kinds of music.
7. Some formerly popular musical artists no longer have recording contracts. Their sales of CDs having dropped drastically.
8. In recent campus concerts, jazz artists have attracted large and enthusiastic audiences. Because of their innovative melodies and sounds.
9. The rhythm section of one group consists of a single unusual instrument. An electronic instrument making sounds like a drum but looking like a guitar.
10. Undecided about whether to sign new groups to long-term contracts. Some companies agree to produce and sell a single CD with an option for future recordings.

40c Partial sentences

In writing of all kinds, you are likely to encounter sentence fragments used correctly and effectively, called **partial sentences.** Used sparingly, partial sentences call attention to details, provide special emphasis for ideas, heighten contrasts, or create powerful images, as in the following passage.

Our house stood apart. A gaudy yellow in a row of white bungalows. We were the people with the noisy dog.   —RICHARD RODRIGUEZ, "Aria"

GUIDELINES FOR CREATING PARTIAL SENTENCES

1. Have a clear purpose, such as highlighting details and ideas or providing strong emphasis and contrast.
2. Make sure readers will recognize the purpose and not mistake the fragment for a detached modifier or word group missing an important element.
3. Take care that readers will be easily able to understand the fragment and any connections among it and other word groups.

Exercise 5

Working with a group, look through a magazine, identify ten sentence fragments, and list them. Share your sets of fragments. Identify those fragments you consider effective partial sentences. Explain how each effective fragment fits the criteria in 40c, and tell what purpose each one fulfills.

Visit mycomplab.com **for more resources and exercises on sentence fragments.**

40c
frag

CHAPTER **41**

Comma Splices and Fused Sentences

You can easily confuse and annoy readers if you inappropriately join two or more sentences using either a comma alone (comma splice) or no punctuation at all (fused sentence).

COMMA SPLICE   CBS was founded in 1928 by William S. Paley, his uncle and his father sold him a struggling radio network.

READER'S REACTION: At first I thought CBS had three founders: Paley, his uncle, and his father. Then I realized that the sentence probably means Paley founded CBS after buying the radio network from his relatives.

EDITED   CBS was founded in 1928 by William S. Paley **;** his uncle and his father sold him a struggling radio network.

FUSED SENTENCE   The city had only one swimming pool without an admission fee the pool was poorly maintained.

READER'S REACTION: I can't decide if the *single* swimming pool in the town is poorly maintained or if the only swimming pool that does not charge a fee is in bad shape.

EDITED   The city had only one swimming pool **,** **but** without an admission fee, the pool was poorly maintained.

 SERIOUS MISTAKE **41a** Comma splices and fused sentences: Recognizing

When you link two sentences *by a comma alone*, you create a **comma splice** (see also 35c).

COMMA SPLICE   Eight inches of rain fell in twenty-four hours, all the creeks swelled rapidly.

READER'S REACTION: I had to read the sentence twice because at first I couldn't tell where one part ended and the next began.

EDITED   Eight inches of rain fell in twenty-four hours **,** **and** all the creeks swelled rapidly.

When you provide *neither a punctuation mark nor a connecting word* to show where one main (independent) clause ends and the next begins, you create a **fused sentence** (often called a **run-on sentence**).

FUSED SENTENCE   That night the river overflowed its banks and spread over the lowlands thousands of people were left homeless by the time the waters receded.

> READER'S REACTION: When I first read that the river "spread over the lowlands thousands of people," I imagined a mass of people being pushed over the land.

EDITED   That night the river overflowed its banks and spread over the lowlands **; as a result ,** thousands of people were left homeless by the time the waters receded.

SERIOUS MISTAKE

41a
cs/fs

STRATEGY   Identify and repair comma splices and fused sentences

- Look for sentences with more than one word group that could stand on its own as a sentence.

COMMA SPLICE   In a typical Navajo family, the husband serves as trustee /, the mother and her children are the real owners of the family's property.

> WRITER'S REACTION: When I drew a line to separate the two word groups that could stand alone, I noticed I had created a comma splice by joining them with only a comma.

FUSED   The engineering and social work programs get the most public attention / the medical technology and marketing programs get the largest enrollments.

> WRITER'S REACTION: Putting a line between the word groups that could be sentences on their own helped me see how the lack of any punctuation between them makes the sentence hard to read.

- Ask, "How many statements are there in this sentence?" A fused sentence is not a single unit but two (or more) units whose relationship is not clearly signaled to readers.
- Notice sentence patterns that may lead to comma splices and fused sentences.

- **Sentences (main clauses) with the same subject**

COMMA SPLICE   **The ice cream cake** had begun to melt, **it** was dripping onto Grandmother's lace tablecloth.

EDITED   The ice cream cake had begun to melt **,** and it was dripping onto Grandmother's lace tablecloth.

- **One sentence (main clause) illustrated by another**

FUSED SENTENCE   Children with Down syndrome feel the same emotions as the rest of us they get sad, puzzled, and playful.

EDITED   Children with Down syndrome feel the same emotions as the rest of us **;** they get sad, puzzled, and playful.

- **Sentences with contrasting or related ideas**

FUSED SENTENCE   Health costs are rising rapidly solutions to the problem are not clear.

EDITED   Health costs are rising rapidly **;** **MOREOVER,** solutions to the problem are not clear.

Exercise 1

A. First, use the strategies discussed in 41a to identify the comma splices in the following passage.

The subarctic region provides little variety in food, therefore, Eskimo diet includes large quantities of meat such as seal and caribou. The cold weather and the available materials determine dressing habits, a loose shirt with a hood, trousers, stockings, and mittens (often made of caribou skin and fur) are a common outfit for men, women, and children alike. Social affairs are important in Eskimo communities, favorite gatherings include carnivals, Christmas parties, and feasts of game brought in by hunters. Children in Eskimo communities begin school at the age of five or six, most quit by the time they are twelve in order to go to work. Boys usually go hunting with their fathers, girls learn to sew and cook.

Next, draw a double vertical line between each of the independent (main) clauses making up the following fused sentences.

EXAMPLE

Casinos used to operate legally in only a few states // they are now springing up all over the country as states make casino gambling legitimate.

1. The gaming industry is one of the fastest-growing industries in some areas it is a major employer.
2. Legalized gambling takes many forms bingo, lotteries, casinos, and video games are run under government supervision in many states.
3. State lotteries are popular they may also encourage people to gamble unwisely.
4. The economic and law enforcement objections to legalized gambling get the most public attention the moral and psychological objections may deserve the most attention.
5. Legalized gambling now goes beyond people in casinos betting on roulette or sports events it includes people playing bingo at a charity event or playing video poker in a family restaurant.

B. Working in a group, decide which, if any, of the sentences in the first passage in Exercise 1A follow sentence patterns likely to lead to comma splices or fused sentences, and identify the patterns.

41b Comma splices and fused sentences: Editing

Here are six strategies for correcting comma splices and fused sentences. As you revise, choose a strategy that brings your ideas into sharper perspective, creates emphasis, and highlights relationships.

1 Create separate sentences

When the ideas in main clauses are loosely related, you can generally express them best in separate sentences.

COMMA SPLICE AND FUSED SENTENCE	Costa Rica's political life has been relatively free of damaging conflict, the same cannot be said of its neighbors El Salvador and Nicaragua, in particular, have long histories of civil unrest.
EDITED	Costa Rica's political life has been relatively free of damaging conflict● The same cannot be said of its neighbors● El Salvador and Nicaragua, in particular, have long histories of civil unrest.

2 Join main clauses with a comma plus a coordinating conjunction

When main clauses convey ideas or information of approximately equal importance, consider linking the clauses with a comma plus a coordinating conjunction (*and, but, or, for, nor, so,* or *yet*) marking their relationship.

FUSED SENTENCE	Schizophrenia is a mental illness its causes may be physical.
EDITED	Schizophrenia is a mental illness● **yet** its causes may be physical.

3 Join main clauses with a semicolon

You can use a semicolon to emphasize the similar importance of two main clauses.

COMMA SPLICE	During flight an airplane tends to drift up or down, left or right because of air turbulence. An autopilot is a device that detects and corrects drift, the system senses changes in the aircraft's motion and reacts accordingly.
EDITED	During flight an airplane tends to drift up or down, left or right because of air turbulence. An autopilot is a device that detects and corrects drift● the system senses changes in the aircraft's motion and reacts accordingly.

4 Join main clauses with a semicolon plus a conjunctive adverb or transitional expression

However, nonetheless, therefore, consequently, moreover, thus, and similar words (conjunctive adverbs) specify relationships between word groups. Transitional expressions such as *for example, in contrast,* and *in addition* have similar purposes. Use them following a semicolon.

SERIOUS
MISTAKE

41b
cs/fs

FUSED SENTENCE	Cattle can reach marketable size within months lobsters must grow for six to eight years.
EDITED	Cattle can reach marketable size within months **;** **in contrast,** lobsters must grow for an average of six to eight years.

Words like *however, nonetheless,* and *thus* and expressions like *for example* and *on the other hand* can appear *within* a second main clause as well as at the beginning. Wherever they appear, the words must be set off with a comma or commas and the clauses themselves joined by a semicolon.

AT BEGINNING	The Great Lakes once supported a thriving fishing industry; **however,** in recent decades pollution has reduced the catch.
IN MIDDLE	The Great Lakes once supported a thriving fishing industry; in recent decades, **however,** pollution has reduced the catch.
AT END	The Great Lakes once supported a thriving fishing industry; in recent years pollution has reduced the catch, **however.**

5 Subordinate one of the clauses

Subordinators such as *although, while, when, because, since,* and *unless* and relative pronouns such as *who, which,* and *that* enable you to specify a wide range of relationships (see 47c).

COMMA SPLICE	Margaret Atwood is best known for her novels, her essays and poems are also worth reading.
EDITED	**Although** Margaret Atwood is best known for her novels, her essays and poems are also worth reading.

6 Join the clauses with a colon

When a clause summarizes, illustrates, or restates a preceding clause, you can join the two with a colon (see 52b).

FUSED SENTENCE	Foreign study calls for extensive language preparation vaccinations and a passport are not enough.
EDITED	Foreign study calls for extensive language preparation **:** vaccinations and a passport are not enough.

Exercise 2

A. Identify and edit in *two* ways each of the following comma splices and fused sentences. Use the methods of revision indicated in brackets after each sentence.

EXAMPLE
Children often fight among themselves, these conflicts pose many challenges for parents. [comma plus coordinating conjunction; semicolon]

41b
cs/fs

Children often fight among themselves, and these conflicts pose many challenges for parents.

Children often fight among themselves; these conflicts pose many challenges for parents.

1. Some parents refuse to become involved in their children's squabbles, they fear the children will resent the interference. [subordination; semicolon]
2. Siblings have special reasons to fight competing for space and playthings or for attention from a parent can turn playmates into rivals. [colon; semicolon plus transitional phrase]
3. Sibling fights offer an opportunity for children to become sensitive to the feelings of others, the arguments pose dangers as well. [comma plus coordinating conjunction; semicolon plus conjunctive adverb]
4. Bickering is common and normal excessive fighting can be a sign of more serious trouble. [semicolon plus conjunctive adverb; separate sentences]
5. By adolescence, most children have worked out compatible relationships with their siblings, they may still occasionally argue. [subordination; comma plus coordinating conjunction]

B. Working with a group, edit each of the following sentences in two ways, using strategies discussed in 41b. You may need to make changes in wording or punctuation.

1. One group claims that cattle raising is hard on the environment another group argues that raising wheat and other cereal grains causes water pollution and destroys topsoil.
2. In Central Florida, cattle waste has polluted Lake Okeechobee runoff from fertilizer has greatly increased the growth of algae in the lake.
3. The waters of Long Island's south shore are also polluted the main culprit is lawn fertilizer.
4. In my state, pesticides from potato farming have polluted the groundwater pig and chicken farming have caused problems.

5. Our large population makes a massive farming industry necessary we are going to have to deal with the problems caused by large-scale farming and livestock raising.

41b
cs/fs

Visit mycomplab.com for more resources and exercises on comma splices and fused sentences.

CHAPTER **42**

Pronoun Reference

Words like *they, it, she, who,* and *which* (pronouns) help you make sentences less repetitive and easier to understand, while linking ideas. For this linking process (called **pronoun reference**) to work, readers must recognize the word to which a pronoun refers, known as its **antecedent.** When the relationship is not clear, readers may be confused.

CONFUSING   Much of my life with the circus consisted of leading the elephants from their cages and hosing **them** down.

                READER'S REACTION: What got hosed down? the elephants? the cages? both?

CLEAR   Much of my life with the circus consisted of hosing the **elephants** down after leading **them** from **their** cages.

42a Unclear pronoun reference: Recognizing and editing

As long as your readers can clearly identify the word or words acting as a single antecedent, pronoun reference will help you tie statements together.

Calvin Klein, Liz Claiborne, and **Donna Karan** started out as clothing designers. **They** now head major corporations bearing their names.

1 Watch for pronouns with several possible antecedents

Look for passages containing a pronoun and two or more words or word groups to which it might *possibly* refer. If your readers cannot easily identify the appropriate antecedent, they will have trouble understanding the meaning.

STRATEGY   Correct ambiguous references

AMBIGUOUS   Detaching the measuring probe from the glass cylinder is a
REFERENCE   delicate job because **it** breaks easily.

          READER'S REACTION: Which is especially fragile, the probe or the cylinder?

1. **Replace** the troublesome pronoun with a noun.

   Detaching the measuring probe from the glass cylinder is a delicate job because **the probe** breaks easily.

2. **Reword** the sentence.

   Because the measuring probe breaks easily, detaching it from the glass cylinder is a delicate job.

SERIOUS
MISTAKE

42a
pr ref

In addition, watch for pronouns that can refer to each of two or more subjects in earlier sentences.

AMBIGUOUS
REFERENCE

Robespierre and Danton disagreed over the path the French Revolution should take. **He** was convinced that the Revolution was endangered by its internal enemies.

EDITED
(ADD NOUNS)

Robespierre and Danton disagreed over the path the French Revolution should take. **Robespierre** was convinced that the Revolution was endangered by its internal enemies.

When you use *said* or *told* to report in a general way what someone has said (**indirect quotation**), you may sometimes create confusion.

AMBIGUOUS

When the project was completed, Jennifer's supervisor said **she** needed a day off because she had been working so hard.

READER'S REACTION: Who needs the time off, Jennifer or her supervisor?

Edit this problem by (1) reporting the person's words exactly (**direct quotation**) or (2) rewriting with nouns rather than pronouns.

DIRECT
QUOTATION

When the project was completed, Jennifer's supervisor said, "**You** need a day off because **you** have been working so hard."

REWRITTEN
WITH NOUN

When the project was completed, her supervisor said that **Jennifer** needed a day off because **she** had been working so hard.

2 Pay attention to pronouns widely separated from their antecedents

When you place a pronoun at a distance from its antecedent, your readers may have a hard time recognizing the connection—even though no other possible referent comes between them.

REMOTE REFERENCE

James Van Allen designed an instrument that the first American space satellite used to detect what are now known to be two doughnut-shaped rings of high-energy particles extending from between several hundred to fifty thousand kilometers above the earth. The belts were eventually named for **him.**

To edit for this problem, either bring the pronoun closer to its antecedent or rename the noun or pronoun to which it refers.

42a
pr ref

EDITED (RENAMED)

James Van Allen designed an instrument that the first American space satellite used to detect what are now known to be two doughnut-shaped rings of high-energy particles extending from between several hundred to fifty thousand kilometers above the earth. They were eventually named **the Van Allen belts after the man instrumental in their discovery.**

Exercise 1

A. Rewrite each sentence to create clear pronoun reference.

EXAMPLE

Someone needs to pick up the weekend shipment ~~at the airport~~ that

at the airport
may arrive late Saturday night.
                    ʌ

1. Both Carlo and Andy agree that he will be responsible for getting the cartons of replacement parts from the air terminal.
2. The accountant has told his client that he will be answerable for any problems with billing.
3. Airfreight offers weekend shipment and is cheaper, which means that work doesn't have to stop on Monday morning while they wait for delivery of the replacement parts.
4. The van used to pick up shipments is the old one the company's owner purchased right after her divorce which is covered with rust.
5. The sales projections used to order supplies are often inaccurate because the sales manager calculates them using a formula on a spreadsheet that is overly optimistic.

B. Working with a group of fellow students, compare the choices each of you made in editing the sentences.

3 Create clear reference chains

You can guide readers through a passage using a chain of pronouns to connect sentences. A **reference chain** begins with an antecedent stating the topic linked to pronouns (or nouns) later in the passage.

1. State the antecedent clearly in the opening sentence.
2. Link the antecedent to pronouns in sentences that follow.
3. Make sure other possible antecedents do not interrupt the chain.
4. Do not interrupt the chain and then try to pick it up later.
5. Call attention to the links by giving the pronouns prominent positions (usually beginning sentences); vary their positions only slightly.

UNCLEAR

Sand paintings were a remarkable form of Pueblo art. An artist would sprinkle dried sand of different colors, ground flower petals, corn pollen, and similar materials onto the floor to create **them.** The sun, moon, and stars as well as animals and objects linked to the spirits were represented in the figures **they** contained. **Their** purpose was to encourage the spirits to send good fortune to humans.

Because the pronouns *them* and *they* are buried at the ends of sentences in the middle of the paragraph, readers can easily lose sight of the paragraph's topic, sand paintings.

EDITED TO CREATE A REFERENCE CHAIN

Sand paintings were a remarkable form of Pueblo art. To create **them,** an artist would sprinkle dried sand of different colors, ground flower petals, corn pollen, and similar materials onto the floor. **They** contained figures representing the sun, moon, and stars as well as animals and objects linked to the spirits. **Their** purpose was to encourage the spirits to send good fortune to humans.

Exercise 2

A. Revise the following sentences so that they form a reference chain giving appropriate emphasis to information provided in the passage. You should emphasize some ideas and details more than others.

When it comes to reading material, Americans have some clear favorites. In terms of circulation, the top five newspapers in the country are *The Wall Street Journal*, *USA Today*, the *New York Daily News*, the *Los Angeles Times*, and the *New York Times*. Sales of softbound books far outnumber sales of hardbound books. Our favorite subject areas for books are medicine, history, fiction, sociology and economics, religion, and technology. The top three magazines in terms of revenue are *Time*, *Sports Illustrated*, and *People*. More people subscribe to *Modern Maturity* and the *AARP Bulletin* than to any other magazines, including *Reader's Digest*, which is number three on the subscription list. *1,001 Home Ideas* and *The Elks Maga-zine* have larger paid circulations than *Vogue, Rolling Stone,* and *Mademoiselle.*

B. Working with a group of writers, share your versions of the pas-sage in Exercise 2A. Choose two versions that give the information dif-ferent emphases. Identify the ways each writer has created a reference chain, and indicate which ideas and details have been highlighted and which have been moved to the background.

42b
pr ref

SERIOUS
MISTAKE

42b Nonspecific pronoun reference: Recognizing and editing

Specific pronoun reference points out for readers the precise rela-tionships among statements. When pronouns refer to antecedents that are implied rather than stated, however, or when pronouns refer too broadly to a preceding passage, readers become confused.

1 Use *it, which, this,* and *that* with care

Used carefully, the words *it, which, this,* and *that* can help you refer ef-fectively to an entire idea, but **overly broad reference** can easily confuse read-ers by failing to make clear the *specific* antecedent of *it, which, that,* or *this.*

OVERLY BROAD REFERENCE

Redfish have been subjected to overfishing, to oil pollution, and to the destruction of their habitat. **That** has led to a recent and rapid decline in the redfish population.

READER'S REACTION: Does *that* refer to the destruction of habitat, to oil pollution, to overfishing, or to some combination?

STRATEGY   Check the reference for *it, which, this,* and *that*

Look for the words *it, which, this,* and *that.* See if you have provided a specific word or group of words to which the pronoun clearly refers. If not, edit by specifying, replacing, or rewording.

- **Specify.** Right after *this, that,* or another troublesome word, add a word or phrase stating the pronoun's referent.

EDITED (SPECIFIES)

Redfish have been subjected to overfishing, to oil pollution, and to the destruction of their habitat. That **combination** has led to a recent and rapid decline in the redfish population.

EDITED (EXPLAINS)

Redfish have been subjected to overfishing, to oil pollution, and to the destruction of their habitat. That **serious set of challenges** has led to a recent and rapid decline in the redfish population.

- **Replace.** Drop the pronoun; use a noun or noun phrase in its place.

VAGUE   One test conducted by the Mars lander discovered some evidence of life on Mars, but the other uncovered no evidence whatsoever. This led many scientists to conclude that there is no life on the planet.

**42b
pr ref**

REPLACED   One test conducted by the Mars lander discovered some evidence of life on Mars, but the other uncovered no evidence whatsoever. **The reliability of the second test** led many scientists to conclude that there is no life on the planet.

- **Reword.** Rewrite so that the pronoun is no longer needed.

REWORDED   One test conducted by the Mars lander discovered some evidence of life on Mars, but the second and more reliable test uncovered no evidence whatsoever, leading many scientists to conclude there is no life on the planet.

2 Look for *it* used in more than one sense

You may confuse readers if you use *it* in more than one sense in a sentence or short passage.

CONFUSING   When I was young, I always found **it** surprising that my father would come home from a hard day at his job and go out to the garden to work in **it,** even when **it** was raining.

EDITED   When I was young, I was always surprised when my father came home from a hard day at his job and went out to work in the garden, even when **it** was raining.

3 Watch for antecedents that are implied rather than stated

Often, writers have an antecedent in mind but fail to communicate it to readers.

IMPLIED   In the West, **they** often prefer Japanese cars.
    READER'S REACTION: I am guessing that *they* means "people in general." But it could mean rich people, people under forty, or some other group.

By stating an antecedent directly, you eliminate both guessing and possible misunderstanding.

EDITED   In the West, **people under forty** prefer Japanese cars.

You **without an antecedent.** When you intend to address the reader directly ("you, the reader"), *you* is acceptable in most writing.

When *you* refers indefinitely to experiences, situations, and people in general, it often leads to confusing and wordy sentences.

MISLEADING   In Brazil, you pay less for an alcohol-powered car than for a gasoline-powered one.

READER'S REACTION: Who is *you*? I'm not likely to be buying a car in Brazil.

EDITED   In Brazil, alcohol-powered cars cost less than gasoline-powered ones.

EDITED   In Brazil, consumers pay less for an alcohol-powered car than for a gasoline-powered one.

SERIOUS MISTAKE

42b
pr ref

Possessive as antecedent. Remember to pair possessive nouns with possessive pronouns: *Kristen's . . . hers*.

UNCLEAR   The **company's** success with a well-known jazz fusion artist led **it** to contracts with other musicians.

EDITED   The **company's** success with a well-known jazz fusion artist led to **its** contracts with other musicians.

When readers encounter the following pattern in academic writing, they will consider it inappropriate because the pronoun refers to the possessive form of a noun. (This pattern is more acceptable in informal writing.)

INAPPROPRIATE   In William Faulkner's *The Sound and the Fury*, he begins the story from the point of view of a mentally disabled person.

William Faulkner, not *William Faulkner's*, should be the antecedent of *he*.

EDITED   In *The Sound and the Fury*, William Faulkner begins the story from the point of view of a mentally disabled person.

Modifier mistakenly treated as antecedent. A modifier (like *experimental*) may *suggest* an antecedent (like *experiment*) without directly stating it. If you mistakenly rely on an implied antecedent of this sort, you force readers to guess at your intentions.

CONFUSING   A product's success may depend on how many demographic studies were conducted. As a result, people trained in it often get good jobs in major corporations.

READER'S REACTION: What field do the people get training in? *demographic*? That's not the name of a field.

EDITED   A product's success may depend on how many demographic studies were conducted. As a result, people trained in **demography** often get good jobs in major corporations.

Antecedent implied by another word. If you make a pronoun refer to a word that is not actually in a sentence but merely implied by some other word, your sentence is likely to be clumsy or hard to understand.

CLUMSY   Growing up in the Southwest, Alice dreamed of studying oceanography, though she had never seen **one.**

READER'S REACTION: One what? An oceanographer? Someone from the Southwest? A dream? An ocean?

EDITED   Growing up in the Southwest, Alice dreamed of studying oceanography, though she had never seen **an ocean.**

**42c
pr ref**

Exercise 3

A. Revise each sentence to eliminate vague pronoun reference and provide specific antecedents.

EXAMPLE

The committee's report

~~In the committee's report it~~ points out that students generally benefit from participating in a music program.

(*or* In its report, the committee points out . . .)

1. Many people study a musical instrument in high school though few students intend to become one.
2. At most secondary schools they offer a variety of music programs.
3. Last February, the town began investigating the quality of its high school band program, but it has not yet been completed.
4. In many regional high schools in the West, the band's large size mirrors the role it plays in the school's social life.
5. In the Northwest you quickly get used to marching and playing in the rain.

B. Compare your revised versions of the sentences with those of other writers. As a group, choose the best version of each sentence and state the reasons for your choice.

42c Matching *who, which,* and *that* to antecedents

Some readers will expect you to use *which* or *who* with **nonrestrictive clauses** and *that, which,* or *who* with **restrictive clauses** (see 51c for discussion of these two kinds of modifiers). Other readers may pay little attention to the distinction. In formal writing, however, you should pay attention to the difference.

RESTRICTIVE (ESSENTIAL, LIMITS MEANING)
Drugs **that** limit tissue rejection are necessary for the survival of transplant recipients.

NONRESTRICTIVE (NONESSENTIAL)
The license, **which** will cost you thirty dollars, permits you to fish anywhere in the state for seven days.

Exercise 4

A. Revise each sentence to correct inappropriate pronoun references. Indicate which sentences, if any, contain appropriate pronoun reference.

42c
pr ref

EXAMPLE

Many scholars ~~which~~ are interested in Buddhism have begun to study Tibetan religious practices.

1. The gathering was addressed by the Dalai Lama, a man which is one of the spiritual leaders of Tibetan Buddhism.
2. Tibetan Buddhism is characterized by large monastic organizations who practice yoga and other spiritual and intellectual rituals.
3. It is also true that this form of Buddhism retains features that it inherited from the folk religions of Tibet.
4. Up until the recent Chinese invasion, that occurred in 1959, Tibetan life was dominated by religious practices.
5. Although Lamaism has its greatest influence in Tibet and in countries who are nearby, such as Nepal and Mongolia, it is beginning to spread its influence in the West, including North America.

B. At a library, find a magazine with somewhat complicated, information-filled articles. Choose an article that interests you, and identify several paragraphs in which the author uses some of the pronoun reference patterns discussed in this chapter. Make copies of these paragraphs to share with a group of classmates. As a group, identify each of the pronoun reference strategies and decide why the author used each one.

Visit mycomplab.com for more resources and exercises on pronoun reference.

CHAPTER **43**

Misplaced, Dangling, and Disruptive Modifiers

The relationship between a modifier and the word(s) it modifies needs to be clear to readers. If it is unclear, it will lead to questions and confusion.

MISPLACED MODIFIER	When I was at the store I only looked at the DVD player.
	READER'S REACTION: Do you mean you just looked and didn't try the DVD player out? You didn't have time to look at other equipment? You were the only person who looked at the DVD player?
DANGLING MODIFIER	Rushing to get to the post office before it closed, my bicycle nearly hit an unwary young woman.
	READER'S REACTION: Who was rushing to the post office—I, the bicycle, or the young woman?
DISRUPTIVE MODIFIER	The chief accountant, **even though her assistant first uncovered evidence that the company president had been embezzling funds,** assumed the responsibility of reporting the crime.
	READER'S REACTION: So many ideas here distract me from the main point about the accountant.

A **misplaced modifier** is not placed closely enough to the word(s) it is intended to modify and appears to modify something else. A **dangling modifier** appears in a sentence that contains no word or phrase to which the modifier can be reasonably linked. A **disruptive modifier** separates closely connected elements such as a subject and a verb, making a sentence difficult to read and understand.

Careful editing can make clear the relationship between a modifier and the word(s) being modified.

EDITED	When I was at the store I looked **only at the DVD player.**
EDITED	Rushing to get to the post office before it closed, **I** nearly hit an unwary young woman while riding my bicycle.
EDITED	Even though her assistant first uncovered evidence that the company president had been embezzling funds, **the chief accountant** assumed the responsibility of reporting the crime.

43a Misplaced modifiers: Recognizing and editing

Misplaced modifiers fail to modify the word(s) you intend and instead appear to modify some other word or group of words.

1 Pay attention to a modifier's location

As you edit, check that modifiers come close enough to the word(s) they are intended to modify so that the relationship is clear.

CONFUSING   It was not a good idea to serve food to the guests standing around the room on flimsy paper plates.

READER'S REACTION: **Surely the guests were not standing on their plates!**

EDITED (MODIFIER MOVED)   It was not a good idea to serve food **on flimsy paper plates** to the guests standing around the room.

ESL ADVICE: CHOOSING THE POSITION OF A MODIFIER

In some languages, the form of a modifier determines its meaning and its role in a sentence. In English, the position of a modifier can be the determining factor. The discussions in this chapter will help you choose a position for a modifier that enables you to communicate your meaning precisely.

2 Pay attention to *only, simply, even,* and other limiting modifiers

Words like *only, almost, hardly, just, scarcely, merely, simply, exactly,* and *even* (called **limiting modifiers**) generally apply to the word that immediately follows, though not always.

During difficult economic times, **only** charities for disabled children maintain their normal levels of support.
They are the sole charities able to maintain normal levels.

During difficult economic times, charities for disabled **only** children maintain their normal levels of support.
The charities are for disabled children from families with one child.

During difficult economic times, charities for disabled children **only** maintain their normal levels of support.
They do not increase the levels of support.

3 Be alert for squinting modifiers

When readers encounter a modifier that appears to modify *both* the word(s) before and the word(s) after, they become understandably confused.

To identify such **squinting modifiers,** read your sentences with attention not just to the meaning you intend but also to other possible readings that a reasonable reader might notice. To edit, move the modifier into a position that repairs the ambiguity.

SQUINTING MODIFIER	People who enjoy listening to Aaron Copland's music **often** claim that he was the finest American composer of the twentieth century. READER'S REACTION: Does this mean that they *listen often* to the music or that they *often claim* something about Copland?
EDITED	People who enjoy **listening often** to Aaron Copland's music also tend to claim that he was the finest American composer of the twentieth century.
EDITED	People who enjoy listening to Aaron Copland's music **will often claim** that he was the finest American composer of the twentieth century.

4 Pay attention to clauses beginning with *who*, *which*, and *that*, or other subordinators

You should generally place a modifying clause beginning with *who*, *which*, or *that* right after the word(s) it is intended to modify. (See 35c-5.)

MISPLACED MODIFIER	The environmental engineers discovered another tank behind the building that was leaking toxic wastes. READER'S REACTION: I know a building can leak, but I'll bet the writer meant to identify the tank as the culprit.
EDITED	Behind the building, the environmental engineers discovered another tank that was leaking toxic wastes.

STRATEGY   Edit misplaced modifiers

- *Move* the modifier closer to the word(s) it should modify.

MISPLACED MODIFIER	After you have installed the fan, follow the directions for the wiring connections on the back of the cover plate. READER'S REACTION: Are the wiring connections on the back of the cover plate?
MOVED	After you have installed the fan, follow the directions **on the back of the cover plate** for the wiring connections.

- *Rewrite* or *modify* a sentence so that the connection between modifier and words to be modified is clear.

MISPLACED
MODIFIER

People who drink frequently have other problems.

READER'S REACTION: Does *frequently* refer to people who drink or the likelihood of their having problems?

REWRITTEN

People who drink excessively tend to have other problems as well.

Exercise 1

A. Identify and correct the misplaced modifiers (words or phrases) in each sentence. You may decide either to move the modifier or to rewrite the entire sentence.

EXAMPLE

in pet store windows.
Puppies spend a lot of time staring at people ~~in pet store windows~~.

1. They decided to buy the beagle puppy confused by the many exotic breeds of dogs.
2. This dog would replace the one killed by a truck running across a busy highway.
3. They forgot to buy a dog bed distracted by the crowd of people in the store.
4. Hurriedly, John sighed and began tearing up newspapers in order to begin house-training the puppy.
5. The parents could hear the children playing outside with the dog yelling and laughing.
6. The coach tossed out the practice balls to the players, wet and soft from yesterday's rain.
7. They worked on hitting and catching for fifteen minutes before the first game which was the only practice time they had.
8. The coach who was known as a strict disciplinarian of the championship Little League team invented a rigorous new set of conditioning exercises.
9. A proposal to follow the infield fly rule was defeated by the coach's committee which no one understood.
10. The coach is unable to present the award given in memory of Father Baker because he is sick.

B. Each of the following sentences contains ambiguity caused by either a squinting modifier or a limiting modifier that should be moved to another position. Indicate the type of problem in each sentence.

EXAMPLE

Adults over age thirty who return to college frequently complete both undergraduate and advanced degree programs. (squinting modifier)

1. Adults entering college after working or raising a family officially are classified "nontraditional students" by many colleges.
2. "Nontrads" defer college entry often until after a major life event.
3. Following divorce or job loss, returning to college temporarily provides a boost to self-esteem.
4. Experts report that nontraditional students earn high grade point averages easily exceeding those of traditional students.
5. Nonetheless, failing to take into account the special needs of "nontrads" causes them to drop out frequently.

43b
nm/dm

SERIOUS MISTAKE **43b** Dangling modifiers: Recognizing and editing

Pay attention to modifying words or phrases that begin sentences. If the modifier does not mention the person, idea, or thing being modified, readers will expect you to name it immediately following as the subject of the main clause. If neither the modifier nor the subject of the main clause mentions clearly what you intend to modify, then the modifier is a **dangling modifier.** Often vague, illogical, or unintentionally humorous, dangling modifiers can needlessly distract readers or leave out important information.

DANGLING MODIFIER	Leaking in several places, the scouts abandoned their tents for the dry cabin.
EDITED	**Their tents leaking in several places,** the scouts decided to spend the night in the dry cabin.
EDITED	The scouts decided to spend the night in the dry cabin **because their tents were leaking in several places.**

A modifier in the body of a sentence can dangle, too, when there is no word or phrase to which it can reasonably refer.

DANGLING MODIFIER	The emergency repairs were completed by noon, having become aware of the problem only at ten o'clock.
	READER'S REACTION: Who became aware of the problem?
EDITED	The emergency repairs were completed by noon, **the telephone company** having become aware of the problem only at ten o'clock.

STRATEGY   Correct dangling modifiers

1. **Add** a subject to the modifier.

   DANGLING   While shopping for a birthday gift for my brother, the stuffed alligator caught my eye.

   EDITED   While **I was** shopping for a birthday gift for my brother, the stuffed alligator caught my eye.

2. **Change** the subject of the main clause.

   DANGLING   Trying to decide where to hold the fundraiser, the new restaurant was attractive.

   EDITED   Trying to decide where to hold the fundraiser, **the committee** was attracted to the new restaurant.

3. **Rewrite** the entire sentence.

   DANGLING   After debating new regulations for months without a decision, the present standards were allowed to continue.

   EDITED   The commission debated new regulations for months without a decision, then allowed the present standards to continue.

SERIOUS
MISTAKE

43b
mm/dm

Exercise 2

A. Rewrite each sentence in the *two* ways indicated in brackets, in order to eliminate dangling modifiers.

EXAMPLE

Marion designed her research poorly.
Unable to meet with an advisor, ~~Marion's research was poorly designed.~~
[change subject of main clause; rewrite]

Because Marion was unable to meet with an advisor, she designed her research poorly.

1. Because of a failure to gather enough data, her study was incomplete. [rewrite; add subject to modifier]
2. Lacking the money to pay skilled interviewers, minimally trained volunteers were relied upon. [change subject of main clause; rewrite]
3. Many subjects were not asked appropriate questions because of poor training. [add subject to modifier; change subject of main clause]
4. Anxious and tired, the two-day attempt to write the research report was unsuccessful. [add subject to modifier; change subject of main clause]
5. After spending over twenty hours writing at the computer, the report was still not satisfactory. [rewrite; add subject to modifier]

B. Compare your edited versions of the sentences with those of another student, and decide which versions are best and why.

43c Disruptive modifiers: Recognizing and editing

Readers generally expect sentence elements like subjects and verbs to stand close to each other. The same is true for verbs and the sentence elements that follow them (objects or complements). Modifiers that come between such elements may be disruptive, making a sentence difficult to understand.

DISRUPTIVE MODIFIER	The researcher, **because he had not worked with chimpanzees before and was therefore unaware of their intelligence,** was surprised when they purposely undermined the experiment he was trying to conduct.

1 Pay attention to separated subjects and verbs

Some modifiers placed between subject and verb are disruptive; others are not. How can you recognize the difference?

- **Not disruptive** (generally). Modifiers providing information related to the subject alone.
- **Disruptive.** Modifiers providing information related to both the subject and the verb.

NOT DISRUPTIVE	The electronics mall **that opened last month** has drawn crowds of customers.
DISRUPTIVE MODIFIER	Contractors, **because house building is a boom-or-bust business,** should be ready to do home repairs when housing starts are down.

Move a potentially disruptive modifier from between subject and verb.

EDITED	**Because house building is a boom-or-bust business,** contractors should be ready to do home repairs when housing starts are down.

2 Pay attention to separated verbs and objects (or complements)

Edit by moving the disruptive modifier.

CLUMSY	Joanne began collecting, **with special attention to survey results,** data for her study of dating preferences.
EDITED	**With special attention to survey results,** Joanne began collecting data for her study of dating preferences.

3 Be alert for split infinitives or verb phrases

Look for words that come between the parts of an infinitive (*to* plus a verb, as in *to run* or *to enjoy*), making it hard for readers to understand the relationship between the parts. Edit by moving the intervening words.

UNCLEAR   The office designer tried **to** respectively **address** each of the workers' concerns.

EDITED   The office designer tried **to address** each of the workers' concerns **respectively.**

43c
mm/dm

Even when a **split infinitive** is easy to understand, you might consider revising it because some readers find split infinitives irritating. At times, however, a split infinitive is the clearest and most concise alternative.

Our goal is to more than halve our manufacturing errors.
The alternatives are more wordy and complicated—for example, "Our goal is a rate of manufacturing error less than half the present rate."

Exercise 3

A. Rewrite each sentence to eliminate disruptive modifiers and to make the sentence easier to read and understand.

EXAMPLE

~~The architect,~~ because she was unfamiliar with eighteenth-century in-
the architect
terior design and furnishings, had to do some research before completing the project.

1. The overall design of a building and its interior decoration ought to thoughtfully and harmoniously work together.
2. Furniture design has at least for the past several centuries been greatly influenced by a handful of designers, including Hepplewhite, Chippendale, Sheraton, and, most recently, Eames.
3. Design in Colonial America, because of economic limitations and social customs, was generally simple and practical.
4. Americans had, by the early 1800s in what is now known as the Federalist period, developed more refined and expensive tastes.
5. Today, magazines like *Architectural Digest* and *House Beautiful* illustrate the tendency for styles in interior design to rapidly change and to add considerably to the cost of a home.

B. Working with a group of fellow writers, compare your revisions of the sentences. Decide which versions you prefer and why.

43d Using absolute phrases effectively

An **absolute phrase** consists of a noun or pronoun, a participle, and modifiers. It modifies an entire sentence rather than a specific word or group of words. Because an absolute phrase provides its own noun or pronoun as subject, it does not dangle.

The water level having risen, people in the valley feared that the dam was about to burst.

The absolute phrase sets the scene for the rest of the sentence.

Visit mycomplab.com for more resources and exercises on misplaced, dangling, and disruptive modifiers.

43d
nm/dm

CHAPTER **44**

Faulty Shifts

In the course of writing, you are likely to ask readers to shift their attention many times—from events in the past to plans for the future, for example, or from what you are saying to what other people have said. As long as such shifts are signaled clearly, your readers should not have trouble following them. Inconsistent and confusing shifts may cause readers to wonder about your meaning, however.

INCONSISTENT   **I** am thinking of taking out a two-year certificate of deposit because **you** can get a high interest rate on it.

READER'S REACTION: I don't think the writer means that *she* may buy the certificate of deposit because *someone else* can get a good interest rate.

EDITED   **I** am thinking of taking out a two-year certificate of deposit because **I** can get a high interest rate on it.

44a Person and number

Person refers to the ways you can use words like pronouns and nouns to shape the relationships among you, your readers, and your subject (see 38a).

1 Pay attention to shifts in person

Look for shifts in person. In particular, watch for inconsistencies created by illogical shifts between **I** and **you** or between **you** and **he, she, it** (or a noun in the third person).

INCONSISTENT   If a **person** is looking for an even higher interest rate, **you** might consider a corporate bond.

READER'S REACTION: I'm confused. Do I consider a corporate bond for someone else?

EDITED   If **you** are looking for an even higher interest rate, **you** might consider a corporate bond.

2 Pay attention to shifts in number

Look for shifts in number, especially with words that identify groups or members of a group, such as *business executives* or *a student,* or with words like *person* or *people*. Check that pronouns and their antecedents agree in number (see 38c).

SHIFT IN
NUMBER

When **a person** has money to invest, **they** should talk to a financial consultant.

READER'S REACTION: I know that *a person . . . he or she* would be correct, but it seems more complicated than necessary.

EDITED

When **people have** money to invest, **they** should talk to a financial consultant.

44b
shift

Exercise 1

A. Rewrite each sentence to make it consistent in person and number.

EXAMPLE

Each person has ~~their~~ *a* favorite fast-food restaurant.

1. A would-be restaurant owner often fails to carefully consider the competition they will face from other restaurants.
2. Good franchise chains survey competition, tell potential owners how much money they will need to open the business, and help you with the many problems a restaurant owner faces.
3. Admittedly, running a doughnut shop or a pizza place gives one less prestige than you get from owning a gourmet restaurant.
4. I would still rather run a successful business than one where you lose money.
5. Not all franchise arrangements are good ones, so people should do some research before he or she decides to open a franchised restaurant.

B. Working with a group of fellow students, write a brief paragraph on a topic of general interest. Then rewrite the paragraph so it contains several nouns and pronouns that do not agree in person and number. Give a copy of the faulty paragraph to another group as a quiz. Correct the paragraph they have created, in turn, for you.

44b Tense and mood

By changing verb **tense** within a sentence or group of sentences, you signal a change in time and the relationship of events (see 36a, 36c, and 36f). When you choose a particular verb **mood,** you indicate an aim or attitude (see 36g).

1 Pay attention to shifts in tense

As you edit, watch out for unnecessary, illogical shifts in verb tense that can mislead readers and contradict your meaning.

ILLOGICAL Paleontologists **discovered** nests and clutches of eggs that **indicate** how some dinosaurs **take care** of their young.

Indicate (present tense) is appropriate because the scientists interpret the evidence in the present. *Take care* (present tense) is inappropriate because the dinosaurs clearly acted in the past.

LOGICAL Paleontologists **discovered** nests and clutches of eggs that **indicate** how some dinosaurs **took care** of their young.

44b
shift

Watch especially for any narration of events in the past tense that shifts suddenly to the present tense.

TENSE SHIFT We **had been digging** at the site unsuccessfully for several weeks when suddenly Tonia **starts yelling,** "Eggs! I think I've found fossil eggs!"

EDITED We **had been digging** at the site unsuccessfully for several weeks when suddenly Tonia **started yelling,** "Eggs! I think I've found fossil eggs!"

2 Be alert for shifts in mood

Choose the *mood* of a verb according to your purpose: to make a command or request (**imperative mood**), to present a statement or question (**indicative mood**), or to offer a conditional or hypothetical statement (**subjunctive mood**). (See 36g.)

INCONSISTENT It is essential that our company **cut** costs and **increases** revenue.

subjunctive   *indicative*

EDITED It is essential that our company **cut** costs and **increase** revenue.

subjunctive   *subjunctive*

Exercise 2

A. Rewrite each sentence to make it consistent in tense and mood.

EXAMPLE

I went to the video store last week, and after half an hour I still ~~can't~~ *couldn't* figure out which movies I ~~want~~ *wanted*.

1. The video store manager said that if I bought two DVDs I will get a third one free, and then he tells me about his favorite DVDs.

2. In the movie *Sacrifice for Glory*, set in World War II, a British Mosquito bomber crashes in the jungle, and only the copilot managed to survive the long walk back to civilization.

3. The hot sun beat on the shoulders of the copilot as he wades through the waist-deep, crocodile-infested swamp.

4. In *The Phantom Menace*, Anakin is a child with the power of the Force, but later he turned to the Dark Side as Darth Vader.

5. In *Ghoulish Lunch*, the main character was reaching into the refrigerator around the guacamole dip for the last piece of apple pie when suddenly a cockroach crawls out from under the crust.

44c shift

B. In a newspaper or magazine, locate a brief review of a movie, performance, book, or recording. Make sure the review contains numerous shifts in tense and mood. Make a copy of the review to share with a group of fellow students. After looking over all the reviews brought in by the group, choose one with particularly complex shifts. As a group, identify each shift and describe its nature. Continue working through as many reviews as you can.

44c Voice

To recognize a verb in the **active voice,** see if the *doer* (or *agent*) of the action acts as the sentence's subject. To recognize a verb in the **passive voice,** see if the *goal* of the action acts as the sentence's subject. (See 36e.)

	subject	verb	object
ACTIVE	The lava flow	**destroyed**	twelve houses.
	doer	action	goal

	subject	verb	
PASSIVE	Twelve houses	**were destroyed**	[by the lava flow].
	goal	action	[doer]

In general, stick to either active or passive voice within a sentence, and be alert as you edit for unwarranted shifts.

	active
INCONSISTENT	Among the active volcanoes, Kilauea **erupts** most frequently, and over 170 houses **have been destroyed** since 1983.
	READER'S REACTION: The first part of the sentence focuses on Kilauea, but the second part doesn't mention it, leading me to wonder if some of the other volcanoes share responsibility.
EDITED	Among the active volcanoes, Kilauea has erupted most frequently in recent years, and **it has destroyed** over 170 houses since 1983.

Occasionally, you may need to shift between active and passive voice to highlight a sentence's subject or to emphasize your meaning.

> passive   active
> Hawaii **was built** by volcanic activity, and the island still **has** active volcanoes.
> The shift between passive and active keeps Hawaii as the sentence's focus.

Exercise 3

A. Rewrite each sentence to make it consistent in voice.

EXAMPLE

and   much
We enjoyed the expedition, ~~and much was~~ learned about fossils.

1. In the morning we dug in the base of the ravine, and during the afternoon the walls were explored.
2. The team found fossils of trilobites, and other fossils were also found at the site.
3. Team members learned about paleontology, and much was learned about the geological history of our area as well.
4. A chart helped in identifying fossils, and we also learned useful identifying strategies from the lecture given by the team leader.
5. After you fill out the application for next month's dig, the form should be given to Bill or sent to his office.

B. Working in a group, use the sentences above as the basis for a brief narrative telling the story of the "dig." Add sentences to fill in the information needed to make the story believable and interesting. Make your narrative consistent in voice.

44d
shift

44d Direct and indirect quotation

In **direct quotation** you present a speaker's or a writer's exact words, set off by quotation marks. In an **indirect quotation** you present the substance of what was said, but in your own words and without quotation marks. Try to avoid mixing direct and indirect quotation within sentences.

MIXED   Writing about the Teenage Mutant Ninja Turtles, Phil Patton names cartoonists Peter Laird and Kevin Eastman as their creators and says, "They were born quietly in 1983, in the kitchen of a New England farmhouse."

EDITED   Writing about the Teenage Mutant Ninja Turtles, Phil Patton says, "Cartoonists named Peter Laird and Kevin Eastman dreamed up the characters," who "were born quietly in 1983, in the kitchen of a New England farmhouse."

Be especially alert for sentences mixing indirect and direct quotations without quotation marks to indicate the difference.

CONFUSING
Before we set out on the hike, the guide told us to stay in line and you should obey all orders immediately.

EDITED TO INDIRECT QUOTATION
Before we set out on the hike, the guide told us to stay in line and to follow every order right away.

EDITED TO DIRECT QUOTATION
Before we set out on the hike, the guide told us, "You should stay in line and obey all orders immediately."

Use the present tense when you summarize or comment on a written work, film, television show, or similar source.

INCONSISTENT	In the novel's opening, Ishmael **arrives** in New Bedford with the intention of shipping out on a whaler, which he soon **did.**
CONSISTENT	In the novel's opening, Ishmael **arrives** in New Bedford with the intention of shipping out on a whaler, which he soon **does.**

Exercise 4

A. Rewrite each of the following sentences twice. First use direct quotation consistently, then use indirect quotation consistently. (Feel free to invent direct quotations in order to complete the exercise. Be sure to change direct quotations into your own words when you present them as indirect quotations.)

EXAMPLE
The article began by saying, "People often fear bees" and that this fear is a result of ignorance.

The article began by saying, "People often fear bees, and this fear comes from ignorance."

The article began by saying that the widespread fear of bees is caused by ignorance.

1. I once heard a beekeeper claim that unless beekeeping becomes more popular as a hobby, "I believe that agriculture in this country may suffer."
2. At a meeting last night, the county agriculture commissioner argued that increased beekeeping would aid agriculture in our area and "We should be willing to provide beekeepers with financial support for their efforts."

3. Having eaten honey every day for sixty years, my grandfather says, "I may not look as good as I did when I was younger," but that he feels just as good.
4. My grandfather also says that he has stayed mentally alert because "I manage a large beekeeping and honey business."
5. My neighbor told me, if you are too busy to sell your honey at a roadside stand I should see if the supermarket in town would sell it for me.

B. Share your edited sentences with a group of classmates. Decide which versions of each sentence are best and why.

44d
shift

Visit mycomplab.com for more resources and exercises on faulty shifts.

CHAPTER **45**

Mixed and Incomplete Sentences

When someone you are talking with switches topics abruptly, you can ask for an explanation. When you are reading, however, you can't ask the author to explain a confusing topic shift that comes in the middle of a sentence.

TOPIC SHIFT   One **skill** I envy is **a person** who can study despite noise and other distractions.

READER'S REACTION: Clearly, a *skill* is not a *person.*

EDITED   One **skill** I envy is **the ability** to study despite noise and other distractions.

Sentences with confusing shifts (called **mixed sentences**) mislead readers by undermining patterns they rely on as they read. An **incomplete sentence** that omits wording necessary to make a logical and consistent statement does the same. For example, if you start by writing "*X* is larger," you should be ready to complete the comparison: "*X* is larger *than Y.*"

(Fragments are incomplete sentences lacking grammatical completeness. See Chapter 40.)

45a Mixed sentences: Recognizing and editing

Mixed sentences shift topics or grammatical structures without warning or reason. They throw readers off track and make illogical statements.

1 Recognizing topic shifts

Keep this basic sentence pattern in mind: The subject *announces a topic*, and the predicate comments on or renames *the same topic.*

You create confusion if you make each part of a sentence address a *different* subject. (The resulting problem is sometimes called a **topic shift** or **faulty predication.**)

TOPIC SHIFT   The **presence** of ozone in smog is the **chemical** that causes eye irritation.

READER'S REACTION: *Presence* is not a chemical, though that is what the sentence says.

EDITED   The **ozone** in smog is the **chemical** that causes eye irritation.

618

STRATEGY Ask "Who does what?" or "What is it?"

TOPIC SHIFT In this factory, **flaws** in the product noticed by any worker **can stop** the assembly line with the flip of a switch.

READER'S REACTION: Who does what? Certainly flaws can't stop the line or flip a switch.

EDITED In this factory, **any worker** who notices flaws in the product **can stop** the assembly line with the flip of a switch.

2 Editing topic shifts

In general, you can eliminate problems with topic shifts by making sure the topic in both parts of a sentence, subject and predicate, is the same.

Rename the subject. When you build a sentence around the verb *be* (*is, are, was, were*) you may choose to have the predicate rename the subject in order to create a definition. When you do, make sure the topics on each side of the verb are roughly equivalent.

TOPIC SHIFT **Irradiation** is **food** that is preserved by the use of radiation.

READER'S REACTION: Irradiation is a process of preservation, not the food itself.

EDITED **Irradiation** is a **process** that can be used to preserve food.

Cut *is when* or *is where*. The phrases *is when* and *is where* make it impossible to balance the topics in a definition built around the verb *is*. Cut them and rewrite to create balance and eliminate a shift in topic.

NOT BALANCED **Blocking** is **when** a television network schedules a less popular program between two popular ones.

EDITED **Blocking** is the **practice** of scheduling a less popular television program between two popular ones.

Omit *the reason . . . is because.* In conversation, the phrase *the reason . . . is because* causes little confusion. In writing, however, a phrase opening with *because* is a modifier that cannot logically rename the topic (subject) of the first part of a sentence.

- Drop *the reason . . . is.*

    ILLOGICAL **The reason** he took up figure skating **is because** he wanted something to do during the long winter.

    EDITED He took up figure skating **because** he wanted something to do during the long winter.

- Change *because* to *that*.

  EDITED   **The reason** he took up figure skating **is that** he wanted something to do during the long winter.

Edit for intervening words. Watch for words and phrases coming between a subject and a verb. You may sometimes mistakenly treat these intervening words as the sentence's topic.

TOPIC SHIFT   Programming **decisions** by television executives generally keep in mind the need to gain audience share.

       READER'S REACTION: I know that network executives can keep an audience in mind, but according to this sentence it is programming decisions that are thinking about the viewers.

EDITED   **Television executives** making programming decisions generally **keep** in mind the need to gain audience share.

Exercise 1

A. Rewrite each sentence to eliminate topic shifts.

EXAMPLE

Hides ~~that are~~ treated with tanning chemicals turn ~~them~~ into leather.

1. Tanning is when animal hide is made supple and resistant to decay.
2. The first step is when the hides are thoroughly scraped and cleaned.
3. The use of diluted acid is the substance that pickles the hides to prepare them for tanning.
4. The reason leather is supple is because it is lubricated with oil after pickling, then dried and impregnated with resins.
5. The final steps are when the leather is dyed and given a shiny surface through compression.

B. Compare your edited sentences with those produced by classmates. Decide which versions you prefer and why you prefer them.

3 Recognizing shifts in grammatical pattern

Occasionally, you may begin a sentence with one grammatical pattern in mind and shift to another partway through. The result confuses readers.

SHIFTED PATTERNS

Because of the rebellious atmosphere generated by protests against the Vietnam war helps explain the often outrageous fashions of the time.

READER'S REACTION: At "helps explain," this sentence seems to start over.

EDITED (MAIN CLAUSE ADDED)

Because of the rebellious atmosphere generated by protests against the Vietnam war, **fashions of the time became outrageous.**

EDITED (REWRITTEN)

The rebellious **atmosphere** generated by protests against the Vietnam war **helps explain** the often outrageous fashions of the time.

STRATEGY   Identify shifts in grammatical construction

45a
mixed

- **Focus on the meaning** by checking that all the elements stand in clear and reasonable relationships to each other. Read aloud sentences that seem potentially confusing.
- **Ask** "What is the topic of this sentence, and how does the rest of the sentence comment on or rename the topic?"
- **Check** that the sentence clearly indicates *who does what to whom.*

SHIFT   By wearing bell-bottom pants, love beads, and tie-dyed T-shirts was how many young people expressed their opposition to mainstream values.

READER'S REACTION: I can puzzle out the meaning, but this sentence really doesn't make clear who did what to whom.

EDITED   By wearing bell-bottom pants, love beads, and tie-dyed T-shirts, many young people expressed their opposition to mainstream values.

---

4 Editing shifts in grammatical pattern

Three kinds of inappropriate grammatical shifts are quite common.

Sentences that begin twice. When you try to give more emphasis to a topic than the structure of a sentence allows, you may mistakenly start the sentence over again, treating the sentence's object as a second subject.

To edit sentences that begin twice, rewrite the sentence, moving most or all of the information in one of the two main clauses to a modifying phrase or clause.

MIXED PATTERNS   **The new procedures for testing cosmetics, we** designed them to avoid cruelty to laboratory animals.

READER'S REACTION: It seems that the writer starts this sentence again with the word *we.*

EDITED   **We** designed **the new procedures for testing cosmetics** to avoid cruelty to laboratory animals.

EDITED   **The new procedures for testing cosmetics** were designed to avoid cruelty to laboratory animals.

Whole sentences used as subjects. Another way you may mistakenly give emphasis to a topic is to put it in a complete sentence (main clause), which you then use incorrectly as the subject of another sentence.

Rewrite so that most (or all) of the information in one of the two main clauses appears instead in a modifying phrase or clause.

> **MIXED PATTERNS**
> In 1872, Claude Monet exhibited the painting *Impression, Sunrise* was the source of the term *Impressionism.*

> **EDITED (PHRASE CREATED)**
> The source of the term *Impressionism* was the painting *Impression, Sunrise,* **exhibited by Claude Monet in 1872.**

> **EDITED (CLAUSE CREATED)**
> In 1872, Claude Monet exhibited the painting *Impression, Sunrise,* **which was the source of the term *Impressionism.***

Clauses and phrases used as subjects. When readers encounter a phrase like "By designing the questionnaire carefully" at the beginning of a sentence, they expect it to be followed by the sentence's subject. They do not expect it to act as the subject.

To edit, either add a new subject or alter the form of the phrase so that it can act as a subject.

> MIXED PATTERNS **By designing the questionnaire carefully** made Valerie's psychology study a success.

> EDITED By designing the questionnaire carefully, **Valerie made** her psychology study a success.

> EDITED The **careful design** of the questionnaire **made** Valerie's psychology study a success.

Exercise 2

A. Rewrite each sentence to eliminate shifts in grammatical pattern.

> EXAMPLE
>
> S
> ~~Many people used to die from infectious diseases was why~~ scientists
>   ^
> worked hard to develop vaccinations.⌐ *because many people used to die from infectious diseases.*

1. By observing that farm workers who had cowpox were resistant to smallpox led Edward Jenner to develop an inoculation for smallpox in the 1790s.

2. Paying attention to Jenner's methods was why Louis Pasteur was able to develop vaccines for chicken pox, rabies, and human anthrax.
3. Vaccinations produce antibodies are the sources of immunity.
4. Because they are not effective against all infections means that vaccinations are not a perfect solution for diseases.
5. Making sure your vaccinations are up to date, you need to do this during your regular medical checkup.

B. In a group, compare your edited sentences with those produced by other writers. Identify the edited versions you consider correct, consistent, and clear.

45b
inc

45b Incomplete sentences: Recognizing and editing

Sentences that fail to complete an expected logical pattern or that leave out words necessary to meaning or logic are called **incomplete sentences.** (Sentences missing a *grammatical* element are fragments; see Chapter 40.)

1 Recognizing and avoiding incomplete or illogical comparisons

When writing a comparison (*X* is greater than *Y*), you will confuse readers if you leave out one element (*X* is *greater*) or if the things you try to compare are not logically comparable.

Recognize missing elements and supply them. Check that you have included both of the items being compared. Omitting one creates an incomplete comparison. To edit, supply the missing element.

INCOMPLETE   The picture quality of the DVDs is much better.

READER'S REACTION: The picture quality is better than what? Than the quality on DVDs used to be? Than the quality was on analog (VHS) tapes?

EDITED   The picture quality of the DVDs is much better than **it was on VHS tapes.**

Look also for places where you have omitted a word or words necessary to complete a comparison or make it clear, and then supply them.

AMBIGUOUS   The most experienced members of the staff respect the new supervisor more highly than their fellow workers.

READER'S REACTION: Do the experienced staff members respect the supervisor more than they respect their fellow workers, or do they respect the supervisor more than their fellow workers do?

CLEAR   The most experienced members of the staff respect the new supervisor more highly **than do** their fellow workers.

CLEAR   The most experienced members of the staff respect the new supervisor more highly **than they respect** their fellow workers.

Watch for illogical comparisons. As you review comparisons, ask, "Can these things be reasonably compared?" If a comparison seems to be illogical, consider using either of these strategies: (1) fill in the missing words or (2) use the possessive.

45b
inc

ILLOGICAL

Even a small hamburger's fat content is higher than a skinless chicken breast.

READER'S REACTION: **The writer probably wants to compare the fat content of two foods, but the sentence actually compares one** *kind* **of food (chicken breast) to the** *fat content* **of the other.**

EDITED (WORDS PROVIDED)

The fat content of even a small hamburger is higher than **that of** a skinless chicken breast.

EDITED (POSSESSIVE USED)

Even a small **hamburger's** fat content is higher than a skinless chicken **breast's.**

2 Recognizing appropriate and inappropriate omissions

Leaving out repeated words or phrases can often make sentences easier to read. So long as omitting these repetitions does not undermine meaning or confuse readers, you should consider cutting them to make writing concise and effective.

LEFT IN   Some presidents spend much time mastering the facts before making a major decision; others spend little **time mastering the facts before making a major decision.**

OMITTED
BUT CLEAR   Some presidents spend much time mastering the facts before making a major decision; **others spend little.**

You can also frequently eliminate the word *that* from sentences where it introduces a noun clause after a verb: "Artists know [that] there is a difference between oil and acrylic paints."

Exercise 3

A. Rewrite each sentence to eliminate any incomplete or illogical constructions.

EXAMPLE

other
Both Shannon and Bill like tennis more than any game.
^

1. His tennis serve has more speed and accuracy than Bill.
2. He also has better sense of where an opponent is going hit ball.
3. Bill's commitment to tennis is greater than his family.
4. He has more fun playing tennis.
5. Like many exercise-addicted people, Bill would be exercising than eating, and he would rather be playing tennis than doing anything else.

45b
inc

B. In a small group, compare the effectiveness of your edited sentences with those of your fellow writers. Make sure the members of your group agree on what is incomplete or illogical in the original version of each sentence.

Visit mycomplab.com for more resources and exercises on mixed and incomplete sentences.

CHAPTER 46

Parallelism

Parallelism is the expression of similar or related ideas in similar grammatical form, as in the following sentence.

I furnished my first apartment

with **purchases**	**from department stores,**
items	**from the want ads,**
and **gifts**	**from my relatives.**

Parallelism enables you to present ideas concisely while highlighting their relationships. Readers generally find a sentence with parallel elements easy to read and understand. They also appreciate the touch of style parallelism can bring even to everyday sentences.

46a Problems with parallelism: Recognizing and editing

To create parallelism with words, phrases, or clauses, you need to make sure all the elements employ the same grammatical form. To recognize a lack of parallelism, look for shifts in grammatical form.

FAULTY PARALLELISM Consider swimming if you are looking for exercise that **aids** cardiovascular fitness, **overall** muscle strength, and probably **will not cause** injuries.

PARALLEL Consider swimming if you are looking for exercise that **aids** cardiovascular fitness, **develops** overall muscle strength, and **causes** few injuries.

1 Check for parallelism in a series

To check for parallelism in a series, mentally isolate each element and verify that each takes the same grammatical form.

NOT PARALLEL patient, tactful, and **to display tolerance**

PARALLEL patient, tactful, and **tolerant**

WORDS (NOT PARALLEL)	To get along with their parents, teenagers need to be patient, tactful, and **to display tolerance.**
WORDS (PARALLEL)	To get along with their parents, teenagers need to be patient, tactful, and **tolerant.**
PHRASES (NOT PARALLEL)	The singer Jim Morrison is remembered for his innovative style, his flamboyant performances, and **for behavior that was self-destructive.**
PHRASES (PARALLEL)	The singer Jim Morrison is remembered for his innovative style, his flamboyant performances, and **his self-destructive behavior.**
CLAUSES (NOT PARALLEL)	We looked for engineers whose work was innovative, **with broad interests, and who had boundless energy.**
CLAUSES (PARALLEL)	We looked for engineers whose work was innovative, **whose interests were broad, and whose energy was boundless.**

46a
//

The final position in a series often receives the greatest emphasis from writers and the most attention from readers. You can create sentences with a strong cumulative effect, directing attention to the final element.

When VG Industries moved, the town was left with abandoned buildings, unused rail lines, and **thousands of unemployed workers.**

2 Decide which words to repeat

In creating parallelism, make sure you repeat all words necessary to the meaning of a sentence, including all the words called for by grammatical structures or idiomatic expressions. You need not repeat a lead-in word, however, if it is the same for all elements in a series.

Mosquitoes can breed in puddles, ~~in~~ ponds, and ~~in~~ swimming pools.

Exercise 1

A. Underline the parallel structures in each sentence.

1. We've told you about the bombs, the fires, the smashed houses, and the courage of the people.
    —EDWARD R. MURROW, "From London, September 22, 1940"

2. She looked at a man because she liked the way the hair was tucked behind his ears, or she liked the question-mark line of a long torso curving at the shoulder and straight at the hip.
    —MAXINE HONG KINGSTON, "No Name Woman"

3. But far below, in the warren of passages on the starboard side forward, in the forward holds and boiler rooms, men could see that the *Titanic*'s hurt was mortal.

—HANSON W. BALDWIN, "R.M.S. *Titanic*"

4. In that context three groups of wounded soldiers are identified: those whose survival depends on their receiving immediate treatment; those who need medical attention but will survive even if they do not get it immediately; and those who are hurt so badly they would not survive even with medical attention.

—RUTH MACKLIN, *Mortal Choices*

46a
//

5. For in each American marriage there is a special code, developed from the individual pasts of the two partners, put together out of the accidents of honeymoon and parents-in-law, finally beaten into a language that each understands imperfectly.

—MARGARET MEAD, *Male and Female*

B. Working in a group, rewrite the following sentences to correct faulty parallelism and create appropriate emphasis. Include all necessary words. If a sentence can be rewritten in several ways, choose the version the group considers most effective.

1. What kind of job would be appropriate for a person who enjoys sailboarding, skiing, and to skydive?
2. The college's career counselor suggested that Rosalie write out her personal goals, read some materials on choosing a profession, or that she might take a career test.
3. Optimism, stamina, and being a good thinker are three traits of a good sales representative.
4. If you wish to choose a career at which you can succeed, you might start by making a list of the things you like to do, anything you are very good at, and also jobs or experiences you always try to avoid.
5. You can locate possible jobs in newspaper ads, friends, and employment agencies.

3 Pay attention to parallelism with paired sentence elements

When you are creating paired sentence elements to emphasize similarities and heighten contrasts, you will call attention to the relationship if you use parallelism—and readers will expect you to present the paired elements in parallel form.

And, but, or, for, nor, so, **and** *yet.* Take notice of sentence elements you have joined with *and, but, or, for, nor, so,* and *yet* (**coordinating conjunctions**). In general, present the words, phrases, or clauses in parallel form, to direct your readers' attention to the relationship of the elements and make the sentence easier to read.

WORDS NOT PARALLEL
Scientists learn to keep detailed lab notebooks and make the entries accurately.

PARALLEL
Scientists learn to keep **detailed and accurate** lab notebooks.

46a
//

PHRASES NOT PARALLEL
First-year chemistry courses are supposed to teach students how to take notes on an experiment and the ways of writing a lab report.

PARALLEL
First-year chemistry courses are supposed to teach students **how to take notes on an experiment** and **how to write a lab report.**

The items you link with correlative conjunctions (*both . . . and, not only . . . but also, either . . . or, neither . . . nor,* and *whether . . . or*) should be clearly related in meaning and similar in grammatical form. If the elements following the first and second connectors do not match, the sentence may be hard to follow or unclear in meaning.

AMBIGUOUS
Leon Blum's election represented a significant change in French politics and society because he was not only the first Socialist premier but also the first Jew.

PRECISE (PARALLELISM ADDED)
Leon Blum's election represented a significant change in French politics and society because he was not only the **first Socialist premier but also the first Jewish premier.**

Comparison and contrast. Be alert for places in your writing where you are comparing or contrasting items, and use parallel forms to help call attention to them.

DRAFT
This new ingredient will reduce the calories in our frozen yogurt, and the yogurt will have more taste.

EDITED
This new ingredient in our frozen yogurt **will reduce the calories** and **improve the taste.**

Exercise 2

A. Rewrite each sentence to eliminate faulty parallelism.

EXAMPLE

$$do$$
In choosing a career, you should plan carefully and ~~also~~ some research
~~is needed.~~

1. Anthony could not decide whether he wanted to be a lawyer or if investment banking was a more promising career.
2. His friends thought Anthony's career plans were not suited to his abilities and his interests didn't fit the plans either.
3. After thinking about his goals, Anthony realized that the two things he wanted most from a career were stability and an income that was reasonable.
4. The counselor suggested that he might consider either working for the federal government or a job with a large, stable corporation.
5. Anthony had been reading about corporations in financial trouble and which had been laying off employees, so he decided to look carefully at government jobs.

B. Working with a group of fellow students, gather a number of pamphlets offering advice. Campus offices, libraries, clinics, banks, and similar places usually provide pamphlets on subjects from health care and home safety to job hunting. Choose one pamphlet, identify those places where parallelism is used effectively with paired sentence elements, and edit to correct any faulty parallelism. Enhance the parallelism when appropriate in order to highlight ideas and their relationships.

46b Parallelism beyond the sentence

As you write and revise, you can create parallelism beyond the sentence level to organize clusters of sentences and even paragraphs. Parallelism of this sort can clarify complicated information or highlight the overall pattern of an argument or explanation.

1 Creating parallel sentence clusters

By adding parallelism to groups of sentences, you call attention to **sentence clusters,** groups of sentences that develop related ideas or information. The parallel elements can link related items or guide readers through an explanation or argument.

Each of us probably belongs to several organizations whose values are in conflict. **You may belong to** a religious organization that **endorses restraint** in alcohol use or **in** relationships between the sexes while at the same time **you belong to** a social group whose activities seem to endorse a contrasting set of values. **You may belong to** a sports team **that endorses** conflict and winning and a club **that promotes** understanding among people and conflict resolution. **You may belong to** a political club whose platform contradicts the policies of your professional organization.

READER'S REACTION: The repetition of certain phrases draws my attention and makes the passage easier to follow.

2 Creating parallel paragraphs

By creating paragraphs that are parallel in structure and wording, you can reinforce the overall pattern of a report or essay and alert readers to your line of argument or explanation. The parallel element can be as simple and unobtrusive as parallel opening phrases for a series of paragraphs.

One reason for acting on this recommendation is that the flooding gets worse every spring. . . .

A second reason for action is that the city currently has a budget surplus that could be spent on drainage improvement. . . .

A third, and most important, reason for taking immediate steps is that the health and safety of city residents is endangered by the floods.

Exercise 3

A. Underline all examples of parallelism in the following passage.

Large computers have some essential attributes of an intelligent brain: they have large memories, and they have gates whose connections can be modified by experience. However, the thinking of these computers tends to be narrow. The richness of human thought depends to a considerable degree on the enormous number of wires, or nerve fibers, coming into each gate in the human brain. A gate in a computer has two, or three, or at most four wires entering on one side, and one wire coming out the other side. In the human brain, a gate may have as many as 100,000 wires entering it. Each wire comes from another gate or nerve cell. This means that every gate in the human brain is connected to as many as 100,000 other gates in other parts of the brain. During the process of thinking, innumerable gates open and close throughout the brain. When one of these gates "decides" to open, the decision is the result of a complicated assessment involving inputs from thousands of other gates. This circumstance explains much of the difference between human thinking and computer thinking.

—ROBERT JASTROW, "Brains and Computers"

B. Working in a group, decide what each example of parallelism in the passage contributes to the effectiveness of the individual sentence or the entire passage. Note any differences of opinion, and discuss whether these differences reveal alternative ways of viewing the meaning or purpose of the passage.

46c Parallelism in lists

46c
//

Lists can summarize key points, instructions, or stages in a process. To avoid confusing readers, make sure the elements in lists are as parallel as possible.

UNEDITED (CONFUSING)

The early 1960s were characterized by the following social phenomena.

1. A growing civil rights movement
2. Kennedy pursued a strongly anticommunist foreign policy.
3. An emphasis on youth in culture and politics
4. Taste in music and the visual arts was changing.
5. Government support for scientific research increased greatly.

EDITED (CLEAR)

The early 1960s were characterized by the following social phenomena.

1. **A growing** civil rights movement
2. **A strongly** anticommunist foreign policy (encouraged by President Kennedy)
3. **A youthful** emphasis in culture and politics
4. **A changing** taste in music and the visual arts
5. **A marked** increase in government support for scientific research

Exercise 4

A. Arrange the following materials into a list whose elements maintain parallel form.

The awards for arts and entertainment for 2005 offer an interesting picture of American culture in the middle of the decade.

Academy Award: *Million Dollar Baby* (Best Picture); Jamie Foxx, *Ray* (Best Actor); Hilary Swank, *Million Dollar Baby* (Best Actress); Morgan Freeman, *Million Dollar Baby* (Best Supporting Actor); Cate Blanchett, *The Aviator* (Best Supporting Actress).

The Emmy Awards went to *Everybody Loves Raymond* (Outstanding Comedy Series), *Lost* (Outstanding Drama Series), and James Spader, *Boston Legal* (Outstanding Lead Actor in a Drama Series), Patricia Arquette, *Medium* (Outstanding Lead Actress in a Drama Series), Tony Shalhoub, *Monk* (Outstanding Lead Actor in a Comedy

Series), Felicity Huffman, *Desperate Housewives* (Outstanding Lead Actress in a Comedy Series).

MTV Video Music Awards: Green Day, "Boulevard of Broken Dreams" (Best Video); Kanye West, "Jesus Walks" (Best Male Video); Kelly Clarkson, "Since U Been Gone" (Best Female Video); Green Day, "Boulevard of Broken Dreams" (Best Group Video).

B. Compare your list with the lists of several other students. Note any differences in the ways your lists are organized.

46c
//

Visit mycomplab.com for more resources and exercises on parallelism.

CHAPTER 47

Coordination and Subordination

You are asked to revise the following passage, which is filled with short, choppy sentences that fail to emphasize the connections among ideas.

> Fresh olives contain a substance that makes them bitter. They are very unpleasant tasting. Farmers soak fresh olives in a solution that removes oleuropein, the bitter-tasting substance. They make sure just enough is left behind to produce the tangy "olive" taste.

You might **coordinate** the sentences, giving equal emphasis to each statement.

COORDINATED

> Fresh olives contain a substance that makes them bitter, **so** they are very unpleasant tasting. Farmers soak fresh olives in a solution that removes oleuropein, the bitter-tasting substance; **however,** they make sure just enough is left behind to produce the tangy "olive" taste.

Or you might try specifying the relationships and relative importance of ideas by using **subordination:** making some sentences modify others by employing subordinating words.

SUBORDINATED

> **Because** fresh olives contain a substance that makes them bitter, they are very unpleasant tasting. **When** farmers soak fresh olives in a solution that removes oleuropein, the bitter-tasting substance, they make sure just enough is left behind to produce the tangy "olive" taste.

47a Creating coordination

When you want to link words or groups of words, the techniques of coordination enable you to give equal weight to the different elements.

WORDS	trims **and** shapes
CLUSTERS OF WORDS	in the shallow water, near the islands, **or** in the middle of the main channel
MAIN CLAUSES	The winter freeze prevents boats from sailing; **however,** the residents are still able to fish through holes in the ice.

CREATING COORDINATION

JOINING WORDS AND CLUSTERS OF WORDS (PHRASES)

1. **Use *and, but, or, nor,* or *yet* (coordinating conjunctions).**

   cut **and** hemmed   smooth **or** textured   intrigued **yet** suspicious

2. **Use pairs like *either . . . or, neither . . . nor,* and *not only . . . but also.***

   either music therapy **or** pet therapy
   not only a nursing care plan **but also** a psychological treatment program

JOINING MAIN (INDEPENDENT) CLAUSES

1. **Use *and, but, or, for, nor, so,* or *yet* (coordinating conjunctions) preceded by a comma.**

   The students observed the responses of shoppers to long lines, **and** they interviewed people waiting in line. Most people in the study were irritated by the checkout lines, **yet** a considerable minority enjoyed the wait.

2. **Use a semicolon** (see 52a).

   The wait provoked physical reactions in some people; they fidgeted, grimaced, and stared at the ceiling.

3. **Use words like *however, moreover, nonetheless, thus,* and *consequently* (conjunctive adverbs) preceded by a semicolon.**

   Store managers can take simple steps to speed up checkout lines; **however,** they seldom pay much attention to the problem.

4. **Use a colon** (see 52b).

   Tabloids and magazines in racks by the checkout counters serve a useful purpose: they give customers something to read while waiting.

47a
coord

By creating effective coordination you can specify and highlight relationships among ideas.

RELATIONSHIPS NOT SPECIFIED	Cats have no fear of water. They do not like getting their fur wet and matted. Cats like to feel clean and well groomed.
CLEAR RELATIONSHIPS	Cats have no fear of water, **but** they do not like getting their fur wet and matted; they like to feel clean and well groomed.

Exercise 1

A. Combine each pair of sentences into a single sentence using coordination. Make sure you use each of the strategies listed in the preceding table for joining main clauses, and do not use any particular conjunction (such as *and* or *however*) more than once. Rewrite the sentences if necessary to avoid awkwardness or confusion.

EXAMPLE

Winter weather makes outdoor exercise difficult. Winter has its own forms of exercise.

1. Ice skating can be enjoyable. It is also physically demanding.
2. Recreational skaters need to be in good shape physically. They should exercise to increase their fitness.
3. Skaters who are not in good shape get tired quickly. These skaters are also more likely to pull a muscle or fall.
4. To get in shape for skating, try a program of regular exercise for at least several weeks. Pay special attention to exercises focusing on knees and ankles.
5. Other areas to exercise are hip and leg muscles. Exercises aimed at each muscle group are best.

B. Working with a group of fellow writers, prepare a brief paragraph (five to seven sentences) offering advice on some subject: fitness, cooking, appliance repair, gardening, or the like. Make sure all but one or two of the sentences are compound sentences containing at least two main clauses. Connect the clauses using a variety of strategies for coordination, making sure they are appropriate for your subject and purpose.

47b Problems with coordination: Recognizing and editing

Problems with coordination generally take two forms: excessive use and the illogical linking of ideas and sentence elements.

1 Look for excessive coordination

If you use words like *and*, *so*, or *but* merely to string together groups of loosely related sentences, you risk boring readers with excessive coordination.

STRINGY   The toy was designed in Japan, **but** its parts are made in Brazil, **and** it is assembled in Mexico, **so** what is the country of origin for tax purposes?

EDITED   The toy was designed in Japan, **but** its parts are made in Brazil, **and** it is assembled in Mexico. What is the country of origin for tax purposes?

2 Check for illogical coordination

To identify loosely related elements (illogical coordination), take on a reader's perspective and question the relationship, perhaps asking "How are these two elements linked?" To correct illogical coordination, try adding information to a sentence or changing its emphasis.

ILLOGICAL	Antarctica is a remote continent with a harsh climate, and scientists are now studying its unique animal life in detail. READER'S REACTION: **What do the remoteness and the climate have to do with either the scientists or the animals?**
EDITED	Antarctica's remoteness and harsh climate **have made exploration difficult,** and scientists are **only now beginning detailed study** of its unique animal life.

Exercise 2

47c
sub

A. Revise the following passage to eliminate excessive or illogical coordination. Use coordination to combine short sentences when appropriate, to clarify relationships, and to eliminate choppiness.

Working for someone else can be unrewarding, and this is also true of working for a large corporation, so many people in their early thirties decide to open businesses of their own, but they often do not have very original ideas, so they open restaurants or small retail stores, for these are the small businesses they are most familiar with, yet they are also the ones that are most likely to fail, and they face the most competition. Franchises are small businesses, and they often provide help to people getting into business on their own for the first time. Enterprising people can own the local office of an armored car service, or they can run a regional unit of a nationwide cleaning service for commercial buildings, and they can open hardware stores with the name of a national chain over the front door.

B. Work with a group of fellow writers to produce two versions of the passage above, each with a different emphasis.

47c Creating subordination

When you want to help readers understand links between ideas or information, you can use **subordination,** in which one clause modifies or comments on another. In using subordination, you create a sentence with unequal elements: one presenting the central idea (main clause), and one or more beginning with a subordinating word like *because, although, who, which,* or *that* and acting as a modifier (subordinate clause).

MAIN CLAUSES	Most first-time home buyers are people in their late twenties or early thirties. They have tired of paying rent.
SUBORDINATED	Most first-time home buyers are people in their late twenties or early thirties **who** have tired of paying rent. READER'S REACTION: **The information after** *who* **adds to the statement presented at the beginning of the sentence and ties the ideas together.**

CREATING AND RECOGNIZING SUBORDINATION

MEANING	SUBORDINATOR
Time	before, while, until, since, once, whenever, whereupon, after, when
Cause	because, since
Result	in order that, so that, that
Concession or Contrast	although, though, even though, as if, while, as though
Place	where, wherever
Condition	if, whether, provided, unless, rather than
Comparison	as
Identification	that, which, who

Subordination enables you to put some information in the foreground (in a main clause) and other information in the background (in a subordinate clause). Thus you help readers distinguish primary statements from secondary statements, new ideas from old, and important information from background.

SECONDARY/ PRIMARY **Although** energy costs are increasing, costs for raw materials have dropped more than 30 percent in the past six months.

OLD/NEW **Though** most biographies of Charles Dickens have spent much time examining his childhood, his latest biographer pays little attention to this period.

IMPORTANT/ BACKGROUND Raymond Carver, **who** died in 1990, created a stir with his "minimalist" short stories.

You can also vary the meaning of a sentence considerably, depending on the subordinating conjunction you choose.

As soon as the copier is repaired, we can print the newsletter.

Whenever the copier is repaired, we can print the newsletter.

If the copier is repaired, we can print the newsletter.

Short, choppy sentences can become smooth and graceful through careful subordination.

CHOPPY For each moon, the Seneca have a name. They draw the name from the season. The sixth moon is called the Strawberry Moon. Strawberries ripen in June.

EDITED For each moon, the Seneca have a name **that** they draw from the season. **Because** strawberries ripen in June, the sixth moon is called the Strawberry Moon.

LOCATING AND PUNCTUATING SUBORDINATION

SUBORDINATING CONJUNCTIONS

You can use a subordinating conjunction such as *although*, *because*, or *since* (see list on page 638) to create a subordinate clause at the beginning or end of a sentence (see 5h).

PUNCTUATION WITH SUBORDINATING CONJUNCTIONS

Use a comma *after* an introductory clause that begins with a subordinating conjunction. At the end of a sentence, do not use commas if the clause is *essential* to the meaning of the main clause (restrictive); use commas if the clause is *not essential* (nonrestrictive). (See 51c.)

47c
sub

BEGINNING	**Once she understood the problem,** she had no trouble solving it.
END	Radar tracking of flights began **after several commercial airliners collided in midair.** Essential
END	The present air traffic control system works reasonably well, **although accidents still occur.** Nonessential

RELATIVE PRONOUNS

You can use a relative pronoun (*who*, *which*, *that*) to create a relative clause (also called an adjective clause) at the end or in the middle of a sentence. (See 5h.)

PUNCTUATION WITH RELATIVE PRONOUNS

If the modifying clause contains information that is *not essential* to the meaning of the main clause, the modifying clause is nonrestrictive and you should set it off with commas. If the information is *essential*, the modifying clause is restrictive and you should not set it off with commas. (See 51c.)

RESTRICTIVE	The anthropologists discovered the site of a building **that early settlers used as a meetinghouse.**
NONRESTRICTIVE	At one end of the site they found remains of a smaller building, **which may have been a storage shed.**
RESTRICTIVE	The people **who organized the project** work for the Public Archaeology Lab.
NONRESTRICTIVE	A graduate student, **who was leading a dig nearby,** first discovered signs of the meetinghouse.

Exercise 3

A. Use subordination to combine each pair of sentences. Choose appropriate subordinating conjunctions, and create emphasis consistent with each sentence's meaning. Rewrite the clauses if necessary to produce effective sentences.

EXAMPLE

Newspapers often contain reports of car accidents. ~~The accidents~~ were preventable.

that ^

1. The comedian Sam Kinison died in a car crash. A pickup truck swerved across the road and hit his car.
2. Kinison was not wearing a seat belt. A seat belt might have saved his life.
3. Driving quickly off the road to the right is one thing you can do. This will help you avoid collisions.
4. Drive a large car. Big, heavy cars and passenger vans are much safer in crashes.
5. Buying a car with front and side impact air bags is an excellent way to reduce your chances of being injured or dying. These cars cost more money.

B. Working with a group of fellow students, conduct research to determine which subordinating words are widely used. Each person should locate a five- to seven-paragraph segment of a magazine article and make a list of all the subordinating words in it, tallying the number of times each word appears. (The list on page 638 and a dictionary can help you decide whether a word is a subordinator.) Pool your lists, and determine how often various words appear in the articles you sampled.

47d | sub

47d Problems with subordination: Recognizing and editing

Problems with subordination generally take two forms: illogical or unclear relationships and excessive use of a strategy.

1 Be alert for illogical or unclear relationships

Sometimes the subordinating word you choose may not specify a clear relationship, or it may indicate an illogical relationship.

STRATEGY **Recognize and edit illogical subordination**

- Ask yourself, "Does the original sentence convey my intended meaning?"
- Ask yourself, "Can the subordinating word I have chosen convey several conflicting meanings?"
- Ask yourself, "Does the main clause present the most important information?"

If your answer to any question reveals a problem, revise the sentence by choosing a more appropriate subordinator (see page 638 for alternatives).

UNCLEAR
EMPHASIS

Since she taught junior high school, Jean developed keen insight into the behavior of adolescents.

READER'S REACTION: I'm not sure whether she developed insights *because* she was a teacher or *after* she quit teaching.

EDITED

Because she taught junior high school, Jean developed keen insight into the behavior of adolescents.

FAULTY

His training and equipment were inferior, although Jim was still able to set a record throwing the discus.

READER'S REACTION: Isn't Jim's achievement the key point?

EDITED

Although his training and equipment were inferior, Jim was still able to set a record throwing the discus.

2 Be careful with troublesome subordinators: *as/while, and which, but that, and who*

The subordinators *as, while, and which, but that,* and *and who* can be especially ambiguous, confusing, or irritating to readers.

As, while. You can use *as* correctly to create a comparison, or you can use it to indicate simultaneous events.

COMPARISON

Our team spent **as much** time on the accounting problems **as** the other, less successful teams did.

TIME

They began interviewing students **as** the semester was coming to an end.

However, if you use *as* to point out a cause-effect relationship, you will probably confuse some readers. Other readers may consider this use of *as* unacceptable in standard written English.

AMBIGUOUS

As the level of achievement in the two classes differed, the researchers looked for possible explanations.

READER'S REACTION: Does *as* mean "while" or "because"?

EDITED   **Because** the level of achievement in the two classes differed, the researchers looked for possible explanations.

Do not use *as* in place of *whether* or *that*. This substitution is always incorrect in writing and formal speaking.

INCORRECT   They were not sure **as** the differences in achievement were significant.

EDITED   They were not sure **whether** the differences in achievement were significant.

EDITED   They were not sure **that** the differences in achievement were significant.

While can indicate events occurring at the same time. *While* can also signal a concession.

SIMULTANEOUS I can get some work done **while** the children are at school.
EVENTS

CONCESSION   **While** she thinks the speech was a success, I am not so sure.

Nonetheless, *while* may be ambiguous in some sentences, and you may need to replace it with another, clearer subordinator.

UNCLEAR   **While** they interviewed the students, the researchers did not come to any conclusions.
              READER'S REACTION: **Does *while* mean "although" or "when"?**

EDITED   **When** they interviewed the students, the researchers did not come to any conclusions.

EDITED   **Although** they interviewed the students, the researchers did not come to any conclusions.

In addition, *while* is never an acceptable replacement for *but* or *and*.

INCORRECT   One researcher claimed that teachers in the morning classes were more effective than those in the afternoon, **while** the other researcher disagreed.

CORRECT   One researcher claimed that teachers in the morning classes were more effective than those in the afternoon, **but** the other researcher disagreed.

3 Watch out for excessive subordination

When you use too much subordination in a sentence, you create a pattern of relationships so intricate that it overloads readers. To clear up such

47d
sub

confusion, separate your ideas into several sentences, and rewrite them so that readers can grasp your meaning more easily.

CONFUSING   The election for mayor will be interesting this year because the incumbent has decided to run as an independent while his former challenger for the Democratic nomination has decided to accept the party's endorsement even though the Republican nominee is her former campaign manager who switched parties last week.

EDITED   The election for mayor will be interesting this year. The incumbent has decided to run as an independent. His former challenger for the Democratic nomination has decided to accept the party's endorsement even though she will have to run against her former campaign manager. He switched parties last week to become the Republican nominee.

**47d
sub**

Exercise 4

A. Revise each sentence to eliminate illogical, incorrect, or excessive subordination. When appropriate, combine short sentences through subordination to clarify relationships and eliminate choppiness.

EXAMPLE

Because
∧Since my doctor said I need more exercise, I have been looking for a sport I might enjoy.

1. As I am not particularly good at athletics, I want a sport that is not too demanding. I would also like a sport that is fun.
2. I enjoy volleyball, although it is a serious, highly competitive sport demanding considerable quickness and coordination. Volleyball is not the answer.
3. Since I have played tennis, I have thought about trying out for the tennis team. I have also thought about talking this idea over with the tennis coach.
4. Some of my friends think I should give the tennis team a try while others think the idea is laughable.
5. What I really want to find is a brand-new sports program, and which will give me the training I need, because I don't have the experience necessary to succeed in established sports, although I am willing to work as hard as I need to in order to bring my skills up to a competitive level.

B. Working in a group, share your revisions of the sentences. Decide which versions of the sentences are the best, and be ready to explain and defend your choices.

ESL ADVICE: GRAMMATICAL STRUCTURES FOR COORDINATION AND SUBORDINATION

Use both coordinators and subordinators, but avoid mixing the two.

| MIXED | **Although** frogs can live on land and in water, **but** they need to breathe oxygen. |

This sentence has a subordinator, *although*, and a coordinator, *but*. Use one pattern, but not both.

| CONSISTENT COORDINATION | Frogs can live on land and in water, **but** they need to breathe oxygen. |

| CONSISTENT SUBORDINATION | **Although** frogs can live on land and in water, they need to breathe oxygen. |

Visit mycomplab.com for more resources and exercises on coordination and subordination.

PART 9

Words and Style

CHAPTER 48

Wordiness

As a writer, you can state similar thoughts in different ways to achieve different effects on your readers. For example, you can create a short, direct sentence.

> Incentive pay improves work quality.

You can then add words to guide the effect of the sentence.

> Incentive pay **often encourages** work **of higher** quality.

Or you can bury the message with unnecessary language that clogs the meaning and frustrates or bewilders your reader.

> **There is evidence that the use of** pay **as an** incentive **can be a causative factor** in the improvement **of the** quality **of** work.

Avoiding **wordiness** does not always mean using the fewest words possible. It means including all the words appropriate for your meaning, purpose, and audience, but no more. To make sure your final drafts are concise, you need to learn how to edit for wordiness.

48a Common types of wordiness

Redundancy can creep into your writing when you use everyday phrases and patterns of expression. Their familiarity disguises their wordiness.

1 Eliminate empty words and phrases

Empty phrases like *at this point in time, totally overcome, due to the fact that,* and *each and every* add length but little meaning. Cut them.

WORDY **At this particular juncture,** the fire damage **makes it incumbent** upon us to decide whether **or not** to rebuild the old plant.

READER'S REACTION: What "particular juncture"? What does "incumbent upon" mean? Doesn't deciding "whether" imply "or not"?

CUT The fire damage **now** forces us to decide whether to rebuild the old plant.

Reduce redundant pairs. English is rich in pairs (and larger groups) of synonyms and near-synonyms. Because they say the same thing twice, **redundant pairs** are always candidates for editing.

above and beyond	each and every	part and parcel
aid and abet	free and clear	ready and willing
any and all	one and only	way, shape, or form

WORDY	To encourage innovation, the manager spoke with **each and every individual** team. Team One made a complex task manageable by dividing it into **bits and pieces.**
CUT	To encourage innovation, the manager spoke with **each** team. Team One made a complex task manageable by dividing it into **pieces.**
REPHRASED	To encourage innovation, the manager spoke with **each** team. Team One made a complex task manageable by **splitting it up.**

48a
wordy

Cut intensifying phrases. Intensifying phrases meant to add force (*for all intents and purposes, in my opinion, all things considered*) carry little meaning. Readers will find your sentences more effective without them.

WORDY	**As a matter of fact,** most archaeological discoveries can be dated accurately.
CUT	Most archaeological discoveries can be dated accurately.

Shorten or rewrite redundant phrases. Redundant phrases say the same thing twice, adding unnecessary words. *True facts, free gifts,* and *final outcomes* are redundant because by definition facts are true, gifts are free, and outcomes are final.

Some redundancies occur when you use a specific word that implies a more general term you've used with it. *Blue,* for example, clearly implies the category *color,* so it is redundant to state both (*blue in color*).

aggressive ~~by nature~~	circle ~~around~~
~~in a~~ clumsy ~~manner~~	~~in a~~ grumpy ~~mood~~
plans ~~for the future~~	small ~~in size~~

WORDY	Because it was sophisticated **in nature** and tolerant **in style,** Kublai Khan's administration aided the development of China.
CUT	Because it was **sophisticated and tolerant,** Kublai Khan's administration aided the development of China.

Edit all-purpose words. They sound important, yet **all-purpose words** like *factor, aspect, situation, type, range, thing, nature,* and *character* are often fillers. Eliminating them makes sentences easier to understand.

WORDY   Viewed **from a** sociological **perspective,** the president's popularity **factor** might be **a type of** result of the changing **nature of** our attitude toward authority.

EDITED   Viewed sociologically, the president's popularity might be a result of our changing attitude toward authority.

    All-purpose modifiers include *very, totally, major, central, secondary, unlikely, peripheral, great, really, surprisingly, definitely, absolutely, marginal, quite, superlative,* and similar terms. They are appropriate when used precisely and sparingly but can easily become clutter.

WORDY   In the short story, Young Goodman Brown is so **totally** overwhelmed by **his own** guilt that he becomes **extremely** suspicious of the people around him and **absolutely** destroys his relationships. [*30 words*]

REWRITTEN   In the short story, Young Goodman Brown's **overwhelming** guilt makes him suspicious **of everyone** and destroys his relationships. [*18 words*]

48a
wordy

Exercise 1

A. Edit each sentence to make it more concise. Use one of the three editing options for wordiness: cut unnecessary words, substitute better words, or rewrite the sentence entirely. Keep track of your changes.

EXAMPLE

~~In spite of the fact that~~ *Although* most ~~ordinary~~ middle-aged people ~~say they generally~~ feel ~~physically~~ healthy ~~and in good shape, severe physical~~ catastrophes such as ~~debilitating~~ strokes ~~and/~~or heart attacks can strike ~~suddenly~~ at any time.

1. As a matter of fact, my uncle had just come back from playing nine holes of golf when he suffered the terrible tragedy of his heart attack.
2. We all thought my aunt was absolutely in the very best of health, but she also died extremely suddenly.
3. For me, the end result of these experiences has been regular periodic visits to the doctor to check on the condition of my health.
4. On account of my last visit to the doctor, I have actually started exercising on a regular basis.

5. A regular exercise program really helps me to a better kind of feeling about myself.

B. In a small group, compare your revised versions of the sentences.
Create a "best" version of each sentence by pooling the changes in
your group. Try to base your decisions on which version gets the
writer's point across most concisely.

2 Edit wordy and repetitive sentences

Some sentence patterns encourage wordiness, which will annoy your
readers. Treat them as likely candidates for cutting and rewriting.

Rewrite sentences with expletive constructions. Beginning a sentence
with a construction like *there is*, *there are*, or *it is* allows you to hold off announcing the subject—sometimes creating emphasis or surprise. You should
use this technique sparingly, however (see 7b). Using strong verbs in place of
expletive constructions can yield shorter, more forceful sentences.

48a
wordy

OVERUSED   **It was** between 1346 and 1350 **that** the bubonic plague
              struck swiftly and horribly. **There were** over 20 million
              deaths from the plague—one-fourth of Europe's population.

REWRITTEN   Between 1346 and 1350, one-fourth of Europe's population—
              about 20 million people—died swiftly and horribly from the
              bubonic plague.

Substitute active for passive constructions. Sentences in the active
voice often strike readers as livelier and more direct than their passive coun-
terparts (see 7c-3). Favor the active voice in your writing unless you have
good reason to use the passive.

PASSIVE   Pictures of Mercury **were taken** from within 300 kilometers.

ACTIVE   *Mariner X* **took** pictures of Mercury from within 300 kilo-
              meters.

Substitute verbs for nominalizations. A **nominalization** is a verb transformed into a noun or an adjective (see p. 69).

VERB	NOMINALIZATION
analyze	analysis
combine	combination
fail	failure
recognize	recognition
vary	variable

Some professions and disciplines heavily nominalize their prose. However, you can create shorter, livelier sentences if you turn nominalizations into verbs.

NOMINALIZED   The committee held **a discussion of** the new regulations for airplane safety. **A limitation on** flammable seat materials now is necessary.

EDITED   The committee **discussed** the new regulations for airplane safety. Airlines now **must limit** flammable seat materials.

Turn clauses into phrases and phrases into words. You can often shorten clauses and phrases or reduce them to single words. Look for clauses beginning with *which, who,* or *that* and phrases beginning with *of.*

CLAUSES   The Comstock Lode, **which was a vein of silver ore,** was named after Henry T. P. Comstock, **who staked one of the first claims.**

CUT TO PHRASES   The Comstock Lode, **a vein of silver ore,** was named after Henry T. P. Comstock, **one of the first claimants.**

PHRASES   Bridge joints **covered with paint** cannot flex to relieve pressure or to avoid **fatiguing of the metal.**

CUT TO WORDS   **Painted** bridge joints cannot flex to relieve pressure and avoid **metal fatigue.**

Eliminate unnecessary repetition. When you write quickly, you may become repetitive. Such careless repetition will tire and annoy your readers. As you revise and edit, look for ideas *already stated or implied* elsewhere in your sentence or paragraph.

WORDY   GPS is a **navigation** system that helps sailors and pilots **navigate.** By getting information **about their position** from **orbiting** satellites, travelers can pinpoint their **global** position **on a chart.**

EDITED   GPS is a system that helps sailors and pilots navigate. By getting information from satellites, travelers can pinpoint their position.

Exercise 2

Rewrite each sentence to make it less wordy.

EXAMPLE

It was an ˄interest in ancient cultures ˄~~that first sparked my interest in~~ ˄an anthropology course~~, taught by~~ Professor Donaldson. ⁵˄

My (above "an")   *attracted me to* (above the struck text)

1. There is much information and detail in this informative course about the civilizations of the pre-Columbian Americas.
2. Anthropologists have spent a great deal of time studying and investigating Machu Picchu, which was the center point of an advanced culture high in the Andes Mountains.
3. There are many excavations in the area that have received support from American universities.
4. It seems to be true that the ruins are a really breathtaking sight.
5. Proposals for further exploration are now being made to funding organizations by several groups of anthropologists.

48b Clichés, generalizations, and overblown language

Many writers in college choose language that is either overused (clichéd) or stuffy or complicated. They may do this because they're unfamiliar with a specialized topic or think they must sound "smart" to their readers. But most readers are more irritated than impressed by such language.

48b
wordy

1 Omit clichés

Much wordiness stems from a lack of tough, careful attention to language. **Clichés** and **vague generalizations** are empty of meaning until the reader plugs in some concrete association. But it's a serious mistake to assume that your reader will do your work for you.

CLICHÉD   In **today's modern world,** college graduates **stumble across a startling discovery** before they **strike out on their own.** The best jobs are not necessarily the ones that give you a **shot at big money** but the ones that **turn you on** personally.

EDITED   Even before they have their diplomas, today's college graduates have begun to rethink the idea of employment. The glamour of high-salary positions is soon replaced by hopes of happiness, job security, and friendly colleagues.

A passage with vague generalizations may be short but still wordy because it offers relatively little information. To revise, *add specific details* or *combine sentences* to eliminate repetition and highlight relationships.

WORDY   Glaciers were of central importance in the shaping of the North American landscape. They were responsible for many familiar geological features. Among the many remnants of glacial activity are deeply carved valleys and immense piles of sand and rock.

COMBINED   Glaciers carved deep valleys and left behind immense piles of sand and rock, shaping much of the North American landscape in the process.

DETAILS ADDED Glaciers carved deep valleys and left behind immense piles of sand and rock, shaping much of the North American landscape in the process. Cape Cod and Long Island are piles of gravel deposited by glaciers. The Mississippi River and the Great Lakes were left behind when the ice melted.

2 Edit overblown language

Overblown language consists of words too formal or technical for your purpose and audience. Rein in your formal diction and technical words, using them only when they contribute directly to your point.

OVERBLOWN Under the **present conditions of** our society, marriage **practices** generally **demonstrate a high degree of** homogeneity.

APPROPRIATE In our culture, people tend to marry others like themselves.

3 Eliminate excessive writer's commentary

**48b
wordy**

In certain contexts, talking directly to readers can be an acceptable strategy. But do so cautiously. You can occasionally use phrases like *as previously stated* or *I intend to demonstrate* to remind your readers of a point you made earlier or to set the stage for what's to come, but such phrases can become superfluous if you use them too often.

IRRITATING **As I have already shown,** considerable research suggests that placebos (pills with no physical effect) can sometimes lead to improvements or a cure. However, **my paper documents the tendency of** experts in medical ethics to question the ethics of placebo use, calling it a form of lying. **I intend to show** that the effects of placebos (**mentioned above**) overcome any moral concerns **such as the one I have just described.**

EDITED Considerable research has shown that placebos (pills with no physical effect) can sometimes lead to improvements or a cure. Experts in medical ethics, however, question the ethics of placebo use, calling it a form of lying. **This paper** will argue that the effects of placebos overcome any such moral concerns.

Exercise 3

A. Rewrite the following passage to eliminate overblown language, unnecessary commentary, vague generalizations, and clichés. As you revise, make the passage more concise.

The social psychologist and student of human behavior Peter Marsh several years ago published a tome entitled *Tribes* in which he set forth the challenging, and for many readers, downright revolutionary, conception that the denizens of our modern world perpetuate the primitive form of social organization known as a tribe. According to Marsh in his book, as a reaction against the tendency of our modern society to break up the social networks characteristic of the more rural lifestyles of earlier decades and centuries, many people form formal and informal groups based on their preferences in food, clothing, recreation, and work. Some of these groupings are of remarkably short duration, consisting of what we might call fads. Let me point out that, in my opinion, Marsh is trying to be critical of many of these groups, particularly those that seek to raise the social status of members by excluding nonmembers from certain privileges. Yet I think that a careful reading of Marsh's book would also indicate that he is favorably predisposed toward the tendency of modern people to form tribes.

B. In a small group, compare your revisions of the passage. What specific changes were especially effective?

Visit mycomplab.com for more resources and exercises on wordiness.

48b
wordy

CHAPTER 49

Style, the Dictionary, and Vocabulary

Dr. Parsippani ——————— Mr. Rollet.

Several words meaning "caused to die" could fill the blank in this sentence, including *killed, slaughtered, assassinated,* and *murdered.* What word will best express your intended meaning? *Assassinate* is usually reserved for important political figures; *slaughtered* usually applies to livestock; and *murdered* indicates foul play. If you meant none of these more specific meanings, *killed* might be the simplest and most precise choice.

Choosing the right words also means choosing words appropriate to your intended purpose, audience, and context. Your choice of words and phrases—your diction—should include terms and a level of formality appropriate to your task as well as language enabling you to write as (un)emotionally, amusingly, objectively, or persuasively as you wish.

Style is largely determined by the *community* you are writing in and for. Academic, public, and work communities also have many subcommunities whose expectations for certain writing styles will differ. As you adapt to the writing of a specific community, study how its writers structure their sentences, how they organize larger pieces of text, how long or short they make their paragraphs, what information they assume to be common knowledge, and what specific words and terminology they use.

WRITING STYLE IN THREE COMMUNITIES

	ACADEMIC SETTINGS	PUBLIC SETTINGS	WORK SETTINGS
TYPICAL STYLE	Complex sentence structures; long paragraphs; specialized terminology; densely packed ideas; high degree of assumed knowledge; in some fields, calls attention to its own language; aimed at specialized, highly trained individuals.	Simple sentence structures; brief paragraphs; often "punchy" to grab attention; common vocabulary; fewer ideas per sentence; aimed at readers with diverse levels of education/reading ability.	Relatively simple sentence structures; emphasis on getting points across concisely and clearly; vocabulary varies by purpose and audience; style is adjusted to readers based on goal (e.g., to sell something vs. to provide sales information to middle managers); may include specialized business language.

WRITING STYLE IN THREE COMMUNITIES *(continued)*		
	ACADEMIC SETTINGS	**PUBLIC SETTINGS**	**WORK SETTINGS**

	ACADEMIC SETTINGS	PUBLIC SETTINGS	WORK SETTINGS
TYPICAL EXAMPLE	"In a sample of patients with a diagnosis of chronic schizophrenia, allocated to receive a course of body oriented group psychotherapy, certain parameters were assessed pre- and post-treatment: (1) Ego-pathology, using the ego-pathology inventory (EPI); (2) Body experiences (size perception/image marking procedure—IMP, body image/body distortion question-naire—BDQ, and body cathexis/ visual-analogue-scales—VAS); and (3) Common symptom factors, using the Positive And Negative Symptom Scale (PANSS)."[1]	"Can't stand seeing trash in Claber Pond? Hate jogging past old cans and bottles along Sillers Creek Trail? Join the CCC (Citizens for a Cleaner Community) THIS SATURDAY, 9:00 a.m.–noon, for a trash cleanup crusade! Meet at the Claber Community Center before 9:00. If possible, wear boots and work gloves. Bags will be supplied. Free donuts and coffee!"	"In late 2008, ITU reported that worldwide cell phone subscriptions had passed the 4 billion mark, creating a ready market for designer cell phone jackets. As a direct result of the surge in cell phone ownership, CellCover has already established a worldwide market base, with shipments expected to increase from 2.1 million in 2009 to 4.3 million by 2011. Our product line, shown on pp. 4–7 of this proposal, includes jackets in a wide range of colors, textures, and patterns, some with animal or sports themes."

**49a
words**

1. Frank, Röhrich, Nina Papadopoulos, Iris Suzuki, and Stefan Priebe, "Ego-pathology, body experience, and body psychotherapy in chronic schizophrenia," *Psychology & Psychotherapy: Theory, Research & Practice*, 82.1 (2009), 19–30.

49a Word choice, readers' needs, and writers' purposes

Whenever you choose specific words while you draft and revise, you base your decisions on your purpose, audience, context, and persona (the image of yourself that you project in your writing).

1 Adjust your diction to your readers' needs

The characteristics of your readers should play a major role in your choice of words (see Chapter 3). When you write for college audiences, maintain a fairly high level of formality (the exceptions being deliberately informal notes, responses, journal entries, and quoted speech).

TOO INFORMAL   The stock market **crash** didn't seem to **faze** many of the investors with **dollars stashed** in property assets.

READER'S REACTION: This seems really casual; I'm not sure I trust the writer's authority.

EDITED   The stock market's fall did not significantly affect investors with extensive property assets.

2 Adjust your diction to your purpose

Your *purpose* plays an important role in determining your diction (see Chapter 3). In much academic writing, your aim will be to inform readers, providing a balanced, detailed assessment of a topic. Using highly emotional, unreasoned, or outrageous language will subvert your purposes.

BIASED   Most proponents of rock-music censorship grew up thinking even wimpy bands like the Beach Boys were a bunch of perverts.

READER'S REACTION: I thought this was a paper weighing the sides of the rock-music censorship debate. This seems too biased and emotional.

EDITED   Proponents of rock-music censorship may unfairly stereotype all of rock-and-roll culture as degenerate or evil.

49a
words

3 Adjust your diction to your persona

Use words that help you create an appropriate persona. Your **persona** as a writer refers to the public role or character you assume. For example, your persona in a clinical experiment will be objective and detached; too many personal references may call into question the accuracy of the experiment. But clinical diction may be too cold and unfeeling for other occasions.

ROBOTLIKE   The river having been reached, a camp was set, and dinner was prepared and eaten. The sunset was observed at the lake. Then eight hours of sleep ensued.

READER'S REACTION This narrative lacks vitality. The characters seem like robots.

EDITED   When we reached the river, we set camp, cooked dinner, enjoyed the sunset at the lake, and slept for eight hours.

4 Use specialized diction appropriately

If you're writing in a specific field or discipline, you need to adjust your diction to your context. In a history course, for example, readers of your papers will expect certain terms and language that might not be appropriate in a physics course.

When you write for general audiences, your readers will find highly specialized language inappropriate. If you use diction too general for readers in a specialized field, however, your writing may seem naive *in that context*. Revise your drafts to include specific terms used in the field (if you understand those terms, and if they add to accuracy and economy).

TOO GENERAL   [*in an analysis of a painting for an art history course*] Tiepolo's *Apotheosis of the Pisani Family* (1761) is a lively painting with lots of action going on in it, with nice colors, and typical of the period when it was painted.

       READER'S REACTION: The diction seems too general for a specialized analysis in my field of art history.

EDITED   Tiepolo's *Apotheosis of the Pisani Family* (1761) shows affinities with typical rococo frescoes of the period, including bright colors with characters in various highlighted actions set against dark border accents.

When you learn new words in one field, you may inadvertently use those words in another field in which they are inappropriate.

49a
words

TOO COMPLEX   [*in an economics paper on the influence of sexuality in the marketplace*] Ego gratification, originating in the neo-erotic domains of the pleasure principle, remains one of the chief factors influencing the attractiveness of sexuality in marketing.

       READER'S REACTION: I'm an economics major, not a Freudian psycho-analyst. Talk in my language, please.

EDITED   Freudian theory can help us to explain why sexuality sells in the American marketplace. According to Freud, humans are biologically caught in a kind of sexual rhythm. This rhythm causes us to seek certain kinds of gratification not always explicitly sexual.

Exercise 1

A. Assume that the following paragraph is part of a brochure on dental hygiene found in a dentist's office. Examine the passage, and circle words and phrases you find inappropriate. Write a paragraph explaining the problems in diction that you identified in the passage. Consider its intended audience, purpose, context, and persona.

Brushing and flossing of human dentin has been shown to be instrumental in the systematic reduction of invasive caries. When brushing, it is advisable to rotate the cusp of the preventive maintenance tool at alternating angles during upward and downward motion. When flossing, it is advisable to insert and retract the flossing material several times between the dentitial spaces.

B. In a group, compare your responses. Which choices of diction did everyone find inappropriate? As a group, try editing the passage.

49b Precise diction

Because you may draft more fluently when you're not weighing every word, you'll find it helpful to work with diction as you edit. Think of this process as adjusting your prose to match your intended meaning.

1 Choose specific words

Try whenever possible to edit for more specific, accurate words.

TOO VAGUE [*in a do-it-yourself brochure describing bathroom remodeling*] Note: Do not place flooring over uneven floor or with wood rot. Remove damaged area first.

READER'S REACTION: The language is vague and imprecise. What do I do with a "damaged area"?

EDITED Note: Do not install any new flooring over existing floors that are weak or uneven or show signs of wood rot. Replace any damaged flooring material before installing new flooring.

2 Choose words with appropriate connotations

English is full of **synonyms,** which are words identical or nearly identical in meaning. When choosing among words, consider the words' **connotations**—the shades of meaning, or associations, that words acquire over time. When editing, look for inappropriate connotations in your choice of words.

IMPRECISE The senator **retreated** from the gathering.

READER'S REACTION: But the senator had no reason to feel attacked or bewildered.

EDITED The senator **left** the gathering.

3 Edit for archaic words and neologisms

The English language changes constantly. Some words are doomed to become obsolete. New words enter the vocabulary by the hundreds. Still others shift their meanings, as in the case of *gay,* which used to mean "carefree" but now almost exclusively means "homosexual."

Most **archaic words**—words that are rarely used any more but are still found in older literature—will be labeled as such in the dictionary. In general, use them only for special reasons. **Neologisms**—words coined very recently—may not be in the dictionary at all. Whenever you suspect that a term is too new to be acceptable in writing, identify it as new and define it, or else avoid it altogether.

ARCHAIC/
NEOLOGIC

Good reviews of our play had been scarce (**save** in *Fanfare*), so the leading actors Shawn and Alexis decided it was time for a staycation, missing two shows.

READER'S REACTION: *Save* seems old-fashioned, and I think I know what a "staycation" is but I'm not sure.

EDITED

Good reviews of our play had been scarce (**except** in *Fanfare*), so the leading actors Shawn and Alexis decided it was time to take a break, missing two shows.

4 Edit for idiomatic and trite expressions

Idioms are words and phrases whose meanings have changed, usually to something quite different from their literal definitions. These terms often have forgotten histories. Here are common idioms.

49b
words

IDIOM	MEANING
get in the fast lane	rise up; lead a fast-paced lifestyle
meet your maker	die
pack it in	quit, resign
take a spin	go for a ride
wipe the slate clean	start over

In most academic writing, idioms are too informal or have become trite from overuse. Replace them with precise words.

IDIOMATIC

The winning team was **placed high upon a pedestal,** while the losers, **wallowing in a slough of despond,** reminded themselves of what a **dog-eat-dog** world it is in sports.

EDITED

The winning team was idolized and cheered by fans, while the losers, despondent and humorless, consoled themselves over their defeat.

Exercise 2

A. Read the following paragraph and identify cases of inappropriate diction. Look for imprecise, misused, stuffy, or trite words, checking in a dictionary if you need to. Then edit the passage by replacing the misused words or expressions with more appropriate ones.

The inaugural time I witnessed someone parachuting from a plane was when I was in college. The parachuting establishment was located in the desert of Arizona. First we apprised ourselves on the diminutive single-prop plane and shackled ourselves into the seats. Three employees of a local business were the jumpers. We circled around until we reached the pinnacle for jumping, about 6,000 feet up. The first customer was about to detort but became lugubrious with fear and couldn't jump. The second man faced us with his back to the open side of the plane and a verecund expression on his face, then fell back deliberately and dejected himself from the craft, spinning downward toward the verdurous desert.

B. In a small group, compare your edited versions of the passage. Discuss all your choices, and then try to reach consensus on the best substitutions.

49c Using a dictionary and a thesaurus

Having a wide-ranging vocabulary—not just *knowing* lots of words, but knowing how to use them appropriately—is clearly helpful for editing your diction. But even the most experienced writers will tell you that when it comes to choosing words, they always search for just the right flavor. Use the following strategies when you think common sense isn't enough.

1 Use a dictionary

Dictionaries give you precise definitions as well as usage notes. When editing your work, circle any words that you have learned fairly recently or have not used often; then look them up to be sure you've used them correctly.

STRATEGY Use the dictionary

Different kinds of dictionaries have different purposes. Some provide etymological information (on the history of a word); others may provide only a basic definition. Learn to look up information in a dictionary based on your own needs. For a test of usage, look at the usage notes in an entry. To be sure that a word captures your precise meaning, read its definition carefully. To test whether the word is grammatically correct in your sentence, look at the information on its part of speech and the variations thereof. (The sample entries in Figure 49.1 provide all these kinds of information.)

in•fer \in-ˈfər\ vb in•ferred; in•fer•ring [MF or L; MF inferer, fr. L inferre, lit., to carry or bring into, fr. in- + ferre to carry — more at BEAR] vt (1528) **1** : to derive as a conclusion from facts or premises (we see smoke and ~ fire —L. A. White) — compare IMPLY **2** : GUESS, SURMISE (your letter . . . allows me to ~ that you are as well as ever —O. W. Holmes †1935) **3 a** : to involve as a normal outcome of thought **b** : to point out: INDICATE (this doth ~ the zeal I had to see him —Shak.) (another survey . . . ~ s that two-thirds of all present computer installations are not paying for themselves —H. R. Chellman) **4** : SUGGEST, HINT (are you inferring I'm incompetent?) ~ vi: to draw inferences (men . . . have observed, inferred, and reasoned . . . to all kinds of results —John Dewey) — in•fer•able also in•fer•ri•ble \in-ˈfər-ə-bəl\ adj— in•fer•rer \-ˈfər-ər\ n

syn INFER, DEDUCE, CONCLUDE, JUDGE, GATHER mean to arrive at a mental conclusion. INFER implies arriving at a conclusion by reasoning from evidence; if the evidence is slight, the term comes close to surmise (from that remark, I inferred that they knew each other). DEDUCE often adds to INFER the special implication of drawing a particular inference from a generalization (denied we could deduce anything important from human mortality). CONCLUDE implies arriving at a necessary inference at the end of a chain of reasoning (concluded that only the accused could be guilty). JUDGE stresses a weighing of the evidence on which a conclusion is based (judge people by their actions). GATHER suggests an intuitive forming of a conclusion from implications (gathered their desire to be alone without a word).

usage Sir Thomas More is the first writer known to have used both infer and imply in their approved senses (1528). He is also the first to have used infer in a sense close in meaning to imply (1533). Both of these uses of infer coexisted without comment until some time around the end of World War I. Since then, senses 3 and 4 of infer have been frequently condemned as an undesirable blurring of a useful distinction. The actual blurring has been done by the commentators. Sense 3, descended from More's use of 1533, does not occur with a personal subject. When objections arose, they were to a use with a personal subject (now sense 4). Since dictionaries did not recognize this use specifically, the objectors assumed that sense 3 was the one they found illogical, even though it had been in respectable use for four centuries. The actual usage condemned was a spoken one never used in logical discourse. At present sense 4 is found in print chiefly in letters to the editor and other informal prose, not in serious intellectual writing. The controversy over sense 4 has apparently reduced the frequency of use of sense 3.

in•fer•ence \ˈin-f(ə-)rən(t)s, -fərn(t)s\ n (1594) **1** : the act or process of inferring: as **a** : the act of passing from one proposition, statement, or judgment considered as true to another whose truth is believed to follow from that of the former **b** : the act of passing from statistical sample data to generalizations (as of the value of population parameters) usu. with calculated degrees of certainty **2** : something that is inferred; esp: a proposition arrived at by inference **3** : the premises and conclusion of a process of inferring

in•fer•en•tial \ˌin-fə-ˈren(t)-shəl\ adj [ML inferential, fr. L inferent-, inferens, prp. of inferre] (1657) **1** : relating to, involving, or resembling inference **2** : deduced or deducible by inference

in•fer•en•tial•ly \-ˈren(t)-sh(ə-)lฺẹ\ adv (1691) : by way of inference : through inference

ESL

49c
dctnry

FIGURE 49.1 Detail from Merriam-Webster's Collegiate Dictionary, 11th ed. Springfield, MA: Merriam-Webster, 2003.

ESL ADVICE: USING DICTIONARIES

Sometimes you want to express an idea or a concept in writing, but you do not know what word or words would express it in English. Bilingual dictionaries are usually a good starting point to find a possible translation. However, for every word, they list several options. It is important that you consult an English dictionary to ensure that you choose the most appropriate word. These dictionaries contain definitions and examples that can help you decide which word best matches your intended meaning and your diction.

TYPES OF DICTIONARIES

collegiate dictionary A full-size academic reference dictionary, generally available in a library, that has not been abbreviated to save space. It provides detailed information about words, including specialized terms, and notes on usage as well as full etymological information.

pocket dictionary An abbreviated or abridged dictionary useful for quick checks on spelling or definitions.

desk dictionary A midsized dictionary suitable for most professional and academic contexts.

thesaurus A dictionary of **synonyms** and **antonyms**—words similar or opposite in meaning to each other. A thesaurus is useful when you want to find an alternative to a word you've already considered, or perhaps to remember a word that has slipped your mind.

specialized dictionary A dictionary that lists terms from a particular field or about a specific topic. For example, dictionaries of colloquialisms, slang, idioms, informal usage, or academic and professional dictionaries.

rhyming dictionary A dictionary that gives rhymes for words.

spelling dictionary A dictionary that gives the spellings of words but not their definitions or etymologies.

online dictionaries and thesauruses Software and online dictionaries and thesauruses are far less bulky and can be upgraded more easily and more quickly than traditional print versions. You can also personalize many computer dictionaries, adding your own special words to the dictionary's memory. Computerized dictionaries also have their limitations. It's more difficult to browse through them, and you won't be able to use your dictionary without a computer.

---

2 Use a thesaurus

A thesaurus provides lists of synonyms that can be useful when you're editing diction and want to replace an existing word. But be careful. Be sure you're familiar with a synonym and its connotations before simply substituting it. Ask yourself whether your new word choice captures your meaning more accurately, gives more flavor, or avoids redundancy more effectively than your original choice. When in doubt, stick with words you know.

ORIGINAL   She was **angered** to the point of frustration.

WRITER'S REACTION: I'm not satisfied with *anger*. My thesaurus suggests the alternatives *vexed, irritated, exasperated, infuriated, inflamed, miffed,* and *enraged.*

IMPRECISE   She was **enraged** to the point of frustration.

WRITER'S REACTION: This word is too strong and does not convey the woman's true feelings.

EDITED   She was **irritated** to the point of frustration.

> **STRATEGY** **Use the slash/option technique**
>
> When you have several alternatives in mind for a particular word, but stopping to weigh the alternatives may break your train of thought, write down the alternative words and separate them with slashes. Later, as you revise and edit, choose the word that most accurately fits your intended meaning.

Exercise 3

Locate a short passage in a newspaper or magazine article and rewrite the passage, substituting words that are inappropriate or inaccurate. Make several copies of the original passage and your version of it. In a group, work on each other's passages to "repair" the damage. Then compare your edited versions with the original passages. How close did you come to the originals? What differences can you see between your repaired versions and the originals?

49d Building vocabulary

A rich, varied vocabulary is the mark of an educated person, and it is essential to effective writing and reading. Clearly, the better your vocabulary, the more easily you'll recognize words as a reader and listener, and the more able you'll be to choose effective words as a writer and speaker.

1 Vocabulary and the writing process

If you don't give yourself many options for word choice, you put a stranglehold on your prose, limiting its variety, its accuracy, and its metaphoric potential. Consider the four versions of one line written by Johanna Vaughan in her paper about food-shelf programs.

> Without the help of local and state government, the food-shelf program in Seattle will become **ineffective.**

> Without the **beneficence** of local government, the food-shelf program in Seattle will die **of starvation.**

> Without the **financial nurturing** of local government, Seattle's food-shelf program will die of **nutritional neglect.**

> Without the financial **sustenance** of local government, Seattle's food-shelf program will **slowly** die of starvation.

Many of Vaughan's choices depend on more than the substitution of individual words, but it's hard to overlook the role her vocabulary plays in her writing process. She can revise more effectively *because she has more options*—she can experiment with words like *sustenance, beneficence,* and *obsolete.*

Although it can become tedious to move back and forth between your emerging sentences and that 1,500-page dictionary on your desk, there is something to be said for even modest vocabulary development during the process of completing each of your writing assignments. Especially while revising, take time to consider alternatives to some of your words, perhaps circling those that seem repetitive or bland, then listing alternatives or using a dictionary or thesaurus.

2 Vocabulary and the reading process

Every time you pick up a book or newspaper, you're exposed to new words. In many cases, the mere exposure to those words, in their contexts, helps you to acquire them as part of your vocabulary. But a few deliberate techniques can help.

- Each day, select one word from something you've read, look up its definition, and check its etymology. Then, without sounding too unnatural, try incorporating the word into your speech at least three times during the day. If that's not possible, just make up sentences on your own, and say them silently to yourself.
- Keep an ongoing list of unfamiliar words, look them up, and review them periodically, crossing them out when they've become part of your vocabulary. The words on your list should come directly from material you're reading and studying, from the daily newspaper to the most complex textbook chapters.
- Every time you look up a word for its meaning, check its etymology. Most English words have Anglo-Saxon, Latin, Greek, or French origins. When you look up a word's roots, you further develop your vocabulary.

Exercise 4

A. To practice studying the etymologies of words, look up the following examples in a full-length (unabridged) dictionary. (The best source will be the *Oxford English Dictionary* in your college library.) Look for anything unusual or interesting about the history of these words.

EXAMPLE: KANGAROO

The OED says that the word probably comes from an indigenous aboriginal language of Australia and meant "I don't know" or "I don't understand," the response given to visitors who asked the aborigines the name of the animal.

barbecue	guillotine	mesmerize	sadist
blimp	juke (box)	muscle	sandwich
blurb	ketchup	OK or okay	serendipity
dollar	laser	robot	voodoo

B. In a group, compare your etymologies for the words above. What surprised you about the origins of these words?

Visit mycomplab.com for more resources and exercises on style, the dictionary, and vocabulary.

49d
vocab

CHAPTER **50**

Appropriate and Respectful Language

What is **sexist language?** People disagree about some common terms. For example, *seminal* is widely used to mean "highly original and influencing future events or developments"—but the literal meaning of the word is "pertaining to, containing, or consisting of semen." As such, it represents a potentially sexist usage: why should originality and creativity be associated with maleness? Some people think the term should be dropped in favor of words like *important* or *influential*; others argue that it's perfectly acceptable.

No matter how you feel about specific issues, as a writer you *must* be concerned with the reactions of readers to the way you represent men and women and members of minority groups. You don't want to alienate your readers, prejudice people against your ideas, or perpetuate unhealthy attitudes.

50a Home and community language varieties

Every language in the world is spoken in a variety of ways called *dialects.* English has hundreds of dialects, which vary in obvious ways between countries, like England and the United States, but also within these countries. The American English spoken in Natchez, Mississippi, differs considerably from the American English spoken in Bar Harbor, Maine. Dialects can also vary by culture, ethnicity, and nationality. Not only do Cuban Americans and Puerto Rican Americans speak different dialects of American English in New York City, but their dialects may vary between the Bronx and Brooklyn. Similar people may have different dialects even though they live just a few miles from each other—or a few blocks.

1 Learn to see dialect variations as "rules"

Linguists point out that all dialects have rules. What conforms to a rule in one dialect may break a rule in another. This is how all language works—the "rules" are the structures and conventions that people within a group unconsciously agree to use in their speech. Pronouncing the word *pen* to rhyme with *hen* is a rule of Northern and much Midwestern speech, but the rule in large parts of the South is to rhyme *pen* with *tin*. Who's right? Each group follows the rules of its own community. To break them is to be seen as an outsider.

2 Understand standard English as a function of power and social prestige

Why *should* it be any more correct to say "There isn't anyone who can tell me anything about what I haven't seen" than to say "Ain't nobody gonna tell me nothing about what I ain't see"? After all, double negatives are acceptable in hundreds of languages around the world, so there is no logical reason why they should be incorrect in English. In fact, they were once perfectly acceptable and were used by Chaucer and Shakespeare.

Around the world, each language has a prestige dialect that is thought to be more "correct" or "proper" than other dialects. How this dialect came to be preferred is almost always a matter of historical, political, and social forces. Some group of people came into power, and before long their language variety became associated with correctness; people who wanted to be thought educated had to learn its rules.

If your home dialect differs from the standard, you may be unfairly stereotyped or discriminated against by people in positions of power. For many, the solution is to learn how to shift between dialects depending on context. Everyone does this to some extent with the level of their formality (they wouldn't speak the same way with their family as they speak in a classroom or on the job). For speakers of nonstandard dialects, shifting involves certain grammatical constructions, word choices, and expressions or uses of language.

50a
discrm

Exercise 1

A. Briefly describe any features of your own home or community language that you're aware of in your speech or writing habits. What kinds of features are they: words? accent? grammar? What are their sources? Have you ever felt stereotyped or discriminated against because of your home or community language, or felt awkward in a situation in which your speech differed from that of others? Is there disagreement within your own community about what's correct? How do you feel about the issue of language authority? Do you want to hold on to your community language? Or do you want to get rid of all traces of that language? If you could do that, how do you think people in your home community would respond?

B. In a group, compare your reflections on your home or community language. Focus specifically on the problems of power, prestige, and language prejudice.

3 Become aware of the grammatical variations in your home dialect

Grammatical variations in your home or community dialect can be tricky to notice in your writing; after all, they may not look the least bit odd or problematic—to you. But someone who isn't a member of your dialect community will see them right away.

HOME VARIETY   Miss Brill know that the lovers making fun of her, but she act like she don't care.

EDITED   Miss Brill knows that the lovers are making fun of her, but she acts as if she doesn't care.

HOME VARIETY   The FDA guy said to Dougherty could he borrow him the test kit, but Dougherty said he would bring it with.

EDITED   A representative of the FDA asked whether Dougherty could lend him the test kit, but Dougherty said he would bring it with him.

HOME VARIETY   The minutes of the last meeting state that unless if RayCorp had ordered the resistors, the shipment was sent out on accident.

EDITED   The minutes of the last meeting state that unless RayCorp had ordered the resistors, the shipment was sent out accidentally.

50a
discrm

STRATEGY Recognize language variations

See variations in your home or community language as rules or patterns, and match them against the rules of the standard dialect. In a notebook, first record examples of rules specific to your community language; then write down the corresponding examples in standard English. Explain the differences in your own words.

RULE IN MY PART
OF KENTUCKY   The lawn needs mowed.

RULE ELSEWHERE   The lawn needs to be mowed.

Everyone in my part of Kentucky leaves out the *to be* and just puts in the verb after *needs*. It's always seemed natural to me, but I learned that it is only done in certain parts of the United States. I can use the "search" function on my computer to look for the word *needs* and then make sure I fix the mistake.

Exercise 2

A. Consider the following excerpt from *Their Eyes Were Watching God*, a novel by the African American author Zora Neale Hurston. This conversation between two characters, Phoeby Watson and Janie Stark, represents the language variety used in the characters' home and community and is therefore the most expressive way for them to relate to each other.

> [Phoeby] found [Janie] sitting on the steps of the back porch with the lamps all filled and the chimneys cleaned.
> "Hello, Janie, how you comin'?"
> "Aw, pretty good, Ah'm tryin' to soak some uh de tiredness and de dirt outa mah feet." She laughed a little.
> "Ah see you is. Gal, you sho looks *good*. You looks like youse yo' own daughter." They both laughed. "Even wid dem overhalls on, you shows yo' womanhood."
> "G'wan! G'wan! You must think Ah brought yuh somethin'. When Ah ain't brought home a thing but mahself."
> "Dat's a gracious plenty. Yo' friends wouldn't want nothin' better."
> —ZORA NEALE HURSTON, *Their Eyes Were Watching God*

The second passage is a letter requesting that a local YWCA suspend the writer's membership until she is able to exercise again. The passage contains features of the writer's home community dialect that are not considered standard. But the letter is written for a general reading public because the YWCA may employ people who do not share the writer's language variety.

50b
discrm

Dear Mrs. Voit,

Like I explain to you when I call last week, I ain't been use my YWCA membership since November because I am pregnant and my doctor be telling me not to work out. Please stop my membership now and I call you when I want it start up again.

Sincerely,

Loretta Saunders

Edit both passages to make them conform to standard written English. Then reflect on the consequences of your changes. Has anything been lost from either passage? Has anything been gained through editing? How appropriate are the changes made to each passage?

B. In a group, compare your changes and your reflections. What does this exercise suggest about the principles of standard English and the idea of flexibility?

50b How dialects influence writing

Along with dialect differences, all speakers of English use differences in **register** in both their speaking and their writing. Register is the form that language takes in a particular context. The variations can be in pronunciation, grammar, or word choice. You might use a *formal* register when being interviewed for an important job, an *informal* register at a ball game, a *technical* register when explaining to a colleague how a piece of electronic equipment works, or a *simplified* register when talking with a toddler.

1 Become aware of oral language influences

Most of the language we produce is spoken. If you haven't been an avid reader, there may be expressions, terms, and constructions that you've *heard* often but haven't *seen* much in print. Your knowledge of the sound can trick you into making an error when you turn that sound into print.

Consider one of the most common mistakes in writing: spelling the phrase *a lot* as one word (*alot*). Why do so many people do this? Partly because they're smart: spoken, this phrase really does sound like one word, with little or no pause between *a* and *lot*. Transcription errors of this kind show up often in unedited prose.

50b
discrm

I should of signed the check	for	*I should have signed the check*
excetera	for	*et cetera*
It's a doggy-dog world	for	*It's a dog-eat-dog world*
expresso	for	*espresso*

The way language sounds in your home or community variety can also end up in your writing, and this may unfortunately (and often unfairly) lead your reader to judge you negatively or doubt your credibility or intelligence. In the first example below, the omission of *-ed* from *ask* is clearly an intelligent mistake: the *-ed* of *asked* is pronounced as a *t*, and the *t* of *Trish* swallows it in speech. In the second example, illustrating the influence of Spanish, *this* sounds like *these* to the writer, leading to another intelligent mistake, while the repetition of *either* is a common feature of the Chicano English of Southern California.

DRAFT   The personnel department ask Trish Walters could she expedite the request.

READER'S REACTION: Why is *ask* in the present tense? Also, when I get to *could*, I'm thrown off track. The writer seems careless.

EDITED   The personnel department asked Trish Walters whether she could expedite the request.

DRAFT   Either the character cause all this events, or either they are coincidental.

EDITED   Either the characters cause all these events, or they are coincidental.

2 Consider your word choices

Usually, writers consciously choose their words to make them appropriate for the occasion—formal or informal, complex or simple. Sometimes, however, writers unknowingly use words that are part of their home or community language but are not shared by a broader community of readers. In such cases, readers may think the text is too informal because it uses "local" words. These words can usually be spotted with a careful editorial eye and the help of a good dictionary.

DRAFT   Our interoffice mail is consistently slow because the mailcarrier has to schlep packages along with the memos and letters.

READER'S REACTION: "Schlep?" Is that some sort of corporate term?

EDITED   Our interoffice mail is consistently slow because the mailcarrier has to deliver packages along with the memos and letters.

3 Distinguish between slang and dialect

Words that are part of a dialect have usually been around in that dialect for some time. People of all ages may use them, and they are known by much or most of the dialect community. Sometimes these words even become part of the standard language—for example, the word *jazz*.

When groups within a dialect community (often young people) create new words that aren't shared by the entire community, those words will be considered **slang.** You should avoid using slang in writing (except perhaps in informal journals or learning logs). Some people may not understand it; others may feel alienated from your prose. Still others, both within and beyond your language community, may not take your ideas seriously. (For more on word usage, see Chapter 49.)

SLANG   The battle scenes in *The Iliad* are phat. Just when Agamemnon chill, someone diss him or jack something up and he wage another war.

4 Recognize hypercorrection

People who use a nonmainstream dialect may become aware of certain language habits that are not considered the norm. When they shift registers in formal situations, they may consciously or unconsciously try to "repair" their speech. Sometimes they may unwittingly create a new error in trying to be correct. Linguists call this phenomenon **hypercorrection.**

Writers create hypercorrection because they're *trying* to be formal. In an urge to be correct, the writer guesses that a construction is wrong and ironically substitutes an error for it.

HYPERCORRECT   Stuart will give the petitions to Mary and I.

EDITED   Stuart will give the petitions to Mary and me.

50b
discrm

The concept of hypercorrection can also apply to the style and structure of your sentences. If you try too hard to be formal and sophisticated, you may end up writing tangled prose.

CONVOLUTED   That the girl walks away, and the showing of the parrot to the restaurant owner who, having closed shop, is not about to let her inside, is indicative of that which characterizes the novel throughout, i.e., denial and deception.

EDITED   The central theme of denial and deception is illustrated when the girl tries to show the parrot to the restaurant owner and is turned away.

50c Sexist language: Recognizing and editing

As you edit your writing, try to read what you've written from the perspective of a person of the other gender or another culture. Be especially sensitive when you're characterizing groups, discussing occupational roles, or referring to all human beings.

1 Avoid implying stereotyped views

Your readers are likely to object to language that demeans women or plays into negative stereotypes of women's behaviors, roles, and attributes.

DEMEANING   Driving **like a typical woman,** Susan backed her car into the shopping cart.
READER'S REACTION: This unfairly stereotypes women as incompetent.

EDITED   Susan **inadvertently** backed her car into the shopping cart.

2 Avoid gender-stereotyping roles and occupations

Our use of language has not entirely kept pace with social changes in men's and women's roles, especially in the area of occupation. Be on the lookout for unfair or inaccurate stereotyping.

STEREOTYPED   The most important thing **a mother can do** to facilitate language growth in **her** child is to read aloud to **him** as much as possible.
READER'S REACTION: I'm the father of a little girl. I object to the implications that only mothers can care for children and that all children are boys.

EDITED   The most important thing **parents can do** to facilitate language growth in **their children** is to read aloud to **them** as much as possible.

3 Beware of male terms used generically

The most common form of sexist language uses *mankind* or *men* for humankind; *he*, *his*, or *him* for all people; and a host of words that imply male roles for occupations (*fireman*, *policeman*, and the like). Most cases are easily edited: *police officer* for *policeman*, *garbage collector* (or *sanitation worker*) for *garbageman*. Editing out the generic *he*, however, may prove more difficult. When possible, try first to make the construction plural. For example, you can substitute *their* for *his* or for the clumsy *his or her*.

SEXIST   Every child should bring **his** lunch money to school with **him** each day.

AWKWARD   Every child should bring **his or her** lunch money to school with **him or her** each day.

BETTER   All children should bring **their** lunch money to school with **them** each day.

Exercise 3

50c
discrm

A. The following list of words and proposed replacements ranges from the obviously sexist (and therefore inflexible and in need of revision) to the highly debatable and even absurd. For each word, decide whether you would accept the alternative term, and explain why. (Tip: Consult a dictionary when in doubt.)

1. *Persondible* for *mandible*
2. *People-eating tiger* for *man-eating tiger*
3. *Personic depressive* for *manic depressive*
4. *Face-to-face talk* for *man-to-man talk*
5. *Sanitation employee* for *garbageman*
6. *Actor* for both *actor* and *actress*
7. *"Our parent, who art in heaven . . ."* for *"Our Father, who art in heaven . . ."*
8. *Chair* or *chairperson* for *chairman*
9. *Waitperson* or *waitron* for *waiter* and *waitress*
10. *Flight attendant* for *steward* and *stewardess*

B. Compare your responses with those of your fellow writers. (And, while you're at it, add *fellow* to your list.)

4 Avoid implying sexist views

Whenever you revise your prose, pay special attention to the ways you characterize men and women and their roles and relationships. Avoid making offhand remarks that could be interpreted as sexist.

SEXIST

Being a girl, Sondra was chosen to be at the top of the cheer-leading pyramid.

READER'S REACTION: I'm not comfortable with what's being implied about girls' abilities here.

EDITED

Being the lightest person on the team, Sondra was chosen to be at the top of the cheerleading pyramid.

SEXIST

Naturally, Mike wrestled with the flat tire while Natasha **tried to seduce someone into pulling over and helping.**

READER'S REACTION: This stereotypes men as inherently strong and capable and women as sex objects.

EDITED

Mike **struggled to change the tire** while Natasha **tried to flag down a car for help.**

5 Avoid making unwarranted claims

50c
discrm

Much sexism finds its energy in misunderstandings about the biological and intellectual nature of men and women. Men are assumed to be stronger, more agile, and more aggressive. Women are assumed to be weaker, worse at math and science but better at language, and less able to manage and negotiate. Many of these assumptions are either unfair or unsubstantiated. In your writing, avoid reinforcing such unfair and incorrect notions.

STEREOTYPED

The anti-abortion protest became more heated when several people appealed to the **instinctive nurturing emotion of the women** in the crowd.

READER'S REACTION: Aren't men nurturers too?

EDITED

The anti-abortion protest became more heated when several people appealed to the **feelings of nurture among the parents** in the crowd.

STEREOTYPED

Behaving like a wimp, Roger chose to stay home and read instead of playing football with his friends.

READER'S REACTION: This attaches negative stereotypes to men who engage in intellectual activities.

REVISED

Roger chose to stay home and read instead of playing football with his friends.

Exercise 4

A. Examine the following paragraph. Then revise its sexist language. Add to the original if you wish.

Preschool programs for children in poor families have always been underfunded and at best only a stopgap measure for more permanent educational reform. This was the message delivered by the man-and-wife team, Dr. and Mrs. Herbert Kline, Ph.D.s, at the Eleventh Regional Conference on Preschool Education. About seven hundred elementary school teachers came to the conference to hear the Klines debunk some old wives' tales about education. The Klines also focused on what the future holds for those interested in becoming public school teachers, including the need to balance work with attending to one's husband and family. Every teacher of young children, Mrs. Herbert Kline pointed out, must not only practice her craft well but also keep abreast of new theory and research which she can then integrate into her classroom in a way rewarding to her and to her students.

B. In a small group, compare your responses. What strategies did you use to revise the sexist language?

50d Discriminatory language: Recognizing and avoiding

Members of minority groups often suffer from discriminatory practices, especially those that are manifested in language. Most readers won't tolerate racism, and as soon as they encounter **discriminatory language,** they'll stop reading or throw the material away.

1 Avoid derogatory terms

You may be used to hearing certain derogatory terms and epithets in others' speech. Make sure that they don't appear in your writing, or you may anger and alienate your readers.

RACIST
> The economic problems in the border states are compounded by an increase in the number of **wetbacks** from Mexico, some of whom are illegally trying to rip off jobs from good, taxpaying citizens.
>
> READER'S REACTION: I object to characterizing a group of people this way. This derogatory name is offensive.

EDITED
> The economic problems in the border states are compounded by an increased number of illegal immigrants from Mexico, some of whom are able to get jobs in this country.

HOMOPHOBIC
> The talk show included a panel of **fags** who spoke about what it's like to be a **homo.**
>
> READER'S REACTION: Using emotionally loaded names for people doesn't encourage reasonable discussion. You'll have to be more objective than this if you want me to pay attention to your ideas.

EDITED   The talk show included a panel of gay and lesbian guests who shared their thoughts about homosexuality.

DEROGATORY   In a typically **white-male** fashion, the principal argued against the schoolteachers' referendum.

                READER'S REACTION: The fact that the principal is in position of authority doesn't give you permission to stereotype all white males negatively.

EDITED   The principal argued against the schoolteachers' referendum.

DISCRIMINATORY The Johnsons **welshed on** their response.

                READER'S REACTION: What made you think that you could say this without offending people of Welsh descent? Casual stereotyping is just as offensive as deliberate insults.

EDITED   The Johnsons were not true to their word.

2 Revise unfair stereotypes

50d
discrm

Some racial and cultural stereotypes are so ingrained in our society that you may not notice them at first. Try to maintain a critical consciousness about these stereotypes, and edit sentences or words that run the risk of unfairly stereotyping groups. Don't rely on your intentions here; think first about how your reader *might* construe your words.

RACIST/ELITIST The streets in St. Paul are so confusing that they must have been planned by a bunch of **drunken Irishmen.**

                READER'S REACTION: I object to the off-hand acceptance of this stereotype and the condescending attitude toward a group of people.

EDITED   The streets in St. Paul are so confusing that no one appears to have done any planning.

3 Choose appropriate group names and terms

Just as the issue of sexism in language continues to evolve, the representation of various groups, especially minorities, cannot be seen as "finally" corrected. Making informed decisions about how to identify different groups may require some thought or consultation. The term *American Indian* is still widely accepted, but a preferred form, *Native American*, has entered the vocabulary. Some Native American groups prefer their tribal names (*Hopi, Navajo, Havasupai*). In the 1960s, the word *Negro* gradually gave way to *black*, but not without considerable overlap in usage and much debate in both the black and white communities, including whether the terms should be capitalized. The term *colored* has been out of use for some time, but *people of color* is now preferred for members of any "nonwhite" minority group. (Many people also object to the term *nonwhite*.) *African American* itself has been gaining popularity in place of *black*, though even African

Americans do not agree on which is preferred. Terms for people of Hispanic descent can also be confusing, from *Chicano* (and its feminine form, *Chicana*) for Mexicans to *Latino* and *Latina* for people from South and Central America more generally.

STRATEGY   **Decide on terms for describing members of groups**

1. Whenever possible, use the term preferred *by the group itself.*
2. When there is disagreement within the group itself about the preferred name or term, choose the *most widely accepted term* or the one favored by a majority of the group's members.

Exercise 5

A. The chief editor of a large city newspaper received several complaint letters from readers about a sportswriter's use of the word *niggardly* to characterize the owner of a major football team who was reluctant to pay the salary asked by a new superstar player. In a column, the chief editor explained that the word *niggardly* means "stingy" or "cheap" (from Old Norse) and has absolutely no etymological connection with any racial terms. Yet some readers were offended. And, he argued, as long as they were simply *reminded* of a more offensive word, he had a duty to avoid it. He subsequently asked all reporters and editors to use alternative words. In your judgment, did the chief editor do the right thing? What issues are at stake here? Write a position statement.

50d
discrm

B. Share your position statement with your classmates.

Visit mycomplab.com for more resources and exercises on appropriate and respectful language.

PART 10

Punctuation, Mechanics, and Spelling

CHAPTER 51

Commas

Of all the punctuation marks in the English language, the comma is probably the one writers most often misuse. Confusion about commas also occurs because sometimes they are mandatory and other times they are optional. The following sentence uses no commas.

> During interviews avoid dominating the discussion because doing so especially with reticent subjects can affect whatever they say cut off the free flow of their ideas and contaminate your data.
>
> READER'S REACTION: I can't understand this sentence; it seems all jumbled together.

In the following version, commas are correctly used and make the sentence easier to read and understand.

> During interviews, avoid dominating the discussion because doing so, especially with reticent subjects, can affect whatever they say, cut off the free flow of their ideas, and contaminate your data.

51a Joining sentences

Whenever you wish to use *and, but, or, for, nor, so,* or *yet* (coordinating conjunctions) to link two word groups that can stand alone as sentences (main clauses—see 35c), you need to use a comma before the conjunction.

> He heard the dog barking **,** **so** he decided to investigate.

> The ground was rough **,** **yet** the dog still ran quickly through the grass.

Remember: join main clauses with a comma *plus* a coordinating conjunction. If you join the clauses with only a comma, you create a comma splice, a serious sentence error (see 41a).

If the main clauses you plan to join are quite short or there is no danger of misreading, you can sometimes omit the comma.

> The temperature dropped **and** the snow began falling.

STRATEGY   **Use commas appropriately**

When you use a comma plus a coordinating conjunction to join main clauses, make sure you do not distract readers by adding commas at these inappropriate places.

- After *and, but, or, nor, so, yet,* or *for* linking main clauses (rather than before).

INCORRECT   I coated the table with varnish **and**, I sanded it again.

EDITED   I coated the table with varnish, **and** I sanded it again.

- Between sentence elements other than main clauses—words, phrases, or clauses—that are linked by a coordinating conjunction.

INCORRECT   We sanded, and stained the old oak table.
   The comma splits parts of a compound verb that belong together.

EDITED   We sanded and stained the old oak table.

INCORRECT   I bought a wood stain that was inexpensive, and that cleaned up easily.
   The comma comes between subordinate, not main, clauses.

EDITED   I bought a wood stain that was inexpensive and that cleaned up easily.

SERIOUS
MISTAKE

Exercise 1

51a
∧
,

A. Combine each sentence pair into a single sentence, using commas and coordinating conjunctions.

EXAMPLE

, and it
Shopping by mail can be convenient. ~~It~~ sometimes helps save money.

1. Jim wanted to buy paper for his copier. He went to all the office supply stores in town.
2. The stores had plenty of paper. It cost more than Jim was willing to pay.
3. Jim then heard about a mail-order office supply company. He called the company for a catalog.
4. The catalog contained more than fifty kinds of reasonably priced copier paper. The paper was available in packs of one thousand sheets. For an even greater discount, the paper came in bulk orders of five thousand sheets.
5. He ordered five thousand sheets of medium-quality paper. It lasted for three months.

B. Compare your versions of the new sentences with those produced by a group of classmates. Decide which versions are the most effective and why.

51b   Setting off introductory phrases

A comma can help your readers sort sentence parts that might otherwise run together and create confusion. The simplest sentences need no comma.

noun   verb phrase
Jessica mowed the lawn.

When you add another layer to this basic sentence—a word or a word group—you may need to signal the addition with a comma.

Tirelessly, Jessica mowed the lawn.

After running five miles, Jessica mowed the lawn.

In spite of the throbbing pain in her ankle, Jessica mowed the lawn.

In general, you need to put a comma at the end of a long introductory element to let readers know where the main sentence begins.

CONFUSING   When Ruane came home and saw the chopped pieces of hose she was furious at Jessica.

CLEAR   When Ruane came home and saw the chopped pieces of hose, **she** was furious at Jessica.

You can insert a comma to tell readers which of two possible meanings you intend.

Well, over there was where I saw him, officer.

Well over there was where I saw him, officer.
Well over there is a location.

In contrast, the following sentences are easy to understand without a comma.

CLEAR   By noon Jessica will be finished mowing the lawn.

CLEAR   Suddenly it started raining and Jessica quit mowing.

You may occasionally wish to open a sentence with an interjection, such as *yes*, *no*, *well*, or *oh*. When you do, follow it with a comma unless an exclamation mark is more appropriate as a way to express strong emotion.

51b
∧
,

Yes , I cleaned the beakers and the test tubes.

No ! I do not want to attend any more meetings on the problem.

Exercise 2

A. Edit the sentences by placing commas after introductory elements where necessary.

EXAMPLE

In the past , mailboxes usually had simple designs.

1. In contrast mailboxes today come in many surprising designs.
2. Occasionally people in the suburbs choose an unusual mailbox, but residents of small towns generally display the most imagination.
3. On a recent trip through rural Iowa I noticed mailboxes in the shape of log cabins, igloos, Eiffel Towers, cows, cats, and even parrots.
4. One morning I drove down a block on which each mailbox took the shape of a different kind of fish, including bass, trout, bluegill, shark, pike, and salmon.
5. Whenever you start thinking that people in big cities or suburbs are more creative than people in small towns remember the mailboxes.

B. Working in a group, combine each of the following pairs of sentences by making one an introductory element for the other. Insert commas when appropriate.

EXAMPLE

Because
~~The~~ morning was gray and foggy , Many people woke up late.

1. People felt sleepy. They still had to go to their offices and plants for a full day's work.
2. People were trying to get to work on time. They jammed the highways and commuter trains.
3. Avi felt rested and alert. The gloomy weather did not bother him.
4. Avi worked hard throughout the afternoon. The other people in Avi's office were exhausted by two o'clock in the afternoon.
5. Avi still felt lively in the evening. He went to see a movie.

SERIOUS
MISTAKE

51c
^
,

51c Setting off nonrestrictive modifiers

Modifiers qualify or describe sentence elements. You can change the meaning of a sentence considerably by deciding whether to set off a modifier with commas. You use a **restrictive modifier** to present information that is essential to the meaning of a passage. You use a **nonrestrictive modifier** to add information that is interesting or useful but that is not essential to the meaning (see 42c).

1 Recognize nonrestrictive and restrictive modifiers

When the information in a modifier adds to a passage but is not essential to its meaning, it is a nonrestrictive modifier; set it off with commas so that readers will regard it as providing helpful but not necessary detail.

NONRESTRICTIVE The charts **,** **drawn by hand ,** were hard to read.

> READER'S REACTION: This sentence says that all the charts were hard to read. It adds the detail that the charts were hand-drawn but doesn't indicate that this was necessarily related to the problem with legibility.

When the information in a modifier is essential to the meaning of a passage, it is a restrictive modifier; present it without commas so that readers will regard it as a necessary, integral part of the sentence.

RESTRICTIVE The charts **drawn by hand** were hard to read.

> READER'S REACTION: This sentence implies that other charts were easier to read than the hand-drawn ones.

SERIOUS
MISTAKE

51c
∧
,

STRATEGY Identify nonrestrictive modifiers

Try eliminating the modifier from a sentence. If you can do so without altering the sentence's essential meaning, then the modifier is nonrestrictive and you should use commas with it.

UNEDITED SENTENCE Their band **which performs primarily in small venues like clubs** has gotten many fine reviews for its music.

WITHOUT MODIFIER Their band has gotten many fine reviews for its music.
The meaning is retained, though the sentence does not offer as much interesting information. The modifier is nonrestrictive.

EDITED Their band **,** **which performs primarily in small venues like clubs ,** has gotten many fine reviews for its music.

If eliminating a modifier changes a sentence's meaning, the modifier is restrictive. Do not set it off with commas.

UNEDITED SENTENCE Executives **,** **who do not know how to cope with stress ,** are prone to stress-related illness.

WITHOUT MODIFIER Executives are prone to stress-related illness.
The intended meaning of the original sentence is that *some* executives are susceptible to stress-related problems; the shortened sentence says *all* are. The modifier is restrictive.

EDITED Executives **who do not know how to cope with stress** are prone to stress-related illness.

2 Pay special attention to modifying clauses, phrases, and appositives

In recognizing nonrestrictive (and restrictive) modifiers as you edit, keep in mind that they can be clauses, phrases, or words (see 42c).

Look for modifying clauses beginning with *who* and *which*. Pay special attention to clauses beginning with *who, which, that, whom, whose, when,* or *where* (see 35c-5 and 42c), and decide whether they should be set off with commas. These common modifying elements can appear in the middle or at the end of a sentence.

NONRESTRICTIVE   Preventive dentistry **,** **which is receiving greater emphasis ,** reduces the number of visits to a dentist's office.

RESTRICTIVE   Dentists **who make a special effort to encourage good oral hygiene** often provide helpful pamphlets and samples of toothbrushes and floss.

Watch for modifying phrases. Be alert as well for phrases (word groups lacking a subject, a predicate, or both) that are nonrestrictive and should be marked with commas. These modifying elements can appear at the beginning, middle, or end of sentences.

NONRESTRICTIVE   **Occupying the local newspaper headlines for the last two weeks ,** our city's budget crisis now threatens to spread to the state budget.

RESTRICTIVE   City services **popular with voters** are seldom cut from the budget.

Look for appositives. An **appositive** is a noun or pronoun that renames or stands for a preceding noun. Since most appositives are nonrestrictive, you generally need to set off appositives with a comma. Be on the lookout for the occasional restrictive appositive, however, and do not use commas with it.

NONRESTRICTIVE   Amy Nguyen **,** **a poet from Vietnam ,** recently published her second collection of verse.

RESTRICTIVE   The terms *cognitive* and *neural pathways* are familiar to anyone involved in brain research.

Exercise 3

A. Edit each sentence to set off all nonrestrictive modifiers with commas and to eliminate any commas that unnecessarily set off restrictive modifiers.

EXAMPLE

My mother who is ninety lives in the retirement residence called South Bay Manor.

1. Fifty years ago, a residence that served retired people, was called an old folks' home.
2. These homes which provided few services for residents were apartment buildings with dining rooms.
3. A retirement residence today offers many things to do including recreational activities, fitness programs, trips, classes, and social events.
4. The image of infirm people, sitting in rocking chairs, has been replaced by one of senior citizens, who are vigorous and involved.
5. Retirement residences often known as retirement communities are small towns, where people go to lead active lives.

B. Have each member of a small group bring in a paragraph from a magazine article, both in original form and rewritten to eliminate the commas setting off all nonrestrictive modifiers. Working as a group, first restore the commas to the rewritten versions, then check the originals to see if you agree with their punctuation.

51d Setting off parenthetical expressions

51d

The basic structure of a sentence can be interrupted with all sorts of words and word groups that add information or modify the sentence's various elements. Use commas to set off words like *however* and *moreover* (see 35a-6, 41b). Do the same with transitional expressions like *on the other hand* and *for example* and with parenthetical remarks like *in fact* and *more important* (sometimes called **interrupters**).

TRANSITIONAL EXPRESSION	The hailstorm **,** **in contrast** **,** caused severe damage.
INTERRUPTER	**In fact** **,** the hailstorm was so powerful that it broke a dozen priceless stained glass windows on the west side of the church.
CONJUNCTIVE ADVERB	We should not be surprised **,** **therefore** **,** if someone takes up a collection for the windows' repair.

You should also use commas to set off tag questions, statements of contrast, and words indicating direct address.

TAG QUESTIONS	We should be ready to contribute to the cause even if we don't attend the church **,** **shouldn't we?**

STATEMENT
OF CONTRAST   The windows' beauty touched all of us in the community**,** **not just the church members.**

DIRECT ADDRESS   Please remember**,** **friends of beauty,** that your contribution will help restore the windows to their former magnificence.

Exercise 4

Edit each sentence to add or delete commas as appropriate.

EXAMPLE

Scheduling may be ^in fact^the toughest job any manager faces.

1. Project schedules need to be arranged so that the job gets done on time of course.
2. Moreover meetings need to be set up so they do not interrupt people's work, unnecessarily.
3. Most staff members are cooperative however, and may even offer suggestions for scheduling.
4. Management training programs should, I think offer instruction in scheduling techniques.
5. Remember your staff's time is too valuable to be wasted.

SERIOUS
MISTAKE

51e Using commas in a series

Whenever you list items in a series and give each item roughly equal status, you should separate the items with commas. In one sense, commas take the place of a repeated *and*, which appears only before the last item in the series.

51e
^
,

HARD TO READ   Harvey's favorite novels are *Moby-Dick* **and** *The Awakening* **and** *Jane Eyre* **and** *Things Fall Apart.*

EDITED   Harvey's favorite novels are *Moby-Dick***,** *The Awakening***,** *Jane Eyre***,** **and** *Things Fall Apart.*

Placing a comma before the *and* that introduces the last item in a series helps avoid confusion. Many readers prefer this practice, especially in academic and professional writing. Editors of newspapers and some magazines, however, do not use this comma.

A numbered or lettered list that is part of a sentence should be punctuated as a series.

To make sure your analysis is complete, you should (1) check the bottom of the container for residue**,** (2) measure the salinity of the water**,** (3) weigh any organic waste in the filter**,** and (4) determine the amount of dissolved oxygen in the water.

If the items in a list are long and complex or if they contain commas, separate the items with semicolons rather than commas (see 52a).

CONFUSING The company is marketing a line of jigsaw puzzles of cities, like San Antonio, Texas ⌐ states, like Michigan and Montana ⌐ and countries, like Mexico, Japan, and France.

EDITED The company is marketing a line of jigsaw puzzles of cities, like San Antonio, Texas ⦂ states, like Michigan and Montana ⦂ and countries, like Mexico, Japan, and France.

51f Separating coordinate adjectives

In a pair of **coordinate adjectives,** each adjective modifies a noun on its own. Thus, you need to separate coordinate adjectives with commas.

COORDINATE (EQUAL) These drawings describe a **quick ⌐ simple** solution to the drainage problem.

With **noncoordinate adjectives,** the first adjective modifies the entire noun phrase formed by the next adjective plus the noun.

NONCOORDINATE (UNEQUAL) We can use **flexible plastic** pipe to carry water away from the building.

STRATEGY Identify coordinate adjectives

If the answer to either of the following questions is *yes*, the adjectives are coordinate and should be separated with a comma.

- Can you place *and* or *but* between the adjectives?

COORDINATE Irrigation has turned dry infertile [*dry and infertile?—yes*] land into orchards.

EDITED Irrigation has turned dry ⌐ infertile land into orchards.

NOT COORDINATE Five percent of the budget goes to new telecommunications [*new and telecommunications?—no*] equipment.

- Can you easily invert the adjectives without creating an awkward sentence?

COORDINATE We moved from our small cramped [*cramped small?—acceptable*] apartment.

EDITED We moved from our small ⌐ cramped apartment.

NOT COORDINATE We moved to a small Manhattan [*Manhattan small?—awkward*] apartment.

51f
∧
⌐

Exercise 5

A. Edit each sentence so that any series and any coordinate adjectives are correctly punctuated. Let any correct sentence stand.

EXAMPLE

McDonald's$_\wedge^,$ Burger King$_\wedge^,$ and Wendy's are worldwide symbols of American culture.

1. McDonald's and the others offer quick appetizing meals and clean pleasant surroundings.
2. In the late 1940s, the McDonald brothers opened a restaurant serving a limited inexpensive menu, including fifteen-cent hamburgers french fries and shakes.
3. The brothers did not want to expand their modestly successful restaurant into a chain.
4. Ray Kroc, a manufacturer of milkshake machines, recognized the potential of the brothers' innovations joined their business to help it expand and, frustrated by their lack of ambition, eventually bought them out.
5. Kroc continued to develop innovative imaginative ways to serve customers, and these fast efficient practices have come to characterize today's fast-food restaurants.

B. Working with a partner, exchange your current papers. Edit your partner's draft so that all series and coordinate adjectives are correctly punctuated.

51g
$\wedge$
,

51g Dates, numbers, addresses, place names, people's titles, and letters

Separate the elements in dates, place names, long numbers, and addresses according to conventional practice.

1 Dates

Put a comma between the date and the year and between the day of the week and the date.

The first computer in this office arrived on August 17$_\wedge$ 1985.

The workshop will begin on Wednesday$_\wedge$ September 23.

In the middle of a sentence, follow the year with a comma when you are giving the full date.

On February 4, 1961, my mother was born in a snowstorm.

Use no commas when giving only month and year or a month and a day.

A test version of the software will be available in January 2010.

Likewise, do not use commas with dates stating a season and a year.

The fall 2009 issue of the magazine arrived late.

Do not use commas with the elements of a date in inverted order (MLA style): 5 July 2011.

2 Numbers

To help readers understand long numbers, use commas to create groups of three, beginning from the right. With four digits, you may choose whether or not to use the comma, but keep your practice consistent.

During the livestock census on the ranch, we counted 1,746 sheep.

The combined income for people in our rural town is $8,543,234.

The best high-speed server costs $3,525 at Electronics World.

Omit commas in addresses and all page numbers.

18520 South Kedzie Drive   page 2054

ESL

51g
∧
,

ESL ADVICE: NUMBERS

Use commas to create groups of three. Periods are used only to indicate decimals.
1.000 = one   1,000 = one thousand

---

3 Addresses and place names

Separate names of cities and states with commas. Within a sentence, place a comma between all elements *except* the state and zip code.

Kansas City, Missouri, is a larger town than Kansas City, Kansas.

You can order the zucchini and carrot seeds from Fredelle and Family, Seed Brokers, Box 389, Holland, Michigan 30127.

4 People's names and titles

Place a comma before a title or initials that come after a person's name. If the name and title come at the beginning of a sentence or in the middle, use a comma after the title as well.

We hired **Crystal Bronkowski**, **A.I.A.**, to design the new building.

When you give a person's surname (last name) first, separate it from the first name with a comma: **Shamoon**, **Linda K.**

5 Salutations and closings of letters

Use a comma after the salutation of personal or informal letters.

Dear Tiffany,   Dear Volleyball Players,

Use a colon after the salutation in business and formal letters.

Dear Specialty Metals Customers :   Dear Sir or Madam :

Use a comma after a letter's closing, just before the signature.

Sincerely,   Best wishes,   With affection,   Regards,

Exercise 6

A. Edit each sentence by adding or eliminating commas as appropriate.

EXAMPLE

My mother remembers assembling her first jigsaw puzzle in autumn, 1985, several months before my birth on January 22, 1986.

1. Puzzles have fascinated me for the last thirty years, and last year I spent exactly $2479.83 on them.
2. For my birthday this year, one cousin gave me a map of Chicago Illinois in the form of a jigsaw puzzle, and another cousin gave me a puzzle of a seventeenth-century print from the Beinecke Library at Yale University New Haven Connecticut.
3. I have ordered a puzzle map of Atlanta Georgia from Buffalo Games, Inc. P.O. Box 85 601 Amherst Street Buffalo New York 14207 and a puzzle of Edward Hopper's painting, *Nighthawks* from Galison Books 36 West 44th Street New York New York 10036.
4. From January through June 2001, I assembled one puzzle a week, with the puzzles ranging from 500 to 1250 pieces each for a total of somewhere between 10500 pieces and 26250 pieces.
5. I am planning to have a business card made up with both my official and unofficial titles, Jessica Montoya Ph.D. Puzzle Assembler.

51g
∧
,

B. Working in a group, share copies of magazine or newspaper articles that contain numbers, addresses, people's names and titles, or openings and closings of letters. Check the articles to see whether they follow the same conventions for comma use as those described here. If not, or if the author uses commas inconsistently, edit each article so that it agrees with the recommendations for comma use in 51g.

51h Commas with quotations

When you introduce or conclude a quotation by indicating its source, separate your explanation and the quotation itself by using commas.

> At the grand opening, he said, "This facility is dedicated to the physical and mental health of the citizens of Oakdale."

> "Some books are meant to be chewed," said Francis Bacon, "and others to be digested."

> "The fire doors need to be replaced before the school can be reopened," the commissioner wrote.

When a quotation ends with a question mark or an exclamation point, keep this punctuation even if your sentence continues.

SERIOUS
MISTAKE

51h
∧
,

> "We can't afford the $30,000 to replace the doors right away!" the schoolboard president responded angrily.

> "Why can't you understand the paramount importance of fire safety?" the commissioner retorted.

If your explanation ends with *that* just before the quotation (either direct or indirect), do not include a comma.

| DIRECT QUOTATION | David James testified that "I did not damage the machinery as a protest during the strike." |
| INDIRECT QUOTATION | David James testified that he did not damage the machinery as a protest during the strike. |

Exercise 7

A. Edit the following passage by adding, deleting, or moving commas so that quotations are appropriately punctuated.

"Ice cream is virtually the only food we eat frozen, which means that its flavor, which we define as a composite of taste and smell, is only fully released upon melting" explains Arun Kilara, a 43-year-old professor of food science at Penn State and one of the world's acknowledged authorities on ice cream.

Not surprisingly, few true ice cream connoisseurs are fond of the industry's use of fat substitutes, such as the complex protein found in NutraSweet's Simplesse. "The search for the perfect fat substitute" Kilara says "is like a contemporary version of alchemy—lots of useful discoveries, but they'll never turn lead into gold." While some protein-based fat substitutes approximate fat's texture, or "mouth feel" he explains, they cannot dissolve flavor compounds in the same way.

"The smaller the ice crystals, the smoother the ice cream" says Kilara. "You get the smallest crystals when the drop in temperature is the most rapid and when agitation is most vigorous."

"There's one basic truth about ice cream—its quality begins deteriorating from the moment it is made" Kilara concludes. "Over the product's lifetime, ice cream's air escapes, its fat clumps, its ice melts, and its water freezes."

—LAWRENCE E. JOSEPH, "The Scoop on Ice Cream"

B. Working in a group, write a paragraph that presents information drawn from a newspaper or magazine article. Include several quotations from the article in your paragraph. Indicate the source or context for the quotations, and use commas appropriately to introduce or conclude the quoted material.

51i   Commas to make your meaning clear

Even when no rule specifies a comma, you may still include one in a sentence if it is necessary to make your meaning clear to readers, to remind them of deleted words, or to add emphasis.

HARD TO READ	Anyone who can afford to buy this high-speed file management program should.
EDITED	Anyone who can afford to buy this high-speed file management program **,** should.
	The comma reminds readers that *should* means "should do so."
UNEMPHATIC	Stocks go up and down.
EMPHATIC	Stocks go up **,** and down.
	The comma emphasizes the contrast.

51j   Commas that do not belong

When they are not sure precisely where to put commas, some writers insert them at every possible point. The result is confusing and irritating to readers. If you are not sure whether to add a comma, leave it out until you have checked to make sure one is required.

1 Do not insert a comma after words like *although* and *because* that introduce a clause

Words like *although*, *when*, and *since* (subordinators; see 47c) introduce an entire subordinate clause and should not be set off with commas.

INCORRECT   **Although** , Jim had just started to learn how to ski, we took him to the most expert slope on his first trip up the mountain.

EDITED   **Although** Jim had just started to learn how to ski, we took him to the most expert slope on his first trip up the mountain.

2 Do not insert a comma between a subject and a predicate

Don't insert a comma between subjects and predicates unless they are separated by a modifying clause (see 51c-2).

INCORRECT   Cézanne's painting *Rocks at L'Estaque* , hangs in the Museu de Arte in São Paulo, Brazil.

EDITED   Cézanne's painting *Rocks at L'Estaque* hangs in the Museu de Arte in São Paulo, Brazil.

SERIOUS MISTAKE

51j

∧
,

3 Do not overuse commas

Today readers generally prefer a style in which commas are not used heavily. Whenever possible, avoid sentence structures that call for a large number of commas. If necessary, edit and rewrite.

TOO MANY COMMAS   Samantha, always one, like her mother, to speak her mind, loudly protested the use of force, as she called it, by two store detectives, who had been observing her while she, looking for bargains, absentmindedly slipped a pair of gloves into her jacket pocket.

EDITED   Always one to speak her mind, like her mother, Samantha loudly protested what she considered the use of force by two store detectives who saw her absentmindedly slip a pair of gloves into her jacket pocket while she was looking for bargains.

Exercise 8

A. Edit each sentence in two ways: (1) by removing any unnecessary commas and (2) by rewriting to create a sentence structure that contains fewer commas, all of which are necessary.

EXAMPLE

When̸ they realized they had no job prospects, the five friends̸ formed̸ a company, which they called Home Restorers, Inc.

When they realized they had no job prospects, the five friends formed Home Restorers, Inc.

1. Because, she likes the outdoors, Sandy, a devoted gardener, takes care of landscaping, grass cutting, and outdoor cleanup.
2. Strong, tireless Jun, does roofing, paving, and similar work.
3. Interior design was, Padmaja's major, so she, everyone agrees, is the person best qualified to do interior decorating.
4. Having painted, her parents' house one summer, Rachael was, chosen, by her partners, as the company's painting supervisor.
5. Desperate, for a place in the company, Joel decided that, marketing, because it would draw on his undergraduate work in sociology, was the best thing for him to do.

B. Exchange draft papers with another writer, and edit each other's work to eliminate unnecessary commas. When you encounter a sentence that might be rewritten to reduce the number of commas, underline it. When your partner returns your paper, check over the editorial changes and consider rewriting any underlined sentences.

SERIOUS
MISTAKE

51j
∧
˒

CHAPTER **52**

Semicolons and Colons

Semicolons and colons help you connect words, word groups, or sentences in useful and varied ways.

> On April 12, 1861, at 4:30 a.m., one of Beauregard's batteries fired upon Fort **Sumter.** **The** Civil War had begun.

> On April 12, 1861, at 4:30 a.m., one of Beauregard's batteries fired upon Fort **Sumter;** **the** Civil War had begun.

> On April 12, 1861, at 4:30 a.m., one of Beauregard's batteries fired upon Fort **Sumter:** **the** Civil War had begun.

READER'S REACTION: Each version has a different effect. In the first, I don't see a necessary connection between the sentences. In the second, the semicolon implies that the firing of the gun started the Civil War. In the third, the colon makes that connection even stronger.

52a Using semicolons

A semicolon joins two main clauses that could act as complete sentences on their own. The semicolon indicates that the clauses are linked logically; at the same time, it creates a brief reading pause between them.

1 Try joining two sentences with a semicolon

You signal a relationship between main clauses by joining them with a semicolon, though you do not explain that relationship as you might by joining them with a word such as *and, but,* or *yet* (see 47a). A semicolon can highlight the close relationship of ideas or dramatically emphasize a contrast.

TWO SENTENCES   The demand for paper products is at an all-time high. Businesses consume millions of tons of paper each year.

ONE SENTENCE   The demand for paper products is at an all-time high; businesses consume millions of tons of paper each year.

When you join such units with a semicolon, make sure readers will be able to recognize the relationship without having to puzzle over the sentence.

STRATEGY Test both sides of the semicolon

Check for correct use of a semicolon by making sure the unit on each side of the semicolon can stand on its own as a sentence.

INCORRECT   The demand for recycled paper has also increased greatly **;** with manufacturers looking for new supplies of scrap paper.

TEST   The demand for recycled paper has also increased greatly.
                The first clause is a complete sentence.

                With manufacturers looking for new supplies of scrap paper.
                The second part is a sentence fragment.

CORRECT   The demand for recycled paper has also increased greatly **;** manufacturers are looking for new supplies of scrap paper.

2 Use a semicolon with words such as *however, on the other hand*

When you use a semicolon by itself to link sentences, you ask readers to recognize the relationship on their own; in contrast, when you use a word like *however* or an expression like *on the other hand*, you specify the relationship. The effect on readers is something like this:

assertion	→	semicolon	→	transition	→	assertion
		(*pause*)		(*consider relationship*)		
I like apples		**;**		**however ,**		I hate pears.
assertion		pause		contrast		assertion

52a
;

To specify the link, you can choose a **conjunctive adverb** such as *however, moreover, thus,* or *therefore* (see 47a) or a **transitional expression** like *for example, in contrast,* or *on the other hand*. The linking words can appear between the units (just after the semicolon), within a clause, or at the end of a clause.

BETWEEN   Joe returned from the Arctic **;** **however ,** Alan was never found.

WITHIN   Joe returned from the Arctic **;** Alan **,** **however ,** was never found.

AT END   Joe returned from the Arctic **;** Alan was never found **,** **however.**

Consider joining a series of short to medium-length sentences with semicolons when (1) the sentences are logically linked; (2) as a group, the unlinked sentences seem choppy or disconnected; and (3) commas do not separate the elements enough to encourage readers to consider each one fully.

CHOPPY   The shelty took first prize. The German shepherd took second. The poodle walked away in third place.

BETTER   The shelty took first prize, the German shepherd took second, **and** the poodle walked away in third place.

MOST EFFECTIVE   The shelty took first prize; the German shepherd took second; and the poodle walked away with third.

3 Use a semicolon with deleted structures

There are exceptions to the rule that semicolons must join units that can stand on their own as sentences (main clauses). In some cases, you can delete elements in a second clause if they "match" elements in the first.

ELEMENTS   In winter, **the hotel guests enjoy** the log fire in the dining
INCLUDED   room; in summer, **the hotel guests enjoy** the patio over-
                 looking the river.

ELEMENTS   In winter, **the hotel guests enjoy** the log fire in the dining
DELETED   room; in summer, the patio overlooking the river.

4 Use a semicolon with a complex series

Most of the time, you can use commas to separate elements in a series with no risk of confusion (see 51e). When some of the items themselves contain commas, however, readers may struggle to decide which commas mark series parts and which ones belong within items.

52a
;

CONFUSING   For the project, I interviewed Debbie Rios, my roommate,
                 Liza Marron, my former employer, and my calculus instructor.
                 READER'S REACTION: How many people were interviewed? three,
                 four, or five?

To avoid confusion, put semicolons between elements in a series when one or more of the elements contain commas or some other internal punctuation such as a dash, parentheses, or a colon.

EDITED   For the project, I interviewed Debbie Rios, my roommate; Liza
                 Marron, my former employer; and my calculus instructor.

Exercise 1

A. The following passage contains some semicolons used correctly and some used incorrectly. It also contains sentences that might be more effective if joined with semicolons and others that would be better as separate sentences. Rewrite the passage, adding or eliminating semicolons and making any other changes necessary to create a more effective piece of writing.

    The Grateful Dead came back into my life recently; largely because of my children's interest. My daughter has been *associated* with the group; I find it difficult to apply the common description of a fan as a Deadhead; since she was fifteen. Her school band; the Cosmic Country Sound, was patterned after the Grateful Dead; she was its lead singer and tambourine player.

    I had no idea that my son, four years younger; had any interest in the group. His room is decorated with posters of Boris Becker and Albert Einstein. But then a year ago he let his hair grow into a mane; started wearing beaded necklaces and rope wristlets, and, sure enough; turned up one day at my study door to announce, "Dad; there's this concert I'd like to go to. . . ."

    Both of my children have urged me to go to a Grateful Dead concert. I hadn't taken them up on the offer until this summer; when by chance I met someone way up in the band's hierarchy who gave me not only some tickets to a concert at the Meadowlands in New Jersey; but also a backstage pass. I told my son. His eyes widened at the news. He invited three of his friends. His sister; with a job on the West Coast, was devastated that she couldn't be on hand.

    —Adapted from GEORGE PLIMPTON, "Bonding with the Grateful Dead"

B. The passage above can be rewritten in many ways, depending on the focus and stylistic effect a writer wishes to create. Share your version of the passage with a group of fellow students. Each group member should be ready to explain the reasons for his or her choices when they differ from those of other writers in the group. As a group, rewrite the passage, and share that version with the class.

52b
:

52b Using colons

    You can use a colon to introduce or set up an example, illustration, list, or quotation.

1 Use a colon to introduce examples, statements, and lists

    You can use colons to introduce examples and concluding generalizations. Commonly, a colon comes after the first part of a sentence, which offers a statement or generalization that the remainder of the sentence (following the colon) illustrates, explains, or makes concrete and particular.

    Mulholland said the growing city at the desert's edge would need another source of water **:** the Owens Valley, several miles away.

    Remember this important selling guideline **:** Know your customer!

By asking readers to pause partway through a sentence, a colon calls attention to the second half and avoids the run-together effect a comma may create.

RUN TOGETHER   After saving for eleven years, the Cranes finally had enough money to get what they wanted **,** a ranch in Wyoming where they could live out their own version of self-reliance.

EDITED   After saving for eleven years, the Cranes finally had enough money to get what they wanted **:** a ranch in Wyoming where they could live out their own version of self-reliance.

A colon can also introduce a more formal series or list.

Though baseball doesn't reign in England, the British enjoy a wide variety of sports **:** soccer, rugby, cricket, tennis, croquet, polo, and billiards, to name just a few.

When a complete sentence follows a colon, you can choose to begin it with either a capital or a lowercase letter. Stick to one style or the other throughout an essay.

CORRECT   The airline lost my bag **:** **our** vacation was ruined.

ALSO CORRECT   The airline lost my bag **:** **Our** vacation was ruined.

When the word group following a colon is not a sentence, begin it with a lowercase letter.

52b
:

LOWERCASE   The symptoms are as follows **:** **sore** throat, joint pain, fever, and headache.

2 Use a colon to introduce quotations

You can use a colon as a convenient way to introduce quotations, either short ones that you integrate into your own words or longer ones that you set off from the body of your text (see Chapter 27). The word group before the colon must be a complete sentence; if it is not, use a comma instead.

Ms. Johnson responded to criticism of the sales campaign **:** "For a program launched in the middle of a recession, sales were quite strong."

3 Use a colon to separate titles and subtitles

Colons separate main titles from their subtitles.

Ballroom Dancing for the Absolute Novice **:** *An Introduction*

Freddie's Dead **:** *The Final Nightmare*

Colons are also used in separating hours from minutes (10:32); in certain chapter and verse notations, such as those in the Bible (John 8:21–23); and in some reference styles (see Chapters 29–33).

4 Use a colon to join sentences

Use a colon to join complete sentences (main clauses) when the second sentence focuses, sums up, or illustrates the first (see 41b).

Hearing a sound like rushing water and ripping cloth, she knew it was too late to abandon her house : The mud slide had begun.

5 Avoid overuse and misuse of colons

Because colons add emphasis to examples and assertions, you may be tempted to use them often. Don't. Vary your style.

COLON
OVERUSED

Suzanne had an obsession for books : there were bookshelves in her kitchen, her bathrooms, and even her closets. She read voraciously : in the morning, at lunch, after dinner, and late at night. And she liked everything : classics, mysteries, pulp romances, autobiographies.

EDITED

Suzanne had an obsession for books. There were bookshelves in her kitchen, her bathrooms, and even her closets. She read voraciously **from morning to** late at night. And she liked everything : classics, mysteries, pulp romances, autobiographies.

The colon and the words introduced by it should appear only at the end of a sentence, not in the middle.

INCORRECT

Keep in mind these elements : introduction, body, and conclusion, while preparing your presentation.

EDITED

Keep in mind these **elements**—introduction, body, and conclusion—**while** preparing your presentation.

52b
:

Exercise 2

A. Edit each sentence by deleting misused or overused colons, adding colons where needed, and retaining any colons that are appropriate. You may need to rewrite some of the sentences.

EXAMPLE

For the Hirsches, retirement meant a trip to France.

1. They prepared for the trip by: first looking for inexpensive hotels in Paris.
2. The Residence Rivoli seemed like a good value clean, centrally located: private bath.
3. Mr. Hirsch, however, wanted to splurge: He argued that an upper-bracket hotel would be so much more enjoyable: a shining marble bath, plush dining room, and elegant meals. There would be parking as well: essential for anyone with a car.
4. But Mrs. Hirsch wasn't impressed: the expensive hotels would be comfortable, but she wanted atmosphere: and small, charming hotels would have that in abundance.
5. Finally, they reached a compromise; they would: stay in a chateau near the Loire, which would be cheaper than a fancy Paris hotel but afford plenty of atmosphere. Then they could: drive into Paris; enjoy the sights; and have a peaceful night: all without driving more than an hour or so each way.

B. Share your edited versions of the sentences with a group of class-mates. For each sentence, choose one version the group considers correct and effective. Then share your chosen sentences with other groups to see how often you have made similar and different choices.

---

mycomplab

Visit mycomplab.com for more resources and exercises on semicolons and colons.

52b

CHAPTER **53**

Apostrophes

The apostrophe may seem trivial, but without correctly used apostrophes, your readers would stumble over your sentences.

MISUSED OR LEFT OUT James horse cant canter, but two months rest and his leg's will heal, and then well see him in race's again.

> READER'S REACTION: I really stumbled reading this sentence. At first I didn't know if the horse was James's, and I thought the horse's legs had a will of their own!

CORRECTED James **'**s horse **can'**t canter, but two **months'** rest and his **legs** will heal, and then **we'**ll see him in **races** again.

  53a Marking possession

A noun that expresses ownership is said to be a **possessive noun.** In writing, you must mark possessive nouns to distinguish them from plurals.

1 Add an apostrophe plus -*s* to mark possession in singular nouns

In general, when you write a singular possessive noun, you will follow it with an apostrophe plus -*s*.

Bill**'s** coat   the dog**'s** collar   New Mexico**'s** taxes

When a noun ends with -*s*, showing possession may be tricky. Writers follow one of two conventions in such circumstances. Choose one of these conventions and stick to it throughout an essay.

1. Add an apostrophe and another -*s*, just as you would do with any other noun. This is the more common and preferred method.

   Chris**'s** car   Elliott Ness**'s** next move

2. Alternatively, simply add an apostrophe to the final -*s*.

   Chris**'** car   Elliott Ness**'** next move

To avoid awkward possessives for nouns ending in *-s* ("the pass'**s** success"), try revising the construction ("the success of the pass").

Be careful with personal pronouns. You may be tempted to add an apostrophe plus *-s*, but they're already possessive.

INCORRECT   If the car was **your's,** why did you tell Jose that it was Lida's and then take **her's** and dent **it's** fender?

EDITED   If the car was **yours,** why did you tell Jose that it was Lida's and then take **hers** and dent **its** fender?

Be especially wary of confusing *it's* and *its*. Practice expanding the contraction *it's* (*it* + *is*) whenever you use it in writing, and you'll locate such slips more easily.

DRAFT   **Its** not the muffler shop employees who were responsible for the fraud, but **its** managers.

EXPANDED   **It is** not the muffler shop employees who were responsible for the fraud, but **it is** managers.

EDITED   **It'**s not the muffler shop employees who were responsible for the fraud, but **its** managers.

SERIOUS
MISTAKE

53a
'
V

2 Add an apostrophe to mark possession in plural nouns

Most plural nouns end in *-s* or *-es*. Add an apostrophe after the *-s*.

POSSESSIVE   The **Solomons'** house had its lead paint removed.

POSSESSIVE   The **roses'** petals had begun to wither.

Some irregular nouns form their plurals differently (*mice, children, fish*). Mark possession by adding an apostrophe plus *-s* to the plural, even if the word does not change in the plural (*deer/deer, fish/fish*).

PLURAL   The livestock show included several **oxen.**

PLURAL
POSSESSIVE   The livestock show featured the **oxen'**s plowing abilities.

Even though third person singular verbs end in *-s*, remember that these are not possessive nouns, so they don't require an apostrophe.

INCORRECT   The *Enterprise* **speed's** out of the galaxy.

EDITED   The *Enterprise* **speeds** out of the galaxy.

3 Add an apostrophe plus *-s* or an apostrophe to only the last word in a noun phrase

Hyphenated and **multiple-word nouns** are becoming increasingly common in English. As a general rule, treat the entire noun phrase as a single unit, marking possession on the last word.

HYPHENATED
NOUN

My **father-in-law** 's library is extensive.

MULTIPLE-WORD
NOUN

The **union leaders** 'negotiations fell through at the last minute.

With two or more nouns connected by *and* or *or*, you'll need to decide whether these nouns function as separate items or as a single unit.

SEPARATE ITEMS

Billy 's and **Harold** 's lawyers were ruthless.

READER'S REACTION: Billy must have one lawyer and Harold another, since the possessive is marked on both.

SINGLE UNIT

Billy and Harold 's lawyers were ruthless.

READER'S REACTION: Billy and Harold must have shared the same team of lawyers, since the entire noun phrase is marked as possessive.

Exercise 1

A. Edit the possessive forms in the following sentences so that each uses apostrophes correctly. You may have to add or move apostrophes, but do not change any correct forms.

EXAMPLE

France ˅'ˢ longest river, the Loire, has its source in Vivarais and winds its way some six hundred miles to the Atlantic.

1. The rivers name is especially associated with the many chateaux that line its bank's.
2. Serious sightseers visits to the Loire Valley should include tours of several of this regions beautiful castles.
3. The Loires reputation is also founded on its renowned cuisine and its sophisticated wines.
4. Barton and Jone's wine import businesses have flourished in the United States ever since Jones came up with the companys award-winning advertising campaign.
5. Several other companies have found an eager market for Frances excellent wine's.

B. In a small group, compare your corrections and discuss any especially difficult cases.

SERIOUS
MISTAKE

53a
˅

53b Marking contractions and omissions

You can use an apostrophe to indicate the omission of one or more letters when two words are brought together to form a **contraction.**

1 Use an apostrophe to contract a verb form

You can contract pronouns and verbs into a single unit by "splicing" them, eliminating the first part of the verb and substituting an apostrophe.

it	+	is	=	it's
who	+	is	=	who's
they	+	are	=	they're
can	+	not	=	can't
you	+	will	=	you'll
you	+	are	=	you're

When writing informally, you can splice nouns followed by *is*.

INFORMAL **Shoshana's** going to the ballet, but her **seat's** in the very last row of the theater.

MORE FORMAL **Shoshana is** going to the ballet, but her seat is in the very last row of the theater.

Edit your papers *very* carefully for contractions before turning them in. Take note of these often-confused forms.

they're	=	they + are
there	=	an adverb
their	=	a possessive pronoun
you're	=	you + are
your	=	a possessive pronoun
who's	=	who + is
whose	=	a possessive pronoun
it's	=	it + is
its	=	a possessive pronoun

2 Use an apostrophe to mark plural letters

To make individual letters plural, add an apostrophe plus -*s*.

Mind your **p's and q's.**   The **x's** mark the spots.

You can omit the apostrophe in the plurals of numbers.

I'll take two size **5s** and two size **7s**.

They walked out in **twos** and **threes**.

The apostrophe is often omitted from the plural form of abbreviations, especially when it might make the word look like a possessive. "I took all my freshman courses from **TAs**" might be just as acceptable as "**TA** ' **s**" because the abbreviation is capitalized.

3 Use an apostrophe to abbreviate a year

You can abbreviate years by omitting the first two numbers of the century as long as the century is understood by your reader. Such contractions represent informal usage.

INFORMAL   Sam has an '**85** Johnson class M sixteen-foot sailboat for sale.

UNCLEAR   Victorian details on houses in our neighborhood remained popular throughout the '**90s.**

REUDER'S REACTION: Does this mean the 1890s (in the Victorian period)? I'm confused.

EDITED   Victorian details on houses in our neighborhood remained popular throughout the **1990s.**

4 Use an apostrophe to show colloquial pronunciation

When quoting people, you can use apostrophes to indicate certain omissions and other features of colloquial speech and dialects.

DIALECT   I'm **a-goin** ' to the post office first **an** ' then home.

53b

Exercise 2

A. The following paragraph contains sentences with some contracted words that require apostrophes and some lookalikes that do not. All these words appear in italics. Insert apostrophes where they belong.

Many medical scholars believe that the age of molecular biology *didnt* really begin until April 1953 when Watson and Crick's article on the double helix appeared in a scientific journal. These researchers *werent* sure at that time how influential their ideas would become. *Its* generally thought, for example, that if several important researchers *hadnt* immediately seen the underlying brilliance of the double helix, the whole idea *wouldnt* have gained such a quick following. "*Your* basic educator," Professor Ewell Samuels asserts, "*couldnt* have seen beyond what was already a given in biology. *Its* when *youre* presented with many scholars *whose* ideas agree that things really begin to happen. *Whos* going to argue with a whole *fields* jumping on the bandwagon of a new theory?"

B. In a small group, compare your corrections to the passage. After reaching agreement on which cases are errors, try to decide as a group which contractions in the passage, if any, are too informal. Would you use no contractions in this passage? some?

Visit mycomplab.com for more resources and exercises on apostrophes.

53b

CHAPTER **54**

Quotation Marks

Consider this exchange:

I was in the back of the store when I noticed the gunman come in. The officer was taking notes. What did he look like? He had the demeanor of someone who would never give up. He was about six feet tall and had a beard. He saw you, you said?

READER'S REACTION: I have no idea what's going on here. Did the gunman look determined? Was the officer taking notes when the gunman came into the store?

Now consider this version, punctuated correctly with quotation marks:

"I was in the back of the store when I noticed the gunman come in."

The officer was taking notes. "What did he look like?" He had the demeanor of someone who would never give up.

"He was about six feet tall and had a beard."

"He saw you, you said?"

As this passage demonstrates, quotation marks play an important role in dialogue. They are also essential when you incorporate other people's words and ideas in your writing. To write effectively, you need to keep track of the conventions for their use.

 ## 54a Marking quotations

Use quotation marks whenever you quote someone else's words. Quotation marks tell readers which words are someone else's.

1 Direct quotations

Whenever you quote someone directly, use double quotation marks (" ") both before and after the quotation—unless the quotation is long or needs special emphasis (see 54b). Make sure that the words within the quotation marks are the exact spoken or written words of your source.

DIRECT QUOTATION (SPOKEN)
⁶⁶The loon can stay beneath the water for several minutes,⁹⁹ the park ranger told us as we walked along the shore.

DIRECT QUOTATION (WRITTEN)
Samuel Gross has written that ⁶⁶every generation looks with scorn upon its offspring's own developing culture.⁹⁹

As you edit, check that you have placed quotation marks around all directly quoted material.

QUOTATION NOT FULLY MARKED
"Had it not been for the flight navigator," the pilot said, we wouldn't have been able to make the emergency landing.
READER'S REACTION: The second part of the sentence doesn't have any quotation marks, so at first I didn't notice that it was something the pilot said.

EDITED
⁶⁶Had it not been for the flight navigator,⁹⁹ the pilot said, ⁶⁶we wouldn't have been able to make the emergency landing.⁹⁹

2 Indirect quotations

Whenever you **paraphrase** or **summarize** someone else's speaking or writing, do not use quotation marks.

INDIRECT QUOTE (PARAPHRASE)
The pilot told us that if it hadn't been for the flight navigator, the plane would not have made a safe landing.

INDIRECT QUOTE (SUMMARY)
Samuel Preston believes that after just one generation, the social consequences of a major war have almost completely vanished.

3 Quotations inside quotations

Whenever a direct quotation contains another quotation, use single quotation marks (' ') for the inside quotation and double quotation marks (" ") for the one enclosing it.

Goddio became interested in searching for the sunken ship *San Diego* after reading an account by De Morga who ⁶⁶wrote of a struggle ⁶obstinately and bitterly waged on both sides so that it lasted more than six hours,⁹ until the pounding of the battle caused his ship to ⁶bust asunder at the bows.⁹ ⁹⁹

ESL ADVICE: QUOTATION MARKS

Conventions for using quotation marks vary from language to language, and British conventions vary from American ones. Check the advice in this section carefully, and proofread your work to make sure you are using quotation marks correctly.

54b Block quotations

When you quote more than four typed lines of prose, you should use a **block quotation** rather than quotation marks. To create a block quotation, begin on a new line after the sentence preceding the quotation, indent one inch (or ten spaces), and present the quotation double-spaced without quotation marks.

> According to Postman, we can no longer ignore the profound effects of technology on all aspects of American life:
>
> > To be unaware that a technology comes equipped with a program for social change, to maintain that technology is neutral, to make the assumption that technology is always a friend to culture is, at this late hour, stupidity plain and simple.

In a quotation of more than one paragraph, indent one-fourth inch (three spaces) for the first line of each full paragraph. In addition, include any quotation marks that appear within the original, but do not add any at the beginning or end of the block quotation.

> Clifford Geertz's discussion of cockfights on the island of Bali illustrates the personal, almost informal tone of much contemporary anthropology:
>
> > My wife and I were still very much in the gust-of-wind stage, a most frustrating, and even, as you soon begin to doubt whether you are really real after all, unnerving one, when, ten days or so after our arrival, a large cockfight was held in the public square to raise money for a new school.
> >
> > Now, a few special occasions aside, cockfights are illegal in Bali under the Republic (as, for not altogether unrelated reasons, they were under the Dutch), largely as a result of the pretensions to puritanism radical nationalism tends to bring with it. The elite, which is not itself so very puritan, worries about the poor, ignorant peasant gambling all his money away, about what foreigners will think, about the waste of time better devoted to building up the country. It sees cockfighting as "primitive," "backward," "unprogressive," and generally unbecoming an ambitious nation. And, as with those other embarrassments—opium smoking, begging, or uncovered breasts—it seeks, rather unsystematically, to put a stop to it.
> >
> > —CLIFFORD GEERTZ, "Deep Play: Notes on the Balinese Cockfight"

54b
" "

(See Chapter 30 for a discussion of parenthetical documentation with block quotations; see 52b-2 for the use of colons to introduce block quotations.)

When you are quoting more than three lines of verse, present them in a block quotation, beginning on the next line after an introductory sentence and indented one inch from the left margin. If the verse contains quotation marks, include them, but do not add any of your own at the beginning or end of the quotation.

Donald Hall also uses lines of uneven length and varying rhythm in his poem
"The Black-Faced Sheep."

> If one of you found a gap in a stone wall,
> the rest of you—rams, ewes, bucks, wethers, lambs;
> mothers and daughters, old grandfather-father,
> cousins and aunts, small bleating sons—
> followed onward, stupid
> as sheep, wherever
> your leader's sheep-brain wandered to.
> My grandfather spent all day searching the valley
> and edges of Ragged Mountain,
> calling "Ke-*day*!" as if he brought you salt,
> "Ke-*day*! Ke-*day*!"

54c Dialogue

When writing dialogue, use the conventions for direct quotations (see
54a-1). Whenever a new person speaks, indent as if you're beginning a new
paragraph, and begin with new quotation marks.

> Finally the old man woke.
>
> "Don't sit up," the boy said. "Drink this." He poured
> some coffee in a glass.
>
> The old man took it and drank it.
>
> "They beat me, Manolin," he said. "They truly beat me."
> —Ernest Hemingway, *The Old Man and the Sea*

When a character in a written dialogue speaks for more than one paragraph with no interruption, begin each new paragraph with quotation marks,
but don't end with them. End only the *last* paragraph with quotation marks.

> "And then that imbecile crowd down on the deck started
> their little fun, and I could see nothing more for smoke.
>
> "The brown current ran swiftly out of the heart of darkness,
> bearing us down towards the sea with twice the speed of our upward
> progress. . . ."
> —Joseph Conrad, *Heart of Darkness*

54d Titles of short works

Use quotation marks to enclose titles of short works, such as articles,
essays, stories, songs, and short poems; parts of a larger work or series, such
as chapters in a book, episodes in a television series, or sections of a musical
work; and unpublished works, such as doctoral dissertations or speeches.

QUOTATION MARKS WITH TITLES

ARTICLES AND STORIES

"TV Gets Blame for Poor Reading"	newspaper article
"A Political Identity Crisis"	magazine article
"The Idea of the Family in the Middle East"	chapter in book
"Baba Yaga and the Brave Youth"	story
"The Rise of Germism"	essay

POEMS AND SONGS

"A Woman Cutting Celery"	short poem
"Evening" (from *Pippa Passes*)	section of a long poem
"You're Beautiful"	song

EPISODES AND PARTS OF LONGER WORKS

"The Promise" (from *Cold Case*)	episode of a TV series
"All We Like Sheep" (from Handel's *Messiah*)	section of a long musical work

UNPUBLISHED WORKS

"Renaissance Men—and Women"	unpublished lecture
"Sources of the Ballads in Bishop Percy's Folio Manuscript"	unpublished dissertation

---

Never put the title of your own paper in quotation marks. This is a common mistake that irritates many teachers. If your title contains quoted material, place that material, not the entire title, in quotation marks.

INCORRECT   "The Theme of the Life Voyage in Crane's 'Open Boat' "

EDITED   The Theme of the Life Voyage in Crane's "Open Boat"

54e
" "

54e Special meanings of words and phrases

You can use quotation marks to set off words and phrases you are using in a special sense or to indicate terms that are part of a technical vocabulary or that are unusual in some way. In using quotation marks to call attention to words and phrases, remember an important principle: Go lightly to avoid distracting readers with too many highlighted words.

The term "FSBO" (sometimes pronounced as "fizbo") is generally used in the real estate industry to refer to a home that is "for sale by owner."

When deciding whether to use quotation marks to set off specialized terms, ask yourself whether the term is likely to be known to your readers.

Ask also whether the term is unusual enough to require highlighting or will seem clear to readers.

Exercise 1

A. Add quotation marks to the following passage as appropriate.

The shame of illiteracy—or so Robert Cullany puts it—affects millions of adults in the United States alone, but the problem is not nearly as prevalent as innumeracy, Cullany's term that means being unable to use numbers. Cullany writes, illiteracy and innumeracy are a national blight on our intellectual landscape, and cannot be tolerated. He also points out that they cripple our productivity, lead to familial dysfunction (poor family structures), and deny people the ability to become what Cullany calls self-learners. The ALVC, or Adult Literacy Volunteer Corps, is made up of dedicated people who believe they can help this so-called mind plague.

B. Working in a small group, share your edited versions of the passage. Which quotation marks did you all agree on? Which ones did members of your group miss or disagree on?

54f   Irony, sarcasm, and authorial distance

You can—*sparingly*—use quotation marks to indicate irony or sarcasm or to show disapproval of a specific term or expression.

To the people who oppose animal rights, the suffering of helpless animals is somehow justified by the "great medical advances" that are encouraged by what they view as "legitimate research" on animals.

This strategy is easy to misuse or overuse, and careful word choice is generally a more effective way of conveying disapproval (see 49b-1 and 2).

Exercise 2

A. Edit the following passage by adding or deleting quotation marks as appropriate. Leave in place any quotation marks that are correctly used.

On April 12, 1633, Galileo was interrogated by the Inquisitor for the Holy Roman and Universal Inquisition. The focus was Galileo's book, the "*Dialogue on the Great World Systems*," in which he posited the theory of a "spinning" earth that "circulated" around the sun. The theory itself was "bad" enough given the Pope's "beliefs," but one of the "characters" in the book's "dialogue" was cast as a "simpleton," and the Pope thought that perhaps it referred to him because he didn't go along with Galileo's "theory." At one point, the Inquisitor asked Galileo, "Did you obtain permission to write the book? To which Galileo replied, I did not seek permission to write this book because I consider that I did not disobey the instruction I had been given. "Did you disclose the Sacred Congregation's demands when you printed the book?" asked the Inquisitor. "I said nothing, Galileo replied, when I sought permission to publish, not having in the book either held or defended opinion. In the end, "Galileo" had to retract his "book," and was also shown instruments of torture "as if" they were going to be used—a "scare tactic," to be sure.

—Adapted from Jacob Bronowski, *The Ascent of Man*

B. Working in a small group, share your edited versions of the passage. Discuss each change and note any that gave you trouble. Indicate whether all group members agreed about each change.

Visit mycomplab.com for more resources and exercises on quotation marks.

54f
66 99

CHAPTER **55**

Periods, Question Marks, and Exclamation Points

When you speak, you mark boundaries between sentences with changes in pitch or with pauses. When you write, you must mark these divisions with visual symbols because your reader can't "hear" the boundaries. When you want to mark the end of a sentence, you will use one of three symbols: a period, a question mark, or an exclamation point.

55a Periods

Use a period to mark the end of a sentence. Periods can also be used in abbreviations.

1 End a sentence with a period

No matter how long or complicated, all sentences that are *statements* must end with periods. However, sometimes a sentence will contain embedded clauses that appear to be something other than statements. Use a period to end a sentence when the main, or outer, sentence is a statement.

INCORRECT   Naomi kissed her little brother on the forehead but wondered whether he really knew that she was sorry for startling him?

READER'S REACTION: The sentence as a whole is a statement; the question in the second half is being reported in the sentence, but the sentence doesn't ask the question.

EDITED   Naomi kissed her little brother on the forehead but wondered whether he really knew that she was sorry for startling him.

2 Use periods in abbreviations

Periods are also used to punctuate abbreviations and to mark decimal points in numbers. Most abbreviations require periods to let the reader know that something has been eliminated from the word or term (see Chapter 61).

Dr.	Mrs.	a.m. (or A.M.)
pp.	in.	abbr. (for *abbreviation*)
Jr.	Ph.D.	B.C. (or B.C.E.)

When an abbreviation that requires a period occurs at the *end* of a sentence, that period will also end the sentence.

CORRECT   Before he became a freelance writer, Richard Rodriguez earned a Ph ● D ●

If the abbreviated word occurs in the *middle* of a sentence, the period may be followed by another punctuation mark, such as a comma, dash, colon, or semicolon.

EDITED   Officials from the paper industry testified until **10 p ● m ●**, well before the meeting adjourned.

Exercise 1

Edit each sentence so that periods are used correctly, adding or omitting punctuation as appropriate.

EXAMPLE

Every two years the French department at St ⊙ Joseph's College organizes

a group trip to a foreign country ⊙

1. On our trip to France, we visited the medieval city of Carcassonne
2. As we approached the inner city, which was surrounded by high walls and a real moat, we wondered whether we were still in the twentieth century?
3. "Have we fallen into a time warp or something" Trish said?
4. As we climbed up to the ramparts at 10 p.m, we decided that the experience was almost as good as watching a N.A.S.A. space shuttle launch.
5. Mr Siefert, the hotel manager, told us that the Bastille Day fireworks would begin at 9:30 p.m.

**55b
?**

55b Question marks

A question mark indicates that something has been asked, either directly or hypothetically.

1 End a direct question with a question mark

Always end a direct question with a question mark.

DIRECT   When is the train leaving ❓

End **indirect questions** with a period. These are sentences whose main clause is a statement and whose embedded clause asks a question.

INDIRECT   Phil wondered whether to support the department's proposal to create a new program ●

When you present the exact words, your quotation is *direct* rather than *indirect*, and you need to include the question mark.

QUOTED   It was Laitan who asked, "Why is the temperature in the solution rising so quickly?"

2 Watch for other uses of question marks

In various kinds of informational writing, a question mark may signal a date or other fact that is uncertain or that has been questioned.

David Robert Styles, 1632?–1676

Occasionally writers will include a parenthetical question mark to indicate genuine doubt, lack of information, or sarcasm.

SARCASTIC   We dispute R & D's finding that the lubricant burns off (?) under high heat.

Such a use of question marks is usually colloquial or informal; in general, try to find other ways to convey the same message in academic writing.

Unless you're writing very informally (in a note to a friend, for example), avoid using more than one question mark for emphasis or combining question marks and exclamation points.

INAPPROPRIATE   Can you believe they arrested him for parking in front of the building?! How can they do that?????

EDITED   Can you believe they arrested him for parking in front of the building? How can they do that?

55b ?

Exercise 2

A. Edit the following passage by removing any inappropriate question marks and adding any that are required.

Are you bat-phobic. Although bats have been hated and feared for centuries, most species are harmless to humans and beneficial to the environment. In his article "Are We Batty over Bats," Harlan Sneed wonders whether our destruction of bats is really justified? Should we be smoke-bombing caves that are breeding places for thousands of bats, just because we are afraid of them. Sneed also gives examples of cultures that are contributing to the extinction of bats not through fear but through excessive trapping—for food; they are a delicacy (!?) in some parts of the world. Sneed ends his article with a reminder: "Environmental protection is as much a matter of the way we think as the way we act. Maybe you have never *acted* against your environment but are you entirely inculpable in your thoughts and attitudes."

B. In a small group, compare your edited versions of the passage. Create one collaboratively edited version.

55c Exclamation points

When you use an exclamation point, you make your statement emphatic. You can also use exclamation points to indicate commands or, in quotations, words that are shouted.

1 End an emphatic statement with an exclamation point

Exclamation points are often used to end emphatic statements such as commands or warnings.

EMPHATIC   Keep all the camp children away from the precipice!

Avoid overusing exclamation points to do the work that should be assigned to strong, carefully chosen words.

OVERUSED   I couldn't believe it! Andrea and I were face to face with a small black bear! We were terrified!

REVISED   Suddenly, out of the shadows, just three feet from the front of our tent, appeared the black nose and sharp, glinting teeth of a small black bear.

Also avoid using more than one exclamation point at the end of any sentence. A single exclamation point is worth exactly as much as a hundred.

INCORRECT   The bear was grunting right outside our tent!!!!!

EDITED   The bear was grunting right outside our tent!

2 Watch for other uses of exclamation points

Like question marks, exclamation points can be used parenthetically or marginally in casual writing to express dismay, outrage, shock, or strong interest. In formal contexts, look for other ways to add emphasis.

INAPPROPRIATE   Emergency rescue workers spent several hours (!) trying to reach the stranded toddler.

EDITED   Emergency rescue workers spent several **agonizing** hours trying to reach the stranded toddler.

55c
!

When you quote people's words directly, you can use exclamation points to indicate emphatic statements or commands.

QUOTED   Halfway to the airport, Sybil suddenly shouted, "Oh, no! We forgot the plane tickets!"

Use exclamation points sparingly and realistically in quotations and dialogue. Few people continue to speak emphatically for very long.

Remember that when you use an exclamation point, you are punctuating the end of your sentence. Don't add another mark, such as a comma, when you write an emphatic sentence within an outer sentence. (This same rule applies to the question mark.)

INCORRECT   "Stop!," yelled Steve.

EDITED   "Stop!" yelled Steve.

Exercise 3

A. Edit the following passage by removing or adding exclamation points to make them correct and stylistically acceptable.

> Seventy-five miles (!) from anywhere, Frank's old Buick decided to sputter and stall out on the edge of Route 61. Meanwhile, the temperature had fallen to 16 below!!!! To make matters worse, the wind had whipped up to 30 miles per hour! That's an incredible wind chill of around 75 below zero!!!!! "Hey," yelled Bill, "don't anyone leave this car. If we stay put, maybe the highway patrol will spot us." "Who are you kidding!!??," shouted Frank. "It's 3 a.m.!"

B. In a small group, compare your edited versions of the passage. Discuss any differences, and create one collaboratively edited version.

55c
!

PEARSON

Visit mycomplab.com for more resources and exercises on periods, question marks, and exclamation points.

CHAPTER **56**

Special Punctuation

Punctuation symbols make up a kind of toolbox for writing. Five special punctuation marks—parentheses, brackets, dashes, ellipses, and slashes—can be useful strategies for guiding readers through complex sentences and for providing emphasis appropriate to your purpose for writing.

56a Parentheses

Parentheses *enclose* a word, a sentence, or a clause: you can't use just one. Whatever you write between two parentheses takes on the quality of an aside—something in a softer voice than that of the rest of a sentence. It becomes something presented in the background rather than the foreground.

1 Use parentheses to set off words or sentences

With parentheses, you can set off a word, a group of words, an entire sentence, or groups of sentences from the rest of your text. By using parentheses to place some information in the background, you can direct your readers' attention to the main assertions and facts in a passage without having to omit worthwhile (though potentially distracting) secondary material.

INFORMATION SET OFF WITHIN A SENTENCE
Although most of the team always eats a hearty and varied breakfast (if a little high in fats and cholesterol), Jim feels he performs much better with less food in his stomach.

INFORMATION SET OFF IN A SEPARATE SENTENCE
Consuelo had tried for two years to get a hearing about her immigration status. (Her employer, during this time, was unsympathetic to her pleas.) Then, in June, she finally received a letter.

Use parentheses sparingly and carefully. Too many parenthetical statements can clutter your sentences and obscure your main assertions.

DISTRACTING   Handico, Inc., decided (early in 1993) to use its waste milling chips (which had been warehoused in Detroit) to manufacture pencils (described as "environmentally friendly") to donate to public schools (which gave the company a tax credit).

CLEAR   Handico, Inc., decided to use its waste milling chips (warehoused in Detroit) to manufacture "environmentally friendly" pencils. These they donated to public schools, resulting in a tax credit for the company.

2 Watch for special uses of parentheses

You can use parentheses to present information that is not essential to the content of a sentence. You can also use parentheses in numbered lists.

NUMBERS   Harry's Bookstore has a fax number (349-0934) for (1) or-
AND LISTS dering books, (2) inquiring about the availability of specific items, or (3) requesting publication information.

STRATEGY   Punctuate parenthetical statements correctly

Don't use a comma *before* a parenthetical statement placed in the middle of a sentence. *After* the closing parenthesis, use whatever punctuation would occur if the parenthetical statement were not there.

When you sign up for Telepick (and list up to four commonly called numbers), you are eligible for free long-distance calls.

When a parenthetical statement *inside a sentence* comes at the end of the sentence, always place the sentence's end punctuation *after* the closing parenthesis.

People on your Telepick list can also call you at the same discounted rate (as long as they, too, use Coombs Communication as their long-distance carrier).

When parentheses enclose an entire freestanding sentence, place the end punctuation *inside* the closing parenthesis.

You can sign up for Telepick's "Free Hour" program until August 10. (This offer does not include international calls.)

56b
[ ]

56b Brackets

Use brackets to indicate that you have added words of your own to a quotation, or to act as parentheses within parentheses.

1 Use brackets for interpolations

Sometimes you need to introduce your own words into a quotation to help clarify a word or a statement for readers, or to provide important background information. To indicate that the words are your own, and not those of the writer or speaker being quoted, enclose the **interpolation** in brackets.

My friends Paula and Kent decided to have their wedding on a sailboat off Key West. When I asked them if the ceremony would take place at a specific place offshore, ⌊Kent said, "It's a surprise even to us. Captain Sims ⌈ the boat's owner ⌉ has chosen a special place within two hours of Key West."

2 Use brackets within parentheses

When you need to include a parenthetical statement *within* a parenthetical statement, use parentheses first, and then use brackets for the inner statement. Try to limit your use of brackets because they can make your writing seem unnecessarily complex.

You can contact Rick Daggett ⎛Municipal Lumber Council ⌈Violations Division⌋, Stinson County Municipal Center⎞ to report violations of the rules governing logging of old-growth trees.

56c Dashes

You can use dashes, like parentheses, to set off material within a sentence. Dashes call more attention to a word or group of words than parentheses do; use them to create emphasis or to indicate a change in tone. Dashes differ in function from hyphens, which are used to connect words or to separate words into parts (see Chapter 59). On keyboards, dashes appear as two unspaced hyphens, with no space before, between, or after them: --. In professional typesetting, the dash is represented by a single line: —. (Some word-processing programs automatically convert two hyphens to a dash, while some provide a choice to insert a dash under "Insert" then "Special Characters.")

56c

1 Use dashes for emphasis

Use dashes to highlight a word or group of words.

MATERIAL SET OFF IN THE MIDDLE
After picking out two pet mice—**one brown with white spots and one white with a brown forehead**—the little boy realized he had only enough money to buy one of them.

MATERIAL SET OFF AT THE END
Heartbroken at the thought that someone might buy the mouse, the boy offered his six quarters as a deposit—**along with his Mickey Mouse watch and his school notebook.**

ITEMS SET OFF IN OPENING
Extended TV hours, better meals, and more physical exercise— these were the inmates' three major demands for prison reform.

2 Avoid overuse of dashes

The use of dashes can become addictive, resulting in sentences and paragraphs that seem to be clusters of fragmented statements.

OVERUSED   There had been some interest—chiefly by Stockton—in an automated navigation system—a way to track cars by telecommunication and let drivers know if they are going in the right direction—or give them directions.

READER'S REACTION: This sentence highlights so many points with dashes that it is hard to tell what the writer considers the most important point.

MORE EFFECTIVE   There had been some interest, chiefly by Stockton, in an automated navigation system—a way to track cars by telecommunication and let drivers know if they are going in the right direction or give them directions.

Exercise 1

A. Dashes and parentheses have been added to the following paragraph. Edit the paragraph to make it more effective, deciding which punctuation marks should stay and which should be replaced. Change sentence structure and strategy if necessary.

The next morning—their donkeys carried them—to the site of the excavation. Carter and his assistant—A. R. Callender—had already begun clearing the stairway (again). As more of the doorway was exposed, the seals (of Tutankhamun) could be seen—in addition to those of the royal necropolis. When all sixteen steps had been cleared (and the entire doorway could be seen), Carter got a jolt—holes had been cut into the (upper) part of the door. The damage had been repaired— and bore the seals of the necropolis, but the question remained—had this tomb, too, been pillaged?
—Metropolitan Museum of Art, *The Treasures of Tutankhamun*

B. Compare your edited version of the passage with those created by some of your fellow students. Remember that there will be no single— or "most correct"—answer. Compare the relative strengths and weaknesses of each version.

56d
· · ·

56d Ellipses

The **ellipsis** (from Greek *elleipsis,* "an omission") is a series of three *spaced* periods telling your reader that something has been left out. You will use ellipses chiefly for two purposes: to omit parts of a quotation and to suggest gaps in a sentence, either in dialogue or in quoted speech.

STRATEGY Place and space ellipses correctly

- Use three spaced periods • • • for ellipses within a single sentence. Occasionally, an instructor may ask you to indicate omitted material by placing brackets around the ellipsis marks.[• • •]
- Use a period before an ellipsis that falls at the end of a sentence • • • •
- Leave a space before the first period • • • and after the last period of all ellipses.
- When another punctuation mark occurs before omitted words, you can eliminate it if it is not necessary to the grammar of the sentence, but you must retain it if it is necessary to the grammar.

EXAMPLE The newspapers reported that "Officer Hatt testified solemnly, • • • often staring at his hands and slowly shaking his head."

1 Use ellipses for omitted words in quotations

Ellipses are especially useful when you want to quote some (but not all) words in a passage. You may wish to omit a portion because it doesn't offer relevant ideas or information, because it makes the quotation too long for your purposes, or because you want to skip from one part of a long quotation to the next without including everything between.

ORIGINAL QUOTATION "We've always played well against Duke. Year before last, we creamed them. Last year their defense fouled us up, but we still won. This year we've got a deep bench. I bet we'll take them to the cleaners, for sure."

56d
• • •

EDITED When I pressed him to predict his team's performance, Coach Harms paused for a minute, then said with determination, "We've always played well against Duke. Year before last, we creamed them. Last year • • • we still won. This year • • • we'll take them to the cleaners • • • •"

2 Use ellipses for other gaps

Occasionally you may want to indicate a pause or a gap in your own writing, not just in quoted material. In fiction and personal narrative, for example, ellipses are often used to show suspense, hesitation, or uncertainty, or to suggest continuing action.

FOR SUSPENSE When we returned to our campsite, we were stunned. The tent was in a shambles. Our food was strewn all over the place. Our water jug was fifty yards away. Muddy claw marks were everywhere • • • •

56e   Slashes

You will use slashes mainly to indicate alternatives. You can also use slashes to mark quoted lines of poetry when those lines are not set off from your text.

1 Use slashes with alternative words

When used to indicate alternative words, the slash translates as "or" or "and." It is a shorthand often used in technical documents and manuals.

Be certain that the **on / off** switch is in the vertical position.

There is no exemption from the Composition **101 / 102** sequence.

Combinations such as *he/she* and *him/her* are not entirely acceptable in formal writing. Many good alternatives for these combinations are available. (See 50c.) The term *and/or* appears primarily in legal writing, but it can be used in moderation elsewhere. Different fields or professions may have particular functions for the slash or may use the slash in specific terms.

2 Use slashes when quoting lines of poetry

When you quote lines of poetry *within* your text rather than setting off the material in a block quotation, separate the lines of verse with a slash. Type a space before and after the slash.

The speaker in Sir Philip Sidney's sonnet addresses the moon by saying, "With how sad steps, O Moon, thou climb'st the skies, **/** How silently, and with how wan a face."

56e
/

Exercise 2

A. Find or create a short paragraph that uses as many of the punctuation marks described in this chapter as possible: parentheses, brackets, dashes, ellipses, and slashes. Choose one example of each case, and explain what purpose it serves in the paragraph.

B. Write or type out another version of the paragraph, stripped of its special punctuation. Make two copies to exchange with classmates. Ask the members of your group to edit the two copies, which lack parentheses, brackets, dashes, ellipses, and slashes. They should insert these punctuation marks wherever they think the marks are appropriate. Then compare your original and the versions punctuated by your classmates. Decide which marks of punctuation you consider effective and ineffective, and give reasons for your judgments.

CHAPTER **57**

Capitalization

Capital letters call attention to themselves and to words containing them. Your readers expect capitalization to signal the start of sentences or to identify specific people, places, and things. Capitalization that follows convention not only makes reading easier but also reflects a general sense that certain people and things deserve the kind of recognition that capital letters can provide.

The general rules for capitalization are easy to remember.

- Use a capital letter at the beginning of a sentence.
- Capitalize proper nouns, proper adjectives, and most words in titles of works.

Specific conventions are often harder to keep in mind, and sometimes you may need to consult this chapter for answers to your questions: When should I use *president* and *President*? How can I recognize when a noun is "proper" and requires capitalization?

57a Beginning a sentence

Sentences begin with capital letters. This rule applies to regular sentences and sentence fragments used as partial sentences. (See 40c.)

Two national parks, Yellowstone and Grand Teton, are in Wyoming.
Are camping spots in the parks hard to get in the summer?
No camping without a reservation.

1 Capitalize the opening word in a quoted sentence

Capitalize the first word in the quotation when it is a complete sentence or when it begins your own sentence.

COMPLETE
SENTENCE
QUOTED
Speaking of *Blind Man with a Pistol*, James Lundquist says, "**T**he novel begins with an opening chapter that, without exaggeration, is one of the strangest in American literature."

If you interrupt a quotation with your own words, do not capitalize after the interruption.

QUOTATION
INTERRUPTED

"The novel," claims James Lundquist, "begins with an open-ing chapter that, without exaggeration, is one of the strangest in American literature."

Also drop the capitalization if you integrate the quotation into the structure of your own sentence (see 27e).

INTEGRATED
QUOTATION

On the other hand, James Lundquist claims that "the novel begins with an opening chapter that, without exaggeration, is one of the strangest in American literature."

If you are quoting only part of someone else's sentence, capitalize the quoted material when you use it to open your sentence but not when you place it in the middle or at the end. (Indicate any changes in capitalization in brackets.)

OPENING
QUOTATION

"[O]ne of the strangest in American literature" is how Lund-quist describes the first chapter.

The first word is not capitalized in the source, so the writer indi-cates the change in brackets.

2 Capitalize a freestanding sentence in parentheses

Capitalize the first word of any sentence that stands on its own within parentheses.

FREESTANDING
SENTENCE

By this time, the Union forces were split up into nineteen sections. (Grant was determined to unite them.)

57a
cap

However, when you place a sentence within parentheses (or dashes) inside another sentence, do not begin the enclosed sentence with a capital.

ONE SENTENCE
INSIDE ANOTHER

Saskatchewan's economy depends heavily on farming (over half of Canada's wheat crop comes from the province), though oil production and mining are also important.

3 Decide whether to capitalize following a colon

When a complete sentence follows a colon, you can choose to capital-ize it or put it in lowercase (see 52b on colon use). Since either choice is cor-rect, you might make your decision on the basis of style or emphasis. But be consistent.

CORRECT

New Brunswick is bilingual: One-third of the population is French-speaking and the remainder English-speaking.

ALSO CORRECT

New Brunswick is bilingual: one-third of the population is French-speaking and the remainder English-speaking.

In general, do not use a capital letter when the word group following the colon is not a sentence.

Foremost among the educational issues in New Brunswick is another problem related to language: bilingualism in the schools.

4 Decide whether to capitalize elements in a series or list

You can treat questions in a series or elements in a list in various ways.

Questions in a series. You can choose whether to use capital letters to highlight the opening of each question in a series. Stick to one style throughout an essay.

CORRECT Should we spend our limited campaign funds on television ads? On billboards? On smaller signs and posters? On flyers?

ALSO CORRECT Should we spend our limited campaign funds on television ads? on billboards? on smaller signs and posters? on flyers?

Run-in lists. In the items in a **run-in list** (a list whose items aren't placed on separate lines) capitalize the first letters of sentences standing alone. Don't capitalize words, partial sentences, or a series of embedded sentences.

In estimating the project's costs, remember the following: (1) lab facilities must be rented; (2) light, heat, and other utilities need to be charged to the project's account; (3) measuring equipment should be leased.

In estimating the project's costs, remember the following: First, lab facilities must be rented. Second, light, heat, and other utilities need to be charged to the project's account. Finally, measuring equipment should be leased.

57b
cap

Vertical lists. You may choose whether to capitalize the elements in a **vertical list** when they are either words or partial sentences. Use the same pattern of capitalization in all the lists in a paper, and make sure the items in each list are parallel in form (see 46c). You must use capitalization with a list of complete sentences.

1. **Lab** facilities 1. lab facilities
2. Utilities 2. utilities
3. Measuring equipment 3. measuring equipment

57b Proper nouns and adjectives

To capitalize a word is to highlight its importance. Readers pay special attention to words naming specific persons, places, and things (proper nouns) and to adjectives created from these nouns (proper adjectives). Capitalizing a title also helps call attention to it.

1 Capitalize proper nouns and adjectives

You should capitalize the names of specific persons, places, and things (**proper nouns**) as well as adjectives derived from them (**proper adjectives**).

PROPER NOUNS	PROPER ADJECTIVES
Brazil	Brazilian music
Dickens	Dickensian portrait

All other nouns and adjectives are **common nouns** and **common adjectives.** Do not capitalize them except in special contexts, such as at the beginning of a sentence, in titles of works, or as parts of proper nouns.

COMMON NOUN (LOWERCASE)	PART OF PROPER NOUN (CAPITALIZED)
lake	Lake Jackson
computer company	Mesa Computer Company

People writing documents under the auspices of an institution (for example, a memo to university staff or a corporate report) may decide to capitalize the common noun when used as a shortened name for the institution.

Sandberg University announced plans for renovating Smith Hall.

The University has contracted with Azar Construction for the project.

CAPITALIZATION OF NOUNS AND ADJECTIVES	
CAPITALIZED	**LOWERCASE**
INDIVIDUALS	
President Obama	the president
Lebron James	her husband
Georgia O'Keeffe	my teacher's neighbor
RELATIVES	
Aunt Rosa; Cousin Jack	an aunt; my cousin Jack
Mother; Dad	my mother; your dad
GROUPS OF PEOPLE AND LANGUAGES	
Caucasian; Japanese; Hopi; Hispanic;	white
African American; Russian;	black (preferred in general usage)
Native American	

(continued)

CAPITALIZATION OF NOUNS AND ADJECTIVES (*continued*)

CAPITALIZED	LOWERCASE
TIME PERIODS, HOLIDAYS, AND SEASONS	
Thursday; October	spring; summer; fall; winter
Easter; Ramadan; Yom Kippur	holiday
RELIGIONS AND RELATED SUBJECTS	
Judaism, Jews; Christianity,	
Christians; Islam, Muslims; Catholic;	catholic (meaning "universal")
Protestant; Hinduism	
Buddhist practices	
Talmud; Bible	talmudic; biblical
God; Jesus Christ	a god, goddess; godly
ORGANIZATIONS, INSTITUTIONS, AND MEMBERS	
Chicago Bulls, the Bulls	the team
Democratic Party, Democrat	democratic (referring to democracy)
Heritage Foundation; Conservative Party; Tory	conservative (referring to a political philosophy)
Metropolitan Opera	the opera
Rolling Stones	the band
Florida State Police	the police, the state police
Coast Guard; Virginia Board of Ethics	the sailors; the board
House of Commons; U.S. Senate	a member of parliament; a senator
PLACES, THEIR RESIDENTS, AND GEOGRAPHIC REGIONS	
Malaysia, Malaysian	the country; the citizen
Cape Verde Islands, Cape Verdean	the state; the resident
PLACES, THEIR RESIDENTS, AND GEOGRAPHIC REGIONS	
Berlin, Berliner	the city; the resident
Erie County; Nassau Avenue	the county; the street
South China Sea; Volga River	the sea; the river
Amazon Basin; Mars	the region; the planet
the Southwest, the East; East Coast	southwest, eastern (directions)
BUILDINGS AND MONUMENTS	
Taj Mahal; Peace Bridge	Jim's garden; our backyard
Tower of London; Busch Stadium	the tower; a stadium
HISTORICAL PERIODS, EVENTS, AND MOVEMENTS	
Thirty Years' War; Dorr's Rebellion	the war; the rebellion
Ming Dynasty	a dynasty
Romantic period; Impressionism	the period or style
Jazz Age; Renaissance	a cultural epoch
ACADEMIC INSTITUTIONS AND COURSES	
Auburn University; Utica College	a university; the college
English Department	an English department

57b
cap

(*continued*)

CAPITALIZATION OF NOUNS AND ADJECTIVES (*continued*)

CAPITALIZED	LOWERCASE
Department of Chemistry	chemistry department
Sociology 203; English 101	sociology or English course
VEHICLES	
Airbus A300; Pontiac Grand Prix	a passenger plane; a car
COMPANY NAMES AND TRADE NAMES	
Samsung; Monsanto Chemical	the company
Intel; Fuji Heavy Industries; Xerox	a manufacturer; an employer
Luvs; New Balance; Kleenex; Toblerone	diapers; shoes; tissues; chocolate
SCIENTIFIC, TECHNICAL, AND MEDICAL TERMS	
Big Dipper; Earth (planet)	the stars; earth (ground)
Surrealism; Heisenberg's	surreal
uncertainty principle	
Alzheimer's disease; Down syndrome	tuberculosis
Pistacia vera; *Gazella dorcas*	pistachio tree; gazelle

ESL ADVICE: CAPITALIZATION

Rules for beginning words with capital letters can vary considerably from language to language, often differing markedly from those in English. In German, for example, nouns and pronouns are capitalized: *Ich werde Sie ihrer Blumen zuruckgeben* (I will give you your flowers back). In Spanish, pronouns and the names of days and months are not capitalized: *Almuerzo con ella los lunes* (I lunch with her on Mondays).

ESL

57c
cap

2 Capitalize the pronoun *I* and the interjection *O*

Whenever **I** try to argue with my parents, they make me feel as if **I'm** still a child.

Trust in him, **O** people, and pour out your heart.

Although *oh* would seem to be capitalized by analogy with *O*, convention requires that *oh* remain in lowercase unless it begins a sentence or is capitalized in material you are quoting.

57c Titles of works

In titles, you should capitalize the first word, the last word, and all words in between *except* articles (*a, an,* and *the*), prepositions under five letters (such as *in, of,* and *to*), and conjunctions under five letters (such as *and* or *but*). These rules apply to titles of long works, short works, and parts of works as well as titles for your own papers. If a colon divides the title, capitalize the first word after the colon.

> *The Mill on the Floss*
> "Factory of the Future: A Survey"
> *Reservoir Dogs*
> "Politics and the English Language"
> *Fragile Glory: A Portrait of France and the French*
> "Just like Romeo and Juliet"
> "The Civil Rights Movement: What Good Was It?"
> "Sumer Is Icumen In"
> Developing a Growth Plan for a Small Retail Business [your paper's title; see p. 713]

(For the rules governing the use of italics and quotation marks in titles, see 58a and 54d.)

Exercise 1

A. Add capitalization wherever necessary in the following sentences. Replace unnecessary capitals with lowercase letters. Circle the number before the cases that seem difficult to figure out.

EXAMPLE

Over the next ten years, india will become an increasingly important trading partner for north america.

1. Located on a subcontinent in the southern part of asia, the republic of india has a territory of about 1.2 million Square Miles.
2. India's population of almost 800 Million falls into two main groups, dravidians and indo-aryans, which in turn are made up of many other cultural groups.
3. Dravidians live mainly in the south, an area that is dominated geographically by the deccan plateau.
4. The religion of the Majority is hinduism, though other religious groups such as sikhs and muslims are important.
5. Recently, religious conflicts have broken out in the provinces of kashmir and uttar pradesh.
6. Indian History is long and complicated, but in Modern Times it has been dominated by the british rule over the Country and by attempts to escape that rule and found a democratic State.
7. British Rule over most of the country began after the sepoy rebellion of 1857–58.
8. It ended after world war II with the independence movement led by mahatma gandhi.
9. The move toward industrialization has been the main goal of indian leaders since Independence, though this movement has at

57c
cap

times been complicated by the problem of overpopulation and by conflicts stemming from the hindu social (or caste) system.

10. The dominant political Party since Independence has been the congress Party, with leaders such as jawaharlal nehru, indira gandhi, and rajiv gandhi.

B. In a small group, compare your list of difficult cases. What did you do to figure out your answer to each difficult case? Compare your answers.

Visit mycomplab.com for more resources and exercises on capitalization.

CHAPTER **58**

Italics (Underlining)

Type that slants to the right—***italic type***—gives special emphasis to words and ideas. In handwritten or typed texts, *underlining* is the equivalent of *italic* type: <u>The Color Purple</u> = *The Color Purple*.

> Walker's novel *The Color Purple* has been praised since 1982.
> READER'S REACTION: I can spot the title right away.

58a Following conventions

Convention requires you to use italics (or underlining) to give distinctive treatment to titles of full-length works, foreign words, names of vehicles, and words named as words. (Titles of shorter works or parts of works require quotation marks; see 54d.)

1 Italicize titles of long or major works

Italicize or underline titles of most long works, such as books, magazines, and films, and of artworks such as paintings and sculptures. For parts of works, however, and for short works such as stories, reports, magazine or newspaper articles, and episodes in a television series, use quotation marks rather than italics. Some titles, such as those of sacred books (the New Testament, Pentateuch, Koran), require neither italics nor quotation marks.

TREATMENT OF TITLES

ITALICIZE OR UNDERLINE	USE QUOTATION MARKS
BOOKS AND PAMPHLETS	
	"Boomers" (book chapter)
Maggie: A Girl of the Streets (novel)	
Beetroot (collection of stories)	"The Purloined Letter" (story)
The Wild Flag (collection of essays)	"Once More to the Lake" (essay)
Tracing Your Family's History (pamphlet)	"List Your Relatives" (pamphlet section)
POEMS	
Paradise Lost (long poem)	"Richard Cory" (short poem)
	(continued)

TREATMENT OF TITLES (*continued*)

ITALICIZE OR UNDERLINE	USE QUOTATION MARKS
PLAYS	
Angels in America	
MOVIES AND TELEVISION PROGRAMS	
Saving Private Ryan (film)	
Queer as Folk (TV show)	"The Long Suit" (episode)
PAINTINGS AND SCULPTURE	
Nude Descending a Staircase (painting)	
MUSICAL WORKS	
Nixon in China (opera)	"Luck Be a Lady" (song)
Nutcracker Suite (work for orchestra)	"Waltz of the Flowers" (section of a longer work)
Some Kind of Blue (album)	"Big Money" (song on an album)
MAGAZINES AND NEWSPAPERS	
Discover (magazine)	"What Can Baby Learn?" (article)
Review of Contemporary Fiction (scholarly journal)	"Aesthetic Discourse in the Fiction of Ishmael Reed" (scholarly article)
the *New York Times* (MLA style)	"Asbestos Found in Schools" (newspaper article)

NO ITALICS, UNDERLINING, OR QUOTATION MARKS

SACRED BOOKS; PUBLIC, LEGAL, OR WELL-KNOWN DOCUMENTS
Bible, Qur'an, Talmud, Bhagavad Gita, United States Constitution

TITLE OF YOUR OWN PAPER
   Verbal Abuse in *The Color Purple* (title of a work being discussed is italicized)

58a
it/und

Italicize any punctuation *only* when it's part of the title.

INCORRECT   What did he think of *Jumanji?*

CORRECT   What did he think of *Jumanji*?

CORRECT   The book *What's Up, Doc?* provides a history of cartoons.
             The question mark is part of the title, so it needs to be italicized.

2 Italicize names of specific vehicles

Italicize or underline the names of specific ships, airplanes, trains, and spacecraft, but not the names of *types* of vehicles. Note that USS and SS are not italicized. (See also 61a-2.)

SPECIFIC VEHICLES
Voyager VI
Orient Express
USS *Corpus Christi*

TYPES OF VEHICLES
Boeing 767
Arctic Cat snowmobile
Chevrolet Impala

3 Italicize foreign words and phrases

Foreign words and phrases pass through stages of familiarity. When a word or phrase is not used commonly and still seems foreign, highlight it with italics or underlining. Extremely common words and phrases—for example, "quiche," "junta," "taco," and "kvetch"—have lost their foreignness. You need not italicize such words. When you can't decide whether to treat a word or phrase as part of the language, look it up in a dictionary.

FOREIGN   The code of *omertà* supported a kind of order in the criminal world.

FOREIGN   The seaweed *Chrodus crispus* turns up in processed form in ice cream, in nondairy creamer, and even in hamburgers.

COMMON   I served the vegetables grilled on skewers like shish kebab.

4 Italicize words, letters, and numbers named as words

When you focus attention on a word, a letter, or a number by discussing it as itself, you should italicize it.

DISCUSSED   In several Boston accents, *r* is pronounced *ah*, so that the words car and park become *cah* and *pahk*.

Also italicize a word or phrase you are defining.

DEFINED   Electricity can also be generated from a *piezoelectric crystal*, a piece of quartz or similar material that responds to pressure by producing electric current.

58a
it/und

Exercise 1

The following sentences contain words that need to be highlighted by italics (underlining) or by quotation marks. Edit each by supplying any necessary italics or quotation marks. Star the items that are the most challenging to edit.

EXAMPLE

The well-known <u>Old Farmer's Almanac</u> contains information about the weather and articles on various topics.

1. I first learned about this famous American almanac from a newspaper article, You Can Look It Up There, that appeared in my local paper, the Record-Advertiser.
2. GQ and Cosmopolitan probably would not print an article like Salt: It's Still Worth Its Salt, which appeared in a recent edition of the almanac.
3. According to this article, the word salary comes from the Latin term for wages paid to some soldiers, salarium argentum, that is, salt money.
4. In an essay on the historic effects of weather, the author points out that freezing temperatures on January 28, 1986, led to the space shuttle Challenger disaster.
5. If you are interested in learning about the ocean, you can find out that high tides occur twice a month at syzygy, the times when the sun and moon are lined up on the same side of the earth or on opposite sides.

58b Emphasis

By italicizing or underlining a word or phrase, you give it special emphasis. Use this strategy on a *very* limited basis, however. Readers become annoyed when you rely too often on italicizing to do the work your words should be doing on their own.

EMPHASIZES CONTRAST

A letter of recommendation mixing strong praise with a few reservations seems direct and realistic; a letter filled with *faint* praise makes the endorsement seem lukewarm.

HIGHLIGHTS IMPORTANT INFORMATION

Whenever you start the generator, *make sure there is sufficient oil.*

Exercise 2

A. For each sentence, add italics or underlining as required by convention or needed for appropriate emphasis. Circle words that are underlined but should not be. Star items that are challenging to edit.

EXAMPLE

In 1957, Chevrolet produced the Bel Air, a model now considered a classic.

1. As David Halberstam points out in his book The Fifties, automobiles from the period were so hot they were cool.
2. Cars from that period, with enormous tailfins and lots of chrome, are still eye-catchers today.

3. The musical Grease is set in the same era.
4. Television shows from the period included the Ed Sullivan Show and Lassie.
5. Readers could choose from such now-defunct publications as the Herald Tribune newspaper and Look magazine.

B. In a group, compare your corrections. Which were the hardest to make, and why?

Visit mycomplab.com **for more resources and exercises on italics.**

58b
it/und

CHAPTER **59**

Hyphens and Word Division

Hyphens divide words and tie them together as well. A hyphen (-) tells readers to treat the divided word as one word, not two.

59a Dividing words

To make your readers' job easier, use a hyphen to split a word at the end of a line. Also hyphenate words that may be misleading or hard to read without a visual break.

If your writing makes use of many long words, such as the names of chemicals, your word-processing program will create lines that look jagged. However, all word processors now have functions that allow you to turn hyphenation on or off. The program will know where to divide long words correctly and will even out the spaces at the ends of lines through a process called *word wrapping*. To create a reasonably even margin, locate the hyphenation function in your word-processing program and turn it on.

DISTRACTING   The rate of change in home appliance manufacturing has accelerated rapidly over the past decade. Increasingly sophisticated consumers, international competition, and the need for an ozone-safe refrigerant to replace CFCs (chlorofluorocarbons) have provided the impetus.

HYPHENATED   The rate of change in home appliance manufacturing has accelerated rapidly over the past decade. Increasingly sophisticated consumers, international competition, and the need for an ozone-safe refrigerant to replace CFCs (chlorofluorocarbons) have provided the impetus.

STRATEGY   Divide words with hyphens

When hyphenating words, use the following principles.

- Divide words only between syllables. Readers have a hard time recognizing words that are split irregularly.
- Consult a dictionary to determine where to divide a word.
- Leave more than one letter at the end of a line and more than two at the beginning of a line.

INCORRECT　Two designers announced they are considering an **a-greement** to produce a line of affordable clothes for professional women.

EDITED　Two designers announced they are considering an **agree-ment** to produce a line of affordable clothes for professional women.

- Don't divide one-syllable words (such as *drought* or *through*).
- Don't split abbreviations, numerals, or contractions (such as *NASA, 100,000,* or *didn't*).
- Divide words to prevent misreading

In the spirit of **reform** politics, the party sought to **re-form** a defunct citizens' action committee.

Exercise 1

A. Look at each hyphen in the following sentences and decide whether to retain it, to change the division within the word, or to eliminate it in favor of placing the entire word on the next line. Use your dictionary if you need to, and keep track of the toughest cases.

EXAMPLE
Although receiving a present can be very pleasant, gift-~~giv~~-
giving
~~ing~~ can be equally rewarding.
∧

1. Looking for a job that would be challenging, Jen thou-ght about taking the position at Hammond's Gift Shop.
2. By the next Saturday, however, she was unpacking a truck-load of the exquisite vases and figurines that the gift shop sells.
3. Hank wanted only one thing for his birthday: an ornamental Chi-nese vase that was way beyond Rachel's budget.
4. When he came home one afternoon and saw the vase on the man-tle, Hank went right out to get flowers as a way of saying "thank you."
5. The bouquet was lovely, redolent of roses, tulips, and baby's-breath.

B. In a small group, compare your edited sentences. Which were the most difficult, and why?

59b
-

59b Joining words

Instead of *dividing* words, hyphens are often used to *tie together* the elements of compound words and phrases. The conventions for linking compounds, however, tend to be mixed; for example, should the mechanical heart regulator be written as *pacemaker, pace maker,* or *pace-maker*?

1 Check hyphens in compound words

A compound word combines two or more words. Some compounds are hyphenated (*double-decker, time-lapse*), some treated as one word (*backfire, timekeeper*), and some treated as separate words (*mail carrier, time bomb*). A dictionary will tell you how to treat a particular compound. Make sure the dictionary is up to date, however, because usage changes.

2 Hyphenate familiar compounds correctly

Some familiar compounds generally require hyphens.

Numbers. Hyphenate numbers between twenty-one and ninety-nine when they are spelled out.

forty‑one   eighty‑six   twenty‑five

This rule holds even when the number is part of a larger number.

fifty‑eight thousand   twenty‑three million

Use a hyphen to show inclusive numbers.

pages 163‑78   volumes 9‑14

Fractions. Hyphenate fractions when you spell them out.

five‑eighths   three‑fourths

Prefixes and suffixes. Hyphenate a prefix attached to a capitalized word or a number.

Cro‑Magnon   non‑Euclidean   post‑Victorian   pre‑1989

Hyphenate a capital letter and a word that together form a compound.

A‑frame   I‑beam   T‑shirt

Some specialized terms, such as those used in music, do not require a hyphen.

A minor   G sharp   C clef

The prefixes *ex-*, *self-*, and *all-* and the suffixes *-elect* and *-odd* should generally be hyphenated in compounds.

all‑encompassing   self‑centered   president‑elect
ex‑partner   self‑denial   twenty‑odd

59b
‑

3 Hyphenate compound modifiers correctly

When you ask two or more words to work as a single modifier and you place them *before* a noun, hyphenate them.

BEFORE NOUN   The **second-largest** supplier of crude oil to the United States is Nigeria.

BEFORE NOUN   Ayn Rand's works are among the most popular **twentieth-century** novels.

When the modifiers come *after* a noun, you generally do not need to hyphenate them.

AFTER NOUN   Many of the drugs used to treat cancer are **nausea inducing.**

Remember that modifying compounds can mean something quite different from the sum of their independent meanings. Hyphens help readers to know which meaning to assign the compound.

The director needed three **extra wild** monkeys for the scene.
READER'S REACTION: Does this mean that the director needed three additional monkeys that were wild?

The director needed three **extra-wild** monkeys for the scene.

Do not hyphenate compound modifiers containing *-ly* adverbs or comparative and superlative forms.

The new products were developed by the company's **highly regarded** research team.

Nigeria is the **most populous** country in Africa.

(Compound modifiers differ from coordinate adjectives, which are joined with a comma. See 51f.)

4 Use hyphens to create new compounds

To add vividness and emphasis to your writing, you can occasionally create (or "coin") a new compound word or phrase. Join the elements in such a compound with hyphens to indicate its original, temporary nature.

She entered the program with a **prove-it-to-me** attitude.

59b
-

Exercise 2

A. Insert hyphens in the following sentences wherever appropriate. Consult a dictionary if necessary.

EXAMPLE

The company hired a well‾regarded accounting firm as part of its financial reorganization.
ˆ

1. Alejo enjoys painstakingly exact work, such as building scale model ships.
2. While working, he likes to listen to Francis Poulenc's jazz influenced classical music.
3. One fourth of all his model ships are sold at auction.
4. Tony, his assistant, keeps track of the profits in a pre and post auction sale log.
5. Although his creations are awesome, Alejo harbors many insecurities that are mostly selfinflicted.

B. In a small group, compare your edited versions of the sentences. Which were the most difficult decisions, and why? Did your dictionaries give all members of the group the same advice?

Visit mycomplab.com for more resources and exercises on hyphens and word division.

59b
-

CHAPTER **60**

Numbers

You can convey numbers in several ways in your writing—as numerals (37; 18.6), as words (eighty-one; two million), or as a combination of numerals and letters (7th, 405 million). Understanding the appropriate ways to present numbers is important because unconventional or inconsistent usage can mislead your readers.

60a Spelling out or using numerals

Whenever you use numbers in your writing, you need to decide whether to spell them out (twenty-five) or use numerals (25). Conventions for the use of numbers may vary according to academic discipline and profession, however, so check with your instructor or with one of the style sheets describing conventions for specific fields (see Chapters 30–33).

1 Spell out numbers of one or two words

Spell out a number if you can write it in one or two words.

CORRECT   We are ordering **twenty-seven** personal computers.

CORRECT   Folktales have been popular for the past **two hundred** years.

Treat a hyphenated number (see 59b-2) as a single word.

CORRECT   Last year, our farm produced **seventy-eight thousand** eggs.

2 Spell out numbers that begin a sentence

Readers expect every sentence to begin with a capital letter. To avoid unsettling your readers, spell out any number that opens a sentence, even if the number contains more than two words. If the number is long enough to be distracting, rewrite so that it appears elsewhere in the sentence.

INAPPROPRIATE   **428** of the houses in Talcottville are built on leased land.

DISTRACTING   **Four hundred twenty-eight** of the houses in Talcottville are built on leased land.

EASY TO READ   **In Talcottville, 428** houses are built on leased land.

3 Express related numbers in a consistent form

When the numbers in a sentence or a passage refer to the same category, treat them consistently by sticking to either words or numerals.

INCONSISTENT Café Luna opened with a menu of **twenty-six** items, which soon expanded to **eighty-five** and then **104** items as word spread about the good food.

CONSISTENT Café Luna opened with a menu of **26** items, which soon expanded to **85** and then **104** items as word spread about the good food.

60b Special conventions

In using numbers as part of dates, measurements, addresses, and the like, you need to follow some special conventions.

1 Use numerals when appropriate

ADDRESSES AND ROUTES
1005 Avenue of the Americas   Interstate 6   Route 102

DATES
September 7, 1989   2002   1880–1910
class of '01 (informal)   the '80s (informal)   1930s
486 B.C. (or BC or BCE)   A.D. 980 (or AD 980   from 1955 to 1957
                           or 980 CE)

PARTS OF A WRITTEN WORK
Chapter 12   page 278
Macbeth 2.4.25–28 (or act II, scene iv, lines 25–28)
Genesis 1:1–6 (reference to the Bible)

MEASUREMENTS USING SYMBOLS OR ABBREVIATIONS
128 MB   65 mph   6'4"

PERCENTAGES, DECIMALS, AND FRACTIONS
7 5/8   27.3   67 percent (or 67%)

TIME OF DAY
10:52   2 p.m.   6:17 a.m.

EXCEPTION
seven o'clock, not 7 o'clock

MONEY (SPECIFIC AMOUNTS)
$7,883 (or $7883) $4.29 $7.2 million (or $7,200,000)

7 out of 10   3 to 1   a mean of 23

CLUSTERED NUMBERS
paragraphs 2, 4, 9, and 13–15 (or 13 through 15)

2 Spell out numbers when appropriate

DATES AND TIMES
the sixties   October seventh   the nineteenth century
four o'clock (or four in the morning)   half past eight

ROUNDED NUMBERS OR ROUNDED AMOUNTS OF MONEY
about three hundred thousand citizens
sixty cents (and other small dollar or cent amounts)

RANGES OF NUMBERS

LESS THAN 100   9–13   27–34   58–79   94–95
Supply the full second number.

OVER 100   134–45   95–102 (not 95–02)   370–420
1534–620 (not 1534–20)   1007–09
Simply supply the last two figures of the second number unless more are needed to prevent confusion. Do
not use a comma in page numbers.

YEARS   1890–1920   1770–86   476–823   42–38 B.C.
Supply both years in a range except when they belong
to the same century.

LARGE NUMBERS   75 million years   2.3 million new automobiles
For especially large numbers, combine numerals and
words.

60c
num

60c Too many numbers

Using too many numbers in a sentence or passage can confuse readers. If numbers come next to each other, first check for any needed hyphens
(see 59b).

CONFUSING   For the company picnic we can buy either **forty six packs**
of soda pop or **twenty two liter** bottles.

HYPHENS ADDED   For the company picnic we can buy either **forty six-packs**
of soda pop or **twenty two-liter** bottles.

When a passage contains so many numbers that readers might have
trouble keeping track of the relationships, consider organizing the numbers

in a table or chart. This alternative is appropriate only when the numbers identify comparable categories.

DETAILED DESCRIPTION

The origins of Canada's population include the British Isles (40%), France (27%), other European regions (20%), and Indian (indigenous) or Eskimo (1.5%).

CHARTED NUMBERS

Canadian Population

ORIGIN	PERCENTAGE
British Isles	40.0
France	27.0
Other European	20.0
Indian (indigenous) or Eskimo	1.5

Exercise 1

A. In the following sentences, correct any errors in the use of numbers. Circle the number before any especially difficult items. You may need to rewrite some sentences.

EXAMPLE

When the list of cities for the Rock and Roll Hall of Fame was narrowed down to 1̸ *one*, the choice was Cleveland.

60c
num

1. Of the groups and individuals elected to the Rock and Roll Hall of Fame from 1986 to 1990, 5 were female and 68 were male.
2. The Hall of Fame is increasing its membership goals from nineteen thousand to twenty-one thousand five hundred.
3. 411 of the 2000 questionnaires about favorite rockers were returned by the deadline.
4. The Hall of Fame museum purchased twenty-six articles of clothing, 127 signed memorabilia, and 232 unused concert tickets.
5. Although subscribers were told the museum would open by 10:30 in the morning on the twelfth, the personnel weren't ready for the large crowd until about 2 o'clock.

B. In a small group, compare your edited sentences. Which cases gave you the most trouble? How did you resolve them?

Visit mycomplab.com for more resources and exercises on numbers.

CHAPTER **61**

Abbreviations

When they are understood and agreed upon by both writer and reader, abbreviations make a sentence quicker to write and easier to read.

Knowing when to use abbreviations and when to spell them out will make your sentences easier to read and understand.

ORIGINAL   In her course Rep. Econ. Iss., new fac. member Doctor Marian Hwang will draw heavily on her prior employment at both the Internal Revenue Service and the National Broadcasting Company.

READER'S REACTION: **Am I supposed to know these abbreviations? And what's the National Broadcasting Company?**

EDITED   In her course Reporting Economic Issues, new faculty member Dr. Marian Hwang will draw heavily on her prior employment at both the IRS and NBC.

61a Familiar abbreviations

Many abbreviations are so widely used that readers have no trouble recognizing them. These abbreviations are acceptable in all kinds of writing as long as you present them in standard form.

1 Abbreviate titles with proper names

When people's titles come right before or after their names, you should use standard abbreviations such as *Dr.*, *Rev.*, *Ms.*, and *Prof.*

BEFORE NAME   **Dr.** Antoinette Plocek; **Mr.** William Choi; **Ms.** Rutkowski; **Mrs.** Stephanie Chenier; **Rev.** Richard Valantasis.

AFTER NAME   Christine Carruthers, **M.D.**; Cathy Harrington, **D.V.M.**; Angelo Iacono, **Jr.**; Jane Berger, **M.A.**; Rosemary Anzaldua, **C.P.A.**

When you give a person's entire name, you may abbreviate the title, but if you use it *as part of your reference to the person*, spell out the entire title.

INCORRECT   The list included **Prof.** Levesque, **Brig. Gen.** Washington, and **Rep.** Schroeder.

ACCEPTABLE	The list included **Professor** Levesque, **Brigadier General** Washington, and **Representative** Schroeder.
ALTERNATIVE	The list included **Prof. Roland** Levesque, **Brig. Gen. William** Washington, and **Rep. Patricia** Schroeder.
EXCEPTIONS	**Rev.** Mills and **Dr.** Smith were not invited.

Spell out a title when it does not come next to a proper name.

INCORRECT	You should consult the **Dr.** about that knee.
EDITED	You should consult the **doctor** about that knee.
EDITED	You should consult **Dr. Boyajian** about that knee.

Use only one form of a person's title at a time.

INCORRECT	**Dr.** Vonetta McGee, **D.D.S.**
CORRECT	**Dr.** Vonetta McGee
CORRECT	Vonetta McGee, **D.D.S.**

Academic titles such as *M.A.*, *Ph.D.*, *B.S.*, *Ed.D.*, and *M.D.* can be used on their own in abbreviated form.

ACCEPTABLE	The university offers an **Ed.D.** specifically designed for schoolteachers who want to become administrators.

61a
abbrev

2 Abbreviate references to people and organizations

Your readers may be more familiar with some abbreviations (3M, IBM) than with the names for which they stand (Minnesota Mining and Manufacturing, International Business Machines). Such abbreviations are almost always acceptable, as are those that simplify complicated names (AFL-CIO for American Federation of Labor and Congress of Industrial Organizations).

In some abbreviations the letters are pronounced singly (YMCA, USDA). In others, called **acronyms,** the letters form a pronounceable word (AIDS, NATO). Abbreviations and acronyms in which each letter stands for a word are usually written in capitals without periods.

ORGANIZATIONS	NAACP, AMA, NBA, FDA, NCAA, UNESCO, IBEW
CORPORATIONS	USX, PBS, GM, CNN, AT&T, PBS, BBC
COUNTRIES	USA (*or* U.S.A.), UK (*or* U.K.)
PEOPLE	JFK, LBJ, FDR, MLK
THINGS OR EVENTS	FM, AM, TB, MRI, AWOL, DWI, TGIF

> **STRATEGY** **Use unfamiliar abbreviations without confusion**
>
> If your reader won't recognize an unfamiliar abbreviation, you can still use it in your document as long as you first give the full name or phrase followed by the abbreviation in parentheses. From then on, you can use the abbreviation without confusion.
>
> The **American Library Association (ALA)** has taken stands on access to information. The **ALA** opposes book censorship and favors privacy for records of borrowing.

This technique is especially useful in academic or technical writing because it enables you to shorten complicated and often-repeated terms.

3 Abbreviate dates and numbers correctly

Abbreviations of dates and numbers may be used only when you specify a number or an amount; they are not a substitute for the general term.

ABBREVIATION	MEANING
A.D. or AD	*a*nno *D*omini, "in the year of Our Lord"
B.C. or BC	*b*efore *C*hrist
B.C.E. or BCE	*b*efore *c*ommon *e*ra, used in place of *B.C.*
C.E. or CE	*C*ommon *E*ra, used in place of *A.D.*
a.m.	*a*nte *m*eridiem, "morning"; some writers use *A.M.* or small capitals
p.m.	*p*ost *m*eridiem, "after noon"; some writers use *P.M.* or small capitals
no.	number
$	dollars

You may use either *a.m.* and *p.m.* or *A.M.* and *P.M.* in hand- or typewritten papers. Book and magazine printers generally set these abbreviations in small capitals (A.M., P.M.). Your word processor may allow you to do this.

61b
abbrev

61b Using abbreviations sparingly

In most formal writing, your readers will expect words spelled out except for certain familiar abbreviations (discussed in 61a). In special situations, such as research papers and scientific or technical writing, you can draw on a wider range of appropriate abbreviations to save space, particularly in documenting sources.

1 Avoid inappropriate abbreviations

The following lists should help alert you to inappropriate abbreviations.

DAYS, MONTHS, AND HOLIDAYS

AVOID	Thurs., Thur., Th.	Oct.	Xmas
USE	Thursday	October	Christmas

PLACES

AVOID	Wasatch Mts.	Lk. Erie	Phil.	Ont.	Ave.
USE	Wasatch Mountains	Lake Erie	Philadelphia	Ontario	Avenue

EXCEPTION   988 Dunkerhook Road, Paramus, **NJ** 07659
Use accepted postal abbreviations in all addresses with zip codes.

COMPANY NAMES

If an abbreviation is officially part of a company name, you may use it. Otherwise, spell out the entire name.

QUESTIONABLE   **LaForce Bros. Electrical Conts.**

EDITED   LaForce Bros. Electrical Contractors

PEOPLE'S NAMES

AVOID   Wm. and Kath. Newholtz will attend.

EDITED   William and Katherine Newholtz will attend.

DISCIPLINES AND PROFESSIONS

INCORRECT	econ.	bio.	poli. sci.	phys. ed.	OT
EDITED	economics	biology	political science	physical education	occupational therapy

PARTS OF WRITTEN WORKS

IN DOCUMENTA-TION	ch.	p.	pp.	fig.
IN WRITTEN TEXT	chapter	page	pages	figure

Use symbols such as @, #, =, ~, and + only in tables or graphs, not in the text of a paper. You may use @ when it is part of an email address.

Write to her at jmjones@adcorp.com

SYMBOLS AND UNITS OF MEASUREMENT

In general, spell out units of measurement such as *quart* and *mile* when you use them in sentences. You may, however, abbreviate phrases such as *rpm* and *mph*, with or without periods.

AVOID	pt.	qt.	in.	mi.	kg.
USE	pint	quart	inch	mile	kilogram

CORRECT   Above 5600 **rpm,** viscosity breaks down.

CORRECT   Above 5600 **r.p.m.,** viscosity breaks down.

61b
abbrev

2 Limit Latin abbreviations

Limit your use of Latin abbreviations such as *et al.* and *e.g.* to documenting sources and making parenthetical comments.

e.g.	for example (*exempli gratia*)	et al.	and others (*et alii*)
etc.	and so forth (*et cetera*)	i.e.	that is (*id est*)

Exercise 1

A. Revise each sentence, adding or correcting abbreviations when appropriate and spelling out or rewriting any inappropriate abbreviations. Assume that these sentences are all written in a fairly formal academic context.

EXAMPLE

New York, Los Angeles,
People think of ₐN̶Y̶,̶ ̶L̶A̶, and Montreal as international cities, but many small- to-medium-sized towns are just as cosmopolitan.

1. At a drugstore in a small Montana town, I talked with a clerk who told me about the Wine Appreciation Guild, Ltd. (155 Conn. St., San Francisco, CA 94107), which publishes books on food, wine, etc., e.g., *Wine Technology and Operations* by Yair Margalit, PhD.
2. According to a study by Ernest D. Abrams Consulting, smaller towns like Sioux City, IA, and Vero Bch., Fla., are even more likely to be the homes of inventors and innovators.
3. In one town in upstate NY, an engineer, Chas. D'Angelis, has created a device that measures rpms by counting the # of times a gear with a single tooth interrupts a laser beam.
4. While I was driving through the rural Midwest, I visited Rich. Forer, D.O., who examined my sore back, prescribed a new exercise rout. he had developed, and gave me an Rx for a mild painkiller.
5. In a city of twenty thou. people in eastern Tenn. I came across a health coop. that is pioneering a new phys. therapy program.

B. Meet in a small group and compare your editing of the sentences. Which ones seemed the hardest? Why?

61b
abbrev

CHAPTER **62**

Spelling

Consider the fact that the sound represented by the word *see* can be spelled in at least a dozen different ways, as illustrated in the words *see, senile, sea, scenic, ceiling, cedar, juicy, glossy, sexy, cease, seize,* and *situ.* Or consider the six different pronunciations of the letters *ough* in the words *cough, tough, bough, through, though,* and *thoroughfare.* English spelling is often difficult, and unless you have been gifted with a marvelous visual memory for the way words are spelled, the best you can do is to develop some practical strategies.

62a Spelling and the computer

You're no doubt aware of the virtues of the spell checker, a program that searches your document for misspellings and asks you whether they're correct. But spell checkers need to be used with care.

1 Understand how spell checkers work

Most spell checkers on personal computers work in conjunction with a dictionary that must be present in the computer's memory. When you ask the computer to screen your document for spelling errors, it compares each word in your text with the words in the dictionary. If the word matches a word in the dictionary, the computer moves on to the next word.

When the computer encounters a word that does *not* match any word in its dictionary, it asks you whether the word is misspelled. A typical program also allows you to add words to its dictionary. In this way, you can personalize the dictionary so that an unusual word or technical term won't be flagged every time the computer finds it in your paper.

2 Use a spell checker cautiously

Using a spell checker, especially on longer documents, is likely to reveal at least one or two errors. But whatever you do, don't rely *entirely* on a spell checker to fix your writing.

A spell checker can't reveal words that are properly spelled but used incorrectly. The computer may flag a word as misspelled and then, on command, offer you other correct spelling options. If you're not careful, you can mistakenly choose the wrong word as a replacement.

62b Recognizing and correcting spelling errors

As you edit and proofread, use one or more of the following methods to recognize and correct misspellings.

1 Pause to think

When you suspect for whatever reason that a word might be misspelled, pause to check the spelling. Think about the sequence of letters, concentrating especially on sequences that are likely to be misspelled.

2 Look it up

If you have some idea of how a word is spelled, especially how it begins, you can usually locate it in a dictionary with a little looking around. If you know how a word sounds but are not sure about the spelling, you can use the lists of correspondences between sound and spelling that some dictionaries offer. If you still can't find your word, you may wish to use a specialized dictionary or a handheld electronic speller designed for people who have considerable trouble with spelling. These dictionaries list words both under the correct spelling (*phantom*, for example) and under likely misspellings (*fantom*). Electronic spellers work like computer spell checkers.

As shown in the samples from *Merriam-Webster's Collegiate Dictionary*, 11th ed. (see Figure 49.1 on page 661), a dictionary entry will tell you a word's correct spelling and also the spelling of its various forms. The entry will indicate preferred spellings and alternative forms, and it will contain listings for related words. It will also provide information about the word's roots and history, and this information may help you remember the spelling.

62b
spell

STRATEGY Try alternatives to the dictionary

When you want to use a particular word and you can't find the correct spelling in a dictionary, try these alternatives.

- List as many possible spellings as you can, even if they seem odd. Look them all up. Often you will locate the word with just a little more searching.
- Try a thesaurus (see 49c) if you know a suitable synonym; the word may be listed there in its correct spelling.
- Ask friends or classmates if they know the spelling, especially for technical terms; then look up the word in the dictionary to be sure you got good information.
- Check the indexes of books that deal with the topic the word relates to.
- Check your textbook, class notes, or handouts to see whether the word appears there.

Exercise 1

A. Assume that you've circled the following words in italics in one of your papers. You're done with your draft, and now you want to double-check your spellings. Look up each word, make any necessary corrections, and then write out one way to remember each correct spelling. Do this whether or not you already know how to spell the word.

EXAMPLE

       pal
school *principle*

  The school principal is not always every kid's "pal."

coal *minor*   *precede* to the gate   *stationery* car
vacume the rug   she was *lieing*   *likelyhood*

B. In a group, share your devices for remembering the spellings. Write out those the group thinks are best, and share them with the rest of the class.

---

3 Be alert for common patterns of misspelling

Many words contain groups of letters that can trip up even the best spellers. Other words have plural or compound forms that may be confusing, and others add suffixes and prefixes that need special attention.

Plurals. For most words, you can form a plural simply by adding *-s* (*novel, novels*; *experiment, experiments*; *contract, contracts*). Watch out for words that end in *-o* preceded by a consonant; they often add *-es* for the plural.

62b
spell

ADD *-ES*   potato, potatoes   hero, heroes

ADD *-S*   cello, cellos   memo, memos

When a vowel comes before the *-o*, add *-s*.

ADD *-S*   stereo, stereos   video, videos

For words ending in a consonant plus *-y*, change *y* to *i* and add *-es*.

etiology, etiologies   gallery, galleries   notary, notaries

Exception: Add *-s* for proper nouns (*Kennedy, Kennedys; Tanury, Tanurys*).

For words ending in a vowel plus *y*, keep the *y* and add *-s*.

day, days   journey, journeys   pulley, pulleys

For words ending in *-f* or *-fe*, you often change *f* to *v* and add *-s* or *-es*.

hoof, hooves   knife, knives   life, lives   self, selves

Remember, however, that some words simply add -*s*.

belief, beliefs   roof, roofs   turf, turfs

Words ending with a hiss (-*ch*, -*s*, -*ss*, -*sh*, -*x*, or -*z*) generally add -*es*.

bench, benches   bus, buses   bush, bushes
buzz, buzzes   fox, foxes   kiss, kisses

A number of one-syllable words ending in -*s* or -*z* double the final consonant: *quiz, quizzes*.

Though most plurals follow these simple rules, some do not, and you need to be alert for their irregular forms. Words with foreign roots often follow the patterns of the original language, as is the case with the following words drawn from Latin and Greek.

alumna, alumnae (female)   criterion, criteria
alumnus, alumni (male)   datum, data
bacterium, bacteria   vertebra, vertebrae

Some familiar words form irregular plurals: *foot, feet*; *woman, women*; *mouse, mice*; *man, men*. (If you suspect that a word has an irregular plural, be sure to check a dictionary for its form.)

For compound words, use the plural form of the last word except in those few cases where the first word is clearly the most important.

basketball, basketballs   snowflake, snowflakes

Exception: sister-in-law, sisters-in-law.

62b
spell

Word beginnings and endings. Prefixes do not change the spelling of the root word that follows.

precut   dissatisfied   misspell   unendurable

The prefixes *in*- and *im*- have the same meaning, but you should use *im*-before the letters *b*, *m*, and *p*.

USE *IN*-	incorrect	inadequate	incumbent
USE *IM*-	immobile	impatient	imbalance

Suffixes may change the spelling of the root word that comes before, and they may pose spelling problems in themselves.

Retain the silent -*e* at the end of a word when you add a suffix beginning with a consonant.

KEEP -*E*   fate, fateful   gentle, gentleness

Exceptions: words like *judgment, argument, truly,* and *ninth.*

Drop the silent *-e* when you add a suffix beginning with a vowel.

DROP *-E*	imagine, imaginary	define, definable

Exceptions: words like *noticeable* and *changeable.*

Four familiar words end in *-ery*: *stationery* (paper), *cemetery, monastery, millinery.* Most others end in *-ary*: *stationary* (fixed in place), *secretary, primary, military,* and *culinary.*

Most words with a final "seed" sound end in *-cede*: *precede, recede,* and *intercede,* for example. Only three are spelled *-ceed*: *proceed, succeed,* and *exceed.* One is spelled *-sede: supersede.*

The endings *-able* and *-ible* are easy to confuse because they sound alike. Add *-able* to words that can stand on their own and *-ible* to word roots that cannot stand on their own.

USE *-ABLE* charitable, habitable, advisable, mendable

Drop the e for word roots ending in one e (*comparable, detestable*), but keep it for words ending in double e (*agreeable*).

USE *-IBLE* credible, irreducible, frangible

Words containing *ie* and *ei*. Here is an old rhyme that tells you when to use *ie* and *ei.*

62b
spell

I before *e*
Except after *c,*
Or when sounding like *a*
As in n**ei**ghbor and w**ei**gh.

Most words follow the rule.

USE *IE* believe, thief, grief, friend, chief, field, niece

USE *EI* receive, deceit, perceive, ceiling, conceited

Exceptions: weird, seize, foreign, ancient, height, either, neither, their, leisure

4 Watch for commonly misspelled words

Words that sound alike but are spelled differently (*accept/except, assent/ascent*) are known as **homophones.** Writers often confuse them, creating errors in both spelling and meaning.

INCORRECT The city will not **except** any late bids for the project.

EDITED The city will not **accept** any late bids for the project.

The list of homophones and other often-confused words that follows will help you recognize errors in spelling or meaning as you proofread.

COMMONLY MISSPELLED OR CONFUSED WORD PAIRS

WORD	MEANING	WORD	MEANING
accept	receive	discreet	tactful, reserved
except	other than	discrete	separate or distinct
affect	to influence; an emotional response	elicit	draw out, evoke
effect	result	illicit	illegal
all ready	prepared	eminent	well known, respected
already	by this time	immanent	inherent
allusion	indirect reference	imminent	about to happen
illusion	faulty belief or perception	fair	lovely; light-colored; just
assure	state positively	fare	fee for transportation
ensure	make certain		
insure	indemnify	forth	forward
bare	naked	fourth	after *third*
bear	carry; an animal	hear	perceive sound
board	get on; flat piece of wood	here	in this place
bored	not interested	heard	past tense of *hear*
brake	stop	herd	group of animals
break	shatter, destroy; a gap; a pause	hole	opening
		whole	complete
capital	seat of government; monetary resources	its	possessive form of *it*
capitol	building that houses government	it's	contraction for *it is*
cite	quote an authority	later	following in time
sight	ability to see; a view	latter	last of two
site	a place	lessen	make less
complement	to complete or supplement	lesson	something learned
		loose	not tight
compliment	to praise	lose	misplace
desert	abandon; sandy wasteland	meat	flesh
		meet	encounter
dessert	sweet course at conclusion of meal	no	negative
		know	understand or be aware of

62b
spell

(continued)

COMMONLY MISSPELLED OR CONFUSED WORD PAIRS (continued)

WORD	MEANING	WORD	MEANING
passed	past tense of *pass*	road	street
past	after; events occurring at a prior time	rode	past tense of *ride*
		scene	section of a play: setting of an action
patience	calm endurance		
patients	people getting medical treatment	seen	visible
		stationary	fixed in place or still
peace	calm or absence of war		
		stationery	paper for writing
piece	part of something	straight	unbending
plain	clear, unadorned	strait	water passageway
plane	woodworking tool; airplane	than	compared with
		then	at that time; next
persecute	harass	their	possessive form of *they*
prosecute	take legal action against		
		there	in that place
personal	relating to oneself	they're	contracton for *they are*
personnel	employees		
precede	come before	to	toward
proceed	go ahead, continue	too	in addition, also
principal	most important; head of a school; invested money	two	number after *one*
		waist	middle of body
		waste	leftover or discarded material
principle	basic truth, rule of behavior		
rain	precipitation	which	one of a group
reign	to rule; period of ruling	witch	person with magical powers
rein	strap for guiding an animal	who's	contraction for *who is*
raise	lift up or build up	whose	possessive of *who*
raze	tear down	your	possessive of *you*
right	correct	you're	contraction for *you are*
rite	ritual		
write	compose; put words into a text		

5 Get help

All writers make some spelling errors that they simply can't fix because they don't know the word is misspelled. If at all possible, ask members of a revision group to identify any spelling errors you haven't caught. But first clean up all the errors you already know, as a sign of consideration.

STRATEGY Improve spelling with practice

- Use memory devices and pronunciation aids, such as "all right is spelled like all wrong," or "a lot is the opposite of a little."
- Read more and attend to spellings. When reading, keep a list of words with difficult spellings.
- Build your own speller. If you keep track of words you commonly misspell, perhaps in a notebook, you'll spend less time looking them up and you'll learn them more quickly.

Exercise 2 ───────────────────

A. Without using a dictionary, circle the words that are misspelled.

supercede	conceed	procede
idiosyncracy	concensus	accomodate
dexterous	impressario	irresistable
rhythym	opthalmologist	diptheria
anamoly	afficianado	caesarian
grafitti	judgement	liason

B. Working with a partner or in a small group, compare your answers and *then* resolve any debates with a dictionary.

62b
spell

Visit mycomplab.com **for more resources and exercises on spelling.**

Glossary of Usage and Terms

Three kinds of entries are found in this glossary: grammatical terms (such as *irregular verb*), rhetorical terms (such as *freewriting*), and words that writers frequently find confusing or difficult (such as *farther* and *further*). The latter entries, which deal with matters of usage, are indicated by an arrow (→).

→**a, an** When the word that follows the article *a* or *an* begins with a vowel, use *an*: *an apple.* Use *a* before consonants: *a banana.* (*See 35a.*)

absolute phrase A phrase consisting of a noun, a pronoun, or a word group acting as a noun followed by a present or past participle and any modifiers; it is used to modify a noun or an entire clause. (*See 35c-2, 43d.*)

> **Their lungs burning from the acrid smoke,** the firefighters pressed ahead into the burning building.

abstract A concise summary of a paper, sometimes used as an overview or preface at the beginning of the paper itself. (*See 19i.*)

academic community The interacting population of individuals involved in scholarly pursuits, from teachers to researchers to students, both within one institution and outside in the broader arena available through publication and the Internet. (*See 1a.*)

→**accept, except** Use *accept* to mean "to take or receive." Use *except* to mean "excluding."

> Everyone **accepted** the invitation **except** Larry.

acronym An abbreviation whose letters begin some or all of the words in the full version: *NASA* (National Aeronautics and Space Administration). (*See 61a-2.*)

action verb A verb that indicates an action or activity: *swim, analyze.* (*See 35a-3.*)

active voice The verb form in which the doer (or agent) takes the position of the main subject, before the main verb. (*See 7c-3, 35a-3, 36e, 44c; compare* **passive voice.**)

ad hominem A **fallacy** in which an argument is based on personal attack rather than rational support and evidence. (*See 11i.*)

ad populum A **fallacy** in which an argument appeals to an audience's biases instead of using rational support. (*See 11i.*)

adjective A word that modifies a noun, pronoun, or word group acting as a noun by answering such questions as "How many?" "What kind?" and "Which one?" (*See 35a-4, 39a, 39b.*)

adjective clause (*See* **relative clause.**)

adjective phrase A phrase that modifies a noun. (*See 35c.*)

adverb A word that modifies a verb, an adjective, an adverb, or an entire sentence by answering such questions as "When?" "Where?" "Why?" "How often?" "Which direction?" "What conditions?" and "What degree?" (*See 35a-5, 39a, 39b.*)

adverb clause A clause that acts as an adverb. (*See 35c.*)

→**adverse, averse** Someone opposed to something is *averse* to it; if conditions stand in opposition to achieving a goal, they are *adverse.*

Bill wasn't **averse** to going on the ski trip unless the warm temperature would be **adverse** to good skiing conditions.

→**advice, advise** *Advice* is a noun meaning "counsel" or "recommendations." *Advise* is a verb meaning "to give counsel or recommendations."

Professor Raul wanted to **advise** his students, but they didn't want his **advice.**

→**affect, effect** *Affect* is a verb meaning "to influence." *Effect* is a noun meaning "a result." More rarely, *effect* is a verb meaning "to cause something to happen."

It is thought that CFCs **affect** the ozone layer. The **effect** on global warming is uncertain. Lawmakers need to **effect** changes in public attitudes toward our environment.

→**aggravate, irritate** *Aggravate* means "to worsen"; *irritate* means "to bother or pester."

He was **irritated** that the hotel had no humidifiers because the dry air **aggravated** his skin condition.

agreement The correct matching, in **person, number,** and **gender,** of subjects and verbs or pronouns and their antecedents. (*See Chapter 38.*)

all-purpose modifier A modifier that adds little or no meaning to a sentence and often can be cut: *very, totally, major, central.* (*See 48a-1.*)

→**all ready, already** *All ready* means "prepared for"; *already* means "by that time."

Sam was **all ready** for the kickoff, but when he had climbed to his bleacher seat, the game had **already** started.

→**all right** This expression is always spelled as two words, not as *alright.*

→**all together, altogether** Use *all together* to mean "everyone"; use *altogether* to mean "completely."

→**allude, elude** Use *allude* to mean "hint at" or "refer to indirectly"; use *elude* to mean "escape."

Francis **alluded** to the time the fugitive **eluded** the police for fifteen years.

→**allusion, illusion** An *allusion* is a reference to something; an *illusion* is a vision or false belief.

Peter found an interesting **allusion** to UFOs in a government document. It turned out that the UFOs were just an **illusion.**

→**a lot** This expression is always spelled as two words, not as *alot.* Even when spelled correctly, *a lot* may be too informal for some academic writing. Use *many, much,* or some other modifier instead.

→**a.m., p.m.** These abbreviations may be capital, lowercase, or small capital letters. (*See 61a-3.*)

→**among, between** Use *between* to describe something involving two people, things, or ideas; use *among* to refer to three or more people, things, or ideas.

A fight broke out **between** the umpire and the catcher; then there was a discussion **among** the catcher, the umpire, and the team managers.

→**amount, number** Use *amount* to refer to a quantity of something that can't be divided into separate units. Use *number* to refer to countable objects.

A large **number** of spices may be used in Thai dishes. This recipe calls for a small **amount** of coconut milk.

→**an, a** (*See* **a, an.**)

analogy A comparison between two things, often on the basis of shared characteristics. (*See 11i, see also* **false analogy.**)

analysis Writing that analyzes or "takes apart" a topic, often looking at how the parts relate to one another. (*See 18d–f.*)

analyze To divide or break something up into its constituent parts to examine their relationships. (*See 3a-2.*)

→**and/or** Although widely used, *and/or* is usually imprecise and may distract your reader. Choose one of the words, or revise your sentence.

annotated bibliography A bibliography that includes short descriptions of each entry, sometimes with accompanying evaluative comments. (*See 17d.*)

annotations Notes written about (or sometimes directly on) a draft or a published text. (*See 9d–f.*)

antecedent The noun or pronoun to which another word (usually a **pronoun**) refers. (*See 35a-2, 38c, Chapter 42.*)

antecedent   pronoun
Jean presented **her** proposal to the committee.

antithesis The use of parallelism to emphasize contrast within sentences. (*See 7d-4, 46a–b.*)

antonym A word opposite in meaning to another word: *hot* and *cold*. (*See 49c.*)

→**anyone, any one** *Anyone* as one word is an indefinite pronoun. Occasionally you may want to use *any* to modify *one*, in the sense of "any individual thing or person." (The same distinction applies to **everyone, every one;** *somebody, some body*; and *someone, some one*.)

Anyone can learn to parachute without fear. But the instructors are told not to spend too much time with **any one** person.

→**anyplace** Avoid this term in formal writing; use *anywhere* or revise your sentence.

→**anyways, anywheres** Avoid these incorrect versions of *anyway* and *anywhere*.

APA documentation style The style of documentation suggested by the American Psychological Association and described in its manual. (*See Chapter 31.*)

appositive A noun or pronoun that stands for a preceding noun (*See 51c-2.*)

appositive phrase A phrase consisting of an appositive (usually a noun) along with its modifiers, used to rename a noun in order to add information to a sentence. (*See 35c-3.*)

Ken Choi and Stephanie Almagno, **my classmates,** won an award.

→**apt, likely, liable** Use *apt* to mean "a tendency to." Use *likely* to mean "probable." Use *liable* only to imply risk, or, in a legal context, obligation or responsibility.

Claude was **apt** to ski the most treacherous slopes when he was young, but he will **likely** keep to the moderate slopes now because he is **liable** to hurt himself again if he skis the expert slopes. The ski resort was **liable** for Claude's injuries because it did not mark the location of the cliff.

argue To prove a point or persuade a reader to accept or entertain a particular position. (*See 3d; see also* **argument.**)

argument Not a disagreement, but the reasons, evidence, and explanations used in an attempt to resolve a disagreement by encouraging readers (listeners) to agree with the writer (speaker). (*See Chapters 9–12.*)

glos

argumentative thesis Statement of opinion or proposition in the presentation of an argument. (*See 3d.*)

article One of three words that precede a noun: *a*, *an*, or *the*. An **indefinite article** (*a* or *an*) precedes a general noun (one that does not refer to a specific thing). The **definite article** *the* precedes a specific noun. (*See 35a.*)

→**as, like** Used as a preposition, *as* indicates a precise comparison. *Like* indicates a resemblance or similarity.

> Remembered **as** a man of habit, Kant would take his walk at exactly the same time each day. He was **like** many other philosophers: brooding, thoughtful, and at times intense.

→**as to** *As to* is considered informal in academic contexts and should be avoided.

INFORMAL	The media had many speculations **as to** the skater's involvement in the attack against her rival.
EDITED	The media had many speculations **about** the skater's involvement in the attack against her rival.

→**assure, ensure, insure** Use *assure* to imply a promise; use *ensure* to imply a certain outcome. Use *insure* only when you imply something legal or financial.

> The surgeon **assured** the world-renowned pianist that his fingers would heal in time for the performance. To **ensure** that, the pianist could not practice for three weeks. In case of an even worse accident, the pianist had **insured** his hands with Lloyd's of London.

→**at** In any writing, avoid using *at* in direct and indirect questions.

COLLOQUIAL	Jones wondered where his attorney was **at**.
EDITED	Jones wondered where his attorney **was**.

audience The implied or intended readers for a particular piece of writing. (*See Chapter 3, 22f.*)

auxiliary verb (*See* **helping verb.**)

→**awful, awfully** Use *awful* as an adjective modifying a noun; use *awfully* as an adverb in verbal structures.

> Sanders played **awfully** at the U.S. Open Golf Tournament. On the sixth hole, an **awful** shot landed his ball in the pond.

→**awhile, a while** *Awhile* (one word) functions as an adverb; it is not preceded by a preposition. *A while* functions as a noun (*while*) preceded by an article (*a*) and is often used in prepositional phrases.

> The shelter suggested that the homeless family stay **awhile**. It turned out that the children had not eaten for **a while**.

→**bad, badly** Use *bad* as an adjective that modifies nouns or with a linking verb expressing feelings. Use *badly* as an adverb.

> The summit was scheduled at a **bad** time of year for some delegates. The British prime minister felt **bad** that some countries weren't represented. Several heads of state spoke **badly** of East–West relations.

bandwagon argument A **fallacy** in argumentative writing in which the writer tries to convince the reader that everyone else feels a particular way about a topic and that the reader ought to as well. (*See 11i.*)

base form The present tense form of a verb. (*See* **tense**; *see 36a.*)

→**because, since** In general, avoid using *since* in place of *because*, which is more formal and precise. Use *since* to indicate time, not causality.

> **Because** the meeting was canceled, Sam gave his nonrefundable plane tickets to a friend. **Since** then, Sam has avoided buying nonrefundable tickets for meetings.

begging the question In argument, a **fallacy** in which assumptions are presented as facts, sometimes using words like *obviously* or *clearly*. (Also known as *overgeneralization* or *hasty generalization*.) (*See 11i.*)

→**being as, being that** Avoid using *being as* or *being that* in academic and other formal writing when you mean *because*.

→**beside, besides** Use *beside* as a preposition to mean "next to." Use *besides* as an adverb meaning "also" or an adjective meaning "except."

> Betsy placed the documents **beside** Mr. Klein. **Besides** being the best lawyer at the firm, Klein was also the most cautious.

→**better, had better** Avoid using *better* or *had better* in place of *ought to* or *should* in formal writing.

| COLLOQUIAL | Fast-food chains **better** realize that Americans are more health-conscious today. |
| EDITED | Fast-food chains **ought** to realize that Americans are more health-conscious today. |

→**between, among** (*See* **among, between.**)

bibliography A list of the sources used by the writer of a research paper, an article, or a book, prepared so that a reader can easily find the same materials. (*See, for instance, the formats in Chapters 30–33; see also* **annotated bibliography.**)

block quotation A quotation of sufficient length to justify separating it from the body of a text in an indented block of prose. (*See 27e-1.*)

blog Short for "Web log," a kind of interactive journal that invites readers to respond to the blog owner or writer's ideas. (*See 15d-2, 25c-3.*)

body The main section of a paper or written document. It is preceded by an **introduction** and followed by a **conclusion**. (*See 4a-2.*)

Boolean logic An electronic search strategy whereby you use *and, or,* and *not* to link terms in a subject you are searching for; usage selected will expand or limit your search. (*See 25b.*)

brainstorming A technique for generating material for possible use in a written document. Brainstorming involves concentrating on a topic, thinking associatively, and finding connections among ideas.

→**bring, take** *Bring* implies a movement from somewhere else to close at hand; *take* implies a movement in the opposite direction.

> Please **bring** me a coffee refill, and **take** away these leftover muffins.

→**broke** *Broke* is the past tense of *break*; avoid using it as the past participle.

| INCORRECT | The computer was **broke.** |
| EDITED | The computer was **broken.** |

glos

→**bust, busted** Avoid the use of *bust* or *busted* to mean "broke."

COLLOQUIAL   The senator's limousine **bust** down on the trip to Washington.

EDITED   The senator's limousine **broke** down on the trip to Washington.

→**but however, but yet** These are **redundant pairs;** choose one word of each pair, not both.

→**calculate, figure, reckon** These three terms are sometimes used informally to mean "imagine" or "think." When in doubt, avoid them.

INFORMAL   John **figured** he had never seen such a large pike.

EDITED   John **thought** he had never seen such a large pike.

→**can, may** *Can* implies ability; *may* implies permission or uncertainty.

Bart **can** drive now, but his parents **may** not lend him their new car.

→**can't hardly, can't scarcely** Use these pairs positively, not negatively: *can hardly* and *can scarcely*, or simply *can't*.

→**capital, capitol** *Capital* refers to a government center or to money; *capitol* refers to a government building.

case The grammatical role that a pronoun or noun plays in a sentence (as subject, object, direct object, and the like). *Subjective case* refers to the role played as the subject of a sentence. *Objective case* refers to the role played as the object of a sentence. *Possessive case* refers to the role played in a sentence to indicate possession or ownership. (*See 37a.*)

cause-effect paragraph A paragraph explaining why something has occurred and exploring consequences. (*See 6e.*)

→**censor, censure** *Censor* means the act of shielding something from the public eye, such as a book or movie. *Censure* implies a punishment or critical labeling.

The school board **censored** *Catcher in the Rye*, but a group of parents **censured** the school by naming it on a list of "anti-intellectual" schools.

→**center around** Something can't center *around* something else. *Use center on* or *focus on* instead, or reword as *revolve around*.

chain of reasoning The path a writer takes and asks others to follow. (*See 8c.*)

→**chairman, chairperson, chair** The use of *chairman* is now considered sexist. *Chairperson* is an awkward but acceptable substitute. *Chair* is now a common nonsexist alternative.

chat rooms Informal real-time communities hosted by private Internet services or available via the Internet Relay Chat (IRC) network. (*See 15d-3.*)

→**choose, chose** Use *choose* for the present tense form of the verb; use *chose* for the past tense form.

chronological order A pattern for structuring writing in which elements of an event are presented in the order in which they happened. (*See also* **sequential order.**)

circular reasoning In argumentative writing, a fallacy in which an assertion is supported with the assertion itself. (Also known as *tautology.*) (*See 11i.*)

→**cite, site** *Cite* means to acknowledge someone else's work; *site* means a place or location.

Phil decided to **cite** Chomsky's theory of syntax as evidence for his thesis.
We chose the perfect **site** to pitch our tent.

claim (*See* **data-warrant-claim reasoning.**)

glos

clarifying sentence (*See* **limiting sentence.**)

classification The organization of information into groups, categories, or parts.

classification paragraph A paragraph in which several subjects are sorted into groups based on their similarities or relationships. (*See 6e.*)

cliché An overused or trite word or expression: *right off the bat, out of the blue, needle in a haystack.* (*See 48b-1.*)

→climactic, climatic *Climactic* refers to culmination of something; *climatic* refers to weather conditions.

clustering A planning strategy in which groups of ideas are related graphically to a kernel topic. (*See 2c-1.*)

CMS documentation style The style of documentation described in *The Chicago Manual of Style.* (*See Chapter 32.*)

coherence Writing in which each sentence or paragraph follows clearly from the one before and leads clearly to the next in a recognizable, easy-to-understand arrangement. (*See 6c, 6d.*)

collective noun A kind of noun that refers to a unit composed of more than one individual or thing: *group, board of directors, family.* Such nouns generally take a singular form even though they refer to more than one thing. (*See 35a, 38b-2, 38c-3; see also* **noun; count noun; mass noun.**)

comma splice Two or more sentences (independent or main clauses) incorrectly joined with a comma. (*See Chapter 41, 51a; compare* **fused sentence.**)

COMMA SPLICE   The human eye is not like that of the cat, it has many more color-sensitive cells.

EDITED   The human eye is not like that of the cat; it has many more color-sensitive cells.

common adjective Any adjective that is not a **proper adjective.** (*See 57b-1.*)

common knowledge Information that most readers of a document will know, making it unnecessary to cite a source for it. (*See 27d.*)

common noun Any noun that is not a **proper noun.** (*See 35a-1, 57b-1.*)

comparative form One of three forms taken by an adjective or adverb to indicate that the noun or verb modified is being compared to something else. The comparative form adds *-er* or *more* to the adjective or adverb. (*See 39c; compare* **positive form** and **superlative form.**)

ADJECTIVE   This oven is **cleaner** than mine.
She is the **more imaginative** designer of the two.

ADVERB   Sometimes you can travel **faster** by foot than by car.
Peggy designs **more imaginatively** than Horace.

→compare to, compare with Use *compare to* when you want to imply similarities between two things. Use *compare with* to imply both similarities and differences.

CORRECT   To help the child understand his virus, the doctor **compared** it **to** a tiny army in his body.

CORRECT   **Compared with** his last illness, this one was mild.

comparing and contrasting A technique for organizing an entire paper or for developing individual paragraphs or sentences. Opinions, characteristics, or objects are compared for similarities and differences, which often are presented in alternating form. (*See 46b on* **parallelism;** *see also* **point-by-point organization** and **subject-by-subject organization.**)

glos

complement A word (noun, pronoun, or adjective) or phrase tied by a linking verb to a subject. (*See 35b-2, 37b, 39b-2.*) *A subject complement* "completes" the linking verb by describing the subject or renaming it. An *object complement* renames or describes the *direct object.*

→**complement, compliment** *Complement* means "an accompaniment"; *compliment* means "words of praise."

The diplomats **complimented** the ambassador on her choice of opera.

The theater's grand ceiling **complemented** the theme of the opera perfectly.

complete predicate (*See* **predicate.**)

complete sentence A sentence that contains both a subject and a complete predicate and is therefore grammatical. (*See Chapter 40; compare* **sentence fragment.**)

complete subject (*See* **subject.**)

complex sentence A sentence with one **main clause** and one or more **subordinate clauses.** (*See 35d, 47b-1; compare* **compound sentence; compound-complex sentence; simple sentence.**)

compound antecedent A group of words to which a pronoun or noun refers. (*See 42a; see also* **antecedent.**)

compound-complex sentence A sentence with two or more **main clauses** and one or more **subordinate clauses.** (*See 35d; compare* **compound sentence; complex sentence; simple sentence.**)

compound predicate A predicate that contains two or more complete verbs, usually connected with *and.*

The car **struck and injured** the bystander.

compound sentence A sentence with two or more **main clauses** and no **subordinate clauses.** (*See 35d; compare* **complex sentence; compound-complex sentence; simple sentence.**)

compound subject Two or more subjects joined with *and* or *both . . . and.* (*See 37c, 38b.*)

Jim and the rest of the Boy Scouts were responsible for the rescue.

conditional statement A sentence that expresses something improbable or hypothetical, often beginning with *if.* Conditional statements use the *subjunctive* form of the verb. (*See 36g.*)

conjunction A word that joins two elements in a sentence. (*See 35a-7, 38b, 46a-3, 51a.*) *Coordinating conjunctions* (*and, but, or, nor, for, yet, so*) link grammatically equal elements such as parts of compound subjects, verbs, objects, and modifiers. *Subordinating conjunctions* (*because, although, while, if, since*) create a **subordinate** (or *modifying*) **clause.**

conjunctive adverb An adverb such as *however, moreover, thus,* or *therefore* that joins sentences or elements within sentences and indicates a logical relationship between them. (*See 35a-5, 51b, 52a-2.*)

connotation The associative or affective shades of meaning conveyed by a word, as opposed to its literal meaning. If someone is said to have *retreated* from a gathering, the word connotes that the person was feeling attacked or bewildered. (*See 49b-2.*)

content The specific ideas or information presented in a piece of writing. (*See 8c.*)

→**continual, continuous** *Continual* implies that something is recurring; *continuous* implies that something is constant and unceasing.

The **continual** noise of landing jets didn't bother the homeowners as much as the foul odor that drifted **continuously** from the landfill near the airport.

glos

contraction A form in which two words are brought together, usually by eliminating one or more letters and adding an apostrophe to mark the omission(s): *it's, they're, can't. (See 53b-1.)*

controlling idea (*See* **thesis statement.**)

coordinate adjectives A pair of adjectives, each modifying a noun on its own and therefore separated by a comma. In *noncoordinate adjectives*, which are not separated by commas, the first adjective modifies the second, which modifies the noun. (*See 51f.*)

COORDINATE   These drawings show a **quick, simple** solution to the problem.

NONCOORDINATE   **Flexible plastic** pipes carry water away from the building.

coordinating conjunction (*See* **conjunction.**)

coordination A sentence structure that links and equally weights main clauses using *coordinating conjunctions.* (*See 51a; compare* **subordination.**)

correlative conjunctions Pairs of conjunctions (*not only . . . but also; either . . . or; neither . . . nor; both . . . and; whether . . . or*) that join sentence elements that are grammatically equal. (*See 35a-8, 46a-3* on **parallelism.**)

→**could of, would of** These incorrect pairs are common because the correct verb forms *could have* and *would have* are often pronounced that way.

INCORRECT   I **could of** majored in psychology.

EDITED   I **could have** majored in psychology.

count noun A type of noun that refers to individual ("countable") items: *chair, bean, cup.* Most count nouns can be made plural by the addition of an *-s.* (*See 35a-1; see also* **noun; collective noun; mass noun.**)

counterargument A claim or opinion opposed to the one being supported in an argumentative paper. (*See 11b–c.*)

→**couple, couple of** These terms are used colloquially; in formal writing, use *a few* or *two* instead.

COLLOQUIAL   Watson took a **couple of** days to examine the data.

EDITED   Watson took **a few** days to examine the data.

critical synthesis Brings together perspectives, interpretations, and evidence from a variety of sources and explores their potential connections. (*See 22j.*)

critique A paper that summarizes and presents a critical reaction to a specific work, such as a speech or book. (*See 17i.*)

CSE documentation style The style of documentation suggested by the Council of Science Editors and described in its guide. (*See Chapter 33.*)

cumulative sentence A sentence that begins with the main clause and then adds modifying phrases, clauses, and words. (*See 7c.*)

dangling modifier A sentence that contains no **headword** or **phrase** to which a modifier can be correctly linked. (*See Chapter 43; compare* **disruptive modifier** and **misplaced modifier.**)

DANGLING   Staring from his study, **Paul's stomach** lurched.

EDITED   Staring from his study, **Paul** felt his stomach lurch.

→**data** Although now widely used for both the singular and plural, *data* technically is a plural noun; *datum* refers to a single piece of data. If in doubt, use the more formal distinction between the two, and make sure your verbs agree in number.

glos

data-warrant-claim reasoning A reasoning or argumentative strategy in which data (indisputable facts) lead to a claim (or conclusion) through a mental process involving probable facts and assertions (warrants). Also called Toulmin reasoning. (*See 11g.*)

database A computerized (CD-ROM or online) collection of resources available to researchers. Databases contain a wide variety of materials such as articles, graphics, bibliographies, and statistics and usually focus on a particular area of study or a particular topic. (*See 23b, Chapter 24.*)

declarative sentence A type of sentence that makes a statement. (*See 35d; compare* **exclamatory sentence; imperative sentence; interrogative sentence.**)

The motor is making a rattling noise.

deductive argument An argument that begins with an explicitly stated premise and goes on to support that premise, using **syllogism** as the basic logical format. (*See 11e; compare* **inductive argument.**)

definite article (*See* **article.**)

demonstrative adjective (*See* **demonstrative pronoun.**)

demonstrative pronoun A pronoun (*this, that, these,* or *those*) that points out or highlights an antecedent. (*See 34a-2, 35c-3.*)

dependent clause (*See* **subordinate clause.**)

diction The choice of words and phrases in a piece of writing. (*See Chapter 48.*)

→**different from, different than** Use *different from* when an object follows, and use *different than* when an entire clause follows.

Jack's quiche recipe is **different from** Marlene's, but his cooking method is **different** now **than** when he was an apprentice.

direct object (*See* **object.**)

direct quotation A quotation that presents a speaker's or writer's exact words, set off by quotation marks. (*See 44d.*)

→**discreet, discrete** *Discreet* means "reserved or cautious"; *discrete* means "distinctive, different, or explicit."

Emmons was as **discreet** as an anthropologist could be, but he violated some of the **discrete** codes of research when he lived among the tribe.

discussion group A type of electronic bulletin board with a specialized membership in a specific academic, work, or public community. (*See 25c-6.*)

→**disinterested, uninterested** *Uninterested* implies boredom or lack of interest; *disinterested* implies impartiality or objectivity.

It wasn't that Reagan was **uninterested** in environmental issues; he was simply a **disinterested** party when it came to special-interest groups.

disruptive modifier A sentence in which two closely connected elements such as a noun and a verb are inappropriately disrupted by a modifier. (*See 43c; compare* **dangling modifier** and **misplaced modifier.**)

DISRUPTIVE   The engineer, **even though he could have become trapped in the burning plant,** was able to shut off the gas valve and prevent millions of dollars in damage.

EDITED   **Even though he could have become trapped in the burning plant,** the engineer was able to shut off the gas valve and prevent millions of dollars in damage.

documentation The process of citing the source or reference for an idea, sentence, passage, or text in a research paper. (*See Chapters 29–33.*)

→**done** Avoid using *done* as a simple past tense; it is a *past participle*. (*See 36b.*)

INCORRECT	The skater **done** the best she could at the Olympics.
EDITED	The skater **did** the best she could at the Olympics.

→**don't, doesn't** These and other contractions may strike some academic readers as too informal. Check with your reader, or err on the side of formality (*do not, does not*) when in doubt.

double negative Avoid the incorrect use of two negative forms. (*See 39d.*)

INCORRECT	The state **hasn't** done **nothing** about it.
EDITED	The state **has** done **nothing** about it.
EDITED	The state **hasn't** done **anything** about it.

→**due to** When meaning "because," use *due to* only after some form of the verb *be.* Avoid *due to the fact that,* which is wordy.

INCORRECT	The mayor collapsed **due to** campaign fatigue.
EDITED	The mayor's collapse <u>was</u> **due to** campaign fatigue.
EDITED	The mayor collapsed **because** of campaign fatigue.

editing The process of fine tuning a rough draft for problems in grammar, wording, style, sentence rhythm or length, and other details. (*See Chapter 5.*)

→**effect, affect** (*See* **affect, effect.**)

→**e.g.** From a Latin term meaning "for example," this abbreviation is common in much writing but should be avoided when possible.

either/or strategy In argumentative writing, a **fallacy** in which an issue is oversimplified, usually into two sides or positions. (*See 11i.*)

electronic indexes Computerized (CD-ROM or online) indexes to articles in magazines, newspapers, or scholarly journals. Indexes enable researchers to identify possible sources. (*See Chapter 25b; see also* **printed indexes.**)

electronic mailing list The most common type of subscriber-based mailing list. (*See 21e.*)

electronic research Research conducted using electronic media or technology, such as CD-ROM databases, online resources, or electronic card catalogs. (*See Chapter 25; see also* **research.**)

ellipsis A series of three evenly spaced periods telling a reader that something has been left out of a quotation. (*See 56d.*)

As Fielding describes it, Allworthy's house had "an Air of Grandeur in it, that struck you with awe . . . as commodious within, as venerable without."

elliptical construction The omission of an otherwise repeated element in a sentence; appropriate omissions are not misleading or confusing. (*See 45b-2.*)

LEFT IN	Some car owners invest lots of time caring for their cars; others **invest little time caring for their cars.**
OMITTED BUT CLEAR	Some car owners invest lots of time caring for their cars; others **invest little.**

glos

embedded quotation A quotation used within a sentence you have written, as contrasted to a **block quotation.**

→**emigrate from, immigrate to** People *emigrate from* one country and *immigrate to* another.

emoticons Faces drawn with keyboard characters. (*See 15c-2.*)

emotional strategy In argumentative writing, a focus on the values, attitudes, systems of beliefs, and emotions that guide people's lives and are central to most decision-making processes. (*See 11f.*)

empty phrase A phrase that adds little or no meaning to a sentence and can be cut or reduced: *at this point in time, due to the fact that, each and every.* (*See 48a-1.*)

→**ensure, assure, insure** (*See* **assure, ensure, insure.**)

→**enthused** Avoid *enthused* to mean *enthusiastic* in formal writing.

equivocation (*See* **misleading language/misleading evidence.**)

→**especially, specially** *Especially* implies "in particular"; *specially* means "for a specific purpose."

It was **especially** important that Nakita follow the workouts **specially** designed by her coach.

→**etc.** Avoid this abbreviation in formal writing by supplying a complete list of items or by using a phrase like *and so forth.*

etymology The history of a word. (*See 49c.*)

evaluation The process of deciding the relative worth of a source, phenomenon, or opinion, including the credibility or authority of a researched source. (*See 22i, 25d.*)

evaluative summary (*See* **summary.**)

→**eventually, ultimately** Use *eventually* to imply that an outcome follows a series of events or a lapse of events. Use *ultimately* to imply that a final or culminating act ends a series of events.

Eventually, the rescue team managed to pull the last of the survivors from the wreck, and **ultimately** there were no casualties.

→**everyday, every day** *Everyday* is an adjective that modifies a noun. *Every day* is an adjective followed by a noun.

Every day in the Peace Corps, Monique faced the **everyday** task of boiling her drinking water.

→**everyone, every one** *Everyone* is a pronoun; *every one* is an adjective followed by a noun. (*See also* **anyone, any one.**)

Everyone was tantalized by **every one** of the items on the dessert menu.

evidence Information that gives readers reasons for accepting the accuracy, value, or importance of conclusions. (*See 9b-2.*)

→**except, accept** (*See* **accept, except.**)

exclamatory sentence A type of sentence that expresses something emphatically. (*See 7d-2, 35d-2; compare* **declarative sentence; imperative sentence; interrogative sentence.**)

The car is on fire!

expletive construction In indirect sentences, the use of opening expletives such as *there is, there are,* or *it is* to delay the actual subject until further into the sentence. (*See 7b, 48a-2.*)

This is the case in which the man bit the dog.

explication A line-by-line analysis of a text. (*See 18c.*)

→explicit, implicit *Explicit* means that something is outwardly or openly stated; *implicit* means that it is implied or suggested.

The conductors **explicitly** assured the passengers that all was well, but **implicit** in their voices was the danger ahead.

extend In writing assignments, to take an idea or concept and apply it more extensively. (*See 3a-2.*)

fallacy Any flaw in reasoning, particularly in the context of persuasive or argumentative writing. (*See 11i.*)

false analogy A **fallacy** in which two things that are presented as comparable are actually not. (*See 11i.*)

→farther, further *Farther* implies a measurable distance; *further* implies something that cannot be measured.

The **farther** they trekked into the wilderness, the **further** their relationship deteriorated.

faulty cause-effect relationship A **fallacy** in which one event is assumed or implied to have caused another event. (*See 11i.*)

faulty parallelism (*See* **parallelism.**)

faulty predication A sentence in which the second part comments on or names a topic different from the one announced in the first part. (*See 45a-1; see* **shift.**)

FAULTY   The **presence** of ozone in smog is **the chemical** that causes eye irritation.

EDITED   The **ozone** in smog is the **chemical** that causes eye irritation.

→female, male Use these terms only when you want to call attention to gender specifically, as in a research report. (*See Chapter 50.*)

→fewer, less Use *fewer* for things that can be counted, and use *less* for quantities that cannot be divided.

Obama had **fewer** supporters for the bill than before, but there was much **less** media coverage this time.

field research (*See* **research.**)

field resources Original documents, interviews, surveys, questionnaires, and personal observations gathered during the process of **research.**

figure, calculate, reckon (*See* **calculate, figure, reckon.**)

→finalize Some readers object to adjectives and nouns that are turned into verbs ending in *-ize* (*finalize, prioritize, objectivize*). When in doubt, use *make final* or some other construction.

→firstly Use *first, second, third,* and so forth when enumerating points in writing.

first person (*See* **person.**)

focused paragraph (*See* **paragraph.**)

format A general plan for the organization, such as length, level of formality, and the actual appearance of a document. (*See Chapter 13.*)

→former, latter *Former* means "the one before" and *latter* means "the one after." They can be used only when referring to two things.

fragment (*See* **sentence fragment.**)

glos

freewriting A technique involving writing as quickly as possible without concern for style or grammar. Freewriting is often used to avoid writer's block, to "warm up" for more formal writing, or to generate ideas for a paper. (*See 2a; see also* **focused freewriting.**)

→**freshman, freshmen** Many readers consider these terms sexist and archaic. Unless you are citing an established term or group (such as the Freshman Colloquium at Midwest University), use *first-year student* instead.

full-text database A database that provides access to complete texts, such as articles or papers, instead of just abstracts or summaries. (*See 25b.*)

further, farther (*See* **farther, further.**)

fused sentence Two or more complete sentences incorrectly joined without any punctuation. (*See Chapter 41; compare* **comma splice.**)

> FUSED   Frank Lloyd Wright's Robie House exemplifies his architectural principles it embodies the idea of "space, not mass."
>
> EDITED   Frank Lloyd Wright's Robie House exemplifies his architectural principles; it embodies the idea of "space, not mass."

future perfect tense (*See* **perfect tense.**)
future progressive tense (*See* **progressive tense.**)
future tense (*See* **tense.**)

gender Labeling of nouns and pronouns according to whether they are masculine, feminine, or neuter. Pronouns must agree in gender with the nouns to which they refer. (*See 35a-2, 42a.*)

> **Harry** put on **his** shirt.

general pattern of development A type of paragraph development such as **narration, comparison,** or **cause-effect,** used to shape a paragraph's content and arrangement. (*See 6e-2.*)

general reference A reference to the main ideas in a source or to information presented throughout the work, not in a single place. (*See 30a; compare* **informational reference** and **specific reference.**)

general-to-specific pattern (*See* **logical order.**)

generalizations Conclusions reached on the basis of facts (*see Chapter 9*) and summing up their meaning or qualities, or broad conclusions about what your research has to say about your topic. (*See 22l.*)

genre The form, or category of discourse, to which a work conforms (e.g., poem, play, novel, novella, film). (*See 18c.*)

gerund An *-ing* form of a verb that acts as a noun. (*See 35a-3, 35c-4, 34b-4; see also* **verbal phrase.**)

> **Running** can be enjoyable.

→**get** Avoid imprecise or frequent use of *get* in formal writing; use more specific verbs instead.

> INFORMAL   Martin Luther King, Jr., had a premonition that he would **get** shot; his speeches before his death **got** nostalgic at times.
>
> EDITED   Martin Luther King, Jr., had a premonition that he would **be** shot; his speeches before his death **waxed** nostalgic at times.

glos

→**goes, says** In very informal contexts, some speakers use *go* and *goes* colloquially to mean *say* and *says*. This usage is considered inappropriate in all writing.

Hjalmar **says** (said) to Gregers, "I wanted to make a clean break."

→**gone, went** Do not use *went* (the past tense of *go*) in place of the past participle form *gone*.

| INCORRECT | The players **should have went** to their captain. |
| EDITED | The players **should have gone** to their captain. |

→**good and** This is a colloquial term when used to mean "very" (*good and* tired; *good and* hot). Avoid it in formal writing.

→**good, well** *Good* is an adjective meaning "favorable" (a *good* trip). *Well* is an adverb meaning "done favorably." Avoid colloquial uses of *good* for *well*.

| COLLOQUIAL | The Vikings played real **good** in the playoffs. |
| CORRECT | A **good** shot in the game of golf is a shot that is placed **well**. |

→**got to** Avoid the colloquial use of *got* or *got to* in place of *must* or *have to*.

| COLLOQUIAL | I **got to** improve my ratings in the opinion polls. |
| EDITED | I **must** improve my ratings in the opinion polls. |

→**great** In formal writing, avoid using *great* as an adjective meaning "wonderful." Use *great* in the sense of "large" or "monumental."

| INFORMAL | Our trip to Stone Mountain was **great**. |
| APPROPRIATE | A **great** carving appears on the rock face of Stone Mountain. |

→**hanged, hung** Use *hanged* exclusively to mean execution by hanging and *hung* to refer to anything else.

The convict was **hanged** at dawn.
The farmer **hung** the dead pheasant upside down for a day before cooking it.

hasty generalization (*See* **begging the question.**)
→**have, got** (*See* **got to.**)
→**have, of** (*See* **could of, would of.**)
→**he, she, he or she, his/her** When you use gender-specific pronouns, be careful not to privilege the male versions. Look for ways to avoid awkward alternations of *he* and *she* or *his* and *her* by revising structures that require them. (*See 50c.*)
headword The word a modifier refers to. (*See introduction to Chapter 42.*)
helping verb The forms of *be, do,* and *have* that link to main verbs and create complex verb forms. Helping verbs are sometimes called **auxiliary verbs** or **modal auxiliaries**. (*See 35a-3, 36c.*)

helping   main
verb   verb

The tourist agency is planning to make a video of the local attractions.

homophones Words that sound like each other but are spelled differently (*accept/except; assent/ascent; principal/principle; stationary/stationery*). (*See 62b-4.*)
→**hopefully** Although the word is widely used to modify entire clauses (as in "Hopefully, her condition will improve"), some readers may object. When in doubt, use *hopefully* only to mean "feeling hopeful."

glos

Bystanders watched **hopefully** as the rescuers continued to dig.

→**hung, hanged** (*See* **hanged, hung.**)

hyphenated noun A single noun that consists of two or more words linked by hyphens: *father-in-law*. (*See 59b.*)

hypothesis A tentative assertion to be explored in an argument. (*See 11e.*)

idiom A common expression that typically means something different from its literal interpretation (e.g., *kick the bucket*). (*See 49b-4.*)

→**if, whether** Use *if* before a specific outcome (either stated or implied); use *whether* when you are considering alternatives.

If holographic technology can be perfected, we may soon be watching three-dimensional television. But **whether** any of us will be able to afford it is another question.

illogical comparison (*See* **incomplete sentence.**)

→**illusion, allusion** (*See* **allusion, illusion.**)

→**immigrate to, emigrate from** (*See* **emigrate from, immigrate to.**)

imperative mood (*See* **mood.**)

imperative sentence A type of sentence that makes a request or command. (*See 7d-2, 35d; compare* **declarative sentence; exclamatory sentence; interrogative sentence.**)

Do your chores immediately.

→**implicit, explicit** (*See* **explicit, implicit.**)

incomplete sentence A sentence that fails to complete an expected logical or grammatical pattern. An *incomplete comparison* leaves out the element to which something is being compared. An *illogical comparison* is worded so that it seems to be comparing things that cannot be reasonably compared. (*See 45b.*)

INCOMPLETE COMPARISON	The sound quality of digital tapes is much better.
EDITED	The sound quality of digital tapes is much better **than that of analog tapes.**

indefinite article (*See* **article.**)

indefinite pronoun A pronoun that refers to people, things, or ideas in general rather than to specific antecedents. Indefinite pronouns include *all, another, any, anybody, anyone, anything, both, each, every, everyone.* (*See 35a-2, 37b.*)

independent clause (*See* **main clause.**)

indicative mood (*See* **mood.**)

indirect object (*See* **object.**)

indirect question A sentence whose main clause is a statement and whose embedded clause asks a question. Such sentences usually behave as statements, not as questions. (*See 55b-1.*)

Phil wondered whether he could handle an additional course.

indirect quotation A quotation in which a writer reports the substance of someone's words but not the exact words the person used. Quotation marks are not needed. (*See 44b-2, 44d.*)

inductive argument An argument that does not explicitly state a premise but leads the reader through an accumulating body of evidence to a conclusion. (*See 11e; compare* **deductive argument.**)

inferences Conclusions reached on the basis of facts. (*See 50b-2.*)

infinitive The "root," tenseless form of a verb. In English, infinitives are preceded by *to*: *to live*, *to abolish*. (*See 35c-4*; *see also* **split infinitive** and **verbal phrase.**)

infinitive phrase A phrase that uses the *to* form of a verbal. It can be used as an adjective, an adverb, or a noun. (*See 35c-4.*)

informants In field research, people interviewed or surveyed. (*See 26c.*)

informative thesis A thesis used when writing to present and explain information. (*See 3d.*)

informative writing Writing whose content and strategies are shaped by the purpose of conveying, explaining, or analyzing information. (*See Chapter 17.*)

→**in regard to** Although it may sound sophisticated, *in regard to* is wordy and unnecessary. Use *about* instead.

WORDY	The cruise company was adamant **in regard to** its docking rights at Christiansted.
EDITED	The cruise company was adamant **about** its docking rights at Christiansted.

→**inside of, outside of** When you use *inside* or *outside* to mark locations, do not pair it with *of*.

INAPPROPRIATE	**Inside of** the hut was a large stock of rootwater.
EDITED	**Inside** the hut was a large stock of rootwater.

→**insure, assure, ensure** (*See* **assure, ensure, insure.**)

intensifying phrase A phrase that is meant to make a sentence more forceful but carries little or no additional meaning; *for all intents and purposes, in my opinion, all things considered*. (*See 48a-1.*)

intensive pronoun A **reflexive pronoun** used to give emphasis to, or intensify, a sentence. (*See 35a-2, 37c-6.*)

He was able to move the heavy refrigerator **himself.**

intentional fragment (*See* **partial sentence.**)

interjection An emphatic word or phrase used to convey a strong reaction or emotion, such as surprise (*Hey!*) or disappointment (*Oh no!*). (*See 35a-8.*)

interpolation The introduction of your own words, marked with brackets, into a verbatim quotation from someone else. (*See 56b-1.*)

Kent said, "Captain Sims **[the boat's owner]** has chosen a special place within two hours of Key West."

interpretation The process of reading into or adding your own understandings to a source, concept, or phenomenon. (*See 9f.*)

interpretive reading A kind of **critical reading** to determine the meaning, perspective, and purposes, both explicit and implicit, of a text. (*See 9d–f.*)

interrogative pronoun The pronouns *who* and *which* when they are used to introduce questions. (*See 35a-2.*)

interrogative sentence A type of sentence that poses a question. (*See 35d-2*; *compare* **declarative sentence; exclamatory sentence; imperative sentence.**)

interrupters Parenthetical remarks such as *in fact* or *more important*. (*See 48a.*)

in-text citation In research writing, a citation that is placed within the text of the paper rather than at the end in a works cited page or bibliography. (*See 26f.*)

glos

intransitive verb A verb that is not followed by an **object** or **complement**. (*See 35b-2; compare* **transitive verb.**)

verb   no object

The president **dreamed.**

invention A term from classical rhetoric referring to the process of generating and exploring ideas before writing a draft. (*See Chapter 2; see also* **brainstorming; prewriting strategies.**)

inverted sentence order A sentence in which the normal subject-verb-object/complement word order is shifted by placing a subsidiary element at the beginning of the sentence in order to call attention to it. (*See 7d-3.*)

NORMAL	**The director's voice thundered** from the darkness near the rear of the auditorium with criticisms of our acting.
INVERTED	**From the darkness near the rear of the auditorium thundered the director's voice** with criticisms of our acting.

→**irregardless** Avoid this erroneous form of the word *regardless*, commonly used because *regardless* and *irrespective* are often used synonymously.

irregular verb A verb that does not follow the usual pattern for distinguishing forms for the present, past, and past participle. (*See 36a-1.*)

	PRESENT	PAST	PAST PARTICIPLE
REGULAR VERB	bake	baked	baked
IRREGULAR VERB	swim	swam	swum

→**irritate, aggravate** (*See* **aggravate, irritate.**)

issue A subject about which there are two (or more) differing opinions. (*See 10a.*)

italic type Type that *slants to the right* and is the equivalent of <u>underlining</u> for emphasis or for some titles. (*See Chapter 58.*)

→**its, it's** Use *its* as a possessive pronoun and *it's* as a contraction of *it* and *is*. (Some readers may also object to *it's* for *it is* in formal writing.) (*See 53b.*)

The porcupine raised **its** quills threateningly. **It's** a shame that dogs must learn about porcupines the hard way.

→**-ize, -wise** Some readers object to the process of turning nouns or adjectives into verbs by adding *-ize* at the end (*finalize, itemize, computerize*). When in doubt, opt for different verbs. Also avoid adding the suffix *-wise* to words, as in "Weather*wise*, it will be a chilly night all over the region."

keywords Most **database** resources and other electronic sources of information such as **online catalogs** and **electronic indexes** allow researchers to retrieve information and listings by typing in important (key) words identifying the subject or important ideas or details related to the subject. (*See 25b.*)

→**kind, sort, type** These words are singular nouns; precede them with *this*, not *these*. In general, use more precise words.

→**kind of, sort of** Considered by most readers to be informal, these phrases should be avoided in academic and professional writing.

lab report A paper that summarizes the methods and results of a laboratory experiment. (*See 19h.*)

→**latter, former** (*See* **former, latter.**)

→lay, lie *Lay* is a transitive verb requiring a direct object (but not the self). *Lie,* when used to mean "place in a resting position," refers to the self but takes the form *lay* in the past tense. (*See 36d.*)

INCORRECT	I was going to **lay** down for a while.
EDITED	I was going to **lie** down for a while.

→less, fewer (*See* **fewer, less.**)
→liable (*See* **apt, likely, liable.**)
→lie, lay (*See* **lay, lie.**)
→like, as (*See* **as, like.**)
→likely, apt, liable (*See* **apt, likely, liable.**)

limiting modifier A **modifier** such as *only, almost, hardly, just, exactly,* or *even* that limits or qualifies a word, usually the one that follows it. (*See 43a-2.*)

limiting sentence A sentence that limits, or narrows, the focus of a **topic sentence.** (*See 6b-2.*)

linking verb Verbs that express a state of being or an occurrence: *is, seems, becomes, grows.* Also known as **state-of-being verbs.** (*See 35a-3, 35b-2.*)

listserv (*See* **electronic mailing list.**)

→literally Avoid using *literally* in a figurative statement (one that is not true to fact). Even when used correctly, *literally* is redundant because the statement will be taken as fact anyway.

INCORRECT	The scholars **literally** died when they saw their hotel.
REDUNDANT	The scholars **literally gasped** when they saw their hotel.
EDITED	The scholars gasped when they saw their hotel.

literature review A paper or part of a paper that provides a **synthesis** of existing literature or research on a specific topic. (*See 17e.*)

logical order A pattern for paragraph development in which details and generalizations are arranged according to a *question-answer pattern,* a *problem-solution pattern,* a *general-to-specific pattern,* or a *specific-to-general pattern,* suggesting an internal logic to the flow of sentences and ideas.

logical strategies The arrangement of ideas and evidence in ways that correspond with patterns that most people accept as reasonable and convincing. (*See 11e.*)

→loose, lose Commonly misspelled, these words are pronounced differently. *Loose* (rhyming with *moose*) is an adjective meaning "not tight." *Lose* (rhyming with *snooze*) is a present tense verb meaning "to misplace."

I was afraid that I would **lose** my ring because it was very **loose.**

→lots, lots of, a lot of (*See* **a lot.**)

main clause A word group that contains a subject and a verb and can act as a complete sentence. Also called an *independent clause.* (*See 35c; compare* **phrase.**)

main verb The central verb (word showing action or state of being) in a sentence; it can stand alone or be accompanied by one or more **helping verbs.** (*See 35a-3.*)

major premise (*See* **premise.**)

major revision (*See* **revision.**)

→man, mankind For many readers, these terms represent sexist usage when they refer to all humans. Use *people, humanity,* or some other substitute. (*See 50d.*)

glos

mass noun A kind of noun that refers to material that cannot be counted, or divided into separate units to form a usual plural. (*See 35a-1; see also* **noun; collective noun; count noun.**)

COUNT NOUNS	Chair + *s*, cake + *s*, shadow + *s*, pea + *s*
NONCOUNT NOUNS	Flour, rice, sugar, steel, sunlight, earth, water

→**may, can** (*See* **can, may.**)

→**maybe, may be** *Maybe* means *possibly; may be* is part of a verb structure.

The President **may be** addressing the nation tonight, so **maybe** we should turn on the news.

→**media, medium** Technically, *media* is a plural noun requiring a verb that agrees in number, but many people now use *media* as a singular noun when referring to the press. *Medium* generally refers to a conduit or method of transmission.

The **media** *is* not covering the story accurately.

The telephone was not a good **medium** for reviewing all the budget figures.

metasearch site A site that allows you to conduct a search using several search engines simultaneously. (*See 25b.*)

→**might of, may of** (*See* **could of, would of.**)

→**mighty** Avoid this adjective in formal writing.

INFORMAL	It was a **mighty** proud moment for NASA.
EDITED	It was a **very** proud moment for NASA.

minor premise (*See* **premise.**)

minor revision (*See* **revision.**)

misleading language/misleading evidence A **fallacy** in which a writer deceives a reader through the use of language or information. Using misleading language, the writer shifts the meaning of a term from one sense to another but still gives the erroneous impression of supporting the argument. Using misleading evidence, the writer uses faulty statistics, survey results, and other material slanted in favor of only one side of an argument. (*See 11i.*)

misplaced modifier A modifier incorrectly placed relative to its intended **headword,** giving the impression that it modifies something else. (*See Chapter 43; compare* **dangling modifier** and **disruptive modifier.**)

MISPLACED	In *Walden*, Thoreau describes how he **simply** lived.
EDITED	In *Walden*, Thoreau describes how he lived **simply.**

mixed sentence A sentence with mismatched topics or with a shifted grammatical structure. (*See 45a; see* **faulty predication.**)

MLA documentation style The style of **documentation** suggested by the Modern Language Association and described in its guide. (*See Chapter 30.*)

mnemonic An aid to memorization, for example, of correct spellings.

modal auxiliary verbs (*See* **helping verbs.**)

moderator The person who decides which messages will be posted on an electronic mailing list. (*See 15d.*)

modifier A word or word group, functioning as an adjective or adverb, that qualifies or adds to a noun or verb. (*See Chapter 43.*)

mood The verb form that indicates the speaker's attitude in a sentence. *Indicative mood* characterizes statements intended as truthful or factual. *Imperative mood* characterizes statements that function as commands. *Subjunctive mood* characterizes statements expressing uncertainty. Many **conditional sentences** require the subjunctive mood. (*See 36g.*)

INDICATIVE MOOD	It will rain today.
IMPERATIVE	Beware of lightning!
SUBJUNCTIVE MOOD	Were it to rain, we would not play golf.

→**Ms.** To avoid the sexist labeling of women as married or unmarried (a condition not marked in men's titles), use *Ms.* unless you have reason to use *Miss* or *Mrs.* (for example, when giving the name of a character such as *Mrs. Dalloway*). Use professional titles when appropriate (*Dr., Professor, Senator, Mayor*). (*See Chapter 50d.*)

multiple-word noun A noun consisting of two or more words that are treated as a single unit when marking plurality or possession. (*See 53a-3.*)

The **union leaders'** negotiations fell through.

→**must of, must have** (*See* **could of, would of.**)

narrowing The process of taking a more specific perspective on a chosen topic. (*See 3c-4.*)

neologism A word that has entered into general use very recently, sometimes not yet having been put into any dictionaries. (*See 49b-3.*)

netiquette Commonsense guidelines for online communication. (*See 15a-3.*)

nominalization A verb or an adjective that has been (sometimes inappropriately) turned into a noun: *completion* (noun) from *complete* (verb), *happiness* (noun) from *happy* (adjective). (*See 7a-2, 48a-2.*)

noncoordinate adjectives (*See* **coordinate adjectives.**)

noncount noun (*See* **mass noun.**)

nonrestrictive clause (*See* **restrictive modifier.**)

nonrestrictive modifier (*See* **restrictive modifier.**)

→**nor, or** Use *nor* in negative constructions and *or* in positive ones.

NEGATIVE	Neither rain **nor** snow will slow the team.
POSITIVE	Either rain **or** snow may delay the game.

→**nothing like, nowhere near** These phrases are considered informal when used to compare two things (as in "Gibbon's position is **nowhere near** as justified as Carlyle's"). Avoid them in formal writing.

noun A word that names a person, place, or thing and is often preceded by an **article** (*a, an,* or *the*). (*See 35a-1; see also* **collective noun; count noun; mass noun.**)

noun clause A clause that functions as a noun. (*See 35d.*)

noun string A string of nouns used as modifiers (usually adjectives) of a main noun. Such strings are grammatically correct but may seem overly abstract or technical. (*See 7a-4.*)

The **area computer network downlink access program** failed.

glos

→**nowheres** Use *nowhere* instead.

number A grammatical concept referring to whether a noun or pronoun is singular or plural. Pronouns must agree in number with the nouns they modify, and subjects and verbs must also agree in number. (*See 35a-2, 37a, 38a, 38b.*)

→**number, amount** (*See* **amount, number.**)

object A noun, pronoun, or group of words functioning as a noun to which the action of a verb applies. *Direct objects* receive the action of **transitive verbs;** *indirect objects* are affected indirectly by the action of a transitive verb. (*See 35b-2; see also* **complement.**)

object complement (*See* **complement.**)

object of a preposition The noun or pronoun that follows a preposition. (*See 35c-1.*)

object pronoun A pronoun that is the **object** of a verb. (*See 35c-1.*)

objective case (*See* **case.**)

objective description Description that emphasizes physical details and avoids attention to their emotional impact. (*Compare* **subjective description.**)

objective summary (*See* **summary.**)

observation A kind of ethnographic research involving firsthand research (*onsite visiting and note taking*) of people, events, or settings. (*See 26e.*)

→**of, have** (*See* **could of, would of.**)

→**off of** Use simply *off* instead.

→**OK** When you write formally, use *OK* only in dialogue. If you mean "good" or "acceptable," use one of those terms.

→**on account of** Avoid this expression in formal writing. Use *because* instead.

online database File of information available through the Internet or Web, or, occasionally, on CD-ROM. (*See Chapter 24.*)

online (electronic) periodicals Periodicals available through the Internet, with past issues or selected articles sometimes available in archives. (*See 25c-4.*)

outline A list, usually hierarchical, showing the main contents of a paper. (*See 2c-5.*) A *working outline* shows the general sequence of information in a paper and the relationships among the segments of information.

→**outside of, inside of** (*See* **inside of, outside of.**)

overblown language **Diction** that is too formal or technical for the writer's purpose and audience, often used out of a misguided attempt to impress the reader. (*See 48b-2.*)

overgeneralization (*See* **begging the question.**)

paragraph A unit of prose marked by an indent at the left margin and consisting of a topic and its **development.** (*See Chapter 6.*)

paragraph development The examples, facts, concrete details, explanatory statements, or supporting arguments that make a paragraph informative and give it a sense of structure. (*See Chapter 6.*)

parallelism The expression of similar or related ideas in similar grammatical form. (*See Chapter 46.*) In paragraphs, parallelism refers to a technique in which grammatical structures are repeated in order to highlight similar or related ideas. (*See 6d.*)

paraphrase A rewriting of an original sentence or passage in your own words, preserving the essence and level of detail of the original. (*See 22l, 54a-2.*)

partial sentence An effective sentence fragment used for emphasis. (*See 40c.*)

participle The form a verb takes when it is linked to a helping verb. Verbs can take either the *present participle* or the *past participle*. (*See 35b-4, 36b.*)

particle   (*See* **phrasal verb.**)

passive voice   The form of a verb in a sentence in which the doer takes the position of the direct object. (*See 7c-3, 36e, 44c, 48a-2; compare* **active voice.**)

subject   verb
The ball was caught by the outfielder.

past participle   (*See* **participle.**)

past perfect tense   (*See* **perfect tense.**)

past progressive tense   (*See* **progressive tense.**)

past tense   (*See* **tense.**)

peer group   A group of fellow writers, usually in a classroom, who participate in collaborative writing activities. (*See 3g-2.*)

→per   Use *per* only to mean "by the," as in *per hour* or *per day.* Avoid using it to mean "according to," as in "per your instructions."

→percent, percentage   Use *percent* only with numerical data. Use *percentage* to imply a statistical part of something.

Ten **percent** of the sample returned the questionnaire.

A large **percentage** of the revenue from the parking meters was stolen.

perfect tense   A tense used to indicate that something happens before something else happens. Three perfect tenses can be marked in verb phrases: present perfect, past perfect, and future perfect. (*See 36c.*)

PRESENT PERFECT   **I have reported** the fire already.

PAST PERFECT   The fires **had burned** for an hour before the brigade arrived.

FUTURE PERFECT   Nancy **will have finished** by the time the dentist is ready.

periodic sentence   A sentence structured so that subsidiary phrases, clauses, or other elements are piled up at the beginning, delaying the sentence's main clause. (*See 7c-2.*)

Because she knows that inspired designs often spring from hard work, because she loves perfection yet fears failure, and because she believes that risk-taking ought to be accompanied by attention to detail, Janelle is working up to eighteen hours a day on the clothing for her fall collection.

periodical   A recurring publication that contains articles by various authors. Periodicals include magazines, scholarly journals, and newspapers. (*See 23b-2.*)

person   The form that a noun or a pronoun takes to identify the subject of a sentence. *First person* is someone speaking (*I, we*); *second person* is someone spoken to (*you*); *third person* is someone being spoken about (*he, she, it, they*). Verbs must agree in person with their subjects. (*See 35a-3, 38b, 44a.*)

persona   The way a writer chooses to characterize himself or herself through the choice of words and phrases, voice, and other devices. (*See 15a-2.*)

personal pronoun   A pronoun that designates persons or things. (*See 37b-2.*)

SINGULAR   I, me, you, he, him, she, her, it

PLURAL   we, us, you, they, them

phrasal verb   A verb plus a closely associated word (**particle**) that looks like a preposition (*run down, burn up, call up, clear out*). Unlike prepositions, particles can be moved from a position after the verb to a position after a direct object. (*See 35a-3.*)

glos

BEFORE OBJECT	Mr. Sims **burned up** all the wood.
AFTER OBJECT	Mr. Sims **burned** all the wood **up.**

phrase A word group lacking one or more elements (such as a subject or a predicate) that would make it a complete sentence. (*See 35c*; *compare* **main clause.**)

plagiarism The unethical practice of claiming that another writer's words or text are your own, or citing another person's words or text without credit, thereby giving the illusion that that person's words are your own. (*See 15b, Chapter 27.*)

plot The chain of events in a work of fiction. (*See 18b.*)

→**plus** Avoid using *plus* as a conjunction joining two independent clauses.

INFORMAL	The school saved money through its "lights off" campaign, **plus** it generated income by recycling aluminum cans.
EDITED	The school saved money through its "lights off" campaign and also generated income by recycling aluminum cans.

Use *plus* only to mean "in addition to."

The wearisome campaign, **plus** the media pressures, exhausted her.

→**p.m., a.m.** (*See* **a.m., p.m.**)

point-by-point organization A strategy for arranging paragraphs that make use of **comparing and contrasting.** Comparable features of two different or opposed subjects are described one by one. (*See 6e-2*; *compare* **subject-by-subject organization.**)

point of view The perspective from which something (particularly a work of fiction) is told. (*See 18b*; *see also* **person** and **persona.**)

policy In argumentative writing, a position that a particular course of action is one that should be undertaken or avoided. (*See 10c.*)

position paper A short, often documented paper that defines an issue, considers an audience, and draws on evidence and logical strategies to make its point.

positive form One of three forms taken by an adjective or adverb to indicate whether the noun or verb modified is being compared to something else. The positive form is used when no comparison is indicated. (*See 39c*; *compare* **comparative form** and **superlative form.**)

ADJECTIVE	She is an **imaginative** designer.
ADVERB	Peggy designs **imaginatively.**

possessive case (*See* **case.**)

possessive noun A noun that expresses ownership. Possession is usually marked with an apostrophe to distinguish the form from a plural. (*See 53a.*)

The bird's call is becoming fainter.

possessive pronoun A pronoun that shows ownership. (*See 35a-2.*)

SINGULAR	my, mine, your, yours, her, hers, his, its
PLURAL	our, ours, your, yours, their, theirs

post hoc **fallacy** (*See* **faulty cause-effect relationship.**)

→**precede, proceed** *Precede* means "come before"; *proceed* means "go ahead."

The Mickey Mouse float **preceded** the mayor's car. The parade **proceeded** down Fifth Avenue.

predicate In a sentence, the word or words indicating an action, a relationship, consequence, or condition. A predicate typically takes the form of a **verb phrase** and is preceded by the subject of the sentence. A *simple predicate* consists only of a verb or verb phrase; a *complete predicate* consists of a verb or verb phrase plus any modifiers and other words that receive action or complete the verb. (*See 35b-2.*)

prefix An affix, such as *un-* in *unforgiving*, placed before a word. (*See 62b-3.*)

premise A claim or assertion that serves as the foundation of an argument. **Syllogistic reasoning** includes both *major* and *minor premises*—assertions or claims on which conclusions can be based. (*See 11e.*)

preposition A word that indicates a location, direction, or time (for example, *to, from, with, under, in, over*). (*See 35a-6; see also* **object of a preposition.**)

prepositional phrase A phrase, created from a preposition plus a noun phrase, that can add information to a sentence. (*See 35a-6.*)

A faint smell **of grilled onions** came **through the window.**

prereading strategies A set of reading strategies in which the reader previews, skims, and samples a reading before working through it more formally. (*See 9e-1.*)

present participle (*See* **participle.**)

present perfect tense (*See* **perfect tense.**)

present progressive tense (*See* **progressive tense.**)

present tense (*See* **tense.**)

→**pretty** Avoid using *pretty* (as in *pretty good, pretty hungry, pretty sad*) to mean "somewhat" or "rather." Use *pretty* in the sense of "attractive."

prewriting strategies A set of writing strategies used to explore ideas and information in order to generate material for a formal paper. (*See Chapter 2; see also* **brainstorming; invention.**)

primary sources (*See* **research.**)

→**principal, principle** Principal is a noun meaning "an authority" or "head of a school" or an adjective meaning "leading" ("a *principal* objection to the testimony"). *Principle* is a noun meaning "belief or conviction."

printed indexes Books listing articles that appear in magazines, newspapers, or scholarly journals. Indexes help researchers locate useful sources. (*See 23b; see also* **electronic indexes.**)

problem-solution sequence A piece of writing in which a problem is presented followed by a proposal for one or more solutions, perhaps with their advantages and disadvantages. (*See 2c-4.*)

→**proceed, precede** (*See* **precede, proceed.**)

progressive tense A tense used to show an ongoing action in progress at some point in time. Verb forms can show three types of progressive tense: *present progressive, past progressive,* and *future progressive.* (*See 36c.*)

PRESENT PROGRESSIVE	The carousel **is turning** too quickly.
PAST PROGRESSIVE	The horses **were bobbing** up and down.
FUTURE PROGRESSIVE	The children **will be laughing.**

glos

pronoun A word that takes the place of a noun, such as *them, his, she,* and *it.* Pronouns are often used to avoid repeating the nouns used in the sentence. (*See 35a-2, 38c.*)

Jim changed **his shirt** after spilling gravy on **it**.

pronoun-antecedent agreement (*See* **agreement.**)

pronoun reference The connection between a pronoun (*its, him, them,* etc.) and its antecedent, or the noun or person to which it refers. (*See Chapter 42.*)

proofreading The process of reading a draft in order to identify and correct distracting and usually minor errors in spelling, punctuation, incorrect hyphenation, and word division. (*See 5h; compare* **editing.**)

proper adjective An adjective derived from a proper noun, used to modify a noun: *Brazilian music, Dickensian portrait.* (*See 57b-1.*)

proper noun A noun that refers to specific people, places, titles, or things and is capitalized: *Miss America, New Orleans, Xerox Corporation.* (*See 35a-1, 57b-1.*)

proposition A **thesis statement** offering an opinion or conclusion that the writer wishes readers to accept or agree with. A proposition is supported or made convincing by an **argument.**

purpose The writer's rhetorical goals or aim. (*See Chapter 3, 10a, 49a.*)

purpose structure A series of statements briefly describing the function of each paragraph or section of a paper. (*See 3b.*)

quantifier A word like *each, one,* or *many* that indicates the quantity of a subject. (*See 38b.*)

question-answer pattern (*See* **logical order.**)

→**quote, quotation** Formally, *quote* is a verb and *quotation* is a noun. *Quote* is sometimes used as a short version of the noun *quotation,* but this may bother some readers. Use *quotation* instead.

→**raise, rise** Raise is a transitive verb meaning "to lift up." *Rise* is an intransitive verb (it takes no object) meaning "to get up or move up."

He **raised** his head from the newspaper and watched the fog **rise** from the lake.

→**rarely ever** Use *rarely* alone, not paired with *ever.*

reader The intended or imagined **audience** for a piece of writing. (*See Chapter 3.*)

→**real, really** Use *real* as an adjective modifying a noun; use *really* as an adverb.

Emmons drove **really** well in the race because she was in a **real** stock car.

real time Electronic discussions that take place without delay. (*See 15d-3.*)

→**reason is because, reason is that** Avoid these phrases in formal writing; they are wordy and awkward.

reciprocal pronoun A pronoun (*one another, each other*) that enables a writer to refer to individual parts of a plural antecedent. (*See 35a-2.*)

The two kinds of birds compete for territory by destroying **each other's** nests.

→**reckon, calculate, figure** (see **calculate, figure, reckon.**)

red herring A **fallacy** in which some fact or information distracts a reader from the real argument. (*See 11i.*)

redrafting Part of the revision process that involves writing unworkable material over again. (*See* **revision.**)

redundancy The use of unnecessary or repeated words and phrases that can be reduced through **editing.** (*See Chapters 5, 48.*) *Redundant pairs* are two words used when only one is needed: *aid and abet, one and only, part and parcel, kith* *and kin. Redundant phrases* say the same thing twice: *each individual, fresh news, free gifts.* (*See 48a.*)

redundant pair (*See* **redundancy.**)

redundant phrase (*See* **redundancy.**)

reference chain A chain of pronouns whose antecedent is stated in the opening sentence of a passage. Reference chains can help to guide readers through a passage and remind them of the controlling topic. (*See 42a-3.*)

reference list List of sources found at the end of a document. (*See Chapter 31.*)

reflexive pronoun A pronoun that enables a subject or doer of an action also to be the receiver of the action. (*See 35a-2.*)

> **He** paid **himself** for the work.

→**regarding, in regard, with regard to** (*See* **in regard to.**)

→**regardless, irregardless** (*See* **irregardless.**)

register In communication, the form language takes in a particular context, showing variations in pronunciation, grammar, or word choice. (*See 50b.*)

relative clause An adjective-like clause that modifies a noun or pronoun and begins with a **relative pronoun.** (*See 35a-2, 37d.*)

> I reminisced about all the shellfish **that I had bought in Seattle.**

relative pronoun A pronoun (*who, whom, whose, which, that*) introducing a subordinate clause that modifies or adds information to a main clause. (*See 35a-2, 35d, 37d, 47c.*)

remote reference Placing a **pronoun** at a distance from its **antecedent.** (*See 42a-2.*)

research The process of investigating a topic, either through *primary sources* such as interviews or observations or through *secondary sources* such as other writers' books and articles on the same topic. *Library research* is conducted primarily using the print and electronic materials in libraries; *field research* is conducted in settings where the subject of the research can be found in primary form. (*See Chapter 22.*)

research file A detailed set of records for a research project. (*See 22a.*)

research plan An anticipated sequence of activities that guides the work of a research paper. (*See 22f.*)

research question A specific question that drives a research project, giving it focus and purpose. (*See 22g–h.*)

→**respectfully, respectively** *Respectfully* means "with respect"; *respectively* implies a certain order for events or things.

> The senior class **respectfully** submitted the planning document. The administration considered items 3, 6, and 10, **respectively.**

restrictive clause (*See* **restrictive modifier.**)

restrictive modifier A midsentence clause that presents information essential to the meaning of a passage. In contrast, a *nonrestrictive modifier* adds information that is not essential to the sentence's meaning. (*See 47c, 51c.*)

> RESTRICTIVE MODIFIER   The charts **drawn by hand** were hard to read.
>
> NONRESTRICTIVE MODIFIER The charts, **drawn by hand,** were hard to read.

resumptive modifier A modifying clause or phrase used to extend a sentence that appears to have ended, adding new information or twists of thought. (*See 7d-4.*)

glos

People who are careful about what they eat may lead healthier lives, **healthier, though not necessarily longer.**

review A critical appraisal of an event, object, or phenomenon, such as a show, a concert, or a book. Most reviews are both descriptive and evaluative. (*See 17j.*)

revision The process of improving rough or preliminary versions of a document by making large-scale changes, additions, or deletions in the material. *Major revision* involves redrafting, reorganizing, adding, or deleting significant material; *minor revision* involves changes within paragraphs, often at the sentence level. (*See Chapter 5; see also* **editing** and **proofreading.**)

rhetorical purpose (*See* **purpose.**)

rhetorical question A question asked not in expectation of an answer but for the purpose of providing the answer. (*See 7d-2.*)

→**rise, raise** (*See* **raise, rise.**)

Rogerian argument A strategy for argument that calls for acknowledging the reasonableness of the opposing point(s) of view rather than strong opposition to alternative perspectives. (*See 11h.*)

rough draft A preliminary version of a paper. (*See Chapter 4.*)

run-in list A list whose items aren't placed on separate lines. Such lists can present items in full or partial sentences. (*See 57a-4; compare* **vertical list.**)

run-on sentence (*See* **fused sentence.**)

→**says, goes** (*See* **goes, says.**)

scholarly journals Journals that appear approximately four times a year; the page numbering may or may not run continuously throughout the separate issues making up an annual volume. (*See 23b-2.*)

screen name A self-identifier the email user chooses. (*See 15c-1.*)

search engines Software dedicated to indexing and sorting Web pages for user convenience. (*See 13f, 25b.*)

search strategy A strategy for research papers in which you identify the type of research you are conducting, the sources you might consult, and the tasks you need to perform. (*See 22g.*)

second person (*See* **person.**)

secondary sources (*See* **research.**)

sentence A group of words containing a complete subject and a predicate. (*See also* **compound sentence; compound-complex sentence; declarative sentence; exclamatory sentence; imperative sentence; interrogative sentence; simple sentence.**)

sentence adverb An adverb used to modify an entire sentence. (*See 35a-5.*)

sentence cluster A group of sentences that develop related ideas or information, often arranged using **parallelism.** (*See 46c.*)

sentence fragment A part of a sentence incorrectly treated as a complete sentence with a capital letter at the beginning and a period at the end. (*See Chapter 40.*)

FRAGMENT   They got the pump started again. **By replacing the filter.**

EDITED   They got the pump started again by replacing the filter.

sequential order One way to organize information in a pattern within a particular perspective or focus, such as spatially or chronologically. (*See 6e-2.*)

→**set, sit** *Set* means "to place"; *sit* means "to place oneself."

The researcher **set** the sample near the centrifuge and then **sat** down on the stool.

setting The physical and temporal context of a work of fiction. (*See 18b.*)

sexist language Language that implies or reinforces unfair, misleading, or discriminatory stereotypes on the basis of gender. (*See Chapter 50.*)

shift An incorrect or inappropriate switch in **person, number, mood, tense,** or **topic.** (*See Chapter 44, 45a-4.*)

→**should of** (*See* **could of, would of.**)

simple predicate (*See* **predicate.**)

simple sentence A sentence with one main (independent) clause and no subordinate (dependent) clauses. (*See 35d-1; compare* **complex sentence; compound sentence; compound-complex sentence.**)

simple subject (*See* **subject.**)

→**since, because** (*See* **because, since.**)

→**sit, set** (*See* **set, sit.**)

→**site, cite** (*See* **cite, site.**)

slang New words not yet, possibly never to be, shared by the general population, but used by a limited social group. (*See 50b.*)

slanted statistics (*See* **misleading language/misleading evidence.**)

→**so** Some readers object to the use of *so* in place of *very.*

INFORMAL	The filmmaker is **so** thoughtful about casting.
EDITED	The filmmaker is **very** thoughtful about casting.

→**somebody, some body** (*See* **anybody, any body.**)

→**someone, some one** (*See* **anybody, any body.**)

→**sometime, some time, sometimes** *Sometime* refers to an indistinct time in the future; *sometimes* means "every once in a while." *Some time* is an adjective (*some*) modifying a noun (*time*).

The probe will reach the nebula **sometime** in the next decade. **Sometimes** such probes fail to send back any data. It takes **some time** before images will come back to us from Neptune.

→**sort, kind** (*See* **kind, sort, type.**)

spatial order In paragraph development, a pattern for arranging descriptive sentences based on the spatial or visual arrangement of a scene, work of art, person, mechanism, or phenomenon (left to right, top to bottom, and so on).

specialized sources Focused, often complex or technical resources for research that provide detailed information on narrow topics and often include the latest scholarly findings. (*See 23b-2.*)

→**specially, especially** (*See* **especially, specially.**)

specific pattern of development A preferred way of developing paragraphs reflecting reader and writer coming from a specific community; compare with **general pattern of development.** (*See 6e-2.*)

specific pronoun reference Using pronouns to clearly specify the relationships between statements. (*See 42b.*)

specific reference A reference that documents the exact location of a word, idea, or fact in a source (for example, on a specific page or in a chart or drawing). (*See 27f; compare* **general reference** and **informational reference.**)

specific-to-general pattern (*See* **logical order.**)

speculative writing Writing that explores a topic without taking a position on it.

split infinitive An **infinitive** in which a word separates *to* from the verb. Some readers object to split infinitives. (*See 43c-3.*)

SPLIT INFINITIVE	The office designer tried **to** respectively **address** each of the workers' concerns.
EDITED	The office designer tried **to address** each of the workers' concerns respectively.

squinting modifier A modifier that incorrectly appears to modify both the word or phrase that comes before it and the one that comes after it. (*See 43a-3.*)

SQUINTING	Those who smoke **seldom** seem concerned about the potential health hazards.
EDITED	Those who **seldom** smoke seem concerned about the potential health hazards.

state-of-being verb (*See* **linking verb.**)

→**stationary, stationery** *Stationary* means "standing still"; *stationery* refers to writing paper.

structure The arrangement of ideas, sections, or paragraphs in a paper or other text. (*See 3g-1; see also* **outline** and **purpose structure.**)

structured observation Carefully planned and focused observation of events, people, or situations intended to produce research data from which conclusions can be drawn. (*See Chapter 26.*)

style The distinctive choice of words (**diction**), sentence structures, and **persona** in a piece of writing. (*See 3g-1.*)

subject In a sentence, the doer or the thing talked about—typically the first noun phrase followed by a verb phrase. A *simple subject* consists of one or more nouns (or pronouns) naming the doer or the topic. A *complete subject* consists of the simple subject plus all its modifying words or phrases. (*See 35b-1.*)

subject-by-subject organization A strategy for arranging paragraphs that make use of **comparing and contrasting.** The writer considers one subject in its entirety and then the other, instead of presenting one point for both and then the next point. (*See 6e; compare* **point-by-point organization.**)

subject complement (*See* **complement.**)

subject pronoun A pronoun that is the subject of a clause. (*See 35d.*)

subjective case (*See* **case.**)

subjective description Description that emphasizes the emotional impact of events or phenomena. (*See 6e; compare* **objective description.**)

subject-verb agreement The verb agrees with the subject in grammatical form. (*See 38a, 38b.*)

subjunctive mood (*See* **mood.**)

subordinate clause A word group that contains both a subject and a predicate but cannot stand on its own as a sentence because it begins with a subordinating word such as *because, since, although, which,* or *that.* Also called a *dependent clause.* (*See 35c-5, 35d, 47c.*)

subordinating conjunction (*See* **conjunction.**)

subordination A sentence structure in which one clause modifies another, helping readers perceive the links between ideas and understand the relative importance of information. The **main clause** is accompanied by a **subordinate clause** that modifies, qualifies, or comments on the ideas or the information in the main clause. (*See 47c; compare* **coordination.**)

→**such** Some academic readers will expect you to avoid using *such* without *that.*

Anne Frank had **such** a difficult time growing up **that** her diary writing became her only solace.

suffix An affix added to the end of a word in order to form a derived word (*bold* + *ness*) or to provide a grammatical inflection (*talk* + *ing*). (*See 62b.*)

summarize (*See* **summary.**)

summary A précis in your own words of an original passage, preserving the essence of the original but boiling it down to its essential points. An *objective summary* focuses on the content of the original passage, without any authorial judgment or commentary. An *evaluative summary* contains the author's opinions and comments on the passage. (*See 22l, 27e-2, 54a-2.*)

summary paragraph A transitional or concluding paragraph used to mark the end of a discussion or to help readers remember main points.

summative modifier A modifying phrase or clause that summarizes the preceding part of a sentence and then takes the sentence on a new course. (*See 7d-4.*)

To protect your vegetables against harmful insects, you can use soap sprays, scatter insect-repelling plants among the beds, or introduce "friendly" insects like ladybugs and praying mantises—**three techniques** that will not leave a harmful chemical residue on the food you grow.

superlative form One of the three forms taken by adjectives and adverbs to indicate whether the noun or verb modified is being compared to something else. The superlative form adds *-est* or *-most* to the adjective or adverb and indicates a comparison of three or more objects or actions. (*See 39c; compare* **comparative form** and **positive form.**)

ADJECTIVE   This is the **cleanest** oven I've seen.
             She is the **most imaginative** designer of the three.

ADVERB   You can travel **fastest** in Manhattan if you ride a bicycle.
             Peggy designs **most imaginatively** of the three.

supporting conclusions The links in the chain of reasoning. (*See 9b-1.*)

supporting evidence Material that supports a central claim or **thesis,** including examples from personal experience, examples from other people's experience, quotations and ideas from recognized authorities, technical information and statistics, data from surveys and interviews, background and historical information, and comparisons to similar situations and problems. (*See 11a, 11b.*)

supporting idea Material that supports an assertion or **thesis.** (*See 3c; see also* **supporting evidence.**)

→**sure, surely** In formal writing, use *sure* to mean "certain." *Surely* is an adverb; don't use *sure* in its place.

He is **sure** to pass the exam.
He has **surely** studied hard for the exam.

→**sure and, try and** *And* is sometimes used in place of *to* with *sure* and *try.* Write *sure to* and *try to* instead.

INCORRECT   We will be *sure and* bring our rackets.

CORRECT   Bob will *try to* win the match.

glos

syllabification The correct division of words into their syllables. (*See 49c.*)

syllogism (*See* **syllogistic reasoning.**)

syllogistic reasoning A kind of logical reasoning that includes a *major premise*, a *minor premise*, and a *conclusion*. (*See 11d; see* **premise.**)

MAJOR PREMISE	All landowners in Clarksville must pay taxes.
MINOR PREMISE	Fred Hammil owns land in Clarksville.
CONCLUSION	Therefore, Fred Hammil must pay taxes.

synonym A word that is identical or nearly identical in meaning to another word: *ill* and *sick*, *large* and *big*. (*See 49c-2; see* **thesaurus.**)

synthesis The combining or distilling of separate elements into a single, unified entity. Synthesizing source material for a research paper involves combining concepts and details from a variety of sources to form a unified discussion of a topic. (*See 27e.*)

→**take, bring** (*See* **bring, take.**)

tautology (*See* **circular reasoning.**)

tense The form a verb takes to indicate time—whether the verb's action occurred in the past (*past tense*) or the present (*present tense*). The present tense form is also called the **base form** of the verb. *Future tense* is marked with the use of **helping verbs.** (*See 35a, 36a, 36b, 44b.*)

PAST	Her grandmother **made** possum stew.
PRESENT	Her friends **stop** to pick up "road kill."
FUTURE	Her children **will find** these old customs offensive.

tense sequence The pattern of tenses in a piece of writing. Incorrect tense shifts can confuse or annoy a reader. (*See 36f.*)

text analysis A paper that provides a close, analytical reading of a particular text, often a work of literature. (*See 18d.*)

→**than, then** *Than* is a word used to compare something; *then* implies a sequence of events or a causal relationship.

Last year, Sallie liked history more **than** math; **then,** this year, she changed her mind.

→**that, which** Use *that* in a clause that is essential to the meaning of a sentence (**restrictive modifier**); use *which* with a clause that does not provide essential information (*nonrestrictive modifier*).

THAT	He has the report **that** will vindicate Clareson.
WHICH	He has a penchant for emotionalism, **which** may help him win the jury's favor.

→**theirself, theirselves, themself** All these forms are incorrect; use *themselves* to refer to more than one person, *himself* or *herself* to refer to one person.

→**them** Avoid using *them* as a subject or to modify a subject, as in "*Them* are delicious" or "*Them* apples are very crisp."

theme In literary works, an idea, perspective, or cluster of feelings and insights conveyed to a reader through various fictional devices. (*See 18b.*)

→**then, than** (See **than, then.**)

glos

→**there, their, they're** These forms are often confused in spelling because they all sound alike. *There* indicates location; *their* is a possessive pronoun; *they're* is a contraction of *they* and *are.*

THERE	Look **over there.**
THEIR	**Their** car ran out of gas.
THEY'RE	**They're** not eager to hike to the nearest gas station.

thesaurus A dictionary of **synonyms** and **antonyms**—words similar or opposite in meaning to each other. (*See 49c-2.*)

thesis or thesis statement A sentence, often at the conclusion of an essay's first paragraph, that establishes the point, main argument, or direction of a paper, giving the reader a sense of purpose and an understanding of the essay's contents. (*See 3c, 10c, 22e.*)

third person (*See* **person.**)

→**till, until, 'til** Some readers will find *'til* and *till* too informal; use *until.*

time sequence A planning strategy, particularly for papers involving chronological or temporal structures, in which events are labeled along a timeline. (*See 2c-3.*)

→**to, as** (*See* **as, to.**)

→**to, too, two** *To* is a preposition indicating location. *Too* means "also." *Two* is a number.

> The Birdsalls went **to** their lake cabin. They invited the Corbetts **too.**
> That made **two** trips so far this season.

topic The focus or subject of a piece of writing. (*See 3c-1, 22a–b.*)

topic sentence A sentence, usually located at the beginning of a paragraph, that announces its main idea or perspective. (*See 6b.*)

topic shift (*See* **faulty predication, shift.**)

→**toward, towards** Prefer *toward* in formal writing. (You may see *towards* used in England and Canada.)

transition (*See* **transitional expression.**)

transitional expression Words or phrases (*in addition to, on the other hand, therefore, without a doubt*) that link one idea, sentence, or paragraph to the next, helping readers to see relationships among ideas by connecting them logically. (*See 6d-2, 51b, 52a-2.*)

transitive verb A verb followed by an **object** or **complement.** (*See 35b-2; compare* **intransitive verb.**)

> transitive verb   object
> The President **called** the British Prime Minister.

→**try and, try to, sure and** (*See* **sure and, try and.**)

→**ultimately, eventually** (*See* **eventually, ultimately.**)

uncountable noun (*See* **noncount noun.**)

unified paragraph (*See* **paragraph.**)

→**uninterested, disinterested** (*See* **disinterested, uninterested.**)

→**unique** Use *unique* alone; don't write *most unique* or *more unique* because the word indicates an absolute condition.

→**until, till** (*See* **till, until, 'til.**)

URL Standing for Universal Resource Locator, a standardized notation specifying the address or location of files on the Internet. (*See 25b.*)

glos

→**use to, used to** Like *supposed to*, this phrase may be mistakenly written as *use to* because the *-d* is not always clearly pronounced. Write *used to.*

usenet newsgroups Electronic bulletin boards tending to attract diverse membership from many geographic regions and professions. (*See 25c-6.*)

vague generalization A sentence or passage that offers so little specific information that it is not meaningful. (*See 48b.*)

vague pronoun reference Using pronouns that refer to antecedents that are implied rather than stated, or pronouns that are not connected explicitly to a specific antecedent. (*See 42b.*)

value judgment An argument that an activity, belief, or arrangement is desirable or undesirable. (See *10c.*)

verb The word in a sentence that indicates the action that has occurred, is occurring, or will occur. (*See 35a-3.*)

verb phrase A phrase that consists of a main verb plus a helping verb. (*See 35a-3, 36b.*)

verbal phrase A verbal plus its modifiers, object, or complements. (*See 35c-4.*)

verbals Verbs or parts of verb phrases that are used to function as nouns, adjectives, or adverbs. The three kinds of verbals are **infinitives, participles,** and **gerunds.** (*See 35a-3, 35c-4.*)

vertical list A list whose items are placed on separate lines. (*See 57a-4; compare* **run-in list.**)

visuals Drawings, photos, graphs, and other visuals. (*See Chapters 12 and 13, 27e-4.*)

voice (*See* **active voice, passive voice.**)

→**wait for, wait on** Use *wait on* only to refer to a clerk's or server's job; use *wait for* to mean "to await someone's arrival."

Julie **waited on** the customers while she **waited for** Melissa to arrive.

warrant (*See* **data-warrant-claim reasoning.**)

Web sites Provide text and graphics with numerous links to related sites. (*See 25c.*)

→**well, good** (*See* **good, well.**)

→**went, gone** (*See* **gone, went.**)

→**were, we're** *Were* is the past plural form of the verb *was*; *we're* is a contraction of *we* and *are.*

We're going to the ruins where the fiercest battles **were.**

→**where . . . at** (*See* **at.**)

→**whether, if** (*See* **if, whether.**)

→**which, that** (*See* **that, which.**)

white space In document design, the amount or use of blank (white) space around text or visuals. (*See 13c-2.*)

→**who, whom** Although the distinction between these words is slowly disappearing from the language, many readers will expect you to use *whom* in the objective case. When in doubt, err on the side of formality. (Sometimes editing can eliminate the need to choose.) (*See 37d.*)

→**who's, whose** *Who's* is the contracted form of *who is. Whose* indicates possession.

The man **who's** going to Frankfurt tried to find the man **whose** bag he mistakenly took at the airport.

glos

→wise, -ize (*See* **-ize, -wise.**)

wordiness Use of too many words. (*See Chapter 48.*)

working bibliography An in-progress bibliography or list of references kept during the **research** process.

working outline (*See* **outline.**)

working thesis (*See* **thesis.**)

works cited List of the works to which the writer makes reference in the body of a research paper, either through in-text (parenthetical) citations or through footnotes or endnotes. (*See 30b.*)

→would of, could of (*See* **could of, would of.**)

writer's commentary A writer's direct address of the reader or reference to himself or herself in prose that is not intended to convey personal feelings. (*See 48b-3.*)

→yet, however, but (*See* **but however, but yet.**)

→your, you're *Your* is a possessive pronoun; *you're* is a contraction of *you are.*

If **you're** going to take physics, you'd better know **your** math.

glos

Credits

Text

4CONTROL Media Web site. Copyright 1995–2001, 4CONTROL Media, Inc., Jersey City, NJ. Reprinted by permission.

Abbey, Edward. *Down the River.* (New York: Dutton, 1982).

Abbey, Edward. *The Journey Home.* (New York: Plume, 1991).

American Psychological Association (APA) Home Page (www.apa.org). Copyright © 2009 by the American Psychological Association. Reproduced with permission.

Animal Project Web site. Opening Webpage for Rutgers University School of Law Animal Rights Project. Copyright © 1996–2004. Reprinted by permission of Gary L. Francione and Anna E. Charlton.

Baldwin, Hanson W. From "R. M. S. Titanic." *Harper's Magazine,* 1933.

Bickner, Robert, and Peyasantiwong, Patcharin. "Cultural Variation in Reflective Writing"; and Kachru, Yamuna. "Writers in Hini and English" from *Writing Across Languages and Cultures,* Alan C. Purves, Ed. (Newbury Park: Sage, 1988), pp. 160–174, 109–137.

Blackwell Publishing. Screen shot of search results in html format from Blackwell Synergy online database for article "A Queen for Whose Time? Elizabeth I as Icon for the Twentieth Century" by David Grant, *Journal of Popular Culture,* 39 (2006). Reprinted by permission of Blackwell Publishing.

Blackwell Publishing. Screen shot of search results in pdf format from Blackwell Synergy online database for article "A Queen for Whose Time? Elizabeth I as Icon for the Twentieth Century" by David Grant, *Journal of Popular Culture,* 39 (2006). Reprinted by permission of Blackwell Publishing.

Boyle, Jennifer Finney. From "The Bean Curd Method."

Braun, Cary. "Whenever we went to my grandfather's house . . ." Reprinted by permission of the author.

Brilliant, Sara. "Breakfast cereals can differ . . ." Reprinted by permission of the author.

Bronowsk, Jacob. *The Ascent of Man.* (Boston: Little, Brown, 1973).

Buffet, Jimmy. *Where Is Joe Merchant.* (New York: Harcourt Brace, Jovanovich, 1992).

CBS News, Screen shot from Web site from 11/20/06. www.CBSNews.com. Copyright © 2006 CBS Interactive, Inc. Reprinted by permission of the CBS News Archives.

Consequences. Figure 1. From "Population Reference Bureau estimates and UN (medium series) long range projections of 1992" as appeared in *Global and US National Population Trends,* Vol. 1, No. 2 (1995). www.grico.org/CONSEQUENCES/summer95/fig1.html.

Coontz, Stephanie. "The Way We Weren't." *National Forum: Phi Beta Kappa Phi Journal,* Vol. 75, No. 3 (Summer 1995). Copyright © by Stephanie Coontz. Reprinted by permission of the publisher.

Database Health Reference Center-Academic. Sample of Abstracts. Courtesy of Providence Public Library.

Davis, Mike. "House of Cards." *Sierra* © 1995.

Dawes, Robyn M. from "Why Believe That for Which There Is No Good Evidence," (Fall 1992) from the False Memory Syndrome Web site, www.fmsfonline.org.

DiGregorio, Jessica. Paper in Process (Planning, Drafting, Revising). Reprinted by permission of the author.

EBSCO Publishing. Screen shot for search terms "hydrogenated oils and food" from EBSCOHost *Academic Search Premier* online database. Reprinted by permission of EBSCO Publishing.

EBSCO Publishing. Screen shot for search result "Treatment Approaches for Sleep Difficulties in College Students" from EBSCOHost *Academic Search Premier* online database. Reprinted by permission of EBSCO Publishing.

EBSCO Publishing. Screen shot for search result "Zero in on Hidden Fats" from EBSCOHost *Academic Search Premier* online database. Reprinted by permission of EBSCO Publishing.

Edmondson, Brad. From "Making Yourself at Home."

Elkind, David. "The Family in the Postmodern World." *National Forum: Phi Beta Kappa Phi Journal,* Vol. 75, No. 3 (Summer 1995). Copyright © by David Elkind. Reprinted by permission of the publisher.

Exxon Valdez Oil Spill Trustee Council Web site, excerpts. www.oilspill.state.ak.us/resoration/index.html. Used by permission.

Fine, Doug. Reprint of image of page 66, excerpt from *Farewell, My Subaru*. Villard (Random House), 2008.

Fussell, Paul. *Uniforms: Why We Are What We Wear.* (New York: Houghton Mifflin-Marnier Books, 2003).

Garrett, Laurie. *The Coming Plague.* (New York: Penguin, 1994), p. 199.

Geertz, Clifford. *The Interpretation of Cultures.* (New York: Basic Books, 1973).

GlobalReach. From the GlobalReach Web site (http://global-reach.biz) Reprinted by permission of Global Reach.

Goddio, Frank. "San Diego: An Account of Adventure, Deceit, and Intrigue." *National Geographic*, 1994.

Goleman, Daniel. From "Too Little, Too Late," *American Health*, 1992.

Google Logo and search code. Copyright © 2000 Google. The Google search code and Google Logo used on the main page of this site are provided by and used with permission of www.google.com.

Gore, Al. *Earth in Balance.* (Boston, MA: Houghton Mifflin, 1992).

Gore, Rick. "Dinosaurs." *National Geographic*, January 1993.

Gorman, Christine. Excerpt from "Sizing Up the Sexes," from the January 20, 1992 issue of *Time*. Reprinted by permission of Time Inc.

Green, Kenneth C. Chart from *The Campus Computing Project*. Copyright © 1998 by Kenneth C. Green. Reprinted by permission.

Hall, Donald. Excerpt from "The Black-Faced Sheep" from *Old and New Poems*. Copyright © 1990 by Donald Hall. Reprinted by permission of Houghton Mifflin Company. All rights reserved.

HELIN Consortium. Screen shot of search results for keywords *Afro-Cuban music* from HELIN Library Catalog. Used by permission of the HELIN Consortium.

HELIN Consortium. Screen shot of detailed information for one entry under *Afro-Cuban music* from HELIN Library Catalog. Used by permission of the HELIN Consortium.

Hemingway, Ernest. From *The Old Man and The Sea*. (New York: Basic Books, 1973).

Hunter, J. Edward. Abstract from "Trans Fatty Acids: Effects and Alternatives," *Food Technology*, December 2002. Reprinted by permission of *Food Technology* Magazine.

Hurston, Zora Neale. Page 4 from *Their Eyes Were Watching God*. Copyright ©1937 by Harper & Row, Publishers, Inc., renewed ©1965 by John C. Hurston and Joel Hurston. Reprinted by permission of HarperCollins Publishers Inc.

Jastrow, Robert. *The Enchanted Loom.* (New York: Simon & Schuster, 1981).

Joseph, Lawrence E., "The Scoop on Ice Cream," *Discover*, August 1992.

Journal of Broadcasting & Electronic Media. One page from *Journal of Broadcasting & Electronic Media*, June 2006. Copyright 2006. Excerpt from "Judging the Degree of Violence in Media Portrayals" by Karyn Riddle et al., *Journal of Broadcasting & Electronic Media* 50(2), 2006, p. 270. Reproduced by permission of Taylor & Francis Group, LLC, http://www.taylorandfrancis.com.

Journal of Cultural Geography, Reprint of magazine page from *Journal of Cultural Geography* with excerpt from "Forget the Alamo: The Border as Place in John Sayles' *Lone Star*" by Daniel D. Arreola, *Journal of Cultural Geography*, Fall/Winter 2005. By permission of JCG Press, Oklahoma State University.

Kingston, Maxine Hong. *The Woman Warrior.* (New York: Alfred A. Knopf, 1976).

Kitwana, Bakari. *Hip Hop Generation: Young Blacks and the Crisis in African-American Culture.* (New York: Perseus Book Group, 2002).

Kowinski, William Severini. *The Malling of America.* (New York: Morrow, 1985).

Lehrer, Jonah. Excerpt from *How We Decide*. Boston: Houghton, 2009, p. 175.

Levine, Robert. *Geography of Time: The Temporal Misadventures of a Social Psychologist, or How Every Culture Keeps Time a Little Bit Differently.* Copyright © 1997 by Perseus Books Group in the Textbook Format via Copyright Clearance Center.

Lundquist, James. *Chester Himes.* (New York: Random House, 1988).

Macklin, Ruth. *Mortal Choices.* (Boston: Houghton Mifflin, 1987).

Mead, Margaret. *Male and Female.* (New York: Morrow, 1949).

Mellix, Barbara. "From The Outside In." *The Georgia Review*, Vol. 41 (Summer 1987).

Merriam-Webster, Incorporated. By permission, from *Merriam-Webster's Collegiate® Dictionary, Eleventh Edition* © 2009 by Merriam-Webster, Inc. (www.Merriam-Webster.com).

MountainLion Foundation Website (www.mountainlion.org) Reprinted by permission.

Mungo, Paul, and Clough, Bryan. "The Bulgarian Connection." *Discover*, February 1993.

Murrow, Edward R. *In Search of Light.* (New York: Alfred A, Knopf, 1967).

Neal, Bill. "How to Cure a Pig." *Esquire* © 1991.

Neutralize. Global Reach, pie graph "Online Language Populations" found at www.glreach.com. Reprinted by permission of Neutralize, United Kingdom.

Noda, Kesaya. "Growing Up Asian in America," as it appeared in *Making Waves by Asian Women United*. Reprinted by permission of the author.

Open Society Institute, *Gun Control in the United States: A Comparative Study of Firearm Laws*, April 2000.

Ortiz, Alfonso. "Some Concerns Central to the Writing of Indian History." *The Indian Historian*.

Petfinder.com. Screen shot of homepage (accessed 8/9/2009.)

Phillips Park Zoolennium Fall Festival 2004! Web site. Reprinted by permission of City of Aurora, IL Parks Department, www.aurora-il.org/parks.

Plimpton, George, "Bonding with the Grateful Dead," *Esquire*.

Popenoe, David. "The American Family Crisis." *National Forum: Phi Beta Kappa Phi Journal*, Vol. 75, No. 3 (Summer 1995). Copyright © David Popenoe.

Postman, Neil. *Amusing Ourselves to Death*. (New York: Penguin, 1985).

Preeth, Samuel J. "Incident at Lake Nyos." *The Sciences* © 1992.

Providence Public Library. From the online catalog of the Providence Public Library, Health & Wellness Resource Center. Reprinted by permission of the Providence Public Library, Providence, RI. Screen shot powered by InfoTrac from the online database Health Reference Center-Academic. Copyright © 2007. Reprinted by permission of Thomson Gale, a division of Thomson Learning: www.thomsonrights.com. Fax 800-730-2215.

Rodeghier, Mark. From "The Center for UFO Studies Response to the Air Force's 1997 Report 'The Roswell Report: Case Closed.'" www.cufos.org/airforce.htm.

Rodriguez, Richard. *Hunger of Memory*. (Boston: David R. Godine, 1983).

Rohrich, Frank, Nina Papdopoulos, Iris Suzuki, and Stefan Priebe. From "Ego-pathology, body experience, and body psychotherapy in chronic schizophrenia." *Psychology & Psychotherapy: Theory, Research & Practice*, 82.1 (2009), 19–30.

Sankey, Jay. *Zen and the Art of Stand-Up Comedy*. Copyright © 1998 by Jay Sankey. Reproduced by permission of Routledge/Taylor & Francis Books, Inc.

Save the Children. From "Save the Children" Web site, www.savethechildren.org. Text and photo reprinted by permission of Save the Children U.S. Headquarters.

Soy Expansion and deforestation in the Brazilian Amazon, 1990–2005. http://news.mongabay.com/2009/0415-amazon_soy.html.

Stacey, Judith. "The Family Values Fable." *National Forum: Phi Beta Kappa Phi Journal*, Vol. 75, No. 3 (Summer 1995). Copyright © Judith Stacey. Reprinted by permission of the publisher.

Student Affairs On-Line. Screen shot from *Student Affairs On-Line*, Summer 2006, Vol. 7, No. 2 with excerpt from article "Student Affairs and Podcasting: The New Frontier?" by Stuart Brown. http://studentaffairs.com/. © 2007 StudentAffairs.com. All rights reserved. Used by permission of StudentAffairs.com LLC.

Tannen, Deborah. *You Just Don't Understand: Women and Men in Conversation*. (New York: Morrow, 1990).

Thomas, Lewis. "Clever Animals" from *Late Night Thoughts on Listening to Mahler's Ninth*. (New York: Penguin, 1992).

Treasures of Tutankhamon. (Washington, D.C.: National Gallery of Art, 1976).

University of Florida Web site (www.ufsa.edu). Reprinted by permission of University of Florida.

Wagner, Richard H. *Environment and Man*. (New York: Norton, 1978).

Werner, Dave. Screen shot of homepage from okaydave.com.

Wideman, John Edgar. *Philadelphia Fire*. (New York: Henry Holt, 1990).

Zimmer, Carl. "The Body Electric," *Discover*, February, 1993.

Student Acknowledgments: Erica Abed, David Aharonian, Summer Arrigo-Nelson, Heloise Benet, Roy Bipin, Katie Bohan, Amy Braegelman, Nicholas Branahan, Carey Braun, Sara Brilliant, Evan Brisson, Katherine Buck, Zachary Carter, Chris Colavito, Paul Copass, Kimlee Cunningham, Jessica DiGregorio, Liv Dolphin, Jason Fester, Nelson Arrigo-Figliozzi, Olivia Garbedian, Daisy Garcia, Lily Germaine, Chantele Giles, Jen Halliday, Andrea Herrmann, Maha Krishnasami, Jenny Latimer, Fredza Leger, Jake Lloyd, Tyson Mao, Reid Nelson, Jennifer O'Berry, Alphonso Ortiz, Michael Perry, Ian Preston, Paul Pusateri, Sam Roles, Dahzane Roninson, Sharon Salamone, Amy Singh, Ted Wolfe.

Photos

p. 136, George D. Lepp/Corbis; p. 160, *all images*, National Park Services; *except bottom right*, NASA; p. 164, *left*, Ted Levine/Corbis; *right*, Richard Gross/Corbis; p. 249, NASA; p. 352, *top*, General Motors; p. 353, Erich Lessing/Art Resource, NY/Kunsthistorisches Museum, Vienna, Austria.

Index

general, 294
specialized, 294–295
Wikipedia, 286
End punctuation
exclamation points, 719–720
with parentheses, 722
periods, 716
question marks, 717–718
Endnotes
CMS in-text citations, 452–460
MLA documentation style for, 380
English
spoken versus written, 574, 707
standard, 667
English as a second language (ESL)
adjective clauses and, 523
adjective forms, 508
adjectives in series and, 572
adverb clauses and, 523–524
apostrophes and possessive pronouns, 546
articles and, 542–543
capitalization, 732
conditional statements and, 540
coordination and subordination, 644
critical thinking in academic contexts, 94
demonstrative adjectives and pronouns, 567
dictionary use, 661
gerunds and infinitives, 519
helping verbs and, 530
noun clauses and, 524–525
numbers and, 690
paired conjunctions, 559
paragraph conventions, 55
passive voice and, 536
peer readers, 41
position of modifiers, 603
prepositions and, 511–512
quantifiers and, 563–564
quotation marks, 710
sentence variety, 78
separated subjects and verbs, 559
simple present and present progressive tenses, 532
subject-verb agreement, 554–555, 559, 563–564
verb forms, 529–530
verbs and verb phrases, 530
ensure, assure, insure, 759, 766
enthused, 774
Envelope, for business letters, 263
Episodes, quotation marks with titles of, 713
Equivocation, 127
-er endings, 572–574
ERIC (FirstSearch), 306

Errors. *See* Documentation, mistakes in; Grammatical mistakes; Sentence problems
-es endings, 529
in forming plurals, 541
forming plurals with, 756
ESL. *See* English as a second language (ESL)
especially, specially, 774
Essay exams, 195–197, 201–202
Essays, unpublished, MLA works cited list, 386–387
Essential (restrictive) clauses, 683–684
-est endings, 572–574
et al. (and others), 376, 383, 388, 417, 421, 753
etc., 753, 774
Ethics. *See also* Plagiarism
email use, 169–171
informed consent in field research, 329
Ethnic stereotyping, 676
Ethnographies, 223–224, 330–331, 333
Etymology, 661, 774
Evaluation, 774
in argumentative writing, 107–108
database, 309
source, 320–323; Internet, 320–323; library, 285–286, 299–300
Evaluative summary, 192
even, as limiting modifier, 603
Events, abbreviating, 750
eventually, ultimately, 774
every
with compound antecedent, 566
subject-verb agreement, 557
everybody, subject-verb agreement, 560–561
everyday, every day, 774
everyone, every one, 774
Evidence
in argumentative writing, 116
in chain of reasoning, 95
defined, 95, 774
integrating into papers, 342
supporting, 793
variety of, 116–119
in visual argument, 138–141
writing about literature, 208, 209
ex- prefixes, 742
exactly, as limiting modifier, 603
Examples
in argumentative writing, 116–117
colons to introduce, 699–700
in concluding paragraphs, 67
to develop stance, 110
in developing introductory paragraphs, 66
integrating into papers, 342
in paragraph development, 60

index

index

GUIDE TO ESL ADVICE

If your first language is not English, look for special advice integrated throughout the handbook. Each ESL Advice section is labeled and highlighted so it's easy to spot. *The Longman Handbook* offers special help on these topics.

ADJECTIVES AND ADVERBS

Adjective Forms (**35a**)
Adjective Clauses (**35a**)
Adjectives in a Series (**39b**)
Adverb Clauses (**35c**)
Demonstrative Adjectives or Pronouns
(**38c**)

AGREEMENT

Pronoun-Antecedent Agreement (**38c**)
   Demonstrative Adjectives or Pronouns
    (**38c**)
   Number, Person, and Gender (**38c**)
Subject-Verb Agreement (**38b**)
   Other, Others, and *Another* (**38b**)
   Paired Conjunctions (**38b**)
   Present Tense Verb Agreement (**36b**)
   Quantifiers (*each, one, many, much,*
    most) (**38b**)
   Separated Subjects and Verbs (**38b**)
   Words Affecting Subject-Verb
    Agreement (**38b**)

ARTICLES, NOUNS, AND PRONOUNS

Articles: *A, An,* and *The* (**35a**)
Demonstrative Adjectives or Pronouns
   (**38c**)
Noun Clauses (**35c**)
Number, Person, and Gender (**35c**)

PREPOSITIONS

Prepositions (**35a**)
For and *Since* in Time Expressions (**35a**)
Prepositions of Place: *At, On,* and *In* (**35a**)
Prepositions of Time: *At, On,* and *In* (**35a**)
Prepositions with Nouns, Verbs, and
   Adjectives (**35a**)
To or No Preposition to Express Going to a
   Place (**35a**)

PUNCTUATION AND MECHANICS

Capitalization (**57b**)
Quotation Marks (**54a**)

SENTENCES

Choosing the Position of a Modifier
   (**43a**)
Coordination and Subordination (**47d**)
Sentence Variety (**7d**)
There is and *There are* (**7b**)

VERBALS

Gerunds (**35c**)
Gerunds vs. Infinitives (**35c**)
Infinitives (**35c**)

VERBS

Verb Forms (**36b**)
Conditionals (**36b**)
Helping Verbs (**36b**)
Passive Voice (**36e**)
Simple Present and Present Progressive
   Tenses (**36c**)
Subject-Verb Agreement (**38a, 38b**)
Third Person *–s* or *–es* Ending (**36b**)
Verb Tense and Expressions of Time (**36c**)

WRITING

Critical Thinking in Academic Contexts (**9c**)
Drafting (**4b**)
Paragraph Conventions (**6b**)
Peer Readers (**5c**)
Using Dictionaries (**49d**)

ESL   ESL exercises can be found on MyCompLab.